Intergroup Processes

Intergroup Processes

A Micro–Macro Perspective

Hubert M. Blalock, Jr.
Paul H. Wilken

THE FREE PRESS
A Division of Macmillan Publishing Co., Inc.
NEW YORK

Collier Macmillan Publishers
LONDON

THE FREE PRESS
A Division of Macmillan Publishing Co., Inc.
866 Third Avenue, New York, N.Y.   10022

Collier Macmillan Canada, Ltd.

Library of Congress Catalog Card Number: 78-19856

Printed in the United States of America

printing number

1   2   3   4   5   6   7   8   9   10

Library of Congress Cataloging in Publication Data

Blalock, Hubert M., Jr.
  Intergroup processes.

  Includes bibliographical references and index.
  1. Social groups—Case studies.   2. Organizational
behavior—Case studies.   3. Sociology—Methodology.
4. Social psychology.   I. Wilken, Paul H., joint author.
II. Title.
HM131.B585 1979   301.15   78-19856
ISBN 0-02-903620-8

To Our Children:
Kristina and Stephanie Wilken
and
Susan, Katie, and Jim Blalock

CONTENTS

Acknowledgments, ix

Chapter 1   Building General Theories of
Complex Social Processes, 1

**Part One   Micro-level Processes:
The Subjective Expected Utility Approach**

Chapter 2   The Significance of Utilities
for Intergroup Processes, 27

Chapter 3   Subjective Probabilities, 78

Chapter 4   Subjective Expected Utility
and Decision Strategies, 122

Part Two   Exchange, Equity, and Power as Social Processes

Chapter 5   Exchange Relationships, 175

Chapter 6   Equity and Distributive Justice, 222

Chapter 7   Contextual Effects:
Theories and Processes, 288

Chapter 8   Social Power I:
Its Nature and Sources, 324

Chapter 9   Social Power II: Degree and
Efficiency of Mobilization, 361

Part Three   Allocation and Approach–Withdrawal Processes

Chapter 10   Allocation I: Allocation Processes
and Discrimination, 413

Chapter 11   Allocation II: The Measurement of
Discrimination and Inequalities, 451

Chapter 12   Allocation III: Eligibility Pools and
Candidate Selection Processes, 484

Chapter 13   Approach and Withdrawal I: Segregation,
Integration, and Related Concepts, 515

Chapter 14   Approach and Withdrawal II: Some Models
of Intergroup Interaction, 545

Part Four   Dynamic Theories

Chapter 15   Toward the Formulation of Dynamic
Models of Macro Processes, 589

References, 614
Name Index, 630
Subject Index, 635

ACKNOWLEDGMENTS

THIS MATERIAL IS BASED upon work supported by the National Science Foundation under grant Soc 72 05601-A01. Without NSF support, and especially that of Donald R. Ploch, formerly director of the sociology program at NSF, this book would no doubt have remained an unrealized goal. All opinions, findings, and conclusions expressed in this publication are, of course, those of the authors and do not necessarily reflect the views of the National Science Foundation.

As for contributions to the content of the book, we wish to thank George Beal, Jr.; Pennie Greene; and Adolph Rosenfeld for the ideas they provided in the early stages of the project. Jim Fendrich provided helpful feedback at various points in the project, and Karen Cook's meticulous comments on an earlier version of chapter 6 were most beneficial. Numerous persons also commented constructively on a previous paper on power that became the basis of chapters 8 and 9.

A number of staff persons at the University of Washington have also been very helpful to us in completing the project. We are especially indebted to Nancy Wallace, whose cheerful administrative assistance brightened many gloomy Seattle days, and to Beulah Reddaway, who typed a large portion of the lengthy manuscript. We also appreciate the assistance of Barbara Davis, Alice Fowler, and Karen Wayenberg, who also typed several chapters; Bruce Moburg and Lois Ellis, who drew the numerous and sometimes complicated figures scattered throughout the book; and the University of Virginia, which made a small grant toward publication costs.

We are certain that the theoretical models we present herein are not the last word regarding intergroup processes. Rather, we hope that they will constitute takeoff points for our colleagues who are also interested in intergroup processes, the relationship between micro- and macro-levels of analysis, and the current fragmentation of the discipline of sociology. Perhaps they will profit from whatever errors in interpretation or logic they may uncover, for which we assume full responsibility.

This project has been a totally joint one in every respect, including the writing, which has been shared equally. Our names appear in alphabetical order. One of us happens to be a bit older than the other but fully admits to having received as much as he gave—in an equitable exchange—and wishes to emphasize that the two authors are equal partners, for better or worse!

CHAPTER 1

Building General Theories of Complex Social Processes

SOCIAL SCIENTISTS agree on very few things, but if there is one fact upon which there is a high degree of consensus it is that social reality is extremely complex. From that point on, however, there are basic disagreements as to how to cope with and study this complexity. Since the present work constitutes one more effort to tackle this reality by means of a particular kind of theory-building strategy, it seems essential in this introductory chapter that we outline the major working assumptions upon which our later discussion will be built. Actually, we shall find ourselves confronted with a number of issues that ideally ought to be handled more or less simultaneously. One of our major objectives will be to bring at least a reasonable number of these problems out into the open where they may be stated explicitly, examined for their implications, and then handled as best one can.

Our ultimate aim, which we assume is shared by most other social scientists, is to achieve a better linkage between micro-level theories concerned with individual motives, behaviors, and interactions and much more macro-oriented theories dealing with interrelationships among large units such as complex organizations, nation-states, or other corporate groups, as well as with loosely organized groupings such as racial or ethnic groups, social classes, and other kinds of interest group. We accept as valid the arguments of those who claim that subjective variables, or "meanings" that actors attach to objective events, must be an integral part of any micro- or macro-level theory that purports to explain social reality. But we reject the implication that some social scientists draw from this that it is therefore impossible to analyze this reality in a systematic manner or to apply scientifically oriented methodological approaches to provide a cumulative knowledge base.

Instead, we shall argue that we need to accommodate our methodology to this admitted complexity and to accept whatever limitations are implied by

1

the presence of a large number of unknowns in any theoretical system. In brief, if reality is complex we must learn to develop complex theories to deal with it, but at the same time we must also study the implications of these complexities for testing and evaluating these theories. Such a complexity calls for a great deal of methodological sophistication, rather than a rejection of the goal of achieving scientific maturity. We take this position because we frankly do not see any other way of proceeding that has anything really positive to offer.

We also accept the position that our theories must be reasonably general but also capable of explaining, as special cases, a number of particular phenomena with sufficient precision that the insights they yield go considerably beyond those generated either by common sense or by an extrapolation of past trends into the present. These theories must also be capable of implying specific falsifiable predictions that would not otherwise have been suggested. Our knowledge in most fields of social science is obviously not of this quality, a fact that has stimulated numerous discussions and debates as to possible inherent limitations and alternative ways of proceeding. We again assume that there is basic agreement about the ideal state of affairs concerning this knowledge, though admittedly there is also a realistic concern about how such knowledge would be *used*, if and when it became available. For our purposes, the major practical question boils down to that of asking whether or not there are some reasonably systematic steps we may take to improve this knowledge base, and if so, how we can go about the task of specifying precisely what they may be.

The orientation we shall take in the remainder of this work is that of beginning with the individual actor and explicitly allowing for subjective factors to account for behaviors, even in instances where these subjective variables can be measured only indirectly and very imperfectly. We shall then turn to several kinds of social process involving interactions among actors, including exchange and power relationships and allocation and approach–withdrawal processes. In each instance we shall be concerned with how these actors cope with complexities by making simplifications and how we, as analysts, may move from highly simplistic situations to much more complex ones involving aggregated individuals, quasigroups, and corporate groups as actors. The essential point is that our macro-level theories need to be given behavioral underpinnings, even in instances where micro-level data may not be available. In order to pass back and forth between the micro and macro levels on a systematic basis it is necessary to state one's assumptions explicitly, and this, of course, implies that we need micro-level theories to justify our macro-level assumptions, and perhaps vice versa.

One of our primary goals is that of convincing macro-oriented sociologists and other social scientists of the desirability of formulating micro-level theories, even in instances where there are insufficient data to test these theories directly. Our own approach can be described as being on an intermediate level, one that might be called the micro–macro level. Most of our models are perhaps best characterized as "contextual-effect" models, provided one thinks of that term in a very broad sense and not merely as involving the kinds of simple contextual effect that have been discussed in the methodological debates on the subject.[1] We see these micro–macro models as providing the behavioral assumptions necessary for truly macro-level theories.

It is our fundamental assumption that macro-level theories will tend to be inadequate to the degree that they ignore the fact that human motivations and behaviors constitute important driving forces or causes of social phenomena. These driving forces are to a large extent given their direction as a result of their interaction with contextual variables, some of which are nonhuman in nature. But we do not see these motivational and behavioral variables as being mere "intervening variables" or dependent variables in micro-level models.

Interestingly enough, behaviors that are usually taken as dependent variables in such micro-level theories—variables such as degree of deviance, discrimination, or political participation—are likely to be taken as independent, or exogenous, variables when aggregated and used in macro-level models. Thus even such a variable as "level of technology" is clearly a function of human inventions, both technical and organizational. Likewise, one of the exogenous variables influencing minority behaviors is the existing level of discrimination, or perhaps the level of economic inequality, that has resulted from a large number of individual behaviors. If one simply takes these variables as givens on the macro level, the resulting theory will be very incomplete, at best, and perhaps even highly misleading in terms of the assumptions being made about the basic causal mechanisms that are at work.

All of this means that our general theories, which are intended to apply to a wide variety of situations, must be highly complex, at least in the sense that they *allow for* possible complications that do not necessarily arise in each specific application. That is, when we consider special cases of the general theory we may be willing to assume that certain variables are effectively held constant or that they appear with zero coefficients. Therefore they may be ignored in these instances, even though in other situations they may turn out to be highly important as explanatory factors. Ideally, then, we would like to formulate a number of reasonably general theories, each of which simplifies to allow for important special cases that are more easily handled in terms of actual empirical research. If the more general theories were available, one could then begin to fit together the pieces of the empirical puzzle. Lacking these theories, and especially not knowing precisely what implicit assumptions are being made, it is often extremely difficult for the social scientist to "add up" a series of empirical findings in any systematic fashion.

But, clearly, our theories will have to be simplified if they are to be testable in the sense of their implying rejectable assertions about the real world. One of the most important contributions coming from the econometrics literature is the notion of identifiability (Koopmans 1949). This refers to the conditions under which an equation system simply contains too many unknowns for solution, even in the presence of perfect data. In brief, a theory that is too complex and that introduces too many such unknowns will yield a hopeless situation in which none of the coefficients in the equations can be estimated by *any* means. This, of course, implies that there will be no empirical way of resolving disputes over the relative importance of the variables involved. It will be necessary to modify the theory in some essential way. This means that the theorist has to straddle the fence between two desirable characteristics of a theory: realism and testability. The theory can be made increasingly realistic by adding to its complexity. But at some point it becomes too complex to be tested, not just in the sense of becoming unwieldy in a practical way but in the more fundamental sense of containing too many unknowns. At this point simplifications must be reintroduced. But this can at least be done on a systematic basis through a process of making assumptions explicit, so that they may each be questioned and evaluated in terms of alternative possibilities.

What makes matters even more difficult is that there will practically always be missing variables or unknown measurement errors in any given piece of research. As a general rule the more variables we can measure, and the better the measures we have of each variable, the more plausible our untested assumptions can be. Clearly, certain kinds of empirical research tend to omit specific kinds of variable on a rather systematic basis. For instance, survey research usually favors attitudinal variables over behavioral responses, neglects earlier values of many variables because of the recognition that memory is often faulty, and also ignores a whole host of contextual variables that are sometimes constant across the individuals being studied, but sometimes not. Macro-level studies, in contrast, are often based on officially collected data sources, highly aggregated data, or data that have been collected with some very different purpose in mind.

It is often convenient to believe that the variables that happen to be missing from one's own empirical analysis are unimportant in a causal sense. But one would hardly expect nature to be so kind to us! Not only do such data gaps lead one to incorrect conclusions, but the omissions are usually so glaring to others having different intellectual persuasions that the studies are sometimes dismissed out of hand as being entirely inadequate. This seems to be one of the mechanisms that inhibit the accumulation of knowledge through a process of incremental additions and that help to sustain rather fruitless debates concerning the superiority of one approach over another.

The only resolution to this very real practical problem that we can visualize is through a theory-construction process that allows for many more complexities than possibly can be handled in any single piece of research. In effect this implies that our theories must "lead" our data-collection capabilities by a reasonable amount and must be sufficiently flexible to allow for additional complications introduced whenever measurement is crude or highly indirect. Furthermore, such theories need to be explicit, so that previously hidden assumptions are brought into the open. Then, for any given test or application of the theory, it will be necessary to introduce further restrictive assumptions required by data limitations, the time span of the study, or imperfections in our theoretical knowledge.

Given the more complete and more general theory, a critic of any particular piece of empirical research may then see more easily just where the shortcomings lie and how the necessarily incomplete knowledge based on one study may be fitted together with that derived from other similarly incomplete studies. This, of course, makes the job of the critic much easier, but it also facilitates the process of linking the results of diverse pieces of research, each of which may have its own unique combination of shortcomings. Also, if one has available a reasonably complete theoretical model it becomes much easier to decide upon a division of labor or sequencing of empirical studies that can be planned in advance to yield cumulative results.

If an investigator begins with a very specific empirical problem, as, for example, the study of racial segregation in large urban areas, the tendency is to look for good sources of data, where available, or to apply for a research grant to collect the data on one's own. Either way, the temptation is to work with a theoretical model that is primarily confined to the list of variables that one can actually measure, rather than a more complex theory that also contains a large number of unmeasured variables. This indeed seems reasonable for the individual investigator because it will later be necessary to omit most of these unmeasured variables at the analysis stage.

But variables will be omitted with varying degrees of faith in the assumptions being made about them. When these omitted variables are not explicitly identified and linked theoretically with the other variables in the model, it becomes virtually impossible to say anything about the possible sources of bias being produced or how the results might have been altered had they been included. For example, in any causal model that is being evaluated empirically it is necessary to make certain assumptions about so-called disturbance, or error, terms. These disturbance terms must be assumed uncorrelated with at least certain of the variables that are explicitly included in the theory. It is tempting to go ahead on the basis of convenience and necessity and to make these assumptions more or less blindly. Had other (unmeasured) variables been explicitly included in a more general theory, however, the investigator might at least be more uncomfortable about making such assumptions. Furthermore, a reader would be in a much better position to reinterpret the conclusions and even to improve upon the study by obtaining supplementary measures of these neglected variables.

The major point, then, is that from the standpoint of the cumulation of knowledge based on individually incomplete empirical studies, it is essential to state our theories in such a way that we allow for many more complexities than will ever be handled in any single piece of research. If we add to this the point previously made, namely, that we desire our theories to be sufficiently general to cover a wide range of special cases, we can begin to see the difficulty of the task that lies ahead. Furthermore, as we have also implied, there will often be a trade-off between the goals of generality and measurement precision, so that tests of reasonably general theories may have to be both partial and relatively crude. When we come to our more detailed discussions of specific social processes these points will become patently obvious, if they are not already so. Our main task, however, is not so much that of learning to live with these difficulties as it is to find ways of slowly overcoming them, while not becoming either overwhelmed with their magnitude or overly tempted to impose undue simplicity prior to a careful study of just how to proceed.

THE MICRO LEVEL OF ANALYSIS

As can readily be inferred from our table of contents, our presentation will move from a somewhat detailed consideration in part 1 of the subjective expected utility perspective, aimed toward explaining the behaviors of individual actors, to discussions of social processes involving multiple actors whose behaviors may be coordinated to varying degrees. As already noted, our micro orientation will be one that treats behaviors as goal directed and based on imperfect information and uncertainty.[2] We shall also need to take the histories of actors into consideration, as well as a number of factors that may operate to distort their perceptions, memory, or expectations concerning the future.

The models we use involve two basic kinds of postulated internal state, namely, subjective probabilities and utilities or subjective values attached to the importance of goals. Thus our primary orientation will be both subjectivistic and rationalistic, but this does not mean we can afford to ignore a number of important kinds of complication and the possible defects of such a perspective on human behavior. In particular, we shall have to cope with the obvious fact that subjective states must always be measured indirectly, though there may be considerable differences among alternative auxiliary measurement theories needed to justify different approaches to such indirect measurements. In brief, certain procedures are much more direct than others. Some are preferable in very simple situations but much less satisfactory in more complex settings (Wilken and Blalock 1979).

We must also cope with the obvious fact that actors will almost always take shortcuts and make simplifying assumptions that on the face of it seem incompatible with a rational model of human behavior. Furthermore, they will be influenced by strong emotions that may, for example, temporarily make certain goals all-encompassing or that may so distort their subjective probabilities that the resulting behavior, as judged by an outsider, appears to be totally irrational and shortsighted. For instance, in situations in which intergroup tension is high, and where fear of and hostility toward members of another group are extreme, actors may engage in violent and possibly sadistic forms of behavior that would never even be considered under other circumstances. Our theoretical framework will need to be sufficiently broad to allow for these possibilities, while still enabling the social scientist to *analyze* this behavior as though it were goal directed and in some sense rational, given the actor's particular set of working assumptions and immediate priorities.

One problem with subjectivistic orientations toward human behavior is that, because of the obvious complexities of human motivations, there is a tendency to remain totally on this subjective level, or at least to give only passing attention to the stimuli that impinge on the actor from the outside environment. This is in fact a limitation of our discussion in part 1 and more generally, we believe, of many psychological and social psychological studies that are confined to very simple laboratory settings. These subjective processes are so complex and difficult to pin down empirically that it is only natural that those who attempt to study them carefully must leave it to others to broaden the contexts and to speculate as to how the theories will have to be modified once situational complexities are introduced. In contrast, those social scientists who are primarily concerned with studying the settings themselves tend to despair of the possibility of ever being able to bring these subjective variables into their theories in a systematic fashion. This apparently leads either to a rejection of systematization in favor of strictly descriptive or literary accounts of the processes or to a rejection of subjective variables as integral parts of the theories.

We shall thus find ourselves on the horns of several dilemmas that, ideally, we would prefer not to have to face. We believe that it is necessary to introduce subjective variables into our theories. Yet we readily admit that this may lead to difficult measurement problems and a degree of complexity that becomes overwhelming once we begin to study the kinds of real-world situation we wish to understand. As we have already implied, our own efforts to resolve this kind of dilemma will involve the introduction of only a very small number of distinct kinds of subjective variable, the assumption of essentially rational behavior, and the argument that other kinds of subjective variable can be subsumed under our basic model. If this turns out to be unrealistic, then our effort would have to be turned in the direction of defining a small number of additional subjective variables of a sufficiently general nature that the resulting modified model would be capable of handling the inadequacies of the previous model.

An alternative strategy would be that of being much less selective in the introduction of subjective variables but also less concerned with problems of measurement, generalizability, and explicit theory formulation. The difficulty we see with this alternative approach, however, is that it is more likely to lead to a lack of concern with stating theories in such a fashion that they imply rejectable assertions that can be made in advance of data collection. It seems to us that testability, measurement, and rigor are far too important criteria to permit this to happen. However, we are painfully aware of the possibility that, if taken as absolutes, these latter criteria may prematurely stifle serious efforts to introduce realism into our theories and to extend the range of our empirical inquiries into topics that involve a large number of simultaneous complexities.

The reader will shortly become aware of our efforts to struggle with these dilemmas as we begin to introduce complexities into the subjective expected utility model. At times it will seem as though no human actor could possibly calculate these subjective expected utilities in the fashion that seems to be implied, and indeed this will be true. There will obviously be a need to simplify, both on the part of the actor and the observer who is attempting to understand his or her behavior. The crucial question then becomes that of what *kinds* of simplification are being made and *how* the actor goes about this process. Here, our general formulation in part 1 will be merely suggestive, and we must turn to the kinds of more specific situation that are discussed in the remaining sections of the book. That is, we shall assume that actors tend to simplify in different ways that will depend, in part, on the kind of situation in which they are placed.

Sometimes actors will rely on tradition or the experiences of others, presumably on the grounds that if a situation has not altered in basic ways it is sensible to proceed in much the same fashion that others have done in the past. On other occasions important kinds of simplification will be suggested by ideological systems that tell the actor what is or should be most important, that provide simple working theories of complex causal processes, or that help one predict how other actors can be expected to behave. Actors may also drastically simplify their calculations by restricting themselves to a very short list of goals while neglecting the rest or by setting subjective probabilities at either zero or one, thereby ruling out uncertainties. Or they may shorten their time perspectives so as to rule out long-term consequences, particularly those whose probabilities would be extremely difficult to calculate. Also, as we shall later suggest, they may simplify the diversity of other actors in their environments either by assuming them to be all alike or acting in concert (as in conspiracy theories) or by treating them as totally irrelevant to their own behaviors. In brief, we shall assume that *some* types of simplification must occur, but it remains for more specific theories to predict which types of simplification will occur under a given set of conditions.

THE MACRO LEVEL OF ANALYSIS

Whereas the focus of attention of the social psychologist is usually, though not always, the individual as a unit of analysis, those sociologists and other social scientists who hold themselves distinct from social psychologists seem to agree on at least one thing, namely, that *groups* of various kinds are also legitimate units of analysis in their own right and that group properties are distinct from those of individual members. They would argue that macro-level, or group-level, theories must supplement those at the micro, or individual, level of analysis. There is probably also a high degree of consensus among social scientists that the two levels of analysis should not lead to logically incompatible interpretations of social reality and that, ideally at least, the two perspectives should be mutually reinforcing. Yet there has been surprisingly little systematic attention given to specifying the exact linkages between levels or to exploring the methodological difficulties one encounters when one attempts to move back and forth between them.

Obviously, such a complex topic cannot be handled adequately in a single work of this scope. Nevertheless, if we were to neglect it completely we would be guilty of much the same practice of which we have by implication been critical in the above paragraph. Therefore it is essential that we attempt to sketch in some of what we consider to be the basic methodological issues involved. Perhaps the most serious difficulty encountered in actual empirical work is that of missing information that produces such huge gaps in our knowledge that it becomes exceedingly difficult to piece the puzzle together. Rarely, for example, can macro-level investigators obtain the kinds of measure of group properties that they would really need in order to test and refine theories at this level. Instead, they must rely on very crude and highly indirect indicators that are related to the basic theoretical constructs in complex ways. But the issues are more complicated than this, so that even under much more favorable data conditions we would still be faced with a number of methodological problems necessitating a series of a priori simplifying assumptions. In the present section we shall merely mention a few of the problems that will later concern us in more detail, beginning with the question of aggregation and degrees of "groupness."

Let us consider three illustrative kinds of group. The first, which is often referred to as a "corporate group," may be characterized by a well-defined structure and what might even be termed a "group behavior" in the form of a definite output that cannot be associated with a single actor or set of actors who are members of such a group. Thus we may speak of the outputs of a legislative body in the form of a set of laws, expenditures, or policies. A college or university produces a number of graduates, and a construction company builds houses. Here, if we wish, we may treat the group as though it were a single actor and then proceed in much the same fashion as we would in the case of an individual person.

The second type of group may also be characterized by a high degree of interaction, group norms and sanctions, and so forth, but for the purposes at hand it may make much less sense to think in terms of a collective product or of corporate action. For instance, a religious denomination, a country club, or an informal clique may provide certain services, but these may be of much less interest to the investigator than their internal and informal interaction patterns and their diverse influences on the individual members. Third, we recognize quasi groups that are hardly distinct from categories, though they may have been called groups at one time or another or for certain purposes. For example, are blacks a group or a category? Sociologists? Residents of the same metropolitan area, neighborhood, or city block?

We encounter here a basic problem that does not arise on the micro or individual level, namely, that of defining the boundaries of a unit and deciding upon the criteria to be used in making that definition. A major difficulty we face in this connection is that most defining criteria we might use are, themselves, continuous variables, so that any simple categorization becomes arbitrary. If, for example, a group is to be distinguished from a category by virtue of the fact that there must be interaction among members of a true group, precisely how much and what kinds of interaction are required? If a group is to be distinguished on the basis of normative consensus, then how much consensus is needed? Clearly, there will be varying degrees of groupness—even where a single defining characteristic is used.

Given this fact, there will often be a certain degree of arbitrariness in group boundaries, and this in turn will have methodological implications for the properties of any aggregated measures of variables such as residential segregation, inequality levels, or degree of consensus. This can be seen from the fact that the very same statistical measures can be constructed for both groups and aggregates, so long as these are aggregated measures of individual scores. Thus we may calculate means, standard deviations, and rates for such diverse populations as residents of a city, black residents over fifty years of age, friendship cliques, persons whose surname begins with B, and persons whose names in a city directory fall on pages ending with the digit 7. A sociologist interested in suicide rates may compute these rates for real groups, but they could also be computed for such categories as persons listed as "psychologically insecure," persons with IQ's over 150, or persons whose fathers had committed suicide. The fact that one is dealing with rates rather than individual scores does not imply that one is necessarily using a macro focus, but merely that these scores have been aggregated in some way.

Our position will be that theories must explicitly allow for varying degrees of groupness, including the limiting possibility that some kinds of behavior may best be treated as completely noncoordinated acts of similar persons. At this extreme, we could link our macro and micro theories very simply by aggregation, and it would be unnecessary to formulate a distinct theory on the one level if one already existed on the other. Presumably, we could all agree that the micro-level theory enables us to explain the relationships between the comparable rates. Thus we could explain the relationship between suicide rates and unemployment rates by means of theories that linked individuals' exposures to unemployment risks to their propensities to suicide.

In terms of statistical aggregation, if we have a number of individuals whose behavior Y is linked to two causes X_1 and X_2 according to the micro-level law

$$Y = \alpha + \beta_1 X_1 + \beta_2 X_2 + \epsilon,$$

where *all* individuals can be characterized by exactly the same coefficients α, β_1, and β_2, then it can easily be shown that for this linear model we shall also have for any aggregates of these individuals

$$\bar{Y} = \alpha + \beta_1 \bar{X}_1 + \beta_2 \bar{X}_2 + \bar{\epsilon},$$

provided that the micro-level model has been perfectly specified and that the criterion for aggregation does not belong in the equation for Y.[3] In other words, for the linear case, at least, we could arrive at the law in question either from the individual data or by aggregating and taking group means. This is a simple illustration of what has been called the consistency criterion in the econometrics literature (see Hannan 1971:18-22). The size of the groupings is irrelevant except for the matter of sampling errors, although the magnitudes of *correlation* coefficients will in general be affected by the size of the groupings.

Obviously, most sociologists do not believe that such a simple translation across levels is usually legitimate, and we have come to refer to the problem involved as the "ecological fallacy." But, as Hannan (1971: 9-10) has noted, when we call something a fallacy we immediately give it a label as something to be avoided without further ado, and without regard to how serious the possible distortions might be under varying circumstances. The "ecological fallacy" cannot be dismissed this simply because under some circumstances this kind of aggregation operation is perfectly legitimate. It also seems obvious that if one adheres to the extreme position that *no* simple aggregation makes sense, then we are going to be in real difficulty in arriving at rational criteria for interrelating micro- and macro-level theories.

When persons are aggregated we generally have some reason for placing them in one category rather than in another. If we are interested in inferring causal laws or processes that are appropriate to both the micro and macro levels, then the key consideration in forming aggregates is that persons grouped together are assumed to be characterized by the same values of the causal parameters. In the above example this means that the individuals lumped together should all have the same numerical values for α, β_1, and β_2. Notice that individuals might have also been grouped according to their similarity with respect to the *levels* of Y, X_1, or X_2, regardless of similarity of the coefficients. If so, we cannot be assured that they will respond in the same ways if, say, an exogenous force threatens to change X_1 or X_2.

In much the same way, human groups may be formed on the basis of similarity with respect to either levels of the variables or parameter values, and the nature of their similarity may make a considerable difference in terms of the way they may organize their responses to exogenous changes. Let us consider a hypothetical example. Suppose there is an economically homogeneous white upper-middle-class community that experiences a substantial in-migration of lower-income blacks. This homogeneity with respect to income does *not* assure us that these persons will react in the same way. Some may feel threatened, others may be delighted, and still others indifferent. In contrast, we might imagine a much less economically homogeneous community in which all persons are united in terms of the perceived threat as indicated by the homogeneity of their coefficients. Prior to the in-migration, neither residential area may have been characterized by anything more than very superficial interaction, so that their initial individual behaviors may have been explained adequately in terms of a micro-level model using only individual traits as predictors of the reaction. Once the migration materialized, however, the first community might be expected to split into rival factions whereas the second would be more likely to be characterized by a high degree of solidarity. The essential point is that both groups and aggregates can be characterized by at least two kinds of homogeneity: homogeneity with respect to *levels* of the variables and homogeneity with respect to the *coefficients* in the laws that connect these variables. In some instances the two kinds of homogeneity may be found together, but this will not necessarily be the case.

This example also points to another respect, in addition to the determination of unit boundaries, in which macro-level theories may differ from micro-level theories. As long as the former involve only *average* levels (or proportions) there remains the possibility that the two may be very simply related in terms of aggregating functions. But when we deal with matters of dispersion, consensus, coordination, division of labor, measures of skewness, and the like we necessarily introduce variables into the macro-level model that enter into the theory in an entirely different way. A measure of dispersion or group consensus can be used as a contextual variable to help explain individual behavior, as, for example, when a person perceives that there is a high degree of consensus within the peer group and therefore anticipates a highly coordinated response to any deviant behavior. But on the macro level homogeneity variables may affect the efficiency of the group's responses or the nature of the means that can be used in a political conflict with another group.

Whenever these group properties are expected to play distinctly different roles in the causal models on the two levels, we cannot move from the one level to the other through a simple process of aggregation or disaggregation. Factors such as the size or homogeneity of the group belong in the sociological theory and cannot be treated as simple artifacts of the aggregating operation. Thus "sociological size" affects such variables as the nature of face-to-face interactions, the probability of subgroup formation, the nature of social control within the group, and many other organizational features. Somehow, then, we must find ways of separating out the statistical artifact of size from the sociological effects of size.

Given these complications in moving back and forth between the micro and macro levels, how can we proceed? It is clear that our macro-level models must allow for the operation of what might be called sociological variables, or group properties that are not appropriate for statistical aggregates. But at the same time they must also allow for the possibility that, in some instances, such group properties are irrelevant or that, for all practical purposes, behavior rates can be explained without having to refer to any organized groups whatsoever. In other words, we must leave open the possibility—seemingly implied in most survey research—that individuals respond in essentially the same ways to similar stimuli purely as a result of their individual characteristics rather than through organized activities. Of course, few sociologists would anticipate that there will be many realistic situations that can adequately be explained in such simple terms, but our models must at least permit this possibility.

Perhaps a simple model will illustrate the point. Let us consider a situation in which actors are responding to some rate of behavior at time $t - 1$, as represented by $\bar{Y}_{t-1}$ in figure 1.1. The actual behavior rate (say, a homicide or an unemployment rate) at $t - 1$ is assumed to affect the average level of perceived

Figure 1.1

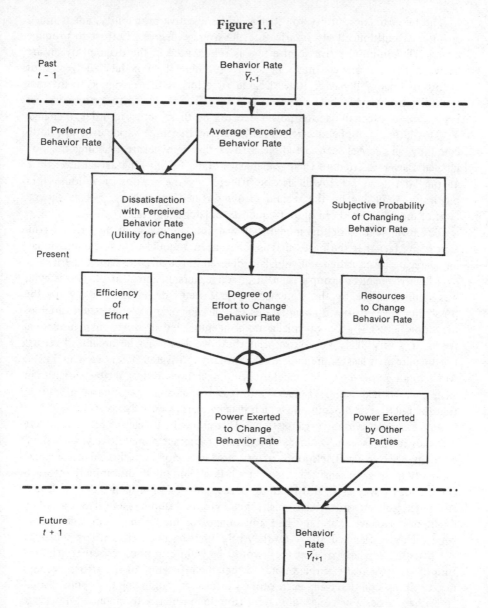

rates, which will, of course, be affected by other variables as well. The discrepancies between perceived rates and those that are desired, or that would be treated with indifference, are then assumed to affect the average level of dissatisfaction or the utility attached to the goal of changing these rates. But motivation alone is not enough, and the actors will presumably assess the probability of achieving the change at a given cost, with these subjective probabilities being functions of the resources for producing the desired change.

The two variables, utility for change and subjective probability, are assumed to interact multiplicatively in affecting the average degree of effort to produce change. This multiplicative joint effect is represented in the diagram by an arc between the two arrows that join before reaching the box labeled Degree of Effort to Change Behavior Rate. Degree of effort is then assumed to interact multiplicatively with two other variables, efficiency of effort and level of resources, to affect the actual power exerted by these actors in order to change $\bar{Y}$. This latter multiplicative relationship among the three variables is also indicated by an arc between the three arrows that join before reaching the box labeled Power Exerted to Change Behavior Rate. Finally, the actual level of $\bar{Y}$ at the later time $t + 1$ will also be affected by the actions of various other parties, as indicated by the second arrow directed toward $\bar{Y}_{t+1}$. This general type of model will be used quite frequently in later chapters.

The main feature of this model that warrants discussion in the present context is the fact that the party that is reacting to $\bar{Y}$ could be a single individual, an aggregate of unrelated individuals subjected to roughly the same experiences, or a highly organized group with centralized leadership and control. This is what was implied above by the statement that it seems desirable to allow for the possibility that efforts to change rates of behavior or other contextual variables may not necessarily be organized or conceptualized in other than individual terms. It is very likely, of course, that there would in fact be organized efforts on the part of at least some individuals similarly motivated. If so, we would need to elaborate upon the basic model by bringing in organizational-type variables in such a way that the model's main features were unchanged—assuming, of course, that the micro-level model upon which it is based is essentially correct.

For example, certain organizational factors might be causes of some of the variables in the system, whereas others might interact nonadditively with them or be involved in feedback loops of various kinds. Some groups might organize primarily in order to sensitize persons to $\bar{Y}$ levels and might disseminate information in such a way as to distort these perceptions or to influence desired levels. Although isolated individuals might be concerned about these $\bar{Y}$ levels, they might not perceive that they had any chance of modifying them unless there were such an organized effort. Or they might not be aware that others perceived the situation similarly or that they would be willing to pool resources. The nature of groups already formed could affect the efficiency of the effort, perhaps negatively by counteracting each other's efforts or mobilizing the opposition of still other parties. Certain groups could function primarily to increase knowledge and to assess alternative means, whereas others served mainly to stir up emotions. Coalitions among interested groups might or might not be formed. If efforts on a particular scale were not effective (say, on the community level), there might be an attempt to deal with the problem at a more macro level (say, by the federal government).

Ideally, complications such as these can be added to the model in such a way that one can also allow for special cases that are much simpler. This can be done by setting some of the organizational-type variables at zero levels in instances where the actors appear to be only very loosely coordinated. In other words, instances in which it is realistic to ignore "group properties" and to replace them with summarizing measures for statistical aggregates can be treated as special cases of the more general theory that also allows for the operation of organizational variables. Since the model of figure 1.1 does not include organizational variables, we would thus have to take this very simple model as appropriate only for these special cases. A somewhat more complex model might be constructed that treated certain kinds of organizational variable as constants but that allowed for variation in others. In the ideal, we would strive to construct a very general model that subsumed all of these particular variants as special cases. Such a general model would be considerably more complex than any model that contained only simple aggregate variables such as means and proportions.

SOME STEPS IN ANALYZING SOCIAL PROCESSES

Since much of the discussion in the remainder of this work will be rather general and abstract in nature, and illustrated primarily in terms of examples that may not be of special interest to the reader, it may be advisable to approach these materials with one or two very specific examples in mind. To facilitate such an analysis of concrete processes it may be helpful at this point to list a number of specific steps one may follow in attempting to conduct what amounts to an analysis of the kinds of decision-making process with which we will be concerned. Obviously, many steps will need to be carried out more or less simultaneously and with the recognition that revisions will continually be necessary. Nevertheless, it does seem possible to suggest a sequence of steps that parallels rather closely our own table of organization.

1. *Identification of Parties.* The rather obvious first step in any analysis of decision-making processes is that of identifying the relevant parties, but it does not follow that this step is necessarily a simple one. Of course, in one sense it is, if one is willing to consider *all* individual actors as though they were distinct parties. But in complex situations this will obviously be impossible from a practical standpoint, so simplifications become necessary. At this point considerations of homogeneity and degrees of groupness become very relevant. As we have already implied, one may have to aggregate individuals according to the assumptions one is willing to make about their homogeneity—if they are acting more or less as uncoordinated actors—or their group memberships—if they are acting in concert. Furthermore, certain actors will have to be eliminated from consideration through simplifying assumptions to the effect that their behaviors are either irrelevant to the process under consideration or perhaps such that in the aggregate they can be assumed to cancel one another out. The important point is that the theoretical system must be "closed" with respect to number of distinct actors being considered, though it may often be possible to include

a consideration of third and fourth parties that have only rather ill-defined boundaries.

2. *Identification of Outcomes, Goals, and Utilities.* Insofar as is feasible the analyst should attempt to delineate a set of possible outcomes, as these are defined by the actors themselves. Quite often such outcomes will be multi-dimensional when examined from the standpoint of actors' goals. That is, a given outcome may satisfy two or more goals or help satisfy one goal but decrease the probability of achieving another. Goals, in contrast, should be easier to dimensionalize, and we shall provide several illustrations of our own attempts to do so in later chapters. The basic problem in this connection is to suggest lists of goal dimensions that represent the actors' own thinking and at the same time are sufficiently general that the analysis does not degenerate into a description of a unique set of events. It must also be recognized that, because of their complexity, outcomes may be delineated or perceived in different ways by the various parties involved. Therefore it may often prove analytically more useful to develop theories in terms of goal dimensions rather than in terms of typologies of outcomes.

It may also be discovered that one's original delineation of sets of actors results in situations in which individuals who were considered homogeneous with respect to certain characteristics do not have approximately the same utilities or goal hierarchies. In this case it may become necessary to make further distinctions among them and, for certain purposes, to treat them separately. For example, coalition partners will almost certainly have somewhat different interests in the outcome of a power contest against another party, and this divergence may affect their ability to coordinate activities, share knowledge, or combine their resources efficiently. Thus, after having examined lists of possible outcomes and goals, it will undoubtedly be wise to return to the question of the optimal delineation of actors.

At this stage it also makes sense to attempt a preliminary assessment of goal compatibility and the relationship between possible courses of action and the costs they entail, such as the consumption of resources. Compatibility may be examined from several perspectives. For a single actor, goals may be incompatible in the sense of being logically inconsistent (e.g., killing and not killing) or of requiring the expenditure of the same scarce resources. If so, it will become necessary for the actor to resolve the problem in some fashion, whether by redefining the goals, by rationalizing the incompatibilities with the aid of ideological supports, or by obtaining additional resources. There will also be goal incompatibilities between actors, as for example the possibility that actor A's achievement of a given objective implies a reduction in B's chances of also achieving it. Such incompatibilities may or may not be perceived and acted upon by the parties concerned. Especially in the case of retrospective or historical analyses, it becomes crucial for the analyst to distinguish his or her own assumptions and knowledge from those of the actors concerned. An outcome that seems to have been inevitable from the perspective of the historian (who usually lacks or ignores many kinds of information available to the actors) may have been very much in doubt at the time the various parties involved were engaging in interaction or making their decisions.

Obviously, few social scientists will ever be in a position to assess accurately the goals and utilities of the actors being studied, nor will the actors themselves be able to make the kinds of exact calculation that seem to be required under a fully rational decision-making model. One must often make very rough kinds of assessment, perhaps involving a rank ordering of goals with respect to their relative importance or even a more crude categorization into three or four levels, such as "very important," "moderately important," and "negligibly important." Presumably, also, utilities may change in magnitude during the interval being studied, so that the social analyst may find it convenient to distinguish several stages in the process so as to take these changes qualitatively into account.

Our point in this connection is that actors' goals and utilities are often *assumed* in one's analysis, sometimes without the reader's being made aware of this fact. Or they may be stated in such a way that the reader is expected to take them for granted, as, for example, when a historian writes that "the peasants were unhappy over land reforms" or that "King X was hungry for power." One often does not know whether there is independent empirical evidence for such statements or whether the motivations were merely assumed after the fact in order to account for the actor's behaviors in terms of motivations that would be understandable to present-day readers.

3. *Assessment of Subjective Probabilities.* Although social scientists are well aware of the fact that virtually all nontrivial decisions must be made in the face of uncertainty, and although we commonly refer to notions such as expectations, future plans, predictions, misunderstandings, secrecy, and many other ideas connoting uncertainty, we have made remarkably little *systematic* use of probabilities in our formal theories. Of course, it will again be difficult for both the actors themselves and any outside observers to pin down subjective probabilities in very precise terms. In many instances, however, it may be possible to make crude judgments as to whether outcomes are thought to be extremely likely or unlikely, or have an approximately 50-50 chance of occurring. More important, perhaps, are judgments concerning whether or not a given course of action will increase (or decrease) the probability of an outcome's occurring, and if so whether the likelihood is thought to be sufficiently improved that the behavior in question is worth the added cost involved. Does an actor believe that the probability of the outcome is basically unaffected by his or her own actions? Is its occurrence thought to be jointly conditional on the actor's behavior and that of some other party, as for example an exchange partner? Is the action expected to have a boomerang, or backlash, effect by producing negative reactions on the part of other parties?

In stressing that subjective probabilities are important ingredients in actors' decision processes we do not imply that so-called objective factors do not enter into the picture in important ways. It becomes important in this connection to assess not only the (approximate) subjective probabilities held by each actor but also the question of how these are anchored to real-world experiences and objective events. Here the analyst must ask not only how past events have influenced the actors' assessments but also how the future expected behaviors of other parties may affect these estimates. Again, it becomes important to recognize that actors are typically involved with uncertain situations, even though the analyst may in retrospect replace many of these unknowns with assertions as to what, in fact, has actually occurred. One of the important reasons for explicitly emphasizing subjective probabilities is to help the analyst place himself or herself in the position of the actors themselves. In particular, it will be important to learn or at least speculate about the nature of the simplifications the actors make concerning these uncertainties and how these simplifications may be influenced by ideological systems, the degree of familiarity with the other actors, the complexity of the setting, and other environmental factors.

As we shall later indicate, it may also be necessary to take into consideration how utilities may affect subjective probabilities, and vice versa, and how biases in these probability estimates may develop. Ideally, the analyst should attempt to develop a reasonably closed list of goals or outcomes, to which both utilities and subjective probabilities may be attached. Our own models will involve the fundamental assumption that all exogenous variables operate through one or more of these two kinds of intervening variable in the case of all decision-making processes. But both utilities and subjective probabilities may, of course, also be influenced by processes internal to the actor, such as recurrent biological needs and "psychological" factors affecting perceptions, learning processes, and so forth.

4. *Study of Decision Processes.* Actors obviously must put together their various combinations of utilities and subjective probabilities and arrive at some specific course of action (or nonaction). This is usually assumed to involve some sort of maximizing operation, but we shall later note several other possibilities. Whenever there are multiple actors we must anticipate complications in these decision processes, since each actor must attempt to assess the motivational structure of the other actors and may also have a set of utilities that relate directly to these actors. For example, actor A may have as a goal the satisfaction of B's objectives as well as his or her own goals. Or A may wish to injure C but may miscalculate through an ignorance of C's utility structure. When we discuss power relationships we shall see that A's power over B depends upon B's goals and resources, which may, of course, be unknown to A. If coalitions involving third parties are being considered, calculations become even more difficult and the need for simplifications more pressing. As we have already noted, it therefore becomes important to study the ways in which these simplifications are made in the process of arriving at concrete decisions.

5. *Assessment of the Most Important Kinds of Interaction Process.* There will be many different kinds of interaction pattern that take place among actors,

only some of which are discussed in the present work. An investigator may choose to select only one or two of these—for example, power and exchange—as the paramount processes, while relegating the remaining ones to a minor position in the overall account. Here the intellectual biases of the social scientist may be such as to give the reader a very one-sided impression of the picture by playing up one or another process as being much more fundamental than the others. In particular, conflict-oriented scholars may, by emphasizing power and the divergence of interests among parties, give a basically different flavor to the account than those who tend to emphasize consensus and exchange.

As we shall note in several places, nearly all instances of human interaction involve a number of processes simultaneously. Yet this does not imply that all are equally important under all circumstances. Indeed, one of our most important theoretical tasks is that of discovering the conditions under which exchange, equity, power, allocation, and approach–withdrawal processes are most likely to predominate over other processes. Obviously the mix of actors' goals, resources, and situational constraints will in part determine which of these processes are primary and which secondary in any given instance. If actor A has an excess of something B wants, and vice versa, we may expect an exchange to occur, with the rate of exchange being affected by the distribution of power as well as their respective utilities. But where there is an extreme asymmetry with respect to resource distribution, the exchange may be such as to be considered a highly exploitative one. Whether or not this leads to overt conflict will again depend upon a number of additional factors, including the roles played by interested third parties.

This step in the analysis obviously constitutes the core, or central focus, of our own attention, but it is highly dependent upon the assumptions made in each of the preceding steps. In our own treatment of several admittedly selected processes, we have tried to be evenhanded, at least in the sense of not implying that any one process is more fundamental than the others. But although this may be true in general, it does not follow that in various special cases it will be wise to pay equal attention to each. In fact, we have ourselves selected only those processes we believe to be most relevant for the study of intergroup relations as typified by racial and ethnic group relations. We have also submerged our discussions of concepts such as exploitation and conflict under the headings of equity and power respectively. Perhaps the most we can hope for, then, is that social scientists will be alerted to the desirability of at least *examining* a number of distinct processes and then selecting among them according to the nature of the interaction that is being analyzed.

6. *Search for Exogenous Variables.* Our own very general discussions of social processes involve a certain number of independent, or exogenous, variables, but we have found that it is difficult to locate exogenous variables with a sufficient degree of generality to include in many of our models. Presumably, in more specific settings it will be easier to identify more complete lists of exogenous variables and to relate these in less ambiguous ways to the endogenous variables of the type that are more likely to be included in our own

models. We believe that this search will be aided and made more systematic to the degree that intervening variables can be explicitly identified, even in instances where the latter variables remain unmeasured.

It seems especially characteristic of macro-level studies that individual actors, and their motives and expectations, are either treated as interchangeable or ignored altogether. In the absence of individual-level data, this does no special harm in connection with *tests* of the theory, once it has been developed and refined. But in *locating* the appropriate macro-level exogenous variables and in specifying how and why they are interrelated, we believe it will be helpful to apply the kind of micro–macro analysis attempted in the present volume. This will, of course, mean that there will be unmeasured variables in one's model. But especially in models where these are variables that intervene between macro-level contextual variables and actors' response rates, it will still be possible to bypass them in our actual tests, while taking advantage of them to help us refine our predictions and conduct a more fruitful search for additional explanatory variables that can be measured at this macro level.

7. *Formulation of Dynamic Models.* Whenever the analyst can observe one actor responding to others, and can follow sequences of such actions and responses over time, it becomes relatively simple to represent such processes in a dynamic model in which time plays an important role. That is, one can assess not only the temporal sequences but also the duration of lag periods, possible cyclical patternings that may either explode or dampen, and perhaps even extrapolate these patterns into the future. Whenever such time-series data are missing, or whenever nearly every variable is undergoing continuous change, it becomes much more difficult to sort out causes and effects and even to formulate a dynamic model that contains estimable parameters. Put another way, one may discover that there are a great many possible dynamic formulations all of which imply the same equilibrium results, so that it becomes impossible to choose among them unless data have been collected in a very special manner. Given the fact that in most instances there will be measurement errors superimposed on what are called specification errors in the theoretical models, the situation may seem empirically hopeless.

Nevertheless, there may be some situations in which it is possible to test the adequacy of alternative dynamic models, or at least make choices among those that also seem theoretically plausible. To the degree that one can observe actors actually responding to one another, in sequence, the situation indeed seems reasonably hopeful—perhaps much more so than in the case of totally macro-level models in which everything is changing more or less simultaneously. In any event, it seems desirable to attempt to formulate dynamic models whenever feasible. On the simplest level, we may certainly take present behaviors, utilities, and subjective probabilities as functions of past levels of other variables, with these behaviors in turn affecting the future levels and behaviors of other parties. Refinements may then become possible, as, for example, those that link behaviors to events or patterns of events that have occurred in the more remote past or those that specify something about differential rates of change.

AN OVERVIEW OF THE VOLUME

The three chapters in part 1 are concerned with presenting a micro-level framework based on the very extensive literature on the subjective expected utility (*SEU*) approach stemming largely from psychology and to a lesser extent economics. Since sociologists do not appear to have made much use of this literature it will be necessary to discuss a number of specific empirical issues, as well as points of agreement and disagreement, to a much greater extent than will be required or possible in later chapters. Given our objective of concentrating primarily on theoretical and methodological problems and constructing tentative causal models of a number of social processes, it will obviously be impossible to go into detail concerning empirical findings, but in these early chapters we have felt it more important to do so. This is not only because we assume that sociologists are less familiar with this literature but also because the empirical studies in this area appear to be relatively more closely interlinked and therefore more likely to provide the basis for a cumulative body of knowledge. At the same time, however, they tend to be highly constricted in terms of their coming to grips with problems that arise in complex settings outside the laboratory of the social experimenter.

Our aim, of course, is to attempt to extend the utility of this approach as an explanatory tool for studying the kinds of social process that are of interest to macro-level social scientists. A "pure" macro-level theory, we presume, would deal only with variables that pertain to macro units and would never dip down as it were, to the level of individual decision making. For example, the macro sociologist might study the relationship of organizational size to the ratio of administrators to production personnel or to the number of hierarchical levels within these organizations. Or the macro-level student of national development might study the relationships among technology, energy consumption, the system of production and distribution of goods and services, the nature of the political system, and so forth.

In parts 2 and 3 we move to discussions of selected social processes that are of special interest to students of intergroup relations in general, and race and ethnic relations in particular. Part 2 is concerned with exchange relationships and inequity and with power confrontations between groups and individuals. Our discussions of exchange and equity theory involve a direct extension of the subjective expected utility approach treated in part 1. When we turn to power confrontations and to allocation and discrimination and to approach–withdrawal processes as discussed in part 3, we shall find it necessary to introduce a very large number of complications, and therefore we have inserted a more methodologically oriented chapter on contextual effects (chapter 7) prior to the chapters on power, allocation and discrimination, and approach and withdrawal.

Thus as the reader progresses through the book he or she will notice a number of changes in style and manner of presentation. In some chapters our references to the empirical and theoretical literatures will become more uneven because of gaps in our knowledge and a lack of supporting data. Throughout the book there will be a heavy emphasis on problems of conceptualization and measurement, and in certain places, as, for example, in the case of the measurement of discrimination, we shall dwell on questions of measurement in some detail because they appear to constitute the crux of the theoretical problem at issue. In these and other instances we shall see that a careful look at what appears to be a simple measurement problem actually leads to a rather involved causal model of a highly complicated social process.

Throughout the book we tend to select our illustrations from the field of race and ethnic relations, but since the arguments in parts 1 and 2 are intended to be much more general, these examples are introduced primarily for the purpose of clarification or to anchor the discussion to empirical reality. As we move from part 2, involving highly general discussions of exchange and power, to part 3, which deals more specifically with processes of immediate interest to students of race and ethnic relations, it will become necessary to give our discussion a more narrow focus. Nevertheless, we have attempted to state our arguments in such a way that they will have greater applicability. Thus, although our primary focus in the first half of part 3 is on the notion of discrimination, we have attempted to draw parallels with more general allocation processes in which an actor allocates rewards and punishments to two or more other actors on the basis of a number of different kinds of criterion. Likewise, our principal concern in the final chapters of part 3 is with the processes of segregation and integration, but we shall see that these processes can also be seen as special cases of more general approach-withdrawal processes.

Finally, in the single chapter of part 4 we focus very explicitly on the construction of macro-level dynamic models capable of explaining change processes. We illustrate the issues in terms of changes in the levels of segregation, as well as the mechanisms by which segregation may feed upon itself to inhibit changes. But our intent is also to outline a much more general strategy for conceptualizing macro-level processes and for formulating specific dynamic models representing these change processes.

Thus throughout the book we move back and forth along several dimensions: (1) micro versus macro, (2) general versus specific, (3) methodological versus substantive, and (4) static versus dynamic. Our methodological discussions will be interspersed whenever they seem most appropriate. Otherwise, the usual order of presentation will be from micro to macro, from the general to the more specific, and from static formulations to dynamic ones. However, we have not always found it possible to adhere to this order of presentation—since the issues we shall encounter are clearly multidimensional—and we therefore beg the reader's indulgence.

Even though this book is very long, it does not include a number of topics that we believe could also be handled in terms of the general approach we are recommending. These include processes such as socialization and attitude formation, conflict resolution, coalition formation, negotiation (e.g., Strauss 1978), and attribution. We have also not attempted to deal with the various strictly macro-oriented race and ethnic relations literatures involving such matters as cultural pluralism, acculturation and assimilation, colonialism and neocolonialism, economic exploitation, or what used to be referred to as the field of race and culture contacts. Thus, our own effort should be viewed as complementary to more macro and comparative works such as those of Mason (1970), Schermerhorn (1970), or van den Berghe (1967).

It is our major purpose to highlight difficult issues, to indicate the ways in which complexities of many kinds enter into both our theories and our research, and to suggest ways in which we believe these problems can be attacked in a systematic fashion. We have attempted to do this by actually committing ourselves on a number of reasonably specific concepts, propositions, and causal models of complex social processes. We hope that the same basic frameworks can be applied to other processes that we have been unable to examine.

Our primary aim is not so much that of presenting models or theories that are themselves adequate to explaining this complex reality. Instead, our purpose is mainly that of serving as catalytic agents in posing a set of questions and suggesting some tentative resolutions that will stimulate the development of theories capable of mounting a cumulative effort to put together the pieces of a gigantic puzzle. Many others have made similar efforts, and we are merely attempting to build upon these works in what we hope will be a fruitful manner. The message we wish to convey is that the overall effort is not only worthwhile but also absolutely essential and not entirely a utopian dream.

NOTES

1. Although there is now a rather extensive literature and debate on the subject of contextual effects, the kinds of model usually discussed contain only simple means and proportions to represent these contextual effects. See Blau (1960), Davis, Spaeth, and Huson (1961), Tannenbaum and Bachman (1964); Campbell and Alexander (1965); Valkonen (1969), Farkas (1974); Hauser (1974); and Przeworski (1974). Many of these models will be discussed in chapter 7.
2. In this respect our orientation is similar to the very general approach referred to by Parsons (1949) as the "voluntaristic theory of action." Our concern, however, will be to bring this kind of orientation much closer to the operational level than is exhibited in the work of Parsons.
3. These assumptions will usually be violated if the micro-level equation contains any contextual-effect terms and/or if individuals have been aggregated by spatial criteria such as county or SMSA. See Blalock (1971), Hannan (1971), and Irwin and Lichtman (1976).

PART ONE

Micro-level Processes: The Subjective Expected Utility Approach

CHAPTER 2

The Significance of Utilities
for Intergroup Processes

IN OUR INTRODUCTORY REMARKS we noted that our strategy in this volume will be to move from a detailed consideration of individual behavior to an analysis of the major processes characterizing interaction among a variety of more or less structured aggregates of individuals, that is, from the micro to the macro level. In the three chapters of part 1 we discuss the components of a micro-level model of individual behavior. This chapter is devoted to a study of the significance of utilities, or the subjective values held by human actors, for their behavior. In chapter 3 we present a comparably detailed description of the part played by actors' subjective probabilities, or their expectations regarding the consequences of their behavior. Chapter 4 combines these two basic components of our micro-level model and describes the decision strategies used by actors in making behavioral choices.

Development of an adequate micro-level theory of behavior is obviously a valid objective in its own right. However, achievement of this objective is of secondary concern to us. Our primary concern is with the development of a model of individual behavior that can provide the theoretical underpinnings for models of macro-level processes, which all too often fail to pay heed to the actions of the individual actors who make up the groups or aggregates that are included in such models. We are not advocating psychological reductionism in the sense that processes involving aggregates of individuals can be explained *solely* by individual behaviors. But we clearly are advocating a place in macro-level theories for variables that have generally been considered the province of micro-level models.

Our basic premise is that micro- and macro-level theories *each* need to make some provision for variables located at the other level. Many of the influences that impinge upon the individual actor involve macro-level groups or aggregates. One needs only to mention such common sociological concepts as norms, sanctions, subculture, and reference group to validate that assertion. Therefore a micro-level model that does not take into account the ways in which influences from the macro level affect behavioral choices at the micro level will only be a partial theory. In this and the following chapter we shall describe how these macro-level influences are transmitted to individual actors via their utilities and subjective probabilities.

Requirements for a Micro-level Model

The micro-level model we present in this and the next two chapters was designed with three basic questions in mind. These are the questions that we feel a micro-level model should answer at minimum. The first involves the basic issue of choice: why does an actor in a given situation choose one course of action rather than another? Why, for example, do individuals choose to become butchers, bakers, or candlestick makers? The second concerns a closely related issue, that of persistence in an action or, conversely, that of change to an alternate action. Why does an actor continue to enact a particular behavior instead of switching to a different behavior, or why does another actor make that change? One may be puzzled, for example, by the tendency of some actors to continue following a course of action despite its apparent lack of rewards. The third issue is somewhat more difficult to handle and pertains to the intensity of an actor's action: why does a given actor pursue a particular action with a high degree of intensity while another actor enacts it much less intensively? If persistence in an action is measured by the length of time an actor devotes to an activity, then intensity can be conceptualized in terms of the amount of energy, or perhaps the proportion of his or her resources, that an actor devotes to the action throughout its duration or per unit of time. Professors are often perplexed by the great variance in the intensity of studying on the part of their students, for example.

As we shall show, these questions are answered in our micro-level model by means of our three major components: utilities, subjective probabilities, and decision strategies.

The micro-level models that have been developed to provide answers to these three questions as well as other related questions can be separated into two categories, sometimes designated as behavioral and cognitive. Coleman (1973) has used the terms *causal process* and *purposive action* to refer to these two categories of models respectively. Causal process models, exemplified by current operant or stimulus-response models, tend to portray actors as relatively powerless conduits for stimuli bombarding them and responses emanating from them. Depending upon the version of this general approach to which one subscribes, the cognitive processes that occur within actors as they interpret these stimuli and formulate responses are regarded as either unmeasurable or irrelevant for explaining their behavior.

In purposive action models actors are not seen merely as conduits but as synthesizers of information and devisers of responses. Whether or not the cognitive processes that intervene between the reception of information and the enactment of behaviors are regarded as merely correlative with undiscovered underlying neurological processes (Atkinson and Birch 1970) or as a significant causal force, advocates of this approach argue that they should be taken into account in explaining behaviors and that they provide at the very least valuable clues regarding actors' responses. Many behaviorists would no doubt admit that they are aware of the occurrence of such cognitive processes within themselves. The major difference between the two approaches, therefore, can be seen to reside in the relative importance given to cognitive processes. Whereas causal process models acknowledge them and simultaneously ignore them, purposive action theories make explicit provision for them as an intervening link between prior conditions and subsequent behaviors.

The reader will have undoubtedly guessed by this point that our micro-level model lies far closer to the group of purposive action theories than it does to causal process theories. Utilities and subjective probabilities are obviously cognitive phenomena. We have several reasons for adopting this approach in the face of apparent increasing interest among some social scientists in causal process models.

First, as we shall show at several places in this volume, a consideration of internal states is necessary for an adequate conceptualization of many general sociological concepts. Most conceptualizations of discrimination, for example, include assumptions about individuals' motivations at least implicitly if not explicitly.

Second, even if internal states are excluded from conceptualizations, one often confronts the need to consider them when determining the most satisfactory way to operationalize a concept. We shall show, for instance, that measurements of physical segregation of groups or collectivities involve assumptions regarding the utilities and subjective probabilities of the parties involved. In many cases these assumptions may not reach the investigator's level of consciousness. We prefer to make these assumptions explicit rather than to ignore them.

Third, internal-state variables cannot be safely excluded from causal models of intergroup processes. They may ultimately constitute unmeasured variables in these models, but their inclusion is nevertheless necessary in order to enable one to explain processes that have different underlying individual dynamics despite their apparent outward aggregate similarities. Causal models of power processes clearly exemplify the need for including the internal-state variables.

Assumptions of Our Micro-level Model

In addition, purposive action models are based upon assumptions regarding human behavior that we find more congenial than the assumptions underlying causal process models. These assumptions can be specified as follows:

First, we see human beings basically as goal-seeking animals. The goals they seek are ultimately translatable into reinforcement or reward–punishment terminology no doubt, but too limited a focus on reinforcement levels obscures the vast multiplicity of consequences that humans may seek.

Second, we assume that humans prefer some goals to other goals. Which goals they prefer is also undoubtedly a function of their relative rewards and punishments, but knowing that alone does not enable us to predict very precisely what their behaviors are likely to be without a great deal of additional information about their perceptions of the relative reward and punishment potentials of alternative actions.

Third, we further assume that humans are able to anticipate the consequences of their actions. The vast majority of this foreknowledge is a result of learning, as causal process models emphasize, but we also allow for the possibility that humans, with their vastly superior mental faculties compared to other animals, are able to anticipate the consequences of their actions in situations in which they have not acted before as well as the consequences of actions they have not enacted previously.

Fourth, we also assume that humans *direct* their behaviors toward their preferred anticipated consequences. It is in this sense that our model assumes human rationality. Behavior that some outside observers might describe as irrational or nonrational we prefer to regard as rational. Actions may appear irrational at times simply because outside observers are not aware of the totality of consequences that individuals may be anticipating from their behavior or because the consequences they are anticipating may not appear as possible consequences to outside observers. The important point is that it is the consequences anticipated by actors that influence their behaviors, even though an outsider may see no way in which a particular consequence can follow from a given behavior. Perhaps a variant of the self-fulfilling prophecy expresses this point succinctly: "if consequences are believed to result, they will have consequences for behavior."

Lastly, we assume that humans are able to create innovative behaviors that are aimed toward the consequences they desire. Causal process models typically allow for this possibility by emphasizing imitation of models and vicarious learning in addition to "learning by doing." We include these possibilities under this assumption, but we also believe it is possible for humans to create totally new behaviors that are not dependent upon observation of others. Human evolutionary history provides ample evidence of substantial behavioral innovation in our opinion. So does the birth of fads, such as the selling of pet rocks. This last assumption perhaps carries us farthest from a strictly behaviorist point of view.

Thus the crux of our assumptions regarding human behavior is that it is oriented to its anticipated preferred consequences. The causal process theories of behavior have maintained that the appropriate way to determine these preferred consequences is by studying the reinforcement histories of actors. Behaviors that have resulted in rewarding consequences in the past will be preferred in the future, assuming that these consequences will be repeated in the future and an actor is not satiated with them. This approach therefore would require complete reinforcement histories of actors to explain and predict their behavior adequately. That is a virtually impossible task, unless one concentrates on very simple behaviors.

The purposive action models have looked to actors' evaluations of their preferred consequences and their perceptions of the linkages between their actions and those consequences. To utilize this approach in order to explain and predict their behavior it is therefore necessary to have a complete accounting of the consequences they prefer and the actions they believe will lead to those consequences. This may also appear to be a hopeless task, but we do not feel that it is as hopeless as it may appear at first glance, nor do we feel that its potential has been fully explored.

We are not claiming that this approach is a simple and problem-free one. As we shall see presently, determination of the utilities and subjective probabilities operative for individuals in a decision situation becomes quite complex rather quickly. We believe that the individuals who are making choices among behaviors solve this problem by introducing various simplifications. Therefore, the investigator using this approach must also leave room for these simplifications in his or her model, and later in this chapter we shall discuss several major types of cognitive simplification. Serious measurement problems with this approach are discussed in this chapter as well.

A major asset of this approach, however, is the fact that it is possible in most cases for humans to *communicate* their preferences and the consequences they anticipate. Thus the researcher is not restricted to the indirect measurement procedures one must use with animals unable to verbalize. As we shall argue later in this volume, we believe there is room for substantial expansion of methodologies that measure cognitive variables, such as utilities and subjective probabilities.

We also believe that a major reason that existing procedures to measure such cognitive variables have appeared inadequate is that they have been used with inadequate information. We shall emphasize repeatedly throughout this volume that human behavior is extremely complex and that it is foolish to expect accurate measures and predictions to follow from simplistic theoretical models and methodologies. At any point in time actors are considering a variety of goals and a multiplicity of alternatives to attain those goals. Omitting most of these, by restricting attention to simple two-alternative models, as is done both theoretically and methodologically, may guarantee quite accurate predictions in the types of unrealistic situation generally devised for laboratory experiments. But it is difficult to see that it will lead to very accurate predictions in real-life situations outside the laboratory. It appears far more desirable to develop models capable of handling the complexities of behavior, and *then* to make appropriate simplifying assumptions in order to test them. If one stays at a very simple level, then one will have no way of knowing whether crucial variables have been neglected.

Laboratory procedures and too simple behavioral models are also often unable to deal with the fact that actors' utilities and subjective probabilities are likely to change over time. Complex models will be necessary to account for the processes underlying such changes, and, despite the serious measurement problems involved, it may be possible to measure these changes only by means of nonlaboratory procedures.

THE SUBJECTIVE EXPECTED UTILITY MODEL

The subjective expected utility approach has been a major paradigm among the purposive action micro-level models of behavior (Edwards 1961; Davidson, Suppes, and Siegel 1957; Luce and Suppes 1965; Becker and McClintock 1967; Siegel, Siegel, and Andrews 1964). Although there are several variations of the approach, the basic idea of the model is that actors take into account two main aspects of their behavior: the subjective value, or utility, of the consequences of their behavior and the likelihood, or the subjective probability, that a given consequence will result from a given behavior. These two elements are combined to yield a subjective expected utility for a behavioral alternative, or an indicator of the amount of utility they expect to achieve from enacting that alternative. Thus, if members of a group consistently withdraw from contact with members of another group, the inference to be made is that the subjective expected utility of contact with the latter group has a different subjective expected utility than noncontact for the former group. In most instances the inference would be that the subjective expected utility of the chosen behavior is greater than that of the alternative that is not chosen. We shall not make so precise an inference at this point, but we shall discuss it and other possibilities in more detail as we examine our model more closely.

The subjective expected utility model can be simply depicted as follows:

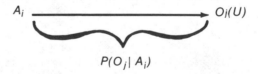

$$A_i \longrightarrow O_j(U)$$
$$P(O_j| A_i)$$

This indicates that an actor believes that a behavioral alternative, A_i, is likely to lead to an outcome, O_j, with utility, U. The likelihood of O_j happening if A_i is enacted is represented by the probability $P(O_j|A_i)$.

We assume that at any point in time actors are considering at least two behavioral alternatives, only one of which we have depicted. At the very least they are considering whether to continue the action they are engaged in or to switch to a different activity. Each alternative will be judged to lead to some outcome; in most cases an alternative will lead to more than one outcome, but for simplicity we have included only one outcome in the diagram. Outcomes will have some utility for actors, depending upon the degree to which they desire them or wish to avoid them. And actors will also have subjective expectations of the probability that the alternatives they are considering will yield those outcomes.

According to the model, the subjective expected utility of an *alternative* will be the *product* of the utility of the outcomes believed to result from the alternative and the subjective probabilities of those outcomes' occurring. Thus a behavioral alternative will have high subjective expected utility only if utilities and probabilities are both relatively large. If an outcome is not highly valued even though an actor believes that it is likely to result from a given alternative, or if the actor believes that an alternative has a low probability of bringing about an outcome that is highly valued, then the subjective expected utility of that alternative will not be very great.

An example will help to clarify the model. Let us assume that a white employer is considering hiring a black job candidate. An outcome the employer is no doubt desirous of obtaining is an employee who will be a productive member of the work force. Therefore the employer will assign a subjective value, or utility, to that outcome. He or she will also have an expectation regarding the likelihood that hiring the black applicant will bring about that outcome. According to the model, hiring the black applicant will have a high subjective expected utility for the employer only if obtaining a productive worker has high utility and if he or she thinks it quite likely that the black applicant will be that kind of worker. In this case the subjective probability is in all likelihood the crucial value, since it is our assumption here that the designated outcome will have high utility. So if the employer places a low probability on the black's being productive, then it is likely that hiring a black applicant will have lower subjective expected utility than another alternative, such as hiring a white applicant.

We have presented only the most elementary situation here to illustrate the model. The complexity of social life does make things more difficult for the model. At any point in time actors are very likely considering several behavioral alternatives that they expect to yield a variety of consequences. In the case of employers, we could consider hiring and not hiring each individual applicant as two behavioral alternatives; thus employers would be confronted by twice as many alternatives as applicants. In this case also it is doubtful that the only outcome of interest to employers would be that the workers they hired were productive. They would likely also want them to relate well with their fellow workers and not have high rates of absenteeism.

This complexity can be described as involving the consideration by actors of multiple *alternatives* that lead to multiple *outcomes* that have multiple *dimensions*. Thus it is necessary to break down the subjective expected utility model into its basic components and examine them closely. The other side of the coin, however, is that the complexity of the model increases its potential for explaining diverse behaviors, even though simplifying assumptions may be necessary. Thus we believe that the model has great promise as a basic micro-level model. We shall first examine the component of the utility of an outcome in detail.

Utility of an Outcome

The concept of utility has had a long and torturous history at the hands of economists and psychologists. Much ink has been devoted to the explication and analysis of this deceptively simple concept. The early economists discovered that the economic choices of people did not correspond with the objective values, as measured by money, of the outcomes they achieved as a result of those choices. The classic Bernoulli paradox illustrated, for example, that ship owners purchased insurance even though they lost money in the long run by doing so (Edwards 1962b). Thus the conclusion the economists reached was that there was not a one-to-one correspondence between objective economic values and the subjective values people assigned to outcomes. In the case of the ship owners the security provided by the insurance they purchased had a value for them that surpassed the value they lost through the payment of premiums. *Utility* was the term they assigned to this subjective value that did not necessarily correspond with objective economic value.

It is understandable, although somewhat unfortunate from our viewpoint, that economists were the first to deal systematically with this problem. The result has been that *utility* has been used to refer to a phenomenon that, to our sociological eyes at least, is simply subjective value.[1] Furthermore, in dealing with economic values it is meaningful to make a distinction between subjective and objective values of a medium such as money, which can be measured very accurately in terms of the goods and services for which it can be exchanged. But in dealing with social commodities, such as status, approval, and liking, the objective–subjective distinction is less meaningful. These commodities become media that are bartered, so to speak, in social interaction, and it is difficult to conceive of an objective rate of exchange. Instead it is the subjective values that are assigned to them by individuals that determine such exchange rates. So we would prefer to label our micro-level model as a subjective expected value model, but the weight of precedent of the utility terminology is sufficiently great to dissuade us.

Values and Utilities

Among sociologists the concept of value has corresponded roughly to the concept of utility as used by economists. But sociologically the value term has been used for at least two different purposes, and precise definitions have not always been provided for it. Some writers refer to values essentially as the goals that a person desires (Rokeach 1973). Thus if a person is said to value friendship, this can be translated into goal terminology by saying that the goal is to attain friendship. The term has also been widely used at the macro level to refer to cultural phenomena. Thus Williams (1960) and others have described the values of American culture. In this context the term has become imbued with normative connotations. Values are not seen simply as the aggregated goals of individuals, but by virtue of their universality or by virtue of the social identity of the actors who hold them—for example, a ruling class—they become viewed as goals that all actors *should* desire. An important sociological issue therefore is the extent to which the values of individuals correspond to or differ from these cultural values. Our use of the term *utility* to refer to subjective value introduces yet a third sense of the term. In our usage, *value* refers to the *degree* to which something is desired, or what might be called the value of a value in the first case described above.

This confusion may be allayed by noting that utility can be applied to two different phenomena: outcomes and alternatives. The utility of an outcome is simply the subjective value of that outcome to an individual. As we shall see, the *amount* of utility of an outcome will be determined by goal-related variables. Hence if goals are considered values, and outcomes are considered goals, then the value of an outcome will be a value of a value. A behavioral alternative can also be regarded as having utility because of the outcome(s) that result from it. Under conditions of certainty, where the alternative always leads to the outcome, one might refer to the utilities of the alternative and the outcome synonymously. However, under conditions of uncertainty or risk it is necessary to refer to the *expected* utility of the alternative. And if one is concerned with an individual's belief in the likelihood of the outcome, i.e., the subjective probability of the outcome rather than its objective probability, then one must refer to the *subjective expected utility* of the alternative. In all these cases, though, utility means subjective value.

Goals and Utilities

We are assuming that humans are goal seekers, and we define goals approximately as many sociologists have defined values; that is, a goal is simply a desired state of affairs. Actors will have a repertoire of goals, some of which will be uniquely theirs and some of which will be shared with others in their particular sociocultural setting. We also assume that these goals are not of equal weight for actors, but that they prefer some of them to others. Depending upon their generality, over time some goals will retain quite constant levels of preference whereas others will fluctuate in importance.

We further assume that individuals' actions are goal oriented; i.e., individuals direct their behavior toward their goals. Thus their behavior is not random but constitutes means to the goals they desire. To these assumptions we now add another, namely, that the outcomes of behaviors will be judged by individuals in terms of their goals. These outcomes will be valuable to the extent that they bring them closer to the goals they deem important or take them farther from the negative goals they wish to avoid. Thus the utility of an outcome is derived from the outcome's relationship to an individual's goals.

This relationship between utilities and goals can be represented as

$$U(O_j) = u_{j1} + u_{j2} + u_{j3} + \cdots + u_{jn}.$$

$U(O_j)$ represents the total utility of an outcome, O_j. Total utility consists of some combination of individual utilities, the u_{jk}, where the k's refer to the goals the actor believes are affected by the outcome. Thus the u_{jk} can be interpreted as the utilities of the outcome for these goals, and the total utility of the outcome is derived from all the goals on which it has an impact. We will soon look more closely at the determinants of the u_{jk} and how they may be combined to yield the total utility of an outcome. What we have presented here can also be seen as an example of multidimensional utilities, exemplifying the situation in which an outcome has relevance for more than one goal or dimension. If a given outcome affects only one goal, then we have $U(O_j) = u_{jk}$, the unidimensional case.

The subjective expected utility of an alternative thus can be represented by

$$SEU(A_i) = \sum_{j=1}^{n} P(O_j|A_i) \times U(O_j).$$

The *total* subjective expected utility of alternative A_i will depend on all the O_j that are believed to result from A_i and their respective subjective probabilities.

If it were possible to derive from individuals the utilities that they assign to outcomes as well as a comprehensive listing of the outcomes they anticipate from their actions, it would not be necessary to bring in their goals. One could simply plug the outcomes and their utilities and the actor's subjective probabilities into the model and test it. However, in many instances this may not be possible, so it may become necessary to infer these utilities from other variables. We suspect that this is the situation one is likely to confront in the construction of macro theories of complex social processes.

In such a situation it will be necessary to predict actors' utilities from their determinants, and this will further necessitate a consideration of their goals, as we have noted. This, too, will be complex for the outside observer because of the similarity of outcomes and goals. One might distinguish between outcomes that constitute goals and outcomes that lead to goals. Some psychologists have distinguished between consummatory and instrumental goals to refer to these two cases respectively, and this distinction might be adopted (Atkinson and Birch 1970). But since it is the individual actor's perception of the relationship between outcomes and goals that is of significance for the model, it hardly seems possible to test the model without some measures of the perceptual "causal models" or "working theories" used by individual actors.

Most attempts to determine actors' utilities for outcomes have used effect measures, in which the utilities are deduced from the actual choices actors make. These utilities are then applied to different situations under the assumption that they have not changed in the interim. Here we are suggesting that it may also be feasible to measure utilities by means of cause indicators, that is, by means of their determinants. These determinants are intimately related to actors' goals. In the next section we analyze how the relationships of outcomes to goals determine the utilities of outcomes.

DETERMINANTS OF UTILITIES

An outcome's utility essentially depends upon the goal or goals it fulfills and the extent to which it fulfills that goal or those goals. In our discussion we shall assume that an outcome fulfills only one goal; outcomes that fulfill multiple goals will follow the same principles but will present much more complex situations. We also assume that all goals can be represented as continuua. Some goals will have more clearly demarcated points marking different degrees of goal fulfillment than will other goals. For example, if we regard getting an education as a goal, then graduation from high school and graduation from college represent degrees of goal fulfillment that are much more distinctive than the numerous gradations into which a goal such as making money can be divided. Nevertheless, both of these goals may be heuristically viewed as continuous. Our goal terminology therefore will differ somewhat from the manner in which people often refer to goals. A person may say, for example, that his or her goal is to receive a college education or to make a million dollars, a manner of speaking that imparts discreteness to the outcome being referred to. In our terminology a college education or a million dollars are considered outcomes that provide the individual with some degree of goal fulfillment on a more general goal or very likely on several goals.

The relationships among outcomes desired by actors may become quite complex. The successful completion of a college course may be considered an outcome that provides a degree of goal fulfillment for the goal of obtaining a college education. In turn, passing the midterm exam in a course may be seen as an outcome that facilitates the outcome of successfully completing the course. Distinguishing which outcomes constitute goals and which constitute means to those goals is an endemic problem in means–ends analyses. We believe the most satisfactory way to resolve this problem is to visualize actors as having a limited number of quite general goals, which, as we shall discuss presently, can be ranked into hierarchies. They will be estimating the utilities of a large number of outcomes, however, that will very likely provide fulfillment for more than one of these goals.

An additional assumption we make is that all goals may be considered as positive. Getting an education and making money are clearly positive goals in the sense that they describe states of affairs that actors desire to achieve. However, humans also orient their behavior toward undesirable states of affairs that they wish to avoid. Rather than treating such goals as somehow different from positive goals, we will also regard them as positive. Thus actor A may be desirous of intimacy in a relationship with another, whereas actor B may wish to avoid such relationships. These two opposite possibilities may both be represented as positive goals and the degree of goal fulfillment achieved by the two actors determined by the extent to which they achieve their respective objectives. Obviously what will constitute goal fulfillment for A will constitute a lack of goal fulfillment for B.

The crux of our approach is the assumption that actors have different utility curves, relating goal fulfillment and utility, for their different goals. Therefore the utility of an outcome can be represented by means of such curves, specifically in terms of segments of the curves. Actors will estimate the utilities of outcomes on the basis of their positions on utility curves at specific points in time—hence they will essentially be making decisions regarding the relative marginal utilities of different outcomes.

The marginal utility of an outcome will be determined basically by two factors: the amount of utility per unit of goal fulfillment for a given goal and the number of units of goal fulfillment on that goal provided by the outcome. We shall refer to these as the goal importance (GI) and degree of goal fulfillment (DGF) determinants respectively. The outcome providing the largest number of units of goal fulfillment on the goal that yields the largest amount of utility per unit of goal fulfillment will have the greatest marginal utility. Thus, $U = GI \times DGF$.

Three other factors will be significant determinants of the utility of an outcome as well, through their influence on the GI and DGF determinants. An actor's current level of goal fulfillment ($CLGF$), or the point at which he or she is on a particular utility curve at the time he or she is estimating the marginal utility of an outcome, will determine the segment of the utility curve that the outcome encompasses. This will be significant because we anticipate important nonlinearities in utility curves. An actor's desired level of goal fulfillment ($DLGF$) represents the region of the utility curve at which decreasing marginal utility occurs as the result of satiation effects. And the temporal immediacy of goal fulfillment (IGF) offered by the outcome has an independent effect on the utility of the outcome resulting in a diminution of utility for outcomes that are postponed. It may also affect goal importance and the degree of goal fulfillment, but we do not include that stipulation in the model.

Figure 2.1 represents the relationship among these five determinants of the marginal utility of an outcome. As in the previous chapter (see figure 1.1) and in succeeding chapters, the nonadditive effects of variables in figure 2.1 (the effects of DGF and GI on $U(O_j)$) are represented by arrows that are joined into a single arrow before reaching a box. We shall look at the influence of each of these determinants in detail.

Degree of Goal Fulfillment

The utility curve for a specific goal essentially represents the relationship between different degrees of goal fulfillment for that goal and the amount of utility yielded by them. Generally the greater the degree of goal fulfillment provided by an outcome, the greater will be the utility of that outcome, as shown in figure 2.2, in which the segment OB of the horizontal axis represents an outcome providing a greater degree of goal fulfillment and hence greater utility than the outcome represented by the segment OA. We assume that for all goals zero degrees of goal fulfillment equals zero utility.

**Figure 2.1. Relationship among the Determinants
of the Marginal Utility of an Outcome**

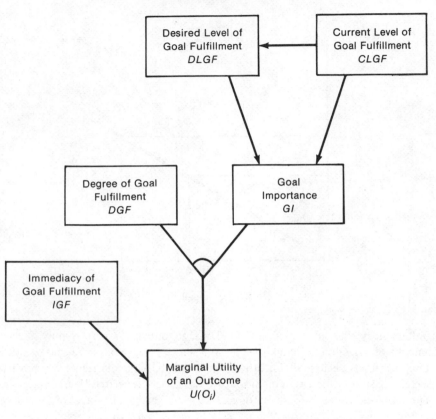

Figure 2.2 represents a linear relationship between *DGF* and utility. It is probable, however, that utility curves are characterized by significant nonlinearities. These occur most likely at either end of the utility curve. At very low levels of goal fulfillment there appear to be two very different possibilities. On the one hand, the first units of goal fulfillment may yield greater utility than subsequent units of goal fulfillment so that the utility curve is already characterized by decreasing marginal utility in its lower regions. Actors who have very little, if any, goal fulfillment at a specific point in time will very likely regard a given outcome as more valuable than if they have at least a moderate degree of goal fulfillment at that point in time. For example, a given amount of food will no doubt have greater utility for people when they are starving than when they are only moderately hungry.

On the other hand, for some goals threshold effects may be operative. Some minimal amount of goal fulfillment may be necessary before additional goal

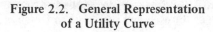

Figure 2.2. General Representation
of a Utility Curve

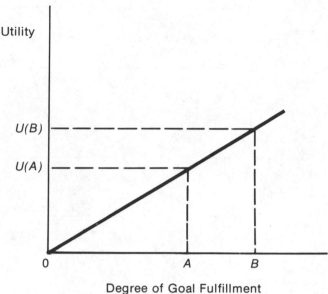

fulfillment yields substantial utility. Thus an individual may require a given amount of affection from another person before it registers, so to speak. In this case the lower region of the utility curve will be characterized by a positive increasing slope, whereas in the prior case it will have a positive decreasing slope. Threshold effects are also likely for goals, such as getting an education, that have definite "passage" points. A grade school education, for example, may offer little goal fulfillment, and it may not be until a person nears completion of high school that he or she will have a sense of the goal being noticeably fulfilled.

At the highest levels of goal fulfillment we anticipate that satiation effects will occur for all goals. Individuals will desire additional goal fulfillment up to a point beyond which it will have decreasing marginal utility. Additional food will have little appeal for the person who has eaten his or her fill. Even a person who is extremely desirous of affection is likely to reach a point beyond which additional affection is less valuable than it has previously been. We will discuss satiation effects more fully in conjunction with the *DLGF* determinant; for now we simply note that all utility curves will have positive decreasing slopes in the region of highest goal fulfillment.

Therefore, utility curves may be represented by the two possibilities in figure 2.3, where curve *A* represents constantly decreasing marginal utility and curve *B* represents threshold effects at the lowest levels of goal fulfillment, approximately constant marginal utility at intermediate degrees of goal fulfillment, and decreasing marginal utility at the highest degrees of goal fulfillment.

Figure 2.3. Nonlinear Utility Curves

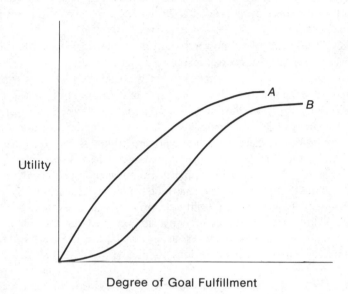

One must also allow for the possibility that a given outcome will *decrease* an actor's degree of goal fulfillment for a particular goal. For example, it may move the actor from *B* to *A* or from *A* to 0 in figure 2.2. We assume that any outcomes that decrease the degree of goal fulfillment will yield negative utility. These outcomes can be represented as downward movement on the utility curve.

So the marginal utility of an outcome is first of all a function of the degree of goal fulfillment that it provides. It will next depend upon the amount of utility yielded per unit of goal fulfillment, which is represented by the slope of the utility curve. As we have seen, these slopes can be considered as constant for only limited segments of the utility curve. Thus the marginal utility of a specific outcome will depend upon the particular segment of the utility curve that it covers.

Goal Importance
The slope of the utility curve will be determined by the relative importance of the goal for which goal fulfillment is to be provided by an outcome. To the extent that it is meaningful to speak in terms of *units* of goal fulfillment, the more important a goal is to an actor, the more utility a unit of goal fulfillment on that goal will offer in comparison with the utility per unit of goal fulfillment of less important goals. Therefore, the more important a goal, the steeper the slope of the utility curve for that goal, as is shown in figure 2.4 where

curves A, B, and C represent goals ranking in that order of relative importance. A unit of goal fulfillment on goal A will yield more utility than will a unit of goal fulfillment on goals B and C. This means that we can represent the marginal utility of an outcome by $U = GI \times DGF$, with a nonconstant GI, or by a power function $U = DGF^{GI}$.

Representing utility as a power function of the degree of goal fulfillment, with goal importance constituting the exponent of this function, has several advantageous features. Exponents between zero and 1 may be used for goals characterized by constantly decreasing marginal utility, one of the two major possible nonlinearities we have noted. The greater the exponent of the function for these goals ($GI < 1.00$), the greater the utility yielded per unit of goal fulfillment. In addition, the greater the exponent, the closer to linearity the curve will be, indicating that more important goals are less susceptible to satiation effects. This, too, is in keeping with our notion of goal importance.[2]

Goals characterized by threshold effects may be represented by a nonconstant exponent. Regions of the utility curves of these goals that have increasing marginal utility may be represented by an exponent greater than 1; regions in which marginal utility increases at a constant rate will have exponents approximately equal to 1; and regions of decreasing marginal utility resulting

Figure 2.4. Utility Curves for Goals Varying in Importance

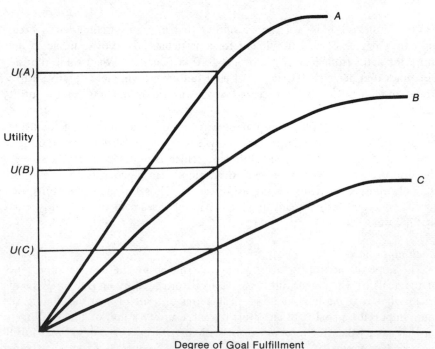

Degree of Goal Fulfillment

from satiation will have exponents less than 1. For such goals, therefore, we anticipate that goal importance will gradually decrease as the degree of goal fulfillment increases. For goals that have constantly decreasing marginal utility, goal importance will remain relatively constant at varying degrees of goal fulfillment.

Our representation of utility as a power function of the degree of goal fulfillment corresponds closely with empirical evidence also. Hamblin (1971), for example, has derived exponents of .67 and .63 for positive utilities and an exponent of 1.6 for negative utilities of wages. These indicate that monetary gains have decreasing marginal utility whereas monetary losses have increasing marginal disutility. Clairmont has found an exponent of .8 for winnings in a gambling experiment (Hamblin 1974). And Stevens (1959) has claimed that the utility of money is a power function of dollars with an exponent of .5.

It may appear that we should represent the goal importance determinant by the *level* of the utility curve rather than by its slope. Thus two goals of differential importance might be represented as in figure 2.5 with curve *A* representing the more important goal. This implies, however, that on some goals of an actor zero goal fulfillment will yield nonzero positive utility, which is contrary to our previous assumption that zero goal fulfillment equals zero utility. Different

Figure 2.5. Utility Curves for Different Actors on the Same Goal

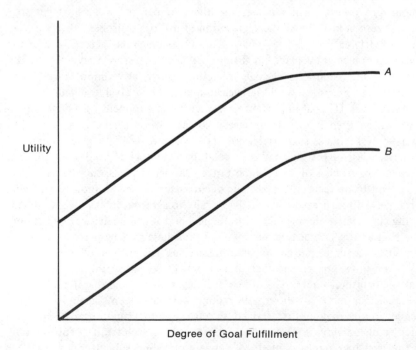

Utility

Degree of Goal Fulfillment

slopes of utility curves will obviously result in different levels for an actor's utility curves, but representing goal importance in terms of slopes enables us to represent differences in the utility of outcomes when the degree of goal fulfillment is held constant. That is, a unit of goal fulfillment will yield more utility on a more important goal. If we represent goal importance in terms of levels, however, a unit of goal fulfillment will yield equal amounts of utility on goals that differ in importance if the slopes for the two utility curves are equal.

If one is interested in comparing utility curves for the *same* goal for different actors, though, then it may be more appropriate to represent differences between them in terms of levels rather than slopes. Thus we can use A in figure 2.5 to represent actor A's utility curve for a given goal and B to represent B's utility curve for the same goal. In this case the different levels and equal slopes of the curves indicate that A's and B's zero utility points are not equal, assuming that the utility axis represents an underlying utility scale. Since the utility curves have equal slopes, an increase in goal fulfillment of one unit will yield equal amounts of utility for both A and B, *as measured from their respective zero points*. But since their zero points are not equal, one unit of goal fulfillment will yield more utility for A *as measured by B's utility scale* than it will for B. By contrast, the amount of utility gained by B is far less than that received by A when measured on A's scale.

This may be seen as part of the general problem of the interpersonal comparability of utilities. Utility curves for different goals for the same person will have common zero points. Utility curves for different persons will not necessarily have equal zero points: hence the aggregation of utilities is problematic.

Without delving into the reasons for it, we assume that actors vary in the relative importance they place on different goals. Therefore they may be described as having hierarchies of goals reflecting their relative importance. Theoretically, these hierarchies should be measurable at the interval level and possibly at the ratio level. (If goal importance represents the exponent of a power function of utility, then it will be necessary to measure it at the ratio level. See below.) Some scholars, such as Maslow (1954), have tried to give content to these hierarchies, suggesting that goals relating to biological needs rank highest, with social goals being of lesser importance. Biological goals, such as satisfying hunger, tend to be recurrent goals, and recurrence may be an indicator of goal importance. Although we are inclined generally to agree with Maslow's argument regarding the relative importance of biological and social goals, we shall simply assume that actors have goal hierarchies and that these may be partially similar.[3]

We further assume that actors' goal hierarchies will have an element of constancy over time, due to the fact that they will be partly influenced by the actors' sociocultural contexts. Actors are likely to have goal hierarchies similar to the goal hierarchies of those with whom they have been socialized. In fact, reference groups may be ascertained in terms of the similarities of the goal hierarchies of individuals. Thus actors whose goal hierarchies differ substantially from the goal hierarchies of their reference groups and subcultures will be the exception. At the same time, it is necessary to acknowledge the possibility that the unique psychological characteristics of individual actors are likely to make any one actor's goal hierarchy at least slightly different from any other actor's. He or she may not place exactly the same importance upon a goal, such as attaining prestige, as another actor, but that goal is likely to hold the same rank in their goal hierarchies if the actors have been subjected to similar sociocultural influences.

Over the long run an individual actor's goal hierarchy may change. Particular goals may change ranks, or the relative "distances" between them may change. These changes will tend to be rather gradual for most actors, although some may experience quite rapid "conversions." In the short run, we have seen that goals having threshold effects will have gradually increasing goal importance as the degree of goal fulfillment increases. We have also assumed that other goals will have constantly decreasing marginal utility. It is conceivable that some goals may be characterized by nonconstant decreasing marginal utility, although that possibility does complicate our model. If this is the case—for example, if marginal utility decreases at a more rapid rate when satiation effects appear than when the degree of goal fulfillment is low—then the goal importance of such goals would vary depending upon the current level of goal fulfillment. If there is a rapid diminution in marginal utility after the point of satiation, then it is possible that the goal importance of a goal ranking higher in an actor's goal hierarchy may briefly drop below the goal importance of a lower-ranking goal on which an actor has little or no goal fulfillment.

It is important to distinguish between these long-run and short-run changes in goal importance. Long-run changes will be reflected in a gradual increase or decrease in the value of the goal importance determinant. They will show up as a steepening or flattening of the entire utility curve relative to other utility curves. Short-run changes, however, will fluctuate in accord with an actor's movement up and down the utility curve over time. They will show up as fluctuations in the value of *GI* within a given range and produce only negligible changes in the *GI*, whereas long-run changes in *GI* will show up as changes in the curves themselves.

The goal importance determinant may have another ramification in our model. It may very well determine the goal that an actor is pursuing at any point in time, if it can be assumed that actors first attempt to fulfill their most important goals and pursue less important goals only after the former have been fulfilled to a satisfactory degree. In chapter 4 we shall discuss this possibility more fully when we consider actors' decision strategies.

So we have seen that the value of the goal importance determinant at any point in time will be partly the result of a given goal's ranking within an actor's hierarchy of goals and partly the result of the actor's position on the utility curve for that goal. The most important determinants of the actor's position on the utility curve are the current level of goal fulfillment, which determines the portion of the utility curve used in the estimation of the marginal utility of an outcome, and the desired level of goal fulfillment, which at least partially determines the point on the utility curve at which satiation effects appear.

Current Level of Goal Fulfillment

The current level of goal fulfillment, symbolized as *CLGF*, simply refers to the point at which actors are on their utility curves at the time they are making utility estimates for various outcomes. Actors located at point *B* in figure 2.2 have higher *CLGF*'s than they have when they are located at point *A*. Generally, the higher an actor's *CLGF*, the more likely it is that an outcome will cover a segment of the utility curve characterized by decreasing marginal utility, and hence the lesser will be the utility of the outcome because of the diminution of the goal importance determinant.

If we assume that the *CLGF* at any point in time *equals zero utility*,[4] then outcomes offering an increase in the degree of goal fulfillment will yield *positive* utility (i.e., reward), whereas outcomes providing a decrease in the degree of goal fulfillment will yield *negative* utility (i.e., punishment). Therefore, the progression of actors' experiences over time may be represented in terms of movement along the utility curve and a continuous equating of the *CLGF* with zero utility, or, to put it slightly differently, continual resetting of the utility scale at zero. Such a progression is shown in figure 2.6. We assume here that at time t_1 the actor has no goal fulfillment, so that $CLGF = U = 0$. At this point in time, therefore, outcome *A* offering the degree of goal fulfillment represented by the distance 0*A* offers the amount of utility represented by the distance 0*V* on the utility axis. This is U_{t_1}.

Assuming that the actor receives outcome 0*A* and it yields the amount of utility anticipated, at time t_2 the actor will be at point *A* on the degree of goal fulfillment axis and point *V* on the utility axis—hence at point *AV* on the utility curve. Therefore *V* represents *zero* utility at time t_2. To emphasize this point we have redrawn the coordinates for the horizontal axis by means of dotted lines. At time t_2, therefore, an outcome with the degree of goal fulfillment *AB* will yield utility *VW*. So $VW = U_{t_2}$. At this point in time, furthermore, an outcome involving a decrease in goal fulfillment represented by a move from *A* to 0 would yield the *negative* utility *V*0.

Thus over time, as the actor represented in figure 2.6 receives outcomes increasing his or her degree of goal fulfillment (i.e., as he or she moves from 0 to *E* along the *DGF* axis), he or she moves along the utility axis from 0 to *Z*. Each of the points along the utility axis becomes the point of zero utility for the subsequent time period and hence for the subsequent utility estimate. Figure 2.7 represents a similar progression over time for a goal having threshold characteristics. In this case we can see the increasing marginal utility of outcomes received at and after time t_4.

Depending upon the nature of the goal and depending upon an actor's experiences, the current level of goal fulfillment may remain relatively stable over time or it may change rather rapidly. If an actor is receiving continual fulfillment of

Figure 2.6. Utility Curve for Goal
with Constantly Decreasing Marginal Utility

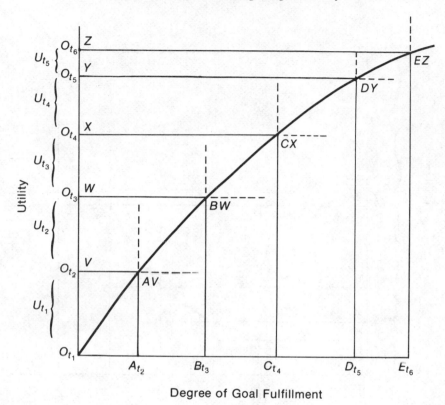

Degree of Goal Fulfillment

a particular goal over time, the *CLGF* for that goal will remain quite stable, but if fulfillment is received only infrequently, then the *CLGF* will follow a cyclic pattern. The rate at which the current level of goal fulfillment for a particular goal declines over time will also vary among goals. We refer to this rate as the *goal decomposition rate*. Goals may be visualized as varying in terms of the length of time that goal fulfillment holds, so to speak, or the rate at which goal fulfillment "decomposes." Fulfillment of some goals will continue over a longer period of time than will fulfillment of other goals. Those goals for which fulfillment lasts relatively long can be described as having low decomposition rates. Those goals for which fulfillment decomposes very rapidly have high decomposition rates, or, goal fulfillment lasts only a relatively short time. Hence goals with high decomposition rates will be periodically recurrent goals whereas goals with low decomposition rates may also recur, but their cycles of recurrence will be much longer. Whether or not a goal has a high or low decomposition rate is ultimately determined by the needs of actors, a subject we shall not discuss here.

Figure 2.7. Utility Curve for Threshold Goal

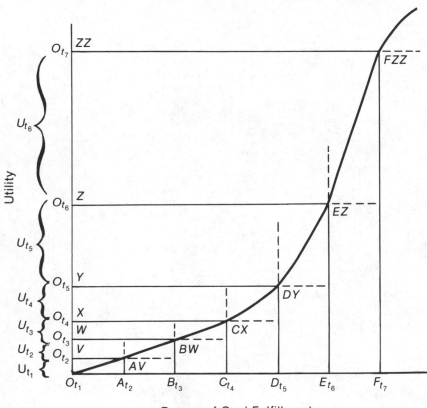

Degree of Goal Fulfillment

A prime example of a goal with a high decomposition rate, and hence one that recurs frequently, is that of satisfying hunger. Immediately after eating, actors' current levels of goal fulfillment are likely to be approximately equal to their desired levels of goal fulfillment. If they consumed more than their desired levels, they are likely to be satiated, and additional food offered at that time would have little utility for them. But over the relatively short period of several hours their current levels of goal fulfillment will have decomposed, or dropped, to a much lower level, and the goal of satisfying hunger will recur. (We shall discuss later the precise mechanisms that cause the goal to recur.) For most people the goal of sexual satisfaction has a somewhat lower decomposition rate and hence the goal recurs less often. At the other extreme is a diffuse goal, such as obtaining an education, which appears to have a very low or zero decomposition rate. If actors attain a given level of fulfillment of this goal, it is doubtful that this fulfillment will decompose so that at a later time their current levels of goal fulfillment will be significantly lower. As we shall see, however, they may increase their desired levels of goal fulfillment for that goal.

So there may be wide variance among goals in the rate at which the current level of goal fulfillment changes, depending partly upon their decomposition rates. Of course goals will also vary in the rate at which goal fulfillment is received, or the rate at which the current level of goal fulfillment increases. It is possible for the *CLGF* to increase quite rapidly. Eating a meal provides a relatively rapid increase in the *CLGF*, as does receiving a substantial monetary gift in one lump sum.

Desired Level of Goal Fulfillment

The desired level of goal fulfillment (*DLGF*) is simply the amount of goal fulfillment desired by actors for specific goals. We will also refer to it as the actor's *aspiration level*. We anticipate that it will be more significant for goals characterized by threshold effects than for goals characterized by constantly decreasing marginal utility. For the former, it will more clearly mark the region of the utility curve at which satiation effects occur. If, for example, a college degree represents the aspiration level of an actor on the goal of getting an education, we believe it likely that once that aspiration level has been attained additional outcomes (i.e., additional college courses completed) will have decreasing marginal utility unless attainment of the *DLGF* results in an increase in that level. In addition, we believe it is probable that marginal utility will be increasing as the actor gets closer to his or her *DLGF*. This means that the goal will become more important when "the end is in sight" than when attainment of the *DLGF* is still far off in the future. In fact, the goal may dominate other goals in the period just prior to the attainment of the *DLGF*.

The aspiration levels of actors may also be significant for goals for which marginal utility is constantly decreasing. Marginal utility may decrease more rapidly once the aspiration levels for these goals have been attained. Again, of course, once an actor has attained his or her aspiration level, he or she may raise its level.

The *DLGF* will also be one of the major determinants of the behavioral alternatives that actors are considering at any point in time. We shall look at its role in that regard in chapter 4.

The levels of goal fulfillment that actors desire on particular goals will be partially influenced by factors unique to them, and they will also be partially influenced by cultural values and norms. Most individuals are likely to desire levels of goal fulfillment quite similar to the levels desired by others with whom they have been socialized, though there is always the possibility of some deviating markedly from their sociocultural peers. Generally, however, we expect that the degree of goal fulfillment on a goal, such as prestige, that is sought by an actor will be partly influenced by his or her own psyche and partly by the degree to which prestige is sought within his or her culture.

Actors who appear to have either unusually high or unusually low aspiration levels have received much attention from behavioral scientists. The former case is represented by the achievement motivation and need-achievement literature (McClelland 1961; McClelland and Winter 1969). According to this school of thought, actors with extremely high need-achievement levels play crucial roles in initiating social and economic change. Achievement constitutes a goal, and high need-achievers are simply those who desire a very high level of fulfillment for that goal. Their high levels of desired goal fulfillment are primarily attributed to their socialization experiences. Although there is substantial controversy surrounding the existence and origins of this phenomenon, it can be meaningfully described in terms of the *DLGF* variable.

By contrast, certain "social problem" areas are often analyzed in terms of extremely low levels of aspiration among certain groups for certain goals. The problem of poverty, for example, is sometimes portrayed as resulting from the low desired level of goal fulfillment among the poor for conventional goals such as money and success. Similarly, members of minority racial and ethnic groups are occasionally described as having below average aspiration levels on these same goals. This point of view has, of course, aroused heated criticism from those who regard it as blaming the victims of misfortune for their situations. We simply present it here as an example of an area of social scientific investigation that can be handled with the model we are presenting. The essential point is that there will be differences among actors and groups in their desired levels of goal fulfillment for various goals, and these differences will yield differences in the utilities of outcomes. Ultimately these differences will be revealed in the diverse behaviors that are enacted.

Generally we expect that actors' aspiration levels will remain relatively stable over time, in all probability more stable than their current levels of goal fulfillment. But under certain conditions it is likely that their aspiration levels will increase or decrease, and consequently the relationship between the degree of goal fulfillment and utility will be modified. For example, someone aspiring to an income of $10,000 a year will likely set his or her sights higher if he or she receives that amount in the first six months of a year. But if satiation occurs when the desired level of goal fulfillment is attained, then he or she is likely to take the rest of the year off. By contrast, someone aspiring to that income who makes only $5000 year after year may well lower his or her aspiration level.

We cannot do justice to the issue of the causes of changes in aspiration levels in this context. We will simply discuss briefly the major ways in which these changes appear to come about. First, as our examples imply, they may result directly from changes in actors' current levels of goal fulfillment. To the extent that actors succeed in attaining levels of goal fulfillment equal to their aspiration levels, they are likely to increase their aspiration levels. Becker and Siegel (1962) and Siegel (1957) have shown this relationship to exist in their studies of students' grade aspirations. In these studies desired levels of goal fulfillment, or aspiration levels, were measured in terms of grades. Those students who succeeded in attaining the grades to which they aspired subsequently revealed greater utilities for grades *above* the levels to which they had previously aspired. But the students who failed to attain their desired grades subsequently revealed utility increases for grades *below* their previous aspiration levels. Although these studies dealt with utilities rather than with goal fulfillment, they do indicate that attaining one's aspiration level results in an increase in that level, whereas failure to attain it often results in a decrease.

We have previously noted that the aspiration level (i.e., the *DLGF*) is the approximate point at which satiation begins. Now we are suggesting that when that level is reached the *DLGF* is likely to be raised to a higher level. In this case satiation would not result from additional goal fulfillment. Thus in order to estimate the utilities of outcomes it will be crucial to know whether attainment of the *DLGF* results in diminishing marginal utility or in an increase in the *DLGF*.

Second, a change in aspiration level may also be interpreted in terms of an effect of an actor's subjective probabilities. The desired level of goal fulfillment may be partly determined by subjective probabilities. For example, it may be the level of goal fulfillment that has some minimal subjective probability of being attained. Actors may desire higher levels of goal fulfillment on a particular goal, but the probabilities of achieving those higher levels may be so low that they do not constitute effective aspiration levels. Many actors may desire to receive a million dollars, but their subjective probabilities for receiving that amount of goal fulfillment may be so low that their operative aspiration levels are really much lower.

Achievement of their aspiration levels, particularly achievement with relative ease (as in the case of the party making $10,000 in six months), may therefore result in a change in their subjective probabilities. The likelihood of attaining higher levels of goal fulfillment will be perceived as greater than it was previously, and hence the effective aspiration level will be raised. Conversely, failure to attain the aspiration level would result in a decrease in subjective probabilities over time and consequently the effective aspiration level would be lowered.

Third, actors' desired levels of goal fulfillment may change as a result of their observations of *others*. This may involve observed changes in the aspiration levels of others who are deemed similar to oneself by an actor, that is, changes in the aspiration levels of members of one's reference groups. Or it may result from observed changes in the current levels of goal fulfillment of these others. Thus if these levels increase for an actor's reference group, that actor is likely to increase his or her desired level of goal fulfillment so that it is approximately equal to the group's current level of goal fulfillment. Or, if actors wish to stay one jump ahead of their reference groups, they are likely to raise their *DLGF*'s above the perceived *CLGF*'s of those reference groups. Veblen's classic discussion (1912) of "conspicuous consumption" vividly portrayed this phenomenon. In terms of our model, consumption constituted a widely held cultural goal that individuals fulfilled by consuming. But consuming as a means of personal goal fulfillment was not sufficient; it was necessary that the consumption be obvious to others. Consequently it was easy for others to see how well they were succeeding at achieving this goal, and these others then could adjust their aspiration levels accordingly. In such circumstances, therefore, the relationship between an actor's *DLGF* and the *CLGF*'s of others was undoubtedly more clear-cut than it would have been otherwise.

The phenomenon of relative deprivation, which occupies a key position in a variety of sociological theories, can also be described in these terms. Actors can be described as experiencing relative deprivation if their desired levels of goal fulfillment are approximately equal to the current levels of goal fulfillment of their reference groups and if their own current levels of goal fulfillment are significantly below their *DLGF*'s and hence also significantly below their reference group's *CLGF*.

Thus a number of factors may determine the *DLGF*'s of actors—unique psychological traits, their reference groups, and both their own experiences and those of their reference groups. Whatever the level of an actor's *DLGF* may be for a particular goal, it will be of importance in our model in influencing the relationship between the degree of goal fulfillment and utility.

Immediacy of Goal Fulfillment

The fifth and last determinant of the utility of an outcome, the immediacy of goal fulfillment (*IGF*), incorporates the phenomenon of "deferred gratification" into our model. Although it is not completely clear, this concept appears to refer to changes in the utilities of outcomes that aren't received immediately. When actors are said to be unable to defer gratification, the implication appears to be that outcomes lose utility for them if they are not received relatively soon. Often it is further implied that these actors are not acting "rationally." Hence they will choose behaviors that bring them outcomes that have less utility than the deferred outcomes but that are received without waiting. If the deferred outcomes were not postponed, the assumption is that they would be preferred.

The decrease in the utility of an outcome when its reception is anticipated at some future time may be conceptualized as a *discount rate* that actors apply to outcomes. Thus actors who appear unable to defer gratification may be applying a higher discount rate than those who appear able to defer it. The discount rates applied by them are very likely influenced both by individual psychological and by sociocultural factors. If differences in the ability to defer gratification simply reflect differences in discount rates, then those who are described as not deferring gratification can be seen as acting on the basis of their subjective expected utilities; that is, they are choosing those alternatives that have the highest subjective expected utility for them, given their high discount rates. In this case, therefore, we would expect varying discount rates among actors that were some function of the amount of time elapsed between estimating the utility of an outcome and when actors believe they will receive it.

A second possibility is that the ability or inability to defer gratification may simply reflect the influence of actors' current levels of goal fulfillment. If they have very little or no goal fulfillment at the time of estimation, they may discount the utility of future outcomes substantially, whereas if they have a high *CLGF*, they may not discount the future outcome appreciably. Or actors with a very low *CLGF* may select an immediate outcome rather than a deferred one for fear that no utility will be forthcoming from other outcomes in the interim between estimation and reception of the deferred outcome.

Third, deferred gratification may reflect the judgments of actors that the other determinants of the utility of an outcome will change between the time they make a utility estimate and the time they actually receive the outcome. If, for example, their *CLGF*'s are so high that they are completely satiated, it is conceivable that the utilities of outcomes to be received in the future, when the *CLGF* is anticipated to be much lower, will be "marked up" rather than discounted. Or if actors anticipate changes in their desired levels of goal fulfillment over time, then outcomes received at a time when the *DLGF* is higher or lower will likely have a different amount of utility than outcomes received at the current level of *DLGF*.

Judgments regarding changes in goal importance and the degree of goal fulfillment may also be involved. If the outcome in question provides fulfillment for a goal that is expected to increase in importance, then receiving that outcome in the future would yield greater utility than receiving it in the present. Or if actors anticipate a different amount of goal fulfillment being provided by the outcome in the future than at present, then their utility estimates will likely reflect that judgment on their part. They may, for example, anticipate "inflation," (i.e., the same outcome providing a smaller degree of goal fulfillment in the future), in which case postponing the outcome would result in decreased utility. But if they anticipate "devaluation," so that the same outcome will provide more goal fulfillment at a future time, then there would be an opposite effect on their utility estimates.

Lastly, deferred or nondeferred gratification may be primarily the consequence of the subjective probabilities of actors. Thus the utilities of outcomes may remain constant over time, but their subjective probabilities of receiving an outcome in the future may be lower than their subjective probabilities of receiving it immediately. If an actor has a very high subjective probability for receiving a low-utility outcome immediately and a very low subjective probability of receiving a high-utility outcome in the future, then it is quite possible that the former will yield greater subjective expected utility. Actors choosing the former may be regarded as unable to defer gratification. Which of the two components—utilities or subjective probabilities—is more significant for the deferred gratification phenomenon can obviously only be discovered empirically. However, the literature on the subject seems to pay little attention to the possible role played by subjective probabilities.

So, the immediacy of goal fulfillment appears to be an important determinant of the utility of an outcome, but incorporating it in a behavioral model is no simple matter. In order to simplify our model, we shall assume it generally operates as a discount rate, so that future outcomes will be estimated as yielding some fraction of the utility of the same outcomes received immediately. We will further assume that although these discount rates may vary among actors, they will be some approximately linear function of time. Therefore, the longer the time believed to elapse between the estimation of the utility of an outcome and the perceived reception of that outcome, the greater will be the decrease in that outcome's utility.

Summary of the Determinants of Utility

We have shown how the utility of an outcome is basically determined by the degree of goal fulfillment that it provides and the importance of the goal that it fulfills. Our device for representing this has been a utility curve relating *DGF* and utility. We have suggested two major types of utility curve—one characterized by constantly decreasing marginal utility and one having threshold character- istics, with marginal utility increasing relatively slowly up to a point beyond which it increases more rapidly. We have suggested that goals that have clearly defined levels or institutionalized "passage" points are likely to have threshold characteristics. All goals, we anticipate, will be subject to satiation effects. For goals with constantly decreasing marginal utility, satiation is likely to result in a relatively more rapid decrease in marginal utility. Satiation effects for thresh- old goals are likely to occur only after the desired level of goal fulfillment has actually been attained.

Generally, therefore, the greater the degree of goal fulfillment provided by an outcome, the greater will be the utility yielded by that outcome, unless the outcome encompasses a segment of the utility curve where marginal utility is minimal. The relative importance of the goal being fulfilled will be of equal importance in determining the amount of utility resulting from the outcome, however. We have maintained that actors have goal hierarchies and that the importance of a particular goal in an actor's goal hierarchy can be represented as the exponent of a power function relating *DGF* and utility, with $0 < GI < 1$. The more important a goal is in an actor's hierarchy, therefore, the greater will be the exponent, the more utility that will be yielded per unit of goal ful- fillment, and the more nearly linear will be the utility curve. Goals with thresh- old characteristics may be represented by exponents greater than one for regions in which marginal utility is increasing.

In order to simplify the estimation of the marginal utilities of outcomes at any one point in time, and in order to account for the fact that reductions in the level of goal fulfillment will yield negative utility, we have argued that over time an actor's current level of goal fulfillment is constantly set equal to zero utility. Goals will vary in the stability of the *CLGF* or in their decomposition rates. Short-run fluctuations in the *CLGF* may be reflected as variation in the goal importance determinant within a limited range of values, whereas long-run changes in the relative importance of goals will be revealed by gradual increases or decreases in the exponent of the power function relating *DGF* and utility.

The desired level of goal fulfillment, or the aspiration level, of an actor will be of major significance for threshold goals by determining the region of the utility curve beyond which marginal utility begins to decrease. It may also indicate the segment of utility curves with constantly decreasing marginal utility beyond which the rate of decrease becomes more rapid. We have also noted the circumstances in which *DLGF*'s are likely to be raised or lowered as the result of actors' experiences in attaining or not attaining an existing *DLGF*.

Lastly, we have suggested that the time at which actors anticipate receiving outcomes will influence their estimates via the immediacy of goal fulfillment determinant. Our general expectation is that the postponement of outcomes diminishes their utilities. After discussing several possible reasons for this, we have suggested that the *IGF* determinant be represented as a discount rate that is an approximately linear function of time elapsed between the estimation of utilities and anticipated reception of an outcome. We believe that this discount rate may vary substantially among actors and may be influenced by both personal and social factors, as are most of the other determinants of utility.

COMPLICATIONS IN ESTIMATING UTILITIES

At this point a brief review of the subjective expected utility model may be beneficial. We have suggested that in the simplest case actors are making choices between two behavioral alternatives on the basis of their subjective expected utilities. The subjective expected utility of an alternative is the *product* of the utilities of the outcomes resulting from that alternative and the subjective probabilities of those outcomes occurring as a result of an alternative being enacted. Actors, therefore, are essentially estimating the marginal utilities of outcomes (i.e., the additional utility an outcome will bring them) and weighting these marginal utilities by their expectations that the outcome will occur. The estimation procedure is simplified somewhat by our assumption that at any point in time an actor's current level of goal fulfillment equals zero utility, and thus marginal utilities are estimated from that baseline.

The simplest choice situation can be represented as a comparison of two equations representing two action alternatives:

(1) $SEU(A_1) = P(O_1|A_1) \times U(O_1) + P(O_2|A_1) \times U(O_2)$

and

(2) $SEU(A_2) = P(O_1|A_2) \times U(O_1) + P(O_2|A_2) \times U(O_2)$.

If we assume that $P(O_1|A_1) + P(O_2|A_1) = 1$ and that $P(O_1|A_2) + P(O_2|A_2) = 1$, then these four probabilities may be represented by p, $1 - p$, q, and $1 - q$ respectively. This choice situation can therefore be diagramed as shown below. In this situation the actor is choosing between two alternatives that lead to

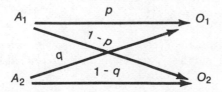

the same outcomes. If we assume that the actor will choose the alternative with the greater subjective expected utility, then relative subjective expected utility may be determined by subtracting equation (2) from equation (1). Incorporating the alternative subjective probability terms, this yields

$$SEU(A_1) - SEU(A_2) = (p - q) \times U(O_1) + (q - p) \times U(O_2).$$

If we then let $(p - q) = P'$, the right-hand side of the equation further reduces to

$$P'[U(O_1) - U(O_2)].$$

If the product of these terms is positive, then the first alternative will have greater subjective expected utility; if it is negative, then the second alternative's subjective expected utility will be greater. Basically, the alternative with the greater probability of producing the higher-utility outcome will have the greater subjective expected utility.

This relatively simple situation involving two alternatives and two unidimensional outcomes requires a comparison of only two of the subjective probabilities and of the utilities of the two outcomes. If the outcomes provide goal fulfillment on the same goal, then the latter comparison reduces simply to one involving the degrees of goal fulfillment offered by the two outcomes. In most instances, however, choice situations will be more complex. Outcomes are likely to provide goal fulfillment on more than one goal, and behavioral alternatives may involve more than two outcomes. Dilemmas are especially likely for actors when a given alternative yields both positive and negative utility. For example, it may bring the actor personal happiness but it may simultaneously result in the disapproval of others. In these situations the problem of combining the utilities resulting from the fulfillment of different goals to yield the total utility of an outcome will become especially significant.

Multidimensional outcomes (i.e., outcomes that yield utility on more than one goal) become problematic already in the fairly simple choice situation described above.[5] To show the complexity these outcomes cause, we can first represent the total utility of a two-dimensional outcome as

$$U(O_1) = u_{11} + u_{12},$$

where $U(O_1)$ represents the total utility of outcome one, u_{11} represents the amount of utility derived from goal fulfillment on goal one, and u_{12} represents the amount of utility derived from goal fulfillment on goal two. We have here represented total utility as an additive function of the individual utilities; we shall presently consider the appropriateness of this additive function.

The relationship between total utility and the component utilities may be alternatively represented by

$$U(O_1) = D_{11}^{G_1} + D_{12}^{G_2},$$

where the D_{jk} represent the degree of goal fulfillment offered by the outcome on each of the goals and the G_k represent the exponents of the power functions relating DGF and utility.[6]

Or if we assume that the utility curve may be regarded as linear within a limited range, then we may express the relationship between total utility and the individual utilities as

$$U(O_1) = G_1 D_{11} + G_2 D_{12} ,$$

where the G_k become slopes, or regression coefficients, in an additive linear equation.[7]

The estimation of the difference in the utilities of outcomes one and two from the choice example we are describing can then be represented as

(3) $$U(O_1) - U(O_2) = (D_{11} - D_{21})G_1 + (D_{12} - D_{22})G_2 .$$

In this equation D_{11} represents the degree of goal fulfillment offered by outcome one on goal one; D_{21} the *DGF* of outcome two on goal one; D_{12} the *DGF* of outcome one on goal two; and D_{22} the *DGF* of outcome two on goal two.

In this situation, therefore, if $D_{11} > D_{21}$ and if $D_{12} > D_{22}$, then the utility of outcome one will be greater than the utility of outcome two. Conversely, if the opposite inequalities hold, then outcome two will have greater utility. In either case it will not be necessary for the actor to estimate the value of the G terms (i.e., the importance of the goals being fulfilled). If, however, outcome one provides a greater degree of goal fulfillment on one goal than does outcome two (i.e., $D_{11} > D_{21}$), but outcome two provides a greater degree of goal fulfillment on the other goal (i.e., $D_{22} > D_{12}$) then estimates of G_1 and G_2 will be necessary in order to determine the relative values of $U(O_1)$ and $U(O_2)$.

More terms in the subjective expected utility equations will have to be estimated as choice situations become more complex. If, for example, the choice is between two alternatives that lead to the same outcomes, but the outcomes provide goal fulfillment on *different* goals so that

(4) $$U(O_1) = G_1 D_{11} + G_2 D_{12}$$

and

(5) $$U(O_2) = G_3 D_{23} + G_4 D_{24} ,$$

then all eight terms must be estimated, since

(6) $$U(O_1) - U(O_2) = G_1 D_{11} + G_2 D_{12} - G_3 D_{23} - G_4 D_{24} .$$

The estimation process becomes even more complex if the choice is between two alternatives that lead to *different* outcomes, with the outcomes providing goal fulfillment on either the same or different goals, or if more than two outcomes are believed to result from either or both of the alternatives. Clearly actors must introduce major simplifications in the estimation process in all but the least complex situations, and we shall look at the content of these simplifications shortly.

As indicated, we have assumed an additive relationship between individual utilities and the total utility of an outcome. This raises the question as to whether some other function is more appropriate in many, if not all, situations.

An additive relationship indicates that utility yielded by an outcome on one goal can compensate for a lack of utility on another goal, and that an outcome will have zero utility only if there is no goal fulfillment on any goals or if positive and negative utilities exactly balance.

Shinn (1971), for example, found that a multiplicative function represented the relationship between individual utilities and total utility better (in terms of variance explained) than did an additive function in a study of housing characteristics. He further argued that a multiplicative function is more satisfactory as the general form of this function because an extremely large amount of utility on one dimension (in the case of his study, a housing characteristic such as living space) cannot compensate for an extremely low utility on another dimension (such as cost or distance from work).[8]

For several reasons we believe an additive function that allows for nonlinearities in the variables is more satisfactory for the general relationship between individual utilities and total utility. First, in the Shinn study, at least, the superiority of the multiplicative model was not substantially greater, $R^2 = .88$ versus $R^2 = .83$. Second, although it is probably true that in many cases a very large amount of utility on one dimension cannot compensate for a lack of utility on another dimension, the relevant comparison is between the degrees of goal fulfillment offered by an outcome. In our model an outcome offering a very high degree of goal fulfillment will not yield a proportionately large amount of utility if it carries an actor into the portion of the utility curve where satiation effects are manifested by a decreasing or horizontal slope. Thus an outcome may offer a high degree of goal fulfillment but will not yield sufficient utility in most cases to compensate for a lack of utility, or negative utility, on another goal simply because beyond some point additional goal fulfillment does not yield very much additional utility.

Third, and most important, when we allow for negative utilities, which the Shinn study does not, an additive model appears clearly superior. With an additive model the positive utility yielded by an outcome may surpass the negative utility yielded by that outcome on another goal, so that total utility of the outcome is positive. Or the negative utility of an outcome may be sufficiently great to detract from its positive utility and to yield a total negative utility. In the multiplicative model, however, all outcomes yielding a combination of positive and negative utility would also yield negative total utility. In some cases this may be true—any negative utility perceived to result from an outcome may be sufficiently distressing to make the outcome's total utility negative—but this appears to be the exception rather than the rule. Furthermore, two wrongs generally do not make a right in folk wisdom, nor do outcomes yielding negative utility on two goals yield a total utility that is positive, but this would be an additional implication of using a simple multiplicative function.

So representing total utility as an additive function of the individual utilities seems more satisfactory. However, an additive model does assume that the D_{jk} are independently related to the total utility of the outcome. In other words, the degree of goal fulfillment on goal one is independent of the degree of goal fulfillment on goal two. In situations where this assumption cannot be met, a nonadditive model may be necessary. Insofar as we are attempting to represent the estimation procedures followed by individual actors, though, it is also probable that a multiplicative function, with interaction terms, gives us a level of complexity that is unnecessarily great. We doubt whether the utility estimations made by most people go beyond the additive model. This, of course, is an issue that can only be determined empirically, but the appropriate starting point of such analyses appears to be the additive rather than the multiplicative model.

SIMPLIFICATIONS IN ESTIMATING UTILITIES

In an intriguing article, Miller (1956) has suggested that the maximum number of bits of information that individuals can process is 7 ± 2. Although we haven't attempted to assess the precision of that claim we are well cognizant of the fact that humans do not, and very likely cannot, make the subjective expected utility estimates that are involved in complex choice situations. Nevertheless, we are convinced that all of us *do* make choices on the basis of the outcomes we desire to attain and our expectations that our actions will influence the likelihood of occurrence of those outcomes. This, of course, raises a very critical question: how do humans simplify the complexities characteristic of most choice situations and thereby make choices and act on the basis of those choices, rather than being immobilized by the difficulty of the estimations involved?

This is a major theoretical and empirical question that appears not to have received the attention it deserves. Those who have concentrated on the extremely simple choice situations that can be handled in laboratory settings have perhaps avoided the problem to a large degree. But if one is not content to model only very simple choice situations, as we are not, then the issue must be faced squarely. Therefore in this section we discuss what appear to constitute the major simplifications that are imposed by actors upon the choices confronting them.

Probably the major development in utility theory to deal with the problems resulting from the complexity of choice situations has been the development of various probabilistic choice models (Lee 1971; Becker and McClintock 1967; Luce and Suppes 1965). The main characteristic of these models is the assumption of a probabilistic relationship between actors' choices and the utilities of outcomes. These models vary primarily in their assumptions regarding the constancy of actors' utilities and the processes determining their ultimate choices among outcomes. A major problem with these approaches, though, has been the difficulty of subjecting them to experimental tests (Luce and Suppes 1965:377).

From our perspective it appears that actors introduce at least three types of simplification in the choice process. First, they make relative rather than absolute estimates of subjective expected utility whenever possible. Second, they may set certain terms in the subjective expected utility equations equal to each other. Third, they may assume certain terms in the equations are equal to zero. Each of the last two simplifications will generally convert absolute estimates into relative ones. We shall generally ignore subjective probabilities in this discussion except to note that the same simplifications are no doubt applied to them.

Relative utility estimates will be facilitated when outcomes provide goal fulfillment on the same goal or goals. If two outcomes provide goal fulfillment on the same goal, we have seen that the relative amounts of goal fulfillment provided by them can be compared without considering the importance of the goals, providing that one outcome offers greater goal fulfillment than the other outcome on both goals. Thus if an actor makes this judgment, then he or she will only additionally need to estimate which of the two alternatives being considered is more likely to bring about that outcome. But when outcomes provide goal fulfillment on different goals, or a combination of the same and different goals, then relative utility estimates will be more complex, and one or both of the other two simplifications is probable.

Instances in which the other two simplifications are most likely can be seen clearly by looking at several common cases.

Same Outcomes, Same Goals

We have shown in equation (3) that a comparison of the utilities of two two-dimensional outcomes that fulfill the same goals can be simplified to

$$U(O_1) - U(O_2) = (D_{11} - D_{21})G_1 + (D_{12} - D_{22})G_2 .$$

In this case an actor may simplify by setting two of the D_{jk} equal to each other, e.g., $D_{11} = D_{21}$. This would result in $(D_{11} - D_{21}) = 0$, so that the relative utilities of O_1 and O_2 could be determined simply by a comparison of D_{12} and D_{22}. The simplification involves the actor's assuming that the two outcomes provide the same degree of goal fulfillment on goal one.

Or an actor may decide to set the degrees of goal fulfillment provided by an outcome on the two goals equal to each other, i.e., $D_{11} = D_{12}$ and $D_{21} = D_{22}$. Thus outcome one provides the same degree of goal fulfillment on goal one as it does on goal two, and outcome two does likewise. If we let $D_1. = D_{11} = D_{12}$ and $D_2. = D_{21} = D_{22}$ then the difference between the utilities of outcomes one and two simplifies to

$$U(O_1) - U(O_2) = (D_1. - D_2.)(G_1 + G_2),$$

and a determination of relative utility can be made solely on the basis of a comparison of $D_1.$ and $D_2..$

Since we are assuming that the actor is at zero utility at the time he or she is estimating the additional utility to be derived from an outcome, it is plausible to assume further that negligible amounts of goal fulfillment will be ignored or that the least important goals in his or her goal hierarchy will not be considered if so doing will overly complicate the estimation procedure. This may be accomplished by setting the appropriate D_{jk} or G_k terms equal to zero. Therefore if

O_1 offers very little goal fulfillment on G_2, and O_2 offers very little on G_1, then equation (3) can be simplified to

$$U(O_1) - U(O_2) = D_{11}G_1 - D_{22}G_2.$$

In addition G_2 may rank sufficiently low in the actor's goal hierarchy so that it, too, is set equal to zero. This will mean that the actor will only have to determine which alternative is most likely to lead to outcome one.

We have already seen that setting two terms such as D_{11} and D_{21} equal to each other makes the difference between them zero and results in an entire term dropping out of the equation. We suspect that this is a very common simplification, occurring in situations where the difference in goal fulfillment provided by two outcomes is "too close to call." If this is the case, then judgments of relative subjective expected utility will be made on the basis of only one of the goals even in the two-dimensional case. Conceivably this could mean that actors will end up making estimates on the basis of their less important goals if two outcomes provide approximately the same degree of goal fulfillment on more important goals.

Same Outcomes, Different Goals

Simplifications will be more essential but also more difficult in situations in which the outcomes being compared provide goal fulfillment on different goals. Equations (4), (5), and (6) have previously represented a situation of this sort. It is difficult to predict which simplifications are most likely in this case. In all probability these will involve setting small amounts of additional goal fulfillment or less important goals equal to zero. For example, G_2, D_{12}, G_4, and D_{24} may all be reduced to zero, in which case the relative utilities of the outcomes can be ascertained by comparing goal fulfillment on goals one and three. Or if an actor were unable to determine whether, for example, the utility yielded by outcome one on goal two was greater or less than the utility yielded by outcome four on goal two, then he or she would set $G_2 D_{12} = G_4 D_{24}$ and the effect would be the same.

If the differences in goal fulfillment between two outcomes are impossible to estimate, so that, for example, the degree of goal fulfillment provided by outcome one on goal one is set equal to the degree of goal fulfillment provided by outcome two on goal three ($D_{11} = D_{23}$) and D_{12} is set equal to D_{24}, then equation (6) can be simplified, if we let $D_1 . = D_{11} = D_{23}$ and $D_2 . = D_{12} = D_{24}$, to

$$U(O_1) - U(O_2) = D_1 .(G_1 - G_3) + D_2 .(G_2 - G_4).$$

If only increments in goal fulfillment, and hence positive utilities, are involved, then the comparison that is necessary to determine the relative utilities of the two outcomes becomes one between goals. If goal one is more important than goal three and goal two more important than goal four, then the utility of outcome one will necessarily be greater than that of outcome two. Of course, any inconsistency in the inequalities (e.g., $G_1 > G_3$ and $G_4 > G_2$) will mean that the D_1. and D_2. terms must also be estimated.

Same Outcomes, Same and Different Goals

The last possibility we shall consider involves outcomes providing goal fulfillment on both the same and different goals. For example, an actor may confront the two following equations:

$$U(O_1) = G_1D_{11} + G_2D_{12}$$

$$U(O_2) = G_2D_{22} + G_3D_{23}.$$

The difference between the utilities of the two outcomes in this case is

$$U(O_1) - U(O_2) = G_1D_{11} + G_2(D_{12} - D_{22}) - G_3D_{23}.$$

Outcome one will have greater utility in this situation unless $D_{22} > D_{12}$ and the sum of the second and third terms in the right-hand side of the equation is greater than G_1D_{11}. What simplifications are likely here? Mainly we suspect that actors will be unable to compare meaningfully G_1D_{11} and G_3D_{23} and so will set them equal to each other, which means that they can be ignored. The relative utilities of the two outcomes will then depend solely on the relationship between D_{12} and D_{22}. Or G_3 may be set equal to zero, so that if $D_{12} > D_{22}$, then $U(O_1) > U(O_2)$).

The same types of simplification will no doubt be made by actors in cases of even greater complexity, such as alternatives leading to different outcomes. In most cases we believe that the degree of goal fulfillment determinant more likely will be manipulated than the goal importance determinant, primarily because we assume that actors have a limited number of goals, and their values remain relatively constant over time. In addition, simplifications are especially likely when degrees of goal fulfillment are being compared on different goals. Comparing the amounts of additional goal fulfillment being provided by two outcomes on the same goal appears manageable, but when different amounts of goal fulfillment are being compared across goals, so that different segments of different utility curves are being considered, we believe that actors introduce simplifications as a matter of course.

Negative Utilities

Outcomes that yield negative utilities as a result of declines in goal fulfillment may also be problematic, particularly when actors are attempting to estimate how the decline in goal fulfillment on one goal compares with the increment in goal fulfillment on another goal. If both outcomes offer additional goal fulfillment on one goal and a loss of goal fulfillment on another goal, then the determination of relative utilities is much simpler.

Let us look at the latter case first. We shall assume that we have two outcomes, both offering positive utility on goal one and negative utility on goal two. They may therefore be represented by

$$U(O_1) = G_1 D_{11} - G_2 D_{12}$$
$$U(O_2) = G_1 D_{21} - G_2 D_{22}.$$

Furthermore,

$$U(O_1) - U(O_2) = G_1(D_{11} - D_{21}) + G_2(D_{22} - D_{12}).$$

Thus the utility of outcome one will be greater than the utility of outcome two if both $D_{11} > D_{21}$ (i.e., outcome one offers a greater degree of goal fulfillment on goal one than does outcome two) and $D_{22} > D_{12}$ (i.e., outcome two offers a greater loss of goal fulfillment on goal two than does outcome one). If, however, $D_{11} > D_{21}$ and $D_{12} > D_{22}$, it will mean that outcome one offers both a greater gain in goal fulfillment and a greater loss than does outcome two. The individual estimating utilities in this case would then have to take the relative importance of the two goals into account in order to determine which outcome had greater utility.

Now consider the case in which the two outcomes provide increases and losses in goal fulfillment on different goals, such that

$$U(O_1) = G_1 D_{11} - G_2 D_{12}$$
$$U(O_2) = G_2 D_{22} - G_1 D_{21}.$$

Here outcome one provides positive utility by adding to goal fulfillment on goal one and negative utility by diminishing goal fulfillment on goal two, whereas outcome two depletes goal fulfillment on goal one and increases it on goal two. Representing the difference in the utilities of the two outcomes as before we get

(7) $$U(O_1) - U(O_2) = G_1(D_{11} + D_{21}) - G_2(D_{12} + D_{22}).$$

This indicates that if the amounts of goal fulfillment received and lost on goal one equal the amounts of goal fulfillment received and lost on goal two, the utilities of the two outcomes will be equal. And for outcome one to have greater utility than outcome two the amounts of goal fulfillment received and lost on goal one weighted by the importance of goal one must be greater than the amounts of goal fulfillment received and lost on goal two weighted by the importance of goal two. That, we feel, is not immediately obvious to either the outside observer or the actor making a utility estimate. Some type of simplification must be made in situations like this.

It is possible in such cases that actors will be more concerned about estimating negative utilities fairly accurately than about the positive utilities to be gained. Thus an actor may set the positive-utility terms both equal to zero so that equation (7) becomes

(8) $$U(O_1) - U(O_2) = G_1 D_{21} - G_2 D_{12}.$$

Outcome one will have greater utility if outcome two threatens a greater loss of goal fulfillment on goal one than outcome one does on goal two. Or if the goal fulfillment the actor anticipates losing is minimal on both goals, the negative-utility terms may be set equal to zero and an estimation made solely on the basis of $G_1 D_{11}$ and $G_2 D_{22}$.

Another possibility is that actors go through a two-step process in estimating the utilities of outcomes offering both positive and negative utility. In the case we are describing they may first compare negative utilities, as in equation (8). On the basis of that comparison a new term, D_{1-2}, could then be included in the equation for the positive-utility outcomes, where $D_{1-2} = G_1 D_{21} - G_2 D_{12}$. Comparing only the positive-utility terms and including the D_{1-2} term we have

$$U(O_1) - U(O_2) = G_1 D_{11} + D_{1-2} - G_2 D_{22}.$$

If $G_1 D_{21} > G_2 D_{12}$ (i.e., outcome two involves a greater loss of goal fulfillment on outcome one than outcome one does on goal two), the D_{1-2} term will be positive and O_1 will have greater utility than O_2 unless the positive utility yielded by $G_2 D_{22}$ is greater than the positive utility resulting from outcome one plus the advantage outcome one has in terms of lesser negative utility (i.e., $G_1 D_{11} + D_{1-2}$).

This two-step process could just as well proceed with a comparison of positive utilities first. Which is considered first will very likely differ among people. Perhaps pessimists will be inclined to consider negative utilities first while optimists will look first at positive utilities. We have looked at two very simple situations. In situations with greater complexity an estimation process involving more than two steps may be necessary. As was the case with outcomes offering only positive utilities, comparisons will be relatively easier to the extent that outcomes provide goal fulfillment on the same goals.

Other Simplifications

Our discussion has more or less assumed that actors consider their goals simultaneously in estimating the utilities of outcomes. This assumption may not be satisfactory for all situations. It may be more accurate in some cases, or for some actors, to allow for the possibility of a sequential consideration of goals. This assumption appears to be basic to lexicographic ordering, a decision model that has been applied to multidimensional utilities in situations of certainty. Fishburn (1974:1443) describes its basic principle: "One alternative is 'better' than another if the first is 'better' than the second on the most important criterion on which they differ." This method may be visualized as involving a sequential considering of goal dimensions by actors, starting with the most important goal. If outcomes differ in the degree of goal fulfillment they provide on that goal, then the estimation process is terminated. A somewhat similar model has been described as "elimination by aspects" by its originator (Tversky 1972a, 1972b). In this approach, dimensions are also considered sequentially with outcomes being successively eliminated from further consideration if they do not offer a certain degree of goal fulfillment on a goal dimension. Presumably this sequential consideration of outcomes also begins with the most important goal. We shall consider sequencing issues in chapter 4 when we discuss actors' decision strategies.

It is quite plausible that the simplifications applied by actors to utility estimates will depend upon their perceptions of the subjective probabilities associated with the outcomes for which utilities are being estimated. One might expect that utility estimates are more likely to be simplified when actors perceive significant differences between subjective probabilities than when these differences are minimal. To some extent this is true, but not uniformly so, since two quite different situations may be involved. We shall consider only the case in which a choice is being made between two alternatives, A_1 and A_2, each of which leads to either O_1 or O_2. First, if the subjective probability for O_2 is substantially less than the subjective probability for O_1, given either A_1 or A_2, then it is probable that actors will not bother to estimate the relative utilities of O_1 and O_2. They will be primarily concerned with subjective probability estimates, so as to determine which alternative is more likely to lead to O_1.

But if the significant difference in subjective probabilities is between $P(O_1|A_1)$ and $P(O_1|A_2)$, so that A_1 is much more likely to lead to O_1, and A_2 is much more likely to lead to O_2, then actors will necessarily need to be concerned with making accurate estimates of the utilities of O_1 and O_2 and it is less likely that they will make simplifications. Similarly, if the difference in the utilities of O_1 and O_2 is substantial, actors will be concerned about making accurate subjective probability estimates in order to choose the alternative with the greater likelihood of the higher-utility outcome's occurring.

Possibly the most common simplification made by actors will be merely to ignore outcomes and/or goal dimensions that are too difficult to estimate, effectively setting them equal to zero. This will no doubt depend upon the decision strategies of individual actors. Some will be more determined to maximize subjective expected utility than will others, hence the former will undoubtedly be less willing to "throw in the towel" on the estimation procedure. If individuals are merely attempting to "satisfice" rather than maximize, however, a comparison of outcomes on the basis of one goal dimension may be adequate for them. Other goal dimensions may be considered only if they offer very large amounts of additional goal fulfillment or the threat of major losses of goal fulfillment. We will discuss these possibilities in depth in chapter 4.

Sociocultural Simplifying Mechanisms

The process of simplifying utility estimates is often itself simplified for actors via certain sociocultural mechanisms. We may think of an ideology as such a device, affecting not only utilities but also subjective probabilities. Ideologies offer their adherents simplified versions of the world, or definitions of the situation that generally gloss over the rough edges of reality. They may be described as collectively created and collectively held versions of "what is" and "what ought to be," or of the real and the ideal.

The components of an ideology that define "what is" would appear to have their greatest effects on actors' subjective probabilities. It is the ideology's definition of the ideal that will most likely help to simplify actors' estimates of the utilities of outcomes. It may do so by making certain goals top priority in the goal hierarchies of "true believers." Thus scientists may be obsessed with the goal of seeking truth, revolutionaries with the goal of overthrowing the establishment, and born-again Christians with the goal of obtaining salvation. These respective goals may so dominate these individuals' goal hierarchies that any outcomes offering even a minimal amount of goal fulfillment on them will automatically overshadow outcomes offering goal fulfillment on other goals. Or individuals holding these goals may have such extremely high aspiration levels on them that satiation effects are minimal and additional goal fulfillment on them is constantly being sought.

Ideologies may also serve to inflate actors' perceptions of the amount of goal fulfillment that certain outcomes will provide, thereby causing them to overestimate the utilities of these outcomes and to underestimate the utilities of other outcomes. This in itself will simplify the estimation process. Thus the scientist may believe that the successful completion of an experiment will result in a quantum leap in the search for truth. The revolutionary may believe that one more victory will result in the establishment's collapse. The seeker after salvation may believe that the results of witnessing to another will put him or her well on the road to the eternal prize. One cannot help thinking about the advertising world, also, with its hyped-up promises regarding the ecstasy that results from the use of the latest kitchen appliance or beauty treatment.

A very significant effect of ideologies may be upon what we have called the immediacy of goal fulfillment determinant. They may convince their followers that utility will not be diminished if outcomes are not received immediately and that in fact it may be increased by the postponement. If, for example, one were to obtain salvation immediately rather than somewhere in the undefined future, then life might lose its meaning. Or if the revolution is assured tomorrow, then the satisfaction of the struggle may be lost.

So ideologies appear to be a potent sociocultural force influencing the utilities of those holding them and simplifying the choices that these individuals make. By making certain goals all-encompassing or by promising extraordinary degrees of goal fulfillment from specific outcomes they help all of us to keep from being bogged down by the implications of our actions.

Given the very rapid increase in the complexity of choice situations as one takes into consideration additional outcomes of one's actions and additional goals affected by those outcomes, it becomes clear that a rational solution to the situation is the adoption of simplifying procedures. These may not be as extreme as those used by the ideologue, but they are undoubtedly utilized to some degree by all who have learned to cope with the world. One may think, for example, of the personality disturbances characterizing individuals unable to deal with the complexities confronting them and who "cop out" by means of bizarre behaviors.

Therefore a thorough analysis of the simplifications used by actors in choice situations will be necessary before a comprehensive theory of individual behavior can be developed.

THE MEASUREMENT OF UTILITIES

The continuing interest in utilities has spawned a voluminous literature on the measurement of this elusive phenomenon. In this section we shall briefly discuss the major issues that have arisen in regard to utility measurement and the strategies that have been adopted by researchers attempting to measure utilities.

Methodologists and utility theorists have adopted several approaches to measuring utilities. Most common have been attempts to measure them indirectly by means of effect indicators; that is, investigators have utilized the choices made by subjects in carefully structured situations to infer the utilities lying behind these choices. Somewhat less common have been attempts at indirect measurement that rely upon subjects' verbal or written estimates of the utilities of various outcomes. And some researchers have essentially given up trying to measure utilities, relying instead upon general tests of axiomatic utility theories by means of a body of data. A fourth conceivable approach, that of *predicting* utilities from their determinants rather than *measuring* them by means of their effects, has not been attempted to our knowledge.

A second major issue that has been extensively discussed in this respect is that of the level of measurement that is obtained by the several techniques for measuring utilities. This issue is usually analyzed in conjunction with a third— the level of measurement that is required by different formulations of utility theory.

Measuring Utilities by Means of Effect Indicators

Researchers have most often measured the utilities of actors by means of the choices they make between different objects, generally different amounts of money. This approach has largely been based on the assumption that individuals are unable to provide meaningful verbal estimates of utility. If asked a question such as, "How much money will make you twice as happy as twenty dollars?" they are presumed unable to provide any answer except "forty dollars," rather than responding in terms of the utilities of specific monetary amounts. Therefore individuals have been confronted with choices between extremely simple outcomes in tightly controlled laboratory situations. Mosteller and Nogee (1951) initiated the use of such techniques, based on von Neumann and Morgenstern's seminal axiomatization of utility theory (1944). The Mosteller–Nogee strategy, and that of many of its successors, can be described as an "indifference point" strategy. A key assumption is that a subject's indifference between two choices can be interpreted as an equality of the subjective expected utilities of the two choices.

The Mosteller–Nogee approach involves presenting subjects with a series of choices between a gamble and an event that occurs with certainty. The gambles involve either winning a given amount of money with a probability, p, or losing a specific amount of money with a probability, $(1 - p)$, and the event occurring with certainty involves neither losing nor winning money. By presenting subjects with a variety of amounts of money and of values of p and $(1 - p)$ the researcher is able to determine the situations in which they will be indifferent between taking the gamble and receiving the certain outcome. Since indifference is assumed to indicate equality, this procedure yields equations of the form (Edwards 1968:37)

$$p(u(\$X)) + (1 - p)(u(\$Y)) = u(\$Z).$$

And since the probabilities and the monetary values have already been specified, one can then estimate any one of the u terms by providing values for the other two. Utility functions then can be calculated on the basis of a large number of such choices.

A second well-known approach that uses the indifference–equality assumption is that of Davidson, Suppes, and Siegel (1957). They modified the Mosteller–Nogee technique by incorporating subjective probabilities in their model and by using indifference between gambles rather than between a gamble and an event that occurs with certainty. To ensure that their subjects used subjective rather than objective probabilities they derived an equiprobable event, a die with two nonsense syllables. Then by giving their subjects choices between two gambles they were able to set up equations of the form

$$.5(u(\$W)) + .5(u(\$X)) = .5(u(\$Y)) + .5(u(\$Z)),$$

which can be converted into an equality of differences:

$$u(\$W) - u(\$Y) = u(\$Z) - u(\$X).$$

In this case it is possible to derive estimates for two of the u's by arbitrarily assigning values to the other two u's. Thus this technique is based on the equality of differences between utilities. Other researchers have followed the general pattern set forth by Mosteller and Nogee and by Davidson, Suppes and Siegel with slight variations. Lindman, for example, asked subjects to give the selling price they would want for a gamble in order to derive the basic equalities (Edwards 1968).

A second approach to the measurement of utilities by means of effect indicators that has not relied on the indifference–equality assumption has simply used preferences between gambles. This procedure has been used by Coombs and Komorita (1958) and by Hurst and Siegel (1956), who have then converted these preferences into ordered-metric scales by means of Coombs's unfolding technique or derivations thereof.

The effect-indicator approach to the measurement of utilities has worked reasonably well in the types of elementary situation that can be constructed in laboratories. But it has broken down rather quickly when researchers have attempted to use it in more complex situations. The reasons for this become quite clear when one considers the assumptions on which the measurement strategy is based. It can be shown that these assumptions can only be met in the most simple choice situations and that when one tries to transfer them to situations with even less complexity than is commonly found in social situations they rapidly become untenable.

Assumptions of the Effect-indicator Approach

We have identified at least eight basic assumptions of the effect-indicator approach that we shall discuss briefly in this context.[9]

1. *Maximization.*   First, all the effect-indicator approaches we have described require the assumption that actors consistently strive to maximize their subjective expected utilities. Hence, if two alternatives differ at all in subjective expected utility, actors will not be indifferent between them but will choose the one with greater subjective expected utility. In relatively complex social situations it is likely that decision strategies other than maximization are operative. (We shall discuss decision strategies in chapter 4.) It is also possible that actors will take the utilities of other actors into account. For example, they may wish to maximize their own utility and minimize the utility of others simultaneously.

2. *Equality of Objective and Subjective Probabilities.*   Even though researchers using the effect-indicator approach have attempted to incorporate subjective probabilities in their experimental designs they have still been forced to present objective probabilities to their subjects. Thus Davidson, Suppes, and Siegel attempted to set all subjective probabilities equal to .5 by creating an equiprobable event, but they had to assume that their subjects were making the appropriate interpretation. There is substantial experimental evidence, from studies designed to measure subjective probabilities, that subjects do not equate subjective and objective probabilities. (We shall note the evidence from these studies in chapter 3.) So we suspect that this assumption has a shaky foundation, particularly in more complex situations. Furthermore, as we will also observe in chapter 3, in real-world situations it is impossible to determine what the objective probabilities of most outcomes are. Consequently it is difficult to see how an effect-indicator approach using this assumption will be feasible in such situations.

3. *Independence of Utilities and Subjective Probabilities.*   A third necessary assumption is that utilities and subjective probabilities are independent determinants of subjective expected utility (i.e., that there are no causal linkages between p and U in the basic equation). This has proven to be a shaky assumption, too, even in simple laboratory situations. Two types of interrelationship between utilities and subjective probabilities have been detected (Edwards 1962b). First, outcomes with high utilities have been assigned subjective probabilities higher than their objective probabilities; this might be called the "wishful thinking" bias. Second, the utility of outcomes has been higher when their probability of occurrence has been low, indicating a possible effect of the scarcity of outcomes on utility. So two opposite effects are apparent—a positive

influence of utilities on probabilities and a negative influence of probabilities on utilities—either of which confounds the measurement approach.

4. *Equal Weights of Utilities and Subjective Probabilities.* A less obvious assumption is that all of the terms in the subjective expected utility model have equal significance. In the case of a gamble, for example, it is assumed that the probability of winning has the same amount of influence as the probability of losing on individuals' estimates of subjective expected utility. But there is evidence from gambling experiments that this is not the case (Slovic and Lichtenstein 1968*b*). Thus it may be more accurate to represent the basic subjective expected utility equation as follows, where W_1 represents the winning and W_2 the losing weight:

$$SEU = W_1 p_1(U_1) + W_2(1 - p_1)(U_2).$$

5. *Knowledge of Signs.* It is also necessary with the effect-indicator method to assume that the outcomes have positive or negative utility. With monetary outcomes this may not be an especially difficult assumption to make, but when one goes beyond monetary outcomes to the variety of nonmonetary outcomes characteristic of social situations the assumption becomes more tenuous. Martyrdom is an extreme example of an apparent punishment being perceived as rewarding by the recipient.

6. *Missing Outcomes.* A sixth assumption is that the outcomes controlled by the investigator are the only outcomes having utility for the subject. But even in a simple laboratory situation it is possible that subjects will perceive other outcomes contingent upon their choices. For example, they may anticipate that the choice they make will result in approval or disapproval from the experimenter. If such additional outcomes are overlooked by the researcher, then the estimates of utility derived by the approach will include the biasing influence of the utilities of the missing outcomes.

We have repeatedly emphasized in this chapter that behaviors in social situations are likely to have multiple outcomes. A subject playing a gamble may be safely assumed to expect *either* to win *or* to lose, but in more complex situations individuals may expect *both* to win *and* to lose. For example, offering assistance to another may simultaneously gratify the recipient and alienate a nonrecipient. Or individuals may anticipate that an action will have both immediate and future outcomes. It is cases such as these, which are clearly very common in real-world social situations, that make this assumption a difficult one to sustain.

7. *Unidimensional Utilities.* The effect-indicator approach as it has generally been used has presumed that the outcomes presented to subjects have been unidimensional. In a gambling situation, for example, it is assumed that the monetary outcome is the only source of utility. If, however, the monetary outcome yields utility from a source in addition to the gain or loss of money (e.g., utility connected with winning or losing), then the estimate of utility of money for the subject will be biased.

A given outcome therefore may provide utility on different goals. A common example is that of outcomes that have both consummatory and status value, as the exchange and status value theorists have emphasized (Cook 1975). Since we have extensively discussed multidimensional utilities earlier in this chapter we shall not extend our discussion at this point. It should be clear that multidimensional utilities will preclude use of an approach assuming unidimensional utilities.

8. *Constancy*. Finally, it must also be assumed that utilities are constant over some period of time. The effect-indicator approach typically involves measuring utilities by one set of choices and then applying them to another set, so it must be assumed that they remain constant over this period of time at least.

In some cases (e.g., Ofshe and Ofshe 1970), such predictions have been quite accurate. But as we have emphasized in our previous discussion in this chapter, it is probably more realistic to assume that most utilities are constantly changing, as levels of current goal fulfillment decline or increase, for example. And it is probable that this is even more likely in complex real-world situations.

Conclusions Regarding the Effect-indicator Approach

Utility investigators have not been unaware of the difficulty of meeting these assumptions and the biases that result from failure to do so. Some have attempted to deal with the problem by including terms in the estimation equations to represent the different sources of error. These have included taking into account utilities for gambling (Luce and Suppes 1965; Tversky 1967*a*) and for choice variability (Siegel 1959), equity (Ofshe and Ofshe 1970), and the variance of gambles (Lee 1971; Coombs and Pruitt 1960; Slovic and Lichtenstein 1968*a*). But these additional terms appear to be interrelated as well, so it has not been possible to specify their influence accurately.

Consequently, it appears as if the effect-indicator approach offers little promise as a viable method of measuring actors' utilities in nonlaboratory situations. We have noted that even under laboratory conditions it is questionable whether the assumptions of the approach have been met. They are even less likely to be met in complex situations where people confront multiple behavioral alternatives with multiple multidimensional outcomes. It is not surprising therefore that attempts to solve the utility measurement problem have moved in two quite different directions in recent years.

Utility Measurement by Means of Verbal and Other Indicators

One group of researchers with methodological roots in the work of S. S. Stevens (1959, 1966) in psychophysics have refused to buy the assumption that individuals are unable to provide meaningful utility estimates either verbally or by means other than choices. These researchers therefore have attempted to measure utilities indirectly by indicators that are relatively more direct than the choices made by subjects. In other words, whereas the choice is

the indicator of utilities for the effect-indicator approach, these other researchers have assumed that non-behavioral indicators of utilities can be tapped.

Stevens's basic argument (1959) was that utility is similar to other perceptual
phenomena, which he described as prothetic continua. According to him,
individuals are not able to estimate equal intervals for such continua, but they
are able to estimate ratios between stimuli. These ratios are represented by the
basic equation $p = ks^n$, in which p represents a psychological magnitude, k an
empirical constant, s the stimulus magnitude, and n the exponent of the power
function. In other words, equal psychological magnitude ratios are some power
of equal stimulus magnitude ratios. And the same procedures that Stevens used
to measure other phenomena, such as loudness and brightness, he believed to
be applicable to the measurement of utility. Therefore he believed utility to be a
power function of objective values.

Stevens's colleague Galanter (1962) was apparently the only researcher to
pick up on this approach. He simply asked subjects questions such as, "How
much money would make you twice as happy as ten dollars"? Combining the
utility functions derived in this manner with subjective probabilities derived in
the same way, he tested the subjective expected utility model and obtained a
high degree of fit ($r = .88$) between choices between paired alternatives and their
differences in subjective expected utility.

This approach seems to have lain dormant until quite recently, having been
revived primarily by Hamblin (1971, 1974), who has used magnitude estimation
techniques to measure the utility of money. Earlier in this chapter we noted the
exponents that he and Clairmont have derived in their studies of wages and
gambling respectively. Shinn (1971) has used magnitude estimation techniques
to measure the utility of housing, and Terhune and Kaufman (1973) have
analyzed family size preferences by the same approach.

The results that have been obtained by measuring utilities in this manner
appear to be sufficiently promising to warrant much more extensive experimentation with it. In fact, this approach may be the only feasible means of obtaining utility scales for social variables and/or complex situations. Since social
variables lack the underlying objective metric of money, using the effect-indicator approach to measure their utilities lacks the guidance that this objective
scale provides for the construction of the choices required by the effect-indicator approach. At the same time, this lack of an underlying scale may prove
beneficial for the use of magnitude estimation techniques to estimate utilities,
because subjects' responses will not be biased by the presence of such a scale.
It should be noted, however, that Galanter's study suggests that the presence of
such a scale does not hinder subjects from responding in terms of utilities
rather than simply in multiples of monetary amounts. Magnitude estimation
techniques may also be more suitable for aggregated data. Stevens's findings,
for example, are based on the medians of grouped data. This is no doubt due
to the averaging out of random measurement error, but it has hopeful implications for anyone interested in measuring the utilities of aggregates.

The Axiomatization of Utility Theory

Another group of investigators has responded to the problems faced by the effect-indicator approach in quite a different manner. They have been less concerned with measuring utilities and instead have opted for refining axiomatic theories of utility that are then tested against a body of data (Luce and Suppes 1965). The attempt by Coombs, Bezembinder, and Goode (1967) to test utility theory without measuring either utilities or subjective probabilities exemplifies this orientation. Within this general approach several investigators have attempted to measure utilities via a procedure known as *conjoint measurement* or *simultaneous conjoint measurement*. (For an extensive discussion of this approach, see Krantz, Luce, Suppes, and Tversky 1971.)

The conjoint measurement approach essentially involves the creation of matrices from values derived from equations of the form

$$p(u(\$X)) + (1 - p)(u(\$0)) = u(\$Z).$$

Z represents the selling price or bid for the gamble represented in this equation, and the Z values derived from subjects for all combinations of p and X are entered into a matrix. If the utility of \$0 is zero, then the equation for any one bet becomes (Edwards 1968:38)

$$\log p + \log u(\$X) = \log u(\$Z).$$

If the matrix is additive (i.e., if the row, column, and cell entries can be rescaled so as to preserve the rank order of the cell entries and if each rescaled entry equals the sum of its row and column components), then values for p and $u(\$X)$ can be found by the solution of a system of inequalities (Edwards 1968; Tversky 1967*a*). Using this approach, and testing to see whether the matrix of bids was *strictly* additive (i.e., each rescaled entry equals the original cell entry), Tversky (1967*b*) has also concluded that utility is a power function of objective values. We find this particularly intriguing since it is the same position advocated by Stevens and Hamblin. Thus it appears that researchers operating from entirely different models and assumptions have come to the same conclusion. Tversky's estimates for the exponents of positive and negative outcomes are approximately 1.0 and 1.2 respectively.

Rapoport and Wallster (1972:135) claim that conjoint measurement provides a complete test of the subjective expected utility model, making it possible to either accept it or reject it. Therefore they regard it as the most satisfactory model available. It is difficult to see, however, how this approach might be utilized in complex social situations. A comparison of this approach with the effect-indicator approach reveals that virtually the same set of assumptions must be made for both approaches, and we have already noted the impossibility of sustaining these assumptions in complex situations.

Utility Measurement by Means of Cause Indicators

We indicated in our introductory comments to this section that one might conceivably approach utilities from a direction opposite to that followed by the researchers who make use of effect indicators. This approach would most likely involve including utilities as unmeasured variables in theoretical models, but attempting to predict them and the choices based on them from their determinants. In this chapter we have presented a model of the determinants of utility. Hence this approach would necessitate measuring some or all of these determinants: degree of goal fulfillment, current level of goal fulfillment, desired level of goal fulfillment, goal importance, and immediacy of goal fulfillment.

Since this approach has not been tried, to our knowledge, it is difficult to know exactly what problems one would face. It appears reasonable that for certain outcomes, such as monetary ones, one could derive measures for each of these determinants—the amount of money being offered, the subject's current amount of money, the subject's desired amount of money, the relative importance of obtaining money, and the time at which the money is to be received. Perhaps then by combining the measures of these determinants and actual choices made by subjects one could derive utility estimates. But this approach would very likely break down, too, if one encountered situations with any complexity. We find the relative simplicity of magnitude estimation techniques much more appealing.

Levels of Utility Measurement

What types of utility scale are obtained by the various means of measuring utilities that we have described? There appears to be fairly widespread agreement now that the effect-indicator approaches based upon the von Neumann–Morgenstern axiomatization yield interval scales—i.e., scales that are unique except for positive linear transformations[10] (Lee 1971).

The researchers who have used preferences between gambles to measure utility have sought to derive ordered-metric scales of utility. These include Coombs and Komorita (1958); Davidson, Suppes, and Siegel's linear and non-linear programming models (1957); and Hurst and Siegel (1956). Such scales lie between interval and ordinal scales (i.e., they are subject to more transformations than the positive linear transformation but fewer transformations than the positive monotonic transformations possible with ordinal scales). Both Coombs and Komorita and Hurst and Siegel found that their scales predicted choices quite well, but Stevens (1959) has criticized the ordered-metric scale as a "kind of unfinished interval scale."

The renewed interest in more direct measurement of utilities (e.g., by magnitude estimation techniques) has been associated with an equally strong interest in deriving *ratio* scales of utility. Stevens's power functions of phenomena such as utility constitute ratio scales. Hamblin (1971) has carried on this argument, claiming that ratio scales of utility are possible and that ratio scales are more accurately characterized as having a *relevant origin* rather than an absolute zero, the usual distinguishing characteristic of a ratio scale. He describes this relevant origin as the point from which a relationship between a stimulus and the scale designed to measure that stimulus begins.

We have suggested above that an actor's current position on a utility curve represents zero utility, an argument also advanced by Edwards (1962a:122). If this assumption is correct, then it appears that a ratio scale of utilities would be feasible, providing that a means of determining equal intervals *from that origin* is found. The magnitude estimation techniques used by Hamblin and others appear to provide this means. Furthermore, if utility is a power function of the degree of goal fulfillment, as we have suggested, and if it constitutes a ratio scale, then it may also be feasible to measure utilities, or to validate magnitude estimations of them, by means of cross-modality matching techniques, such as force of handgrip on a dynamometer. As Hamblin (1971) points out, Stevens's original magnitude estimation techniques were substantiated in this way. Numerical estimates and force of handgrip have been shown to be themselves interrelated by a power function in which the exponent is different from unity.

The investigators working with axiomatic utility theories have taken a somewhat different approach to the level of measurement issue, namely, specifying the conditions that must be met by the data in order to enable inferences regarding different levels of measurement. Particularly important in this regard is the degree of transitivity present in the data (Restle and Greeno 1970).

Level of Utility Measurement Required
by Subjective Expected Utility Theory

The level of measurement yielded by the various techniques for measuring utilities is really an academic issue unless seen in the context of the level of measurement required by the subjective expected utility model. Here we find much disagreement among experts. According to Lee (1971) and Ferguson (1965), Pareto showed that it was possible to derive interval measures of utility but that they were not necessary, at least for economists who could utilize preference orderings and indifference curves. However, Luce and Suppes (1965: 281–84) point out that ordinal utilities are not satisfactory in situations of uncertainty and advocate a scale of utilities somewhere between the ordinal and interval levels.

An ordered-metric scale fits these qualifications, and we have previously noted the attempts of several researchers to derive such scales (Siegel 1956; Hurst and Siegel 1956). Luce and Suppes (1965:279) suggest using the unfolding technique to measure utilities, and Coombs himself (1964) has discussed its use to derive measures of social, or aggregate, utility.[11] However, we have also noted Stevens's criticism of such scales.

Edwards (1962a:111–12) has introduced an additional complication, claiming that in some cases utilities may be measured on an interval scale while in other situations they must be measurable at the level of a ratio scale. If the subjective probabilities in the subjective expected utility model are required to add up to a constant, then interval-level utilities are satisfactory. If they are not required to add up to a constant, then ratio-level utilities are necessary, because linear transformations of the utilities in such models may change equal subjective expected utilities to unequal ones.

In light of the model of utilities that we have presented in this chapter it would appear that in cases where *individual* actors are making estimates of *relative* utilities, ordinal measures of utility will be sufficient. We have suggested that actors will invariably try to simplify subjective expected utility estimates by reducing absolute estimates to relative ones where possible. In cases where this is not possible higher levels of measurement will be necessary, and the assumption that the actor's current position equals zero utility facilitates such measures. We anticipate that magnitude estimation techniques used in conjunction with this assumption will very likely yield ratio scales of utility. Ratio scales of utility will be necessary if utility constitutes a power function of the degree of goal fulfillment. They will also be necessary if one wishes to go beyond the utilities of the individual actor. Even ratio scales may not solve the problem of the interpersonal comparison of utilities, however. Since actors' current levels of goal fulfillment will vary, their zero points will also vary, and it will not be possible to derive a common utility scale representing an aggregate of actors. In such cases, therefore, ordered-metric scales may be the highest level obtainable. These scales can be derived from aggregates, providing there is a relatively high degree of agreement regarding an underlying ordering of outcomes (Long and Wilken 1974).

Thus, when we take into account a variety of contingencies, including the complexity of social situations and the desirability of being able to measure utilities for aggregates as well as individuals, it appears that researchers should devote their energies to a comprehensive analysis of the potentials of techniques for deriving either ordered-metric or ratio scales of utilities.

SUMMARY

We have explored an extensive and forbidding territory in this chapter, ranging from the determinants of the utilities of behavioral outcomes to possible ways of measuring these utilities. At this point the faint-hearted reader may suggest retitling the chapter "The Futility of Utility," or may suspect us of rushing in where the proverbial angels fear to tread. Before turning to a consideration of subjective probabilities let us simply reiterate a point made earlier and one that will be made several more times in the course of this book: we cannot hope to represent complex social processes by simple theoretical models. Parsimonious models are clearly the objective we are seeking, but we believe they can only be attained after a thorough analysis of the manifold complexities of human behavior.

NOTES

1. Siegel, Siegel, and Andrews (1964:9) use *utility* and *subjective value* as synonyms: "The term *utility* might be used interchangeably . . . with the term *subjective value*." (Emphasis in the original.)

2. The notion that more important goals are less subject to satiation effects is very similar to the concept of inelasticity in economics. One might say that more important goals are characterized by an inelasticity for goal fulfillment, for example.

3. The economist Georgescu-Roegen (1968) makes a similar argument with his principle of the Irreducibility of Wants. According to this principle, actors have some wants in common, particularly if they come from the same culture, but they will also have differing wants, i.e., goals in our terminology (Taylor 1970:422).

4. Edwards (1962*a*) suggests that zero utility is the point at which an individual currently is, although he makes this statement in regard to the measurement of utilities.

5. They are not problematic in a choice between two alternatives that lead to the same two outcomes when one of those outcomes is simply a nonoccurrence of the other outcome, if it is assumed that nonoccurrence has zero utility. In that case a choice can be made between the alternatives solely on the basis of their subjective probabilities.

6. This may also be represented as $\log U_1 = G_1 \log D_{11} + G_2 \log D_{12}$. However we doubt that humans estimate utilities by means of logarithms, so we have chosen not to use this representation.

7. We have omitted the intercept term from this equation under the assumption that $X = 0 = U$.

8. The additive and multiplicative models correspond to Einhorn's (1971) disjunctive and conjunctive models respectively.

9. For a fuller discussion, see Wilken and Blalock (1979).

10. According to Taylor (1970:421) this holds true if individuals can give a complete weak ordering of all the basic alternatives and of all the probability combinations of those alternatives, and if they make choices so as to maximize expected utility.

11. For a simplified presentation of this technique, see Long and Wilken (1974).

CHAPTER 3

Subjective Probabilities

THE SECOND MAJOR COMPONENT of the subjective expected utility model is the actor's assessment of the likelihood of a particular outcome's resulting from action or nonaction on his or her part. Probability theorists' descriptions of personal or subjective probabilities, as indicating an individual's degree of belief about the occurrence of an event (Hays and Winkler 1971:69), reveal the difference between this type of probability and objective probabilities based on frequency distribution notions. However, we shall see that frequency distributions undoubtedly play a significant role in the determination of actors' subjective probabilities.

Another way of looking at subjective probabilities is in terms of the "causal models" that actors apply to the world. Their "causal models" reflect their beliefs about the relationships between their actions, and the actions of others, and the occurrence of various outcomes. For example, if they assign a probability of 1 to an outcome, given a particular course of action on their part, it indicates a belief that this action is certain to produce that outcome. Or if the probability they assign is zero, it indicates certainty on their parts that the action will not bring about the outcome. In most social interaction situations, however, actors will most likely consider the probabilities of outcomes to lie somewhere between these two limits.

Furthermore, the orientations of actors to the world and their beliefs regarding the significance of their actions for desired outcomes may also be expressed in terms of their subjective probability estimates. For example, they may be described as having different degrees of *perceived efficacy*. Those who regularly assign higher subjective probabilities to an outcome, given an action rather than a nonaction, i.e., for whom $P(O_j|A_i) > P(O_j|\bar{A}_i)$, may be regarded as having a high degree of perceived efficacy.[1] This may be further differentiated into *positive* and *negative* perceived efficacy, depending on the utilities of the outcomes involved. Actors persistently perceiving high probabilities of positive-utility outcomes, given their actions, may be described as having a strong sense of positive efficacy, whereas those tending to estimate high probabilities of negative-utility outcomes, given their actions, can be depicted as perceiving themselves to have negative efficacy.

Similarly, if we consider a low degree of perceived efficacy as synonymous with fatalism, so that actors perceive their actions as having little effect on outcomes, we can also describe this orientation to the world in terms of subjective probabilities. For such actors outcomes will be perceived as having approximately equal subjective probabilities of occurring, given action or nonaction, i.e., $P(O_j|A_i) \approx P(O_j|\bar{A}_i)$. If these actors perceive that positive-utility outcomes are likely to occur regardless of whether or not they act, an orientation we would describe as "positive fatalism," then this could be represented by $P(O_j|A_i)$ and $P(O_j|\bar{A}_i)$ being approximately equal and both close to one. Contrarily, actors reflecting the orientation more commonly referred to as fatalism, but which we would label as "negative fatalism," namely, a tendency to anticipate negative-utility consequences whether or not they act, can be characterized by a similar equality of subjective probabilities for negative-utility outcomes. So rather subtle but significant differences between actors' orientations to the world can be easily represented in terms of their subjective probabilities.

The frequency distribution and causal models approaches to subjective probabilities suggest two different ways of analyzing and estimating these probabilities. The former involves specification of the determinants of actors' subjective probabilities, as we have specified the determinants of their utilities, and attempting to estimate these probabilities on the basis of the determinants. The determinants will be found primarily in actors' experiences, but particular characteristics of the situations in which they are making subjective probability estimates will also be influential.

The latter approach attempts a more direct assault upon subjective probabilities by analyzing the causal models that actors typically use in situations in making their subjective probability estimates. Hence it will necessitate ascertaining the action alternatives they are considering and all the outcomes they believe conditional upon those action alternatives in a given situation. We shall see that this approach becomes unmanageable rather quickly as choice situations become complex, and therefore we shall devote much attention, as we did in the case of the estimation of utilities, to the simplifications that actors impose on such situations.

These two approaches to subjective probabilities are clearly not mutually exclusive but merely represent attacking the problem at different points in a causal sequence. Figure 3.1 shows the relationship between the two approaches. If we regard actors' causal models as being influenced by their experiences and the characteristics of the situation in which they are estimating subjective probabilities, then we can see that the frequency distribution approach concentrates on the determinants of these causal models while omitting this intervening construct. The causal models approach, by contrast, pays relatively little atten-

Figure 3.1

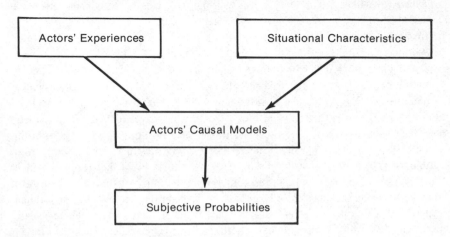

tion to actors' experiences and situational characteristics and focuses instead upon the actual "working theories" used by actors that are constructed from these influences. So the difference between the two approaches is the result of selectivity of the features to be emphasized.

THE FREQUENCY DISTRIBUTION APPROACH
TO SUBJECTIVE PROBABILITIES

Objective probabilities may be visualized in terms of empirical frequency distributions of outcomes. Thus an empirical distribution of outcomes, e.g., the number of times different numbers of heads come up in an extremely large number of tosses of five coins, can be converted directly into objective probabilities. The probability of a specific outcome, e.g., five heads, is assumed to be equal to the proportion of times that five heads come up in the tosses of five coins. This assumption, of course, constitutes one of the bases of modern probability theory.

The idea of frequency distributions can be extended to the analysis of subjective probabilities if we visualize individuals as having similar sorts of frequency distributions involving action alternatives and their outcomes. A given action alternative may be viewed as being linked to a specific set of outcomes, with frequencies for each of the outcomes in the set. Learning, therefore, can be seen as comprising the acquisition and refinement of such frequency distributions, the enlargement of individuals' repertoires of action alternatives, and the differentiation of action–outcome linkages. The infant human is born with a limited set of action alternatives and, to our knowledge at least, no awareness of the outcomes that are linked to these actions. In the process of maturation individuals gradually expand their repertoires of action alternatives and they also gradually discover which outcomes tend to be linked with which actions.

Reinforcement theorists make this the foundation of their theories of behavior—the organism learns that certain actions bring either pleasant or unpleasant outcomes—and they extend the idea further to account for motivation. Thus the actor is motivated to enact those alternatives that have led to pleasant outcomes in the past and to avoid those alternatives that have led to unpleasant outcomes simply because of the pleasantness or unpleasantness of the outcomes. We do not quarrel with this general orientation to the dynamics of human behavior; however, we believe, as we have indicated earlier, that it oversimplifies many of the complexities of behavior. The possibility that an actor may occasionally select an unpleasant outcome should not be excluded, nor should one overlook the variables that account for the anticipated rewards or punishments in particular situations.

So we can conceptualize actors as having stored in their memories a very large number of frequency distributions of outcomes related to specific action alternatives. They can be simply represented as NO_j/NA_i with NA_i constituting the number of times that alternative A_i has been enacted and NO_j representing the number of times that O_j has occurred when A_i has been enacted. This proportion, of the times an alternative has been followed by a particular outcome, can conceivably be converted directly into a subjective probability, $P(O_j|A_i)$, by an actor and then applied in a current situation. (In a moment we shall note several factors that make the correspondence between this proportion and a subjective probability estimate less than perfect.)

Thus if an actor has enacted an action alternative ten times and a particular outcome has occurred five of those times, the experienced proportion would be .5 and the actor would likely estimate the subjective probability of the outcome's occurrence, given the same action alternative, as .5. These frequency distributions will be constantly subject to revision as a result of the actor's experiences. If the action alternative is enacted again, then its consequences will feed back upon the frequency distribution and revise it accordingly. If A_i is followed by O_j then the proportion will become $6/11$ and the new $P(O_j|A_i)$ will be .55; if O_j does not occur following enactment of A_i then the proportion will become $5/11$ and $P(O_j|A_i)$ will be .45. Extinction of a specific action–outcome linkage is likely to occur when the NO_j/NA_i term drops below some threshold level, which will no doubt vary among actors. If the NA_i term should reach 100, for example, without any more occurrences of O_j, the proportion would drop to .05 and probably only the most stubborn actor would continue perceiving a linkage between O_j and A_i.

Generally, therefore, we expect that the greater the proportion of times a particular action alternative, A_i, has led to a particular outcome, O_j, the more likely actors will believe, and the higher their subjective probability estimates, that A_i will result in O_j the next time it is enacted, other things being equal. Conversely, the lower the proportion of times that A_i has resulted in O_j, the lower will be the subjective probability estimates for the occurrence of O_j, given A_i.

Indirect Learning

This discussion of frequency distributions of outcomes as the basis of actors' subjective probabilities makes it appear as if they were only derived from their direct experiences. Provision must be made, however, for learning that occurs through the observation of others, or vicarious learning. Thus the NO_j/NA_i proportion used by actors undoubtedly represents the sum of their experiences and the experiences of others with whom they are familiar. This introduces a potential complication because it is questionable whether the experiences of others carry as much weight in the learning process as actors' own direct experiences. Perhaps not as much credence is given to the experiences of others, so that more than one occurrence of an outcome, given a particular action, for another actor equals one such occurrence of the outcome for the actor who is making the estimate. Young children, for example, often have to "see for themselves." The extent to which this takes place can clearly only be determined by research.

Which others will be considered by actors is also a relevant issue. We expect that their "reference" others, or actors similar to themselves, will be the ones whose experiences are given most weight, but all actors have a number of reference others, each of whom may be given varying degrees of credence. The experiences of some of these may serve as a substitute for actors' own direct experiences, while the experiences of others may be discounted and not accepted at face value. Again, these complexities can only be sorted out through extensive research.

Unique Situations

Also problematic are situations in which actors are contemplating action alternatives with which they have no direct experience, in other words, where the denominator in the NO_j/NA_i term is zero. In most instances it is unlikely that they are completely without evidence on which to base subjective probability estimates, because they possibly have been influenced to consider the alternative as a result of observing others acting in that manner. However, we think it is necessary to retain the possibility of actors' thinking up entirely novel alternatives rather than restricting them to what they have already experienced or observed. In such cases we anticipate that they will not be left without a subjective probability. Instead it is likely that they will be influenced by the NO_j/NA_i for a similar action alternative. Operant theorists refer to a process of stimulus generalization, and we expect that a similar process takes place in regard to subjective probabilities. If actors are familiar with an alternative, A_i, that is similar to the untried alternative, A_k, then it is likely that the subjective probabilities of a particular outcome for the two alternatives will be approximately equal, i.e., $P(O_j|A_i) \approx P(O_j|A_k)$. The more similar the two alternatives are, the closer to equality will be the two subjective probabilities.

The process of response generalization no doubt takes place too. If actors are interested in an outcome they have not received before, then they may very well apply to it a subjective probability estimate approximately equal to the subjective probability estimate for a similar outcome, given an alternative that leads to the known outcome. Thus if O_j constitutes an experienced outcome and O_k an unexperienced one, we anticipate that $P(O_j|A_i) \approx P(O_k|A_i)$. Again, the greater the similarity between the outcomes, the greater the similarity of the two subjective probabilities.

Factors Modifying Subjective Probability Estimates

This has been a relatively simplistic conceptualization to this point. We have suggested that subjective probability estimates may be derived directly from actors' experiences of alternative-outcome relationships, from their observations of other actors, or from the subjective probabilities of similar alternatives and outcomes. But we must also consider factors that make for a less than one-to-one correspondence between the frequency distributions of outcomes and subjective probability estimates. In this context we shall consider two characteristics of the *patterning* of outcomes in actors' experiences. The basic idea behind these factors is the simple fact that equal frequency distributions may be derived through different patterns of outcome reception and nonreception.

Consistency of an Outcome. On prior occasions when actors have enacted a given alternative they have either received or not received a given outcome. These experiences, of course, constitute the data for the frequency distributions we have described. Now the question is: did these outcomes occur randomly, or were there sufficient regularities in their pattern of occurrence to suggest nonrandomness? Random occurrences of outcomes constitute a basic assumption for equating frequency distributions and objective probabilities. If outcomes do not occur randomly, however, then modifications must be introduced into the linkage between frequency distributions and probability estimates. Gamblers confronted with ostensibly random events supposedly make inferences of nonrandomness, perceiving a run of good luck, for example. Thus we would expect that actors making subjective probability estimates on the basis of their experiences would be almost certain to assume nonrandomness in the patterning of outcomes. Only an unusual few are likely to regard their experiences as the result of totally random influences.

We use the term *consistency* to refer broadly to all possible types of nonrandomness that actors perceive in their experiences. They may perceive that outcomes tend to alternate with nonoutcomes (an $O, \bar{O}, O, \bar{O}, O$ pattern) or that outcomes and nonoutcomes tend to occur in runs (an $O, O, O, \bar{O}, \bar{O}, \bar{O}$ pattern). In either case their current position in the perceived sequence will be relevant. In the former pattern, with a subjective probability of .6, it will make a difference whether the previous occasion on which the alternative was tried resulted in an outcome or a nonoutcome. With the latter pattern (a subjective probability of .5) several immediately previous occasions on which the alternative was enacted will be relevant. Not only will it be important to know whether the last enactment of the alternative resulted in an outcome or a nonoutcome, but the patterning of outcomes before that time will also be significant. Like gamblers, actors in the real world may anticipate that a run of nonoutcomes is bound to change to a run of outcomes, and thus they may raise their subjective probabilities above the value of the NO_j/NA_i term. Or they may revise their subjective probabilities downward if they have experienced a sequence of outcomes and anticipate that that sequence cannot continue.

It appears that the more consistency, or nonrandomness, actors perceive in the patterning of outcomes, the more precise will be the subjective probability estimates they are able to make. Or, if their estimates are not necessarily more precise, we anticipate that they will have greater confidence in their estimates to the extent that they have perceived nonrandomness in the sequencing of outcomes and have deduced the nature of the nonrandomness. So perceived nonrandomness will result in modifications of NO_j/NA_i values rather than using them directly to estimate subjective probabilities. Nonrandomness may result in a subjective probability's being either greater or less than the corresponding NO_j/NA_i term, depending upon its nature and on an actor's position in a sequence of outcomes and nonoutcomes.

The evidence from experimental research regarding the efficacy of intermittent reinforcement in maintaining behavioral patterns does suggest the possibility that randomness, or a lack of consistency of outcomes, will lead to an inflation of subjective probabilities. This research indicates that animals, at least, are likely to continue enacting a type of behavior, even though they are only reinforced occasionally, if that reinforcement is done randomly. If this pattern is generalizable to humans, then it may be interpreted in subjective probability terms. If actors have received O_j sufficiently often to keep the linkage between O_j and A_i above the extinction threshold level, and if they perceive that outcomes occur randomly, then they may be revising their subjective probabilities upward, guessing that they will get lucky the next time they enact the alternative. (This phenomenon may also indicate that utilities and subjective probabilities are not independent. We discuss that issue later in this chapter.) So we may tentatively say that the effects of randomness in the patterning of outcomes are somewhat more clear-cut than the effects of perceived nonrandomness. Randomness appears to increase subjective probabilities for positive-utility outcomes, whereas nonrandomness either increases or decreases them.

Recency of an Outcome. We have noted that recent cases in which actors have enacted alternatives will be of significance for estimating subjective probabilities if the actors perceive nonrandomness in the occurrence of outcomes. Relatively more recent outcomes will also be of importance in another way, by virtue of the fact that they may be accorded more weight than outcomes that were received in the distant past. We anticipate that items of information will lose their informational value as they are succeeded by new bits of information. One can conceive of a decay curve representing this phenomenon, with each instance of an A_i leading to either O_j or $\bar{O}_j$ becoming gradually less influential in influencing $P(O_j|A_i)$ and ultimately becoming insignificant. This may be due to the item's being lost in actors' memories. Or it may be due to the fact that more recent situations reflect actual or perceived changes in the world.

Exactly how one would determine the limits of this process or the rate at which bits of information lose their relevance for actors is difficult to determine at this time. Actors will no doubt vary in their rates of decay since some will have better memories than others. These rates will also likely vary in accord with personality predispositions of different actors. For example, it is possible that actors differ in their orientations to the past, just as they are presumed to differ in the extent to which they are future oriented. Some actors will be more likely to hold on to past experiences and accord them greater weight in analyzing their current situations.

So, in general, more recent outcomes will be more influential in the subjective probability estimation process than will less recent ones. Will the recency of outcomes also affect the actual values of the subjective probabilities involved? The effects of recency would appear to be similar to those of consistency. It seems reasonable that the more recently outcomes have been received, the more likely actors are to anticipate their occurrence upon the next enactment of a given alternative, on the grounds that the more recent occurrences carry greater weight and in this case they involve outcomes rather than nonoutcomes. If this is the case, then the influence of the recency of an outcome upon a subjective probability will be the opposite of its influence on utility. We noted in the previous chapter that the current level of goal fulfillment is generally negatively related to the marginal utility of an outcome. If we can further assume that the more recently an outcome has been received, the higher will be the $CLGF$, then recency and utility will also be negatively related. Now we are suggesting that the more recently an outcome has occurred, the more likely it will be expected to occur again.

Combining these two possibilities results in a prediction of increased subjective probability and decreased marginal utility. Or, in other words, the more recently an outcome has occurred, the more likely actors will be to expect it to recur, but its recurrence will be less valuable to them than if its prior occurrence had been less recent. Later we will discuss the evidence that indicates actors place lower utilities on outcomes to which they assign higher probabilities. Our comments on recency suggest that it may be partially responsible for this nonindependence between utilities and subjective probabilities.

However, it seems equally reasonable that actors will believe that outcomes that haven't occurred recently are overdue and hence that they will inflate their subjective probability estimates. In this case less recent outcomes would have higher subjective probabilities. We may very well have a curvilinear relationship on our hands, with the most and the least recent outcomes tending to have subjective probabilities somewhat higher than their corresponding NO_j/NA_i terms, and outcomes of intermediate recency having somewhat lower subjective probabilities.

The influences of consistency and recency are probably not independent. For example, the effect of recency will depend upon the degree of consistency of outcomes and actors' positions in sequences of outcomes and nonoutcomes. If the recent occurrence of an outcome inflates the subjective probability of the outcome, given a particular alternative, then the subjective probability may be simultaneously deflated by a perception that there is nonrandomness in the sequence of occurrences and that a nonoccurrence is due on the next occasion of the alternative's enactment. Moreover, the combination of an outcome that has not occurred for a long time and of randomness in the occurrence of outcomes is likely to produce a relatively high subjective probability estimate for the next enactment of an alternative. Messick's finding (1970) that the "runs structure" of a sequence of events was more important than the most recent outcome in influencing subjective probabilities suggests that, of the two, consistency is more influential.

Therefore our general supposition is that the frequency distributions of NO_j/NA_i terms based upon actors' direct experiences and their observations of others will be modified by both the consistency with which A_i has led to O_j and the recency of the occurrence of that linkage. In addition, at least three characteristics of the situation in which actors are making subjective probability estimates will be influential.

Situational Determinants of Subjective Probabilities

The characteristics of situations, as perceived by actors, will probably be of equal importance to the actors' experiences in influencing their subjective probability estimates for those situations. We believe that actors do not blindly apply their experiences to the future, but that they ascertain the extent to which they can be applied to new situations.

Generally we expect that the greater the similarity between a situation, Z, in which actors are making a subjective probability estimate, and previous situations, Y_n, in which an action alternative, A_i, has actually led to an outcome, O_j, the greater will be the actors' estimates of the likelihood that A_i will lead to O_j in situation Z, i.e., the greater will be $P(O_j|A_i)$. Likewise, the greater the perceived similarity between the new situation, Z, and previous situations in which A_i has led to $\bar{O}_j$, the lower will be the actors' estimates of the subjective probability $P(O_j|A_i)$. (We are assuming here that the consistency and recency factors are not operative.) We can account for these generalizations by utilizing a determinant we shall call the degree of cue similarity.

Degree of Cue Similarity. If actors were fully knowledgeable of all of the linkages, both direct and indirect, between A_i and O_j, they could determine why on some previous instances A_i has led to O_j while on other instances it has led to $\bar{O}_j$. In most cases the difference has likely been due to the particular combination of other factors that were present in a specific situation. By estimating the probabilities of these other factors' being present in the new situation they could thereby revise their NO_j/NA_i terms accordingly in estimating $P(O_j|A_i)$. However, they will surely never have complete knowledge in this regard, except possibly in the most elementary situations.

They are not left totally without guidelines, though, because in past situations when A_i was tried both the $A_i \rightarrow O_j$ and the $A_i \rightarrow \bar{O}_j$ sequences were undoubtedly accompanied by a variety of distinguishing *cues*. These cues will often consist of characteristics of other actors who were involved in previous situations. Rather than attempt to analyze all the possible characteristics of such cues we simply include the *degree of cue similarity* in our model as a major situational determinant of subjective probabilities. Of course it is a determinant that resides in actors' perceptions, but it specifically involves the situation in which an action alternative is to be enacted.

Ignoring for the time being the influence of the recency and consistency determinants, we may visualize actors as approaching situations armed with a basic NO_j/NA_i proportion. Assuming that O_j and $\bar{O}_j$ represent discrete, mutually exclusive outcomes, we may also visualize them as possessing a $N\bar{O}_j/NA_i$ proportion that is equal to $1 - NO_j/NA_i$. We can further visualize them as possessing sets of cues corresponding to each of these two proportions that are "matched" to the cues available in the situation for which the subjective probability estimate is being made. The basic NO_j/NA_i proportion therefore will be modified in arriving at $P(O_j|A_i)$, depending upon the relative correlations between the cues available in the new situation and the two sets of cues available from the past. If, for example, there is a rather high correlation between the present cues and the set of cues associated with NO_j/NA_i, so that the current situation is very similar to past situations in which A_i was followed by O_j, then it is probable that $P(O_j|A_i)$ will be greater than NO_j/NA_i. If, however, the cues for the current situation are more highly correlated with the set associated with $N\bar{O}_j/NA_i$, then it is likely that $P(O_j|A_i)$ will be less than NO_j/NA_i. At the limit, if there is a perfect correlation between the set of cues for the new situation and either of the sets of past cues, then it is conceivable that $P(O_j|A_i)$ will be set equal either to 1 or to zero. For example, if the cues for the current situation are identical to the cues that were present when A_i led to O_j in the past, the actors are likely to be certain that O_j will result the next time they enact A_i.

Change in Expected Support from Others. Many of the cues that will be relevant will pertain to the responses of other actors in a situation who may either increase or decrease the likelihood of occurrence of an outcome through their actions. In a new situation the question of concern to actors will be whether or not these actors, or other similar actors, will act the next time the way they have in the past. The actor making a subjective probability estimate will be particularly concerned about whether the other actors will be supporting or opposing him or her, and whether their degree of support or opposition will be greater or less than it was in the past.

We can include this aspect in our model by referring to the change in expected support from others. (We will consider opposition from other actors as negative support.) If actors perceive no change in previous levels of support or opposition from these other actors, then their basic NO_j/NA_i terms will not be influenced by this determinant. In this case, their actions would be handled adequately by the degree of cue similarity factor. But if actors anticipate greater support from other actors for the occurrence of outcome O_j, given alternative A_i, than they have received in the past, then their subjective probability $P(O_j | A_i)$ will be greater than the corresponding NO_j/NA_i term. If a lesser amount of support, or opposition, is expected, then $P(O_j | A_i)$ will be less than NO_j/NA_i. Actors' judgments regarding this variable will be dependent primarily on cue similarity, but we believe this factor is sufficiently important to isolate its influence from that of cue similarity. Cue similarity will still retain a direct effect on $P(O_j | A_i)$ to account for factors other than expected behaviors of other actors. Generally speaking, it subsumes all the changes that may have occurred since the last commission of A_i.

Perceived Limits on an Outcome. Subjective probabilities will also be modified to the extent that actors perceive that the outcomes to be received are not limitless. We consider this to be a situational determinant since it will largely depend upon the number of other actors in the situation vying for the particular outcome. This factor therefore takes into account the influence of relative scarcities of outcomes upon subjective probabilities. Generally we might anticipate that scarcity would have a greater influence upon the utilities of outcomes, with relatively scarce outcomes having greater utility than relatively abundant ones. We did not emphasize that characteristic in our discussion of utilities, but we shall take it into account in subsequent chapters in our analyses of exchange and power processes.

In this context we are simply noting that the greater the relative scarcity of an outcome, the lower will be actors' estimates of subjective probabilities for that outcome. Thus their NO_j/NA_i terms will likely be modified by their perceptions of the number of competitors for the outcome and the extent to which the outcome is divisible. Students, for example, may perceive that only a limited number of A grades will be given in a course, in which case their expectations of receiving an A will very likely be lower than if they perceive that it is possible for all those taking a course to receive an A. Thus an individual student may have a very high NO_j/NA_i proportion, but if he or she enters a course where the number of A grades to be given is severely limited, the subjective probability will very likely be modified so that $P(O_j | A_i)$ will be less than NO_j/NA_i.

Figure 3.2 summarizes the determinants of actors' subjective probabilities that we have discussed. All of these determinants are "located" in actors' perceptions. However, we have made a distinction between experiential and situational determinants in the model to make clear the different sources of these determinants. All five of the determinants we described operate to modify the basic relationship between a NO_j/NA_i proportion and the subjective probability $P(O_j | A_i)$ associated with it.

Figure 3.2. Model of Determinants of Subjective Probabilities

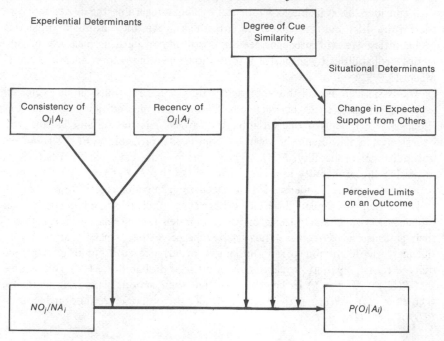

THE CAUSAL MODELS APPROACH TO
SUBJECTIVE PROBABILITIES

We have described in some detail the various factors that we believe influence actors' subjective probability estimates. In this section we explore the potential of analyzing subjective probabilities by means of their more immediate determinant, the causal models, or working theories, actually used by actors in estimating subjective probabilities. We are assuming that these perceptual constructs intervene between the determinants we have described and actual estimates of the subjective probability of a specific outcome, given enactment of a specific alternative. They simply represent the way in which actors combine the information they have available from their experiences and the perceived characteristics of the situation in which they will be enacting the alternative.

To our knowledge this approach to subjective probabilities has not been tried before. Nevertheless we feel that there are fruitful similarities to be investigated between the models of causation that actors apply to their worlds and the causal models that have been developed in the social sciences to represent relationships among variables. Our discussion, therefore, is based upon our familiarity with these models as well as upon the mathematical rules for combining probabilities. We do not claim that actors use these rules in estimating their subjective probabilities, but rather that they represent a model from which to start. Later we shall consider the available experimental evidence regarding the deviations from these rules that humans appear to introduce when they estimate subjective probabilities. We will also consider the possibility of deriving measures of subjective probabilities by means of information regarding actors' operative causal models.

The basic idea behind this approach is that causal relations can be expressed in terms of differences between conditional and unconditional probabilities (Suppes 1970). Thus if one variable, X, "causes" another variable, Y, this will be reflected in a difference between the conditional probability, $P(Y|X)$, and the unconditional probability, $P(Y)$. X may be a positive cause, as Suppes calls it, increasing the probability of Y's occurrence, so that $P(Y|X) > P(Y)$. Or it may be a negative cause, hindering Y from occurring, in which case $P(Y|X) < P(Y)$.

We anticipate similar differences between conditional and unconditional probabilities will characterize actors' causal models for the relationships between their actions and outcomes. Thus if they perceive that a particular action influences the likelihood of an outcome's occurrence, the conditional probability, $P(O_j|A_i)$, will not equal the unconditional probability, $P(O_j)$. (We assume that $P(O_j) = P(O_j|\bar{A}_i)$.) If they perceive that their actions make O_j more likely, then $P(O_j|A_i) > P(O_j)$. If their actions hinder the outcome from occurring, then $P(O_j|A_i) < P(O_j)$.

Direct and Indirect Effects

The familiar distinction between direct and indirect effects of one variable upon another can easily be applied to actors' causal models and expressed in terms of inequalities between conditional and unconditional probabilities. Thus an actor's perception that an action has a direct effect upon an outcome, as shown by the following simple diagram in which X_n represents an extraneous variable, can be represented by means of the indicated inequalities.

$$X_n$$
$$A_i \longrightarrow O_j$$

(i) $P(O_j|A_i) \neq P(O_j);$

(ii) $P(O_j|X_n) = P(O_j);$

(iii) $P(X_n|A_i) = P(X_n);$

(iv) $P(O_j|A_iX_n) = P(O_j|A_i);$

(v) $P(O_j|A_iX_n) \neq P(O_j|X_n).$

The first inequality simply indicates the actor's perception that A_i has an effect upon O_j. The second equation shows that X_n has no influence on O_j, and the third shows that A_i has no influence on X_n. The fourth and fifth equations are superfluous since they are implied by the previous three; however, we include them here for sake of contrast with the next two examples.

We can compare the case in which A_i is perceived to have only a direct effect on O_j with the case where the only perceived effect is indirect, via X_n, as shown by the following diagram and equations:

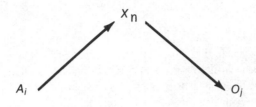

(i) $\qquad\qquad P(O_j|A_i) \neq P(O_j);$

(ii) $\qquad\qquad P(O_j|X_n) \neq P(O_j);$

(iii) $\qquad\qquad P(X_n|A_i) \neq P(X_n);$

(iv) $\qquad\qquad P(O_j|A_iX_n) \neq P(O_j|A_i);$

(v) $\qquad\qquad P(O_j|A_iX_n) = P(O_j|X_n).$

As before, the first inequality shows an effect of A_i on O_j. But now the second equation indicates that X_n also has an effect on O_j, while the third equation indicates an influence of A_i on X_n. The fourth equation reveals that X_n's influence on O_j is a direct one, while the fifth equation indicates that there is no direct influence of A_i on O_j.

If an actor perceives a combination of direct and indirect effects, as in the following diagram, then similar comparisons of conditional and unconditional probabilities may be made. An example of combined effects is the case in which an actor perceives that an action will influence the occurrence of an outcome, but that it will simultaneously influence another party to act, possibly in opposition. If this is the case, then the direct effects will be positive, in the sense of making O_j more likely, whereas the indirect effects will be negative, making it less likely.

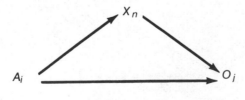

(i) $\qquad\qquad P(O_j|A_i) \neq P(O_j);$

(ii) $\qquad\qquad P(O_j|X_n) \neq P(O_j);$

(iii) $P(X_n|A_i) \neq P(X_n);$

(iv) $P(O_j|A_iX_n) \neq P(O_j|A_i);$

(v) $P(O_j|A_iX_n) \neq P(O_j|X_n).$

This set of equations differs from the previous set only in that the fifth equation indicates that A_i has a direct influence on O_j in addition to its influence through X_n.

We have worked only with inequalities since both A_i and X_n may either increase or decrease the likelihood of occurrence of outcomes. Thus an actor's action may make an outcome more likely to occur, or it may hinder it from occurring. Actors likely will be particularly concerned about the effects of their actions on negative-utility outcomes. Likewise the intervening X_n may make outcomes either more or less likely, and actors may make these X_n either more or less likely by their actions, the A_i. As a result a given action may have contradictory effects upon the occurrence of an outcome. At this point, however, we are primarily concerned with representing actors' perceptions of those effects rather than in the specific nature of the effects.

The combination of direct and indirect effects can be also represented by means of a somewhat different causal diagram; see figure 3.3. Here we represent the indirect effects of A_i on O_j by means of the usual path through X_n. But now we represent the direct effects by means of a "path" through $\bar{X}_n$, since we are assuming that either X_n or $\bar{X}_n$ may result from A_i. The subjective probability $(O_j|A_i)$, therefore, can be represented as the sum of these two paths:

(1) $P(O_j|A_i) = P(X_n|A_i) \times P(O_j|X_n) + P(\bar{X}_n|A_i) \times P(O_j|\bar{X}_n).$

Here we specify that a direct effect will be represented by a nonzero "path" through $\bar{X}_n$.[2] The crucial probability here is $P(O_j|\bar{X}_n)$. If that equals zero, i.e., there is no possibility of O_j, given $\bar{X}_n$, then A_i cannot have a direct effect upon O_j.

Equation (1) will yield an absolute estimate of subjective probabilities. Thus it will not be especially helpful for actors attempting to determine whether or not to enact a particular alternative. If we assume that at the very least actors

Figure 3.3

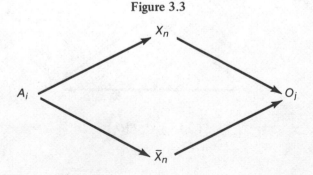

are trying to decide whether to enact an alternative or to do nothing, i.e., a choice between A_i and $\bar{A}_i$, then it is probable that they are primarily concerned with the *relative* subjective probabilities of the alternatives. If a given outcome is equally likely whether or not an actor enacts an alternative, then undoubtedly virtually all actors will choose to do nothing.

Equation (2) represents the subjective probability for O_j, given nonenactment of A_i:

(2) $P(O_j|\bar{A}_i) = P(X_n|\bar{A}_i) \times P(O_j|X_n) + P(\bar{X}_n|\bar{A}_i) \times P(O_j|\bar{X}_n).$

This equation represents a causal diagram identical to that presented just previously, except that $\bar{A}_i$ is substituted for A_i. The indirect effect of $\bar{A}_i$ on O_j is represented by the path through X_n, while its direct effect involves the path through $\bar{X}_n$.[3] This equation indicates that $P(O_j|\bar{A}_i)$ will have a nonzero value if X_n can occur in the absence of A_i and X_n influences O_j, and/or if X_n has some nonzero probability of not occurring when A_i does not occur and X_n's nonoccurrence influences O_j.

By subtracting equation (2) from equation (1), we can represent a comparison of the subjective probabilities of the alternatives A_i and $\bar{A}_i$. This will also enable us to show more clearly the effects of actors' perceptions of direct and indirect effects upon their subjective probabilities. Our strategy is similar to that we followed in the previous chapter in which we indicated how actors simplify their estimations by making relative rather than absolute utility estimates. Equation (3) represents the difference between the two subjective probabilities, based upon equations (1) and (2):

(3)
$$
\begin{aligned}
P(O_j|A_i) - P(O_j|\bar{A}_i) = &\; [P(X_n|A_i) \times P(O_j|X_n) + P(\bar{X}_n|A_i) \\
&\times P(O_j|\bar{X}_n)] - [P(X_n|\bar{A}_i) \times P(O_j|X_n) \\
&+ P(\bar{X}_n|\bar{A}_i) \times P(O_j|\bar{X}_n)].
\end{aligned}
$$

This can be simplified to

(4)
$$
\begin{aligned}
P(O_j|A_i) - P(O_j|\bar{A}_i) = &\; \big[P(O_j|X_n) \times [P(X_n|A_i) - P(X_n|\bar{A}_i)]\big] \\
&+ \big[P(O_j|\bar{X}_n) \times [P(\bar{X}_n|A_i) \\
&- P(\bar{X}_n|\bar{A}_i)]\big].
\end{aligned}
$$

These equations are not so complex as they appear at first glance. They might be described as providing an estimate of the *marginal* subjective probability associated with action rather than nonaction. If these equations yield a positive value, then they indicate how much the likelihood of O_j can be increased by enacting A_i. If there is no difference between the two subjective probabilities, then the actor might as well save resources and energy and do nothing, assuming that O_j is a desired outcome. Of course, if O_j were a negative-utility outcome, then actors would likely be interested in the alternative that had the lower subjective probability. A subjective probability that was greater for $\bar{A}_i$ than for A_i would indicate an actor's perception that by enacting A_i he or she could prevent or reduce the chances of the occurrence of O_j in this case.

We can relate equation (4) to the three cases we have described—direct effects only, indirect effects only, and combined direct and indirect effects. We can also simplify the notation by making the following substitutions:

$$a = P(X_n|A_i); \qquad d = P(O_j|\bar{X}_n);$$
$$b = P(O_j|X_n); \qquad e = P(X_n|\bar{A}_i);$$
$$c = P(\bar{X}_n|A_i); \qquad f = P(\bar{X}_n|\bar{A}_i).$$

The equation can then be represented as

(5) $$P(O_j|A_i) - P(O_j|\bar{A}_i) = b(a - e) + d(c - f).$$

Direct Effects. Equation (i) (p. 90) for the case in which only direct effects of A_i on O_j are perceived to be operative indicates that equation (5) will yield a nonzero value. We can see from the other equations in that set exactly how that will result. Since equation (iii) for the direct-effects case indicates that $P(X_n|A_i) = P(X_n|\bar{A}_i)$ the $(a - e)$ term in equation (5) will be zero and the difference between the subjective probabilities will reduce to $d(c - f)$. If c is greater than f, signifying that $\bar{X}_n$ is more likely to result if A_i rather than $\bar{A}_i$ occurs, then the subjective probability for O_j, given A_i, will be greater than $P(O_j|\bar{A}_i)$. The d term will not be relevant for a comparison of the subjective probabilities, even though it will equal the b term in the direct-effects case.

Indirect Effects. If only indirect effects are operative, then equation (5) will also have a nonzero value. In this case the path from A_i through $\bar{X}_n$ to O_j will have a zero value. The most likely way that this will happen will be if $P(O_j|\bar{X}_n)$ equals zero, indicating that O_j cannot occur if X_n does not occur. In that case the d term will be zero in equation (5), and whether A_i or $\bar{A}_i$ is more likely to result in $\bar{X}_n$ will be immaterial. The difference between the subjective probabilities will completely depend upon whether A_i or $\bar{A}_i$ is more likely to result in X_n. If the d term is not zero, then a perceived absence of direct effects of A_i on O_j will be indicated by a zero value for the c term, or $P(\bar{X}_n|A_i)$. If that were the case, then all other probabilities in the equation would have to be estimated to make a relative comparison of subjective probabilities.

Combined Effects. If direct and indirect effects are perceived to be operative for both A_i and $\bar{A}_i$, then it will be necessary to estimate all the probabilities in equation (5). This essentially involves determining the likelihood of O_j, given X_n, next determining whether A_i or $\bar{A}_i$ is more likely to promote X_n, then determining the probability of O_j, given $\bar{X}_n$, again determining whether A_i or $\bar{A}_i$ is more likely to result in $\bar{X}_n$, and finally comparing the relative direct and indirect effects of the two alternatives. This can easily become quite complex, and later in this chapter we shall discuss the simplifications we believe actors introduce into this estimation process.

We can exemplify the way in which causal models of actors can be used to estimate subjective probabilities by considering the interesting case of combined direct and indirect effects in which the effects, for a given alternative, are opposite. Let's assume that an actor is interested in enacting an alternative, A_i, in order to receive an outcome, O_j. He or she anticipates that enacting A_i will make the occurrence of O_j more likely, but he or she also anticipates that enacting A_i will influence another actor, X_n, to act in opposition. Consequently the actor is interested in estimating whether action is likely to result in O_j or whether X_n's opposition is sufficiently great to make reception of the outcome less likely than if he or she simply did nothing. We will assume that the actor had made the following conditional probability estimates, and we are attempting to predict the actor's estimate of the relative subjective probabilities of the two alternatives:

$$P(X_n|A_i) = .6; \qquad P(X_n|\bar{A}_i) = .2;$$
$$P(O_j|X_n) = .4; \qquad P(O_j|\bar{X}_n) = .8;$$
$$P(\bar{X}_n|A_i) = .4; \qquad P(\bar{X}_n|\bar{A}_i) = .8.$$

From these elemental probabilities we can see that the actor believes that A_i is more likely to promote X_n rather than $\bar{X}_n$, that the occurrence of X_n makes O_j less likely, and that X_n is less likely to occur if A_i is not enacted. These probabilities can also be shown in terms of a causal diagram; see figure 3.4. We are assuming here that all outcomes and actions are dichotomous and mutually exclusive and that in all cases they sum to 1, i.e., either O_j or $\bar{O}_j$ occurs.

By inserting these probabilities into equation (5) we get

$$\begin{aligned}
P(O_j|A_i) - P(O_j|\bar{A}_i) &= .4(.6 - .2) + .8(.4 - .8) \\
&= .4 \times .4 + .8 \times (-.4) \\
&= .16 - .32 \\
&= -.16.
\end{aligned}$$

Figure 3.4

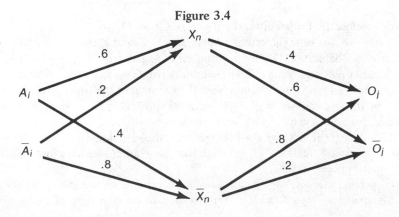

From this we see that enacting A_i will make the occurrence of O_j less likely. The actor would be well advised in this case not to act and arouse actor X_n. Using equations (1) and (2) to estimate the absolute subjective probabilities of A_i and $\bar{A}_i$ we get

$$P(O_j|A_i) = .24 + .32 = .56 \quad \text{and} \quad P(O_j|\bar{A}_i) = .08 + .64 = .72.$$

For each of these the first term represents the indirect effects and the second the direct effects. Thus we can see that the difference between the two alternatives comes in primarily in regard to the latter. The "direct" effect of $\bar{A}_i$ on O_j is substantially greater than the direct effect of A_i. X_n is not very likely to act if the actor does not enact A_i, and O_j is very likely to occur if X_n does not occur. The difference between $P(O_j|\bar{X}_n)$ and $P(O_j|X_n)$, .8 versus .4, indicates the actor's perception of the extent to which X_n can reduce the likelihood of O_j's occurring through action. And since X_n is more likely to occur than $\bar{X}_n$ if the actor acts, he or she would be smart to "let sleeping dogs lie." Again, we should point out that we are not claiming that actors will make this precise an estimate of their subjective probabilities. But we do anticipate that in this situation they will estimate that $P(O_j|\bar{A}_i)$ is greater than $P(O_j|A_i)$.

Another way to view this example is in terms of the actors' perceptions of the relative likelihoods of different sequences of events. By looking at the values of the indirect- and direct-effect terms for the two alternatives we can see that the actor sees the $\bar{A}_i \rightarrow \bar{X}_n \rightarrow O_j$ sequence as the most likely. The $A_i \rightarrow \bar{X}_n \rightarrow O_j$ sequence is perceived somewhat less likely than the prior one. And the $A_i \rightarrow X_n \rightarrow O_j$ is perceived to be not very likely at all. Furthermore, the gap between the first two sequences is sufficiently great to make $\bar{A}_i$'s overall subjective probability of obtaining O_j greater than A_i's. This suggests the intriguing possibility that actors' subjective probabilities may be estimated by having them compare the relative likelihood of different sequences of events. If enough comparisons of enough different sequences were made, it is conceivable that not only could their causal models be represented but relatively precise estimates of their subjective probabilities could be obtained.

Deriving Subjective Probabilities from Actors' Causal Models

We have shown how the causal models of actors can be used to estimate their subjective probabilities. The more important question is "If we do not know their basic conditional probabilities, can we derive them from the actors in some manner, create their causal models, and then estimate their subjective probabilities?" In this section we shall explore the feasibility of this approach, using a series of paired comparisons between conditional probabilities and elements of the unfolding technique for the construction of ordered-metric scales (Coombs 1964; Long and Wilken 1974). We shall use the example we have just discussed to make the process clearer.

The general strategy we shall follow is to assume we are asking an actor a series of questions regarding his or her estimates of conditional probabilities. For example, we might ask, "Which is greater, the likelihood of O_j, if A_i occurs, or the likelihood of O_j, if A_i does not occur?" This of course represents a comparison of $P(O_j|A_i)$ and $P(O_j|\bar{A}_i)$. We shall do this separately, first for the linkage between A_i and X_n, and then for the linkage between O_j and X_n. We shall then convert the results of these paired comparisons into a rank ordering of conditional probabilities, one of A_i, given X_n, and the other of O_j, given X_n. We shall then compare several conditional probabilities from the two sets with each other to determine the overall ordering. Finally we shall assign numerical values to the conditional probabilities and test them in equation (5) to see how closely they correspond to the values we calculated previously.

Suppose that we obtained the following inequalities from a respondent through questions similar to the one mentioned above:

1. $P(X_n|A_i) > P(\bar{X}_n|A_i)$

2. $P(X_n|A_i) > P(X_n|\bar{A}_i)$

3. $P(X_n|A_i) < P(\bar{X}_n|\bar{A}_i)$

4. $P(\bar{X}_n|A_i) > P(X_n|\bar{A}_i)$

5. $P(\bar{X}_n|A_i) < P(\bar{X}_n|\bar{A}_i)$

6. $P(X_n|\bar{A}_i) < P(\bar{X}_n|\bar{A}_i)$

The reader will see that we have simply taken the four possible probabilities of X_n, given A_i, and formed all possible combinations of them. These six comparisons can then be presented spatially, with larger conditional probabilities above smaller ones, as shown in figure 3.5. This gives us the ordering

$$P(\bar{X}_n|\bar{A}_i) > P(X_n|A_i) > P(\bar{X}_n|A_i) > P(X_n|\bar{A}_i).$$

Now we can assign approximate values to these four conditional probabilities.

Figure 3.5

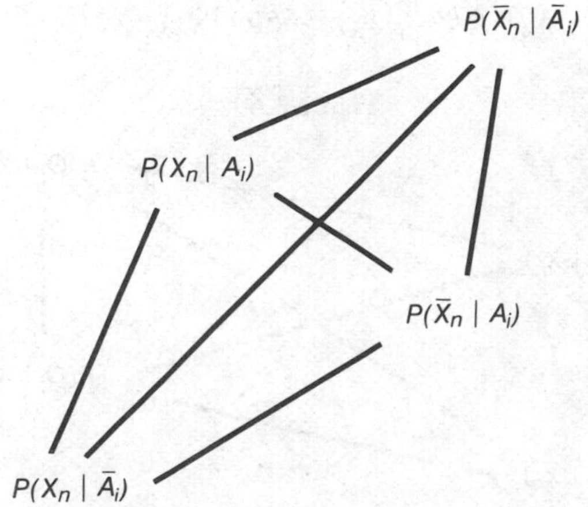

It appears reasonable to start in the middle of the ordering, with a value of about .5, and work outward, and to express probabilities in tenths as far as possible. This suggests that $P(X_n|A_i)$ should have a value greater than .5 and $P(\bar{X}_n|A_i)$ a value less than .5. (If our respondent had indicated that they were equal we would assign .5 to each.) Furthermore, we can see that these two probabilities involve the two mutually exclusive outcomes of A_i. Consequently, under the assumption that they should sum to 1, we assign the value of .6 to $P(X_n|A_i)$ and .4 to $P(\bar{X}_n|A_i)$. Following the same logic, we set $P(\bar{X}_n|\bar{A}_i) = .7$ and $P(X_n|\bar{A}_i) = .3$.

Comparing all possible combinations of the probabilities of O_j, given X_n, suppose we get the following inequalities and the rank ordering shown in figure 3.6.:

$$1.\ P(O_j|X_n) < P(O_j|\bar{X}_n)$$
$$2.\ P(O_j|X_n) < P(\bar{O}_j|X_n)$$
$$3.\ P(O_j|X_n) > P(\bar{O}_j|\bar{X}_n)$$
$$4.\ P(O_j|\bar{X}_n) > P(\bar{O}_j|X_n)$$
$$5.\ P(O_j|\bar{X}_n) > P(\bar{O}_j|\bar{X}_n)$$
$$6.\ P(\bar{O}_j|X_n) > P(\bar{O}_j|\bar{X}_n)$$

Therefore, $P(O_j|\bar{X}_n) > P(\bar{O}_j|X_n) > P(O_j|X_n) > P(\bar{O}_j|\bar{X}_n)$.

On the basis of the procedure we have discussed we assign the following values as first approximations: $P(O_j|\bar{X}_n) = .7$; $P(\bar{O}_j|X_n) = .6$; $P(O_j|X_n) = .4$; $P(\bar{O}_j|\bar{X}_n) = .3$. The next step is to make comparisons between our two rank orderings in order to estimate the probabilities more precisely. At this point we have the following:

$$P(\bar{X}_n|\bar{A}_i) > P(X_n|A_i) > P(\bar{X}_n|A_i) > P(X_n|\bar{A}_i)$$
$$\quad .7 \qquad\qquad .6 \qquad\qquad .4 \qquad\qquad .3$$
$$P(O_j|\bar{X}_n) > P(\bar{O}_j|X_n) > P(O_j|X_n) > P(\bar{O}_j|\bar{X}_n).$$

Figure 3.6

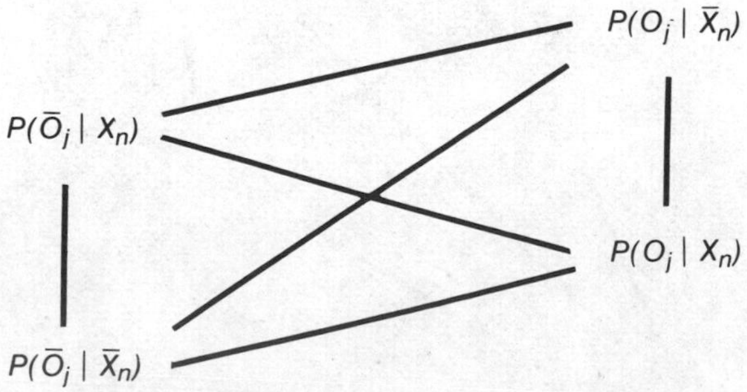

$P(O_j | \bar{X}_n)$

$P(\bar{O}_j | X_n)$

$P(O_j | X_n)$

$P(\bar{O}_j | X_n)$

The appropriate comparisons to make are between the probabilities occupying the same rank in the two orderings in order to determine what adjustments are necessary in the values we have assigned. This is probably the trickiest part of the whole procedure since it requires respondents to answer rather difficult questions, e.g., "Which is more likely, that X_n will not occur if A_i does not occur or that O_j will occur if X_n does not occur?" However, as we shall see shortly, complete accuracy on the part of respondents is not essential.

Since we are working with the conditional probabilities we originally provided for our example, we shall assume that we derived the following from our comparison of the two orderings:

1. $P(\bar{X}_n | \bar{A}_i) = P(O_j | \bar{X}_n)$

2. $P(X_n | A_i) = P(\bar{O}_j | X_n)$

3. $P(\bar{X}_n | A_i) = P(O_j | X_n)$

4. $P(X_n | \bar{A}_i) = P(\bar{O}_j | \bar{X}_n)$

On this basis we leave the probability values as they are. Checking back to the original values, we see that we have deviated only for the extreme probabilities. By using the values we have assigned in equation (5) we can see just how serious that deviation is. Doing so, we get the following:

$$P(O_j | A_i) - P(O_j | \bar{A}_i) = .4(.6 - .3) + .7(.4 - .7)$$

$$= .4 \times .3 + .7 \times (-.3)$$

$$= .12 - .21$$

$$= -.09.$$

Our value of $-.09$ is not far different from the original value of $-.16$. On this basis we would estimate that our actor will assign a slightly higher value to $P(O_j | \bar{A}_i)$ than to $P(O_j | A_i)$.

We can show that even if a respondent makes moderate-sized errors in the comparisons between the two rank orderings the resultant deviation will not be great. We shall assume that we got the following responses:

1. $P(\bar{X}_n | \bar{A}_i) > P(O_j | \bar{X}_n)$

2. $P(X_n | A_i) < P(\bar{O}_j | X_n)$

3. $P(\bar{X}_n | A_i) > P(O_j | X_n)$

4. $P(X_n | \bar{A}_i) < P(\bar{O}_j | \bar{X}_n)$

and assigned the following values: $P(\bar{X}_n | \bar{A}_i) = .8; P(O_j | \bar{X}_n) = .7; P(\bar{O}_j | X_n) = .6;$ $P(X_n | A_i) = .55; P(\bar{X}_n | A_i) = .45; P(O_j | X_n) = .4; P(\bar{O}_j | \bar{X}_n) = .3; P(X_n | \bar{A}_i) = .2.$ Inserting these values in equation (5) we derive a value of $-.085$ for the difference between $P(O_j | A_i)$ and $P(O_j | \bar{A}_i)$.

Like many other scaling techniques, this procedure will undoubtedly be susceptible to intransitivities in responses. Thus it will break down if probability a is greater than probability b, b is greater than c, but c is greater than a. This problem is likely to show up in more complex models but should not be too troublesome in models of the complexity we have described. The procedure is facilitated by the fact that we can assume that subjective probabilities have limits of 0 and 1. Consequently, the values to be assigned are within a delimited range. Using a similar procedure to derive utility estimates would be handicapped by the fact that they have no known limits.

Earlier we mentioned the possibility of using differences in the perceived likelihood of action-intervening factor-outcome sequences to derive actors' subjective probabilities. After some experimentation with that possibility, using the same example, it appears that is not a practical approach by itself. If used in conjunction with the procedure we have described, however, it might enable one to cut down on the number of comparisons between probabilities that are required of respondents.

Thus we have shown that it is possible to derive estimates of subjective probabilities by constructing actors' causal models from relatively simple comparisons between probabilities. Now it is time to consider some problems that procedure, and the estimation of subjective probabilities in general, are bound to encounter.

COMPLICATIONS ENCOUNTERED IN ESTIMATING SUBJECTIVE PROBABILITIES

Both the actor attempting to estimate the subjective probabilities of his or her actions and the researcher attempting to predict behavior will encounter problems to the extent that the causal models become relatively complex. To this point we have looked only at situations involving a choice between an action and a nonaction, which may or may not influence another factor or actor, and one outcome or nonoutcome dependent on that original action. Two complicating characteristics are likely to be present in most real-world situations.

Multiple Indirect Effects

Quite often there will be more than one indirect path between A_i and O_j. That is, actors may anticipate that their actions will influence more than one condition to intervene between A_i and O_j. An action may prompt one actor, X_n, to oppose the actor's receiving the outcome and another actor, Y_n, to assist the actor in obtaining the outcome, for example. These intervening conditions may be independent of each other, or one may be dependent on the other, e.g., Y_n's action may depend upon whether or not X_n acts. We'll look at the former case first.

The situation we have described can be diagramed as shown in figure 3.7. A significant complication that arises in this situation is that there are now more than two mutually exclusive possibilities. Only X_n may occur, only Y_n may occur, both X_n and Y_n may occur, or neither X_n nor Y_n may occur. In this case

Figure 3.7

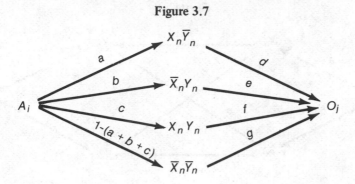

the anticipated direct effects of A_i on O_j are represented by the path through $\overline{X}_n \overline{Y}_n$, indicating the probability that A_i will result in O_j if neither intervening condition occurs.

We have assumed that these four intervening conditions are the only ones possible and that the sum of their probabilities equals one. Hence the last path is labeled $1 - (a + b + c)$. The equation for estimating $P(O_j|A_i)$, therefore, becomes:

$$P(O_j|A_i) = ad + be + cf + [1 - (a + b + c)]g.$$

This reduces to

$$P(O_j|A_i) = a(d - g) + b(e - g) + c(f - g) + g.$$

We can see from this equation that the estimation of the subjective probability of O_j is based on a comparison of the differences between the indirect effects of A_i on O_j through the intervening conditions and the direct effects of A_i on O_j, and by a weighting of those differences by the probabilities of the intervening variables' occurring. Thus for the case where d, e, and f are all greater than g, indicating that both intervening conditions promote O_j, we can predict that the greater the positive influence of these conditions on O_j and the greater their probabilities of occurrence, the greater will be $P(O_j|A_i)$. And, if g is greater than d, e, and f, then the greater those differences, the lower will be the probability.

A comparison of relative subjective probabilities will be even more complex in this situation. We can visualize paths from $\overline{A}_i$ to each of the intervening conditions; the probability of a specific intervening condition, given A_i, will have to be compared with the probability of that condition, given $\overline{A}_i$, and weighted by the path connecting that condition with O_j. For example, it will be necessary to compare $P(X_n \overline{Y}_n | A_i)$ with $P(X_n \overline{Y}_n | \overline{A}_i)$ and weight that difference with $P(O_j | X_n \overline{Y}_n)$. This comparison procedure can only be simplified by setting certain paths equal to zero, 1, or to each other.

Intervening conditions may also be perceived to occur in causal chains. For example, an actor may expect that A_i will influence X_n, which will in turn

Figure 3.8

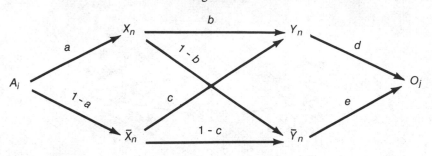

influence Y_n, which will have an effect on O_j. A fairly simple case of this type can be diagramed as shown in figure 3.8. The equation for this causal model is

$$P(O_j|A_i) = ab(d - e) + ac(e - d) + c(d - e) + e.$$

From this equation we can see that the magnitude of the difference $(d - e)$ between $P(O_j|Y_n)$ and $P(O_j|\bar{Y}_n)$ will be of major importance in influencing the size of $P(O_j|A_i)$. The sign of the difference will also be significant. If $d > e$, then Y_n is a condition promoting O_j. Consequently any combination of probabilities prior to Y_n in the model that promote it rather than $\bar{Y}_n$ will make O_j more likely and increase $P(O_j|A_i)$. The two combinations filling that bill are $b > 1 - b$ and $a > 1 - a$, and $c > 1 - c$ and $1 - a > a$. If $e > d$, then Y_n is a condition hindering O_j, and the combinations of prior probabilities that will make O_j more likely are $1 - b > b$ and $a > 1 - a$, and $1 - c > c$ and $1 - a > a$. Other paths through the model will generally result in a lower value of $(O_j|A_i)$. Thus if $d > e$, the prior inequalities of $a > 1 - a$ and $1 - b > b$ will mean that A_i is promoting X_n and X_n is hindering Y_n, thereby decreasing the likelihood of O_j.

Because we can predict the impact of these prior inequalities on O_j, given knowledge of the relationship between d and e, it appears that estimating subjective probabilities will be somewhat easier in situations such as this, where intervening conditions are dependent upon each other, than in situations like the one we have described just before, where the intervening conditions are independent. For example, if we know that an actor perceives d to be greater than e, then we can predict that $P(O_j|A_i)$ will be greater if the actor also perceives that $b > 1 - b$ and $a > 1 - a$ than if he or she anticipates that $1 - b > b$ and $a > 1 - a$. One conceivably could derive a fairly precise estimate of the subjective probability by asking the actor to make a series of comparisons between probabilities, as we did before, and then arbitrarily assigning values to the rank ordering of probabilities that is obtained. This process would of course be facilitated if one is comfortable with the assumption that the sum of the subjective probabilities of exhaustive mutually exclusive outcomes equals 1.

One can derive a rough estimate of actors' subjective probabilities in cases in which multiple intervening factors are involved simply from knowledge of their perceptions regarding the influence of their actions on these intervening factors and the influence of these factors on an outcome of interest. This is accomplished by representing the paths in their causal models by positive or negative signs and then estimating the combined influence of the paths on the outcome. We may start with the simplest case, involving only one indirect path, shown in figure 3.9.

We can use a positive sign to represent the perception that an action promotes, or increases the likelihood of, the occurrence of another action, and a negative sign to represent an action's hindering, or decreasing the likelihood of, the occurrence of that action. Thus in this situation if an actor anticipates that $P(X_n|A_i) > P(X_n|\bar{A}_i)$, the path between A_i and X_n will be positive.[4] If the actor expects that A_i hinders X_n, then the path may be represented by a negative sign. By comparing the combined effects of the two paths in this case one may at least compare the subjective probability $P(O_j|A_i)$ for this case with cases in which the combined effects of the two paths between A_i and O_j are perceived differently.

For example, if all three paths are positive, this indicates that the actor perceives that A_i promotes O_j directly and that A_i also promotes X_n, which in turn promotes O_j. In this case the combined effects of A_i and O_j will be positive. Since we represent an indirect effect as the product of its component direct effects, it will be positive if the number of negative direct paths comprising it is even or is zero. In this situation if either "component effect" is negative, the indirect effect of A_i on O_j will also be negative. Consequently, $P(O_j|A_i)$ will likely be lower than if both the direct and indirect paths were positive. And if both paths have a negative effect, $P(O_j|A_i)$ will be still lower.

This approach can be extended to more complex models, such as that shown in figure 3.10. Here we have five simple paths, each of which can be positive or

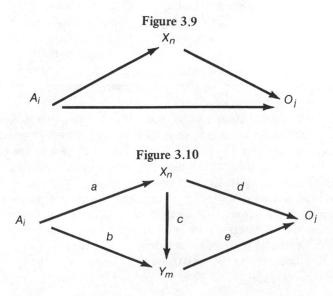

Figure 3.9

X_n

A_i O_j

Figure 3.10

X_n

a d

A_i c O_j

b e

Y_m

negative depending upon whether an action promotes or hinders the action or outcome following it in the model. Thus even though it is relatively simple it can represent $2^5 = 32$ possible sign combinations. The total influence of A_i on O_j can be predicted by observing the combined influence of the paths ad, ace, and be. The path ace is particularly interesting because its total influence on O_i involves three component paths. As a result the indirect effect of A_i on O_j through both X_n and Y_m will be positive if either three or one of the direct paths constituting it is positive. It will be negative if none or two of them is positive. Thus if c were the only positive path of the three, the indirect effect ace would be positive.

We can make two general predictions about the subjective probability $P(O_j|A_i)$ on the basis of this model. First, generally the more paths, both direct and indirect, between A_i and O_j that have positive products, the greater will be $P(O_j|A_i)$. Second, the influence of A_i on O_j along any indirect path, such as ad, will be less than either of the component probabilities, i.e., a or d. It may not exactly equal ad, but we anticipate that it will be closer to a product than to a sum of the component probabilities.

So, merely by determining what factors are included in actors' causal models and by determining whether these factors are perceived to promote or hinder other factors and the ultimate outcome, one may derive approximations of their subjective probabilities that may not differ substantially from the actual subjective probabilities they use in estimating their subjective expected utilities.

Multiple Outcomes

Very similar complications will be created if actors perceive multiple outcomes to be contingent upon their actions. The multiple intervening factors we have just discussed can be regarded as multiple outcomes if they provide utility for actors. However, our general assumption in the previous section has been that they have provided utility only indirectly, by making outcomes that do provide utility either more or less likely. More representative of the multiple-outcome case is the situation in which an actor anticipates that more than one other actor may respond to his or her action with an action that provides utility. For example, he or she may anticipate that more than one actor may offer praise for a particular action.

Two important distinctions can be made in discussing multiple outcomes. The first we shall refer to as the *compatibility* of outcomes. If two outcomes may both occur, we regard them as compatible; if only one or the other may occur, we shall refer to them as incompatible. The second distinction is one we have already made in regard to multiple intervening factors, namely, between simultaneity and sequence. Multiple outcomes may occur either at the same time or sequentially. In the former case we shall assume that they are independent of each other. In the latter case, they may be either independent or dependent, depending in part upon whether or not they are compatible. Thus, if two outcomes are incompatible *and* sequential, we shall assume that the occurrence of one of the outcomes depends on whether or not the other occurs. Combining these two distinctions we have the four possible models displayed in figure 3.11.

In general the estimation of subjective probabilities will be somewhat more complex if outcomes are compatible than if they are incompatible because of the greater number of component probabilities involved. This can be seen by comparing (a) with (b) and (c) with (d) in figure 3.11. Model (a) contains one more path than (b), representing the possibility of O_j and O_k's occurring simultaneously. In model (b) the supposition is that either O_j or O_k or neither O_j nor O_k will occur. Model (d) also has one less path than model (c), indicating the actor's perception of the impossibility of O_k's occurring if O_j occurs. Since we are not assuming that O_k will necessarily occur if O_j does not occur, we have left in the path connecting $\bar{O}_j$ and $\bar{O}_k$.

If we make two assumptions—first, that the utility of $\bar{O}_j\bar{O}_k$ is zero, and, second, that the probability of the joint occurrence of two outcomes is the product of the probabilities of the two outcomes' occurring separately, i.e., $P(O_jO_k|A_i) = P(O_j|A_i) \times P(O_k|A_i)$, then only three probabilities need to be estimated for model (a) and the subjective expected utility equation for that model becomes

$$
\begin{aligned}
SEU(A_i) = \ & P(O_j\bar{O}_k|A_i) \times U(O_j) + P(\bar{O}_jO_k|A_i) \times U(O_k) \\
& + P(O_jO_k|A_i) \times U(O_jO_k),
\end{aligned}
$$

(6)

with $P(O_jO_k|A_i) = P(O_j|A_i) \times P(O_k|A_i)$. For model (b) only the first two terms in equation (6) will be necessary under our assumptions.

Figure 3.11. Four Types of Multiple Outcomes

(a) Compatible Simultaneous

(b) Incompatible Simultaneous

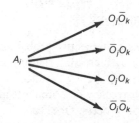

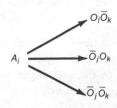

(c) Compatible Sequential

(d) Incompatible Sequential

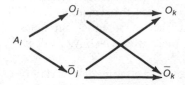

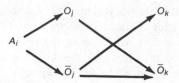

When one of the outcomes is perceived to be dependent on the other, as in model (c), the situation is slightly more complex. Equation (6) constitutes the basic equation for this model as well, but now the subjective probability of O_k is conditional upon O_j, so that $P(O_j O_k | A_i) = P(O_j | A_i) \times P(O_k | O_j)$. And with model (d) the fact that O_k is perceived to be incompatible with O_j is represented by setting $P(O_k | O_j)$ equal to zero. As a result $P(O_j O_k | A_i) = 0$, and the subjective expected utility equation reduces to the equation used for model (b). Thus there probably is little reason for retaining the distinction between models (b) and (d) except for illustrative purposes, unless O_k is sufficiently lagged in time so that there is a diminution in utility as a result of the effects of the immediacy of goal fulfillment determinant.

Again we have looked at the simplest of cases. In the social world things are often more complex. For example, an actor may anticipate more than one possible response from more than one actor. Earlier we mentioned that more than one actor may respond with praise. It is very possible that the actor will anticipate criticism or neither criticism nor praise from one or more actors. If so, then he or she will actually be estimating the probabilities of three different outcomes—praise, criticism, or nothing—from each other actor. In such a situation the probability estimations will become unmanageable quite rapidly, unless simplifying assumptions are made.

It is also quite likely that actors' causal models will include both multiple intervening factors and multiple outcomes. Our attempts to work with such models indicate very clearly that actors must make simplifications in estimating subjective probabilities just as they simplify their utility estimates, if for no other reason than to save the time and resources required to make the necessary estimates.

SIMPLIFICATIONS INTRODUCED IN THE ESTIMATION OF SUBJECTIVE PROBABILITIES

Looking at this issue in terms of the determinants of subjective probabilities, it appears that actors will simplify their estimations by increasing the importance of some of the determinants and/or by setting certain NO_j/NA_i ratios equal to zero or close to 1. For example, the consistency or recency determinants may be given greater weights than usual in the estimation process. Or actors may estimate their subjective probabilities primarily on the basis of cue similarity. If they are anticipating four different possible outcomes resulting from an action, then the NO_j/NA_i ratio for the one of these that has the highest degree of cue similarity between past situations in which it has occurred and the current situation may simply be set close to or equal to 1 and the remaining NO_j/NA_i ratios reduced to approximately zero. The number of potential outcomes to consider may also be reduced by ignoring all those whose NO_i/NA_i values are less than some threshold level.

When we consider this issue in terms of actors' causal models, a variety of simplifications suggest themselves. First, certain paths in these models may be set equal to zero or to 1 or equal to each other. Thus in figure 3.11 (d) the impossibility of O_k's occurring, given O_j, was exemplified by a zero path between those two outcomes. Setting any one of the direct paths between two factors in a model equal to 1 will have the effect of setting all other direct paths between those factors equal to zero, if we assume that the sum of the probabilities of all outcomes or actions contingent upon a particular factor equals 1. It is probable that these adjustments will be made for paths that are already perceived to be relatively close to either zero or 1. Paths will be set equal to each other, of course, if actors perceive that outcomes are about equally likely. If two outcomes, e.g., O_j and $\bar{O}_j$, are involved, then the paths leading from an action, A_i, to them will each equal .5; if three outcomes were involved the paths would each equal .33. In this case the utilities of the outcomes would become more significant than the subjective probabilities in the subjective expected utility estimate.

Second, which paths actors actually estimate and the precision with which they do so will likely be influenced by the utilities of the outcomes that are involved, just as we noted in the last chapter that the necessity and accuracy of utility estimates will be affected by subjective probabilities. For example, we expect that actors will not bother to estimate probabilities for outcomes that promise only minimal increments of utility. These utilities may simply be set equal to zero, thus making estimation of the subjective probabilities associated with them unnecessary. In addition, differences in the utilities of outcomes must be significant. Considering only the two-alternative, two-outcome case, where A_1 and A_2 both lead to O_1 and O_2, it can be shown that if the utilities of O_1 and O_2 are approximately equal it will be rather meaningless to estimate the subjective probabilities precisely, since neither alternative will have significantly greater subjective expected utility than the other. If, however, the utilities of O_1 and O_2 are substantially different, then an accurate estimate of subjective probabilities will be necessary to ensure enacting the alternative that will yield the higher-utility outcome.

Third, in cases in which many different actors are anticipated to intervene between an action and an outcome and to affect the likelihood of that outcome by their actions, it is plausible that simplifications will be made by merely treating them as a group and thereby reducing the number of indirect paths between the action and the outcome. Or it is also plausible that the same probabilities will be assigned to each of them. This may be either the probability that they will act, given the original action, or their probable effect on the outcome. Possibly, also, these two types of simplification will be combined. An actor may assign equal probabilities to each actor's likelihood of action in response to his or her action and then assign a single probability, representing their combined influence, to the linkage between their actions and the outcome.

Fourth, in the last chapter we discussed at length the possibility of simplifying utility estimates by making relative, rather than absolute, estimates. Similar comments are applicable to subjective probabilities. We also noted there that in the two-alternative case in which both alternatives lead to the same two outcomes a relative estimate of subjective expected utility can be made by means of the equation

$$SEU(A_1) - SEU(A_2) = P'[U(O_1) - U(O_2)],$$

where $P' = (p - q)$, $p = P(O_1 | A_1)$, and $q = P(O_1 | A_2)$. Here one needs to assess only the relative values of $U(O_1)$ and $U(O_2)$ and of p and q. If $p > q$, then $U(O_1)$ must be greater than $U(O_2)$ for A_1 to have greater subjective expected utility. If $p < q$, then $U(O_2)$ must be greater than $U(O_1)$ for A_1 to have greater subjective expected utility. Numerical values are not required for either the utilities or the subjective probabilities in this case.

Relative estimates of subjective probabilities will be facilitated by alternatives leading to the same outcomes, as was the case with utilities. This can be shown by comparing the previous case with one in which the two alternatives lead to a common outcome, O_2, and each also leads to a unique outcome, A_1 to O_1 and A_2 to O_3. A comparison of the subjective expected utilities of the two alternatives is given by

$$
\begin{aligned}
SEU(A_1) - SEU(A_2) &= [p \times U(O_1) + (1 - p) \times U(O_2)] \\
&\quad - [q \times U(O_2) + (1 - q) \times U(O_3)] \\
&= [p \times U(O_1)] + [(1 - p - q) \times U(O_2)] \\
&\quad - [(1 - q) \times U(O_3)].
\end{aligned}
$$

In this case relative estimates of subjective probabilities, or of utilities, will not be sufficient to determine which alternative has greater subjective expected utility. If $1 - p > q$ the first and second terms will be positive, but it will be necessary to estimate all terms to see if their value is greater than that of the third term.

Psychological and Sociocultural Simplifying Mechanisms

A major reason actors simplify their estimates of both utilities and subjective probabilities is, of course, the fact that the complexity of many social situations makes estimation impossible without such simplifications. Therefore social scientists who are attempting to model human decision processes must duplicate these simplifications in their models. Their models should also take into account those factors, in addition to sheer complexity, that induce actors to make simplifications. We believe that at least three of these need to be considered.

One of these we have already discussed in conjunction with the simplification of utility estimates. That is the influence of ideologies, or collective definitions of the situation. By providing their adherents with an already formulated causal model of the way the world operates they thereby provide them with subjective probability estimates, thus obviating the need to derive these estimates solely from personal experiences. Socialization processes in general can be viewed as the development of these causal models—"if you do thus and so, then that is bound to happen." Ideologies are therefore helpful socializing devices: "if you do this, you will go to heaven"; "if you do that, you will be happy"; "if you work hard, you will be successful." The world of advertising is a prime example of manipulation of people's subjective probabilities, offering a multitude of rewarding outcomes contingent only upon the purchase of one or another product.

Ideologies clearly offer simplified versions of the "taken for granted" world, to use Peter Berger's phrase (1963). Insofar as subjective probabilities are concerned, their major simplifying contribution is to promote perceptions of certainty or impossibility, i.e., to push these estimates toward 1 or zero. They strive to leave little doubt in their followers' minds, guaranteeing that actions either absolutely will or will not yield particular outcomes. In this chapter we have only scratched the surface of the complexity that would be involved if one were to attempt to estimate accurately all the utilities and subjective probabilities of all the outcomes and the actions of others contingent upon his or her own actions. Thus it is not surprising that ideologies abound, enabling us to function without becoming immobilized by the complex decisions confronting us.

Psychological factors are undoubtedly also significant in influencing the simplifications individuals are likely to make. At the beginning of this chapter we referred to efficacy and fatalism as orientations to the world that can be represented in terms of subjective probabilities. To these can be added others, such as dogmatism. One of the characteristics of persons described as dogmatic, or authoritarian, is the tendency to see things in absolute terms. This clearly involves their value judgments, but it likely will also be revealed in a strong tendency to remove uncertainty from their causal models by seeing outcomes as either certain or impossible (Phillips 1970:263). Actors with a strong sense of personal efficacy are likely to make similar simplifications, assigning quite high subjective probabilities to outcomes contingent on their actions.

Persons supposedly high in need achievement, whom we discussed in conjunction with utilities, can also be described in subjective probability terms. According to McClelland (1961:210-14), a distinctive characteristic of such individuals is the tendency to seek out situations offering moderate risk. This implies that they are likely to select action alternatives that offer a relatively high, but not too high, probability of attaining an outcome. It is not clear that this personality trait influences their subjective probability estimates, but it does suggest that they find some subjective probabilities more rewarding than others. The dogmatic or authoritarian person might also be regarded as receiving some satisfaction from imposing certainty upon an uncertain world.

Finally, the differential levels of knowledge and ranges of experiences of different actors are likely to affect their subjective probability estimates. Those with more knowledge conceivably will be able to make more accurate estimates and will be more aware of the linkages between actions and outcomes. This may not always work to their benefit, however. One who sees too many ramifications of his or her actions may not be able to act.

A lack of knowledge or experience appears more likely to immobilize actors, however. It may result in complete uncertainty, for example, so that the world is seen as a "toss-up" and the probabilities of all outcomes are set equal to one another. As a result action alternatives will not differ in subjective expected utility, and selection among them may occur at random. It may also cause actors to perceive that their actions make no difference in the likelihood of outcomes, so that the probability of an outcome, given an action, is set equal to the unconditional probability of that outcome. In this case apathy would appear to be a likely response.

Grossly inaccurate subjective probability estimates and ignorance of outcomes are probably more serious consequences of limited knowledge. Thus actors lacking knowledge of their worlds may consistently find themselves failing to attain the outcomes they desire or encountering unexpected consequences. Consequently, knowledge may legitimately be regarded as a power resource. Actors possessing it will have an advantage over those who lack it by being able to allocate their energies efficiently to alternatives most likely to yield desired outcomes and by not being caught off guard by totally unexpected consequences. The advantages of a guerrilla force, familiar with a situation, vis-á-vis an invading foreign army come to mind. The failure of the United States military forces in Vietnam stands as a classic example of the effects of erroneous subjective probability estimates, as well as of the power of an ideology to influence these estimates. It seems quite clear in retrospect that the architects of that futile venture consistently overestimated the probabilities of positive-utility outcomes and grossly underestimated the likelihood of negative consequences. Former President Nixon's behavior in regard to Watergate also demonstrates a significant underestimation of the probabilities of others' responses. In fairness to him, and to the military leaders in Vietnam, it should be acknowledged that both were involved in unique situations. Nevertheless neither he nor they made wise use of the available knowledge, thus wasting a major resource.

The canny politician may be taken as the example par excellence of an actor using knowledge as a resource to obtain the maximum in utility. Armed with the knowledge of how a variety of others are likely to respond to different actions, he or she is able to devise courses of action that alienate a minimum and satisfy a maximum of other actors. Successful political operators know their limits, so to speak. An in-depth study of their decision processes would undoubtedly provide a fascinating view of the way in which subjective probability estimates are made.[5]

THE MEASUREMENT OF SUBJECTIVE PROBABILITIES

A variety of methods has been devised for measuring subjective probabilities, and these can be divided into categories similar to those we used in our discussion of utility measurement. Investigators have either made use of verbal or written estimates of subjective probabilities or inferred them from a series of highly structured choice situations. Subjective probability measurement has differed from utility measurement, however, in that the former, more direct, approach has been used more often than the latter, less direct, approach (Lee 1971:60), which we noted earlier to be predominant among utility researchers.

The most direct approach has simply involved asking subjects to give specific point estimates of the subjective probability of a given event or set of events. Galanter (1962) represents one of the earliest attempts to use this approach for estimating the subjective probabilities of everyday events. Other relatively direct approaches that have been used include asking subjects to give odds estimates;[6] marking rating scales ranging from 0 to 10, .00 to 1.00, or 0 to 100; dividing lines into segments; or simply asking subjects the extent to which the likelihood of one event exceeds the likelihood of another (Lee 1971; Wyer and Goldberg 1970). Examples of these types of measurement can be found in Wyer (1970), Beach and Wise (1969), Barclay and Beach (1972), Ford, Huber, and Gustafson (1972), Wyer and Goldberg (1970), Holmstrom and Beach (1973), and Peterson, Ulehla, Miller, Bourne, and Stilson (1965).

In the vast majority of cases, subjective probabilities have been measured expressly to determine the extent to which they correspond with objective probabilities based on frequency distributions or the extent to which subjects utilize the laws of objective probability in manipulating their subjective probabilities. Thus some studies have analyzed the accuracy of predictions of binary events occurring in a sequence, e.g., whether a light will be on or off on the next trial (Lee 1971; Beach and Wise 1969). Others have explored whether subjects follow the laws of objective probability in combining the probabilities of simple events to derive the probabilities of compound events. Barclay and Beach (1972), for example, looked at the relationship between estimates of single events, the unions of mutually exclusive and nonexclusive events, and the intersections of independent and nonindependent events. A third use of relatively direct subjective probability estimates has been in studies of probability revisions, i.e., how does a subject revise his or her subjective probabilities after being given additional information (Lee 1971; Peterson and Beach 1967)? The basis of comparison in these studies has been Bayesian probability theory. In addition, subjects' estimates of the proportions of items in a sample and in populations have been sought. Peterson and Beach (1967) provide an extensive summary of studies of these types.

The less direct and more highly structured techniques that have been used to measure subjective probabilities have been virtually identical to the indirect techniques used to measure utilities. Subjective probabilities are inferred from choices among gambles, or between gambles and events that occur with certainty, and from bids for the opportunity to play gambles, generally using the indifference point strategy described in the previous chapter (Lee 1971; Beach and Wise 1969). The usual strategy has been to derive subjective probability estimates *after* utilities have been estimated, rather than the other way around

(Luce and Suppes 1965). Some evidence suggests that the estimates derived by these more indirect methods are quite similar to estimates derived by the more direct methods described above (Beach and Phillips 1967; Lee 1971; Heinrich 1971; Howell 1972), although Beach and Wise (1969) suggest that subject familiarity with the events being predicted is an important factor in this regard. (For examples of the use of these more indirect techniques to measure subjective probabilities see Bar-Hillel 1973; Davidson, Suppes, and Siegel 1957; Beach and Wise 1969; Halter and Dean 1971).

Quite recently Wise (1970) and Wise and Mockovak (1973) have begun exploring the potential of measuring subjective probabilities by means of multi-dimensional scaling techniques. However, sufficient work has not been done to indicate the feasibility of this approach.

Most of the studies of subjective probabilities involving either of the approaches we have described have been conducted in laboratory settings, involving elementary events under the control of the investigator rather than the subject. We have mentioned Galanter (1962) earlier as one who has measured subjective probabilities of real-world outcomes, which presumably would be under at least some control of the subject. Ford, Huber, and Gustafson (1972) have likewise investigated the subjective probabilities of more realistic outcomes, asking job applicants for their estimates of the probabilities of accepting jobs possessing different characteristics. We think that much more research energy should be devoted to the measurement of subjective probabilities in real-world situations, particularly in regard to outcomes over which actors perceive them-selves to have some influence. An implicit assumption in this chapter has been that actors do not merely respond to chance outcomes but that they anticipate some effects of their actions on outcomes they desire. Hence concentrating solely upon their perceptions regarding the likelihood of outcomes over which they have no influence will not shed much light on the decisions all of us make in the real world. In addition, the fact that the two approaches to the measure-ment of subjective probabilities appear to yield comparable results argues for a more extensive utilization of the more direct techniques that can be more easily adapted to nonlaboratory situations. The ratio scaling techniques we discussed in conjunction with utility measurement will very possibly also be applicable to the measurement of subjective probabilities.

Biases in the Estimation of Subjective Probabilities

Those studies of subjective probabilities for which there is a meaningful basis of comparison in the form of objective probability theory have revealed some fairly common deviations, or biases, in individuals' subjective probability estimates. In most real-world situations, of course, there is no meaningful objective probability to use for comparative purposes. Subjective probabilities essentially represent actors' degrees of belief that certain outcomes will or will not happen. The NO_j/NA_i ratios that we have discussed previously represent our attempt to provide an objective probability on which subjective probabilities can be based. Our discussion of the determinants of subjective probabilities has attempted to delineate the factors we think are most important in revising these objective ratios based on experience to yield subjective probability estimates. Even though the kinds of real-life situations with which we are concerned may lack the objective probabilities of laboratory experiments, an analysis of the manner in which individuals deviate from the laws of probability in cases in which there is a base of comparison should be helpful in developing more accurate models of subjective probability estimation.

The most relevant finding, for our purposes at least, from studies involving the prediction of events in a binary sequence is that subjects apparently are influenced by the patterning of the occurrence and nonoccurrence of outcomes (Peterson and Beach 1967; Messick 1970; Lee 1971). This is revealed in a tendency to vary responses across trials rather than predicting the event with the highest probability on each trial. Siegel, Siegel, and Andrews (1964) have attributed this "nonrational" response primarily to a utility of choice variability. Others, such as Peterson and Beach, and Messick, explain it in terms of subjects' perceiving nonrandom effects as operative even when they are estimating the probabilities of random events. We find the latter explanation persuasive since we have claimed earlier in this chapter that subjects will take sequencing into account in estimating subjective probabilities. The consistency and recency determinants have represented that influence. Thus we would expect that subjects will apply their perceptions regarding the real world, i.e., nonrandomness, to an experimental situation.

A very pervasive bias in the estimation of the probabilities of single and compound events is the underestimation of high probabilities and the overestimation of low probabilities (Wyer and Goldberg 1970; Lee 1971; Coombs, Dawes, and Tversky 1970; Luce and Suppes 1965). There appears to be a universal tendency among subjects to avoid extreme estimates, in other words. According to Luce and Suppes (1965:323–25), it is not clear at what point in the range of probabilities these tendencies become evident. According to some studies, probabilities below .2 are overestimated and probabilities above .8 are underestimated, while according to other studies the dividing line between these tendencies is at .5. Tversky (1967*b*:35) suggests that an overestimation of the relatively low probabilities of winning a sweepstakes or having one's property stolen can account for gambling and buying insurance. If this explains these phenomena, however, it indicates that utilities and subjective probabilities are not independent determinants of subjective expected utility.

In the case of compound events, this tendency shows up primarily in the underestimation of disjunctive events, i.e., the probability of O_j *or* O_k's occurring, and the overestimation of conjunctive events, i.e., the probability of *both* O_j and O_k's occurring (Barclay and Beach 1972; Bar-Hillel 1973). According to Wyer (1970) and Wyer and Goldberg (1970), disjunctive events tend to be estimated more accurately than conjunctive events, while according to the latter, the average rather than the product of the probabilities of single events is often used for the conjunctive case.

The most common deviation, in this case from the Bayesian model, to appear in probability revision studies is that of conservatism in the revised estimates (Peterson and Beach 1967; Edwards 1968; Keeley and Doherty 1972). Peterson and Beach note that subjects tend to be consistent in their estimates, even though conservative, and both they and Edwards suggest that the tendency may be due to the difficulty subjects have in combining information.

There is also some evidence suggesting that individuals have preferences for some probabilities rather than others (Edwards 1960). Probably the most serious deviation from the model of objective probability to show up in these studies, however, is the failure of subjects' estimates of the probabilities of an exhaustive set of events to sum to 1 (Lee 1971; Edwards 1960). Because that problem becomes confounded with the issue of the level of measurement of subjective probabilities we shall defer consideration of it until the next section.

Even though subjects have not followed the laws of objective probability perfectly in making their subjective probability estimates, there is evidence that they are consistent, and not random, in their deviations (Peterson and Beach 1967; Peterson et al. 1965). There is also evidence that their subjective probabilities are a linear function of objective probabilities (Luce and Suppes 1965; Wyer and Goldberg 1970). Coombs, Dawes, and Tversky (1970) claim that this varies among individuals, however, and Tversky (1967b:35) argues that either utilities or subjective probabilities must be nonlinear functions, of objective values and objective probabilities respectively, in the subjective expected utility model.[7] Although we are primarily concerned with subjective probability estimates in situations in which there is *no* objective probability, the fact that individuals appear to bias their responses in consistent ways is somewhat comforting. In a moment we shall note how this can be taken into account in our model.

The evidence that subjective probability estimates derived by current measurement procedures are more accurate for grouped data than for individual data (Wyer 1970; Wyer and Goldberg 1970) is somewhat of a mixed blessing. It is not particularly surprising because we would expect random errors to be averaged out in the aggregation process. On the one hand, it does call into question the feasibility of accurately estimating individuals' subjective probabilities, but, on the other hand, it also suggests that subjective probabilities can be derived from individuals and aggregated to represent relatively accurately the subjective probabilities of a group or collectivity. The latter is, of course, our goal. The greater accuracy of group rather than individual subjective probability estimates appears to be opposite to the case of utility estimates. There is evidence that group utility estimates are less accurate than individual ones (Halter and Dean 1971). No doubt this is partly due to a less serious problem of interpersonal comparison in the case of subjective probabilities, which in turn is partially if not wholly due to the fact that probabilities have limits, of 0 and 1.00, whereas utilities do not.

The simple fact that subjects' subjective probability estimates do differ from objective probabilities is extremely significant since it constitutes a strong argument for the inclusion of subjective probabilities in decision models. It is clearly damaging to models that utilize objective probabilities, such as conditioning models of behavior that make behavior solely a function of past experiences. In such models, what we have described as an NO_j/NA_i ratio is implicitly assumed to be equal to an actor's expectation of reward or punishment in a situation. Furthermore, Tversky (1967*b*) and Luce and Suppes (1965) have claimed that the difference between subjective and objective probabilities is more crucial than the difference between subjective and objective values. In other words, if one can only include one or the other in a behavioral model, greater accuracy will be attained by making the probability component, rather than the value component, subjective.

We have already suggested how the tendency of subjects to perceive sequences in the occurrence of outcomes can be included in our model of the determinants of subjective probabilities, namely, via the consistency and recency determinants. The tendency toward avoidance of extreme probability estimates, which may be a special case of a more general phenomenon in psychological measurement (Lee 1971:61–62), suggests that NO_j/NA_i ratios are being inflated for low probabilities of individual events and for the probabilities of conjunctive events and deflated for high probabilities of individual events and for the probabilities of disjunctive events. It is difficult to see exactly how one might include terms in the determinants model to represent these revisions of NO_j/NA_i ratios, however.

These biases have somewhat less relevance for the causal models approach, because that approach does not rely upon anything like objective probabilities but instead directly utilizes actors' estimates of conditional probabilities. However, the evidence concerning these biases may be helpful in indicating the values that should be assigned to the probabilities in the causal models. The apparent general tendency of subjects to avoid extreme subjective probability estimates for single events suggests that one who uses the procedure we described earlier for assigning values to subjects' subjective probabilities should also avoid extreme values. In our example, we used probabilities ranging from .3 to .7, which would appear to be quite satisfactory, given this conservative tendency. Using values covering the entire 0 to 1.00 range may involve a tradeoff, achieving greater differences between the subjective expected utilities of alternatives at the expense of inaccurately representing actors' actual subjective probability estimates.

The evidence regarding subjects' estimates of compound events, namely, overestimation of conjunctive events and underestimation of disjunctive events, calls into question two assumptions we have been making repeatedly throughout this chapter. The former bias casts doubt upon the validity of the assumption that $P(O_j O_k \,|A_i) = P(O_j|A_i) \times P(O_k|A_i)$. We have noted some evidence that indicates that subjects use the average of the probabilities of the two single events composing the compound event. The latter bias makes one wonder whether the subjective probabilities of two exhaustive mutually exclusive events can be accurately represented by $p + (1 - p)$, as we have also done. Inability to make this assumption would appear to constitute a grave problem for the subjective expected utility model. We shall show shortly that it is intimately related to the level of measurement of subjective probabilities that is required by the subjective expected utility model.

Feedbacks

We noted in the last chapter that utilities will change as the result of goal fulfillment obtained from outcomes. This goal fulfillment may be viewed as a feedback from outcomes to the determinants of utility. Although we have not emphasized the point in this chapter, feedbacks will also be significant for subjective probabilities. From the perspective of the determinants approach, each trial of A_i will result in one or more outcomes, and these consequences will be reflected in the NO_j/NA_i ratios. Likewise the consistency, recency, and degree of cue similarity determinants will be influenced on each trial. Outcomes will also have two major effects upon actors' causal models. One would certainly expect them to lead to revisions in the basic conditional probabilities contained within the causal model, but one must also take into account the fact that the entire causal model may be changed. New intervening factors and outcomes may be introduced as well as new direct and indirect effects. Consequently it is doubtful that one's causal model will remain the same for very long, unless one is in a highly repetitive, structured situation. This constitutes an additional reason for deriving actors' subjective probability estimates by means of relatively direct, and relatively simple, methods, such as verbal estimates. These estimates can be more quickly applied in a particular situation than can estimates derived by more circuitous and indirect methodologies; hence the possibility of subjective probabilities' changing will be less problematic.

Level of Measurement of Subjective Probabilities

There has been less concern regarding the level of measurement of subjective probabilities than has been the case with utilities. The general assumption appears to be that the techniques we have described yield at least interval-level scales, and possibly ratio scales, although Vlek (1970:165) claims that they should not be regarded as ratio scales. A more pressing issue has been that of whether individuals' subjective probability estimates for an exhaustive set of events sum to 1, or some other constant. Both Tversky (1967a) and Edwards (1962a, 1968) claim that this is a problematic area for subjective expected utility models. According to them, these models are characterized by two incompatible requirements. If one requires the subjective probabilities to sum to a constant, normally 1, then one must include a utility for gambling in subjective expected utility equations. If one does not include a utility for gambling, then subjective probabilities cannot be assumed to add up to 1, or any constant. This rather disturbing conclusion is based on evidence that if subjective probabilities are assumed to add to 1, then utilities for specific outcomes are higher when measured under conditions of uncertainty than under conditions of certainty. This discrepancy they interpret as evidence of a utility for gambling.

This problem is actually more relevant for the measurement of utilities than probabilities because, in models in which subjective probabilities do not add to a fixed constant, utilities must be measured at a ratio-scale level, whereas in models in which they are assumed to add to a constant they may be measured at only an interval level. Subjective probabilities, in either case, must constitute ratio scales (Edwards 1962*a*). This problem would also seem more serious for the techniques that measure subjective probabilities only very indirectly and that must assume at some point that subjective and objective probabilities are equal. If more direct verbal techniques are used to derive subjective probability estimates, the major problem that is encountered is the loss of the simplifications achieved by assuming that $p + (1 - p) = 1$. However, the validity of this assumption can be checked quite easily by means of additional questions given to subjects if one is using verbal techniques. So it does not appear to be an insuperable obstacle.

Problems such as this, which crop up in the indirect measurement of subjective probabilities, have motivated some researchers to give up on measuring subjective probabilities. Tversky's simultaneous conjoint measurement technique (1967*a*), which we noted in the last chapter, represents one approach. Coombs et al. (1967) have forgone measurement of either utilities or subjective probabilities and instead have tested the subjective expected utility model against other decision models by means of gambling situations in which both utilities and subjective probabilities are systematically manipulated. And we have earlier noted the attempts by Wise (1970) and Wise and Mockovak (1973) to adapt multidimensional scaling techniques to subjective probability measurement. Hopefully other investigators will continue to explore the potential of more direct measurement techniques in this area because they are more adaptable to real-life situations.

SUBJECTIVE PROBABILITIES AND INTERGROUP PROCESSES

We have discussed subjective probabilities almost exclusively in terms of individual actors. Now, how do they apply to intergroup processes and how does one get from the subjective probabilities of the individual actor to the subjective probabilities of the groups of which he or she is a member?

At the level of the group, subjective probabilities are primarily involved in the collectively held beliefs and attitudes of a group that affect the manner in which that group interacts with other groups. Wyer (1970) and Wyer and Goldberg (1970) have shown how beliefs and attitudes and relationships among them can be expressed in terms of subjective probabilities. Wyer and Goldberg (1970: 102) note, for example, that the belief "Communists support civil disorders" can be expressed as a probabilistic statement, namely, the conditional probability of membership in the category "civil disorder supporter," given membership in the category "Communist," i.e., $P(S|C)$, where S represents "civil disorder supporter" and C stands for "Communist." This can be taken a step further and translated into an expectation that an actor from category C will in fact act in a certain way, in this case to support a civil disorder. This specific conditional probability, and others, therefore may be seen as constituting one's beliefs about individuals who are Communists. Thus one may very well also assign a high value to the conditional probability that one who is a Communist will also be a member of the category "atheist."

When these beliefs are imbued with evaluative content we may refer to them as attitudes. Brim (1955) has suggested that the positiveness or negativeness of one's attitude toward an object or person is a function of one's expectation that that object or person will provide satisfying or unsatisfying outcomes. He has also suggested that the intensity of that attitude will be a function of the degree of confidence one has in his or her subjective probability estimate. Hence the most intense positive attitudes will be felt toward those persons or objects for which one has high subjective probabilities of receiving positive-utility outcomes and a high degree of confidence in his or her subjective probability estimates as well.

More recently, Blumstein (1973) has linked subjective probabilities and evaluations by suggesting that the latter will be affected by the extent to which individuals live up to the expectations one has for them. Actors in certain categories, e.g., clergymen, are expected to do "good" things while actors in other categories, e.g., criminals, are expected to do "bad" things. Consequently if either does not live up to expectations, i.e., the clergyman does a "bad" thing and the criminal a "good" thing, then one's evaluations of them will be more extreme than usual. The clergyman will receive a more negative evaluation for doing a "bad" thing than will the criminal, whereas the criminal will be more positively evaluated for acting in a "good" manner than will the clergyman. Although Blumstein found only partial support for his hypotheses (more negative evaluations of "good" persons behaving badly were evident, but not more positive evaluations of "bad" persons behaving well), his approach suggests an additional way in which attitudes and beliefs can be presented by means of subjective probabilities.

Our supposition is that the subjective probabilities held by members of one group regarding the actions, characteristics, and outcomes offered by members of another group will influence the former's actions toward the latter by affecting the former's choice of action alternatives. These shared subjective probabilities may be succinctly summarized in terms of the attitudes and beliefs of the former group toward the latter. Thus prejudice, a very common phenomenon in intergroup relations, especially relations between racial and ethnic groups, may be represented in terms of subjective probabilities. It may be roughly defined as an encompassing negative attitude toward members of another group, and it will be manifested in a variety of ways. For example, it may appear in the assignment of a very high subjective probability, perhaps 1.00, to the coincidence of the categories "minority-group member" and "lazy person." It will also be evident in the subjective probabilities assigned to specific outcomes. Members of a dominant group may think it very likely that minority-group members will try to harm them physically or that they will try to marry into the dominant group. They may also believe it quite likely that members of their own group will shun them if they associate with minority-group members. Or they may anticipate little likelihood of minority-group members' retaliating against them if they act unfairly toward them, so that exploitation of members of the minority group becomes a viable alternative. Brim (1955:71n) notes that these expectations are clearly not based upon scientific evidence, but that fact does not detract from their significance for the prejudiced individual's decisions. We heartily agree with him.[8]

Another concept that has been used extensively in the area of race relations but which is also applicable to intergroup processes in general, is the self-fulfilling prophecy—if something is believed to be true, it will be true in its consequences. This can also be expressed in terms of subjective probabilities, specifically as constituting a summation of a particular relationship between beliefs and choices of action alternatives. For example, a dominant-group member may assume that the opportunity for education is necessary if one is to be educated, i.e., $P(E|\overline{Opp}) = 0$. He or she may simultaneously assume, however, that minority-group members will not become educated, even if they are given the opportunity to do so, i.e., $P(E|Opp) = P(E|\overline{Opp}) = 0$. In this case there will be little incentive to provide minority-group members with the opportunity to get an education, so that $P(Opp)$ equals zero. Consequently the probability that minority-group members will receive an education will be zero, since $P(E) = P(E|Opp) \times P(Opp) + P(E|\overline{Opp}) \times P(\overline{Opp})$. Conceptualizing this phenomenon in subjective probability terms increases its precision substantially, as well as possibly suggesting additional mechanisms through which exogenous or contextual variables may operate.

Aggregation of Subjective Probabilities

We are not aware of anyone's attempting to aggregate the subjective probabilities of individual actors so as to represent the subjective probabilities of a group. (We have previously noted evidence that averages of individual estimates correspond more closely to the laws of objective probability than do individual estimates, however.) Our comments regarding the representation of subjective probabilities in terms of beliefs and attitudes, or vice versa, suggest that it may be possible to derive aggregate estimates by a conversion process. The degree to which members of a group agreed with certain statements about members of another group might be converted into subjective probabilities, with very strong agreement indicating a subjective probability close to 1.00, uncertainty or neutrality a .5 subjective probability, and very strong disagreement a subjective probability of approximately zero. This conversion procedure would be facilitated by the fact that probabilities have limits of 0 and 1.00, as we previously noted.

Or it may be feasible simply to aggregate individual subjective probability estimates and represent the group's collective expectation by means of some measure of central tendency. This procedure encounters weighting problems, however. Should all members of the group be weighted equally, or should some of them, opinion leaders, so to speak, be given a disproportionate weight? Large-scale opinion polls accord equal weight to all respondents, which may well be an appropriate procedure for the general opinions they survey. If one is interested in the collective views of more or less coherent groups, however, this technique may not be satisfactory. Research regarding this issue would certainly be welcome.

SUMMARY

We have complemented our discussion of utilities in the previous chapter with a discussion in this chapter of subjective probabilities, the other major component in the subjective expected utility model. We have presented two alternative approaches to this component, one a determinants approach comparable to our discussion of the determinants of the utilities of outcomes, the other an approach utilizing the actual "causal models" used by actors in making decisions. We have also discussed the several techniques currently in use for measuring subjective probabilities and have added to these a new methodology whereby the "causal models" of actors might be duplicated.

In this chapter, as in the previous one, we have given extensive consideration to the ways in which actors simplify their subjective probability estimations. Lastly we have described the relevance of subjective probabilities for intergroup processes. It is now possible to combine the utility and subjective probability components and analyze how the subjective expected utilities of action alternatives are estimated as well as how these estimates are in turn used by actors to make choices among these alternatives.

NOTES

1. We consistently use a bar over a letter to represent nonentities. Thus $\bar{O}_j$ represents the nonoccurrence of outcome O_j and $\bar{A}_i$ the nonenactment of alternative A_i. We use the terminology of nonactions and nonoutcomes to represent actors doing nothing and nothing happening, respectively, because we regard the choice between doing something and doing nothing, and a possibility of either something or nothing happening as a result, as the simplest conceivable choice situation and hence best suited to our exposition of the subjective expected utility model. On philosophical grounds

one may choose to regard nonactions and nonoutcomes as actions and outcomes respectively.

2. We represent the direct effect in this fashion for three reasons. First, it avoids the temptation to represent equation (1) as $P(O_j|A_i) = P(X_n|A_i) \times P(O_j|X_n)$. This equation is not correct in the case of combined direct and indirect effects. Second, this representation shows more clearly that there are actually *four* possible outcomes of A_i: X_nO_j, $\bar{X}_nO_j$, $X_n\bar{O}_j$, and $\bar{X}_n\bar{O}_j$. We have omitted $\bar{O}_j$ from the diagram in order to simplify it, hence equation (1) represents only two of the possible outcomes—X_nO_j and $\bar{X}_nO_j$. To estimate accurately the subjective expected utility equation for A_i one would also have to include the other possible outcomes—$X_n\bar{O}_j$ and $X_n\bar{O}_j$—and their subjective probabilities. Third, both $\bar{X}_n$ and $\bar{O}_j$ must be included in the subjective expected utility equation for A_i because there may be utilities associated with them. So their subjective probabilities must be included in the equation also.

3. It may appear strange to talk about the "effects" of nonactions. Normally one thinks only of actions "causing" other actions. In the social world, however, that does not necessarily hold. The failure of others to act may prompt a given actor to act. For example, if I observe an accident, the failure of other observers to report it may prompt me to do so. Similarly, in the case of blocking actions, my action may prompt another actor to act in opposition to me, whereas if I do not act then he or she will also be less likely to act. So both actions and nonactions may be perceived as influencing subjective probabilities.

4. The promotion of one action by another may actually be represented in two different ways. $P(X_n|A_i) > P(X_n|\bar{A}_i)$ simply says that X_n is more likely if A_i occurs than if A_i does not occur. The alternate representation, $P(X_n|A_i) > P(\bar{X}_n|A_i)$, says that X_n is more likely to occur than $\bar{X}_n$ if A_i occurs. We believe the former more clearly represents the idea of one action promoting another action and hence use it in this context. However, both comparisons are necessary to obtain a clear picture of the influences of A_i on X_n.

5. Phillips (1970:262–63) notes that the issue of the influence of social and cultural factors on subjective probabilities has received virtually no attention. Our comments suggest issues in that area that are worthy of exploration.

6. There is some evidence that odds estimates are more accurate than point estimates when compared to objective probabilities (Ford, Huber, and Gustafson 1972).

7. It has been suggested that the overestimation and underestimation biases may be artifacts of the methodology being used (Slovic and Lichtenstein 1968*b*; Beach and Wise 1969).

8. Blumstein's failure to find unusually positive evaluations of "good" acts committed by "bad" people appears very similar to the oft-noted tenacity of prejudice in the face of contradictory information. These two instances may represent special cases of a more general underlying process, conceivably involving cognitive consistency.

CHAPTER 4

Subjective Expected Utility
and Decision Strategies

IN THE PREVIOUS two chapters we have subjected the two major components of the subjective expected utility model—utilities and subjective probabilities—to an in-depth analysis, describing particularly the complications encountered by human actors attempting to estimate these components and the major simplifications they introduce to ease their calculations. As we indicated earlier, the subjective expected utility of an action alternative will equal the sum of the products of the utilities of all outcomes believed to have some possibility of occurring, given that alternative, and the subjective probabilities of those outcomes occurring following enactment of that alternative.

The subjective expected utility of an alternative can be visualized as always being compared with the subjective expected utility of another alternative prior to actors' choices of actions. (In the simplest case the other alternative is to do nothing, represented by $\bar{A}_i$.) Whenever possible, we anticipate that actors will simplify their decisions by making relative, rather than absolute, subjective expected utility estimations. That is, the issue confronting them will be whether A_i or $\bar{A}_i$ has greater subjective expected utility, not the total subjective expected utilities of the two alternatives.

It might seem that the calculation of subjective expected utility, and particularly of relative subjective expected utilities, would be quite straightforward once the problems associated with the estimations of the utilities and subjective probabilities have been resolved. This is not the case, however, and in the beginning segment of this chapter we consider ways in which this estimation process becomes complicated, too. First, we raise the possibility that subjective expected utilities for specific alternatives may be visualized in terms of *ranges* of values rather than point estimates. So far we have generally assumed that actors will make point estimates. In many cases they may be able to, but in others they may only be able to estimate a range of values within which subjective probabilities and/or utilities may lie. Consequently their estimates of subjective expected utilities will also be in terms of ranges of values.

The subjective expected utility of an alternative may also consist of a range of values in cases in which it is possible for actors to vary the *intensity* with which they anticipate enacting that alternative. In such cases we anticipate that greater intensity, in terms of a greater expenditure of energy or resources, is likely to yield greater subjective expected utility. This, too, will result in a range of values rather than a point estimate, but it will depend upon the marginal gains associated with greater intensity rather than upon an inability to estimate utilities or subjective probabilities with sufficient precision to obtain a point estimate.

The intensity with which actors anticipate enacting their action alternatives will in turn involve another problematic area, the effect of current actions upon future ones. We assume that actors take the implications of their current actions upon their potential future actions into account when making subjective expected utility estimates. If resources are expended on an action in the present, they may not be available for future alternatives. This of course presents an additional complication for the subjective expected utility model.

Second, the possibility of different amounts of resources being expended in the enactment of a particular alternative and thereby affecting the enactment of other alternatives impinges upon another issue, the most satisfactory way to deal with positive and negative utilities, or rewards and costs respectively.

In chapter 2 we noted that whether an outcome yields positive or negative utility depends both upon the nature of the goal being fulfilled and the amount of goal fulfillment being attained. We decided at that time to regard goal fulfillment received as always yielding positive utility but to allow for the possibility of quite different types of goals. For example, one's goal may be to avoid another party. To the extent that one achieves that goal positive utility results. Failure to achieve that goal, as would be the case if one were forced to have contact with the other party, is assumed to constitute negative utility. The distinction between positive and negative utility becomes more complex, however, when one takes into account the effect of current actions upon other current actions and upon future actions. In either the present or the future, enactment of one alternative may preclude enacting another alternative. Often this utility forgone has been regarded as an additional cost to the actor, or additional negative utility. We present what we believe to be a unique way of dealing with that problem.

Third, we consider an especially vexing problem that has arisen in numerous subjective expected utility studies: the nonindependence of the utility and subjective probability components of the model. We shall see that different effects of these two components on each other have appeared in empirical investigations.

After our consideration of these additional complications we turn our attention to the selection of action alternatives and the decision strategies used by actors. This process includes not only how actors choose action alternatives, once their subjective expected utilities have been estimated, but also the factors that determine when actors decide to make a choice between alternatives and the alternatives that are actually selected for comparison from their repertories of alternatives.

SOME FURTHER COMPLICATIONS

Point Estimates versus Ranges of Values

Actors may not always make a point estimate, say .3, of a subjective probability or the utility of an outcome. This may be due to their unfamiliarity with a situation, to lack of knowledge regarding the probable actions of other actors, to their own indecisiveness, or a variety of factors. In such cases it is likely they will only be able to make an estimate of a range of values for each or for both—for example, .3 to .4 for a subjective probability and 10 to 12 for the utility of an outcome.

Subjective utility estimates based upon these utility and subjective probability estimates will necessarily also be in terms of a range of values, potentially from 3.0 to 4.8 in the above case. If this range of values does not overlap with a range of values estimated for the subjective expected utility of another alternative, then the choice situation will not be unduly complicated. But if the subjective expected utility estimate for another alternative should overlap, for example, a range from 3.5 to 6.0, then an actor will be faced with a dilemma. He or she might choose the latter alternative in this case, on the grounds that the potential maximum subjective expected utility is greater for it than for the other alternative. But attaining this maximum will depend upon a fortunate conjunction of maximum possible values for both the utility and subjective probability components.

The range of values can be restricted somewhat if one is willing to assume that a trade-off between utility and subjective probability is likely. That is, it seems more likely that the maximum likelihood of an outcome's occurring would coincide with the minimum potential utility of that outcome. In the case of the first alternative above, actors may well combine the .4 subjective probability estimate with the lower utility estimate of 10 and the .3 subjective probability estimate with the other extreme of the utility range—12. This would reduce the range to 3.6 to 4.0. Or they may simply choose to take the midpoint of the two ranges to derive a point estimate of 3.85, i.e., .35 times 11. How actors deal with this problem merits empirical investigation.

In situations where it is possible for actors to make precise estimates of subjective expected utility some alternatives may nevertheless be better represented in terms of a range of values. This will be characteristic of alternatives that may be viewed as continuous rather than discrete phenomena. Actors will be able to enact such alternatives at different *levels* or with different degrees of *intensity*. For example, one may run at different speeds to catch a bus. Or one may work at a job with varying levels of concentration. Students may study with differing degrees of diligence. In each of these cases the basic action alternatives—running, working, studying—can be enacted in varying degrees. Analytically one may treat these differences in degree either as different alternatives or as a continuum representing the same alternative. The latter approach appears the more sensible one, but it means that actors will be confronted not only with choices among different alternatives but also with a decision regarding the level, or degree of intensity, at which to enact the alternative.

Treating alternatives as continuous will have implications for both utilities and subjective probabilities. In most cases we may safely assume that enacting alternatives at different levels will result in different amounts of goal fulfillment attained. And in most cases there will be a positive relationship between the level of the alternative, expressed in terms of energy exerted or resources committed to the alternative, and the amount of goal fulfillment. If an employee desires praise from his or her employer, then it is likely that the more effort he or she devotes to the work, the more praise that will be forthcoming. There will undoubtedly be diminishing returns operative, so that beyond a particular level of effort the amount of praise received will level off. (Of course, there will also be diminishing marginal *utility* if the amount of goal fulfillment received carries the actor to a portion of his or her utility curve where satiation effects are experienced.) Similarly, if a good grade is the outcome desired by a student, then presumably the more effort that is devoted to studying, the better will be the achieved grade. So our general prediction is that there will be a positive relationship—with a decreasing rate of increase beyond some point—between effort or energy exerted by actors and utility received. We will ignore for now the possibility that greater levels of energy exertion will be met by comparably greater efforts to block reception of the desired outcome by other actors.

We have essentially held subjective probabilities constant in this discussion, but a similar relationship can be hypothesized between them and effort exerted in the commission of an alternative. Normally the greater the effort exerted, the greater will be actors' estimates that an alternative will result in a given outcome. Running hard to catch a bus, rather than merely jogging, increases the likelihood that the bus will be caught. Or working hard at a job is more likely to result in praise from one's employer than is a lackadaisical effort. Thus we would generally expect that increased effort devoted to an alternative will result in an increased expectation that the alternative will yield a particular outcome, also with diminishing returns being manifested in a decreasing rate of increase beyond some point.

It would appear that these relationships between energy or resource expenditure and the subjective expected utility of an alternative may be handled via *either* the utility *or* the subjective probability component of the model. That is, either one may predict that the greater the energy expended, the greater will be the subjective probability for a specific outcome, or, the greater the expenditure, the more (in terms of amount of goal fulfillment) of an outcome that will be achieved with the same probability. Only in exceptional cases would we expect increased energy expenditure to have both effects, namely, resulting in an increased probability of a higher-utility outcome. The major implications are therefore that the subjective expected utility of an alternative will be some positive function of *anticipated* energy exertion, and, second, for a given alternative, such as studying, that the subjective expected utility will constitute a range of values, varying with the possible levels of energy exertion. Consequently, one must make provision for the amount of effort actors anticipate devoting to enacting their alternatives.

Provision must also be made for the fact that energy exertion or the expending of resources in the commission of an action alternative will be experienced as a cost by actors. This cost may be experienced both at the time the alternative is enacted and in the future, when the resources are not available for enacting another alternative. Normally we would expect that the greater the energy expenditure, the greater the cost, and that beyond some point additional energy exertion will be accompanied by accelerating costs. We have said that the relationship between energy exerted and both utility and subjective probability will be characterized by diminishing returns at some level of energy exertion. The costs of increased exertion are certain to accelerate at the point at which diminishing returns sets in, and possibly before that point.

Consequently actors will be confronted by a trade-off when they consider the degree of energy or resources to expend in their behavior. The gains in utility and/or subjective probability may be counterbalanced, or even diminished, by the increased costs resulting from the additional expenditure. Generally we would expect the maximizing actor to devote the amount of energy or resources to an alternative that will maximize the utility to be received and minimize the costs to be incurred. A decision on the amount of energy invested in an activity, or in the *intensity* with which the activity is enacted, may therefore very well be made on the basis of marginal considerations. Actors may expend energy up to the point at which an additional expenditure of energy will not yield additional subjective expected utility. This marginal issue is, of course, separate from the issue of marginal utility discussed in chapter 2, namely, the marginal utility associated with an outcome per se.

The impacts of different degrees of energy expenditure upon utilities and subjective probabilities are shown by figure 4.1 in a fashion similar to the indifference curves of economists. In this diagram we have represented the utility and the subjective probability of an alternative as ranges of values, but with constant subjective expected utility. Thus a higher subjective probability estimate is balanced by its combination with a lower utility estimate. Curve SEU_1 represents the subjective expected utility of alternative A. The increased subjective expected utility resulting from an increase in energy expenditure in enacting an alternative is represented by curve SEU_2. We have suggested that this increased expenditure will result in *either* increased utility *or* an increased subjective probability. Thus if an actor is at point A on curve one, representing a

Figure 4.1.   The Effects of Energy Expenditure on Utilities and Subjective Probabilities

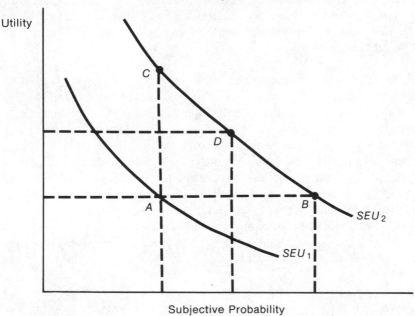

particular combination of utility and subjective probability, an anticipation that increased expenditure of energy will result in an increased probability of receiving an outcome with the same amount of utility will be represented by a move to point *B* on curve two. By contrast an expectation that increased effort will yield an outcome with greater utility but the same subjective probability may be depicted by a movement to point *C* on the second curve. If the increase in effort affects both utilities and subjective probabilities, then the additional subjective expected utility can be shown by a movement to point *D* on curve two.

The increased costs associated with greater expenditure of effort or energy may of course also be represented by curves such as those in figure 4.1. If the increased costs surpass the increase in expected utility, then the curve representing greater effort will move back toward the origin, indicating a loss in subjective expected utility.

So we anticipate that the intensity with which actors contemplate enacting action alternatives, i.e., the amount of energy and resources they expend upon them, will depend upon the gains in subjective expected utility accruing from the increased effort balanced by the additional costs incurred as a result of the greater expenditure. Therefore, actors should not be seen as estimating the subjective expected utility of an alternative independently of a consideration of other alternatives. Rather the crucial question becomes: how do actors apportion their resources among a variety of competing alternatives? Do they sink all of their resources into one, or a few, alternatives in order to obtain a limited number of high-utility outcomes? Or do they spread out their resources among a larger number of alternatives, thereby achieving more outcomes that are likely to have lower utility? This is one of the issues we consider when we look at their possible decision strategies.

The Conceptualization of Rewards and Costs

In our discussion to this point we have simply dealt with positive and negative utilities in terms of goal fulfillment. Outcomes that provide goal fulfillment may be regarded as providing positive utility. Outcomes involving a decrease in goal fulfillment, or downward movement on actors' utility curves, have been conceptualized as yielding negative utility. We shall refer to positive-utility outcomes as rewards and negative-utility outcomes as costs. Thus rewards and costs have been conceptualized *solely* in terms of gains or losses in the amount of goal fulfillment enjoyed by actors. These both involve the actual outcomes anticipated by actors following enactment of action alternatives. If an outcome is expected to increase one's level of goal fulfillment then it yields positive utility; if it decreases the level of goal fulfillment for a particular goal then it provides negative utility.

This conceptualization does not adequately account for all the rewards and costs associated with enactment of a particular action alternative, however. The exchange theorists, particularly Homans (1974) and Blau (1964a), have emphasized that rewards (or positive utilities) forgone should also be considered as part of the cost of an action; that is, if one alternative, A_1, leads to a particular outcome, O_1, while another alternative, A_2, leads to a different outcome, O_2, and if O_2 does not result from A_1, then the utility provided by O_2 will be forgone by an actor if he or she enacts A_1. So whereas our conceptualization of the costs of an action has included only a potential loss in goal fulfillment, this conceptualization includes the failure of goal fulfillment to increase as an additional cost. If one does not enact A_2, then goal fulfillment does not increase by the amount it would have if O_2 had been received. The exchange theorists therefore have measured this cost in terms of the positive utility provided by the outcome that is not received. In fact, they have seemingly overemphasized this cost component and consequently not given sufficient attention to the more direct costs, i.e., actual losses in goal fulfillment, that we have emphasized in our model.

As Simpson (1972) has rightly pointed out, one cannot logically ignore the costs forgone as a result of enacting a particular alternative if one insists upon including rewards forgone. Costs that are not received should constitute a reward. So we can add to our reward component—increases in goal fulfillment or positive utility received—a second reward component: losses in goal fulfillment avoided. Using our above example, if O_2 is an outcome involving a loss in the amount of goal fulfillment, then enactment of A_1 will mean that this loss of goal fulfillment will not be experienced and that one's amount of goal fulfillment will stay the same, except, of course, for the change in goal fulfillment resulting from receiving outcome O_1.

Thus we can reconceptualize rewards to include outcomes that increase goal fulfillment or preclude a loss in goal fulfillment and costs to include outcomes that decrease goal fulfillment or do not provide an increase in goal fulfillment.

Our above discussion of possible differences in resources expended in enacting alternatives and their implications for subjective expected utility estimates relates to the utilities forgone conceptualization of costs. We have suggested that actors are likely to believe they can increase the subjective expected utility of an alternative by investing more resources in it, but that they must also be aware of the fact that use of these additional resources on one alternative may prevent them from using them for another alternative. The value of these resources, and hence the cost associated with expending them, might conceivably be estimated independently of outcomes and goal fulfillment, but it appears much simpler to include them in the utilities forgone component of either rewards or costs. If resources are expended in enacting an alternative and they are used up in the process so that they will not be available for enacting another alternative, then this can be seen as resulting in the loss of any utilities connected with outcomes resulting from that other alternative. Resource expenditure therefore constitutes a cost if it means a loss of future positive utility. Conversely, if resources are saved in the present, so that they will be available in the future, then this means that they should be valued partly in terms of future increases in utility that they may provide. So resource conservation should constitute a reward if it makes possible an increase in goal fulfillment in the future.

The relationship between these two types of reward and cost is displayed in table 4.1, which shows that goal fulfillment may be either increased or decreased

Table 4.1. Types of Reward and Cost

| | | GOAL FULFILLMENT | |
		Decreased	Increased
	Received	Cost	Reward
EXPERIENCE	Forgone: Present	Reward	Cost
	Forgone: Future	Reward	Cost

and that either of these outcomes may be received or forgone. The first row of the table represents the types of reward and cost we have been dealing with primarily, while the second and third rows involve outcomes that are not received. These outcomes are further divided into present and future depending upon the time at which an outcome is precluded. Utilities forgone as a result of resource expenditure can occur in either the present or the future. In the present, expending resources on one alternative may prevent simultaneous expenditure of resources on another alternative. And resources expended in the present may not be available to obtain outcomes that increase goal fulfillment in the future. Defense expenditures may be viewed as a prime example of alternatives that represent a cost in the present, in the sense that the resources devoted to them are not available for procuring other positive-utility outcomes, but a reward in the future, if they prevent one from being attacked, i.e., future decreases in goal fulfillment are forgone. (Some may argue that they represent a cost in both the present and the future since the expenditure on guns precludes expenditures on butter either now or later.)

Utility, either positive or negative, i.e., in terms of goal fulfillment received or not received, will be forgone in the present to the extent that action alternatives are *simultaneously* incompatible. Some alternatives will be simultaneously compatible. One can, for example, eat a meal and read a book at the same time, perhaps with some difficulty. Or one can attend a movie and listen to a basketball game on a portable radio simultaneously. However, very few people can read a book and swim at the same time, and no one can attend a basketball game and a movie concurrently. This, of course, is the usual notion of utility forgone. By attending the basketball game, one does not receive the utility associated with attending the movie. If alternatives are simultaneously compatible, then conceivably one forgoes utility if he or she does not enact such alternatives at the same time. The person who doesn't read while eating might be seen as forgoing utility, although he or she may have judged that enacting the two alternatives together will diminish the utility of each one to the point where their combined utility is less than the utility of either one separately. Most, if not all, discussions of utility forgone have neglected the possibility of simultaneously enacting alternatives, though.

Most action alternatives will be compatible with a variety of nonaction alternatives. This apparently inane observation may have relevance in social situations. For example, an actor may decide that praising actor X and not praising actor Y is the most likely way to bring about the desired responses from both X and Y, and he or she could clearly simultaneously praise X and not praise Y. By so doing, our actor may anticipate that Y will be induced to greater effort on a task.

Simultaneous incompatibilities may be converted into sequential compatibilities quite often. One can eat first and read later, or one can go to a movie after attending a basketball game. But in this case one may encounter limitations because of the resources expended on the prior alternative. One may not have sufficient time to read after eating, or one may not have sufficient time or money to take in both the movie and the basketball game. Hence a *sequential* incompatibility may arise as well. We see these incompatibilities as primarily due to the expenditure of resources or energy. Thus they are of the same class as the cases involving differential intensity of the enactment of alternatives discussed above. Devoting additional resources to the enactment of an alternative in the present so as to increase one's subjective expected utility may diminish the subjective expected utilities of future action alternatives.

Actually both types of incompatibility may be seen as cases of resource limitations. If we consider time and space as basic resources, then a person is not able to do such things as attend movies and basketball games simultaneously because it is impossible to be in two places at the same time. Both types of incompatibility also highlight the significance of actors' resource supplies. The greater the resources possessed by actors, the less likely they will be to confront incompatibilities between action alternatives. The actor with much time available will be able to eat a leisurely meal and read a book afterward. And actors with sufficient financial resources will be able to afford both the game and the movie. Not only will actors with greater resources have more action options available to them, but they will also be able to enact more of them. This fact will obviously have implications for their power and dependence positions relative to other actors with fewer resources.

Including Rewards and Costs in the
Subjective Expected Utility Model

We have shown that rewards and costs should be conceptualized in terms of utilities received *and* utilities forgone, and that these involve both the present and future experiences of actors. Each of the types of reward and cost we have discussed can be incorporated in the subjective expected utility model without too much difficulty. Looking back at table 4.1, we see that outcomes received in the present (the first row) are, of course, the basic components of the subjective expected utility equation, the O_j and their associated subjective probabilities. Rewards and costs in the form of utilities forgone in the present (the second row of table 4.1) are handled by the model through *relative* subjective expected utility estimates, at least for simultaneously incompatible alternatives. If A_1 and A_2 cannot be enacted simultaneously, then one forgoes the subjective expected utility of A_2 if one enacts A_1, and vice versa. Thus it is not necessary to include an additional term in the subjective expected utility equation to represent the present utility forgone type of reward or cost.[1]

Utility forgone in the future presents more problems. We believe that this type of reward and cost (row three) should be included in the subjective expected utility equations for particular alternatives in certain situations, but doing so does create some problems. If two alternatives, A_1 and A_2, differ in regard to the likelihood of occurrence of some future outcome, $O_{2_{t+1}}$, for example, then this future outcome should be included in the subjective expected utility equations for the two alternatives, since enacting one of the alternatives may result in a forgoing of future utility. This future utility forgone should be regarded as part of the cost, or reward, associated with enacting either alternative in the present.

We shall use a relatively simple example for illustration. Let us assume that an actor is attempting to choose between A_{1_t} and A_{2_t}. Let us further assume that he or she believes that enacting either alternative will affect his or her capability of enacting a future alternative, $A_{3_{t+1}}$, which in turn affects the future outcome, $O_{2_{t+1}}$. Figure 4.2 represents this situation for alternative A_{1_t}. A similar diagram could be constructed[2] for A_{2_t}.

We have already said that a relative comparison of A_{1_t} and A_{2_t}, taking only O_{1_t} and $\bar{O}_{1_t}$ into consideration, takes care of present utility forgone. But now, if A_{1_t} and A_{2_t} differ in their effects upon $A_{3_{t+1}}$, then the actor may forgo future utility by enacting one or the other. If, for example, he or she uses more resources in enacting A_{1_t} than A_{2_t}, then he or she may be less able to enact $A_{3_{t+1}}$, i.e., $P(A_{3_{t+1}}|A_{1_t}) < P(A_{3_{t+1}}|A_{2_t})$. Enactment of A_{1_t} therefore will result in a certain amount of future utility forgone, with the amount being determined primarily by the difference in the two probabilities $P(A_{3_{t+1}}|A_{1_t})$ and $P(A_{3_{t+1}}|A_{2_t})$.

Consequently in this case the subjective expected utility of the future outcome should be included in the equations for both A_{1_t} and A_{2_t}. It is very possible that the actor will not forgo present utility by enacting A_{1_t} but will forgo future utility, assuming that all outcomes provide positive utility. Hence a more accurate estimate of subjective expected utility will be obtained if both present and future outcomes are included. In this case, the subjective expected utility equation for A_{1_t} is

$$
\begin{aligned}
SEU(A_{1_t}) = {} & p \times U(O_{1_t}) + (1 - p) \times U(\bar{O}_{1_t}) + [qr + (1 - q)s] \\
& \times U(O_{2_{t+1}}) + [q(1 - r) + (1 - q)(1 - s)] \\
& \times U(\bar{O}_{2_{t+1}}).
\end{aligned}
$$

(1)

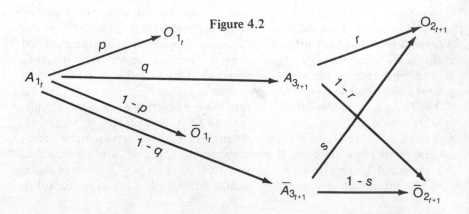

Figure 4.2

A comparable equation could be presented for A_{2_t} and subtraction would yield a relative subjective expected utility estimate. Undoubtedly actors will find it necessary to introduce some of the simplifications we discussed in our chapter on subjective probabilities to make such comparisons.

Several additional points should be made in this regard. First, situations such as the one we have described are *not* the same as our discussion of multiple outcomes in the last chapter. In that context we noted the possibility of future outcomes' being dependent upon present outcomes. Here our concern has been with the dependence of future alternatives upon present ones. Both dependencies may be present in a given situation. For example, if an actor receives a particular outcome in the present, he or she may anticipate that other actors will be mobilized to hinder his or her reception of future outcomes. At the same time, his or her expenditure of resources in attaining the first outcome may deplete his or her resource supply so that he or she will be less able to counteract the opposition of these others and obtain the future outcome. In a case such as this, equation (1) would have to be expanded to take into account the dependence of the future outcome on the present one.

Second, unless actors have substantial resources, we anticipate trade-offs between utility received and utility forgone. Increasing one's present rewards by enacting an alternative with greater intensity, i.e., expending more resources, may increase one's costs through the loss of future positive utility. Most actors are confronted by the need to balance current expenditures against future needs. Bankruptcy may occur socially as well as financially.

Third, although the inclusion of future outcomes in this manner does complicate our model, we believe it more accurately represents human decision processes. An approach that concentrates only upon the utility forgone as the result of the simultaneous incompatibility of alternatives leaves actors jumping from one time point to another and considering only the immediate actions available to them. Some choices between action alternatives can be made with little or no regard to future actions, but probably a majority have the "if X now, then Y later" quality we have tried to represent.

The Independence of Utilities and Subjective Probabilities

There is fairly substantial evidence that utilities and subjective probabilities are not independent determinants of subjective expected utility, but instead that there is a reciprocal relationship between them. Edwards (1962b) has described this most fully. On the one hand, it appears that individuals assign higher subjective probabilities to higher-utility outcomes—a positive influence of utilities on probabilities; that is, the more valuable an outcome, the more likely it is to occur. We have referred to this earlier as the "wishful thinking" bias. On the other hand, it also appears that individuals assign higher utilities to lower-probability outcomes—a negative influence of subjective probabilities on utilities. In other words, the more difficult it is to obtain an outcome, the higher is its utility.[3] In another context, Edwards (1961) has also suggested that the influence of utilities on subjective probabilities involves only the sign of the utility of an outcome, not the amount of utility. This would show up in the form of different subjective probability estimates for the same outcome, depending upon whether it provided positive or negative utility.

A nonindependent relationship between utilities and subjective probabilities is also built into Atkinson's (1957; Atkinson and Birch 1970) theory of motivation (Edwards 1962b). One of the determinants of the valence (or utility) of an outcome in this model, for outcomes that depend on an actor's skill, is the incentive value of success, which Atkinson assumes to be equal to 1 minus the probability of success, i.e., equal to the probability of failure. This theory of motivation has been used by McClelland (1961) to explain differences in risk taking among individuals with varying levels of need achievement.

The reasons for these reciprocal influences of utilities and subjective probabilities are somewhat murky, however. Edwards (1962b) has offered two different explanations for the negative influence of subjective probabilities on utilities. Either, he suggests, this reflects the nature of the world, namely, that scarcer outcomes have greater utility, or it reflects a psychological tendency of individuals to judge outcomes more valuable when they are harder to obtain. Atkinson's model predicts that individuals will have greater motivation to obtain outcomes for which the probability of achievement is moderate rather than extremely low, however. In terms of our model, this influence of subjective probabilities on utilities may be a spurious consequence of other influences in the model. We have suggested that perceived limits on an outcome is one of the determinants of the subjective probability of an outcome, and that this will be a function of objective scarcity of the outcome. Thus the less plentiful an outcome, the greater perceived limits, and the lower the subjective probability estimate. The objective scarcity of an outcome may simultaneously have a positive effect on the outcome's utility through its positive influence on the goal importance determinant. If so, this could lead to the apparent negative relationship between utilities and subjective probabilities, as shown in figure 4.3.

In the last chapter we also suggested that the recency of an outcome may be at least partially responsible for the apparent negative influence of subjective probabilities on utilities. This would result if, as we expect, more recent outcomes will have higher subjective probabilities than less recent ones, but they will also be likely to have less marginal utility than outcomes that have not been received recently.

The "wishful thinking" phenomenon, or the assignment of higher subjective probabilities to higher-utility outcomes, appears more difficult to explain. One may simply make the assumption that outcomes with a low objective probability do in fact have relatively high utility because of the effects of scarcity discussed above. Then one may explain "wishful thinking" in terms of the tendency of individuals to overestimate low probabilities, which we described in chapter 3. This explanation is not very satisfying, however, since it still leaves utilities and subjective probabilities not independent of each other.

Figure 4.3

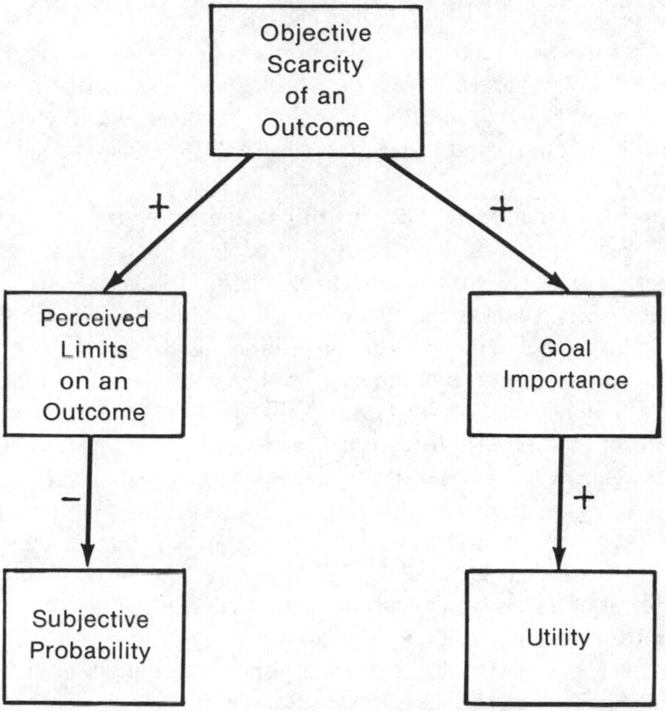

Objective
Scarcity
of an
Outcome

$+$ $+$

Perceived
Limits
on an
Outcome

Goal
Importance

$-$ $+$

Subjective
Probability

Utility

This relationship between the objective probability of an outcome, its subjective probability estimate, and its utility is shown in figure 4.4. Although this explanation removes any causal influence between utilities and subjective probabilities, it does leave them both dependent upon the objective probability of an outcome, and hence not independent of each other.

A partial explanation can also be provided for "wishful thinking" by reference to our previous discussion of differences in energy or resource expenditure.

Figure 4.4

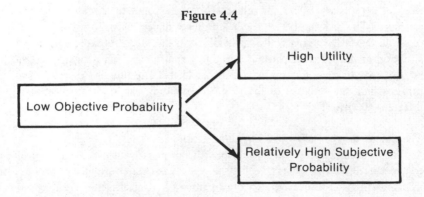

High Utility

Low Objective Probability

Relatively High Subjective
Probability

Because the amount of resources or energy an actor anticipates expending in enacting an alternative is never measured, the assignment of a relatively high subjective probability to a high-utility outcome may simply reflect actors' greater willingness to expend substantial amounts of resources in order to obtain these outcomes. We have assumed that anticipated expenditures will have a positive relationship with subjective probabilities, so this would yield the coincidence of high utility and subjective probability estimates that has been observed.

The apparent nonindependence of utilities and subjective probabilities may also simply be an artifact of the indirect methodologies that have been used with the subjective expected utility model. Edwards (1962b) claims that when choices between two-outcome gambles are tested with the model the variance of a gamble becomes confounded with the utilities of the outcomes.[4] Thus it is impossible to determine whether choices are being made on the basis of utilities or variance preferences. Tversky (1967b), however, suggests that utilities and subjective probabilities tend to appear independent of each other in gambling experiments but not in studies in which they are directly estimated.

So the actual relationship between utilities and subjective probabilities is not at all clear, nor are the reasons for any reciprocal influence that they may have. It seems that their nonindependence will be a somewhat less severe problem for investigators who are using more direct methods to measure utilities and subjective probabilities than for those who rely upon the more indirect methods. One hopes that estimates given in response to a question such as "What is the probability of outcome O_j, given alternative A_i?" will reflect whatever influence the utility of O_j may have on that estimate. Estimates of the utilities of outcomes appear to be more problematic, however, since individuals would typically be asked to estimate utilities without regard to different action alternatives. This implies that relatively direct estimates of utilities should be obtained in conjunction with more than one alternative in a manner similar to the way in which subjective probability estimates are obtained, i.e., "What is the utility of outcome O_j, given alternative A_i?" and "What is the utility of outcome O_j, given alternative A_k?" Because there are no objective probabilities or values against which these estimates can be compared in virtually all real-life situations, this appears to be the closest one can come to a reasonably accurate estimate. The possibility of the nonindependence of utilities and subjective probabilities also suggests the hazards of using the estimates derived in one situation as the operative estimates in another situation. This constitutes another reason for making greater use of more direct methodologies for measuring utilities and subjective probabilities because they can be used more easily in different situations.

The Calculation of Subjective Expected Utility

Since outcomes may have either positive or negative utility it appears simpler to separate these two types of utility and their associated subjective probabilities in calculating the subjective expected utility of an alternative. We may refer to the former as *subjective expected rewards,* consisting of positive utility received and negative utility forgone (in either the present or future). The latter will constitute *subjective expected costs* comprising negative utility received and positive utility forgone (also either in the present or future). The sum of positive and negative utilities, or the difference between subjective expected reward and subjective expected cost, equals the subjective expected utility of an alternative, which may also be referred to as *subjective expected profit.* An estimate of relative subjective expected utility therefore may be considered as an estimate of relative subjective expected profit, if the estimate yields a positive value, or as relative subjective expected loss, if it yields a negative value. Choice of one action alternative rather than another will be perceived as a potential profit or loss by actors, unless of course the subjective expected utilities of the two alternatives are equal.

We believe that this type of progression mirrors quite well the decision processes of actors. The costs of an action are subtracted from its rewards and the resultant anticipated profit (or loss) is then compared with the expected profit (or loss) of a different action. As we have shown in previous chapters, in some cases the estimation processes can be radically simplified, depending upon the outcomes resulting from the alternatives and the commonality of the goals fulfilled by the outcomes.

However, this approach to the calculation of subjective expected utility makes one key assumption: that all components of the subjective expected utility equation are weighted equally. Several investigators have called this assumption into question. For example, Slovic and Lichtenstein (1968*b*), using what they refer to as an information processing approach, have represented the four components of the model—positive and negative utilities and their associated subjective probabilities—as additive "risk" dimensions in a multiple regression equation. In their model the four components are allowed to have different weights, as follows:

$$A(G) = m + w_1 P_W + w_2 U(+) + w_3 P_L + w_4 U(-).$$

Here $A(G)$ represents the attractiveness of a gamble, P_W the probability of winning the gamble, $U(+)$ the amount of positive utility to be gained, P_L the probability of losing, and $U(-)$ the amount of negative utility accompanying loss of the gamble. Their research has shown that, at least in the case of gambles, subjects do not assign equal weights to these four components. P_W is weighted more heavily than P_L, and negative utility has greater weight than positive utility. Payne (1973) has described more complex patterns of weightings of these dimensions in choices among gambles.

These findings are closely related to Edwards's discussion of the relationship between subjective probabilities and the signs of gambles mentioned previously. In either case the implication is that the subjective probabilities of positive-utility outcomes will be inflated and those for negative-utility outcomes will be deflated. This weighting effect may be counterbalanced by the tendency to give greater weights to negative-utility outcomes than to positive-utility ones, however.

One cannot be certain, of course, if a weighting pattern that shows up in studies using gambles will also be present in real-world situations involving positive- and negative-utility outcomes. If differential weights are assigned in these situations, then this can be handled within the confines of our model by using exponents for the probability and utility terms in the subjective expected utility equation. The subjective expected utility equation for an alternative leading to two mutually exclusive and independent outcomes may be represented as

$$SEU(A_1) = p^a \times U(O_1)^b + q^c \times U(O_2)^d.$$

Therefore in this way a greater weight for the subjective probability of a positive-utility outcome could be represented by a larger exponent.

The possibility that individuals do assign different weights to the four components presents an additional reason for keeping positive- and negative-utility outcomes (and their associated subjective probabilities) separate in the subjective expected utility equation.

In figure 4.5 we represent the relationships among the various types of rewards and costs and the basic components of the subjective expected utility

Figure 4.5. Model of the Estimation of Subjective Expected Utility

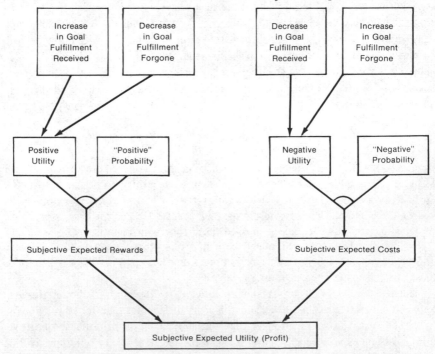

model that ultimately yield the subjective expected utility (or profit) of an action alternative. We use the terms *positive probability* and *negative probability* to refer to the subjective probabilities assigned to positive- and negative-utility outcomes, respectively. We have not included the influence of anticipated energy exertion on the utilities and probabilities in this figure, although it may be assumed to affect both of them.

THE SELECTION OF AN ACTION ALTERNATIVE

We have now brought our hypothetical actors to the point where they can estimate the subjective expected utilities of their action alternatives. We have seen that this is a complex process, but we have also noted a number of simplifications they are likely to make. We must now consider an equally complex issue: the choice process itself. How do actors utilize their subjective expected utility estimates in making decisions regarding which alternatives to enact? Simplifications will also be mandatory in this process if our actors are to keep from becoming immobilized by the sheer complexity of the situation.

The process of actually selecting an alternative to enact can be broken down into a set of components or a series of phases that culminate in the selection of an alternative. First, we must look at the factors that motivate actors to consider enacting alternatives other than the one in which they are currently engaged. We refer to this phase as the initiation of the selection process. It may also be described as the phase in which actors "decide to decide" among potential action alternatives. Second, once actors have initiated the selection process, what determines which action alternatives they include for consideration? It is obviously not possible for them to consider all the action alternatives available to them at any one time, so we must look at the influences that motivate them to select a subset of their repertoire of action alternatives for consideration.

Third, in many instances the *sequence* in which action alternatives are considered by actors will influence the alternatives that are ultimately chosen. We feel that this facet of the selection process is often overlooked, but will be crucial when nonmaximizing decision strategies are being used. The fourth and final phase in the selection process involves the decision of whether or not to switch action alternatives. Actors will either decide to continue enacting their current alternative or to change to one of the other alternatives that has been under consideration. It is in conjunction with this fourth phase that we shall discuss the potential decision strategies available to actors.

Initiating the Selection Process

We start with the basic assumption that actors are constantly either enacting action alternatives or experiencing outcomes that are yielding them positive or negative utility. In some cases of course, two people kissing each other being an obvious example, it is possible for one to simultaneously behave and receive an outcome. But for our purposes we shall assume that these two—actions and outcomes—can be temporally separated. Whether or not actors initiate the process of selecting a different action alternative will depend on what happens in this action-outcome sequence. If the enactment of an alternative is followed by an anticipated outcome, then the search process for another alternative will begin at some point during the reception of that outcome. However, if enactment is not followed by the anticipated outcome, or is followed by an unanticipated outcome, then it is probable that the actor will immediately consider the possibility of enacting another alternative. In both cases, though, the impetus for the selection process is provided by the judgment that greater utility can be obtained through enactment of an alternative other than the one being enacted or the one enacted most recently. We shall first look at these two cases of realized and unrealized expectations.

The Effect of Realized Expectations. We further assume that, in cases in which enactment of a behavior is followed by the reception of an anticipated outcome, this outcome does provide actors with some degree of goal fulfillment and thus utility. In order to explain the reasons for their switching to another alternative it is necessary to introduce a new construct, which we shall call the goal fulfillment deprivation gap (*GFDG*). This is conceptualized as simply the difference between the current level of goal fulfillment and the desired level of goal fulfillment for any goal. In chapter 2 we discussed these levels as determinants of the utility of outcomes, noting that the *DLGF* is likely to mark the approximate point on actors' utility curves at which satiation effects become evident and goal fulfillment has decreasing marginal utility. The goal fulfillment deprivation gap therefore simply constitutes the portion of the utility curve between the amount of goal fulfillment the actor has at any point in time and the amount of goal fulfillment he or she desires. These gaps will also be weighted by the goal importance of the goals they represent. Since, in chapter 2, we suggested that the utility of an outcome is basically equal to DGF^{GI}, this means the influence of the goal fulfillment deprivation gap on initiating the selection process may also be represented by the size of the gap raised to the goal importance power.

As an outcome is being received, we may visualize this gap as gradually being filled or narrowed and possibly becoming completely closed if the outcome reaches the desired level of goal fulfillment. Overfulfillment of the gap will be characterized by satiation and decreasing marginal utility; this overfulfillment may also be represented by a negative value for the *DLGF–CLGF* term. We assume here that attainment of the *DLGF* does not result in an increase in that value, reflecting an actor's increased aspirations, although in chapter 2 we noted that this is a very real possibility.

So the goal fulfillment deprivation gap for any goal that is being fulfilled by a particular outcome may be visualized as becoming smaller as the outcome is received. In the case of discrete outcomes this closing of the gap may be an "all-at-once" phenomenon. At the same time, however, one may visualize the goal fulfillment deprivation gaps *widening* for all those goals for which the given outcome is *not* providing fulfillment. The speed at which this occurs will vary among goals, depending upon their goal decomposition rates. Consequently the utility not being received as the result of lack of fulfillment of these goals can be seen to be increasing at the same time that utility is being received from the goal that is being fulfilled.

We suspect that the process of selecting another action alternative, in this case to provide fulfillment of a different goal than is currently being fulfilled, will be initiated when the goal fulfillment deprivation gap for an unfulfilled goal *surpasses* the goal fulfillment deprivation gap of the goal that is being fulfilled. Because the goal fulfillment deprivation gap is weighted by goal importance a given amount of deprivation on more important goals will be more likely to initiate the selection process than will the same amount of deprivation on less important goals. Or, to put the same idea somewhat differently, actors will devote more of their time to selecting alternatives to provide fulfillment of their more important goals.

We have said that biological goals, such as satisfying hunger, are prime examples of recurrent goals. We have also indicated that such goals are likely to have high decomposition rates. As a result their goal fulfillment deprivation gaps will widen relatively quickly and will signal to actors that they should begin considering alternatives to fulfill such goals. In extreme cases they may become all-encompassing and require actors to refrain from attempting to fulfill virtually all their other goals.

For some actors social goals—for example, obtaining approval from others—may be almost as important and may also have high decomposition rates. If so, then actors having these goals ranked very high in their goal hierarchies will undoubtedly be constantly experiencing deprivation and considering alternatives whereby these goals might be fulfilled.

Comparison of the goal fulfillment deprivation gaps will be complicated if outcomes provide goal fulfillment on multiple goals. However, we anticipate that in virtually all cases the more important goals will have greater influence in motivating actors to begin considering other alternatives. Since the goal fulfillment deprivation gaps can be visualized as segments of utility curves, the amount of utility deprivation may be seen as the basic determinant of the initiation of the selection process in the cases we have described. When that amount for any goal (or goals) surpasses the amount of utility received through the enactment of an alternative, then actors will begin to consider switching to another alternative.

The Effects of Unrealized Expectations.   We have suggested that the reception of expected outcomes ultimately leads to the consideration of alternatives whereby other unfulfilled goals may be fulfilled. In cases in which the outcomes that result from the enactment of alternatives differ from what was anticipated, we suspect that actors' first reactions will be to consider how the originally anticipated outcomes may still be procured. Someone anticipating praise from an employer, for example, will likely be miffed if it is not forthcoming and will probably consider one of two options. He or she may either begin considering other alternatives that might yield that outcome *or* he or she may consider enacting the original alternative at a different level of intensity, i.e., expending greater effort in enacting that alternative. In either case it is the blockage of the anticipated outcome that triggers the selection process, whereas in the case of realized expectations, it is success, and not failure, that leads to an eventual switch to a different alternative. Failure in these cases does not necessarily mean not receiving a particular outcome at all. It may involve receiving only part of the anticipated amount of goal fulfillment. The employer, for example, may not be as effusive with praise as was expected. Or it may involve receiving an unexpected outcome, such as criticism, from the employer.

Goal fulfillment deprivation gaps will also be influential when outcomes do not meet actors' expectations. The more important the goal an actor is attempting to fulfill by means of the blocked alternative and the greater the deprivation gap for that goal, the more likely it is that blockage will initiate the selection process, in this case possibly for a more effective means of attaining the goal. If fulfillment of a relatively unimportant goal is not received, or if there is relatively little deprivation, then it is probable that other goal fulfillment deprivation gaps will be greater and actors will initiate the search for alternatives to meet those goals. In the long run, it is quite likely that continued lack of fulfillment of a goal will result in that goal's becoming less important, so that subsequent blockage of the goal will become less significant.

The other major factor affecting the likelihood of initiating the selection process for another alternative is the extent to which the results of one's actions do not live up to expectations. The greater this disparity, the more likely will actors be to start searching for other possibilities. Thus an outcome that is completely opposite from the anticipated outcome, e.g., criticism rather than praise, is more likely to result in a consideration of other alternatives than an outcome that provides at least some portion of the anticipated amount of goal fulfillment. Therefore the greater the goal fulfillment deprivation gap, the more important the goal, and the less a received outcome meets actors' expectations, the more likely they will be to consider other action alternatives.

The Effects of External Stimuli. This discussion of the beginning of the process of selecting an action alternative has centered primarily on factors internal to actors, such as the goal fulfillment deprivation gap. The failure of outcomes to live up to actors' expectations does involve an external stimulus impinging upon actors, but the effects of this stimulus are partially dependent upon their internal states.

More generally we can think of external stimuli as cues that have been associated with goal fulfillment in the past. The appearance of a baby's mother constitutes an external stimulus with pleasant connotations for the baby, for example. These external stimuli play a major role in the operant model of behavior. According to that paradigm the presence of these stimuli motivates actors to behave in a manner that was rewarded in the past when these stimuli appeared.

We believe it is more accurate to depict their influence as a something less than automatic process and to note the possibility of slippage in this linkage. The occurrences of such stimuli are likely to cause actors to consider other action alternatives than the one they are enacting, but they do not automatically trigger behaviors.

These stimuli may bring to the attention of individuals the possibility of receiving goal fulfillment on a goal that is currently at least partially unfulfilled. Thus they may initiate the selection process even though the *GFDG* for a particular goal is not as large as the *GFDG* for some other goal. A person walking down the street may suddenly spy a dollar bill lying beneath a storm grating. This is likely to prompt him or her to at least pause and consider whether to continue walking or to stop walking and consider alternatives for retrieving it. Such stimuli may of course also threaten actors with negative-utility outcomes, in which case they must decide whether to continue enacting their present alternative or consider alternatives that would enable them to avoid the undesirable outcome.

The external stimuli of greatest concern to us are the actions of other actors, which may either be anticipated or totally unexpected. For example, the movement of a black family into an all-white neighborhood will be a very visible symbol that will possibly cause some of the residents to begin considering whether to remain living there or to move elsewhere. Similarly, any negative response on the part of the residents to the incoming family will no doubt motivate the family to confront the same choices. Or the arrest of a black suspect by a white policeman in a ghetto area will constitute an external stimulus to people in the area and will promote the consideration of action alternatives on their part.

The effect of external stimuli such as these will clearly depend, however, on actors' internal states. If the stimuli suggest the possibility of receiving positive utility on relatively important goals that are currently very unfulfilled, then they are very likely to initiate the process of selecting an action alternative. They will also be very likely to trigger the process if they threaten a loss of utility on very important goals that are relatively well filled. The individual who sights the dollar bill will be more likely to consider alternatives to retrieve it if he or she is destitute than if he or she is wealthy. The black family's moving into a white neighborhood may be perceived by some of the residents as a threat to a sizable financial investment, whereas to others it may be viewed as an opportunity to become acquainted with someone of a different race. In either case the stimulus is likely to prompt the residents to consider new action alternatives, although it is likely that the alternatives they consider will be different.

On the basis of our above comments we can further differentiate among individuals within the two categories. Those for whom financial security is an extremely important goal and/or who feel financially insecure (i.e., deprived on that goal) will be more likely to begin considering the other options available to them than will those for whom financial security is less important and/or who feel more financially secure. Similarly, those whites who are especially desirous of making friends with blacks or who feel deprived on that goal will also be more apt to consider other alternatives, in their case how to best approach the black family.

So we can conclude that individuals will be prompted to begin considering action alternatives other than the one they are currently enacting for quite different reasons, namely, either because their expectations have been met or have not been met. The process may also be initiated by the responses or actions of other actors in conjunction with the individuals' goals and the extent to which these goals are fulfilled. The basic determinant of the initiation of the selection process is the perceived possibility of positive utility or the threat of negative utility in all these cases, but as we have seen this covers a wide variety of situations.

The fact that an actor has initiated the process of considering alternatives in addition to the one being currently, or most recently, enacted does not mean that he or she will necessarily switch to a new alternative. That decision will be made on the basis of the relative subjective expected utilities of the alternatives that are considered and whatever decision strategy the actor is using in a given situation. These two processes—deciding to consider other action alternatives and choosing among the alternatives under consideration—should be kept analytically separate.

Alternatives Considered in the Selection Process

Which of their possible action alternatives will actors consider in the selection process? Generally we would expect them to consider those alternatives that have been most likely to result in outcomes that yielded goal fulfillment on unfulfilled goals in the past. The implications of this are slightly different for the cases of realized and unrealized expectations. In the case of realized expectations, utility deprivation is experienced when the goal fulfillment deprivation gap for a goal that is not currently being fulfilled surpasses the *GFDG* for the goal or goals that are receiving fulfillment. Thus actors will experience deprivation on a particular goal and work backward, so to speak, to the outcomes and then alternatives that brought them fulfillment on that goal formerly. When expectations are not met by an outcome, however, we have suggested that actors' most likely responses are to repeat an enacted alternative at a different level of intensity or consider a different alternative for meeting the same goal.

We have already discussed alternative-outcome linkages in our chapter on subjective probabilities, where we hypothesized the existence of a large number of NO_j/NA_i proportions that are more or less directly converted into subjective probability estimates. These proportions may also be visualized as a matrix of alternatives and outcomes in which the cells consist of these NO_j/NA_i values derived from actors' experiences.

We have also discussed outcome-goal linkages in the context of the utilities of outcomes, suggesting that the utility of an outcome at a specific point in time will primarily be a function of the degree of goal fulfillment provided by that outcome. We may also postulate the existence of an outcome-goal matrix, containing all the actors' goals and the outcomes of which they are aware. In this matrix, the cells can be thought of as containing the expected degree of goal fulfillment offered by the jth outcome on the kth goal. These values, also, will be based on actors' experiences, but they do not represent a proportion convertible into a probability as in the case of the alternative-outcome linkage. Rather they may be represented as the expected value of a frequency distribution of the occasions on which the particular outcome has occurred in the past. If we assume that a particular outcome has provided varying degrees of goal fulfillment for a specific goal in the past, then this can be represented as a frequency distribution representing the number of times different degrees of goal fulfillment have resulted. The expected degree of goal fulfillment (*EDGF*) therefore may be represented by

$$EDGF(O_j|G_k) = \sum_{i=1}^{m} P_i X_i,$$

where X_i represents the different amounts of goal fulfillment, P_i represents the proportion of times a specific X_i has occurred, and there are m different levels of goal fulfillment.[5]

Therefore actors attempting to determine which action alternatives to consider in a selection process will likely first consider which value in the outcome-goal matrix is largest for a specific goal, i.e., they will "look" only in the row or column corresponding to that goal, and will then consider which alternative or alternatives are most likely to bring about that outcome. Their choices of alternatives to consider will be simplified to the extent that there are noticeably superior alternative-outcome and outcome-goal linkages. Thus the expected degree of goal fulfillment for outcome O_2 may be much greater than that for any other outcomes on unfulfilled goal G_3, and alternative A_1 may be much more likely to bring about O_2 than any other of the available A_i. In these cases the estimations of the subjective expected utilities will also be simplified, unless the situation requires substantial modifications of an NO_j/NA_i proportion, or unless the other determinants of the utility of an outcome, such as the immediacy of goal fulfillment, are significant.

If there are no significant differences among alternatives (in terms of their likelihood of bringing about certain outcomes) and/or among outcomes (in terms of the degree of goal fulfillment they provide), then actors' choices will be complicated by the need to consider more than one other alternative. To the set of alternatives derived from their experiences, actors may also add alternatives they have not tried in the past. Or they may suspect that outcomes they have not experienced in the past will in fact provide goal fulfillment for particular goals. These may be alternatives and outcomes they have observed others experience, or they may be ones they themselves have conceptualized. If such alternatives or outcomes are included in the set of alternatives actually considered in the selection process, then we anticipate that actors will assign to them the NO_j/NA_i proportions and expected degrees of goal fulfillment of the alternatives and outcomes perceived to be most similar to them. We must acknowledge, of course, the possibility of grievous errors in either case and resultant unrealized expectations that will serve as the setting for the next choice of alternatives that is made.

If actors are considering other action alternatives because their expectations have not been met by the outcome or outcomes they have experienced, then the consideration of similar alternatives and/or outcomes will be more likely. We have predicted that a likely response to an unanticipated outcome will be the consideration of enacting the same alternative at a different level of intensity.[6] In addition, actors may reenter the outcome-goal matrix to ascertain what other outcomes have brought fulfillment on the yet unfulfilled goal and then look to the alternative-outcome matrix to consider the best alternatives to bring about those outcomes. Or some combination of these may be considered—for example, trying the same alternative in hopes of getting a different outcome that satisfies the same goal, trying a different alternative to get the same outcome, or trying a different alternative in order to get a different outcome that still fulfills the same goal. In all these cases we suspect that actors will first consider alternatives and outcomes most similar to the alternative that was tried and the outcome (or outcomes) that was anticipated originally.

Thus the set of action alternatives that actors consider in the process of selecting an action alternative will largely depend upon their experiences and the reason why they have initiated the selection process, i.e., realized or unrealized expectations. We have suggested that they will utilize their recollections of the outcomes that have brought them goal fulfillment in the past and their causal models of the relationship between alternatives and outcomes to limit the set of alternatives to be considered. The thought processes are somewhat different than those involved in the estimation of subjective expected utility. In estimating SEU actors are faced with the questions "What is the utility of outcome O_j?" and "What is the probability of O_j, given A_i?" In the prior process of determining which alternatives to consider they are faced with the questions "What outcome has brought the greatest goal fulfillment on goal G_k in the past?" and "What alternative has most often resulted in that outcome in the past?"[7]

The Sequence in Which Alternatives Are Considered

This discussion of the set of action alternatives considered by actors suggests the most logical sequence in which these alternatives will be considered, namely, in rank order of the degree of goal fulfillment they have provided in the past. Thus if O_2 brought more goal fulfillment on G_3 than any other outcome in the past, and if A_1 resulted in O_2 more often than any other alternative in the past, then A_1 would be the most logical alternative to consider first. This does not mean of course that A_1 will necessarily have the greatest subjective expected utility of any alternative in the specific situation in which an actor is making a subjective utility estimate; it would simply be the first one considered. This logical sequence is probably quite likely in cases in which the selection process has been induced by goal fulfillment on one goal and increasing goal deprivation on another goal. It is probably much less likely in cases in which an anticipated outcome has not occurred or external stimuli confront actors with unanticipated possibilities for gains or losses of goal fulfillment.

In cases of this latter type we anticipate that the *cues* present in the situation will be quite significant in determining the sequencing of alternatives. They are likely to suggest other alternatives to the actors involved. For example, failure to receive an outcome because of opposition from another actor may be accompanied by behavioral cues or signs given by that actor which imply other alternatives that have been tried in the past with success. If so, then actors are likely to consider first the alternative most closely associated with those cues as discussed in chapter 3. Or the external stimulus, e.g., the black family moving into the neighborhood, may itself constitute the cue that calls to mind previous alternatives. In these cases we expect that actors will consider alternatives in the order of clarity of cues. These cues will be ultimately linked to past goal fulfillment, but we are not sure that actors think in goal-fulfillment terms in these situations.

It is conceivable that actors go immediately to this third stage in the selection process without going through the prior stage of delimiting the set of action alternatives to consider. Whether or not they go through both stages, or just the third, will basically depend upon the decision strategy under which they are operating. Specifying the set of alternatives to be considered will be necessary if they are following a maximization strategy. It will not be necessary if they are following a different strategy, such as satisficing. We defer consideration of these and other decision strategies until after the next section.

Choosing among Action Alternatives

The final phase in the selection process is of course the *choice* among action alternatives. At minimum actors will choose between continuing the alternative they are currently enacting and switching to a different alternative. They may also consider enacting the same alternative at a different level of intensity, and they may be trying to fulfill either the goal they are currently fulfilling or a goal that is substantially underfulfilled. We have consistently assumed that choices among alternatives will be made on the basis of their subjective expected utilities. Generally we expect them to switch to a different alternative if that alternative has greater subjective expected utility than continuation of their current alternative has. This means that actors may continue enacting a given alternative even though they are experiencing severe deprivation on other goals simply because they perceive no alternatives with greater subjective expected utility available to fulfill those other goals.

Actors may also continue enacting a current alternative because of "sunk costs" (Stinchcombe 1968). Resources may have been invested in that alternative, e.g., several years in college, which do not have to be invested again. Or the resources necessary to initiate another action may be so costly, in terms of positive utility forgone, that it is not possible for a new alternative to have greater subjective expected utility. It is conceivable also that changing to a different alternative will itself have a negative utility, the opposite of the utility for gambling that we have discussed previously. In this case, avoidance of change may constitute an important goal for actors. Making a change will represent a loss of goal fulfillment and hence have negative utility.

When the availability of alternatives is not a problem for an actor, then we anticipate that he or she will switch to a different alternative when the subjective expected utility of continuing the present alternative falls below the *SEU* of the other alternative. In the case of realized expectations, the current alternative's subjective expected utility will drop primarily because of the current level of goal fulfillment determinant. Fulfillment of the goal being fulfilled will have brought the actor to a portion of the utility curve with decreasing marginal utility, whereas he or she will be located at a point of constant or increasing marginal utility on the utility curve for another goal. In the case of unrealized expectations, we suspect that the drop in the enacted alternative's expected utility will be primarily the result of a decline in the subjective probability component, if an anticipated outcome is not received at all, or the result of a decreased utility estimate for the outcome, if it did not provide the amount of goal fulfillment that was anticipated. However, failure to receive even a portion of the expected outcome may result in an increased utility estimate for that outcome if the current level of goal fulfillment for the goal that outcome was to fulfill has declined sharply.

Because the actual basis on which the choice is made is quite a complex topic, we discuss it in the next section in the context of decision strategies.

DECISION STRATEGIES

The usual assumption of subjective expected utility theory and the norm of prescriptive subjective expected utility theory has been that actors act so as to maximize their subjective expected utilities.[8] This assumption has two major implications: (1) actors will switch from a current action alternative to another action alternative when the subjective expected utility of the new alternative exceeds the subjective expected utility of continuing the current alternative; and (2) actors will select the action alternative with the highest subjective expected utility. We have made the first assumption in our above discussion of the selection process. The second assumption is a more difficult one to make, and its apparent simplicity hides some complexity. For example, it is not clear whether as commonly used it means that actors select the alternative with the highest *SEU* from all the alternatives that are available to them at a given time or whether they select the alternative with the highest *SEU* in the subset of alternatives they have delimited through the process we have suggested above. The latter seems more logical, but if that is the case, then, given the complexity of decisions, it is likely that maximization is an impossibility for anyone because it is always possible that one has overlooked an alternative with greater subjective expected utility than the one that is chosen. Most serious, however, is the fact that experimental evidence indicates that actors do not consistently maximize their *SEU*'s. This has of course prompted the consideration of other possible decision strategies used by actors.

"Satisficing" as a Decision Strategy

An alternate decision strategy that has not received much attention in the subjective expected utility literature, but that has been developed primarily in the literature on decision making in formal organizations, is that of "satisficing" (Simon 1957). Actors following this strategy do not necessarily select the alternative with the greatest subjective expected utility, but rather any alternative that has a satisfactory level of *SEU*, or any alternative that is "good enough." This strategy has two implications for our model. First, it suggests that actors will continue enacting their current alternatives as long as they are satisfactory to them, even though they may be experiencing deprivation on an unfulfilled goal. Second, if and when they switch to another alternative, they will switch to an alternative promising satisfactory subjective expected utility.

The basic problems one confronts with this decision strategy are determining what constitutes a satisfactory level of subjective expected utility for an alternative and how great deprivation on an unfulfilled goal must become before it is unsatisfactory. Simon (1957) has defined a satisfactory level in terms of actors' aspiration levels. Any outcome that equals or surpasses their aspiration levels is satisfactory. He notes, for example, that a chess player who discovers a move that enables him or her to checkmate an opponent is not interested in other alternatives yielding the same outcome (1957:252–53). But he also notes that actors' aspiration levels are likely to change, depending upon how difficult it is to find alternatives that are satisfying. Consequently the levels of subjective expected utility that would be perceived as satisfactory by them would also be expected to change over time.

We have equated actors' aspiration levels with their desired levels of goal fulfillment in our model. In this context, therefore, any alternatives yielding outcomes that reach or exceed their *DLGF*'s for a particular goal will be satisfactory to them and hence chosen. But this neglects the fact that we are assuming that actors operate in situations of uncertainty, so that the subjective probability of an outcome's occurring must also be taken into account. It is one thing to receive an outcome that surpasses one's aspiration level and be confronted with a decision on whether to accept it. It is quite a different thing when one is not certain whether that outcome will be received. So the satisfactory level must be defined in terms of subjective expected utility and not simply in terms of goal fulfillment. Furthermore, outcomes that surpass the *DLGF*'s on different goals or the same goal may differ very little in utility because of satiation effects.

Differences in subjective expected utility among such alternatives will depend primarily on differences in their subjective probabilities. Thus an alternative will have to have a satisfactory level of subjective probability and the outcome anticipated must also promise a satisfactory level of utility for the alternative to "satisfice."

What constitutes a satisfactory level of subjective expected utility will undoubtedly vary among actors and may well be some function of their aspiration levels. It may also be a function of goal importance, with less subjective expected utility on their more important goals equally satisfactory to more subjective expected utility on less important goals. We can suggest two quite different possibilities for the location of this satisfactory level.

First, the first alternative an actor considers that has higher subjective expected utility than a current alternative may constitute an alternative that satisfices. If no other alternative has higher subjective expected utility, then we would expect the actor to continue the existent action. Other alternatives may have greater subjective expected utility than the first one the actor comes to and selects, but they will not even be considered. If this is the case, then the sequence in which alternatives are considered will be crucial. If alternatives are considered in the order we have suggested previously, namely, in terms of the highest expected values in the outcome-goal matrix and the highest probability in the alternative-outcome matrix, then possibly the choice of the first alternative considered will correspond with the choice that would be made under a maximization strategy. It may not correspond, however, because these matrices are based on actors' experiences. In the actor's current situation that alternative may not have the highest subjective expected utility, or even a satisfactory level.

Second, in some cases any alternative that promises some fulfillment of a goal on which there is severe deprivation may have a subjective expected utility that is satisfactory, even though its *SEU* may not be greater than that of a current alternative or other potential alternatives and even though it does not attain an actor's desired level of goal fulfillment. In this case it will probably be very difficult to ascertain whether an actor is maximizing or satisficing without having measures of all subjective probabilities and utilities. One might assume that the long period of deprivation had increased the importance of a goal so that the actor was maximizing when in fact he or she was simply happy to receive any fulfillment on that goal. We see no easy way to include this possibility in our model.

Maximizing and Satisficing Compared

The maximizing and satisficing strategies may not be as different as they appear at first glance. We have already noted that maximization probably refers to a subset of the action alternatives available to actors; it will be impossible to consider all potential alternatives in all situations. Satisficing undoubtedly also refers to some subset of alternatives, and if the subsets under the two strategies are the same and alternatives are considered in the order we have suggested, then the two strategies are likely to be synonymous. The major difference may simply lie in the amount of information processed by actors. The maximizer will consider all options and then choose the best one, a process that will require more information and probably allow fewer simplifications than will be the case for the actor who satisfices.

This suggests that maximizing may be a more viable option in situations when the necessary information is either available or is not too costly, in terms of time and other resources, to obtain. Satisficing will be more viable in situations in which information is not available and difficult to procure (Coombs, Dawes, and Tversky 1970). Satisficing may also be the only possibility in situations in which alternatives must be considered sequentially, i.e., a decision must be made on one alternative before considering the next one. In such situations it will not be possible to obtain the information necessary for maximizing.

It is perhaps not surprising that satisficing has been related to formal organizations. Actors in such organizations may be under time and resource constraints, for example, that preclude extensive searches for information covering a large number of alternatives. The alternatives they consider may also be available only in sequence. Or the choices they confront may be so complex that maximization will not be feasible even with a limited number of alternatives under consideration.

Both strategies will involve trade-offs for actors. Maximizing will minimize the possibility that substantial utility connected with an unenacted alternative will be forgone because it involves selecting the alternative with the greatest subjective expected utility. But there may be substantial costs involved in making that determination, in both resources and time. Satisficing, by contrast, minimizes the costs of information procurement, but it increases the likelihood that the alternative with greatest subjective expected utility will not be enacted, and hence utility will be forgone.

Consequently we anticipate that actors do not use one or the other decision strategy exclusively in choice situations. Which one they choose will depend on the relative rewards and costs of the two strategies in a situation. We may regard them as asking, "Does the utility that is possibly gained as a result of maximizing justify the additional cost in time and resources that the strategy requires?" In situations in which they cannot make very precise estimates of utilities and subjective probabilities, or if they do not have the resources to consider all alternatives, the increased expenditure that would be required to obtain more precise estimates or to consider more alternatives will very likely not be worthwhile. We also suspect that the greater investment that maximization requires will more likely be worthwhile in choices involving actors' more important goals than in choices involving goals ranking low in their goal hierarchies, unless the latter involve outcomes with very large amounts of goal fulfillment. Our general anticipation therefore is that actors will maximize when they are *able* to—i.e., when the costs of so doing are not too great—and will satisfice when *necessary*, i.e., when the costs of maximization are exorbitant.

It is necessary to make a distinction between maximizing subjective expected utility in a choice among action alternatives and maximizing one's total utility as a result of one's choices. If the costs of maximizing each choice are sufficiently great, it is conceivable that one's total utility will be less than maximum because of the expenditure of resources entailed in obtaining necessary information. Consequently it is conceivable that actors could follow a satisficing strategy for most choices, thereby saving resources, and in the long run maximize their total utility. This, of course, will depend upon the amount of resources they have; actors with substantial resources will be less likely to confront this problem.

It will generally be very difficult for an outside observer to ascertain whether an actor is maximizing or satisficing unless the observer has a measure of the actor's subjective expected utilities. Choices that appear to be based on a satisficing strategy may actually have been the result of maximization. This is likely to occur in cases where alternatives lead to deferred outcomes. If actors radically discount the utilities of future outcomes, then alternatives yielding only current outcomes are likely to have greater subjective expected utility. An outside observer may regard actors choosing alternatives that yield current outcomes rather than future outcomes as following a satisficing strategy or may say they are unable to defer gratification, as we noted in chapter 2, when in fact this is not the case. Similarly, if an actor considers more than one alternative before finding one that surpasses the subjective expected utility of continuation of a present alternative, an outside observer may regard that actor as maximizing, when in fact the actor is satisficing.

Other Decision Strategies

We shall basically restrict our discussion of decision strategies to the maximizing and satisficing strategies. However, we wish to note briefly several other possibilities.

Components Other Than Profits. We have concentrated on decisions made on the basis of subjective expected utility in our discussion of the maximizing and satisficing strategies. Under the former strategy actors choose the alternative with the greatest *SEU*, whereas under the latter they choose an alternative with a satisfactory *SEU*. These two options may also be described as a choice between maximum and satisfactory subjective expected *profits* on the basis of our discussion earlier in this chapter.

However, it is conceivable that actors may not base their decisions upon subjective expected utilities, regardless of which decision strategy they are following. They may choose on the basis of specific components, e.g., subjective expected *rewards* or subjective expected *costs*. Thus they may choose the alternative with the greatest subjective expected rewards or the one with the smallest subjective expected costs, in either case ignoring the other component. They may also make a choice on the basis of one of two ratios—the reward/cost ratio or the profit/cost ratio—choosing the alternative with the best ratio or a satisfactory ratio in either case.

Our guess is that actors are likely to choose among alternatives on the basis of one of the last three of these if they have limited resources and they are concerned about conserving them. Actors with substantial resources may be able to absorb high costs in order to obtain substantially higher rewards and hence great profits. But actors with limited resources, the expenditure of which we have noted shows up as utility forgone, likely will have to settle for lower profits in order to enact an alternative they can afford, so to speak. An example that comes to mind is that of poor families who have not been able to come up with the lump sum of money necessary to buy food stamps and hence have not been able to gain that potential profit.

Making decisions among alternatives on the basis of their profit/cost ratios would be especially helpful for individuals with limited resources because it would indicate where they could get the greatest returns per unit investment. Individuals wishing to allocate their resources most efficiently among a variety of goals could also base their decision on that ratio.

Situations Involving Other Actors.   Choice situations in which an actor's action constitutes an outcome for another actor will be covered in the next chapter under the heading of exchange. In this context we simply wish to note that these situations may involve slightly different decision strategies. We shall assume that two actors, A and B, are in interaction, and that A is the one making a choice among action alternatives. We shall also assume that A perceives that A's action will have utility for B, i.e., that it will constitute an outcome providing goal fulfillment for B. If one of A's goals is to increase, or decrease, B's utility, then the outcome for B should also constitute an outcome for A. If A wishes to increase B's utility and A perceives that A's action will have that result, then this consequence will have positive utility for both A and B (the latter of course from A's perspective).

The important point is that the perceived outcomes to B may enter into A's decision strategy for A's choice of alternatives. For example, A may wish to choose the alternative that maximizes the difference between A's profits and B's profits. This strategy could possibly be labeled as exploitation. Or A may wish to minimize the difference between A's and B's profits, a consequence that may be regarded as equity. A may even wish to minimize A's profits and maximize B's, in which case one would likely label A as altruistic. In all of these cases it will be necessary for A to include B's expected utility as a basis for A's decision, and either maximizing or satisficing will refer to both A's and B's expected outcomes.

Meeker (1971) has discussed these and several other possibilities as decision rules rather than decision strategies, and she does not discuss them in subjective expected utility terms, but her discussion can easily be adapted to our approach. She defines rationality as the exchange rule that assigns to Person the outcome maximizing Person's total payoff. In our terms, this is the strategy of maximizing subjective expected utility on the part of P. Altruism she defines as assigning to Other the outcome that maximizes Other's total payoff; in our terms it constitutes a strategy that strives to maximize O's expected utility (as anticipated by P). She defines group-gain as obtaining the maximum combined payoff for O and P; we would refer to this as maximizing both P's and O's subjective expected utilities (O's again from P's perspective). And what we have suggested might be called exploitation—trying to achieve the maximum difference between P's and O's expected utilities—she refers to as competition.[9]

Meeker also mentions the possibility of multiple motivations of actors but does not go into them in detail. In our model this will involve the simultaneous application of more than one decision strategy. For example, actors may try to find an alternative that will maximize the difference between their and other's expected utilities and that will also maximize their own subjective expected utility. The well-known Prisoners' Dilemma Game represents a situation in which such decision strategies are possible.[10]

Another possibility is that actors will alternate between decision strategies in an exchange situation. At time t they may choose to maximize their subjective expected utility and minimize the expected utility of the other actor, but at time $t + 1$ they may adopt the opposite strategy, minimizing their SEU and maximizing the other's expected utility. This pattern is common to many game-theoretical situations and represents what might be regarded as reciprocity.[11]

So a variety of situations in which the expected utilities of other actors are taken into account by an actor choosing among action alternatives can be represented in terms of actors' decision strategies.[12]

Nonmaximizing Strategies. Some theorists have attempted to deal with the apparent failure of actors to maximize their subjective expected utilities by the introduction of additional components in the decision model or by the postulation of nonmaximizing strategies other than satisficing. We shall lump all of these, some of which have already been mentioned in this chapter or previous chapters, under the heading of nonmaximizing strategies and discuss them briefly. One such attempt has been the inclusion of a utility for choice variability in the model (Siegel 1959; Ofshe and Ofshe 1970) on the grounds that actors vary their choices among a series of alternatives to avoid boredom rather than maximizing subjective expected utility on every choice. Second, a utility for gambling has also been included by some, indicating that choices differ between situations of certainty and uncertainty (Tversky 1967a; Royden, Suppes, and Walsh 1959). Third, some have argued that actors have variance preferences and base their choices on them (Lee 1971; Payne 1973; Coombs and Pruitt 1960). Fourth, a similar argument has been made regarding probabilities (Edwards 1961; Luce and Suppes 1965:327). Fifth, a fairly extensive literature has developed on the concept of risk, including discussions of the differences in risk among choice situations and differences in risk-taking tendencies among actors. The general assumption of this approach is that decisions are made on the basis of the degree of risk characterizing a situation and the preferences for risks characterizing the actors making the decisions.[13]

The experimental evidence regarding these approaches is quite mixed. Although it is possible that each of them may be valid in certain situations, we question their wholesale application to all situations. Furthermore they are all based upon and applied to the experimental studies of utilities and subjective probabilities using very indirect methods of measurement that we have suggested may not be applicable to many real-world situations.

The Choice of a Decision Strategy

We shall limit our discussion of the factors influencing actors' choices of a decision strategy in a given situation to a choice between the maximizing and satisficing strategies. We have claimed earlier that this choice will be based upon the relative rewards and costs of the two strategies in a particular situation. To avoid an infinite regress we shall assume that actors maximize in making this decision, i.e., they choose the strategy that offers the greatest profit in that situation. Most of our discussion will be in terms of the relative costs of the two approaches since we are assuming that actors cannot know (and may never know, if they choose a satisficing strategy) the utility they are going to gain by adopting a particular strategy. This suggests that in some cases actors may choose a decision strategy *after* they have begun considering the subjective expected utilities of alternatives. They may, for example, start out following a maximizing strategy and switch to a satisficing strategy if they discover that the former is too costly. Or they may switch from a satisficing to a maximizing strategy if the first alternatives they consider do not have greater subjective expected utilities than their current alternatives but they are experiencing extreme deprivation on a particular goal.

First, it is probable that the greater the situational constraints confronted by actors in particular situations, the less likely that they will choose a maximizing strategy. These constraints include obstacles to obtaining information to make utility and subjective probability estimates and characteristics of the situation that make it impossible to consider alternatives simultaneously. Constraints can also be expanded to include the anticipated actions of others in the long run. Actors may perceive that if they consistently maximize their subjective expected utility they may stimulate the opposition of others who will prevent their obtaining future goal fulfillment, particularly if their maximizing comes at the others' expense. Thus members of a dominant group may choose to satisfice occasionally so as to not engender the eventual wrath of members of groups subordinate to them. One may include ethical or moral constraints as well. Ideologies stressing altruism may motivate actors to not maximize at times, even though maximizing may be the more profitable strategy for them.

Second, the influence of these constraints upon actors will be mediated by the actors' resources. Actors with substantial resources will find maximizing less costly than will actors with limited resources. The former will be able to invest more in information seeking, and thus the significance of the constraints will be diminished. Of course, even very well endowed actors will only be able to maximize on those alternatives that they think to include in the selection process. They may overlook alternatives that would have even greater subjective expected utilities than the one (or ones) they actually choose.

Third, we anticipate that actors will be more likely to adopt a maximizing strategy in situations where they expect substantial differences in the subjective expected utilities of the alternatives they consider than in situations where they suspect that the alternatives will be relatively similar in *SEU*. This judgment will necessarily be based upon their experiences with these alternatives. If alternatives are nearly equal in *SEU* it is likely that the costs of determining exactly which alternative has greater *SEU* will become too great.

Fourth, we also anticipate that the more complex a choice situation is—i.e., the more alternatives that have multiple outcomes, both current and future, and the more outcomes that fulfill multiple goals—the less likely actors are to maximize. To some extent actors with substantial resources may be able to handle quite complex situations, but even they will no doubt face situations where they are forced to satisfice. Satisficing therefore constitutes a major means of simplifying complex situations.

Fifth, maximizing will be the more likely strategy for choices among alternatives that provide goal fulfillment on actors' more important goals, whereas satisficing will be more likely for decisions involving their less important goals. We base this prediction on the assumption that outcomes fulfilling their more important goals will provide greater utility, all other things being equal, than outcomes fulfilling less important goals, hence the potential gain from maximization is likely to offset whatever additional costs may be incurred.

Sixth, we suspect that the greater the variance of goal importance—i.e., the greater the disperson of goal importance values of an actor's goal hierarchy—the more likely he or she will be to maximize on alternatives fulfilling his or her most important goals. The less the variance of goal importance, however—i.e., the larger the proportion of approximately equally important goals—the more likely he or she will be to select a satisficing strategy so as to obtain a satisfactory level of goal fulfillment for the largest number of goals.

Seventh, to these influences must be added personality factors. Actors probably differ in the extent to which choosing the alternative with the highest subjective expected utility is important to them. If so, those for whom it is very important will be willing to absorb the extra costs associated with maximization.

We regard actors' resources as the major factor influencing their choices of a decision strategy because sufficient resources enable them not only to pay the generally greater costs of maximization but also to maximize on their less important goals. This suggests that individuals, and groups, with markedly unequal resource holdings may very well follow different decision strategies. Differences in behavior between groups, such as racial and ethnic groups or classes, may reflect a difference in decision strategies and not just differences in their utilities and subjective probabilities. However, it is also possible that groups with limited resources may be following a maximizing strategy and that differences between them and those with substantial resources are due to the fact that the former simply have available to them fewer alternatives yielding high utility. They may be maximizing on decisions among a limited number of very poor options. Which of these is the case could only be determined if measures of their utilities and subjective probabilities were available.

THE GENERAL MICRO-LEVEL MODEL

Figure 4.6 presents the general micro-level model of choice behavior that we have discussed in this and the preceding two chapters. The figure represents the process whereby the subjective expected utility of a single alternative is estimated and a choice is made between it and another alternative. (We have not included a similar diagram for the other alternative.) This process involves first the initiation of the selection process, or the decision to consider alternatives in addition to the one currently being enacted; second, the estimation of the utilities and subjective probabilities of the alternatives considered; third, the estimation of the subjective expected utility of each alternative; fourth, the choice of a decision strategy; and fifth, the choice of an action alternative, either the same alternative enacted at the same or a different level of intensity or a different alternative. We shall look at each of these phases in turn in order to summarize the general model.

Initiating the Selection Process

We have suggested that actors start the process of considering other action alternatives under one of three conditions: (1) the goal fulfillment deprivation gap for an unfulfilled goal surpasses the *GFDG* for the goal that is being fulfilled by enactment of the current alternative; (2) they do not receive an anticipated outcome; (3) external stimuli alert them to the possibility of receiving goal fulfillment on an unfulfilled goal. In all these cases actors become aware that they may be forgoing utility by continuing to enact their present alternatives. The goal fulfillment deprivation gap is the most influential of these three determinants, because unexpected outcomes will initiate the selection process only if they result in failure to fill the *GFDG* for some goal, and external stimuli will have an effect only if there is at least some lack of goal fulfillment on a goal.[14] The goal fulfillment deprivation gap is simply the difference between the desired level of goal fulfillment and the current level of goal fulfillment for any goal weighted by goal importance.

Once the selection process has received its initial impetus from one of these three sources, actors decide which alternatives to consider on the basis of their goal-outcome and alternative-outcome matrices, in conjunction with their decision strategies. If they are attempting to maximize it will generally be necessary to consider at least more than one other alternative. If they are satisficing, only one alternative is necessary. Their decision strategy, plus exogenous influences, will also determine the sequence in which alternatives are considered.

Figure 4.6. The General Micro-level Model

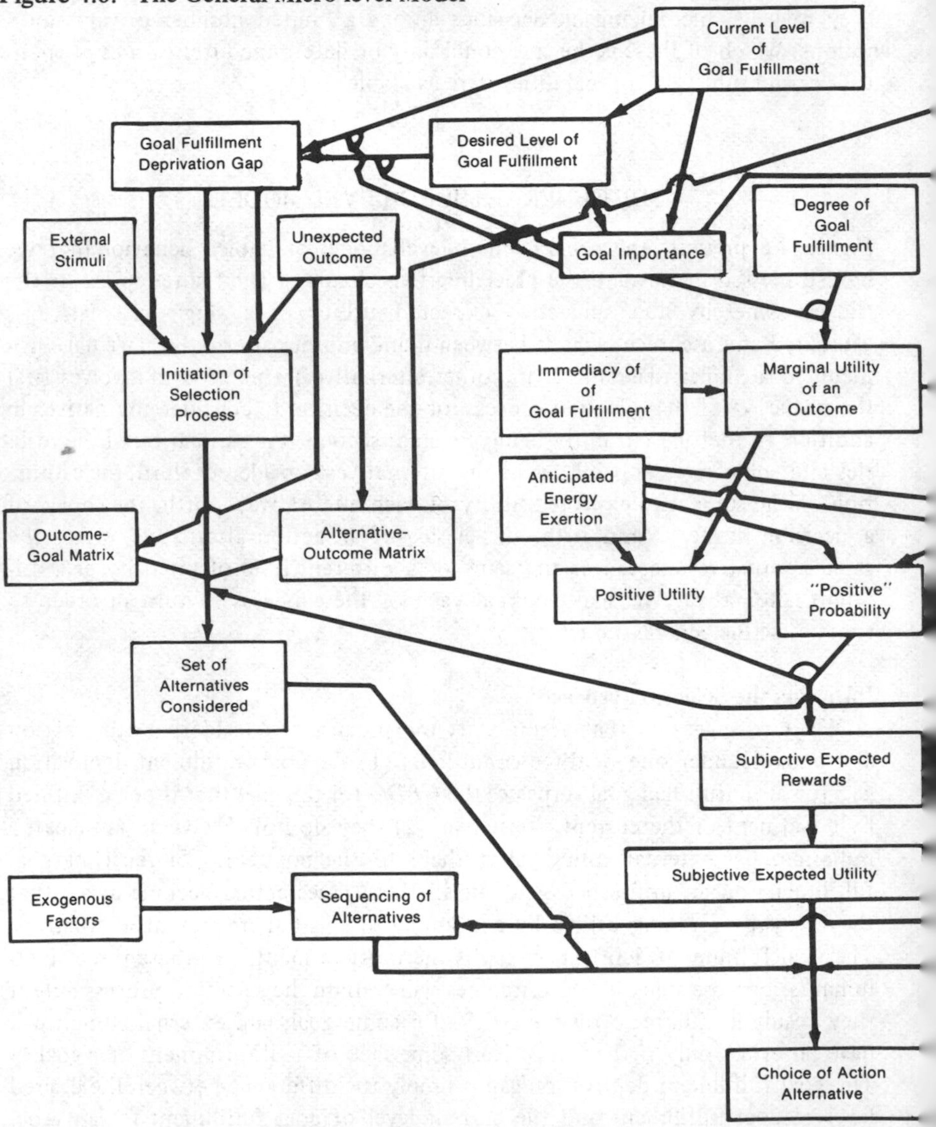

If they are maximizing, this sequence should make no difference; but if they are satisficing it will. Our guess is that they will consider them in the order of their past successes; that is, the alternative that has brought the most utility in the past will be considered first.

The relationships among these factors are shown in the left-hand portion of figure 4.6. Multiplicative influences of variables are shown by arrows joined with an arc.

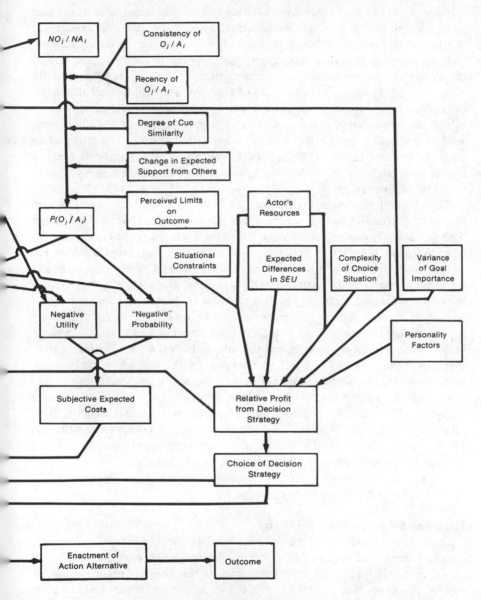

Estimating Utilities and Subjective Probabilities

The next phase involves the processes to which we have devoted the previous two chapters: estimating the utilities of the outcomes that will fulfill goals and the probabilities that those outcomes will occur, given various alternatives. As we suggested in chapter 2, actors will essentially be concerned with the marginal utility offered by an outcome, or with the portion of the utility curve encompassed by that outcome. This in turn will depend upon the degree of goal fulfillment the outcome is perceived to offer and the goal importance of the goal being fulfilled by the outcome. We have further suggested that goal importance can be represented by the slope of the utility curve. Since we anticipate non-constant marginal utility for most goals, goal importance can be represented as the exponent of a power function relating utility and the degree of goal fulfillment, i.e., $U(O_j) = DGF^{GI}$. The value of this exponent will be partially determined by exogenous factors, some of which are unique to individual actors, and by the difference between the desired level of goal fulfillment and the current level of goal fulfillment for that goal. The last factor affecting the utility of an outcome we have called the immediacy of goal fulfillment. Outcomes that are not received relatively soon after enactment of an alternative are likely to have their utilities discounted.

The alternative-outcome matrix that we have discussed in conjunction with the set of alternatives considered by actors in the selection process serves as the basis for actors' subjective probability estimates. Each cell of the matrix consists of an NO_j/NA_i proportion, indicating how often O_j has occurred when A_i has been enacted. These proportions are modified by several other factors to yield the subjective probability estimate $P(O_j|A_i)$. First, the patterning of outcome reception and nonreception is taken into account, particularly its randomness and whether reception or nonreception has occurred most recently. Second, actors compare the cues present in their current situation with the cues that have been present on past occasions when the alternative was enacted to see whether the current cues are more similar to occasions in the past when the outcome occurred or occasions when it did not occur. Cues regarding the actions of other actors will be particularly important. These cues may cause actors to anticipate changes in the amount of support for receiving the outcome expected from others and hence to revise their subjective probability estimates accordingly. Third, if actors perceive that there are limits to the number of times an outcome can occur, they will also revise their estimates on that basis.

The process of estimating utilities and subjective probabilities is shown in the upper-middle portion of figure 4.6.

Estimating Subjective Expected Utility

Once utilities and subjective probabilities have been estimated, actors can combine them multiplicatively to derive the subjective expected utility, or profit, of an alternative. We suggested earlier in this chapter that it is easier to analyze this phase if subjective expected rewards and subjective expected costs are kept separate. The former includes all outcomes resulting from enactment of an alternative that provide increases in goal fulfillment as well as all outcomes yielding decreases in goal fulfillment that are avoided by enactment of that alternative. These outcomes are multiplied by their associated subjective probabilities. Subjective expected costs by contrast include all outcomes yielding decreases in goal fulfillment that are received and all outcomes providing increases in goal fulfillment that are not received as a result of enacting an alternative times their related subjective probabilities. The expenditure of resources in the enactment of alternatives therefore will show up as a cost if it means that subsequent positive-utility outcomes may not be received or negative-utility outcomes cannot be avoided as a result of the expenditure in the present.

In the first part of this chapter we argued that subjective expected utility estimates will also be influenced by the amount of energy or resources actors expect to devote to an alternative. That is, they may perceive that they can either increase the probability that an outcome will occur by enacting the alternative at a higher level of intensity, i.e., devoting more resources to it, or that they can increase the amount of goal fulfillment provided by the outcome, thereby increasing the outcome's utility. An increase in resource expenditure is likely to be accompanied by an increase in costs, however, because the additional resources that are used will not be available for other alternatives. It may constitute a reward, though, if it forestalls the occurrence of later negative-utility outcomes. So it is necessary to also include Anticipated Energy Exertion as a determinant of the subjective expected utility estimate.

We show the estimation of subjective expected utility in the lower-middle portion of figure 4.6.

Choosing a Decision Strategy

An actor's choice of decision strategy for making choices between alternatives is determined primarily by the relative rewards and costs of different strategies in a given situation. We noted in the previous section of this chapter that the actor's resources and constraints under which he or she is operating will be major influences on this choice. Maximization will generally be a more costly strategy than will satisficing, so we predict that maximization will be discarded whenever situations are complex or it is difficult to obtain the information necessary to make subjective expected utility estimates. This is shown in the right-hand portion of figure 4.6.

Choosing an Alternative

Finally, as we see in the lower portion of figure 4.6, the combination of the operative decision strategy, the sequencing of alternatives, and the actor's subjective expected utility estimates will result in the selection of an alternative, which in turn will result in some outcome. The outcome will, of course, feed back upon many of the components of the model. (These feedbacks have been omitted from figure 4.6.) The most immediate feedbacks will be upon the NO_j/NA_i proportion for that alternative and the current level of goal fulfillment determinant. The feedback of the outcome on the current level of goal fulfillment determinant will determine the size of the goal fulfillment deprivation gap for the goal being fulfilled and other goals that are not being fulfilled. (It would feed back a zero value to the *CLGF* for goals not being fulfilled.) Consequently, depending upon how rapidly the outcome provides goal fulfillment, the amount of goal fulfillment it provides, and the rate at which the *CLGF*'s for other goals are declining, this feedback will determine when the actor next initiates the process of selecting an alternative. If the outcome is received quickly and if it provides less goal fulfillment than expected, the actor will be motivated to consider alternatives very soon. We have suggested that in this case he or she will most likely first consider reenacting the same alternative at a different level of intensity.

The NA_i term in the NO_j/NA_i proportion will be increased by 1 by enactment of the alternative. The NO_j term will be increased by 1 if the outcome has occurred, and will not increase if the outcome does not occur. In addition, there will be feedbacks to the other determinants of subjective probability. The consistency and recency determinants will be affected, depending on whether the outcome occurred. Likewise the cues present in the situation will be incorporated into the degree of cue similarity determinant, and, if other actors were involved, will provide information regarding their expected support that will be utilized the next time the alternative is considered. And either occurrence or nonoccurrence of the outcome will influence the perceived limits on an outcome determinant. Nonoccurrence will increase the actor's perception that the outcome does have limits.

We can also visualize a feedback from the outcome to the outcome-goal matrix that is used in selecting a set of alternatives for consideration. The amount of goal fulfillment that is actually received from the outcome will feed information into that matrix that will affect the expected value of the outcome for the next occasion on which that particular goal needs fulfillment. If, for example, the outcome provided very little goal fulfillment, its expected value would decrease and might drop below the expected value of some other outcome. The next time the actor sought fulfillment of that goal he or she would therefore likely look to the latter outcome and possibly to a different alternative, depending upon the information in the alternative-outcome matrix. A feedback from the outcome to the desired level of goal fulfillment determinant is also probable. As we noted in chapter 2, if the outcome attains the *DLGF,* the *DLGF* may be raised by an actor, whereas if it fails to attain that level the actor's *DLGF,* or aspiration level, may decrease.

Comparison of the Model and Our Original Objectives

At the beginning of chapter 2 we said that a micro-level model of behavior should address three major issues: choice, persistence/change, and the intensity of behavior. We can now look briefly at how our general model deals with these issues. First, most of our attention has been devoted to the bases on which actors choose among various action alternatives. We have argued that these decisions are based upon the subjective expected utilities of the alternatives and the decision strategies used by actors in specific situations. They may choose either the alternative with the greatest subjective expected utility in the set of alternatives considered or the first alternative that provides satisfactory subjective expected utility. We have suggested that the choice of a decision strategy will be based upon its relative rewards and costs in a specific situation.

Calculating the subjective expected utility of an alternative is a tremendously complex process, involving determining the utility of all outcomes expected to result from enactment of that alternative and multiplying these by the subjective probabilities that those outcomes will occur. Therefore we have repeatedly suggested ways in which actors simplify this process, including making relative rather than absolute estimates wherever possible, setting utilities of outcomes equal to each other or to zero, and setting subjective probabilities equal to zero, 1, or to each other. We have further suggested that the satisficing decision strategy constitutes a simplifying procedure, since it requires less information than does the maximizing strategy. We are quite certain that actors make choices upon the basis of their utilities and subjective probabilities, but we are also quite certain that they find it necessary to simplify the process for themselves. Hence we have tried to point out the major ways in which simplifications are introduced.

Second, regarding the degree of persistence actors exhibit in enacting alternatives, or, conversely, the factors that induce them to switch alternatives, we have suggested that they will continue enacting an alternative as long as they do not perceive that they are forgoing utility as a result of continuation. They will perceive that they are being deprived of utility in two different situations. On the one hand, if an outcome occurs as they have anticipated and they receive fulfillment on a goal, a point will be reached at which the goal fulfillment deprivation gap for some unfulfilled goal will exceed the goal fulfillment deprivation gap for the goal that is being fulfilled. When this occurs, they will be stimulated to consider other action alternatives. They may continue enacting their current alternatives after they have considered these other alternatives, if they can find no alternative with greater subjective expected utility than their current alternatives, but they will have at least looked at other possibilities.

On the other hand, they will be motivated to consider other alternatives if outcomes do not occur as expected or if external stimuli make them aware of the possibility of receiving goal fulfillment on some unfulfilled goal (or threaten them with the loss of goal fulfillment on goals that are fulfilled). The first case involves primarily situations where outcomes do not occur as anticipated or provide less goal fulfillment than expected. In this case it is likely that the goal fulfillment deprivation gap for the goal an actor hoped to fulfill will remain quite large, and the actor will be confronted with the choice of continuing to pursue that goal or pursuing a different goal. The second case refers to unexpected outcomes that remind an actor that a gain (or loss) of goal fulfillment is possible on some goal. These stimuli will constitute cues that have been associated with outcomes providing gains (or losses) of fulfillment on that goal in the past. If the goal they have been associated with is currently unfulfilled, so that its goal fulfillment deprivation gap is a nonzero value, the actor will be motivated to consider alternatives to provide fulfillment on that goal. If the goal is adequately filled, however, we believe that the actor will be more concerned about potential losses of goal fulfillment than about increasing his or her *CLGF*.

Lastly, we discussed the intensity of behavior in the context of the expenditures of energy or resources anticipated by actors in enacting their alternatives. We made the suggestion that actors will often perceive the possibility of increasing the probability of an outcome or of increasing the utility of an outcome by increasing the degree of goal fulfillment through a greater expenditure of energy or resources. (Increased expenditures will be subject to diminishing returns, however.) If they increase their expenditures, though, they are also likely to increase their costs because the resources used will not be available to enact other alternatives. Therefore the intensity at which an alternative is enacted will be determined by a balancing of these two sets of factors—the greater subjective expected rewards connected with a greater expenditure and the greater subjective expected costs resulting from that expenditure. If actors perceive that they can increase their subjective expected utility markedly with only a minimal increase in energy expenditure, they are likely to do so. But if substantial inputs of resources are required to achieve only a small gain in subjective expected utility, they will probably not make the additional investment.

Other Decision Models

A variety of micro-level models of behavior exist in addition to the subjective expected utility model on which our general model is based. We wish briefly to acknowledge their existence and indicate how they relate to the subjective expected utility model.

Most closely related are several variants that use objective values for either or both of the two major components of the *SEU* model—utilities and subjective probabilities. These include the expected utility model (objective probabilities and subjective values), the expected value model (objective probabilities and objective values), and the subjective expected value model (subjective probabilities and objective values). In one of the few studies comparing the explanatory power of these four models, Coombs et al. (1967) found that the subjective expected utility model explained subjects' choices best. They attribute this to the fact that the model allows for nonlinearity in both components, whereas the other models do not. Tversky (1967a), however, has shown the superiority of the subjective expected value model to the subjective expected utility model. According to Rapoport and Wallster (1972:140–41), the basic issue is not rejection of one model and acceptance of another but rather determination of the conditions under which each model is valid.

The class of micro-level models known as instrumentality or expectancy theory is also quite closely related to the subjective expected utility model. These models are direct descendants of Lewin's work in field theory and they utilize different terms—valences, expectancies, instrumentalities—to refer to the phenomena we have referred to as utilities and subjective probabilities. The basic model characterizing this class of models can be represented by $E \times I \times V$. E refers to the expectancy that a given level of effort will lead to a given level of performance. I, or instrumentality, refers to the probability that this given level of performance will yield a given outcome.[15] V represents the valence of the outcome (Pritchard and Sanders 1973; Pritchard and De Leo 1973). The product of these three variables is considered to constitute a motivational level, the degree of effort an actor will display, or the degree of force impinging on an actor.

The concept of expectancy appears to be identical to our concept of subjective probability, and valence is seemingly synonymous with our use of the term utility. So the major difference between this model and the subjective expected utility model is the instrumentality component included in the former. Pritchard and Sanders (1973) argue that this component is necessary because it allows for a separate assessment of the valence of high performance ($V \times I$) to the actor. Since this class of models has generally been used to predict variables such as work motivation, job performance, and intentions to work (Mitchell and Biglan 1971; Pritchard and Sanders 1973; Pritchard and De Leo 1973; Mitchell and Nebeker 1973; Feldman 1974), it may be that the instrumentality component is necessary in such situations. We do not feel it is necessary to include it in our general model.[16]

A third group of micro-level decision models has developed primarily in response to the difficulties that have been encountered in using the subjective expected utility model. This group consists of several probabilistic, or stochastic, choice or utility models. These models have been developed largely to deal with the problems of inconsistency and intransitivity of choices among alternatives that are found when the subjective expected utility model is tested.[17]

The major characteristic of these models is the specification of a probabilistic relationship between choices and the utilities of outcomes. Rather than assuming an invariant relationship between an outcome's value and an actor's preference for that outcome, these models assume either varying values for outcomes or varying preferences. Random utility models, one of the two main classes of stochastic utility theories, posit a random distribution of utilities, with actors choosing the alternative with the highest utility at a given point in time. Constant utility models, the other major class, posit just the opposite—fixed utilities and a random distribution of preferences (Luce and Suppes 1965).

Theorists working with stochastic utility models have devoted most of their time to axiomatization of the models and tests of their implications, particularly tests of the transitivity assumptions required of different models. It is difficult to see how this class of theories can be applied to nonexperimental, real-world situations. Extensive discussions of these models can be found in Luce (1959), Coombs, Dawes, and Tversky (1970), and Becker and McClintock (1967).[18]

APPLYING THE MICRO-LEVEL MODEL TO MACRO-LEVEL PHENOMENA

Having outlined the basic parameters of our micro-level model, we now confront the issue of applying this model to macro-level groups, or collectivities, and to various intergroup processes. We shall do this first by noting variables that the micro-level model suggests should be taken into account in a macro-level model, and, second, by previewing briefly the implications of the model for the intergroup processes that will be discussed in subsequent chapters. It is our contention not only that micro-level variables can be taken into account in macro-level models but also that they *must* be taken into account if one is to fully understand processes occurring at the macro level.

Micro-level Variables Relevant at the Macro Level

The micro-level model we have presented allows for tremendous variation in the behavior of individuals. We have argued that individuals choose behaviors primarily on the basis of their utilities and subjective probabilities, but we have not placed any restrictions on the outcomes that they may regard as having utility or on the actions that they feel will bring about their desired outcomes. Presumably the behaviors of the Indian holy man lying on a bed of nails and the gray-flannel junior executive can both be explained by the general model. The difference, of course, comes in the outcomes they desire and the alternatives they expect to bring about those outcomes.

Macro-level groups or collectivities will also be characterized by immense variation in the behaviors of the individuals who constitute them. Nevertheless, it is a basic sociological premise that the individuals making up a group or collectivity have a sufficient commonality of characteristics to constitute a group. In other words, they are assumed to be more homogeneous than heterogeneous on some variables. The degree of homogeneity will of course vary among groups; normally one thinks of a collectivity as being less homogeneous than a group, and a large group as likely to be more heterogeneous than a small group. The important point is that a certain degree of homogeneity is assumed when a set of individuals is defined as constituting a group. This assumption is made not only by outside observers but by group members who define themselves as a group, as "we" or "us" rather than "them." Quite often the assignment of individuals to groups by outside observers will be based upon external characteristics, such as age, race, sex, common participation in an organization, e.g., students and faculty, and so forth. Similarity on these characteristics may or may not be highly correlated with homogeneity on other less visible characteristics, such as values, however. Locating individuals within groups is also complicated by the fact that any one individual can likely be located within more than one group. So, all in all, defining the boundaries of groups is an extremely complex matter, requiring a number of simplifying assumptions on the part of the observer. It is clearly a necessary first step in explaining intergroup processes, though.

Assuming that the boundaries of groups can be more or less accurately determined, using the insights provided by our micro-level model to explain intergroup processes is going to require further simplifying assumptions. Because of the severe aggregation problems involved, it may be necessary to assume homogeneity of utilities and subjective probabilities on the part of members of a group. Conceivably one could derive estimates of measures of central tendency and measures of dispersion for both utilities and subjective probabilities from samples of group members. But this procedure will encounter two serious problems. One is the lack of an underlying utility scale that makes interpersonal comparisons of utilities problematic and renders any summarizing measures questionable.[19] The second problem is that of the proper weights to apply to individuals having different amounts of influence within the group. So homogeneity of individuals on basic variables such as utilities and subjective probabilities may have to be assumed.

Despite these serious problems, a number of the variables we have included in our micro-level model will be applicable and necessary at the macro level. First, just as individuals make choices among alternatives, so also may groups be seen as selecting alternatives. Members of one group may choose to interact with or to withdraw from interaction with members of another group. Or the former may attempt to influence the latter to act in accord with the former's wishes. However, the number of alternatives being considered by groups vis-à-vis other groups will undoubtedly be far less than the number of alternatives considered by individual actors.

Second, it is also meaningful to think in terms of group goals. The hypothetical actors in our micro-level model are engaged in goal-seeking behavior and choose behavioral alternatives largely on the basis of whether or not they will enable them to attain their goals. Similarly, groups may be perceived to have goals, which, of course, are some composite of the goals of their individual members. One group's major goal may be domination of another group, while a second group's primary goal may be that of peaceful coexistence. One can also visualize groups having goal hierarchies like those of the individual actors, with those hierarchies having the same implications for choices of behavior as they do for the individual. Group goals will most likely be reflected in group ideologies, which not only reveal to others what a group seeks but, probably more important, also instill in members of the group the appropriate states of affairs to desire.

Third, groups may also be visualized as having utilities for outcomes that are determined by a calculus similar to that used by individual actors. Outcomes that provide immediate and substantial goal fulfillment on the group's most important goals will have highest utility for the group. Outcomes that threaten losses of goal fulfillment, e.g., the threat of domination for a group desiring peaceful coexistence, will have negative utility. Groups may also be characterized in terms of goal fulfillment deprivation gaps (desired level of goal fulfillment minus current level of goal fulfillment). Hitler's call for *Lebensraum* ("living space") comes to mind as a leader's expression of a group's dissatis-faction because of the disparity between its current level of goal fulfullment and its desired level.

Fourth, expectations, or subjective probabilities, are also relevant at the macro level. Again, the ideology of a group and the general belief system shared by members of the group will exemplify the group's expectations. A group desiring to avoid contact with another group will possess expectations regarding how that might best be achieved.

Fifth, we have seen that at various points the amount of resources possessed by actors will be important for their choice of alternatives, influencing, for example, their subjective probability estimates, their estimates of the costs of various alternatives, and their choices of the degree of intensity at which they enact alternatives. Groups' resources will be no less significant for group actions. Power differences between groups may be seen largely in terms of resource differences. A group with ample resources will have a larger array of options from which to choose, will have to worry less about the consequences of resource expenditure, and will be able to enact alternatives with greater intensity than will a group with limited resources. Power differences should not be seen solely in terms of resources, however. It is also necessary to consider a group's goals; it may not wish to use its resources to dominate other groups.

So the variables we have discussed in regard to our micro-level model can also be applied to groups and collectivities at the macro level. Values for these variables cannot be estimated with the same degree of accuracy that they can for individual actors, but the variables can nevertheless be used in macro-level theories of intergroup processes. We shall illustrate this further by looking briefly at several intergroup processes that we shall discuss more fully in the rest of this book.

Major Intergroup Processes and the Micro-level Model

When we look at some of the more common intergroup processes we find that they *must* be explained in terms of some of the variables we have included in our general micro-level model. We shall not look at these processes in detail here but shall simply describe how the micro-level variables are relevant at the macro level.

In the next chapter we shall look at exchange processes between two actors, whether individuals or groups. These processes may involve individuals' exchang-ing gifts or countries' exchanging goods. Exchange processes have two distinctive characteristics. First, it is usually assumed that both actors gain positive utility as a result of the exchange. Second, an alternative enacted by one actor in the exchange process constitutes an outcome for the other actor and vice versa. We shall show that, as a result, decisions by actors on whether or not to exchange with other actors will require each actor to estimate the utilities of *the other actor*, as well as his or her own in order to determine whether a given action will lead to exchange. Thus if one wants to predict whether or not actors will enter into exchange relationships with each other and the length or duration of such relationships, it will be necessary to make estimates of both actors' utilities and subjective probabilities *and* of each actor's estimates of the other actor's utilities.

Judgments regarding equity commonly accompany exchange relationships. Exchanges that are perceived to be inequitable, or exploitative, by one or the other of the participants, are likely to be terminated and may promote conflict between the parties. We shall see in chapter 6 that these judgments regarding the degree of equity in an exchange are based on each actor's estimates of his or her own, and the other actor's inputs to, and outcomes from, the relationship. These input and outcome estimates in turn require actors to estimate both their own and the other actor's utilities. We shall also show the significance of actors' resources for their participation in inequitable exchanges. Actors with limited resources may have little choice except to continue in an inequitable relationship, but they are not always restricted solely to this choice. Thus it may be argued that to some extent they participate in their own exploitation.

Inequity is also a characteristic of the intergroup process that has been labeled as discrimination. We shall show that this term is usually applied to situations of *indirect* exchange, in which specific allocators, often members of a dominant group, dispense outcomes to candidates applying for them. Discrimination is perceived to exist if the allocations result in unequal distributions of the outcomes among members of different groups. We shall see that utilities and subjective probabilities play a significant role in the analysis of discriminatory situations. First, it may be argued that consideration of the candidates' utilities must be taken into account in order to determine whether they have in fact been victims of discrimination. If they have been deprived of outcomes they did not desire anyway, then it is questionable whether the situation is a discriminatory one. Second, the utilities and goals of allocators must also be considered. Discrimination may constitute a goal for some allocators. For others, it may emerge as a means to other goals, if an unequal allocation of outcomes is perceived by them to be correlated with, or to promote, the fulfillment of these other goals. Third, we shall argue that discriminatory allocations will be perceived by participants to them, and by outside observers, as varying in their degree of legitimacy. This judgment regarding legitimacy will also be based on these actors' utilities, subjective probabilities, and goals.

Exchange and power situations share several characteristics. One of these is that one participant's action constitutes an outcome for the other participant. A second is that both involve dependence. In exchange situations the parties tend to be mutually dependent—each depending on the other for an outcome. In power situations, however, the dependence is more one-sided. The party that is more dependent on the other party will be the one more likely induced to act according to the other's wishes. In terms of our model, dependence can be interpreted in terms of goal fulfillment, utilities, and probabilities. If party *A* controls to some degree the means whereby party *B* plans to fulfill his or her goals, and if B's utilities are such that there are no substitute goals that he or she desires, and if B's probabilities are such that he or she anticipates no other means of attaining those goals, then B will be dependent upon A to some degree. And the more dependent B is upon A, the more susceptible B will be to A's power. Actors' or groups' relative resources will be of great significance in defining power and dependence relations. A group's resources will affect its degree of dependence by limiting the number of available alternatives and by influencing its probabilities for fulfilling its goals by means of those alternatives.

Finally, groups may deal with other groups by avoiding them, or segregating themselves from them. This may involve one group's moving itself physically from the presence of another group and/or one group's putting barriers between itself and the other group to prevent the latter from coming into contact with it. As is the case with discrimination, physical segregation from another group may constitute a goal in itself, or it may be perceived as a means to attaining other positive-utility outcomes (or avoiding negative-utility outcomes). Which of these cases holds in a given situation, and which strategy a group adopts in order to ensure segregation, can only be determined by analyzing the goals, utilities, and subjective probabilities of the group members. Most studies of discrimination and segregation have ignored these issues and concentrated instead on the consequences of the processes. We shall argue that this may lead to erroneous conclusions and that it also inhibits a thorough analysis of these two important intergroup processes.

SUMMARY

We have completed the discussion of our general micro-level model in this chapter by analyzing how actors calculate their subjective expected utilities, the factors that motivate them to consider selecting an action alternative, and the bases on which they select the decision strategy to be used in making choices among alternatives. In addition, in the first part of the chapter, we considered several additional complexities in the model: the possibility that utility and subjective probability estimations may be in terms of ranges of values rather than point estimates, the nonindependence of utilities and subjective probabilities, and the various components of rewards and costs. In the next chapters we will use insights from this model to analyze the intergroup processes discussed in the section just preceding.

NOTES

1. Strictly speaking, one may claim that in this case no utility is forgone by enacting the alternative with the larger subjective expected utility and that utility would only be forgone if the two alternatives were simulta-

neously compatible but one only enacted one of them. We shall only deal here with cases of simultaneously incompatible alternatives.

2. We shall assume that alternatives and outcomes occur more or less simultaneously, so as to avoid an excessive use of subscripts.

3. If we are to believe popular psychology or common parlance, a negative influence of subjective probabilities on utilities is also quite usual, in the form of "sour grapes." This may be seen as assigning a low utility to an outcome that has a very low subjective probability.

4. The variance of a two-outcome gamble is equal to $p(1 - p) (A - B)^2$ when p = the probability of winning $\$A$ and $(1 - p)$ = the probability of winning $\$B$ (Edwards 1962b:48). Thus, if probabilities are held constant, then as the difference in the utilities of the outcomes increases, the variance of the gamble will also increase.

5. This formula therefore constitutes the basic determinant of the degree of goal fulfillment determinant discussed in regard to the utilities of outcomes. The formula will undoubtedly be modified by actors' perceptions of the characteristics of situations in which they are making utility estimates, just as their NO_j/NA_i proportions are modified, but we do not have space in this context to discuss the factors that will be responsible for these modifications.

6. In actuality, in many cases the first likely response to an unanticipated outcome will be to repeat the previous alternative at the *same* level of intensity on the grounds that the failure to receive the anticipated outcome was a fluke.

7. We do not have room to discuss the possibility that actors will consider *combinations* of compatible action alternatives for inclusion in the selection process. For example, actors may consider *adding* a compatible alternative to the alternative they are already enacting. See our prior discussion of incompatible and compatible alternatives in this chapter.

8. According to Rapoport and Wallster (1972:147) the maximization assumption technically is not an assumption but is derived from other assumptions of subjective expected utility theory.

9. Meeker also defines status consistency and reciprocity in her discussion, but we shall not discuss those two rules here.

10. McClintock, Messick, Kuhlman, and Campos (1973) describe the four possible strategies in this game as own maximum gain (individualism), joint gain (cooperation), relative gain (competition), and minimization of other's gain (aggression).

11. Meeker's conceptualization of reciprocity differs from this.

12. We shall not consider here other strategies from game theory, such as the sure-thing principle, Pareto optimality, maximin, and regret. For a discussion of them, see Luce and Suppes (1965:300–304).

13. For examples and discussions of risk and risk taking, see Rapoport and

Wallster (1972), Pruitt (1962), Wendt (1970), Lee (1971), Vinokur (1971*a*, 1971*b*), McCauley and Graham (1971), Lupfer and Jones (1971), Cameron and Myers (1966), Jones and Johnson (1973), and Higbee and Lafferty (1972).

14. If outcomes should unexpectedly *overfulfill* a particular goal, then their effect on the initiation process would also come through the *GFDG* factor because this would likely mean that the goal fulfillment deprivation gap for another goal would surpass the *GFDG* for the goal that was overfulfilled. In our previous discussion we concentrated on outcomes that failed to provide as much goal fulfillment as expected; we must also allow for the possibility that they will provide more than anticipated.

15. Mitchell and Biglan (1971) suggest that the instrumentality component represents perceived correlations between levels of performance and outcomes rather than perceived probabilities.

16. For additional discussion of this class of theories, see Vroom (1964).

17. Inconsistency refers to selecting different alternatives at different points in time from the same set of alternatives. Intransitivity in its simplest form is characterized by an actor's choosing *a* over *b*, *b* over *c*, and *c* over *a*.

18. We shall not consider here several other decision theories that are less closely related to the subjective expected utility model. These include information integration theory (Slovic and Lichtenstein 1971) and various multistage decision-making models, such as the Bayesian revision of opinion model, optional stopping, and dynamic decision making (Rapoport and Wallster 1972:152-69; Rapoport 1968; Rapoport and Jones 1970; Rapoport, Jones, and Kahan, 1970).

19. For analyses of the problem of comparing the utilities of different individuals, see Arrow (1963), Coombs (1964:383-99), Stevens (1959), and Simon (1974).

## PART TWO

Exchange, Equity, and Power as Social Processes

CHAPTER 5

Exchange Relationships

INDIVIDUALS ACT so as to obtain the outcomes they desire. That is the premise on which the micro-level model of choice behavior we presented in part 1 has been based. There we described the manner in which choices are made between behavioral alternatives on the basis of subjective expected utility estimates in order to obtain these outcomes. But that model can only be the starting point for a theory of intergroup processes. Obviously the choices made by actors are not made in isolation. In most instances the utilities and expectations of other actors must also be taken into account. In many situations the outcomes desired by one actor are also desired by other actors, or the outcomes desired by one actor may consist of the actions of another actor. Thus in virtually all social situations actors' choices of behavioral alternatives are influenced by their expectations regarding the actions that other actors are likely to take. Hence the logical next step is to include another actor in our model, and in the chapters of part 2 we explore the nature of two common social processes—exchange and power—that involve interactions between two or more parties.

Our discussion is primarily oriented to interindividual rather than intergroup exchange and power relationships. Our rationale for this approach is that the process must be fully understood at the simpler micro level before attempts are made to comprehend macro-level exchanges and power confrontations involving groups and collectivities. Many simplifications will of course have to be introduced as one moves from the micro to the macro level. There will also be serious problems resulting from the necessity of aggregating micro-level utilities and subjective probabilities. However, we facilitate our objective of understanding macro-level processes by first analyzing the micro level, where the nature of the simplifications that are needed can be seen more clearly.

In recent years the model of economic exchange has been adopted by many sociologists to represent what is regarded as one of the most basic social processes (Homans 1961, 1974; Blau 1964a; Emerson 1972a, 1972b). Although there have been scattered criticisms of the suitability of this model for social behavior (Boulding 1962; Abrahamsson 1970; Ekeh 1974), it has developed into one of the major sociological paradigms. According to this paradigm, the outcomes that individuals desire are analogous to economic goods and services and are traded in the social marketplace in accord with the principles characterizing economic transactions. Actors approach each other as "buyers" and "sellers" of social commodities. Most attempts to utilize the model of economic exchange for social interaction have relied upon the psychological base provided by operant theories of behavior. In this chapter we shall depart from that pattern by analyzing the characteristics of exchange relationships using the subjective expected utility model we presented in part 1.

THE NATURE OF EXCHANGE RELATIONSHIPS

Exchange relationships do not comprise the totality of social processes. We define an exchange relationship or situation as one involving "the mutual achievement of desired outcomes through the voluntary enactment of behaviors that have positive utilities for the parties involved." Thus we first limit our perspective to situations in which there is a *mutual* achievement of desired outcomes by the parties involved in the interaction. In its simplest form, and probably also its most common, exchange will involve two parties both achieving their desired outcomes. Exchanges involving more than two parties we will refer to as exchange networks, in accord with Emerson's terminology (1969, 1972b). The important point is that the parties involved both attain the outcomes they desire by means of the exchange. This characteristic distinguishes exchange relationships most clearly from conflict relationships, as we shall show presently. The mutual achievement of desired outcomes does not mean that the outcomes that are received will be equal. In many cases they will be unequal, and in the next chapter we consider the nature of the equity or distributive justice judgments that are made regarding the distribution of outcomes by the parties involved.

Second, following Blau's lead, we also restrict our consideration to situations in which the behaviors that are enacted occur voluntarily, that is, without coercion. Voluntariness of action is undoubtedly extremely difficult to determine, and our inclusion of this characteristic, given our specification of the mutual achievement of desired positive-utility outcomes, may be superfluous. However, we wish to differentiate exchange relationships from power situations, and voluntariness appears to be a crucial characteristic distinguishing these two types of process.

The class of social interactions that we regard as exchange does constitute a very important sector of social phenomena. Many of the more common reciprocal roles, such as employer–employee, husband–wife, parent–child, and teacher–pupil, fall within its scope. Such interactions will often provide outcomes with very high utility for the participants because they provide fulfillment of a multiplicity of important and recurrent goals. In addition, this class of interactions is likely to become regularized, as is indicated by the existence of reciprocal roles. Therefore these interactions will be characterized by relatively high subjective probabilities, i.e., actors will anticipate each other's actions with a high degree of certainty. Thus, over time, particular action alternatives are likely to yield consistently high subjective expected utility estimates for the individuals involved, and rather stable interaction patterns will be created.

These quite common role relationships at the micro level are also duplicated by relationships between groups at the macro level. Combinations of individuals playing similar roles may properly be regarded as engaged in relationships of exchange with other combinations, e.g., employers and employees, teachers and pupils, nations and nations. As societies become increasingly differentiated internally, exchange relationships between such aggregate groups play a more important role in creating bonds of interdependence linking disparate segments of a society. Consequently, a detailed understanding of exchange relationships constitutes a necessary component of any theory of societal structure.

Exchange, Conflict, and Power Relationships

Exchange relationships have some similarities to two other basic social processes: conflict and power. They are most easily distinguished from conflict relationships. We reserve the term *conflict* for situations characterized by a mutual exchange of *negative* utilities, or the mutual infliction of punishments. If the recipient of a negative-utility outcome responds with an action that has negative utility for the actor from whom he or she received the negative-utility outcome, then a conflict relationship has been established. Therefore conflict relationships may be seen as exchanges, but the outcomes that are exchanged are the opposite of the positive-utility outcomes we consider under the heading of exchange.

Exchange and power relationships are not as easily distinguished from each other. This is due to the fact that power may be exerted by means of positive-utility outcomes as well as negative-utility ones. For example, actor A may obtain actor B's compliance by offering B a reward for compliance or by threatening B with a punishment for noncompliance. Therefore the major characteristic differentiating exchange relationships from power relationships is the element of resistance, or involuntariness, characteristic of the latter. Power models, based on physical rather than economic analogies, necessarily include the notion of resistance, or, in terms of our model, a difference in desired outcomes or alternatives between actors. If actor A desires actor B to enact behavior 1, then one has a power situation if actor B desires to enact some behavior other than behavior 1. The exertion of power by actor A is successful to the extent that A overcomes B's resistance and obtains B's compliance in enacting behavior 1. In this situation B will not have enacted behavior 1 voluntarily. This simple example of a power relationship also indicates that such relationships are in general distinguished by a *unilateral* achievement of desired outcomes, compared to the *mutual* achievement of desired outcomes characterizing exchange relationships.

All three of these processes—exchange, conflict, and power—occur in intergroup relations. Their mix in the relationships between any two groups (or individuals) will depend upon a variety of factors, including the goals of the groups, their resources for meeting those goals, and the means they perceive available for obtaining their goals. Although relationships between certain groups, such as racial and ethnic groups, are often regarded as primarily conflict and power relationships, one must allow for the possibility that interaction between them may also be represented in terms of an exchange model. Exchanges between these groups may often be unequal and they may be difficult to distinguish from power relationships in many instances, but it is likely that they play a significant role in promoting the stability of interaction between these groups over long periods of time.

Most of our discussion in this chapter will focus upon the simplest type of exchange relationship, in which the actions of each party constitute outcomes for- the other party. We refer to these cases as *direct* exchanges. They may be represented as

The reciprocal roles we mentioned earlier involve this type of exchange. Employees give their labor to employers and employers in turn reimburse their employees. Or husbands and wives give affection and emotional support to each other. The social commodities that are exchanged may be different, as in the former case, or they may be identical, as in the latter case.

Two parties may also engage in exchanges in which the actions of one, or both, do not constitute outcomes that provide utility directly but instead influence the likelihood of occurrence of outcomes that do provide utility. This possibility can be represented as

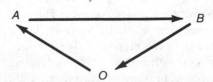

Here *A*'s action is followed by a response by *B,* which affects the probability of outcome *O*'s occurrence. For example, if *A* is a salesman wishing to meet a reluctant businessman (the desired outcome), *A* may give something to a receptionist, *B,* in order to receive that outcome.

A closely related situation that can also be considered in the context of exchange relationships involves *A* and *B*'s giving each other assistance in order to obtain an outcome neither can attain individually. We refer to such cases as *cooperation.*[1] They may be represented by

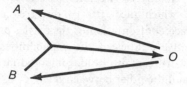

The crucial characteristic marking this as an exchange relationship is that *A* and *B* are both *giving* and *receiving* something that they desire and that has positive utility.

When we move to exchanges involving more than two parties we are in the realm of exchange networks. One common type of exchange network, which has been referred to by Adams (1965) and others, involves two parties, *A* and *B*, each giving something to a third party, *C*, who then allocates outcomes among *A* and *B* as in the following diagram:

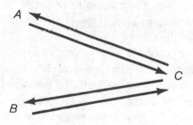

The employment situation exemplifies this type of network, as does a parent's allocating outcomes among children or a teacher's allocating them among students. These situations are especially likely to be accompanied by judgments regarding the equity of the allocation of outcomes by *C*. In chapter 10 we discuss this type of exchange network, which we call *indirect* exchange, in greater detail. It is clear that it can be decomposed into two direct exchanges.

Another type of exchange network is represented in the following diagram:

We refer to this type as *mediated* exchange. The essential feature is that the commodity given by *A* to *B* is not given directly, but is mediated by *C*; the same holds true for the commodity given to *A* by *B*. Thus *C* may transmit the commodities that are being exchanged without modification, or they may be inflated or deflated in value in the course of the transaction. This type of exchange network is exemplified by mediation between labor and management, with the mediator transmitting messages for the parties. In this case the message received by one party may not be a completely faithful reproduction of the message sent by the other party, or it may be less likely to promote conflict if transmitted by a third party. Another situation falling within this type of exchange would be an employment situation involving labor bosses who serve as intermediaries between employers and employees. We anticipate that mediated exchanges will occur in situations in which the costs of direct exchange are too great, for example, if a face-to-face confrontation of the parties produces negative utilities that diminish the positive utilities of the commodities being exchanged. This type of exchange network can also be decomposed into two direct exchanges, one between A and C and the other between B and C.

Implications of Exchange Situations for the *SEU* Model

The inclusion of another actor has several important implications for the subjective expected utility model. First, the fact that another actor's actions constitute the outcomes of interest to either actor may have the effect of simplifying subjective expected utility estimates. These will be simplified to the extent that an actor can assume that the other actor's utilities and subjective probabilities are similar to his or her own. If he or she can make this assumption, then judgments regarding the likelihood of a particular action by the other actor will probably be easier to make. They will also be simplified if exchanges between the two actors become regularized over a period of time, so that each can anticipate the actions of the other.

However, it is also conceivable that subjective expected utility estimates and choices between behavioral alternatives will be more complex in exchange situations. This will occur in one, or both, of two ways. First, goal fulfillment for the *other* actor may constitute one of the goals for an actor in an exchange. If so, it will be necessary for that actor to estimate not only the utility of the other actor's action for himself or herself but also the utility of his or her actions for the other actor. We shall refer to such estimates of the other actor's utilities as *vicarious* estimates of utility.[2] If this is the case, then the process of estimating utilities will be made more complex.

In addition, the choice situation for an actor will also be complicated if he or she uses a decision strategy that takes into account both his or her utilities and those of the other actor. For example, he or she may be trying to select the alternative that maximizes the utility *difference* between the actors. Vicarious estimates of the other's utilities will also be necessary in this situation.

A third implication is that the contexts within which exchanges occur are particularly important for the choices made by actors in those situations. These contextual influences, therefore, will have to be incorporated into the subjective expected utility model. In this chapter we shall be primarily concerned with the influence of context upon the relative *dependence* of the parties in exchanges. The degree of dependence of an actor will influence not only whether he or she participates in an exchange, but also his or her likelihood of withdrawing from the exchange. Norms constitute another contextual influence with significant implications for the choices made in exchange situations, and we shall briefly consider them as well.

APPLYING THE SUBJECTIVE EXPECTED UTILITY MODEL
TO EXCHANGE SITUATIONS

We have said that in direct exchanges the actions of each party constitute positive-utility outcomes for the other party. Therefore a typical direct exchange situation can be represented by figure 5.1, involving actors A and B. This figure shows an exchange situation in which actor A is considering two alternatives, A_1 and A_2, at time t. B's choice is between alternatives B_1 and B_2 at time $t + 1$, and this is followed by another choice for A between alternatives A_1 and A_2 at time $t + 2$.[3]

We shall represent the subjective expected utilities of these alternatives as $SEU(A_{1_t})$, $SEU(B_{2_{t+1}})$, and so forth. The utility of the action of one actor for the other actor—for example, the utility of B's alternative 1 for A—will be represented by $U(B_{1_{t+1}})$. And a subjective probability, such as A's subjective probability for B's enactment of alternative 1, given A's enactment of alternative 1 at time t, we shall represent as $P(B_{1_{t+1}} | A_{1_t})$.

Therefore with this notation we can represent A's and B's subjective expected utility estimates with the following equations:

(1)
$$SEU(A_{1_t}) = P(B_{1_{t+1}} | A_{1_t}) \times U(B_{1_{t+1}}) + P(B_{2_{t+1}} | A_{1_t})$$
$$\times U(B_{2_{t+1}});$$

(2)
$$SEU(A_{2_t}) = P(B_{1_{t+1}} | A_{2_t}) \times U(B_{1_{t+1}}) + P(B_{2_{t+1}} | A_{2_t})$$
$$\times U(B_{2_{t+1}});$$

(3)
$$SEU(B_{1_{t+1}}) = P(A_{1_{t+2}} | B_{1_{t+1}}) \times U(A_{1_{t+2}}) + P(A_{2_{t+2}} | B_{1_{t+1}})$$
$$\times U(A_{2_{t+2}});$$

(4)
$$SEU(B_{2_{t+1}}) = P(A_{1_{t+2}} | B_{2_{t+1}}) \times U(A_{1_{t+2}}) + P(A_{2_{t+2}} | B_{2_{t+1}})$$
$$\times U(A_{2_{t+2}}).$$

These equations can be simplified by representing the subjective probabilities in a different form under the assumption that the sum of the subjective probabilities of a set of exhaustive mutually exclusive outcomes is 1, e.g., substituting p for $P(B_{1_{t+1}} | A_{1_t})$ and $(1 - p)$ for $P(B_{2_{t+1}} | A_{1_t})$.

Figure 5.1. Representation of a Direct Exchange Situation

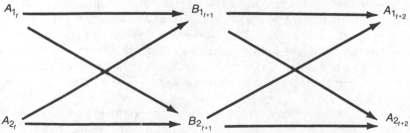

From equations (1) through (4) we see that each actor's actions can be quite easily incorporated as outcomes for the other actor in the subjective expected utility model. As in other cases, the subjective expected utility of an alternative will be determined by the utilities of all outcomes believed to result from that alternative multiplied by their respective subjective probabilities, given enactment of that alternative. In the direct exchange situation this means that the subjective expected utilities of one actor effectively depend upon the utility of the other actor's actions for that actor and that actor's expectations that the other actor will enact those actions.

Estimating the Utilities of Outcomes/Actions

The utility of one actor's action for another, say of B's action for A, will depend, as in our general model, upon the degree of goal fulfillment that it provides A, the importance of the goal that is being fulfilled for A, A's current and desired levels of goal fulfillment, and the immediacy of goal fulfillment provided by B's action. Because we have discussed the operation of these utility determinants in detail in chapter 2, we shall simply consider here how they are affected by exchange situations.

Many exchange situations will involve the fulfillment of quite important goals for both parties to the exchange. We would expect this to be true of parent–child exchanges and husband–wife exchanges, for example. Consequently the goal importance determinant will be weighted quite heavily, or, in terms of our model, the actors' utility curves will be relatively steep. The major implication of this is that rather small outcomes, in terms of their degrees of goal fulfillment, are likely to be quite significant because of the relatively large increments in utility associated with them. Or, by contrast, minimal decrements in goal fulfillment will have disproportionate effects in terms of losses of utility. We expect, therefore, that actors in such exchange situations will be especially alert to fairly subtle differences among outcomes, i.e., among actions of the other party. Seemingly minor differences in the other party's actions may have major import for the recipient of that action.

Perhaps more significant is the fact that these reciprocal exchange relationships are also likely to fulfill a multiplicity of goals. Relationships of this type are often described as primary, as opposed to secondary, and conceivably the number of goals fulfilled for the parties in a relationship may be regarded as a major criterion of the primacy of that relationship. Emerson (1972a), for example, describes the primacy of exchange as a function of the number of domains that it involves, and his use of the term *domains* appears to be synonymous with our use of the term *goals*. If, therefore, *multiple* important goals are involved in these exchanges, then it is probable that the decisions regarding the behavioral alternatives relevant to such exchanges will be weighed very carefully by actors.

The relative significance of decisions involving these alternatives in the totality of choices made by actors will be further increased if, as we suspect, they involve goals with high decomposition rates. In other words, the goals that we believe to be involved in the types of exchange we have described as primary are likely to be recurrent ones. This would appear to be especially true of those goals involving affective and emotional needs, although there will no doubt be variance among actors in this regard. In terms of our model, therefore, this means that current levels of goal fulfillment will decrease quite rapidly, thereby also increasing the potential utility of an outcome by lowering the actor's position on his or her utility curve for that goal.

The goals fulfilled in primary exchange relationships may also be somewhat less subject to diminishing returns than are goals in nonprimary exchanges or goals not fulfilled through exchanges. Affective and emotional goals, for example, may not have as specific a desired level of goal fulfillment as do some other goals. If this is a correct assumption, then larger outcomes will almost always yield greater utility than smaller ones, regardless of an actor's current level of goal fulfillment. The desired levels of goal fulfillment for these goals may also be particularly susceptible to the escalation effect resulting from attainment of those levels, or the reduction effect brought about by failure to attain those levels, which we described in chapter 2, although repeated attainment or failure may be necessary for these effects to appear. One hears, for example, of spouses who over a period of time come to accept the inability of their partners to provide them with more than a given level of emotional gratification, as well as of individuals whose aspirations for gratification increase markedly once they discover that their previous aspirations can be met.

Another distinctive characteristic of social exchange relationships relevant to the estimation of utilities is that the outcomes involved are likely to be of indeterminate size, i.e., in terms of their degree of goal fulfillment. This is one point at which social exchanges differ substantially from many economic exchanges, although "deceptive packaging" may also be characteristic of the latter type of exchange. Generally, economic "buyers" and "sellers" exchange very specific quantities of commodities. But in social transactions the parties often cannot estimate very precisely just how much of a given action the other party is going to enact. For example, a young man on his first date with a young woman may not only be unsure of what reactions she will make to his actions but how intensely she will react. This will complicate the estimation of utilities in such situations and actors may only be able to arrive at a rather wide range of values for a given outcome.

Finally, exchange relationships may often involve outcomes that are not received immediately, so that the immediacy of goal fulfillment determinant becomes significant. The other party's response to one actor's action may very well occur at some unspecified future time. According to Blau (1964a), the lack of specificity regarding timing and the terms of the exchange are two major characteristics distinguishing social exchanges from economic exchanges. Stack's recent study (1974) of family patterns among low-income urban blacks is of great interest not only for her detailed description of the importance of exchange relationships among these families but also for showing that such exchanges rarely are completed immediately. The typical pattern is for the action of one actor to be reciprocated sometime in the future, with no deadline specified. In this case, the open-endedness of the exchange creates a sense of obligation that helps to cement the exchange relationship, and the postponement of goal fulfillment does not appear to diminish the utility anticipated by the initiator of the exchange. The obligation created by deferred reciprocation we suspect to be quite common in exchange relationships, and we shall consider it more fully when we discuss the role of commitments and trust in exchange relationships in conjunction with the estimation of subjective probabilities. However, the apparent disinclination to depreciate the utilities of deferred outcomes that Stack found in her study we suspect to be less common in exchange relationships. Deferred gratification, even in primary exchange relationships, is likely to have less utility than that received relatively soon.[4]

So, although the determinants of the utilities of outcomes in exchange situations are the same as we have suggested to be operative in nonexchange situations, the characteristics of exchange situations have several important influences on the operations of these determinants. A particularly significant difference between exchange and nonexchange situations is that the former are likely to include estimates by an actor of *the other actor's* utilities as well as of his or her own. We have earlier referred to these as *vicarious* estimates of utility.

Estimating the Utilities of One's Actions for the Other Actor. Actors in exchange relationships will make "guesstimates" of the utilities of their actions for the other actor if either the other actor's receiving utility constitutes a goal for them or if both their and the other actor's utilities are relevant for their decision strategies. A parent's receiving satisfaction from observing his or her child receive a positive-utility outcome or a parent's saying "This is going to hurt me more than you" before spanking a child represents evidence that in exchange situations the outcomes the other receives may provide goal fulfillment for the actor enacting them. When this is true this will, of course, greatly complicate the estimation process for an actor. Not only must he or she estimate the subjective probability that a given alternative will yield the outcome he or she desires from the other, but he or she must also estimate how valuable that alternative is to the other. This situation is represented in equation (5), where $U(A_{1_t}.B)$ represents the utility of alternative A_{1_t} for B from A's perspective:

$$SEU(A_{1_t}) = P(B_{1_{t+1}}|A_{1_t}) \times U(B_{1_{t+1}}) + P(B_{2_{t+1}}|A_{1_t}) \times U(B_{2_{t+1}})$$

$$(5) \qquad + U(A_{1_t}.B).$$

The determinants of utility that we have just discussed in regard to the actor's outcomes will no doubt also be operative in the case of vicarious utility estimates. Thus an actor will have to make assumptions about the goal (or goals) his or her action fulfills for the other actor, how important that goal is to the other actor, the degree of goal fulfillment his or her action provides for the other actor, and the other's current and desired levels of goal fulfillment. The immediacy of goal fulfillment determinant will not be operative because we can assume that the other actor will receive the action immediately.

Although we have simply added the vicarious utility estimate to the basic subjective expected utility equation in (5) above, it should be understood that the other actor's receiving utility is best visualized as an additional outcome of one's action, A_{1_t}, in the case of equation (5). The subjective probability for that outcome can be set equal to 1 because that outcome is certain to occur if A_{1_t} is enacted. The utility it provides to the actor, A in the above case, will be determined by the importance to A of B's receiving utility, A's current and desired levels of goal fulfillment on that goal, and the degree of goal fulfillment that B's utility provides. We can assume that $DGF(A) = U(A_{1_t}.B)$, since A's goal is that B receive utility, but we can make no assumptions about the values of the other determinants without further information, except to say that it is probable that the value of the goal importance determinant (the exponent of the utility curve) will probably be greater, the greater the primacy of the exchange relationship between A and B.

The process of vicariously estimating the utilities of one's actions for another actor appears essentially similar to a more familiar sociological concept, "taking the role of the other." This concept, which has been a favorite among social psychologists following a Meadian perspective, can be more precisely defined as "putting oneself in the place of another and looking at the world from his or her perspective." Vicarious estimates of utility involve precisely that process, and by formalizing the process within the subjective expected utility model we can both represent it more accurately and also indicate its implications for exchange relationships.

Emotional identification of one person with another is generally considered part of the role-taking process. A child, for example, first achieves emotional identification with specific significant others and then with a more diffuse generalized other according to this perspective. The capacity to identify emotionally with other actors will no doubt enable an actor to make more accurate vicarious utility estimates. If a particularly high degree of emotional identification is achieved between actors, it is likely that specific outcomes will have very similar degrees of utility for both of them, so that one actor may simply utilize his or her own estimate of the utility of an outcome for a vicarious utility estimate.

Simplifying the Estimation of Utilities. The major factor promoting simplifications in the estimation of actors' utilities in exchange situations will be the predictability resulting from regularization of an exchange relationship over time. As actors become more familiar with each other's repertoire of actions (and hence of outcomes) it is likely that there will be less variance both in one actor's actions and in the other actor's estimates of the utilities associated with those actions. A husband and wife, for example, may develop patterns of providing the same outcome to each other over a period of time. In addition, the importance of certain goals may become fixed and these goals may develop a stable decomposition rate so that the periodicity of the desire for goal fulfillment also becomes fixed. If their aspirations also stabilize, then the same utility estimate may be used repeatedly for a given outcome. What may be lost in such a relationship in terms of excitement and variety may be recouped, therefore, through the simplicity with which utility estimates can be made and the certainty of the partners regarding the accuracy of their estimates.

Vicarious estimates of utility will also be simplified to the extent that exchange relationships become regularized. Participants in an ongoing exchange relationship may very well become familiar with all the likes and dislikes of the other actor, partly as a result of emotional identification, as we have noted above, but possibly more as a result of the repetition of behavioral exchanges. Verbal communication between the participants in an exchange relationship will also facilitate accurate vicarious utility estimates. Actors can inform each other about the amount of utility they receive from certain outcomes. This, of course, does not always happen. One is reminded of the story of the husband who ate oatmeal every morning for breakfast for thirty-five years. One morning his wife apologetically reported that they were out of oatmeal, to which he responded, "That's okay. I don't like it anyway." The incongruity of that response is the exception that supports our assertion about the relevance of verbal communication for estimating other's utilities.

Estimating the Subjective Probabilities of Outcomes/Actions

The basic question facing an actor in an exchange situation is "Which alternative should I enact so that the other actor will enact the action that I desire?" If we assume an actor to be considering two action alternatives at minimum, then this basic question breaks down into two questions, as is shown by equations (1) and (2) for actor A. The first concerns whether a given alternative, e.g., A_{1_t}, is more likely than another, A_{2_t}, to bring about the desired outcome, which we shall assume to be $B_{1_{t+1}}$. Assuming that $P(B_{1_{t+1}} | A_{1_t}) > P(B_{1_{t+1}} | A_{2_t})$, then the question this raises is whether A_{1_t} is also more likely to bring about $B_{1_{t+1}}$ than some other alternative, e.g., $B_{2_{t+1}}$. A_{1_t} may be judged more likely to bring about $B_{1_{t+1}}$ than is A_{2_t}, but it may also be judged more likely to result in $B_{2_{t+1}}$ than $B_{1_{t+1}}$, in which case the actor would likely search for another alternative in order to procure $B_{1_{t+1}}$.

In chapter 3 we presented two different approaches to the analysis of subjective probabilities: a frequency distribution approach and a "causal models" approach. Both of these approaches are applicable to the estimation of subjective probabilities in exchange situations.

Frequency Distribution Approach. The crux of the frequency distribution approach is a set of NO_j/NA_i ratios possessed by an actor as the result of previous experiences and the observations of others' experiences. In unique situations the NO_j/NA_i ratios of similar situations are utilized through a process of generalization. These basic NO_j/NA_i ratios are modified by several factors to yield a subjective probability estimate for a specific situation. Thus in the exchange situation described above we can visualize actor A as having a set of NO_j/NA_i ratios, one for each of the possible combinations of the two alternatives and the two outcomes described, or four in all. These ratios will be modified and a $P(O_j|A_i)$ estimate will be the result.

We labeled the first subjective probability determinant consistency of an outcome, referring to the existence of patterns in the action–outcome sequence in the past. A closely related determinant is recency of an outcome. The consistency determinant can be exemplified by an actor's asking himself or herself "Has Other followed any pattern when I've enacted A_i in the past?" The recency determinant is illustrated by the question "What has Other done the last few times I've enacted A_i?" Both of these determinants are likely to be operative in exchange situations. For example, an employee may ascertain that his or her employer has a pattern of offering praise (a desired outcome) several times in succession and then subjecting him or her to criticism, perhaps to prevent the employee from becoming complacent. Or a husband may note that his wife has gradually been responding more positively to his requests for affection. In these cases this information would no doubt be utilized in anticipating both the employer's and the wife's actions on the next occasion on which the employee or the husband interacted with them.

The cue similarity determinant is also likely to be operative in exchange relationships. Perhaps a child will become aware that a parent tends to honor his or her requests for extra spending money when the parent is in a good mood and to refuse the request when grouchy. If so, the child will undoubtedly attempt to "read" the parent's mood before making such a request. If the various cues available—e.g., facial expressions, tone of voice—are favorable, then the child's subjective probability estimate of receiving the money may be close to 1, whereas if the cues are unfavorable the estimate may plunge to zero.

The generalization process characteristic of unique situations also involves the use of cues. These may be cues present in the situation or cues characterizing the other actor. An actor may have surmised, for example, that, in situations with people he or she does not know, offering a humorous comment generally results in a willingness on the part of the others to converse with him or her, and perhaps enables him or her to gain their approval. Thus if this actor is in a situation with another group of strangers, he or she is likely to generalize and anticipate that another humorous comment will produce the same result. Or the actor may be in a situation that is not unique, but with actors who are. We can visualize, for example, someone attending a cocktail party with a group of entomologists, assuming that they respond in a manner similar to physicists, with whom he or she is familiar, and thus acting accordingly. Such situations obviously carry the potential for embarrassingly erroneous expectations. A man on his first date with a woman may discover too late that she does not find discussions of professional football esoterica very interesting, even though on all previous occasions his dates have been spellbound by his immense store of knowledge.

The three subjective probability determinants we have just discussed exemplify what we called experiential determinants in chapter 3. In that chapter we also discussed two determinants that we regarded as situational. The first of these, change in expected support from others, opens up the possibility of third parties' actions affecting goal attainment. In the exchange situation the influence of this determinant is revealed by the question an actor may ask of himself or herself: "Are there relevant third parties who may persuade, or dissuade, Other from enacting the action I want?" This determinant is not solely situational, since third parties' actions may have been either influential or noninfluential in the past, but the answer to the above question is likely to be based on situational cues. An employee who walks into his or her employer's office to request a raise and discovers the chairman of the board there is likely to make some revision of his or her expectation for receiving the raise. Or a student praising a teacher's course so as to receive approval of a request to postpone taking an examination may well anticipate a different response if that teacher is in the company of another teacher than if he or she is alone.

The other situational determinant, perceived limits on an outcome, involves perceptions regarding the finiteness of Other's actions. The above-mentioned student is likely to estimate his or her chances of avoiding the examination differently if he or she arrives at the teacher's office to discover a waiting line of fellow students than if he or she is the only person there.

Thus exchange situations constitute a particularly fruitful area in which to explore the effects of these subjective probability determinants. All these determinants are more likely to yield relatively accurate subjective probability estimates to the extent that exchange relationships have become regularized over time. Thus the more often an actor has enacted a particular alternative for another actor, the more apparent will be any patterning of the other's responses, the greater will be the repertoire of cues available, the more aware the actor will be of the possible effects of third parties, and the more evidence there will be available for judging whether there are limits on Other's actions.

"Causal Models" Approach. The distinction we have made between perceived direct and indirect effects in our discussion of the "causal models" approach lends itself well to the analysis of exchange situations. *Direct*-exchange situations may be described as those situations in which the actors perceive that they have direct effects on the other actor's actions. Exchange situations in which a third party intervenes in some manner between the actions of the two exchange partners will involve perceived *indirect* effects on the part of the actors. This may involve an actor, A, influencing a third party, C, who in turn influences the exchange partner, B, to give an outcome directly to A. Or it may involve what we earlier called mediated exchange—both actors interacting with a third party who transmits each actor's action to the other actor.

Direct exchanges, involving only direct effects of actors on each other, can be analyzed in a manner identical to the simplest cases discussed in chapter 3. Since the effective choice for an actor is between at least two action alternatives, relative subjective expected utility estimates become significant. And in the direct-exchange case, the difference between two alternatives, A_{1_t} and A_{2_t}, can be reduced to equation (6), in which $p = P(B_{1_{t+1}}|A_{1_t})$, $q = P(B_{1_{t+1}}|A_{2_t})$, and $P' = (p - q)$.

$$(6) \qquad SEU(A_{1_t}) - SEU(A_{2_t}) = P'[U(B_{1_{t+1}}) - U(B_{2_{t+1}})].$$

If $B_{1_{t+1}}$ is the outcome desired by actor A, then A merely has to assess whether A_{1_t} or A_{2_t} is more likely to result in that outcome.

Indirect-exchange situations involving third parties are somewhat more complex, but nevertheless simplifications can be introduced. We shall first consider the case in which an actor is considering two alternatives, one of which, A_{1_t}, has a direct effect on actor B, and the other, A_{2_t}, an indirect effect on B through a third party, C. This situation is diagramed in figure 5.2. The subjective expected utility equations for the two alternatives are

$$SEU(A_{1_t}) = P(B_{1_{t+2}}|A_{1_t}) \times U(B_{1_{t+2}}) + P(B_{2_{t+2}}|A_{1_t}) \times U(B_{2_{t+2}})$$

and

$$
\begin{aligned}
(7) \qquad SEU(A_{2_t}) = \ & P(C_{1_{t+1}}|A_{2_t})P(B_{1_{t+2}}|C_{1_{t+1}}) \times U(B_{1_{t+2}}) \\
& + P(C_{2_{t+1}}|A_{2_t})P(B_{1_{t+2}}|C_{2_{t+1}}) \times U(B_{1_{t+2}}) \\
& + P(C_{1_{t+1}}|A_{2_t})P(B_{2_{t+2}}|C_{1_{t+1}}) \times U(B_{2_{t+2}}) \\
& + P(C_{2_{t+1}}|A_{2_t})P(B_{2_{t+2}}|C_{2_{t+1}}) \times U(B_{2_{t+2}}).
\end{aligned}
$$

Figure 5.2. Exchange Situation Involving Direct and Indirect Effects

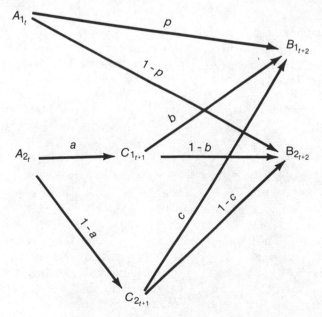

From these two equations we can see that there is only one path from A_{1_t} to $B_{1_{t+2}}$, while there are two from A_{2_t} to $B_{1_{t+2}}$. We shall first simplify by substituting terms for the subjective probabilities and by assuming that all outcomes that are exhaustive and mutually exclusive must sum to 1, so that the following hold:

$$p = P(B_{1_{t+2}}|A_{1_t}); \qquad\qquad 1 - p = P(B_{2_{t+2}}|A_{1_t});$$

$$a = P(C_{1_{t+1}}|A_{2_t}); \qquad\qquad 1 - a = P(C_{2_{t+1}}|A_{2_t});$$

$$b = P(B_{1_{t+2}}|C_{1_{t+1}}); \qquad\qquad 1 - b = P(B_{2_{t+2}}|C_{1_{t+1}});$$

$$c = P(B_{1_{t+2}}|C_{2_{t+1}}); \qquad\qquad 1 - c = P(B_{2_{t+2}}|C_{2_{t+1}}).$$

The difference between the subjective expected utilities for the two alternatives can therefore be expressed as

$$SEU(A_{1_t}) - SEU(A_{2_t}) = [pU(B_{1_{t+2}}) + (1 - p)U(B_{2_{t+2}})]$$
$$- [abU(B_{1_{t+2}}) + (c - ac)U(B_{1_{t+2}})$$
$$+ (a - ab)U(B_{2_{t+2}})$$
$$+ (1 - a - c + ac)U(B_{2_{t+2}})].$$

This can in turn be simplified to

$$= (p + ac - ab - c) \times [U(B_{1_{t+2}})$$
$$- U(B_{2_{t+2}})].$$

The implications of this simplification can be spelled out in more detail. If $B_{1_{t+2}}$ is the outcome desired by actor A, so that $U(B_{1_{t+2}}) > U(B_{2_{t+2}})$, then A will be better off enacting A_{1_t} if $(p + ac) > (ab + c)$. Returning to the original probabilities, this says that

$$P(B_{1_{t+2}}|A_{1_t}) + P(C_{1_{t+1}}|A_{2_t}) \times P(B_{1_{t+2}}|C_{2_{t+1}})$$

must be greater than

$$P(B_{1_{t+2}}|C_{2_{t+1}}) + P(C_{1_{t+1}}|A_{2_t}) \times P(B_{1_{t+2}}|C_{1_{t+1}}).$$

This then becomes more meaningful if we recast $(p + ac - ab - c)$ in a slightly different form, namely, $[(p - c) + a(c - b)]$. Now it can be seen that for this sum to most likely be positive, and thus $SEU(A_{1_t}) > SEU(A_{2_t})$, p must be greater than c and c must be greater than b. If p is greater than c, this means that A_{1_t} is more likely than $C_{2_{t+1}}$ to lead to $B_{1_{t+2}}$, and $c > b$ indicates that $C_{2_{t+1}}$ is more likely to lead to $B_{1_{t+2}}$ than is $C_{1_{t+1}}$. Consequently, $C_{1_{t+1}}$ is more likely to lead to $B_{2_{t+2}}$ than is $C_{2_{t+1}}$. So because neither of the potential actions of the third party, $C_{1_{t+1}}$ or $C_{2_{t+1}}$, is as likely to result in $B_{1_{t+2}}$ as is A_{1_t}, A_{1_t} will have greater subjective expected utility.

These equations, although they look complex, mirror quite well the thought processes of actors in exchange situations. In this case actor A's judgment that neither action taken by actor C has a greater likelihood of resulting in $B_{1_{t+2}}$ than does A_{1_t} leads to the conclusion that A_{1_t} is the alternative to enact.

The thought processes involved can also be shown by a slightly different situation. Let us assume that actor A believes that $C_{1_{t+1}}$ is more likely to lead to $B_{1_{t+2}}$ than is A_{1_t}, but also that A_{1_t} is more likely to lead to $B_{1_{t+2}}$ than is $C_{2_{t+1}}$. In this case we would expect the crucial question to be what the impact of A_{2_t} will be on actor C. If it makes C more likely to enact $C_{1_{t+1}}$, then A_{2_t} would be the appropriate action to take. If, however, it makes $C_{2_{t+1}}$ more likely, then A would be better off with A_{1_t}.

These assumed conditions indicate that $b > p > c$. Consequently $p - c$ will yield a positive number, but $c - b$ will yield a negative number that will be larger than the difference between p and c. Thus the important term becomes a, or $P(C_{1_{t+1}}|A_{2_t})$. If this is relatively large then the relative subjective expected utility estimate is likely to be negative, and A_{2_t} will be the action with greater subjective expected utility.

Next let's consider the situation in which only indirect effects are anticipated, with both actions of A affecting a third party, C, as we see in figure 5.3. We can use equation (7) for the subjective expected utility estimate for A_{2_t}, but the equation for A_{1_t} now becomes

$$
\begin{aligned}
SEU(A_{1_t}) = \; & P(C_{1_{t+1}}|A_{1_t})P(B_{1_{t+2}}|C_{1_{t+1}}) \times U(B_{1_{t+2}}) \\
+ \; & P(C_{2_{t+1}}|A_{1_t})P(B_{1_{t+2}}|C_{2_{t+1}}) \times U(B_{1_{t+2}}) \\
+ \; & P(C_{1_{t+1}}|A_{1_t})P(B_{2_{t+2}}|C_{1_{t+1}}) \times U(B_{2_{t+2}}) \\
+ \; & P(C_{2_{t+1}}|A_{1_t})P(B_{2_{t+2}}|C_{2_{t+1}}) \times U(B_{2_{t+2}}).
\end{aligned}
$$

We add to our previous substituted terms, a, b, and c, the following:

$$
d = P(C_{1_{t+1}}|A_{1_t}) \quad \text{and} \quad 1 - d = P(C_{2_{t+1}}|A_{1_t}).
$$

Figure 5.3. Exchange Situation Involving Only Indirect Effects

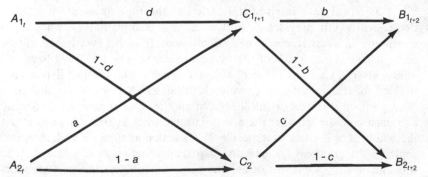

The difference between the subjective expected utilities of the two alternatives can thereby be represented as

$$SEU(A_{1_t}) - SEU(A_{2_t}) = (db + c - cd)\, U(B_{1_{t+2}})$$
$$+ (1 + cd - bd - c)\, U(B_{2_{t+2}})$$
$$- (ab + c - ac)\, U(B_{1_{t+2}})$$
$$- (1 + ac - ab - c)\, U(B_{2_{t+2}}).$$

And this in turn simplifies quite nicely to

$$= (d - a)(b - c)\,[U(B_{1_{t+2}})$$
$$- U(B_{2_{t+2}})].$$

Assuming again that $U(B_{1_{t+2}}) > U(B_{2_{t+2}})$, A_{1_t} will have greater subjective expected utility than A_{2_t}, if $d > a$ and $b > c$ or if $d < a$ and $b < c$. If the former conditions hold, then A_{1_t} is more likely to lead to $C_{1_{t+1}}$ than is A_{2_t}, and $C_{1_{t+1}}$ is more likely to lead to $B_{1_{t+2}}$ than is $C_{2_{t+1}}$.

If the latter conditions hold, then A_{2_t} is more likely to lead to $C_{1_{t+1}}$ than is A_{1_t}, but $C_{2_{t+1}}$ is more likely to lead to $B_{1_{t+2}}$ than is $C_{1_{t+1}}$, so the most probable path would run from A_{1_t} to $B_{1_{t+2}}$ through $C_{2_{t+1}}$. But if only one of these inequalities holds, then A_{2_t} will have greater subjective expected utility. If, for example, $d > a$ and $b > c$, then the most likely path would be from A_{2_t} to $C_{2_{t+1}}$ to $B_{1_{t+2}}$. Again, the model exemplifies the thought processes involved quite well. The $A_{2_t} \rightarrow C_{2_{t+1}} \rightarrow B_{1_{t+2}}$ path choice can be seen as the result of actor A's thinking somewhat as follows: "I'd like B_1 rather than B_2 at time $t + 2$. If C enacts C_2 at time $t + 1$, then B is more likely to enact B_1 than if C enacts C_1. And if I enact A_1, then C is more likely to enact C_1 than if I enact A_2. So my best bet for getting B_1 is to enact A_2 now."

The factors that go into B's decision as to how to respond to A's action can also be illustrated via the causal model approach. Let us assume that B is desirous of obtaining an outcome from A at time $t + 3$ as a result of B's action at time $t + 2$. We shall assume two possible outcomes, $A_{3_{t+3}}$ and $A_{4_{t+3}}$. The major difference between B's choice situation at the time $t + 2$ and A's at time t is that B will have received A's action at the time he or she must decide. Consequently this provides B with additional information on which to base a response so as to receive a desired outcome from A. Two issues will be of concern to B. First, which of the two outcomes at time $t + 3$ will have greater utility, given A's action at time t? This will depend upon the goal that A's action fulfilled for B and the extent to which it fulfilled it. B may desire additional goal fulfillment on that goal or fulfillment of another goal at time $t + 3$. Second, B also must consider whether the action enacted by A at time t has any effect on the action A will enact at time $t + 3$. A's action at time t may have seriously depleted the resources for enacting a particular action at time $t + 3$. If so, B will undoubtedly adjust his or her subjective probability estimates accordingly.

We shall see that, of the two, the utility issue is more relevant for B's choice.

B's choice situation and the effect of A's action at time t are shown by the following two subjective expected utility equations. We are assuming that A enacted A_1 at time t.

$$SEU(B_{1_{t+2}}) = P(A_{3_{t+3}}|B_{1_{t+2}} + A_{1_t}) \times U(A_{3_{t+3}}|A_{1_t})$$

$$+ P(A_{4_{t+3}}|B_{1_{t+2}} + A_{1_t}) \times U(A_{4_{t+3}}|A_{1_t}).$$

$$SEU(B_{2_{t+2}}) = P(A_{3_{t+3}}|B_{2_{t+2}} + A_{1_t}) \times U(A_{3_{t+3}}|A_{1_t})$$

$$+ P(A_{4_{t+3}}|B_{2_{t+2}} + A_{1_t}) \times U(A_{4_{t+3}}|A_{1_t}).$$

Here we have incorporated the information from A's action at time t in both the subjective probabilities and the utility terms. Now the two issues can be posed more precisely: (1) Which has more utility, A_3 or A_4, given that A_1 has been received? (2) Given that A has enacted A_1 already, is A_3 or A_4 more likely to be enacted at time $t + 3$?

We make the following substitutions, again assuming that the sum of exhaustive mutually exclusive outcomes equals 1:[5]

$$a - P(A_{3_{t+3}}|B_{1_{t+2}}); \qquad 1 - a = P(A_{4_{t+3}}|B_{1_{t+2}});$$

$$b = P(A_{3_{t+3}}|B_{2_{t+2}}); \qquad 1 - b = P(A_{4_{t+3}}|B_{2_{t+2}}).$$

The difference between the subjective expected utilities of the two alternatives can thereby be reduced to

$$SEU(B_{1_{t+2}}) - SEU(B_{2_{t+2}}) = (a-b)[U(A_{3_{t+3}}) - U(A_{4_{t+3}})].$$

With this formulation we can see that the first decision B must make is whether A_3 or A_4 has greater utility, given that A_1 has occurred. Then B must simply determine which of his or her alternatives is more likely to result in A's enacting A_3. If A_3 is judged to have greater utility, then B_1 will have greater subjective expected utility if the $(a - b)$ term is positive, which indicates that B_1 is more likely than B_2 to result in A's enacting A_3. And if $U(A_4) > U(A_3)$, then a negative $(a - b)$ term, which shows that B_2 is more likely than B_1 to lead to A_3, will yield a greater subjective expected utility for B_1.

Thus we can see that the causal models approach can be used quite well in analyzing exchange relationships and can handle a fair amount of complexity.

Simplifying the Estimation of Subjective Probabilities. The predictability resulting from prolonged interaction in an exchange relationship will be the major factor simplifying actors' estimates of subjective probabilities. Partners in an exchange relationship will very likely be able to anticipate the responses of each other after a period of time with a high degree of accuracy. In fact, one might regard this predictability as one of the most satisfying features of primary-exchange relationships. The participants are saved the expenditure of resources to obtain subjective probability estimates that may be required in other, less regularized exchanges. Of course, there is always the possibility that "familiarity breeds contempt" in such relationships and that for some individuals a high degree of certainty will be unsatisfying.

In a regularized relationship it is probable that the participants will be able to anticipate behavioral sequences and will not be restricted to anticipating the other party's behavior only at the next time point. Actor A, for example, may know very well that if he or she does one thing actor B will respond in a certain way to which actor A will in turn respond, and so forth.

These observations suggest that role taking will also be an important factor for estimating subjective probabilities. It is possible that the historical use of this concept has applied more to the estimation of subjective probabilities than to utility estimation. The notion of "putting oneself in the place of the other" has been used primarily to mean thinking about how one would act if he or she were in another's position. Thus it is best exemplified by someone's saying, "If I were he [or she], I would do thus and so." If actors actually are able to do this, then their estimations of the relative likelihood of the other's actions will be simplified.

Vicarious estimates of subjective probability do not appear to be as important as vicarious estimates of utility, however, although they may play a part in the estimation of subjective probabilities. In an earlier version of this chapter we attempted to show that one actor's subjective probabilities may be regarded as approximately equal to vicarious estimates of the other actor's subjective expected utilities in an exchange situation. That is, A's subjective probability for a specific action on the part of B may be assumed to be equal to A's estimate of B's subjective expected utility for that action. If this were correct, then A would have to make vicarious estimates of both B's utilities and subjective probabilities. This avenue of thought soon became hopelessly complex, though, and we abandoned it in favor of our present approach.

It is conceivable, though, that some individuals will estimate their exchange partner's subjective probabilities. We can visualize this happening if actors have a utility for surprise, i.e., they receive goal fulfillment by acting differently than they anticipate their exchange partner expects them to act. Actor A may say, for example, "B expects me to enact A_1, but I will surprise him [or her] and enact A_2." The use of the unanticipated response, based on vicarious subjective probability estimates, may actually be quite important in exchange relationships and used to advantage by some individuals. Thus an employer who has constantly criticized an employee may attempt to win the employee's loyalty by suddenly changing tactics. A parent may be pleasantly surprised to find a child's normally chaotic room suddenly transformed into the epitome of order. In cases such as these it is probable that vicarious subjective probability estimates have played a role.

Two characteristics that Blau (1964a) has stressed also help to simplify subjective probability estimates in exchange relationships. The first of these is trust, which involves *unspecified* obligations between the participants. Thus, one actor may indicate to the other that a vaguely defined behavior will be offered at some indefinite future time. If the other actor in the exchange is trusting, then we anticipate that two things are likely to happen. First, the potential recipient of the deferred outcome will not depreciate the value of the outcome. It will have the same utility as if it were received immediately. We have previously noted this characteristic of the exchanges described by Stack (1974). Second, the trusting partner will likely estimate the subjective probability of the outcome close to or equal to 1. This consequence of trust is exemplified by statements such as "I know I can count on you" and "I trust you to do that."

Commitment is the second of these characteristics, which not only serve to buttress exchange relationships but simplify subjective probability estimates as well. It essentially involves the parties to an exchange indicating to each other that they will not withdraw from the exchange relationship. At the very least, this simplifies matters by removing the behavioral alternative of withdrawal from the actors' repertoires of actions. An actor who makes a commitment to an exchange relationship simplifies his or her choice situations in two ways. On the one hand, he or she does not consider withdrawal as a viable alternative to enact in the relationship. And, on the other hand, he or she does not have to take it into account as a possible reaction of the other party, so subjective probabilities will not have to be estimated for that outcome. By contrast, the actors in exchange relationships where commitments are lacking will not be able to dismiss completely the possibility of the other actor's leaving the relationship. If that outcome has great negative utility for them, then any actions that they perceive to have even a remote possibility of promoting that outcome will likely not be considered by them. Therefore commitments are likely to lessen the levels of anxiety of the participants in an exchange relationship.

Norms constitute a last factor simplifying subjective probability estimates. Commitment may itself be regarded as a normative element, since its implication is that withdrawal from an exchange relationship is wrong. Trust likewise has normative overtones, as can be seen when one considers the usual reaction to violations of trust. Virtually all individuals regard such an action as a moral wrong and not merely as a failure to live up to expectations. Later in this chapter we will consider norms as a contextual influence on exchange relationships. At this point we are primarily concerned with the fact that regularization or patterning in an exchange relationship may become imbued with normative connotations. In other words, if individuals in an ongoing exchange relationship continually respond in the same way to a given action by the other party, the other party is likely to develop normative expectations regarding that response. A specific response may not be seen simply as habit, or one's normal way of doing things, but as the way one *should* respond. Thus the husband who suddenly decides he doesn't like oatmeal may find himself the victim of his wife's *moral* indignation. Or the child who responds with anger to a parent's scolding after having been very submissive over a long period of time may also be seen to have violated a norm.

It is very difficult to separate the emergence of norms out of the patterning of exchange relationships from the influence of contextual norms. Thus the wife may feel that there is a norm specifying that husbands should like oatmeal, or should eat what their wives fix for them, and the parent may believe that children should not get angry at their parents. Nevertheless, it seems important to us to make this distinction and note the possibility of the emergence of norms within exchange relationships. Our major point here, of course, is that to the extent they develop they will ease the process of estimating subjective probabilities.

Decision Strategies in Exchange Situations

In our discussion of decision strategies in chapter 4 we concentrated upon the maximization strategy, i.e., choosing the action alternative with the greatest subjective expected utility, although we did give some consideration to the satisficing strategy, i.e., selecting the first action alternative with an acceptable level of subjective expected utility. For both of these strategies our focus was upon the subjective expected utilities of a single actor. Exchange situations, however, create new possibilities for actors' decision strategies, as we have noted previously. There are three basic possibilities in these situations. First, actors may act as they do in nonexchange situations, either maximizing or satisficing their subjective expected utilities. Second, they may go to the opposite extreme and base their choices of alternatives solely upon the utilities of the other actor in the exchange, a strategy we might consider the purest form of altruism. A cynic may question whether this strategy is ever used by humans; we at least allow for the possibility. Third, the decision strategies used by actors may involve some *relationship* between the subjective expected utilities of the two parties. Actors may try to maximize, to minimize, or to satisfice the differences between their own subjective expected utilities and the utility received by the other actor. Or actors may attempt to maximize or satisfice the *combined* utilities of the two actors.[6] In all cases but the first above, vicarious estimates of utility will be required. (We shall here disregard the satisficing strategy.)

Clearly, if actors do not use different decision strategies in exchange situations, then the general strategy we have been following of making relative subjective expected utility estimates will also be applicable to choices made in exchange situations. For those situations in which vicarious utility estimates are used we can start with the simple case of two alternatives that we have used before, as represented in the following two equations:

$$
(8) \quad
\begin{aligned}
SEU(A_{1_t}) = \; & P(B_{1_{t+1}}|A_{1_t}) \times U(B_{1_{t+1}}) \\
& + P(B_{2_{t+1}}|A_{1_t}) \times U(B_{2_{t+1}}) + U(A_{1_t}.B)
\end{aligned}
$$

$$
(9) \quad
\begin{aligned}
SEU(A_{2_t}) = \; & P(B_{1_{t+1}}|A_{2_t}) \times U(B_{1_{t+1}}) \\
& + P(B_{2_{t+1}}|A_{2_t}) \times U(B_{2_{t+1}}) + U(A_{2_t}.B).
\end{aligned}
$$

These equations show the by now familiar case of actor A faced with a choice between two actions, each of which is believed to have some influence on the actions of actor B. A's vicarious estimates of B's utilities resulting from A's actions are included as the last term in each equation. These can be regarded as additional outcomes of each alternative and the subjective probability terms for them can be omitted because it can be assumed that $P(A_{1_t}) = P(A_{2_t}) = 1$.

If an actor is following the pure altruism decision strategy, then his or her choice of an action alternative will be given by the relative utility estimate

$$SEU(A_{1_t}) - SEU(A_{2_t}) = U(A_{1_t}.B) - U(A_{2_t}.B).$$

If B is perceived to receive more utility from A_1, then the positive value of the difference indicates that A_1 should be selected.

The decision strategies using both actors' utilities are slightly more complex and also more interesting. They will necessarily involve the subjective expected utility of the actor making the choice among alternatives and the *utility* received by the other actor, as perceived by the first actor. This is simply due to the fact that the choosing actor does not know with certainty in most cases which outcome he or she is going to receive, whereas the vicarious utility estimates he or she makes are based upon enactment of an alternative. That is, A's vicarious estimate of B's utility assumes that A is going to enact an alternative.

Turning first to the case in which the decision strategy entails maximizing or minimizing the difference between the actors' utilities, how this is achieved can be shown by a modification of equations (8) and (9). If we let D_1 equal the difference between the actor's subjective expected utility and other's utility for A_{1_t}, and let D_2 equal the same for A_{2_t}, then

$$D_1 = SEU(A_{1_t}) - U(A_{1_t}.B) \quad \text{and} \quad D_2 = SEU(A_{2_t}) - U(A_{2_t}.B).$$

A comparison of the absolute values of these differences, i.e., $|D_1| - |D_2|$ can then be used to determine which of the alternatives to enact.

This procedure does not take into account which of the actors benefits from the maximization of differences. Therefore if an actor wishes to maximize the difference by maximizing his or her subjective expected utility and minimizing the other actor's utility, a slightly different procedure will be necessary. In this case he or she can ignore the absolute values of differences as follows:

(10) $\quad D_1 - D_2 = SEU(A_{1_t}) - U(A_{1_t}.B) - SEU(A_{2_t}) + U(A_{2_t}.B).$

If we substitute p for $P(B_{1_{t+1}}|A_{1_t})$ and q for $P(B_{1_{t+1}}|A_{2_t})$ in equations (8) and (9) and assume that the subjective probabilities of each of these outcomes and the other anticipated outcome of a given alternative sum to 1, we can represent equation (10) as

(11)
$$D_1 - D_2 = (p - q) \times [U(B_{1_{t+1}}) - U(B_{2_{t+1}})]$$
$$+ [U(A_{2_t}.B) - U(A_{1_t}.B)].$$

The choice of an alternative in this case will be based upon three relationships between probabilities and utilities: (1) the difference between p and q; (2)

the difference between $U(B_{1_{t+1}})$ and $U(B_{2_{t+1}})$; (3) the difference between $U(A_{2_t}.B)$ and $U(A_{1_t}.B)$. If equation (11) yields a positive value, then A_{1_t} will maximize the difference between utilities in the actor's favor; if it yields a negative value, then A_{2_t} will be the alternative that does so. In the case in which the difference between the actor's subjective expected utility and the other actor's utility is negative for both alternatives, equations (10) and (11) will minimize the difference between the actors' utilities.

A_{1_t} will clearly maximize the difference in the actor's favor if all three of the differences in equation (11) are positive. If they are, this indicates that A_{1_t} is more likely than A_{2_t} to lead to $B_{1_{t+1}}$, that $B_{1_{t+1}}$ has greater utility than $B_{2_{t+1}}$ for A, and that A_{2_t} has greater utility for B than A_{1_t}. The first two of these differences maximize A's subjective expected utility, while the third minimizes B's utility, thus maximizing the difference between A and B.

Another possibility is that the actor attempts to maximize the total utility received in the exchange. In this case the choice between alternatives A_{1_t} and A_{2_t} can be represented as

$$SEU(A_{1_t}) - SEU(A_{2_t}) = SEU(A_{1_t}) + U(A_{1_t}.B)$$

$$- SEU(A_{2_t}) - U(A_{2_t}.B).$$

This can be modified to

$$SEU(A_{1_t}) - SEU(A_{2_t}) = (p - q) \times [U(B_{1_{t+1}}) - U(B_{2_{t+1}})]$$

$$+ U(A_{1_t}.B) - U(A_{2_t}.B).$$

Interpretation of this equation is relatively straightforward, except for the case in which A's subjective expected utility is greater for one alternative and A believes B's utility to be greater for the other alternative. Which alternative is selected will depend upon the relative amounts of utility involved. Since B's utility is not modified by a subjective probability estimate, it is conceivable that maximum total utility may be obtained by selecting the alternative that offers B greater utility than A. (We assume here that A perceives that A's action is B's outcome.)

We have shown how exchange situations affect the estimation of utilities and subjective probabilities and the decision strategies used with the subjective expected utility model. We now consider the implications of the contextual characteristics of exchange situations for the model, and how the model can be used to represent these influences.

CONTEXTUAL INFLUENCES IN EXCHANGE SITUATIONS

Exchange relationships rarely exist in a vacuum. The actors involved in any exchange bring to that relationship ties with the outside world, so to speak. They are likely to be involved in similar exchange relationships with other actors that cannot be isolated from a specific exchange with a given actor. They also carry with them the resources they possess as persons that they may have accumulated by means of previous exchange relationships. And they approach the exchange situation under the influence of ideational phenomena that will affect their orientations to the relationship. In this section we look at two contextual characteristics in some detail. One of these, dependence, is only partially contextual, since it basically involves a relationship between actors' goals and their contexts. The other, norms, is somewhat more completely contextual, although actors are not totally submissive to normative influences.

The significance of dependence for exchange situations has been most strongly emphasized by Emerson (1969, 1972*a*).[7] Dependence, for him, primarily involves the number of alternatives available to an actor (the greater the number of alternative means for goal fulfillment, the less the dependence of an actor on any one other actor for having his or her goals fulfilled) and the value of the rewards offered by an exchange (the more valuable these are, the greater the dependence). According to Emerson, exchange relationships are more likely to be initiated and sustained when each party is dependent upon the other.

We view dependence in a fashion similar to that of Emerson. The concept refers to a state of reliance upon some actor other than oneself for fulfillment of one's goals. Actors will, of course, differ in their degrees of dependence. Some will be able to fulfill a large proportion of their goals without assistance from others, while some will have to rely almost totally on others' actions. We also view the degree of dependence as being partly a function of the number of alternative means an actor perceives for attaining a goal.[8]

The influence of the availability of alternatives on dependence is goal specific. That is, the degree of dependence of an actor must be estimated in regard to a specific goal, and not to goals in general, although some kind of summary measure of total dependence across all goals may be possible. It is necessary to allow for the possibility that actors may have a relatively large number of alternatives available to fulfill certain goals and relatively few available to fulfill other goals.

The second major factor determining the degree of dependence is the degree of *deprivation*, which we define in terms of utility not received. This determinant will also be goal specific, since actors' goals will likely vary in terms of the amount of utility that has not been received as a result of the lack of goal fulfillment. We believe it is preferable to keep the two determinants of the degree of dependence—availability of alternatives and degree of deprivation—separate. The effects of the availability of alternatives for goal fulfillment will primarily be manifested through the subjective probability component of the subjective expected utility model, whereas the effects of deprivation will show up in the utility component.

Since two factors determine the degree of dependence, this means that the degree of dependence will be greatest when both are at an extreme—the availability of alternatives at a minimum and the degree of deprivation at a maximum. Thus actors will be most dependent when they have few alternatives available to fulfill goals on which they are severely deprived. These two factors probably have a multiplicative influence on dependence because intuitively we would expect dependence to be low if only one of them were extreme. An actor may be quite deprived on a particular goal but may have numerous alternatives available to fulfill it, or he or she may lack alternatives to fulfill a goal on which there is little deprivation. Both of these cases will be characterized by limited dependence.

The degree of deprivation, or the amount of utility not received, will primarily be a function of the size of the goal fulfillment deprivation gap for a goal, i.e., the difference between the desired level of goal fulfillment and the current level of goal fulfillment. It is plausible that consistent deprivation will lead to a lowering of the desired level of goal fulfillment, however, so that the deprivation gap, and hence the experienced degree of deprivation, may diminish over time.

The other determinants of the utilities of outcomes will also be of significance for the degree of deprivation. First, we expect deprivation to be more severe the greater the importance of a given goal. A given amount of missing goal fulfillment will translate into a larger amount of unreceived utility on more important goals because of the greater steepness of the utility curves for such goals. Second, it should be noted that a relatively small outcome, in terms of the degree of goal fulfillment that it supplies, may offer relatively large amounts of utility. This will occur if the actor's current level of goal fulfillment is so low that the outcome covers a portion of the utility curve where there is sharply increasing marginal utility. Furthermore, the immediacy of goal fulfillment may have either of two very different effects. On the one hand, we can visualize situations in which a severely deprived actor will not discount deferred outcomes because he or she anticipates an outcome received in the future to be better than no outcome at all. On the other hand, we can also visualize actors applying quite large discount rates to postponed outcomes and as a result accepting immediate outcomes with smaller utility because, for them, a small outcome now is preferable to a large outcome later. We have discussed this possibility in chapter 2 in terms of the alleged inability of certain actors to defer gratification, pointing out there that the choice of alternatives promising immediate outcomes may be very "rational" on their parts, given their discount rates for deferred outcomes.

So the general conclusion we can draw from this discussion is that actors who are suffering from deprivation are likely to be seeking rather high-utility outcomes, particularly if the deprivation is on quite important goals. (The total degree of deprivation of the actor would be a sum of the degrees of deprivation on all goals where there is a lack of goal fulfillment.) We believe it is also a possibility that actors experiencing deprivation will *overestimate* the potential utility to be gained from outcomes, due to the fact that a move from little or no goal fulfillment to some goal fulfillment is probably more difficult to estimate accurately than are increments to an intermediate level of goal fulfillment. This phenomenon may also be the result of an influence of the limited number of alternatives on utility estimates. Again Stack's study (1974) of lower-class black families provides supporting evidence, as she noted the unrealistically high value placed upon friendship relationships by many of the people she studied. Liebow's description (1967) of lower-class black males provides corroborating evidence. Both researchers found that in many instances the friendships simply were not able to bear the weight of the high values placed upon them and disintegrated.

We have said that the influence of a limited number of alternatives available to an actor will be revealed through the subjective probability component of our model. Specifically, actors perceiving a limited number of alternatives available to them will assign zero or very low subjective probabilities to a large proportion of the alternatives they consider. The corollary of this premise is that a small proportion of the alternatives they consider will have quite high subjective probability estimates. If we consider that at the very least each alternative has two potential outcomes—occurrence and nonoccurrence of an outcome—then a high degree of dependence will mean that the subjective probabilities for many of the outcomes of these alternatives will be close to zero, whereas the subjective probabilities for many of the nonoccurrences of the outcomes will be close to 1. Unless an actor is completely fatalistic, i.e., expecting that no matter what he or she does desired outcomes are not going to occur, we anticipate that a very few alternatives will have the opposite pattern, namely, very high subjective probabilities for the occurrence of the outcome, given the alternative, and very low subjective probabilities for the outcome's nonoccurrence. One might call this a "putting all one's eggs in one basket" approach.

The fact that so many of the alternatives considered by an actor in a situation of dependence are assumed to have virtually no probability of bringing about desired outcomes may lead to an overestimation of the subjective probabilities for those alternatives that are perceived to have some possibility of resulting in an outcome. The friendship relations described by Stack and Liebow can also be interpreted in this light. Since these actors had very few friends and since they had few other sources of goal fulfillment available to them, they appear to have had unrealistic expectations about the outcomes they could receive from the friends they did have.

Describing a situation of dependence in subjective probability terms does not fully explain it, of course. At base, actors' subjective probability estimates are a consequence of their resources and their knowledge. Actors with greater resources are better able to afford the expenditure of time and energy necessary to seek out additional alternatives. And, whether we regard knowledge as a separate entity or as a type of resource, actors with greater knowledge of their environment will be more aware of possible action alternatives. So we would expect dependence to be greater among actors with limited resources and knowledge.

Actors in a situation of high dependence may also be victims of a snowball effect. If they perceive a limited number of alternatives available to them, then we would further predict that they will be more likely to develop a *commitment* to a particular exchange relationship than if they believe a relatively large number of alternatives can lead to outcomes they desire (Blau 1964a). And we have already noted that commitment involves rejecting the alternative of with-drawing from an exchange relationship. Consequently that action alternative is not regarded as a feasible one, and actors will continue to be restricted to their current repertoires of alternatives. Thus, whichever spouse is relatively more dependent on his or her partner will be more likely to develop a commitment to the marriage relationship and thus will forego the option of seeking relationships with others that potentially might offer greater goal fulfillment than the rela-tionship with the spouse. Over time this spouse's degree of dependence is there-fore likely to increase.

When we put the two components together, and thus the effects of both a limited number of alternatives and a high degree of deprivation, the picture that emerges is that of dependent actors having in their repertoires of alternatives many alternatives with very low subjective expected utilities and a few alterna-tives with very high subjective expected utilities. We see two implications of this conclusion, one of which may be considered somewhat positive and the other less satisfactory for these actors. On the one hand, it should be easier to make choices between alternatives from a repertoire with these characteristics than from a repertoire with a large number of alternatives with approximately equal levels of subjective expected utility. Thus, individuals in situations of depen-dence may not face many perplexing choices. But on the other hand, it also means that dependent actors are likely to consistently enact the few alternatives with very high subjective expected utilities simply because there are so few, if any, alternatives to compete with them.

If those alternatives that are consistently enacted are alternatives leading to exchanges with others (very likely a specific other), then dependent actors will continue in such relationships over a long period of time even though they may be benefiting very little from them in comparison to their exchange partner. Slavery is probably the prime example of this type of situation, with the slaves being almost completely dependent upon their owners. We would not go so far as to say that the slaves were "committed" to this exchange relationship, but they clearly had few other alternatives available to them that offered positive utility. For most, attempting to escape or revolt involved very high subjective probabilities of outcomes yielding very high negative utility. The slave owners were fully aware of the importance of both resources and knowledge for reduc-ing dependence and effectively prevented the slaves from increasing their sup-plies of either.

Dependence is also likely to have an effect on the decision strategies used in exchange situations. Our previous comments regarding the great disparity between the subjective expected utility estimates for alternatives suggest that maximization will be a likely strategy, simply because of the ease of determining which alternative has greatest subjective expected utility. However, we do not believe that it will be the most probable decision strategy used by actors who are dependent. We anticipate that they will utilize decision strategies that take into account the other actor's utilities. Although dependent actors may strive to maximize total utility, they may be even more likely to maximize the other's utility, or possibly to minimize differences in utilities between themselves and others *and* to maximize others' utilities. We base this prediction on the fact that dependent actors will have more to lose if the other actor withdraws from the exchange relationship than will actors who are not dependent. Consequently, we expect that dependent actors will try to keep the other actor happy, even if it means a loss of utility for them in the short run, so as to prevent the other actor from withdrawing and entering an exchange relationship with someone else. This prediction must, of course, stand empirical testing, but intuitively it seems sensible.

By contrast, independent actors in an exchange relationship with actors they perceive to be quite dependent on them may have few qualms about consistently maximizing their subjective expected utility and/or maximizing the difference between their and the dependent actor's utilities. In other words, they may milk the exchange for all it's worth, giving just enough to the dependent actor to keep him or her from withdrawing and spoiling a good thing. The actions of slave owners may be seen in this light, writers such as Fogel and Engerman (1974) notwithstanding. Many slave owners appear to have given enough food and care to their slaves to keep them from dying or sitting down on the job, but at the same time worked them hard enough to make certain that the utilities (profits) they received from them were maximized. It is precisely at this point where it is difficult to determine whether a relationship between actors is better viewed as an exchange relationship or as a power relationship. On the basis of our previous discussion of these two types of relationship the only relatively foolproof way for making this determination is to find out what actions the dependent actor would enact in the absence of the other actor.

A major conclusion we can draw from this is that exchange relationships characterized by inequalities in degrees of dependence between the participants are liable to be characterized by some amount of tension. Dependent parties will strive to keep the exchange going, whereas independent parties are likely to be continually pulling away from the exchange and considering other alternatives. If each party is about equally dependent on the other, however, the exchange will be more stable.[9] This argument can be applied to a variety of exchanges, ranging from marriages to slavery. It has been repeatedly argued, for example, that the stability of the American system of slavery was largely due to the slave owners' dependence on the slaves to provide them with profits.

Finally, we simply wish to note that there are two main ways whereby an actor's degree of dependence may be reduced. First, he or she may discover that additional alternatives with nonzero subjective probabilities are available or that the subjective probabilities for existent alternatives can be revised upward. This may result from increases in resources that promote a search for new alternatives or the capacity to devote more resources to a present alternative, or it may be the consequence of inputs of information. Second, dependence can also be reduced if deprivation diminishes on a particular goal. This may result from goal fulfillment, or it may be a psychological adjustment by the actor. Deprivation can be reduced if a goal is downgraded in importance ("I really didn't want that anyway"), or if the desired level of goal fulfillment is reduced ("I'm content with what I have"). These changes will lead to changes in the utility curve for a given goal so that the same outcome will have less utility than it would have had previously. Hence the actor will have less of a sense of not having received utility.

NORMATIVE INFLUENCES IN EXCHANGE SITUATIONS

In the next chapter we discuss one of the major norms influencing exchange situations: the equity/distributive justice norm. Here we simply wish to note several ways in which other norms can influence exchange situations.[10]

Normative influences can appear in exchange situations in a variety of ways. At the very outset, they may preclude actors from entering certain exchanges with other actors. For example, the common parental directive to young children not to talk to strangers or not to accept rides from them represents a norm that discourages their becoming involved in such exchanges. Similarly, the norms of a group may prohibit entering exchange relationships with members of another group. Thus in the Indian caste system higher-caste individuals have been forbidden to enter exchanges with Untouchables. Members of one religious group may be discouraged from developing friendship relationships with members of another religious group and absolutely prohibited from marrying them. Or racial groups may have norms against interaction with members of another racial group.

Norms may also proscribe enactment of certain alternatives in exchange relationships. Parents may inform their children that "children do not talk back to parents." Aggression against a child by an adult may be permissible, whereas aggression of a child against an adult may be not allowed. Historically some action alternatives—striking, addressing by one's first name—have been normatively supported for whites in relations with blacks, but blacks have not been allowed to enact the same alternatives in exchanges with whites. Contemporary South Africa offers a wide range of supporting examples. Blacks may enter white areas to work, but they may not enter them to live, for example.

Norms will affect exchange relationships primarily through influencing actors' subjective probability estimates. Thus the major consequence of a norm's prohibiting a particular course of action is the implicit message that dreadful outcomes are very likely to happen if that alternative is enacted. The child who accepts rides from strangers is very likely to be severely harmed. (Quite often the actual nature of the outcome in this case is left undefined, except that it will be bad and very certain to happen.) High-caste individuals who come into contact with an Untouchable are certain to become impure, just as are individuals who interact with members of another race. Children who talk back to their parents or aggress against them are certain to be spanked. In the past blacks who stepped out of line in their exchanges with whites were very likely to be beaten and maybe even lynched.

So a variety of norms operate to constrain the range of alternatives likely to be enacted in exchange situations. An effect of norms on utilities, separate from their effect on subjective probabilities, is difficult to discern, but it is probable that norms also dictate appropriate decision strategies for exchange situations. These norms will simply involve the relative outcomes of the two parties, whereas the equity/distributive justice norm to be discussed in the next chapter will concern both the relative inputs and outcomes of the actors.

In certain groups, for example, norms may specify maximizing one's own outcome and minimizing the outcomes of others. The cutthroat, survival-of-the-fittest orientation supposedly characterizing portions of the business world, which is exemplified by the normative statement "If you don't take advantage of them, they'll take advantage of you," would encourage use of this type of decision strategy. Or members of one racial group may regard it as proper to maximize their outcomes and to minimize the outcomes of another racial group, perhaps on grounds of the inherent inferiority of the other group.

Of course, in certain groups an exactly opposite decision strategy may be normatively specified. In some religious groups, for example, members may be admonished to minimize their outcomes and to maximize the outcomes of others. The American family has historically been characterized by a norm specifying that parents should sacrifice for their children, which can also be viewed in terms of a minimize own, maximize others decision strategy.

Lastly, norms may also prescribe that actors in an exchange relationship seek to minimize the difference between their outcomes. In some cases the implication of this norm is that total utility of the actors in the exchange will be maximized as a result. A major emphasis of the current women's liberation movement has been upon a minimization of differences between the outcomes received by men and women in exchange relationships. This may also be interpreted in terms of equity/distributive justice, if the argument for minimizing the discrepancy in outcomes emphasizes the relative inputs of men and women as well. But for our purposes here it can be viewed as simply involving outcomes. Likewise, there allegedly has been a change in American family relations in recent years, involving a minimization of differences between the outcomes received by parents and children. However, commentators on the American family seemingly have diverse views on the nature of this change. Some call attention to a decline in the willingness of parents always to put their children first—a minimization of difference by increasing parents' outcomes relative to children's. Others emphasize the shift from patriarchal to egalitarian family patterns—minimization of differences in outcomes as a result of an increase in the outcomes of children relative to parents. Probably both changes are taking place, though they may be located in different subgroups in American society.

The most universal norm regulating exchange relationships is the norm of reciprocity described by Gouldner (1960). Its significance for exchange relationships equals that of the norm of equity/distributive justice for the outcomes of exchange relationships. The reciprocity norm can simply be stated as "If you give me something, I should give you something." In other words, the recipient of a positive-utility outcome is obligated to repay the giver of that outcome with a positive-utility outcome at some time in the future. Presumably the outcome that is offered as repayment has equal or greater utility than the outcome that has been received.[11]

The norm of reciprocity applies to virtually all exchange situations. Anthropologists have repeatedly described its effect on gift giving in primitive cultures (Mauss 1954). The potlatch ceremonies of the Kwakiutl Indians described by Benedict (1934) represent a variant on the theme—reciprocation in the form of offering a higher-utility outcome than that which has been received. Probably even the most mundane activities in complex societies bear some influence of this norm. Many people's Christmas card lists reflect its influence. More than a few situation comedies have revolved around a married couple's concern about when they are going to have those "dreadful Smiths" over for dinner.

One of the more interesting aspects of the norm of reciprocity is that it may counteract the effects of dependence. Actors who are relatively independent, and who have little need or desire to enter exchange relationships with more dependent actors, may nevertheless reciprocate and complete the exchange simply because they sense an obligation to do so. Failure to reciprocate may very well be associated with the anticipation of negative-utility outcomes, i.e., the disapprobation of third parties: "What will the neighbors say?" or "What will people think of us if we don't do it?" In this way exchange relationships may be established that would have little likelihood of occurring on other grounds.

EXEMPLIFICATION OF THE SUBJECTIVE EXPECTED UTILITY MODEL IN EXCHANGE SITUATIONS

Having completed our discussion of the ramifications of exchange situations for our micro-level choice model, we turn in this section to illustrate the applicability of the model in such situations. First, we shall consider conditions under which exchanges are initiated. We shall next analyze the reciprocation or nonreciprocation of another actor to the initiation of exchange, and we shall conclude with a discussion of the conditions under which exchanges are maintained or terminated.

The Initiation of Exchange Relationships

Assuming a maximizing decision strategy, the model implies that individuals will initiate exchange relationships (i.e., enact alternatives that they believe will result in reciprocation by an other) if the subjective expected utility of an alternative resulting in action of an other is greater than that of alternatives leading to other outcomes. Whether one of an actor's alternatives has that feature will, of course, depend upon the actor's situation at a given point in time and his or her subjective probability and utility estimates based on that situation.

The degree of dependence of an actor will constitute a primary determinant of whether he or she initiates an exchange relationship. In our previous comments we suggested that the subjective expected utility of an alternative leading to exchange is likely to be appreciably higher than the *SEU* of an alternative not leading to exchange if an actor is in a high-dependence situation. Actors in low-dependence situations are more likely to possess nonexchange alternatives with subjective expected utilities equal to, or greater than, exchange alternatives. Therefore the first prediction we can make is that actors with greater dependence are more likely to initiate exchange relationships.

A distinction should be made here concerning the number of goals on which actors are in a situation of dependence. Actors who are dependent on a number of goals (i.e., experiencing deprivation and having a limited number of alternatives for goal fulfillment on those goals) are more likely to initiate an exchange relationship with no specific other. For example, an actor may be visualized as being dependent on two goals, G_1 and G_2, with one alternative, A_1, available for goal fulfillment on G_1 and one alternative, A_2, available for goal fulfillment on G_2. If A_1 constitutes an action directed toward actor B and A_2 an action toward actor C, then, assuming approximately equal amounts of utility were missing on both goals, it would probably make little difference whether A initiated an exchange with B or C. In contrast, another actor dependent on only one goal, G_3, and having one alternative, A_3, an action directed toward actor D, would be more likely to initiate an exchange with a specific other, namely actor D.

In either case, not only will the more dependent actor be more likely to initiate the exchange, but it is also quite likely that he or she will be inclined to offer the other actor an action assumed to have very high utility to the other party in order to ensure reciprocation of the other party. He or she may "sweeten the deal," so to speak. One thinks, for example, of a young man with few female friends inviting the most popular woman on campus to dinner at a place he really cannot afford so that she will agree to go with him. Dependent actors may thereby diminish their own utility because of the costs imposed by an action, but this may be compensated for by the increased subjective probability of the outcome, so that total subjective expected utility is still greater than that of other alternatives. Thus the young man may anticipate that he is making the young woman an offer she can't refuse, even though her acceptance may put a crimp in his social life for a long time thereafter because of the financial cost. Our young man may also anticipate that acceptance of his offer at this point in time will also increase the likelihood of future acceptances of his requests.

If actors are more evenly matched in their degree of dependence than the couple we have just described, then the more dependent party is still more likely to initiate the exchange relationship, but he or she is not as likely to try to offer the other actor an action that has extremely high utility. These observations suggest that actors considering initiating exchange relationships are likely to make some estimate of their potential partner's degree of dependence, or a vicarious dependence estimate. Since the determinants of utility play a part in the determination of the degree of dependence, a vicarious dependence estimate can be based on vicarious utility estimates along with vicarious subjective probability estimates.

These observations further suggest that actors deciding whether or not to initiate an exchange relationship do not think solely in terms of their own self-interest, i.e., maximizing only their own utility. The suitor attempting to gain the young woman's consent with the offer of a lavish dinner is also taking her self-interest into account. If he correctly anticipates her desire to attend the fancy restaurant and she accepts, then he has fulfilled her desires for goal fulfillment as well as his own. At this point also it is difficult to distinguish exchange from power relationships, since the man has essentially gained the woman's compliance via a positive-utility outcome.

Considerations of both one's own and the other's self-interest are probably made more often by dependent actors than by independent actors, simply because of the former's fewer available alternatives and greater deprivation. Failure to consummate the exchange will have greater negative consequences for them than it will for less dependent actors who have more alternatives to which to turn, plus less deprivation. The young woman, for example, who is not hard up for dates can decide whether or not to accept the offer of the luxurious dinner simply in terms of its utility for her. She will very likely have less interest in keeping the exchange going, so will not be particularly concerned about providing the dependent man with high-utility outcomes.

These considerations concerning one's own and the other's self-interest are likely to involve both immediate and future self-interest. Thus the man may not only anticipate that his inviting the woman to a fancy restaurant will increase the likelihood of her accepting, but that buying her an expensive dinner at that restaurant will make it more likely that she will give him a good-night kiss. Thus he perceives the following sequence of events: I invite her to a fancy restaurant; she accepts; I buy her a fancy dinner; she gives me a good-night kiss. Satisfying her self-interest by the two actions on his part actually serves to satisfy his self-interest.

The woman, whom we have assumed is in a less dependent position, will have less incentive to concern herself with the man's self-interest. She may perceive a sequence of events something like this: I accept his invitation; he buys me a fancy dinner; I give him a good-night kiss; he invites me out again. But if being invited out again by the man is not in her self-interest, possibly because it precludes her going out with men she'd rather date, then satisfying his self-interest by giving him a good-night kiss is counterproductive. Thus her response is likely to be to take the dinner and run.

Reciprocation of the Other

According to our model, an other will respond with an action that constitutes a positive-utility outcome for the initiating actor if that action alternative has greater subjective expected utility than any other alternative, again assuming maximization on the part of the other. And the subjective expected utility of reciprocation will be greater than that of nonreciprocation if both the utilities and the subjective probabilities of the outcomes of reciprocation (one of which will be another action on the part of the initiator) are quite high.

A potential reciprocator's subjective probability for an outcome/action by the initiator in response to the reciprocator's action is likely to be quite high if the outcome constitutes an action the initiator has enacted before. Thus the woman we have been describing will be more likely to anticipate that the man will ask her out after he has already done so than if he had not done so previously. In some situations, though, the reciprocator may not anticipate a particular action because it is perceived to be too costly for the initiator to reenact. The woman may, for example, anticipate that the man will not ask her out to a fancy restaurant again because he cannot afford that action more than once.

The utility of an outcome/action by the initiator in response to the reciprocator's action will most likely be high if it provides fulfillment on a goal that has not been fulfilled recently, all other things being equal. Therefore, repetition of an action by the initiator, in response to an action by the reciprocator, is likely to have lower utility than commission of a new action. This means that repetition of an action will have contrasting effects on utilities and subjective probabilities, decreasing the former and increasing the latter. The woman described above is likely to perceive a greater likelihood for a less desirable outcome. Being asked out again is more probable but less valuable in this case.

This outline of possibilities suggests the importance of actors' varying actions in an exchange relationship. An astute exchange participant will be cognizant of a partner's becoming satiated on a particular goal and will increase the partner's subjective expected utility (and his or her own subjective probability for a desired action by the partner) by somehow letting the partner know that a new action offering utility on some unfulfilled goal is possible in the future.

These effects of the recency and similarity of actions enacted in the past and anticipated in the future will be counteracted by the effect of dependence. Thus a dependent reciprocator will be more likely than an independent reciprocator to remain at least somewhat deprived and lacking in alternatives. Consequently the utility of a repeated outcome will not be decreased to the same extent. Furthermore, we can say that dependent actors will, in general, be more likely to reciprocate than will independent ones, simply because they are less likely to have many alternatives available with high subjective expected utilities. Thus exchange relationships are more likely to be established if both parties have high dependence than if they both have low dependence or if they have sharply differing levels of dependence. We have seen, however, that the effects of dependence may be counteracted by the norm of reciprocity. Thus, if there were not norms still prevalent that proscribed a woman's inviting a man out to dinner, we could visualize the woman we have described inviting the man to dinner at a fancy restaurant at some time in the future, even though she was in a situation of low dependence.

The reciprocator in an exchange relationship does have some advantage over the initiator in that he or she can act on the basis of knowledge of the action already taken by the initiator. The initiator has gone out on a limb, in all probability not knowing with certainty what the response of the other will be. The other, however, has the luxury of knowing the initiator's action, and probably will be able to assess his or her potential outcomes with a greater degree of certainty. The woman we have been describing can be virtually certain that the man, having asked her to an expensive restaurant, will buy her a fancy dinner. The reciprocator can maintain this advantaged position by an equivocal response, thereby keeping the initiator "on the ropes," so to speak. The woman may respond to the dinner invitation with a request for time to think about it, for example. This very possibly will be an unanticipated response for the initiator who may be at a loss for the appropriate response on his part.

Initiators of exchange relationships may compensate for their vulnerability in this respect by themselves initiating exchanges with somewhat vague actions. Thus, instead of initiating the exchange with the woman by means of an invitation to dinner, the man may initiate it with a request for information or assistance regarding some problem. Depending upon the woman's response to that alternative—i.e., whether she is friendly or unfriendly—he can then decide whether or not to enact the original alternative.

Again, a situation of high dependence is likely to restrict the maneuverability of both initiators and reciprocators. Dependent reciprocators will be less likely to make a noncommittal response and thereby decrease their chances of receiving an outcome they desire, and dependent initiators will be more likely to enact an alternative with some probability of getting a desired outcome even though the first response of an other may not be very promising. Thus the relative dependence of the parties to an exchange continues to be an important contextual variable.

Our general discussion also points up the fact that an analysis of exchange situations based upon the subjective expected utility model is much more future oriented than the more common analyses of such situations based upon operant psychological models. The actors we have been describing certainly take their experiences into account in making subjective expected utility estimates, but these estimates are directed to the future. Each actor asks himself or herself: "What action is the other actor most likely to enact if I act in a particular way now, and how valuable will that action be to me?" These estimates of future outcomes are not likely to be simple extrapolations of past situations. The situations we have discussed also show the manner in which an individual can think through a future *sequence* of actions on his or her part and reactions by another actor. Our strong conviction, fortified by experience, is that actors do look ahead in these situations, and that they may allow for the occurrence of unique responses by others. The more regularized an exchange relationship becomes over time, however, the more the participants can base their expectations for the future on what has happened in the past, and outcomes may be anticipated with certainty. Thus operant models of exchange relationships become more useful in the analysis of regularized exchanges.

The Maintenance/Termination of Exchange Relationships

An exchange relationship between two actors will be maintained as long as the subjective expected utilities of actions continuing the exchange are greater for both actors than the subjective expected utilities of other actions. It will be terminated when one or both of the actors discover that other alternatives have greater subjective expected utilities than does the alternative of continuation. It takes two to tango, and it obviously takes two actors to have an exchange relationship, with each giving positive-utility outcomes to the other and receiving them from the other. In some situations, therefore, such as those in which contexts are rapidly changing, exchange relationships may be very tenuous phenomena. In our discussion of maintenance/termination we shall primarily concentrate on the conditions promoting termination of an exchange.

The subjective expected utilities of alternatives continuing the exchange will decline for actors if, on the one hand, the subjective probabilities of certain positive-utility outcomes decline. At the outset of an exchange relationship, the subjective probability of a particular outcome may be quite high, perhaps even equal to 1. If, over the course of the exchange, that outcome rarely if ever occurs, its subjective probability is bound to decline and may even reach zero. Thus actors may become certain that they will not receive particular outcomes from the other party in an exchange.

These subjective expected utilities will also decline, on the other hand, if the utilities of anticipated outcomes decrease as well. This will primarily be the result of satiation on the goals that the outcomes fulfill, perhaps as the result of repetitions of actions by the other party. It may also result from changes in actors' goal hierarchies over time. Goals that may have been most important at the beginning of an exchange relationship may gradually become less important as they are fulfilled, and unfulfilled goals may become more important, so that continued lack of fulfillment of them makes the effects of deprivation more severe.

The likelihood of termination will be increased if, simultaneously with the decrease in the subjective expected utilities of alternatives keeping the exchange going, the subjective expected utilities of the alternative of withdrawal or other nonexchange alternatives increase. This development will take place, first, if the subjective probabilities for desired outcomes, given nonexchange alternatives, increase. Second, the actor may become aware of new alternatives likely to bring about desired outcomes. Third, the utilities of the outcomes received as a result of nonexchange alternatives may also increase. This will be most likely for goals that are not being fulfilled by the current exchange relationship.

These changes can easily be described in terms of changes in actors' degrees of dependence. The more dependent an actor is in a given exchange relationship, the less likely he or she will be to terminate that exchange. Thus termination of exchanges will become more likely as actors become less dependent.

Regularization of an exchange relationship over time may be seen as having mixed effects on an actor's degree of dependence. It will decrease deprivation, thereby decreasing dependence, on goals on which it provides fulfillment, but it will increase deprivation, thereby increasing dependence, on goals that are consistently unfulfilled. It will also increase dependence to the extent that it restricts an actor's search for additional sources of goal fulfillment.

The overall effect may be seen as a *decrease* in dependence upon the specific other in the ongoing exchange, and an *increase* in dependence on some other party in another exchange. Thus an actor experiencing these changes will be more likely to terminate the existing exchange relationship *and* to initiate a new exchange relationship with another actor. These actions will become even more likely if the actor becomes aware of the possibility of new alternatives leading to exchanges with new actors.

We have previously suggested the importance of variation in the actions enacted by participants in an exchange if they desire to maintain the exchange. This prevents or at least decreases the likelihood of the development we have just described—satiation on a few goals and severe deprivation on others. It may well be that exchanges will also have greater longevity if their participants provide each other with satisfactory, but not maximum, goal fulfillment on a large number of goals than if they provide satiation on a few goals and nothing on others. Complete deprivation is likely to induce a search for alternatives that will provide goal fulfillment.

An exchange relationship may not actually reach the point of termination even though the changes we are describing take place. For one thing, a discontented exchange partner may decide to remain with the exchange because of the high probabilities of negative-utility outcomes associated with withdrawal. He or she may regard leaving the exchange relationship as a very serious violation of a major norm, and consequently may fear receiving negative utilities from a number of other actors. Or the dissatisfied party may simply not come up with any alternatives likely to result in fulfillment of the unfulfilled goals. Withdrawal may also not be a viable option if the actor is concerned about the negative utility such an action would have for the exchange partner. In addition, the existence of a commitment to the relationship on the part of the unhappy actor will also reduce the likelihood of termination, since it is probable that the actor will first have to take the step of breaking the commitment before he or she can actually consider whether or not to withdraw from the relationship.

We shall illustrate the process we have been describing by means of the currently rather common phenomenon of the breakup of a marriage relationship, attempting not to be too stereotypical in our comments. One can imagine a married couple developing a highly regularized exchange relationship over a period of years. During this period each party has developed a patterned repertoire of actions and reactions so that each can anticipate the other's actions with virtual certainty. Action alternatives that provided each with minimal utility early in the relationship have gradually been discarded, so that unanticipated responses rarely occur. The increased certainty regarding the other's actions has brought to the relationship a level of comfort that was not present earlier in their relationship when each had to evaluate more actively the probable responses of the other.

In the process the amounts of utility received by each from the other's actions have also become quite standardized. Each knows that the other can be counted upon to provide goal fulfillment within a narrowly defined range on some goals and to provide little or no goal fulfillment on other goals. Dependence on the other has undoubtedly also increased in the course of the relationship, as each has relied upon the other to meet most of his or her goals. The division of labor that has developed in regard to many daily activities and in the rearing of children has also contributed to this situation of mutual dependence. Very likely the marriage ritual itself represented for each party a commitment by the other to the relationship, thus removing concern about the other's departure from the relationship.

This routinized exchange relationship, although perhaps exaggerated, may constitute a secure and satisfying base for many married couples. But for other couples the evidence shows that the security associated with routinization is not sufficiently satisfying to maintain the exchange relationship. Our previous comments suggest that such a relationship will not be maintained when it no longer provides greater subjective expected utility than other alternatives for one or both of the participants. We have also suggested that this will result from a decrease in the utility of outcomes and decreases in the subjective probabilities for some relatively high-utility outcomes. Declines in the utility of outcomes may stem from several causes. The importance of goals that are consistently being fulfilled may decrease. One spouse may discover, for example, that having financial security has become less important. Or the desired level of goal fulfillment may decrease on some goals, so that satiation is more likely to occur. The talkativeness of a spouse may overfulfill one's desire for conversation after a period of time. One's spouse may also simply be providing smaller and smaller amounts of goal fulfillment. The effusive show of affection of the past may have turned into the ritualized peck on the cheek of the present.

The pattern of countless actions and reactions, or failures to react, will have resulted in quite precise subjective probability estimates. A wife may have given up on asking her husband for assistance on various projects because of his consistent failure to respond. A husband may have come to the conclusion that his wife will never show interest in his career. If these are relatively important goals, then increasing deprivation will be experienced by both of these individuals.

Meanwhile the importance of unfulfilled goals may have been increasing. Receiving assistance from her husband may have become increasingly important for a wife, as may having one's wife show interest in one's career for a husband. Consequently the utilities of outcomes fulfilling these goals will be increasing. Both parties may also be inferring that other alternatives providing these outcomes are available to them. A wife may discover that she can perform certain tasks without her husband's assistance and thereby derive a great deal of satisfaction. A husband may discover that other people are much more interested in discussing his career with him. Thus dependence on the spouse will decrease and these other alternatives will gain in subjective expected utility.

Termination of the relationship will be speeded up by the examples of other similarly situated couples successfully terminating their marriage relationships. Our couple may come to estimate the probabilities of positive-utility outcomes as being very high and those of negative-utility outcomes resulting from termination as very low. What at one point in the relationship had not even been considered as an alternative may now become the alternative with greatest subjective expected utility.

Although our scenario has been rather simplistic, it does square with many popular accounts of the causes of increases in the incidence of divorce, particularly among older married couples. Marital dissolutions occurring during the "empty nest" period, for example, often involve some of the changes we have described. Other factors, which can be explained in terms of our exchange model, have also played a part. Thus a decline in public disapproval of divorces has meant that couples run less risk of being stigmatized for ending a marriage. Increasing participation of women in the labor force has decreased their financial dependence upon their spouses, so that withdrawal from the relationship becomes a viable option for them. So, given knowledge of actors' goal hierarchies, their repertoires of alternatives, and their utilities and subjective probabilities, the exchange model we have presented has the potential to predict situations under which exchange relationships, such as marriages, are likely to be maintained or terminated.

EXCHANGE RELATIONSHIPS AND INTERGROUP PROCESSES

Most of our discussion, and accompanying examples, has dealt with interpersonal exchanges. Our model is intended to be applicable to intergroup exchanges as well. Using it for an analysis of intergroup exchanges, of course, requires solution of the problem of aggregating the various components of the model to the macro level. It will always be difficult at this level to speak about actors with the same concreteness that one can speak about actors, and their utilities and subjective probabilities, at the micro level. It will be especially difficult to distinguish between exchange and power processes at the macro level because of the need we have shown to have some knowledge of actors' internal states to make that distinction. Nevertheless, we shall suggest here some general characteristics of intergroup exchanges.

Members of any group will be inclined to initiate exchanges with another group when they perceive that the other group is likely to provide them with high-utility outcomes. Exchange with another group becomes more likely as the likelihood of obtaining desired outcomes by means of unilateral group actions decreases. Thus the early planters in the New World saw rather quickly the limited feasibility of conducting their agricultural enterprises on their own, or with the assistance of wage labor, and the greater viability of using slave labor for these purposes.

Similarly, members of the second group will be more likely to reciprocate the exchange if they too perceive a higher probability of getting outcomes that they desire through reciprocation than through nonreciprocation. It is at this point in the establishment of an exchange relationship that it is most difficult to determine whether the relationship between the two groups is in fact an exchange, or whether it is in actuality a power situation masquerading as exchange. Reciprocation on the part of a group may have greater subjective expected utility than other alternatives, but the alternative of nonreciprocation may carry with it the likelihood of dire consequences carried out by the initiator. Thus it would be stretching the model too much to claim that slaves entered their exchange relationship with slave owners because of the positive-utility outcomes they thought they would realize by doing so.

Exchange relationships between groups will be maintained as long as both groups are satisfied with them. As in a personal exchange, a period of time may be required before the exchange stabilizes into a pattern of actions and reactions and of relative outcomes from the exchange. Both groups will have to find which action alternatives work for them and which do not. Or, to put it succinctly, they have to find out how much to give, in order to get. Since groups do not constitute a specific entity in the sense that individual actors do, exchange relationships between them may never become stabilized to the extent that personal exchanges do. Segments of the groups may settle into routinized patterns, whereas other segments may continue to experiment with a variety of alternatives.

Termination of an exchange relationship between groups will result if one, or both, of the groups sees the possibility of establishing a better exchange with another group or believes desired outcomes can be obtained outside an exchange relationship. For example, when indigenous Indian slaves proved intractable, Caribbean slave owners terminated their exchanges with them (largely by killing most of them off) and instituted a slavery relationship with more malleable blacks imported from Africa.

Dependence will be as important for group exchanges as for individual exchanges. And, for groups, the degree of dependence will be a function, first, of how severely they are deprived and, second, of their resources, which will determine the alternatives available to them. If a group lacks resources but has no unfulfilled goals, then it is not likely to be dependent.

The more dependent a group is, the more likely it will be to initiate an exchange with another group. Likewise, the more dependent a group is, the more likely it is to respond to an exchange initiated by another group. The dependent group's lack of resources will preclude its obtaining unfulfilled goals on its own or seeking out other groups with which to establish exchanges. And, if two groups are dependent on each other, exchange relationships between them will have the greatest probability of being established.

Group exchanges may be characterized by a gross inequality in relative outcomes, a situation that might be regarded as exploitation. But this disparity in outcomes may be consonant with both groups acting so as to maximize their subjective expected utilities. We anticipate that the more dependent of the groups will receive the lesser outcomes, but that these will still surpass the probable consequences of any other alternatives on their part because of their limited opportunities.

Lastly, dependence will also be significant for the maintenance or termination of group exchanges. Exchanges in which the groups are approximately equally dependent on each other will have the greatest staying power. If there are discrepancies in dependence, then the more dependent group will be the one less likely to terminate the exchange, which suggests that the American slave owners were more dependent on their slaves than vice versa.

The characteristics of specific intergroup exchanges clearly need to be more systematically explored than we have been able to do here. But we hope that our general observations in this regard exemplify the applicability of our model of exchange relationships to the macro level.

AN EXCHANGE MODEL

Figure 5.4 presents a simplified summation of the processes we have discussed in this chapter. In this model we see that in an exchange relationship the primary determinant of initiation, of reciprocation, and of maintenance or termination is the relative subjective expected utility of an action alternative intended to result in exchange. This relative subjective expected utility is, of course, combined with the actor's decision strategy, and with vicarious utility estimates in cases in which the other actor's utility is relevant to a decision strategy, to determine an actor's actual choice of an alternative.

Relative subjective expected utility is determined from a comparison of the subjective expected utilities of exchange and nonexchange alternatives. These are determined by the utility and subjective probability determinants described in our previous chapters. (To simplify figure 5.4 we have lumped all the determinants for utilities and subjective probabilities into two blocks. The reader may refer to figure 4.6 to refresh his or her memory concerning these determinants and their interrelationships.)

The model includes the factors and their effects that we have claimed to be significant in exchange relationships. On the utility side of the model (the left-hand side) we see that vicarious utility, or estimates of the utility of one's own actions for the other, enters as an influence on the determinants of utility, specifically influencing the degree of goal fulfillment determinant. The primacy of the exchange is a second factor influencing the utility determinants, affecting goal importance, the desired level of goal fulfillment, and the current level of goal fulfillment. On the subjective probability side (the right-hand side) we see the influence of the presence of third parties on the subjective probability determinants.

Two variables influence both sides of the model. The degree of trust influences utility estimates primarily through its effects on the immediacy of goal fulfillment determinant. It affects subjective probability estimates by decreasing the subjective probabilities of certain outcomes, such as withdrawal, and increasing others, those for positive-utility outcomes.

The degree of dependence, which we have described as a major contextual influence in exchange situations, affects both utilities and subjective probabilities. It is itself a multiplicative function of the degree of deprivation, which is determined primarily by the goal fulfillment deprivation gap, and the number of alternatives available, which is a function of an actor's resources. The degree of dependence's major influence is to increase the relative subjective expected utility of an exchange alternative. It does this by both decreasing the subjective expected utilities of nonexchange alternatives and increasing the subjective expected utilities of exchange alternatives. On the utility side, it does the latter by influencing the goal importance determinant and by affecting the influence of the immediacy of goal fulfillment determinant. On the subjective probability side, it does both by reducing and increasing the subjective probabilities of the outcomes of nonexchange and exchange alternatives respectively. The degree of deprivation also contributes to the ultimate relative subjective expected utility of an exchange alternative through its effects on the degree of goal fulfillment perceived by actors.

The effects of several other significant factors are also represented in figure 5.4. First, the degree of commitment influences the set of alternatives considered by an actor, precluding alternatives like withdrawal. Norms constitute a major contextual influence, affecting the degree of commitment, the set of alternatives considered, the subjective probabilities of certain outcomes, and actors' decision strategies. Finally, the degree to which an exchange is regularized has pervasive effects in the model. Regularization affects vicarious utility estimates directly, and also indirectly, through its promotion of emotional identification with others. It influences the utility and subjective probability determinants and the degree of dependence. And it also partially affects the set of alternatives

Figure 5.4. Model of Exchange Processes

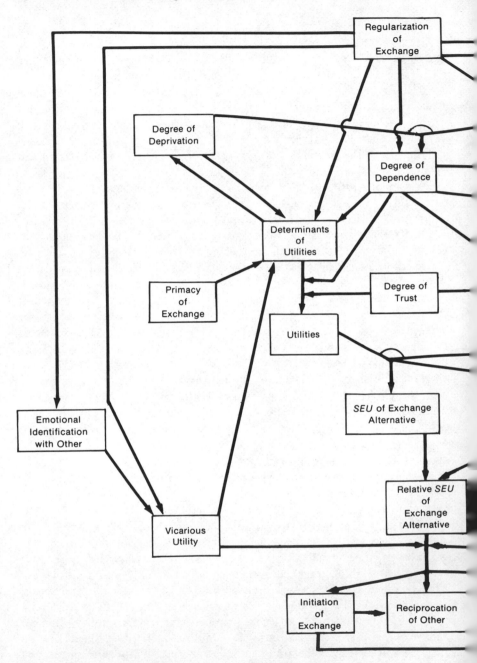

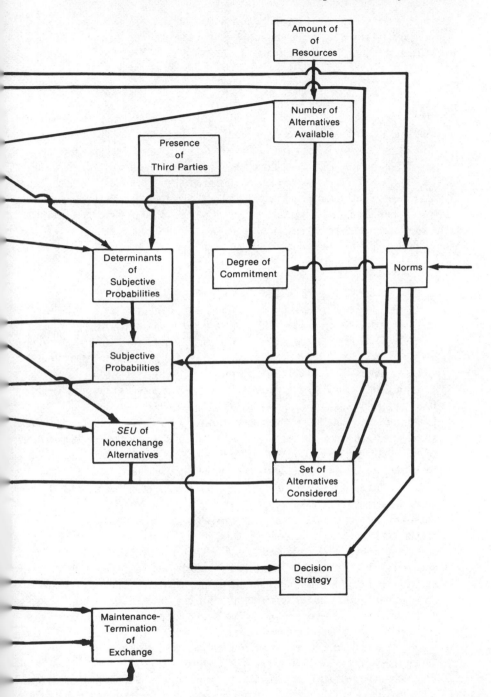

considered by an actor and partially promotes the development of normative expectations influencing the exchange. Other exogenous determinants of such norms are not included in this model.

SUMMARY

In this chapter we have added a second actor to our basic model of choice behavior and have analyzed exchange relationships between actors by means of this model. After specifying the nature of exchange relationships and exemplifying the application of the subjective expected utility model to them, we looked at the effects of two major contextual influences—dependence and norms—on them and on the conditions under which they are most likely to be initiated, established, and maintained or terminated. We have included examples of both interpersonal and intergroup exchanges to show the applicability of the model to both the micro and macro levels.

NOTES

1. Emerson (1969) refers to them as productive exchanges.
2. Our reference to vicarious utility differs slightly from that of Valvanis (1958). He refers to the utility an actor obtains from others' deriving utility as "vicarious utility," while we use the term to refer to any estimates an actor makes of another actor's utilities.
3. Alternatives A_1 and A_2 considered at time $t + 2$ may be the same or different alternatives than were considered at time t.
4. It is interesting that most laboratory studies of exchange situations do not allow for postponing the reception of outcomes for any appreciable period of time. This appears to be a variable that should be taken into account if such studies are to be generalizable to real-world situations.
5. Here we do not represent the entire conditional probability used above because we assume that $P(B_{1_{t+2}}|A_{1_t}) + P(B_{2_{t+2}}|A_{1_t}) = 1$.
6. Different writers use different terms to refer to these decision strategies. Maximizing one's own outcome is called "rationality" by Meeker (1971) and "self-interest" by Lane and Messé (1971). Both Meeker and Lane and Messé regard "altruism" as maximizing other's outcome, and Meeker and Pepitone (1971) both define maximizing the difference between outcomes as "competition." Meeker refers to maximizing total utility of both actors as "group-gain," whereas Pepitone calls it "cooperation" and Lane and Messé label it "reward maximization." Of these writers, only Lane and Messé deal with the strategy of minimizing the difference in outcomes, which they refer to as the strategy of "equality."
7. Emerson (1972b) also emphasizes the similarity of exchange and power relationships. For him one actor's power over another is approximately the same as the other actor's dependence on that actor.

8. One might make a distinction between actual, or objective, dependence, and perceived, or subjective, dependence. The former would refer to the actual objective number of alternatives available to an actor, and the latter to the number of alternatives the actor believes to be available to him or her. Our discussion of dependence is of perceived dependence, since we assume that actors act on the basis of their perceptions rather than of their objective situations. There may, of course, be discrepancies between the two types of dependence. Actors may be unaware of alternatives available to them, or they may believe alternatives are available that actually are not. In either case they will act on the basis of their erroneous expectations and not on the basis of the actual situation.

9. Emerson (1972*b*) makes the same argument in his discussion of balanced and unbalanced exchanges. Balanced exchanges have equal levels of dependence, whereas they are unequal in unbalanced exchanges. Emerson also claims that unbalanced exchanges tend to become balanced. They may do that, but they may also be terminated.

10. Simpson (1972) has argued that exchange theorists have not paid sufficient attention to the effects of norms on exchanges.

11. The ancient maxim "An eye for an eye and a tooth for a tooth" may be described as a norm of *negative* reciprocity.

CHAPTER 6

Equity and Distributive Justice

WE CONTINUE our analysis of exchange relationships in this chapter with an analysis of an aspect that is characteristic of most exchange situations. This involves the equity or distributive justice judgments that are made by the participants in an exchange, or by interested third parties. For this analysis we will use the insights of two bodies of literature that have developed rather independently of each other. The first of these, equity theory, has its basis in exchange theory and, as the name implies, uses the concept of equity. The other, status-value theory, does not generally deal with exchange per se, but its insights regarding distributive justice can be applied to exchange situations. We believe that the concepts equity and distributive justice are sufficiently similar that they can be treated as synonyms. The fact that Homans (1961, 1974), who writes from the perspective of exchange theory, refers to the "rule of distributive justice" in discussing inequitable exchanges shows that there is overlap between the two approaches (cf. Cook and Parcel 1977 for a comparison of these two approaches).

Whether one is talking about equity or about distributive justice judgments regarding exchange relationships, it is clear that neither concept refers simply to the *outcomes* of exchanges. Rather, both concepts are concerned with the *relationships* between each party's outcomes from the exchange and what each party contributes to the exchange. The equity theorists emphasize the relative *inputs* of the two parties to an exchange and compare them with their relative outcomes. The status-value theorists emphasize the relationships between outcomes and the *social characteristics* of actors. In the former case inequity is said to exist when there is an imbalance between relative inputs and relative outcomes. In the latter case distributive injustice is said to exist when there is an imbalance between social characteristics and outcomes.

Inequitable or unjust exchange relationships are assumed to be less stable than equitable or just ones because the participants are likely to be dissatisfied

222

with them and are predisposed to act to decrease the degree of injustice or inequity. This may involve attempting to change the conditions under which the exchange is occurring, or it may lead to termination of the exchange altogether. We shall see, though, that the capacity of the partners in an exchange to effect these changes will be greatly influenced, like their exchange relationship in general, by their relative degrees of dependence. Inequitable exchanges may be maintained for a long period of time if there are substantial differences in the participants' degrees of dependence.

So, whether one refers to these phenomena in terms of equity–inequity or distributive justice–injustice, they constitute a significant component of exchange relationships. Furthermore, these concepts are of particular relevance for *intergroup* relationships, where judgments regarding *collective* injustice may be made, even though they have been most completely analyzed in regard to exchanges between individuals. Groups, like individuals, may develop ongoing exchange relationships characterized by equity or distributive justice, with each group's outcomes in balance with its inputs and/or other characteristics. But they may also become locked into inequitable exchanges, with one group gaining relatively more from the exchange than another group. Exchanges between racial groups, for example, or between classes or occupational categories, may be regarded by their participants as inequitable and yet may continue indefinitely. Thus a detailed analysis of the characteristics of inequitable exchanges at the micro level will provide illumination of the conditions responsible for these phenomena at the macro level.

RELATIONSHIP TO OTHER CONCEPTS

Each of the concepts we are considering is quite similar to several other sociological concepts. The first of these related concepts is status congruence, or its opposite, status inconsistency, which Homans (1974) has related to distributive justice. Status inconsistency arises from individuals' occupying discrepant positions on different dimensions of social status. For example, one may rank relatively higher on the prestige dimension than on the class dimension, where the latter represents the objective amount of monetary wealth and property possessed by an individual. Status inconsistency may involve either a comparison between the positions of one actor and the positions of another specific actor on these dimensions or a comparison between the actor and some general class of actors. We shall see that either type of comparison may be involved in an equity/distributive justice evaluation. And implicit in the status inconsistency case is a norm or standard that says that actors should occupy relatively similar positions on different dimensions of social status. A comparable standard is found in equity/distributive justice situations as well.

Relative deprivation is a second related concept, noted by Zelditch, Berger, Anderson, and Cohen (1970), who refer to inequity as a form of relative deprivation. It, too, may involve a comparison with a specific other actor or with a general class of actors. But in this case the most obvious component of the comparison is the outcomes of the actors. An actor is believed to feel relatively deprived if his or her outcomes are not equal to those of another actor or actors. Nevertheless, other components are also compared, albeit somewhat less obviously than the comparison of outcomes. Selection of the appropriate object of comparison is crucial for the determination of the existence of relative deprivation (as it will also be for equity), and this object will be selected either on the basis of having contributed similar inputs (I worked as hard as he did, so I should get as much as he does) or on the basis of possession of similar social characteristics (I am not getting as much as other people in my position).

The concept of discrimination, which we discuss at length in chapters 10 through 12, is not often linked with either equity or distributive justice. Yet it involves comparative processes similar to those characterizing equity/distributive justice judgments. It also involves a comparison of one's own and others' outcomes, and the other may be a specific other or a generalized class of others. However, it differs slightly from equity/distributive justice evaluations in that a greater emphasis is placed upon actors' social characteristics. Discrimination is perceived to exist when unequal outcomes are believed to result from the social characteristics contributed by actors. It also differs in that it occurs primarily in situations of indirect exchange and the issue of the legitimacy of a distribution rule (topics we shall discuss later) is more relevant (Cook 1975; Leventhal 1976). Equity judgments are characteristic of situations of direct and indirect exchange, and the legitimacy of a distribution rule may be somewhat less problematic for situations involving equity judgments.

Exploitation is the sociological concept that probably relates most closely to the concepts of equity and distributive justice. The Marxian sense of exploitation—the appropriation of the surplus value of workers by the proprietors of capital (Nikolinakos 1973)—implies an inequitable exchange between the proletariat and capitalist classes. Non-Marxist writers (Gouldner 1960; Rapoport 1967; Gergen 1969) have conceptualized exploitation similarly, emphasizing the greater rewards of one party at the expense of another.

The exploitation concept has been widely and loosely used in sociological discussions of macro-level phenomena. Minority groups are described as being exploited by dominant groups, workers by employers, peasants by landowners, and women by men. In some cases the term has accumulated additional connotations. For instance, it is generally applied to situations of long-term inequity, often involving sizable differences between the parties. Second, it sometimes includes the proviso that the inequity is intentionally perpetrated by the party who is benefiting from an exchange. Thus, Walster and Walster (1975) claim that it is conventional to label the party *intentionally* taking the larger relative outcome in an exchange as the exploiter. Third, the concept also sometimes includes the notion that one party is somehow "using" the other party to attain his or her own goals, implying disregard for the other party's goals (Walster, Walster, and Berscheid 1978). Even with the inclusion of these connotations we believe it is possible and preferable to regard exploitation as a type of inequitable situation.

A crucial issue for the concepts of exploitation and equity/distributive justice is whether they can be objectively measured. Marx assumed an objective measure of exploitation was possible, based upon his labor theory of value. Moore (1966: 471) has also argued that exploitation is an objective phenomenon that should be discernible to a detached observer. We agree with Homans (1974:251), however, that an objective measure of exploitation is not possible and that it can only exist at the perceptual level. Since no objective measure is possible, the likelihood of disagreements regarding its presence in specific exchanges is very great, a point we shall have occasion to reiterate later in this chapter.

CURRENT APPROACHES TO ANALYSIS

We said that two bodies of sociological literature are relevant to our topic: equity theory, which has generally emphasized equity or inequity, and status-value theory, which has been more inclined to speak in terms of distributive justice or injustice. We shall look first at their contributions to the current state of the arts regarding these concepts.

Equity Theory and Equity–Inequity

The theoretical approach to equity that has its roots in exchange theory is best exemplified by the writings of Homans (1961, 1974), Blau (1964a, 1964b), and Adams (1963, 1965). Although there are some differences in their approaches, the distinguishing characteristics of equity judgments are quite clear.

Homans's perception of the nature of distributive justice, which he defines as "justice in the distribution of rewards and costs between persons" (1961:74), is summed up in his well-known rule of distributive justice: "A man in an exchange relation with another will expect that the rewards of each man be proportional to his costs—the greater the rewards, the greater the costs—and that the net rewards, or profits, of each man be proportional to his investments—the greater the investments, the greater the profit" (1961:75). It should be noted that this rule actually specifies *two* rules that must be met if distributive justice is to hold. First, rewards must be proportional to costs and, second, profits must be proportional to investments.

In his 1974 revision of *Social Behavior* he lists three components of comparisons that enter into distributive justice judgments: "What a man gives . . . , which includes his perceived costs, what he gets (that is, his rewards) and what we have called his investments" (p. 248). Investments consist of the background characteristics the actor brings into the exchange, both ascribed and achieved. He has also revised his rule of distributive justice in this later work. Now only one rule is presented: investments and what one gives must be proportional to rewards, or what one gets (1974:245, 248).[1] But proportionality of whatever components are compared remains the essential relational characteristic. The rule of distributive justice is presumably a universal standard for Homans. The comparisons an actor makes tend to be with other actors to whom he or she is close or similar and especially with those with whom he or she is in direct exchange.

Homans has also provided a well-known description of the emotional consequences of violation of the rule of distributive justice: "The more to a man's disadvantage the rule of distributive justice fails of realization, the more likely he is to display the emotional behavior we call anger" (1961:75). In other words, the more an actor is the victim of injustice, the madder he or she will be. He does not indicate whether this anger is the result of unfulfilled expectations or of the feeling that a norm has been violated, but he does suggest that anger will result only if the victim of injustice sees it as the result of the action of someone other than himself or herself (1974:257). Homans also suggests two possible behavioral responses to injustice. Victims will try to increase their rewards, and the beneficiaries of injustice will contribute more to the exchange in order to increase their partner's rewards, but only if the cost is not too great for them (1974:268).

Blau's view (1964a, 1964b) of distributive justice differs from Homans's at several significant points. For him, the standard of distributive justice is clearly a relative social norm and not a universal. Thus it will vary in different times and places. He describes the standard as analogous to a fair rate of economic exchange, contrasting it with the going rate of exchange determined by the factors of supply and demand. The distributive justice standard may be viewed as being "superimposed" upon the primary exchange of actions and outcomes within a situation.

Since distributive justice "refers to the relationship between the returns received for services rendered and the investment costs incurred in order to be able to render them" (1964a:68), the variable standard of distributive justice is based on a comparison of rewards and investments. However, Blau is insistent that the investments included in distributive justice considerations do not include actors' ascribed characteristics. They only include the actions contributed by the participants in an exchange. Furthermore, the actual content of the standard will be determined both by the prevalent values and norms in a society and by an actor's reference group, whose average reward provides a baseline for such comparisons.

The existence of a fair rate of exchange (or standard of distributive justice) is necessary for a situation of inequity or distributive injustice to exist, according to Blau. Violation of the going rate of exchange can only result in disappointment, while violation of the fair rate of exchange results in the moral indignation characteristic of normative violations, and hence of situations of distributive injustice.

Of the three equity theorists we are considering, Adams (1965) has emphasized most strongly that the comparison involved in an equity situation is between an actor and a specific other actor. This comparison involves the outcome/input ratios of the actors. Outcomes and inputs are not precisely specified but are determined by the perceptions of the parties involved on the basis of their relevance for a particular exchange. Thus the actors' social characteristics may or may not be included within the ratios. Exchanges are perceived as equitable if the actors' outcome/input ratios are equal. Departures from equality of these ratios constitute situations of inequity. Like Homans, Adams appears to regard the standard of equity as a universal.

Adams (1965) has also discussed the consequences of inequity in detail, and we shall summarize his discussion in detail later in this chapter. Many other theorists and researchers have followed Adams's lead and concentrated upon the consequences of inequitable situations rather than upon the logically prior issue of the conditions under which equity judgments are made (Cook 1973).

Status-value Theory

The status-value approach to equity/distributive justice is represented by theorists such as Anderson, Berger, Zelditch, and Cohen (1969); Zelditch et al. (1970); and Berger, Zelditch, Anderson, and Cohen (1972). These theorists have filled some of the gaps in the exchange approach while they have paid relatively little attention to some of the areas that the exchange approach emphasizes most. They have concentrated upon the nature of equity/distributive justice evaluations and the conditions under which they are made, whereas the exchange theorists have focused upon the resolution of inequitable or unjust situations (Cook 1973, 1975). Thus a combination of the two approaches conceivably offers the potential for a comprehensive synthetic theory of equity/ distributive justice.

The contrast between the exchange and status-value approaches can be seen from an analysis of several major issues. First, the status-value approach regards distributive justice situations as involving comparisons between actors and *generalized* others rather than specific other actors. Comparisons between individuals and specific actors constitute *local* comparisons, which are not sufficient for judgments of distributive justice or injustice. Comparison of oneself to a generalized other constitutes a *referential* comparison, the basis of such judgments.

Second, the comparisons made involve actors' social characteristics and the outcomes they receive, which are termed *states* and *goal-objects* respectively. Moreover, it is the *status* values of the characteristics and outcomes that are significant (hence the designation of the approach as the status-value approach) rather than their consummatory or gratificational values.

Third, the standard of distributive justice applicable in a situation is derived from the referential structure. Specifically, if states and goal-objects are correlated for generalized others in the referential structure, then they should also be correlated in the local system. Or the "is" relationships between states and goal-objects in the referential structure are translated into "ought" relationships between states and goal-objects in the local structure. Thus the rule of distributive justice can be stated as "A state of *distributive justice* exists in S* if and only if all association relations between characteristics and goal-objects coincide with relevance relations in the local system. Otherwise a state of *injustice* exists in S*" (Berger et al. 1972:141).[2] (Italics in the original.) Association relations, or the actual correlation of states and goal-objects, must be the same as the relevance relations, or expectations, created by the perceived correlation between states and goal-objects of generalized others in the referential structure for distributive justice to exist.

Fourth, the failure of outcomes to live up to expectations does not yield a situation of distributive injustice unless the expectations are based upon the referential structure. If outcomes are not correlated with social characteristics in the way that they are perceived in the referential structure the result will be the indignation characteristic of a situation of distributive injustice. This is very similar to Blau's distinction (1964a) between the disappointment resulting from violations of the going rate of exchange and the indignation accompanying violations of the fair rate of exchange, the latter also having a referential basis outside the specific parties in exchange.

Fifth, the status-value approach has taken a somewhat different tack in regard to the behavioral consequences of unjust situations, emphasizing appeals to third parties and the probable tendency of victims and beneficiaries of injustice to prefer interaction with others similar to themselves than with equitables. They have also made an important distinction between individual and collective injustice, suggesting that the two will not be identical (Anderson et al. 1969). Determining the conditions under which a group of actors arrive at a judgment of collective injustice will be of major significance at the macro level.

FRAMEWORK FOR A THEORY

From our preceding discussion of the exchange and status-value approaches to the issue of equity and distributive justice one can see substantial points of agreement between the two approaches. One can also infer the characteristics of situations in which equity/distributive justice judgments are made as well as the nature of these judgments. These can be summarized as follows:

1. They may be made in situations of *direct* or *indirect* exchange.
2. They involve *comparisons* between the actors participating in those exchanges or between an actor and some generalized other. The exchange approach emphasizes the former, the status-value approach the latter.[3]
3. These comparisons involve the *relationships* among the actors' *social characteristics,* the *actions* (or inputs) they contribute to exchanges, and the *outcomes* they receive from exchanges. The approach based on exchange theory emphasizes actions and outcomes (Adams) or all three (Homans and Blau.) The status-value approach concentrates on characteristics and outcomes.
4. The comparison is made on the basis of some *standard,* or rule, of distributive justice.

5. The comparisons result in *emotional responses* of satisfaction or dissatisfaction, depending upon the degree and direction of the inequity or distributive injustice that is perceived to exist.
6. These emotional reactions lead to *behavioral responses* that are intended to modify the existing distribution of inputs and/or outcomes. The equity approach has developed this aspect most fully.

Inadequacies of Current Approaches

Although both of the approaches we have considered have developed substantial literatures, a number of questions regarding equity and distributive justice remain unanswered. Among the most important are the following:

1. Under what conditions are equity/distributive justice evaluations made? Do they occur in all exchanges, or only in exchanges with certain characteristics?
2. What determines whether a specific or a generalized other is the object of comparison?
3. What components are compared in equity/distributive justice evaluations—outcomes and inputs, investments and profits, rewards and costs, or social characteristics and outcomes? Are the same components used in all situations? In addition, what do these components consist of, e.g., what is an "input"?
4. What standards are used under what conditions? Is there a universal standard of equity/distributive justice or do standards vary across situations? Some theorists have referred to the standard as a distribution rule (Cook 1973, 1975; Leventhal 1976). With this terminology the question becomes: Under what conditions are which distribution rules applied?
5. How exactly do emotional responses vary with the degree and direction of inequity/distributive injustice? For example, is anger a linear or a nonlinear function of the degree of inequity? How do the emotional reactions of victims and beneficiaries of inequity differ?
6. Under what conditions do which behavioral responses to inequitable or unjust situations occur?
7. What are the implications of different types of exchange situation, i.e., direct versus indirect, for equity/distributive justice judgments?
8. What are the ramifications of different types and degrees of inequity for the continuation of exchange relationships? Does inequity lead to a termination of an exchange, or are there conditions under which exchanges will be continued even though they are inequitable?

In the following section we will attempt to provide answers to these basic questions by presenting our own theoretical framework for the analysis of equity/distributive justice judgments. We will then look in detail at the responses of exchange participants to situations of inequity–injustice, following which we will explore the implications of inequity for exchange situations. We will see that dependence is an important factor influencing the nature and effects of equity/ distributive justice judgments and promoting inequitable exchanges, as we have previously shown it to be for exchange situations in general. Lastly, we shall show how inequity judgments are incorporated in the subjective expected utility model.

Basic Variables

Seven basic variables that can be used to characterize equity/distributive justice situations are identifiable as follows:

1. *Type of Exchange.* Equity/distributive justice judgments may be made in situations of direct exchange, involving only two actors, or in indirect-exchange situations, involving a third actor allocating outcomes to two other actors in exchange for their inputs (Adams 1965). In this chapter we will primarily consider direct-exchange situations, leaving a discussion of indirect exchanges for chapters 10 through 12, in which we discuss discrimination. A major difference between the two types of exchange is that in direct exchanges the other actor will be perceived as the source of inequity, if it is believed to exist, whereas in indirect exchanges the source of perceived inequity will be the allocator.[4] Consequently actions taken to modify the inequity will probably be directed at different actors in the two situations.

2. *Basis of Judgment.* We have noted that actors may compare themselves to specific other actors or to some generalized other. We shall refer to specific bases of equity/distributive justice judgments in the former case and to generalized bases in the latter case.

3. *Criteria of Judgment.* Three different criteria are available for equity/ distributive justice judgments: (1) actors' outcomes, i.e., the actions, with their associated utilities, that they receive in an exchange; (2) actors' inputs, i.e., the actions they enact in an exchange; and (3) their social characteristics, both ascribed and achieved. We refer to these as outcomes, inputs, and characteristics respectively.

4. *Standard of Judgment.* A relationship among these criteria constitutes the base against which an actual exchange is compared. We shall deal with two different standards: equality, or proportionality, and similarity.[5]

5. *Type of Inequity.* Inequity may be perceived to exist because one or more of the three criteria—outcomes, inputs, and characteristics—are disproportionate for the actors in an exchange. Thus a distinction can be made between inequitable situations on the basis of which one(s) of the criteria is (are) perceived to be unequal, disproportionate, or dissimilar.

6. *Direction of Inequity.* Actors may be either the beneficiaries or the victims of inequitable exchanges. Someone benefiting in an inequitable exchange will be regarded as being in a situation of *positive* inequity; the victim of inequity will be considered to be in a situation of *negative* inequity.

7. *Degree of Inequity.* The extent to which an exchange is inequitable or unjust will be determined by the extent to which it deviates from the standard

being applied to a particular exchange situation by its participants. Obviously the greater the departure from the standard, the greater the degree of inequity.

Later we shall also discuss the emotional and behavioral responses stemming from inequitable situations. Because these responses constitute multidimensional variables we have not included them as basic variables in our theoretical framework. As we shall show, one must consider the emotional, cognitive, and behavioral responses of those experiencing both positive and negative inequity.

COMPONENTS OF A THEORY: BASIS AND CRITERIA

Conditions under Which Equity Judgments Are Made

The first question we have raised regarding equity/distributive justice judgments concerns the conditions that prompt these judgments to be made. The available literature provides little guidance on this issue (Cook 1973; Cook and Parcel 1977; Walster, Berscheid, and Walster 1973). However, several characteristics of exchange situations that increase the likelihood of equity/distributive justice judgments' being made can be suggested. First, we anticipate that such judgments will be more likely in direct exchanges than in indirect exchanges. This may be simply due to the relatively greater visibility of the former. An actor in a direct exchange, since he or she is both giving and receiving action-outcomes, can more easily see what each party is contributing to and gaining from the exchange. In indirect exchanges, the action given by the other actor to the third party and the action received from the third party by that actor are likely to be less obvious. Also the third party may refuse to divulge such information or may misrepresent the contribution of the other actor.[6] An indirect exchange also increases the possibility of misperceptions on the part of actors regarding other actors' inputs and outcomes, so that diverse conclusions regarding the existence of equity or inequity may result.

Second, we anticipate that equity judgments will be more likely to be made to the extent that an exchange relationship has become regularized over time. Once the initial stages of establishing the exchange have been passed, the parties should be able to devote more attention to their relative costs and benefits from the exchange and less attention to determining which alternatives to enact in order to receive rewards. They should also have the opportunity to make a more careful assessment of what they and the other party are actually giving and receiving in the exchange. In status-value terms, the association and relevance relations will have become well defined.[7]

Third, it has also been suggested that the relative dependence of the parties to the exchange will affect whether or not equity judgments are made. Those parties lacking alternatives, and hence being in a high-dependence situation, will likely have less equity concern than those in low-dependence situations (Cook and Parcel 1977). Actors in situations of high dependence presumably will be so involved in the striving for goal fulfillment that concerns about whether the exchange that offers them goal fulfillment is also equitable will be a luxury they can ill afford. By contrast, an actor with low dependence may decide to leave an exchange offering him or her goal fulfillment because it is less equitable than he or she desires.

Most of the analyses of equity/distributive justice judgments have simply assumed that these judgments are made and have concentrated upon the nature and consequences of these judgments. We shall use six of the seven components we have described above for our analysis, discussing mainly direct exchanges, as we noted previously.

Basis of Judgment

A first significant distinction can be made between cases in which equity judgments are based upon comparisons between an actor and a specific other actor, a specific basis of judgment, and situations in which the object of comparison is a generalized other, or generalized basis of judgment. Generalized others may be defined as ideal-type actors having a combination of characteristics representative of particular social categories. In statistical terms, they consist of a combination of central tendencies on a number of variables. One may use a specific person in the social position of father as the basis of comparison, or one may use an ideational generalized other—namely, "fathers"—as the basis.

What determines whether one chooses a specific or a generalized other as the basis of comparison? Also, *which* specific other does one choose? One may think, for example, of a son in exchange with his father. Does the son use the father as the basis of comparison, or does he use the generalized other of "sons"? Or does he perhaps use another son (or daughter) in the family as the basis? The exchange theorists have emphasized comparisons with specific others and the status-value theorists have emphasized comparisons with generalized others without adequately explaining why one and not the other is selected (Cook 1973, Cook and Parcel 1977).

The possibilities confronting the son in this example are shown in figure 6.1. He may make a specific outcome–input comparison with his father—"What am I giving and getting in comparison to what he is giving and getting?" This comparison can be symbolized by

$$\frac{O_s}{O_f} : \frac{I_s}{I_f} \ .$$

Second, he may make a generalized outcome–input comparison, using "sons" as the basis of comparison—"What am I giving and getting compared to what sons in general give and get in exchanges with fathers?" This comparison can be represented as

$$\frac{O_s}{O_{s_g}} : \frac{I_s}{I_{s_g}} \ .$$

Third, he may make a specific outcome–input comparison, using another son in the family as the basis—"What am I giving and getting compared to him?" This can be symbolized by

$$\frac{O_{s_1}}{O_{s_2}} : \frac{I_{s_1}}{I_{s_2}}.$$

As we have said, the equity theorists emphasize the specific son-father (or son-son) comparison. The status-value theorists emphasize the relevance of comparisons in the referential structure, e.g., involving "sons" and "fathers" in figure 6.1, in contrast to expectations in the local structure—e.g., what constitutes distributive justice in the father-son exchange. Our formulation allows for both possibilities. Which basis of comparison is used will depend upon both the characteristics of a specific exchange and the characteristics of the participants.

Type of Exchange. We can provide some suggestions regarding the factors influencing the basis of comparison even though there is little in the way of empirical evidence to support them. The first major factor affecting the basis of comparison will be the type of exchange—direct or indirect. Homans (1974) and others (Walster et al. 1973) have suggested that the most likely basis of comparison in a direct exchange will be the specific other actor involved in the exchange, e.g., the father in the case of the son we have been discussing. This is simply due to the fact that in a direct exchange another specific actor is immediately at hand and usually highly visible. The exchange very likely involves an actual physical relationship with the other party, so that his or her inputs and outcomes are relatively obvious.

In indirect exchanges it appears that a specific other, e.g., another son in the family situation described above, will more likely be used as the basis of comparison the smaller the number of actors involved in an exchange with a third party. Thus in the family situation one son is likely to use another son as a basis of comparison, but in situations where a larger number of actors are involved in exchanges via a third party, e.g., students in a classroom in which the third party is the teacher, the likelihood of one student's using another student as a basis of

Figure 6.1. Example of Possible Bases of Comparison in a Son-Father Exchange

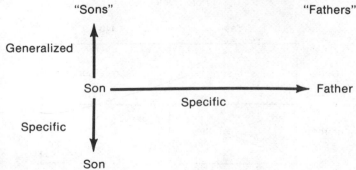

comparison is lessened. In this case, a generalized basis of comparison, "students," becomes more likely.

Role Similarity. The second major factor influencing the choice of a basis of comparison is role (or position) similarity. Similarity has been singled out most often as the factor determining the choice of an other for comparison. Actors supposedly compare themselves to others who are similar to them either in social characteristics (Walster et al. 1973; Homans 1974) or in terms of inputs and outcomes (Pritchard 1969). Homans (1974) suggests that this is largely due to the fact that individuals do not like to compare themselves consistently with others who are either better off or worse off than they are.

We shall make the emphasis on similarity more specific by referring to role (or position) similarity. Actors are most likely to use others in similar roles (or positions) as their basis of comparison, primarily because it facilitates the estimation process. We have noted that equity/distributive justice comparisons are based upon outcomes, inputs, and social characteristics. By comparing oneself to an other, either specific or generalized, in the same or a similar social position, one can effectively hold the social characteristics component of the equity judgment constant, and thus the judgment can be based simply upon outcomes and inputs. This becomes especially important in exchanges involving actors in dissimilar social positions, such as the son in the direct exchange with his father. He is faced with the choice between a specific dissimilar other as the basis of comparison (the father) or a generalized similar other ("sons").

Combined Effects. The influences of the type of exchange and role similarity may have opposing effects at times. Table 6.1 shows the four exchange possibilities created by combining these two factors. In cell (a), two sons are in a direct exchange, and it is quite likely that each will use the other as the basis of comparison. (There is a possibility of using the generalized other "brothers" as the basis, however.) Cell (b) is our son–father example, where the choice is between father and "sons." Cell (c) represents the indirect exchange of actors in

Table 6.1. Cross-classification of Type of Exchange and Role Similarity of Partners

Role Similarity

		Yes	No
Type of Exchange	Direct	son–son (a)	son–father (b)
	Indirect	son son > father (c)	son father > mother (d)

similar positions, i.e., two sons. Here the use of the other son as the basis of comparison is most likely for one of the sons, but a son–"sons" comparison is also conceivable. And the last cell, (d), shows a possible indirect exchange between two actors in dissimilar positions (son and father via mother). In this case either a son-father or a son–"sons" comparison appears likely.

We suspect that similarity is the more influential of the two factors. We anticipate, however, that its influence will be modified by an actor's degree of familiarity with the outcomes and inputs of a specific or generalized similar other. This can occur in several ways. For example, one actor may not know about a specific similar other's outcomes and inputs and therefore switch to a specific dissimilar other. One of the sons in cell (c) of table 6.1 may not know what the other son is giving and getting in the exchange and hence will switch to the father as the basis of comparison. (He may find it simpler to switch to the similar generalized other, "sons," however.)

A second possibility is that an actor will not know which similar generalized other to apply in a specific situation and consequently will use a specific dissimilar other as the basis of comparison. One can visualize, for example, a black student in an exchange with a white teacher not knowing whether to use the generalized other "blacks," "students," or "black students," in which case he or she will be more likely to use the teacher as the basis of comparison.

The confusion regarding which generalized similar other to apply in a specific situation may be seen as primarily a function of the extent to which the exchange is regularized. As an exchange becomes more regularized over time, the most relevant generalized other is likely to become clearer. The black student may discover that in an exchange with one teacher, "blacks" constitutes the most meaningful basis of comparison—for example, if the teacher pays special attention to his or her race. In another exchange, the "students" basis of comparison may be more appropriate.

Regularization of an exchange relationship over time may also have the opposite effect, namely, promoting switching from a generalized similar other to a specific dissimilar other. Thus in the early period of a marriage relationship a husband may judge the equity of exchanges with his wife on the basis of his perceptions of what "husbands" in general give and get in marriages. As the marriage continues he may become less concerned about what he is giving and getting in comparison with "husbands" and more about what he is giving and getting in comparison to his wife, thus using her as the basis of comparison.

Effects of the Choice of Basis. The issue of which other is selected as the basis for an equity judgment is a crucial one, because different bases are likely to provide different information about the presence or absence, or degree, of inequity in a given exchange. Returning to our son-father example, a judgment by the son using father as the basis of comparison may yield different information than a judgment using "sons" as the basis. Thus it is conceivable that in some exchanges actors may utilize *both* specific and generalized bases of comparison, although we cannot say what factors will make that more likely. If both bases are used, then the possibility of discrepant information regarding equity is created, as we have noted, and its occurrence may have interesting implications for actors' responses. For example, a wife may perceive that she is experiencing negative inequity when she uses her husband as the basis of comparison but that she is experiencing equity when she uses the generalized "wives" as the basis. In this case it seems that the information derived from the generalized comparison will modify the dissatisfaction resulting from the specific comparison. The implication, of course, is that she perceives that wives in general experience negative inequity in exchanges with their husbands, so her situation is not unique. If, however, she perceives equity in the exchange when her husband is the basis of comparison and negative inequity when "wives" is the basis of comparison, then the satisfaction resulting from the former perception may well be diminished by the latter one, since it indicates that other wives are better off than she is.

So the choice of the basis of an equity judgment is likely to influence both judgments regarding the existence of inequity and responses to those judgments. The latter effect is also shown by Homans (1974), who, citing a study by Patchen, notes that workers were less dissatisfied when they compared their salaries to those of their relatives than when they compared them with the salaries of workers to whom they were unrelated. We do not have room in this chapter to expand upon all of the possible ramifications of the choice of the basis of judgment but will primarily concentrate upon direct exchanges in which the specific other actor constitutes this basis.[8]

Criteria of Judgment

Regardless of whether a specific or generalized other is used in making an equity/distributive justice judgment, the question of the criteria used in that judgment arises. This is undoubtedly the knottiest problem confronting equity/distributive justice theorists, and it is far from being resolved. Homans's deceptively simple statement of the rule of distributive justice camouflages the extent of the problem.

We have suggested three possible criteria: inputs, outcomes, and social characteristics—the last of which may be regarded as investments. Each of these criteria presents problems for one attempting to apply them in an analysis. First, which of the criteria are the most meaningful ones to use in equity/distributive justice situations? Do these three represent the most parsimonious conceptualization, or can one of them be interpreted in terms of the others? Is it best to assume that all three criteria are operative in all situations or that different criteria are used under different conditions?

Second, when we refer to an "input," what exactly is meant? (Cook 1970; Cook and Parcel 1977.) Third, similarly, what does one mean when referring to actors' "outcomes" from exchanges? Fourth, what social characteristics may be properly regarded as "investments" in an exchange? In what sense is an actor "investing" his or her social characteristics in an exchange? How do actors arrive at an evaluation of the values of their social characteristics that are comparable to their evaluations of their inputs and outcomes?

Again, the existing literature is not particularly helpful in answering these questions. We have noted the differences between the various points of view regarding the criteria that are used. Equity theorists such as Adams deal in inputs and outcomes. Others, like Homans, utilize all three. The status-value theorists work with social characteristics and outcomes and furthermore concentrate upon the status values of these criteria.

Social Characteristics. The crucial issue in this regard concerns the conditions under which social characteristics are taken into account in equity judgments. In other words, when will actors add to their basic equity/distributive justice estimations in terms of inputs and outcomes a consideration of the social characteristics each party is investing in the exchange? Thus we regard an input–outcome comparison as the crux of equity/distributive justice judgments.

As our previous comments indicate, this issue will be problematic only in situations in which the basis of judgment is a *dissimilar* specific other. Choosing a similar other, either specific or generalized, as the basis of judgment can be assumed to solve the problem, since the social characteristics of an actor and the other that is serving as the basis of comparison are equated. A son, using another son or the generalized "sons" as the basis of judgment, need not take the social characteristics of the other into account since the other is chosen precisely because of the social characteristic of "sonness."[9]

Therefore the problem involves only those cases in which a dissimilar specific other is the basis of judgment. And in these cases the gist of the problem involves what it means for social characteristics to be invested in an exchange. If they are not invested, or if they are invested but are judged to have no relative value, then an equity judgment can be based solely on outcomes and inputs.

We regard social characteristics as investments when they are consciously brought into play in an exchange, that is, when an actor participates in the exchange as a possessor of a particular characteristic, or when the actor is perceived by the other participant in the exchange to be acting as the possessor of that characteristic. For example, with some imagination one may visualize two exchanges involving a white person and a black person. In one the white engages in the exchange in the role of "white person" and in the other in the role of "person." Similarly, one can imagine the black person perceiving that the white is acting as a "white person" in one case and as a "person" in the other.

This will, of course, involve very subtle distinctions in some cases, observable only by an ethnomethodologist perhaps. Nevertheless we believe it is a meaningful contrast to draw. One may also think of other examples, e.g., a male acting in the role of male in an exchange with a woman, or a father acting in the role of father in an exchange with his son. In fact, given the widespread sociological belief in the significance of roles for behavior, the investment of social characteristics in exchanges between dissimilars is probably the rule rather than the exception.

One must keep in mind that just because characteristics are invested in an exchange does not mean that they will influence an equity/distributive justice judgment. The values of the characteristics that are invested by the two actors may be perceived to be equal, in which case an equity estimation will involve only outcomes and inputs. One should also keep in mind that there may be disagreements regarding the values of these investments. The white person we have described may assign an equal or greater value to the characteristic of "whiteness" than to the characteristic of "blackness," whereas the black exchange partner may assign equal values to the two characteristics or a lesser value to the characteristic of "whiteness" than to "blackness."

Social characteristics will not be regarded as investments in all exchanges involving actors in dissimilar social roles. We can venture some suggestions regarding the conditions under which they are more likely to be considered as investments. First, it is probable that a threshold effect is operative, so that they will be considered as investments only when they are sufficiently different to be noticeable. Thus race will more likely be considered an investment when a comparison is between a black and a white than between a white and a mulatto. The continuum of color existing in Brazil (Degler 1971), for example, is less likely to result in perceptions that race constitutes an investment than is the racial dichotomy existing in the United States.

Second, it is also probable that social characteristics are more likely to be considered as investments in the early stages of an exchange relationship and that they are less likely to be so considered after the relationship has become established. According to Parcel and Cook (1977) there is evidence that status characteristics are not used in equity judgments when performance information is available. This may be interpreted in terms of information becoming available as an exchange continues that makes it unnecessary to consider social characteristics as investments.

Third, the intimacy or the primariness of an exchange relationship may be the most important factor influencing whether or not social characteristics are considered as investments. The more intimate or primary the relationship, seemingly the less likely that social characteristics will be relevant, as the participants will interact less as role players and more as individuals. One may imagine a husband and wife, for example, only paying attention to their relative outcomes and inputs and ignoring the fact that one is a husband and the other a wife. Likewise, the fact that one has more education than the other, or more prestige in the occupational world, is likely to be ignored. In fact, the disregarding of social characteristics may be more appropriately considered as an indicator of the primariness of an exchange relationship than as a consequence of primariness. In other words, exchanges are more primary the greater the extent to which social characteristics are discarded and individuals interact with each other as persons rather than as role players.

Fourth, the type of value being sought by participants in an exchange may also determine whether social characteristics are considered as investments. Actors seeking status goals may regard them as investments, whereas actors seeking consummatory goals may ignore them. But this may in turn be a consequence of other factors, such as the primariness of the exchange. At base, it will be a function of the goals on which actors are experiencing deprivation, so that those lacking fulfillment of a status goal will be more inclined to regard social characteristics as investments than those lacking fulfillment on nonstatus goals.

Inputs. The question of what constitutes an input is slightly easier to resolve. According to Adams (1965) things will be considered as inputs if they are perceived to be relevant, whereas Walster et al. (1973) describe inputs in terms of assets and liabilities. Neither description is particularly helpful because of its generality. The research tradition has operationalized inputs primarily in terms of time and effort expended by actors, with the size of the input generally assumed directly proportional to the amount of either expenditure. This assumption is clearly questionable.

If we assume that equity/distributive justice judgments are made after the completion of an exchange in which two actors have both given and received actions, then their inputs consist simply of the actions each has enacted in the exchange. The size of these inputs can be estimated most easily and most sensibly in terms of their costs to the actors. We have previously observed that costs include both negative utilities received and positive utilities forgone. Consequently if the action an actor has enacted has resulted in the direct loss of goal fulfillment on any goals, or if it has meant that positive utility cannot be received on some goal (which will almost always be the case because of the existence of possible action alternatives that are incompatible with the one that was enacted), then a utility value can be given to the input criterion.

It is our opinion that both the status value and the consummatory value of inputs (and also of outcomes and social characteristics) will enter into an actor's calculus. In our model both types of value constitute utility; they simply refer to different goals on which utility is received. Of course, their relative importance will likely vary in different exchanges. One exchange may involve status values solely, and another may involve only consummatory values, while others may involve combinations of the two. But these can be reduced to the same metric by referring to them in terms of goal fulfillment and utility.

So inputs consist of actions enacted and their values are measured in terms of costs, which in turn are measured in terms of utilities. This estimation of costs should be easier for actors than their estimations of subjective expected costs prior to their enactment of actions simply because no subjective probability component is involved. Actors know with certainty which outcomes they have received in the exchange. However, the estimation process is complicated by the fact that each actor will necessarily have to estimate the other's costs in order to make an equity/distributive justice judgment. A's input will be the cost of the action A enacted, and B's input will be the cost of B's action (to B). But A's perception of B's input will necessitate a vicarious estimate of B's costs and likewise B will have to estimate A's costs vicariously. These vicarious estimates, of course, open the Pandorean possibilities of erroneous estimates and their implications for equity/distributive justice judgments.

Outcomes. If inputs constitute actions *given* to an exchange, then outcomes constitute the actions *received* by the participants in a direct exchange. A's outcome in an exchange with B is the action enacted by B, and B's outcome is A's action.[10] If inputs are measured in terms of costs, then outcomes are most suitably measured in terms of rewards, or positive utilities received (by A from B's action, for example) *and* negative utilities forgone (by A as a result of enacting one alternative rather than another).[11]

Vicarious estimates of rewards will be necessary also, so that each actor can estimate the other's outcome from the exchange. In addition, the outcome received by the other actor may enter into a given actor's estimation of his or her own outcome if, as we noted previously, providing utility for the other actor provides goal fulfillment for that actor. This creates the rather incongruous situation of A's receiving utility from B's action and also receiving utility from observing B receive A's action. Conceivably this may account for the great rewards derived by some parents from exchanges with their children. Not only do they receive utility from the child's action, but seeing the child enjoy something, e.g., a Christmas present, provides them with additional utility.

Most experimental studies of equity/distributive justice have used monetary rewards as outcomes, simply because of their convenience and quantifiability. These studies do not adequately test these theories, however, because they first of all assume that the objective values of the outcomes equal their utilities and, second, they do not appear to leave room for a consideration of the status value of outcomes. The monetary reward is almost always assumed to have only consummatory value.

Our discussion of inputs and outcomes suggests that the criteria used in an equity/distributive justice judgment by A regarding an exchange with B may be represented as follows: A's outcome $= U(B_i)$;[12] A's input $= C(A_i)$; A's vicarious estimate of B's outcome $= U(A_i.B)$; A's vicarious estimate of B's input $= C(B_i.B)$. Thus, whereas in the estimation of subjective expected utility A calculates anticipated costs and anticipated rewards, in the estimation of equity A calculates actual utility received and actual costs incurred in enacting an alternative. B's estimates can be represented in a similar fashion, which we will not show here.

The Value of Investments. Conceptualizing and measuring inputs and outcomes is a relatively minor problem in comparison with the problems created by trying to include social characteristics/investments in equity/distributive justice models. To include them with outcomes and inputs it will be necessary to give them a utility value. But how does one assign utility to a social characteristic? The literature on the subject does not offer any concrete suggestions regarding how this might be accomplished.

The essential question is "How much utility is a social characteristic worth when invested?" The quick answer to this question is "Whatever one can get for it." But that removes the possibility of making any sort of equity/distributive justice judgment, because such judgments involve the possibility that one may not be able to get what a characteristic is worth by investing it in a particular exchange.

We once more find ourselves in the position of being able only to venture suggestions as to how such evaluations may be made. One possibility is that actors will have some sense of an average utility associated with given social characteristics that they have derived from previous exchange situations. These estimates would very likely be quite imprecise but they could provide a basis for comparing one's own social characteristics with those of other actors. A utility value would simply be substituted for the investment component in an equity comparison and either compared directly with one of the other components, e.g., profits or rewards, or added to one of the components, e.g., costs.

A second, more likely, possibility is that actors work with crude *ratios* of investment values that are not converted into utility terms. Thus they are likely to have a rough idea of the relative worth of different social characteristics, e.g., the ratio of the value of "whiteness" to the value of "blackness." This ratio of the values of the social characteristics invested can then be applied as part of an equity comparison, as we shall show later in this chapter.

This, of course, raises the question of the source of these ratios of values of social characteristics. One possibility is that they are derived from an actor's personal experiences, for example, from a comparison of the average outcomes associated with given social characteristics. Thus the son in our son–father example is likely to have a general idea of the relative outcomes he and his father have received in previous exchanges. If the father's outcomes have been twice as large as the son's on the average, then the son would likely assume that the value of the social characteristic "father" is twice that of the characteristic "son."

The second possibility is that the ratio of values of social characteristics is derived from generalized others, i.e., in the son–father case from the relative outcomes received by "sons" and "fathers" in general. If the outcomes of "sons" are generally half those of "fathers," the implication is that the characteristic "son" has half the value of the characteristic "father." In this case the values of social characteristics would be derived from a larger number of cases than if they were simply derived from the son's own experiences with his father. In either case, i.e., whether derived from personal experiences or from generalized others, the outcome/outcome ratios will be very similar to the outcome/action ratios described in our discussion of subjective probabilities.

It should be remembered that we are dealing here with equity judgments in which the basis of judgment is a dissimilar specific other, e.g., the son–father comparison. In these cases the values of the reward and cost components used in the judgment will be derived from the actions enacted in the exchange, and the values assigned to the investment component will be the ratio of values derived either from an actor's past experiences or from the actor's perceptions of the relative outcomes of generalized others. In cases in which the basis of judgment is a similar other, e.g., the son's basis of comparison is another son or the generalized "sons" in the son-father exchange, the investment ratio may be assumed to be equal to unity because of the equality of social characteristics of the actor and the other that is used as the basis of judgment.

We noted earlier that Homans and Blau disagree on the characteristics that may be regarded as investments in exchanges. We lean toward Homans on this issue and toward the inclusion of both ascribed and achieved characteristics.[13] The relevant issue here is which characteristics actors are likely to include in making equity/distributive justice judgments, and we see no reason why one should assume that actors refrain from including their ascribed characteristics. Parsons (1951), with his pattern variables, and others have pointed out that the relative importance of achievement and ascription represents one of the major dimensions distinguishing different social and cultural systems. Therefore we expect that whether ascribed characteristics are included in equity judgments will depend on the sociocultural value context within which participants in an exchange are operating. In some contexts ascribed characteristics will undoubtedly be considered as legitimate investments. It is obvious that in certain contexts today the color of one's skin counts as a legitimate investment and is presumed to have payoffs that, when not received, create inequitable situations in the eyes of individuals having that color skin. This gets us into the issue of the legitimacy of distribution rules, which we will consider in the next section, but at this point it seems premature to exclude ascribed characteristics from equity/distributive justice situations. Instead, it is more important to determine the conditions under which ascribed characteristics will be considered as investments, and we have suggested the sociocultural value context of the exchange as a primary determinant.[14]

COMPONENTS OF A THEORY: STANDARD AND TYPE

Standard of Judgment

The standard of judgment simply refers to the norm, or distribution rule, relating the criteria of judgment. Here we find substantial agreement—the criteria should be either proportional or similar to each other. Rewards should be proportional to costs; inputs should be proportional to outcomes; investments plus costs should be proportional to profits; or (in the status-value version) individuals with similar social characteristics should receive similar outcomes or rewards. These two standards may be considered synonymous. They can also be phrased oppositely, e.g., disproportionate rewards should be associated with equally disproportionate costs, to show that inequity is not synonymous with an inequality of rewards or costs (Burgess and Nielsen 1974). If the outcomes of an exchange are unequal for the participants, then the standards specify that the inputs should be proportionately unequal. There is also consensus among the equity/distributive justice theorists of whatever persuasion that the standard constitutes a *norm* and not simply idiosyncratic expectations on the part of the participants.

One Standard or Many? However, there are issues regarding the standard of judgment on which there is significant disagreement. The first of these is whether the rule of distributive justice is a universal rule or whether it varies across situations. In other words, is there one distribution rule or many? Homans and Blau again part company on this issue, with the former tentatively suggesting that the rule is universal, whereas the latter argues that the standards of the fair rate of exchange are relative to the situation. Cook and Parcel (1977) have also suggested the possibility of a variety of standards being applied, and Goodman and Friedman (1971) suggest that more than one standard may be applied in a given situation. Deutsch (1975) has listed eleven different rules of justice.

There appears to be some confusion on this issue. Some of the apparent differences in rules actually involve the criteria included in the standard, rather than the standard itself. For example, Cook and Parcel's list of possible distribution rules (Cook and Parcel 1977) includes equality, need, ability or merit, effort, and productive contribution. Of these only equality constitutes a standard, the others constitute criteria. Need and ability or merit may be considered social characteristics, and effort and productive contribution appear to refer to inputs.

Likewise Blau's argument for the relativity of fair rates of exchange essentially refers to the fact that different criteria may be used having different values in different situations. It is doubtful that he is arguing that some standard other than proportionality or similarity is being invoked in certain situations.[15] Therefore it appears most satisfactory to operate with a single standard—proportionality or similarity—and allow the criteria included in distribution rules to vary across situations.

Legitimacy of the Standard. A second problem regarding distribution rules has been raised by Cook (1975), who suggests that a distinction needs to be made between situations where inequity exists because a legitimate distribution rule has been violated and situations where inequity is the result of the application of a distribution rule considered illegitimate by one or both parties. This will complicate equity/distributive justice situations also. Generally we assume that actors will apply distribution rules that each regards as legitimate. It is conceivable, though, that an actor will knowingly violate a distribution rule he or she regards as legitimate. But in this case it will be difficult to discern whether the actor has violated a legitimate distribution rule or is actually applying a different distribution rule than the one he or she is assumed to be applying. Consequently this distinction between legitimate and illegitimate distribution rules is probably more meaningful when applied to an actor's perceptions regarding his or her exchange partner's application of distribution rules than to his or her own application of these rules.

To avoid unduly complicating our discussion we will assume that each actor regards his or her distribution rule as legitimate and that he or she will perceive inequity to exist whenever that distribution rule is violated. We will not distinguish between cases in which inequity is perceived to exist because of the perception that the other actor has violated a legitimate distribution rule and cases in which the perception is based on the other actor's perceived application of an illegitimate distribution rule. Our primary concern is with the fact that there very well may *not* be consensus between the participants to an exchange regarding the existence of inequity, the degree of inequity that exists, or its direction.

Disagreements concerning these issues may become focused around charges that an individual or group is exploiting another individual or group. Such disagreements will be difficult to resolve, because, as we noted earlier in this chapter, it will be impossible to derive objective measures of exploitation. Thus each party to the disagreement can only rely upon his or her own perceptions and attempt to convince the other party of the rightness of those perceptions. Observing third parties may also apply distribution rules and judge whether the exchange is equitable or inequitable, but their judgments will also lack objectivity. So our assumption is that no one perception of inequity or exploitation can be accorded greater objectivity than any other perception, and we further assume that the reactions of both participants and outside observers will be based upon each one's own perception of the presence or absence of inequity.[16]

A Basic Distribution Rule. Given the fact that the criteria used in equity/distributive justice judgments will vary across situations, is it possible that one may nevertheless determine a basic distribution rule from which other common distribution rules can be derived? Our discussion to this point has involved outcomes, inputs, profits, rewards, costs, and social characteristics conceptualized as investments. We have noted Homans's use of several of these terms in his different renderings of the rule of distributive justice and have suggested that there is a discrepancy between his versions of it. Is it therefore possible to represent some of these components in terms of each other so that *the* basic distribution rule can be specified?

By measuring outcomes and inputs in terms of utilities we have effectively equated outcomes with rewards and inputs with costs so that we are left with four basic criteria: rewards and profits—referring to what actors receive from exchanges—and costs and investments—referring to what they contribute. Upon closer analysis one finds oneself on the horns of an interesting dilemma. Two possibilities for developing a basic distribution rule present themselves. On the one hand, one may regard the proportionality of rewards and costs as the basic distribution rule. With the aid of one additional assumption, namely, that investments are proportional to either rewards or costs, one can derive the other distribution rule cited by Homans (1961), namely, profits $(R - C)$ proportional to investments (I), and Homans's (1974) later distribution rule, namely, rewards (R) proportional to investments plus costs $(I + C)$. If $R_A/R_B = C_A/C_B = I_A/I_B$, then $(R_A - C_A)/(R_B - C_B) = I_A/I_B$ and $R_A/R_B = (I_A + C_A)/(I_B + C_B)$.

Both of these seem to be meaningful statements of the comparisons between what actors give to, and receive from, exchanges. Consequently, situations will be equitable or just if rewards are proportional to costs and investments are proportional to either rewards or costs. Of the two, it appears more desirable to set investments proportional to rewards, even though by so doing one also makes them proportional to costs, given the reward–cost proportionality. The reward–cost proportionality represents the distribution rule emphasized by the equity theorists, whereas the reward–investment proportionality is the one emphasized by the status-value theorists.

But, on the other hand, one may start from the opposite direction, so to speak, as Homans does in his 1974 version of the rule of distributive justice, and regard the proportionality of rewards (or profits) to the totality of what an actor gives to the exchange (costs plus investments) as the basic distribution rule. If one does this, then one derives a quite different picture of situations that will be equitable. If $R_A/R_B = (I_A + C_A)/(I_B + C_B)$, then R_A/R_B is not necessarily equal to C_A/C_B or to I_A/I_B. Nor is C_A/C_B necessarily equal to I_A/I_B. Now situations are equitable if the rewards the actors get from them are proportional to the *sum* of actions and characteristics they have contributed, a subtle but significant distinction.

The difference between the two approaches rests upon the *substitutability* of actions and characteristics contributed to the exchange. With the former approach one is in effect saying, "The exchange is equitable if both you and the other actor have received rewards in proportion to the costs you have incurred, and if your rewards have also been proportional to the social characteristics you have invested in the exchange." This means that actors who receive more from an exchange must not only have contributed more in the way of actions but they must also have invested more in terms of their social characteristics. Simply, actors who receive greater rewards should incur greater costs and invest more. Or actors who invest more and incur greater costs should receive greater rewards.

The latter approach allows actors to substitute actions for social characteristics, or vice versa. It says, "The exchange is equitable if the rewards you and the other actor have received are in proportion to the *sum* of actions and characteristics you have given." Consequently an actor contributing a very costly action to an exchange should not have to invest much in terms of social characteristics to receive a given amount of reward. Or he or she may choose to invest substantially but to enact a relatively "cheap" action in order to receive that amount of reward. In other words, varying mixes of actions and investments are consonant with a given reward. As a result rewards may not be proportional to costs nor to investments, considered separately.

If we can assume that status characteristics represent investments, then, from this perspective, an exchange involving a higher-status and a lower-status actor in which equal rewards are received will be equitable only if the lower-status actor contributes a more costly action. The actors' rewards will not be proportional to their costs (the higher-status actor is getting a greater reward for less cost), nor will their rewards be proportional to their investments (the lower-status actor is getting a greater reward for a lesser investment), but the total situation balances out as an equitable one when the comparison is between what they give and what they receive.[17]

This latter approach, therefore, parsimoniously combines the emphases of the equity and status-value approaches. Rewards must not be proportional just to costs (the equity approach) or just to investments (the status-value approach) for a situation of equity/distributive justice. Rather, rewards must be proportional to costs and investments. The equity approach, by not including investments of social characteristics, does not allow for the possibility that actors can *compensate* for their lesser contribution to an exchange by investing more valuable social characteristics than does the other party. The status-value approach, by disregarding inputs, precludes the possibility that actors can compensate for lower-value characteristics by giving more inputs to an exchange. Thus the approach we are suggesting, which combines the equity and status-value approaches, provides a more comprehensive framework for analyzing equity/distributive justice judgments than does either of the approaches taken separately.

Which of these two approaches better represents the essence of equity/ distributive justice judgments: the rewards proportional to costs and also proportional to investments approach, which does not allow for the substitutability of costs and investments; or the rewards proportional to costs plus investments approach, which does allow substitution? This depends, of course, on whether the substitution of investments and costs occurs in such situations, and we believe it is preferable to allow for this possibility by adopting the latter as the basic distribution rule than to foreclose the possibility of these substitutions' being made.

An alternative basic distribution rule to the one we have suggested can be represented as follows, for two actors, A and B:

$$R_A/R_B = (C_A/C_B) \times (I_A/I_B).$$

Although we have previously been discussing the *sum* of costs and investments contributed, the inclusion of investments as a ratio not measured in terms of utilities is represented more advantageously by the *product* of costs and investments. If social characteristics are not invested in an exchange, then the I_A/I_B ratio is assumed to drop out of equation (1). If the investments are equal, as in the case in which a similar other is used as the basis of comparison, $I_A/I_B = 1$, and rewards and costs are the only relevant components. If the investments are unequal, then equation (1) specifies that an excessive investment can be compensated for by a withholding of costs, and vice versa. Thus if $R_A/R_B = 2$ and $I_A/I_B = 4$, then C_A/C_B must equal one-half for the equality to hold.

It is very possible that costs and investments will not be given equal weights in all equity/distributive justice judgments. Their relative importance may vary across both situations and actors. Hence exponents for the cost and investment terms could be included in equation (1) to represent this possibility. For example, if investments are unimportant, the ratio of I_A/I_B can be given an exponent close to zero. We have left these out of equation (1) for the sake of simplicity, and equation (1) can be regarded as a suitable *basic* distribution rule. A generalized version of this distribution rule can be represented as

(2) $$R_A/R_B = (C_A/C_B)^{\beta_1}(I_A/I_B)^{\beta_2}$$

where β_1 and β_2 cannot be negative.

Thus our argument can be summarized as follows. (1) The basic distribution rule applicable to equity/distributive justice judgments states that the rewards of exchange participants should be proportional to the costs and investments each has contributed to the exchange. (2) If social characteristics are not invested in the exchange, then the investment component drops out and the judgment is made on the basis of relative rewards and costs. (3) If social characteristics are invested, but the investments are equal, the judgments will also be made on the basis of relative rewards and costs because the ratio of investments can be assumed to equal 1. (4) If the investments are unequal, then all components—rewards, costs, and investments—will influence the equity judgment.

It should be emphasized once again that what are actually regarded as rewards, costs, and investments and the values placed upon these will vary widely in different situations. Marx's claim that need, and not ability, is the proper criterion for allocating rewards constitutes a momentous difference in criteria, for example. Nevertheless, we believe that the distribution rule we have specified can be regarded as the basic rule in equity/distributive justice judgments. A great deal of theoretical and empirical work needs to be done in specifying the criteria used in this basic rule in different exchanges. The selection of criteria will no doubt be strongly affected by cultural and subcultural values and ideologies. Cook and Parcel (1977) have suggested factors such as type of economy and the total amount of available goods to be distributed as important in the choice of distribution rules, or, in our terms, the standards relating criteria. Undoubtedly others can be unearthed, and their effects need documentation.

Type of Inequity

Equation (1) specifies that inequity will be perceived to exist when the ratio of rewards is unequal to the product of the ratios of costs and investments. Thus inequity will involve the ratio of A's to B's rewards being either greater or less than the product of the ratios of A's costs to B's costs and A's investments to B's investments.

The equity theorists have paid more attention to whose advantage or disadvantage an inequitable situation exists than to the issue of the component or components responsible for the perceived inequity. To facilitate comparisons between different situations we make a differentiation among three primary types of inequity: *reward* inequity exists when the reward ratio does not equal

1, i.e., $C_A = C_B$, $I_A = I_B$, and $R_A \neq R_B$; *cost* inequity refers to a situation in which the cost ratio does not equal 1; and *investment* inequity to the case in which the investments of the actors are not equal, and hence the investment ratio does not equal 1. Obviously, more than one of the components may be responsible for the inequity, so we add to these three basic types four combinations of components: reward–cost, reward–investment, cost–investment, and reward–cost–investment inequity. We will refer to the case in which all three components are unequal as *total* inequity.[18]

Differences in the type of inequity will be associated with the reactions of exchange participants to inequitable situations. We shall spell this out more fully later in this chapter. In the case of reward inequity, for example, actors will have a choice of two basic alternatives to remove the inequity. They may adjust their costs and investments so that they are proportionately unequal to the existing inequality in rewards. Or they may equalize their rewards so that they are in line with the equal costs and investments they have contributed.[19]

COMPONENTS OF A THEORY: DIRECTION AND DEGREE

Direction of Inequity

The most important determinant of actors' responses to inequitable exchanges is undoubtedly whose ox is being gored. Generally we expect the party who benefits from an inequity—by getting greater rewards than justified by his or her actions and investments—to feel guilty and the party who is victimized—by contributing more than he or she gets out of the exchange—to be angry. Several different terms have been suggested to represent this aspect of an inequity situation. Homans (1974) refers to victims and beneficiaries; Gergen (1969) to benign and malignant exchanges; Cook (1975) to equity advantage and disadvantage; and Walster et al. (1973) to victims and harm-doers. We prefer to distinguish between *positive* and *negative* inequity, although we use the victim-beneficiary terminology to simplify our presentation. An actor experiences positive inequity when he or she perceives his or her rewards to be disproportionately higher than the product of his or her costs and investments and negative inequity when the rewards are disproportionately lower. Both of these comparisons are, of course, relative to the other party, and a perception of positive inequity for self necessarily implies a perception of negative inequity for the other participant in a direct exchange when the other actor is used as the basis of judgment.

Congruence of Perceptions

The perceptions of exchange participants regarding the direction of inequity will not necessarily be congruent. In many cases they will agree on which actor is the victim and which the beneficiary, but it is likely that in some cases their perceptions won't match. They may each feel they are the beneficiaries of an inequitable exchange, or, more likely, they may both feel they are being victimized by such an exchange. We can visualize actually five different possibilities in this regard: (1) one perceives equity and the other perceives positive inequity; (2) one perceives equity and the other perceives negative inequity; (3) one perceives positive and the other negative inequity; (4) both perceive positive inequity, i.e., both believe they are beneficiaries; and (5) both perceive negative inequity, i.e., both believe they are victims. Combining these five possibilities with the seven types of inequity described above and allowing for both actors' perceptions gives us fifty-six different situations that could be investigated empirically! In a specific situation, for example, one actor may perceive positive reward and cost inequity, and the other may perceive negative cost and investment inequity.

We clearly do not plan to explore the characteristics of all fifty-six possible situations in this chapter, but later we shall offer some observations concerning differences between *congruent, complementary,* and *incongruent* inequity perceptions. Possibilities (1) and (2) above will be considered to involve incongruent inequity perceptions because only one of the parties perceives inequity. Possibility (3) constitutes the only case of complementary inequity perceptions, where the actors' perceptions match. And the last two possibilities we consider as involving congruent perceptions because both actors perceive the same direction of inequity. Possibility (5) will be particularly important in indirect exchanges, since it represents the situation of perceived *collective* injustice. Both exchange partners believe they are being victimized by the third party involved in the indirect exchange.

Degree of Inequity

A third factor influencing reactions to inequitable or unjust exchanges, and the last basic component in our equity model, is simply the degree, or magnitude, of the perceived inequity. The greater the inequality of equation (1), the greater the degree of inequity. And generally the greater the degree of inequity, the greater the emotional reactions of the participants to the exchange, all other things being equal. Usually one will expect the degree of inequity to be greater in situations in which inequalities between components are in opposite directions than when they are in the same direction but simply differ in their amount of deviation from equality. For example, the degree of inequity will likely be greater if A's rewards are greater than B's rewards and B's costs and investments are greater than A's costs and investments, than if A's rewards, costs, and investments are all greater than B's but the ratio of A's rewards to B's rewards is greater than the ratio of A's costs and investments to B's costs and investments.

Summary of the Components

We have now covered the major components of our equity/distributive justice model. They are briefly the following:

1. type of exchange—direct versus indirect
2. basis of judgment—specific versus generalized

3. criteria of judgment—rewards, costs, and investments
4. standard of judgment—proportionality or similarity
5. type of inequity—reward, cost, investment, reward-cost, reward-investment, cost-investment, and total
6. direction of inequity—positive versus negative
7. degree of inequity

These components provide a framework that can be used in the comparative analysis of inequitable situations. They also represent major variables that when linked in propositional form will yield a reasonably comprehensive theory of equity/distributive justice situations. A number of exogenous variables will be needed and provision must also be made for the major types of consequences of actors' perceptions of inequitable exchanges. In the next section we consider these consequences in detail, and in the subsequent section we explore the factors promoting exchanges that are perceived as inequitable. One of our basic assumptions, stated earlier, is that it is impossible to determine whether exchanges are objectively inequitable. Such judgments are subjective, based on actors' perceptions. Thus we are actually concerned with the factors that promote exchanges that are likely to be *perceived* as inequitable.

THE CONSEQUENCES OF INEQUITABLE EXCHANGES

The bulk of the research on equity has focused on the consequences of inequitable exchanges for the participants. This research has consisted almost entirely of laboratory experiments involving limited aspects of such situations at a time. Much of the research has built upon Adams's (1965) original formulation of means of resolving inequitable situations, which we shall summarize briefly.

In Adams's view inequity creates "tension" that is proportional to the magnitude of the inequity. This "tension" in turn promotes a proportional motivation to remove or decrease the inequity, and the motivation triggers behavioral and/ or cognitive responses. He suggests four major behavioral responses: changing one's inputs, changing one's outcomes, leaving the field (i.e., giving up the exchange), or acting upon the other party to the exchange in a variety of ways. Two cognitive responses are suggested: changing the value, importance, and relevance of one's inputs and outcomes or changing the object of comparison. Adams notes the latter is not possible in a direct-exchange situation, although our conceptual framework allows for the possibility of an actor's shifting his or her judgment from a specific to a generalized basis. Changing one's object of comparison will be difficult in any situation if that other has become a referent for an actor. Adams suggests that cognitive changes may also be difficult, particularly cognitions important to one's self-concept. He also claims that it will be more difficult to change cognitions regarding one's own outcomes and inputs than cognitions regarding the other actor's.

Some of Adams's proposed reactions need to be translated into our terminology. Thus changing one's inputs either behaviorally or cognitively means changing one's costs—by enacting a different action in another round of the exchange or by reestimating the cost of the same action. Similarly, changing one's outcomes will entail receiving a different outcome on the next round or revaluing the same outcome. A change in one's investments, either behaviorally or cognitively, needs to be added to these. This will involve investing different social characteristics or reevaluating the worth of those already invested.

Our basic assumption is that equity/distributive justice is a goal that actors strive to fulfill. Like other goals, the importance of the equity goal will vary among actors. It may also vary across goals for the same actor; inequity in the fulfillment of some goals may be perceived as less serious than inequity in the fulfillment of other goals. The status-value approach to distributive justice, as we have noted, concentrates only on the status value of outcomes. We have earlier suggested that both types of value should be taken into account in a theory of equity/distributive justice. However, it is conceivable that inequity in the fulfillment of consummatory goals may be perceived as less (or more) serious than inequity in the fulfillment of status goals. In addition, inequity in a given exchange may involve both consummatory and status goals, in which case it will likely be perceived as especially serious. We do not believe we can specify at this point which of the two types of goal is likely to promote more intense responses on the part of beneficiaries and victims.

The possibility that inequity is less significant for some actors than for others has not yet been adequately analyzed in experimental studies of reactions to inequity. Generally inequity is assumed to be approximately equally distressing for all, though self-esteem appears to influence victims' responses. Its influence can also be described in our terms. Individuals with high self-esteem may be considered as having the goal of self-esteem relatively well fulfilled. Consequently, it is probable that other goals, such as equity, will be relatively more influential in choices than they would be if there were severe deprivation on the self-esteem goal. In other words, reducing inequity may be too expensive a luxury for some actors. Unless it is extremely important in their goal hierarchies, they will seek to fulfill it only after other goals have been fulfilled.[20]

We also assume that actors' choices of reactions to inequitable situations will be determined by subjective expected utility considerations. They will choose those reactions that they regard as least costly and that have the greatest probability of achieving the desired outcome of reducing the inequity in the situation. These estimations will in turn be dependent on their perceptions of their, and the other party's, relative resources and upon the degree of inequity in the exchange situation. The degree of inequity itself is very likely a function of the actors' relative resources, so that the options available to victims will no doubt be more limited, the greater the degree of inequity in the situation. Beneficiaries, though, are likely to have a greater number of viable options, the greater the degree of inequity in the situation, given their relatively greater resources in such situations.

Consequently, we predict that beneficiaries will be more likely to take actions to reduce the degree of inequity, the greater the degree of inequity, whereas the likelihood of victims' responses will be affected more by their relative resources, as well as the magnitude of the inequity. If victims' relative resources are sufficient, then they will be more likely to take actions to reduce the inequity, the greater the degree of inequity. But if their relative resources are quite limited, then they may be more likely to take such actions, the less the degree of inequity. Laboratory studies that show that the likelihood of victims' reactions is positively related to the magnitude of inequity (cf. Schmitt and Marwell 1972) rarely involve substantial differences in relative resources. In the real world much larger resource differences are likely to prevail, with the effects we have suggested.

These considerations raise another very complex problem. The motivation to reduce inequity may come into conflict with the motivation to maximize utility. This clearly is of greatest relevance for beneficiaries of inequity, for whom a reduction in inequity may involve a simultaneous reduction of utility. A similar problem also confounds the analysis of victims' reactions. For them a *reduction* in inequity is also likely to involve an *increase* in utility. In their case it may be impossible to determine whether given actions involve attempts to maximize utility or to reduce inequity.

Some very general observations can also be made regarding the relative ease of carrying out their various options on the part of both victims and beneficiaries. Generally we expect that it will be easier for actors to change their cognitions than their behaviors. Generally, also, it will be easier for them to change their own behaviors than the behaviors of the other actor involved in the exchange, although it is conceivable that they will find it easier to change their cognitions about the other's rewards, costs, and investments than about their own (Adams 1965). It also appears that changing one's costs and changing the other's rewards will be relatively easier responses than changing one's rewards and the other's costs in a direct exchange simply because the first two are under one's own control. Changing either one's own or the other's investments is likely to be more problematic, because social characteristics are difficult to discard. So cognitive manipulations of this component appear more likely than behavioral adjustments.

In all cases, one must keep in mind that we are dealing with perceptions, not with actual costs, rewards, and investments. These perceptions are most susceptible to error when *another* actor's components are involved rather than an actor's own. An actor necessarily will enact those actions that he or she perceives will change the other's costs, rewards, and investments, even though they may not actually have that effect. This means that an actor's reactions to inequity may reduce the inequity he or she perceives, but they may also backfire and perhaps even increase the inequity in the situation. Therefore it is likely that attempts to reduce inequity will not be one-shot affairs. A sequence of reactions, and reactions to those reactions, will be necessary to get the exchange to a state of equity.

We will attempt to simplify the following discussion by looking at the responses of victims and beneficiaries of inequity separately. Their responses are difficult to analyze in isolation for two reasons. First, a given response is likely to affect both one's own outcomes or inputs and the other's. For example, reducing one's costs is likely to reduce the other's perceived rewards. Second, a given response may be intended to produce a particular response in the other party. Thus one may reduce one's costs with the expectation that it will moti-vate the other actor to increase his or her costs. However, we believe it is prefer-able to analyze the reactions separately first. We shall discuss the hypothesized emotional responses and the suggested cognitive and behavioral responses avail-able to both victims and beneficiaries. In addition, we shall look at the available empirical evidence and call attention to some of the variables that have been suggested by theorists and researchers as intervening between, or interacting with, the reward, cost, and investment components and the reactions to inequity. It is somewhat surprising that much more research has been done, at least by psychologists, on beneficiaries' responses than on victims' responses (Walster et al. 1978). [21]

Cook (1975) has pointed out that the reactions of both victims and benefi-ciaries are necessarily dependent upon their levels of knowledge. If they cannot make a determination regarding the criteria that are appropriate in a situation, or the rewards, costs, and investments of the participants, then they will tend to correlate their expectations regarding the situation with the actual distribution of outcomes. If given control over the allocation of outcomes, they will attempt to maintain the existing distribution. So our discussion of reactions is based on the premise that the participants have sufficient knowledge to make equity judgments.

RESPONSES OF INEQUITY VICTIMS

Emotional Responses

Actors experiencing negative inequity will be dissatisfied or, more likely, angry. That has been the primary generalization guiding researchers studying the reactions of individuals perceiving themselves inequity victims. The emotional distress victims experience is assumed to be greater than that experienced by the beneficiaries of inequitable exchanges (Walster et al. 1973). We have noted the argument of some theorists that the anger stems from the sense that a norm has been violated, but Adams (1963) and Alexander and Simpson (1971) suggest that it is the result of frustration. We prefer to analyze it in terms of a lack of goal fulfillment. Failure to fulfill the equity goal results in anger, and generally the greater the lack of fulfillment of this goal, the greater the anger. The sugges-tion that victims' distress is greater than that of the beneficiaries of inequitable exchanges simply indicates that the utility curve for the equity goal has a steeper curve for negative inequity than for positive inequity.

The distress associated with negative inequity is probably not solely due to lack of goal fulfillment, however, since it appears that victims also take into account the *reasons* for their disadvantaged positions. If they feel they are being intentionally victimized, then their distress will be greater than if they perceive their victimization to be accidental (Walster et al. 1973; Burgess and Nielsen 1974) or their own fault (Homans 1974). We would expect them to perceive intentionality more often in direct exchanges than in indirect exchanges. In direct exchanges the other actor participating in the exchange is the source of one's outcomes, so this perceived responsibility is likely to be transformed into a sense of intentionality. In indirect or mediated exchanges, though, it may not be possible to pin down responsibility precisely on the other party or on the third party intervening between oneself and the other. So the anger associated with victimization is likely to be greater in direct exchanges.

Earlier we have assumed that a victim's anger will be proportional to the degree of inequity he or she perceives. It is time to examine that assumption more closely, since the degree of anger will also depend upon the importance of the equity goal for the particular goals that are being fulfilled in an exchange. We earlier also noted a possible difference between consummatory and status goals in this regard. With either type of goal a small degree of negative inequity can result in very great anger if the equity goal for that type of goal is extremely important. One hears, for example, of business executives (and even professors) becoming livid over small discrepancies in status symbols. Slight differences in the thickness of carpeting or the amount of office space allocated to them may become objects of intense conflict. In this type of situation equity on status goals is apparently very important to the participants, although there may be some minimal consummatory value gained from a slightly thicker carpet or slightly more space. Likewise, most parents are familiar with their children's scrapping over infinitesimal differences in the sizes of pieces of pie. Presumably consummatory goals are more significant in this case and equity on them is very important, although the differences in the sizes may also have status connotations.

Consequently, our inclination is to represent the relationship between the perceived degree of negative inequity and actors' degrees of anger by a curve with a positive but decreasing slope, as in figure 6.2. Anger increases more rapidly at lower degrees of negative inequity and then increases less rapidly at higher degrees of negative inequity. At some point additional negative inequity will not produce additional anger, because there is a limit to the anger an individual can feel. An interesting question is whether this relationship applies to both individuals and groups. It has been argued that conflicts between groups are most likely when the power differences between them are relatively small (Korpi 1974). Ostensibly this is due to the fact that they are more likely to be competing with each other under these conditions than if the power difference between them were greater. If the groups are in an exchange relationship, however, the increased probability of conflict in the situation of near equality may in fact be due primarily to the slight degree of inequity perceived by one of the groups.

Figure 6.2.   **Relationship between Perceived Degree
of Negative Inequity and Anger**

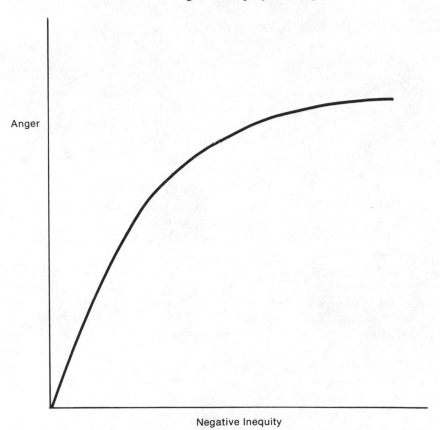

Anger

Negative Inequity

Individuals' reactions to negative inequity are no doubt also influenced by personality characteristics (Burgess and Nielsen 1974). Self-esteem appears to be especially important in this regard (Cook 1973). The degree of self-esteem possessed by a victim may have two very different effects on the amount of anger he or she experiences. One may argue that the higher a victim's self-esteem, the greater will be his or her anger because inequity represents a severe depreciation of that sense of self-esteem. Or one may argue that victims with higher levels of self-esteem will be less angry because their self-esteem is less likely to be damaged by inequitable exchanges. Or possibly it is the sense of security one has about his or her level of self-esteem, regardless of the level, that is most crucial here.

If we assume that victims experience anger roughly in proportion to the degree of inequity they perceive, what alternatives are available to them to reduce or eliminate the inequity? This can be answered in terms of the three basic components of equity estimates—rewards, costs, and investments—that can be changed either cognitively or behaviorally. Cognitive manipulations may be the first line of offense because of their relatively greater ease, or they may be a last resort, when no action alternatives appear viable. There are six adjustments that may be made to three components, plus a couple of alternatives that involve going outside the exchange. As Burgess and Nielsen (1974) and Weick and Nesset (1968) have pointed out, any of these six adjustments can also be explained in terms of the maximization of the victim's utility. So it will be difficult to determine in a specific case whether an individual's attempts to reduce inequity are separate from his or her attempts to maximize utility.

Behavioral and Cognitive Responses

Victims have three basic alternatives available for reducing inequity. First, they can attempt to bring their relative rewards *up,* either by raising their own rewards or lowering the beneficiary's. Second, they can also try to bring their relative costs *down,* by reducing their own costs or raising those of the beneficiary. Third, according to our formulation, they can also reduce inequity by lowering their relative investments, which will result if their investments are decreased and/or the beneficiary's are increased. These alternatives may be regarded as "coping" strategies for victims. They may be enacted behaviorally, or they may simply involve cognitive manipulations. And, as we have noted, we assume that victims will choose an alternative on the basis of its subjective expected utility.[22]

Decrease Other's Rewards. Probably the easiest way for victims to reduce inequity in direct exchanges is to reduce the rewards of the beneficiary, simply because those rewards are dependent upon the victim's actions. By so doing, victims may simultaneously reduce their costs and thereby reduce inequity by means of a two-pronged attack. There are several ways in which a beneficiary's rewards can be reduced, each of which will have likely consequences from which we can infer the relative riskiness of the different courses of action.

A victim may simply enact a less valuable action for the beneficiary. Or a victim may "give" the beneficiary a negative-utility action (a punishment), the response that Walster et al. (1973) refer to as retaliation. A third possibility is to add a negative-utility action to the same positive-utility action and thereby reduce rewards. A victim may add disapproval to another action, for example. Yet a fourth possibility is one that might be called the "dull thud" phenomenon—enacting an action in a manner that reduces its value, generally with limited intensity or enthusiasm. (In chapter 4 we discussed the possibility of enacting a given action with different levels of intensity.) One may respond to a beneficiary's affectionate overtures very impassively, or one may ritualistically thank a beneficiary for a gift so that the extent of appreciation is in doubt. With this tactic a victim cannot be berated by a beneficiary for failure to enact a specific action, and he or she can diminish the beneficiary's rewards to some degree.

How are the beneficiaries in an exchange likely to respond to these actions taken by victims? One possibility is that they will also retaliate by reducing the victims' rewards even further.[23] This can result in a process of escalation that leaves the victim both in a continued state of negative inequity and worse off in terms of utility received. A second possibility of concern to the victim will be that the beneficiary will punish him or her for the decreased reward, thus making the exchange even more inequitable, unless by this course of action the beneficiary also experiences increased costs. Ideally for the victim, the beneficiary will increase the victim's rewards. This alternative may be chosen by the beneficiary because he or she feels uncomfortable with the victim's lower relative rewards, or it may be chosen with the anticipation that it will induce the victim to restore the original level of reward. In either case, the victim's situation will be improved.

It is likely that reducing the beneficiary's rewards by a reduction of positive utility or by the addition of a negative-utility action to a positive-utility one will be less risky for a victim than simple retaliation, and it will also be more likely to bring desired results. Walster et al. (1973) see it as a last-resort option, likely to be enacted if a victim believes the beneficiary is not going to increase his or her rewards. They also suggest it is a satisfactory option only if the beneficiary feels responsible for the inequitable situation. Blumstein and Weinstein (1969) found little evidence of victims overtly reducing beneficiaries' rewards, but they did find victims denying esteem to the beneficiaries, thus diminishing the latter's total rewards. Anderson et al. (1969) suggest that victims must first get the attention of the source of inequity, and in a direct exchange withholding rewards is probably the quickest way to do so.

Cognitively, reducing the beneficiary's rewards will involve a devaluation of one's vicarious utility estimate—"Is that all it means to him [or her]? I thought it meant more than that!" This particular cognitive adjustment may very well diminish victims' liking for beneficiaries. It may also have damaging effects to victims' self-esteem, since they are devaluing the worth of their actions for the beneficiary. In primary exchanges these spin-off effects may be devastating for the stability of the exchange relationship.

Reduce Own Costs. A second response under the direct control of victims is that of reducing their costs. If victims assume a one-to-one correspondence between their costs and the beneficiary's rewards, then this and the previous objective can be achieved at the same time. For analytical purposes we shall keep the two responses distinct, however.

Adams (1965) has predicted this to be a likely response of victims. It is the predicted response in work situations for underpaid workers being paid on an hourly basis, who may reduce either the quality of their work or its quantity (Goodman and Friedman 1971). It can be carried out simply through enactment of a less costly action, or it can be carried out more subtly through enactment of the same action with diminished intensity. Victims may lower their costs surreptitiously, giving the impression of working diligently while actually achieving very little. Observers of military life have noted this phenomenon, which we can call the "Beetle Bailey" phenomenon. It has also been suggested that this was a primary way in which the American slaves coped with their situation.[24]

We anticipate that the latter response will be less risky for victims than the former because it is less blatant. It may also increase the beneficiary's costs because it may be detectable only through close surveillance. A too obvious reduction may be met with responses by the beneficiary that do not improve the victim's situation—reduction of the beneficiary's own costs or reduction of the victim's rewards, either through the diminution of positive utility or the commission of actions entailing negative utility.

Victims will have several objectives in mind with these responses. Hopefully the beneficiary will not require the victim to raise his or her costs to their prior level and will raise his or her own costs instead. Or, if the beneficiary is not aware of the inequity, he or she may choose to increase the victim's rewards as a means of getting the victim's costs back up, thus reducing inequity at least in the short run.

A cognitive reduction of one's costs is likely to be quite difficult for victims. After all, it is their own efforts that are involved, and it would essentially require them to say, "I really haven't been contributing as much to this exchange as I thought." This response may also damage their self-esteem, and it may in fact be a function of their level of self-esteem. Victims with low self-esteem may make this response, whereas victims with high self-esteem may be more inclined to inflate their estimates of the costs of their actions as a result of the anger they are experiencing.

Increase Own Rewards, Increase Other's Costs. It will be more difficult for victims to reduce inequity by changing the actions of the beneficiary than by changing their own actions. Both of the strategies we have just discussed may achieve this result. But victims are not powerless if these strategies under their control are not successful. Three different avenues are open to them to induce beneficiaries to either give them greater rewards or increase their own costs.

The first of these we will call the martyr response, involving victims playing the strings of beneficiaries' sympathy or guilt. They may emphasize the discrepancy in rewards resulting from the exchange and implore the beneficiary to make it right—"Your piece is bigger than mine! Look how much you get and how little I get." Walster et al. (1973) describe this as "seeking restitution" and claim that it is a more likely response than retaliation. If it doesn't work, retaliation can be tried as an alternative.[25] Or victims may choose to concentrate on the discrepancy in costs—"Look how much I've done and how little you've done." Anderson et al. (1969) refer to this as convincing the source of one's high input, and note that it may not be successful because outcomes are more easily observed than inputs.

Either approach, emphasizing relative rewards or relative costs, may be accompanied with shading of the truth. (We don't predict that victims will be guileless.) Children can perceive differences in pieces of pie that rulers cannot detect. Wives and husbands are each likely to feel that their own efforts are greater than the other's.

Threats represent another possible response designed to move the beneficiary to reduce inequity directly. Again victims may emphasize rewards—"I'll reduce your rewards if you don't increase mine"—or costs—"I'll do less if you don't do your share." Victims may also threaten to abandon the exchange or to elicit support of a third party to rectify the inequity. The effectiveness of threats, of course, depends upon the ability of victims to carry them out. Thus they are more likely to be tried in situations where relative power differences between victims and beneficiaries are not great. Their effectiveness also depends upon the value of the exchange to the beneficiary. Victims may find, to their dismay, that beneficiaries don't care if they leave the exchange. Consequently, we expect this tactic to be more common in exchanges where levels of dependence are approximately equal. A third factor influencing the effectiveness of threats is the beneficiary's feeling that he or she is responsible for the inequity (Walster et al. 1978). Our previous comments suggest that victims may jump to the conclusion that beneficiaries will feel responsible.

A victim may also try the tactic of unfulfilled promises. He or she may offer to increase the beneficiary's rewards if only the beneficiary will first increase his or hers, for example. The tactic may be tried with no intention of carrying through on the promise, in which case it is likely to be effective only occasionally, or the intention may be to increase the rewards given to the beneficiary less than the increase in rewards offered by the beneficiary, thereby reducing inequity although not attaining a situation of complete equity.

All three of these general tactics require a certain amount of cunning on the part of victims, and they all involve risks. The martyr response may induce guilt, but it may also have negative consequences for the victim. A beneficiary may be angered by the accusation and respond with actions that increase the degree of inequity. This is especially likely if the beneficiary does not perceive himself or herself as a beneficiary. However, the martyr response is likely less risky than threatening the beneficiary. Promising something one can't (or won't) deliver is also risky. Victims may be able to delude beneficiaries for a while, but when found out they may end up in an even more inequitable situation.

Cognitive adjustments in this case will involve inflating either the value of one's rewards or of the beneficiary's costs. The former is exemplified by a "things aren't so bad after all" attitude and the latter by "He [or she] is really doing more than I thought." It has been suggested that actors will ascribe higher inputs to the other actor if they believe the other to be under involuntary constraints (Goodman and Friedman 1971). So victims may inflate the beneficiary's costs by telling themselves, "He [or she] is doing all he [or she] can."

Neither of these cognitive responses appears particularly easy for victims. Increasing the value of one's rewards cognitively appears to be a truly last resort—after all options that a victim thinks have some possibility of succeeding have been tried. Increasing the beneficiary's costs also is likely to be a last resort, unless the beneficiary has responded to the inequitable situation, or the victim's accusations, by trying to convince the victim of the great contributions he or she is making, or would really like to make, to the exchange.

Combinations of Victims' Responses. Victims may try more than one tactic at the same time, for example, reducing their own costs *and* playing the martyr role. It has been shown in work situations that underpaid workers on a piece-rate basis will both lower the quality of their work, thereby decreasing their costs and/or the other's rewards, and increase their productivity, ostensibly to prove to the other that they deserve greater rewards (Goodman and Friedman 1971). To the extent that an increase in productivity entails an increase in costs, however, they may not come out ahead.[26]

Changes in Investments. We have suggested that investments will be somewhat more difficult to change overtly than will rewards and costs, so that cognitive responses are more probable with them. Behavioral changes involving either the victim's or the beneficiary's investments are possible, however. Victims may decrease their investments by actually withdrawing social characteristics they have already invested. This will require shedding portions of their identities. One may think, for example, of a high-status individual playing down his or her high status and attempting to level with lower-status individuals. This individual may enter a group therapy session, for instance, carrying his or her social credentials and then discard them after discovering they have no value in that particular exchange. This is partly a cognitive adjustment, but it will also have observable behavioral manifestations. Victims may also cognitively devalue their investments rather than withdraw them, saying, in effect, "I thought that was worth more than it was." A young man attempting to make a big impression on a young woman by calling certain of his social characteristics to her attention may find that they do not achieve the desired results and will be forced to reevaluate them.

The two possibilities here should be empirically distinguishable. Either one withdraws an investment, thereby preserving its value for other exchanges, or one continues investing it and sees its "buying power" eroded. This obviously will be more difficult to do with some social characteristics than with others. A white person in an exchange with a black person may find it impossible to interact in the role of "person" and not in the role of "white person," just as the black person may always perceive that the white is acting in the "white person" role. Likewise, the white person may not be able to view the black person in the "person" role, but will always perceive him or her as a "black person."

Victims may also get beneficiaries to invest more of their social characteristics. This can be accomplished by a variant of the "dull thud" response—the "I'm not impressed" response. It may also be achieved by emphasizing one's own social credentials—perhaps with a little poetic license—by name dropping or by well-timed one-upmanship. The danger with these tactics, which are often displayed at cocktail parties, is that the beneficiary may choose to escalate the contest and the victim may remain on the short end.

A cognitive reevaluation of the beneficiary's investments may also take place. This can involve increasing the value of the characteristics being invested by the beneficiary, or perceiving that the beneficiary is investing more characteristics than originally thought—"Why didn't you tell me you went to Harvard?" The response that Pepitone (1971) calls "attribution of merit" may involve either of these. The beneficiary is seen to be more meritorious than he or she was perceived originally, and the inequitable exchange is rendered equitable.

Going Outside the Exchange Relationship. If the options we have discussed prove unsatisfactory, then victims may choose to go outside the inequitable exchange in several ways, either behaviorally or cognitively. First, they may switch to a generalized basis of judgment, comparing themselves with some generalized other. We have already noted that this is likely to be difficult, especially in a direct exchange, and especially in a primary long-established direct exchange (Adams 1965; Cook 1970). Second, they may physically pull out of the exchange. This too may be a difficult option to undertake. They may not be aware of other exchanges offering greater subjective expected utility or less inequity, and there may be serious punishments connected with withdrawing from the exchange. Numerous people have undoubtedly chosen to stay with unsatisfactory marriages for these very reasons.

In certain situations, victims are likely to appeal to third parties who have influence over the beneficiary to remove the inequity (Walster et al. 1973). A theme often appearing in cartoons is that of the unhappy married couple going to a marriage counselor and each spouse imploring the counselor to straighten out the other spouse. Parents often find themselves forced into adjudicating disputes regarding inequities in exchanges between their children that the Supreme Court might be leery of tackling. Organized groups in American society of course attempt to reduce inequitable situations by appeals to third parties, such as the government. Continual disputes between such groups are likely to lead to the establishment of mediated exchanges between them. Lastly, victims may search out other victims in exchanges with a given other and attempt to right the inequity through their collective efforts.

So actors are not without alternatives when they find themselves victimized in an exchange relationship.[27] True, the cards are likely to be stacked in the beneficiary's favor, but winning poker players have not always held the best cards. Knowledge of the beneficiary's resources, intentions, and likely responses can be used effectively by victims to improve their situations. Having sufficient resources, or powerful friends, is surely important for carrying out these responses, but an adroit use of available resources can compensate for resources that are lacking.

Reducing Inequity versus Maximizing Utility

We observed earlier that it will be very difficult to tell whether victims choose their responses so as to reduce inequity or to maximize utility. Increasing relative rewards and decreasing relative costs are consonant with either motivation.

The best way to handle this problem is to include the attainment of equity in exchanges as a goal in actors' goal hierarchies. If it is a goal, then failure to achieve it, i.e., the existence of inequity, provides negative utility.[28] Reducing inequity therefore can be subsumed under the more general motive of maximizing utility for victims.

RESPONSES OF INEQUITY BENEFICIARIES

Emotional Responses

Actors who benefit from inequity do not escape psychologically unscathed. They too experience psychological distress, which Walster and Walster (1975) divide into two types: self-concept and retaliation. Traditionally the emphasis has been upon the former, usually termed guilt because of the violation of the normative standard that has occurred. But Cook (1970) and Pritchard (1969) claim that there is little empirical evidence of this form of psychological distress or its hypothesized behavioral ramifications.

Whether or not beneficiaries feel guilty will depend primarily upon whether they perceive themselves responsible for the inequity. This perception is much more likely to occur in direct exchanges than in indirect ones (Walster et al. 1973; Pritchard 1969). A distinction should be made between responsibility and intentionality, however. Even though beneficiaries may feel responsible for the other party's negative inequity, they may feel it was not intentional. They may have anticipated incurring greater costs from a particular action, for example. We suspect, though, that victims are likely to perceive intentionality in direct exchanges and to be angry even though beneficiaries may not feel guilty.

Actors may also perceive themselves to be beneficiaries of inequity, but they may attribute it to the other party and hence not feel responsible. For example, they may feel that the exchange would have been equitable if the other actor hadn't been so foolish and expended far more than was necessary. In such cases they will not be likely to feel guilt, whereas the victim who realizes too late that he or she has tried too hard is likely to be angry at himself or herself and may turn that anger toward the beneficiary. So one cannot assume that beneficiaries will feel guilty even though victims are angry.[29] Guilt will be greatest when beneficiaries feel they are responsible for the inequity and the inequity was intentional.

What about the relationship between the degree of inequity and the degree of guilt, when it does exist? Is it similar to the nonlinear relationship we previously suggested between the degree of inequity and the degree of anger? Adams's (1965) suggestion that the threshold for overreward is greater than the threshold for underreward implies that the relationship will be positive and nonlinear with an increasing slope, as in figure 6.3. Figure 6.4 combines figures 6.2 and 6.3 into a curve relating both positive and negative inequity with psychological distress by making the perhaps unrealistic assumption that anger and guilt may be treated as extremes along a single continuum. Positive inequity will

**Figure 6.3. Relationship between Perceived Degree of
Positive Inequity and Guilt**

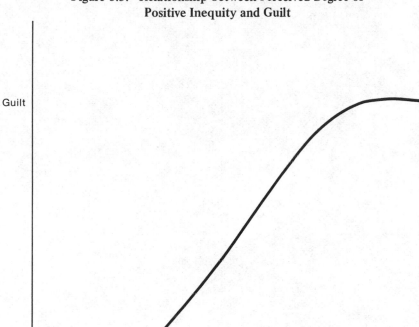

Positive Inequity

produce minimal guilt until some threshold level is reached and then the relationship is likely to accelerate. But Pritchard's (1969) suggestion that distress
will be greater, the greater the similarity of victim and beneficiary on input
and outcome dimensions, implies a relationship identical to the inequity–anger
one: positive nonlinear with a decreasing slope. Goodman and Friedman (1971)
claim that the former has received substantial empirical support, so our inclination is to go with that form of the relationship.

The psychological distress associated with the fear of victim retaliation has
received less attention from equity theorists and researchers than has guilt.
We suspect that it is very likely linearly related to the degree of positive inequity, but that it will be greatly influenced by beneficiaries' perceptions of the
ability of victims to retaliate. It can be best analyzed in the context of the
maximization of utility, which we discuss next.

Reducing Inequity versus Maximizing Utility

One of the major problems predictions regarding beneficiaries' responses have
encountered is the apparent incompatibility between inequity reduction and

Figure 6.4.   Relationship between Perceived Degree of Inequity
and Psychological Distress

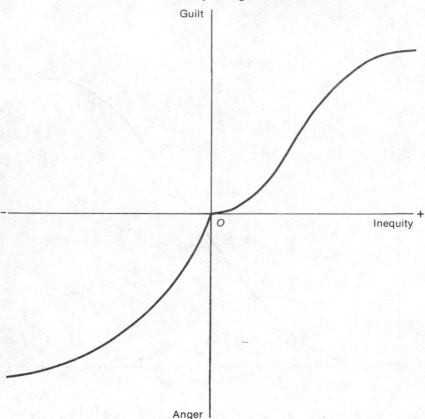

utility maximization. It is generally assumed that the two are in conflict because beneficiaries must lower their relative rewards or increase their relative costs to reduce positive inequity, either of which will diminish their utility. It is also generally assumed that when the chips are down, or in the long run, maximization will win out (Nielsen 1972; Homans 1974; Goodman and Friedman 1971). Walster et al. (1978:16) exemplify this premise succinctly in one of their major propositions: "So long as individuals perceive they can maximize their outcomes by behaving equitably, they will do so. Should they perceive that they can maximize their outcomes by behaving inequitably, they will do so." This problem is a difficult one and can be resolved best by treating equity as a goal, as we have done, so that positive inequity has negative utility and thus reducing inequity will help to maximize utility. Again there will be differences between individuals in the importance of the equity goal. It may have zero importance for the Simon Legrees of the world, but for the St. Francises it may be an extremely important goal, so important that it may seriously distract from the positive utilities of outcomes received on other goals in a positive-inequity situation. Thus the more important the equity goal is for a beneficiary, the greater will be the negative utility resulting from failure to attain that goal, and the more likely it is that the reduction of inequity will be a necessary part of a maximization strategy, and not in conflict with it. Beneficiaries for whom the equity goal is extremely important may attain greater utility from smaller, more equitable outcomes than from larger, less equitable ones.

A maximization strategy will also necessitate the reduction of positive in-equity in those cases in which victim retaliation is anticipated. Continuation of the inequitable exchange in such cases may lead to nonmaximization. Even those for whom equity is not an important goal may be wise to reduce inequity, therefore, lest they end up as victims themselves. They may not restore complete equity to the exchange (Thomas 1973), but it is probable that they will reduce inequity to a level that they think their victims will tolerate if they believe the victims have sufficient resources to hurt them. Many of the concessions the southern slave owners granted their slaves were no doubt the result of their paranoia regarding the likelihood of slave revolts.[30]

Compensation versus Justification

Walster et al. (1978) claim that beneficiaries' responses can be divided into two types—compensation and justification—and that these two types are mutually exclusive. Beneficiaries either restore actual equity (compensation) or restore psychological equity (justification). However, they have not clearly spelled out the relationship between these two response types and the two sources of beneficiary distress: guilt and fear of retaliation. We assume that beneficiaries will more likely compensate victims if either of these two sources of distress is present, and that they will be most likely to compensate if both are present. This means that beneficiaries who do not feel guilty about their advantaged status may end up compensating victims because they fear that the victims are going to punish them.

The justification response appears slightly more complex, and a distinction needs to be made between justification to self, which restores psychological equity for the beneficiary, and justification to the other or third parties, which is designed to restore psychological equity to them rather than to self. We assume that beneficiaries are not likely to justify an inequity to themselves unless they feel guilty. Self-justification therefore can be seen as a way of coping with guilt. We further assume that beneficiaries will most likely justify an inequity to their victims if they fear retaliation. They are essentially saying to victims, "You got what you deserved," and they will most likely be trying to convince them of this if they fear the victim is planning to punish them.

Hence if beneficiaries feel guilty but do not fear retaliation, they have a choice between compensating victims, thus admitting an inequity was present, and self-justification, telling themselves an inequity was not present. If they fear retaliation but do not feel guilty, then the choice is between compensation or other-justification, either of which is designed to minimize the likelihood of their being punished. And if guilt and fear of retaliation are both present, then beneficiaries may compensate, thereby resolving their guilt and avoiding punishment, or they may attempt both self-justification and other-justification to achieve the same two ends.

Further reflection suggests that the compensation and justification responses will not necessarily be mutually exclusive. Compensation may occur with either self- or other-justification. In the first case, beneficiaries may compensate because of a fear of retaliation, but while so doing tell themselves that they were not beneficiaries, in which case they are likely to feel themselves victims of an inequity after they have completed the compensation. In the second case, they may compensate while simultaneously telling the victim, "You really don't deserve this, but I'm giving it to you anyway," thereby possibly inducing guilt in the victim or gaining the victim's gratitude.[31] The effects of guilt and fear of retaliation on beneficiaries' responses are shown in table 6.2.

Determinants of Beneficiaries' Responses

Walster et al. (1978) also propose that beneficiaries' reactions are determined by two considerations: the adequacy of an alternative and its cost. First, alternatives are completely adequate if they restore equity. Excessive or insufficient actions will be less than completely adequate. Second, the less costly an action the more likely it is to be enacted. As we indicated earlier, we prefer to analyze the likelihood of beneficiaries' responses, like victims', in terms of the subjective expected utility model. We have described how inequity reduction is compatible with a maximization strategy. According to the model, the actions of beneficiaries will depend primarily upon the importance of the equity goal to them, the extent to which an action fulfills that goal compared to its effects on other goals, and the associated subjective probabilities.

The costs of an action will, as in the general model, consist of positive utilities forgone and negative utilities received. For beneficiaries the former will primarily involve possible losses of goal fulfillment on goals other than the equity goal. So to the extent that an action restoring equity does not simultaneously fulfill other goals, the greater will be its cost. The negative utilities received will stem either from a failure to fulfill the equity goal or from punishments inflicted by the other or by third parties. The subjective probability of retaliation, given noncompensation, will be a crucial one for beneficiaries to consider.

Rewards consist of positive utilities received and negative utilities forgone. Obviously the former will basically depend upon the importance of the equity goal and the extent to which it is fulfilled. We believe it quite likely that the curve for this goal will have a positive but decreasing slope in the region prior to the desired level of goal fulfillment. It is also possible that for some actors the *DLGF* will not equal complete equity. Responses that restore total equity may

**Table 6.2. Effects of Guilt and Fear of Retaliation
on Beneficiaries' Responses**

		Guilt	
		Yes	No
Fear of Retaliation	Yes	Compensation Self-justification Other-justification	Compensation Other-justification
	No	Compensation Self-justification	No response

not provide significantly more utility than responses that provide almost total equity (and the former may also be much more costly), so that the adequacy of a response should not be equated with complete equity. The negative utilities forgone will involve the lack of fulfillment of the equity goal and the punishments accompanying retaliation that will be avoided by means of compensation. Therefore if the equity goal is very important and severe retaliation is very likely, beneficiaries will receive substantial rewards from compensation.

Behavioral and Cognitive Responses

With these considerations in mind we now turn to the behavioral and cognitive responses available to beneficiaries. We will consider how these responses may be used to compensate or to justify, either to self or to other (or third parties). Compensatory responses will be behavioral, whereas justificatory responses will be primarily cognitive. Other-justification, though, will also include behaviors directed toward the other.

Denial of Responsibility. According to Walster et al. (1973, 1978), a first line of defense for beneficiaries is to justify the results of an exchange to themselves by denying responsibility for it. They may, for example, blame it upon fate. To this must be added an overt denial of responsibility to victims made by those beneficiaries who do not feel guilty about their beneficiary status and who fear retaliation from victims.[32] These individuals will likely attempt to mollify victims by claiming that the results of the exchange are not their fault. This will be rather difficult to do in direct exchanges, unless they can plead that they were themselves victims of circumstances. Thus they may claim that they'd like to give more to the exchange if they could, but they simply can't afford to. Or they may attempt to place the blame on someone else—"If it were up to me, I'd give you more, but my superiors won't let me."

Denial of Intentionality. A second line of defense, which has not been emphasized, to our knowledge, is to accept responsibility for the inequity but to claim that the inequity was not intentional—"I did it, but I didn't mean to" or "I thought that's what you wanted." This, too, is a justificatory response that may be directed toward oneself or toward the exchange partner. It comes under the scope of Walster et al.'s discussion of apologies (1978), but they do not make the necessary distinction between responsibility and intentionality. To the extent that victims accept the explanation, one would expect that their anger will be modified and the likelihood of retaliation reduced. This type of response may even constitute a form of psychological compensation for victims, who will have the satisfaction of seeing the beneficiary admit the legitimacy of their claims, and consequently they may not press for actual compensation. It is probable that this response will also diminish the guilt of beneficiaries more than will the denial of responsibility.

Increase Other's Rewards. Probably the simplest way beneficiaries can reduce inequity is to compensate victims directly by increasing their rewards. This may be accomplished by providing more of the same action or by adding another action to the original action on the next round of the exchange. The added action may be esteem or liking. Blumstein and Weinstein (1969) found greater liking of beneficiaries for victims than of victims for beneficiaries, for example. Overpaid workers on a piece-rate payment basis have been found to display this general response (Goodman and Friedman 1971). They reduce positive inequity by increasing the quality of their work, which we interpret as increased rewards for the other, while decreasing the quantity of work. Presumably the combination of increased quality and decreased quantity does not result in a net decrease in their costs.

Beneficiaries will be most likely to increase victims' rewards if they feel guilty and fear retaliation. Even though they may not feel guilty, increasing the victim's rewards will be the quickest way to resolve a situation in which the victim is making a scene, so to speak, complaining loudly to third parties about the inequity of the exchange. Sticking a piece of candy in a wailing child's mouth comes to mind. However, the costs of this response will be increased and its likelihood reduced by several factors. For example, if a beneficiary is in a situation of positive inequity with a number of other individuals, he or she may be reluctant to give in to the demands of one of them for fear the others will also demand greater rewards. Or a request by a victim for an amount of compensation the beneficiary regards as excessive may result in no compensation at all. Similarly, a beneficiary may regard a victim's threats as blackmail and refuse to compensate, or he or she may be insulted by the victim's calling the inequity to his or her attention. So this relatively simple response may be hedged with a variety of costs.

Self-justification will involve the beneficiary's inflating the victim's rewards in his or her own mind. This response may very well accompany an inflated sense of self-esteem, for example, the "God's gift to women [or men]" syndrome. This cognitive response may also consist of a deflation of the victim's costs, the response that Walster et al. (1978) refer to as "minimizing suffering." Again slaveholder–slave relations provide illustrative material. The southern slave owners were prone to overestimate the benefits the slaves received from the system and to underestimate the damage to the slaves. And many Southerners in the postslavery period apparently genuinely felt that blacks were happy with their lot and became dissatisfied only because of the influence of outside agitators. Other-justification will involve convincing victims how well off they actually are.

Increase Own Costs. Beneficiaries may also indirectly compensate victims by increasing their own costs. If the increase in costs simultaneously increases the victim's rewards, then the beneficiary has also directly compensated the victim. Beneficiaries may increase their costs by enacting a different, more costly, action, or they may enact the same action with greater intensity. They, like victims, may engage in deceptive practices in this regard, such as attempting to convey the impression of greater intensity without actually doing so. For example, a beneficiary may pretend to take great interest in what a victim is doing. One can visualize an employer occasionally circulating among his or her employees and displaying an apparently sincere interest in their work. Such actions may not be very costly for beneficiaries and will constitute good public relations gestures on their part. Beneficiaries may even occasionally step in and perform a task for a victim—"Here, let me do that for you," a response also designed to deflect victim antagonism.

Increasing one's own costs appears to be the most common response of overpaid workers on an hourly-pay basis in work situations. They will increase their costs by increasing the quantity they produce. The possibility has been raised, however, that their responses really reflect the influence of their level of self-esteem or their degree of job security. The greater their self-esteem and the greater their job security, the less likely they will be to increase their costs (Goodman and Friedman 1971). This would also appear a likely response in primary exchanges, particularly if a victim has complained about cost inequity. A husband may agree to take a bigger hand in household chores, for example, if his wife has complained that he has not been doing his part.

We anticipate that this response will be most likely if the costs are not too great for beneficiaries. Husbands who feel that extra time spent around the house will severely conflict with their careers, for example, may feel that it is impossible to sustain additional costs in this area. Such individuals will also be likely to attempt justificatory responses, convincing themselves and their spouses of the tremendous costs they are already experiencing—"I work like a slave at the office all day, and all you do is sit around home." Employers may take a similar approach with employees, telling them how difficult it is to be their employer and to shoulder all the responsibilities of the business. Beneficiaries and victims are both more likely to be impressed with their own contributions to an exchange than with the other party's inputs.

Decrease Own Rewards. Beneficiaries may also indirectly compensate victims quite easily by voluntarily decreasing their own outcomes, the response Walster et al. (1973, 1978) call self-deprivation. The general prediction of equity theorists is that this is a very improbable response on the part of maximizing beneficiaries (Walster et al. 1978; Adams 1965). However, this overlooks the possibility that beneficiaries may be shrewd enough to realize that they can win points with victims by occasional displays of magnanimity. What better way to achieve this result than by voluntarily taking a smaller piece of the pie? This response can be even more effective if coupled with the "victim of circumstances" justification. "Since I'm not allowed to give you more, which I would really like to do, I will take less for myself." Anyone who is willing to do that can't be all bad!

Beneficiaries may also give the appearance of decreased rewards by hiding their actual rewards from victims or by deemphasizing them through a pattern of behavior we will call conspicuous underconsumption. The phenomenon of "dressing down" by the jet set is a prime example of this response. Whereas the parvenu try to call attention to their newly achieved level by conspicuous consumption, those who have already achieved this level, and don't need to prove the fact to themselves or others, can afford to adopt the dress of lower-status individuals. This pattern of behavior has been generally interpreted as a renunciation of materialistic values, but a less charitable construction is that it deflects attention from one's actual level of wealth.

We do expect that beneficiaries will generally be less likely to decrease their own rewards than to increase a victim's rewards. The former response will be most likely if the sense of guilt is very strong and the reward is relatively inconsequential, or if the threat of retaliation is very great and no other option is readily available. It is likely that justification will be tried first, however. In this case it will require convincing oneself that one's rewards really are not that great and then getting that message across to the victim.

Decrease Other's Costs. Perhaps an even more magnanimous gesture than decreasing one's own rewards is to decrease the costs of one's exchange partner— "That's all right; you don't have to do that. I wouldn't expect it of you." This form of direct compensation of a victim is really a two-edged sword, however. It does reduce the inequity in the situation, but it does so with paternalistic overtones. Implicit in the response may be a suggestion, either intentional or not, that the victim is somehow incapable of contributing very much to the exchange. The pros and cons of this response are currently a controversial topic in the area of educational inequities affecting minority groups. Some have argued that the best way to decrease these inequities is to lower the costs of members of minority groups that have not attained the level of educational achievement of the dominant group. This lowering of expectations has been severely criticized by both minority and dominant group members, however, for its implicit racism. Their counterargument has been that the real problem is that the American educational system does not adequately value the inputs of minority-group members.

Justifying inequities by cognitively lowering the victim's costs appears quite common in dealing with educational inequities and inequities in general. Schuman (1975) has found, for example, that the explanation whites are most likely to offer for the disadvantaged status of blacks is that they simply do not try hard enough—"If only they worked as hard as we do, they would be successful." Thus the inputs of blacks are perceived by whites as being less costly than white inputs. Walster et al. (1973, 1978) refer to these responses as "derogating the victim" and justifying suffering. A similar argument has been presented by Ryan (1976) in a recent book regarding American social problems. Derogation and justification of victims' suffering appears a particularly effective means of resolving guilt for beneficiaries. This is no doubt partly due to the fact that their own self-esteem is enhanced by contrasting their characteristics with those of victims. According to Berscheid, Boye, and Walster (1968) derogation is unlikely if retaliation is anticipated, however.

Changes in Investments. Beneficiaries may also revise their investment portfolios in exchange situations in order to reduce inequity. To do so they will obviously have to increase their own investments or decrease those of the other party. Behaviorally, increasing one's own investments will require putting more of one's identity into play in the exchange. This may be accomplished by revealing more of one's social characteristics to the exchange partner—"Well, when I was a student at Harvard . . . ." The intention, of course, is to convince the victim that one's reward level is justified because of the presence of heretofore unrevealed characteristics. The canny beneficiary, therefore, may keep certain investments in reserve so that they can be invested at opportune times when the market is right. Investment strategies of this type, and even more sophisticated ones, can be observed at what is rapidly becoming an American institution, the singles cocktail party. These parties consist to a large extent of series of brief exchanges in which the participants attempt to size each other up primarily on the basis of relative investments. Inputs and outcomes vary little, so that the participants' investments become the main medium of exchange.

In such situations inflation of the value of one's investments is also likely to be used as a strategy. One may conveniently forget that he didn't graduate from Harvard but actually dropped out during the first semester. With this type of response beneficiaries do run the risk of overkill, however. Too great an investment too soon may result in an individual's being unable to establish exchanges with anyone because potential exchange partners will be fearful of becoming involved in exchanges in which they come out as victims.

Beneficiaries may work on the victim's investments rather than their own. If they can persuade the victim to invest less or if they can devalue the characteristics the victim does invest, then equity can be restored. The former may be accomplished by "cornering the market," i.e., convincing the victim that it would be foolhardy to invest all his or her stocks against one's own superior investments. The latter may be accomplished through devaluing the victim's investments—"You only went to State U. I thought you went to Harvard, too."

This response will have to be used carefully by beneficiaries. They may find themselves with egg on their faces if the victim has been concealing an investment. They also increase the risk of retaliation.

We have admittedly taken a rather jaundiced view of beneficiaries in this section. One must keep in mind that the responses we describe will have costs connected with them—in the form of victim retaliation particularly, but also in the fact that if one desires exchange relationships, then one cannot realistically hope always to be the beneficiary of inequity in those exchanges, unless one can coerce others into entering relationships.

Going Outside the Exchange. Beneficiaries may very well find it necessary to leave inequitable exchanges and find exchanges that can be conducted on a more equitable basis with other actors. They may be motivated to do so if they are unable to remove the inequity by means of the responses we have described. If the inequities remain over an extended period of time beneficiaries will likely experience continued psychological stress, either because of guilt or because of the anger directed against them by the victim and the consequent fear of retaliation. If they do leave the exchange, then it is probable that they will seek exchanges with other beneficiaries, just as victims will be more comfortable with other victims (Anderson et al. 1969). Or they may remain with the exchange but change their object of comparison, although this will be difficult in a direct exchange.

Third parties may be relevant to beneficiaries in three ways. First, they may direct their attempts at justification to third parties to convince them that the exchange is in fact equitable. This they will be most likely to do if they anticipate that the third party is considering intervening in the exchange on behalf of the victim. Parents may be used in this manner by children who feel themselves victimized by a sibling, for example. Second, beneficiaries may arrange to compensate the victim through a third party rather than doing so themselves. They can thus avoid admitting to the victim that they were in fact beneficiaries in the exchange, thereby avoiding a loss of face. A child may ask a parent to relay an apology to a sibling, for example. Third, beneficiaries may simply use delaying tactics and let a third party compensate the victim. This, of course, will result in savings for them, and Walster et al. (1973) also suggest it will reduce their guilt.

THE SIGNIFICANCE OF CONFLICTING EQUITY PERCEPTIONS

Earlier in this chapter we observed that the perceptions of inequity of the partners in an exchange will not always "fit" with each other. As a matter of fact, this "fit," or what we have called complementarity of perceptions, i.e., both partners agree on which one is the victim and which the beneficiary, may be the exception rather than the rule. Since there can be no objective standard of equity, and since the situation involves two actors making judgments about the *other* actor's rewards, costs, and investments as well as their own, some difference of opinion appears almost certain in most exchanges. We have previously identified two general classes of noncomplementary perceptions: incongruent, where one perceives equity and the other either positive or negative inequity; and congruent, in which both perceive either positive or negative inequity. We shall very briefly offer some observations regarding the implications of the similarity or dissimilarity of the participants' perceptions.

We can safely assume that when perceptions are complementary there is less likelihood of conflict than if they are noncomplementary. There may still be disputes over the best way to remove the inequity in the former case, but there will be basic agreement on whose situation should be improved and whose diminished so as to render it equitable.

Cases in which perceptions are incongruent are likely to be somewhat more conflictual than cases involving complementary perceptions. In the situation in which one actor perceives equity and the other perceives positive inequity, we can anticipate that the latter will be continually trying to compensate the former and the former will be refusing the compensation, so as to avoid moving to a situation of positive inequity. One may be made to feel guilty by gifts lavished upon oneself by a persistent suitor. Or children may feel uncomfortable if parents constantly are giving them gifts.

Situations in which one of the actors perceives negative inequity and the other equity are likely to be characterized by demands from the former for compensation and refusals from the latter to comply. We have also noted in the previous section that persons perceiving equity in such situations may nevertheless give in to the other's demands simply because the costs of listening to the constant complaints are too great or because of a fear of retaliation.

If perceptions are congruent, then conflict of some form is also likely. This is likely to be more severe and protracted in situations in which both parties perceive themselves victimized than in situations where both perceive themselves as beneficiaries. Two beneficiaries may fight over who pays the check in a restaurant, for example. Or they may become involved in an escalation of rewards, each trying to give the other something slightly more valuable than the other has given. But in direct-exchange situations involving two perceived victims, the conflict may become vicious, since each will be demanding more from the other and each will feel he or she has been shortchanged.

Something of this sort appears to be going on in current relationships between nonwhite and white ethnic groups in the United States. Nonwhites feel they have been victimized by whites in general, and the white ethnics feel they are being victimized by government programs that primarily benefit nonwhites. Although they do not enter into direct exchanges very often, the potential for conflict between the two groups is there. This potential has not been realized partly because the two groups are not in direct exchanges. Each can presently allocate some of the responsibility for the inequity to someone else—nonwhites to higher-status whites and the ethnic whites to the federal government. If these possibilities for diverting anger were not present, and each attributed its position solely to the other, conflict between the groups would be extremely likely.

So we can see that the fit between the perceptions of the parties in an exchange is an extremely important aspect of inequity situations. Unfortunately, to our knowledge, this has not received the attention it deserves. Researchers and, to a lesser extent, theorists have generally assumed that perceptions are complementary. But we doubt that they are very often complementary in real-world situations. The commonness of conflict between individuals and groups weakens the plausibility of that assumption.

THE ESTABLISHMENT AND CONTINUATION
OF INEQUITABLE EXCHANGES

It has been widely observed that, despite the apparent pressures to reduce inequity on the part of both beneficiaries and victims, inequitable exchanges are established and continue, sometimes for years. Why does this happen? Are the supposed pressures to remove inequity really "paper tigers" not relevant to the real world?

We believe these questions are best answered by reference to two factors we have stressed before: power and dependence (cf. Emerson 1972b, for a discussion of these factors). Inequitable exchanges are established primarily because of *differences* in power and *similarities* in dependence between actors and they continue for the same reason. The greater the difference in power between two parties in an exchange, the greater the likelihood that the exchange will be inequitable. If the power difference is coupled with a situation of high dependence for both actors, then the likelihood of inequitable exchange is even greater (Burgess and Nielsen 1974). A power difference provides the capacity for one party to victimize another in an exchange. The greater one's power resources, the more likely one is to be in a situation of positive inequity, and the less one's power resources the more likely one is to be in a situation of negative inequity. Moreover, the greater one's dependence upon a particular exchange, the more likely it is that the exchange will be inequitable. Those with high dependence and great resources will utilize the exchange for goal fulfillment because alternative exchanges are lacking. Those with high dependence and few resources will be forced to submit to victimization in order to attain even a modicum of goal fulfillment, since they, too, lack alternative exchanges to attain fulfillment on important goals.

We have noted that even the most powerful beneficiary's position is not absolute. Victims may have more opportunities for getting back at beneficiaries and reducing inequity than they may imagine. These opportunities will increase with decreases in power discrepancies between them and beneficiaries. Beneficiaries may, as a result, find continuation of the beneficiary status, or the degree of inequity that is present, so damaging that it is more profitable for them to move to a situation of lesser inequity or one of complete equity. The damage accruing to them will come from the guilt associated with failure to fulfill the equity goal, the fear of possible retaliation, and actual punishments inflicted on them by the other or by third parties in the form of retaliation or the withdrawal of rewards. In this way, therefore, the inequity resolution process can work to prevent unlimited maximization by any one party (Alexander and Simpson 1971).

This means that the continuation of inequitable exchanges basically depends upon both the size of the power differences between individuals or groups and their dependence. The greater the power difference and the greater the dependence of both parties on the exchange, the longer the inequity will continue. Slavery and concentration camps are obvious extreme examples. Victims with few power resources will not be able to mount an effective retaliation threat and will have nowhere else to go because of their dependence. They may have become so demoralized that they have even accepted the exchange as equitable. If not, then their only hope is that the withdrawal of rewards or a decrease in inputs on their part will not result in too severe punishment, or that the beneficiary of the exchange will develop a sense of guilt, or that third parties will step in to rectify the situation.

Beneficiaries, however, will be interested in continuing the exchange because they will be receiving rewards that they could not get elsewhere and they will have little fear of retaliation. In extreme cases such as this, maximization will coincide with the maintenance of positive inequity. The only psychological cost may be a sense of guilt, but this may very well be reduced by the social chasm between beneficiaries and their victims, who may be despised and dehumanized. Beneficiaries will very likely have developed an ideology of justification that serves to quell any pangs of guilt.

The picture we have painted is not a pretty one, and we believe it holds in only the most exceptional cases. But it does clearly exemplify the fact that inequity cannot be understood without an understanding of power. It also provides additional support for our earlier contention and that of others (Emerson 1962; Blau 1964a) that exchange and power processes cannot be divorced from each other.

INCORPORATING EQUITY JUDGMENTS IN THE
SUBJECTIVE EXPECTED UTILITY MODEL

Our discussion has concentrated on the equity judgments made by exchange partners after the conclusion of any round of an exchange, a round consisting of an action and a reaction. Therefore equity judgments are based on the actual rewards received by self and the perceived rewards received by other and upon the actual and perceived costs incurred by self and other respectively. However, it is also necessary to include equity judgments as an influence on two other aspects of the exchange: the initiation of the exchange and its continuation. If we regard equity as a goal, then we can assume that whether actors initiate an exchange, and whether they continue an exchange that has been initiated, will depend partly upon the degree of inequity they anticipate in the exchange and whether they anticipate experiencing positive or negative inequity. This means that we must also take into account *subjective expected* inequity, and not just actual perceived inequity. It also opens the possibility that part of the emotional response associated with experiencing actual inequity may be due to a discrepancy between subjective expected inequity and actual inequity.

Estimating Subjective Expected Inequity

We have argued that equity can be considered a goal. Therefore it should be included in the subjective expected utility model as any other goal, contributing to subjective expected utility primarily on the basis of its importance and its degree of goal fulfillment. But this inclusion is complicated by the fact that the degree to which it is fulfilled will depend upon the estimates an actor makes of both his or her own and the other actor's rewards, costs, and investments. Anticipated fulfillment of the equity goal therefore will depend upon anticipated fulfillment of other goals being affected by a particular action alternative, and upon perceptions regarding the extent to which the other actor's goals will be fulfilled, not to mention the costs he or she will incur and the probable characteristics he or she will invest.

This is not the most serious complication, however. Much more vexing is the fact that the equity goal cannot make an independent contribution to the subjective expected utility of an alternative, as other goals can, because the amount of utility derived from the fulfillment of the equity goal will depend upon the subjective expected utility of that alternative. The degree of utility derived from fulfillment of the equity goal will be a function primarily of the importance of the equity goal and the degree of goal fulfillment resulting from an outcome or outcomes. But the degree of goal fulfillment of the equity goal will depend upon the subjective expected utility of that alternative compared with the utility the other actor in the exchange is expected to receive. Consequently the degree of utility derived from fulfillment of the equity goal will, on the one hand, partially determine the subjective expected utility of an alternative, and, on the other hand, be partially determined by the alternative's subjective expected utility.

The only apparent way out of this dilemma is to assume that actors estimate subjective expected utility and subjective expected inequity in a two-stage process, calculating the former first and then modifying that estimate with their subjective expected inequity estimates. But this also presents complications. There are two ways in which this modification may be made. One is to subtract subjective expected inequity from subjective expected utility to give net subjective expected utility. The other is to multiply the subjective expected utility estimate for an alternative by some factor representing the subjective expected inequity associated with that alternative.

If one subtracts subjective expected inequity from subjective expected utility, then it will be necessary to represent a situation of anticipated equity with a zero value and positive and negative inequity with nonzero values. To do so, it will be necessary to represent subjective expected inequity in terms of the *absolute values* of *differences* between own and other's expected rewards, costs, and investments. Throughout this chapter we have found it more meaningful to represent equity judgments in terms of ratios. Another disadvantage of this approach is that it assumes that positive and negative inequity have identical effects on subjective expected utility. Two units of positive inequity will reduce subjective expected utility as much as two units of negative inequity. But we have argued earlier in this chapter that the utility curves for positive and negative inequity may not be the same.

Representing subjective expected inequity *(SEI)* as a factor by which subjective expected utility is multiplied is more satisfactory. To illustrate this approach we first convert equation (1) to a form from which a subjective expected inequity estimate can be derived directly, as follows:[33]

$$(3) \qquad SEI = \frac{R_A C_B I_B}{R_B C_A I_A} .$$

This equation will yield a value of 1 for a situation of equity, values greater than 1 for positive inequity, and values less than 1 for negative inequity.

The subjective expected inequity value so derived can then be given an exponent to represent the importance of the equity goal, in the same way that we have earlier represented the goal importance determinant with an exponent that determines the steepness of the utility curve. Negative inequity will be represented by *positive* exponents, positive inequity with *negative* exponents. Let us assume an actor estimates a .8 subjective expected inequity value, indicating anticipated negative inequity. If an exponent of 1 is used, then the subjective expected utility estimate for an alternative will be multiplied by a factor of .8. If an exponent of 2 is used, indicating greater importance of the equity goal, then multiplication will be by a factor of .64. This clearly shows that the more important the equity goal, the more a given degree of negative inequity will detract from subjective expected utility.

For the positive-inequity situation, let us assume a subjective expected inequity value of 1.2. Using an exponent of negative 1, this will result in the multiplication of the subjective expected utility of an alternative by the factor 1/1.2, or .833. An exponent of negative 2 will result in multiplication by the factor 1/1.44, or .694. Again increased importance of the equity goal results in decreased subjective expected utility for a given degree of subjective expected inequity.

The major disadvantage of this approach is that it only allows for *reductions* of subjective expected utility resulting from anticipated inequity, either positive or negative. It does not allow for the possibility that anticipated equity will *increase* the subjective expected utility of an alternative. This disadvantage does not seem that serious, however, mainly because this factor will be held constant across all the alternatives actors are considering.

Modifying subjective expected utility estimates with subjective expected inequity estimates will complicate the behavioral choices confronting actors even if they work with relative *SEU* estimates, which we have previously suggested are a common means for simplifying choices between alternatives. Therefore it is probable that subjective expected inequity estimates will be taken into account in either of two cases. First, if the relative subjective expected utility estimate reveals that two alternatives are equal or very similar in *SEU*, then subjective expected inequity estimates may be used to tip the balance in favor of one or the other alternative. Second, if an actor anticipates, most likely on the basis of previous experience, that two alternatives will differ greatly in their subjective expected inequities, then *SEI* estimates will also be made, lest the difference in subjective expected inequity counteracts the difference in subjective expected utility. Even in this case subjective expected inequity estimates may be disregarded if the inequity difference is in a direction consistent with the utility difference. For example, if $SEU(A_1) > SEU(A_2)$ for actor A, then a difference in subjective expected inequity will be crucial only if $SEI(A_1) > SEI(A_2)$.

Discrepancies between Subjective Expected Inequity and Actual Inequity

Relatively little attention has been given to the implications of differences between actors' subjective expected inequity estimates for alternatives and their estimations of actual inequity made after completion of an action and reception of an action from the other party in an exchange. It seems likely that differences in these estimates will have both emotional and behavioral consequences. In this context we can only note briefly some of the possible implications.

First, if actual inequity experienced equals subjective expected inequity, then we suspect that actors' emotional responses will be affected to some degree. Actors experiencing positive inequity will probably feel less guilt than if their beneficiary status had not been anticipated. Those experiencing negative inequity will be less angry than they would be if they had not been expecting to be victimized. These responses appear more likely than an intensification of emotion, although perhaps a case could be made for that consequence instead.

Second, cases in which actors experience inequity that differs in degree or type from that which was anticipated are more complex because of their greater variety of possibilities. Looking first at actors anticipating positive inequity, we expect that they will be satisfied, or relieved, if they actually experience equity or a smaller degree of positive inequity than they had expected. If they experience negative inequity, however, we suspect they will be angry and that their anger is likely to be greater than if they had been expecting equity or positive inequity. This unanticipated switch from beneficiary to victim is likely to make them the angriest of all inequity victims.

Actors anticipating equity and experiencing inequity are also interesting. If they experience positive inequity they may feel guilt, particularly if they feel they are responsible for the inequity, e.g., by not incurring as many costs as the other party. If they do not feel responsible, however, but attribute the inequity to the other party's lack of discretion in giving rewards, then their sense of guilt will undoubtedly be modified. Similarly, they are likely to be angry if they experience negative inequity. If they feel responsible, the anger is likely to be directed at themselves. If they feel the other party responsible—e.g., by failing to invest what had been expected—then the anger will be directed at that other party. In both cases—unexpected positive and negative inequity—it is likely that the emotional responses will be more intense than if the inequity has been correctly anticipated.

Finally, actors expecting to be victims who wind up as beneficiaries should be quite satisfied, but possibly not as satisfied as those who wind up in an equitable situation. The latter are likely to be relieved, whereas the former's satisfaction may be tempered by a sense of guilt for coming out ahead of the other party. The perceived responsibility for the discrepancy will again be significant. Those who attribute responsibility for their unexpected good fortune to the other party are likely to feel less guilt, if they reach a situation of positive inequity, than if they hold themselves responsible. Their liking for the other party will also probably increase. And those who find themselves in an equitable exchange are likely to have good feelings for the other party, if he or she is perceived responsible, and for themselves, if they feel they achieved it on their own.

SUMMARY

In this chapter we have completed our analysis of exchange relationships by analyzing the equity/distributive justice judgments and subjective expected inequity anticipations that are characteristic of exchange participants. We have presented the basic framework for the comparative analysis of equity/distributive justice and have discussed the factors leading to inequitable exchanges as well as the predicted reactions of exchange participants to situations of inequity. Our focus in this chapter has been mainly on direct exchanges. In chapters 10 and 11 we raise the equity issue once again, where we concentrate upon indirect exchanges, allocation mechanisms, and discrimination.

Figure 6.5 presents a general summary of the framework we have described in this chapter. This model is intended to represent one actor in an exchange situation; a similar model could be provided for another actor. Consequently, several of the matters discussed in this chapter have been omitted from the model, such as the response of the second actor to the first actor's inequity reduction response (or lack of such response) and its implications for the continuation or termination of the exchange relationship. We have also omitted the influences of the factors that we have suggested make equity judgments more likely, and the variety of possible feedbacks from the actor's actual response to earlier variables in the model. We assume maximization in the model.

The model can be viewed as consisting of two parts: the top half, which includes the factors influencing an equity estimation, and the bottom half,

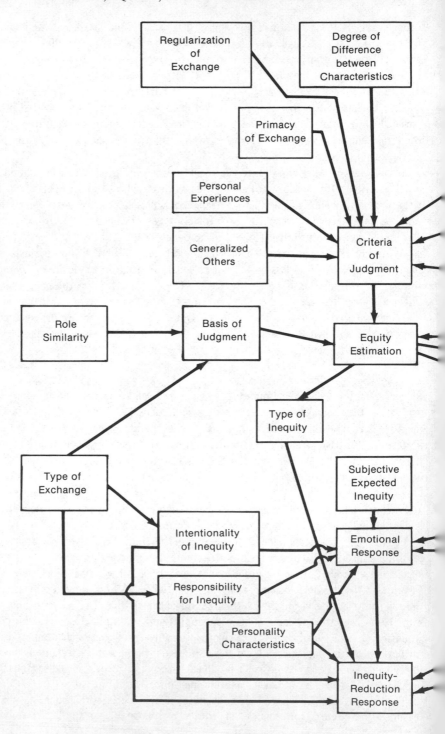

**Figure 6.5.   Model of Equity/Distributive Justice
Judgments and Responses**

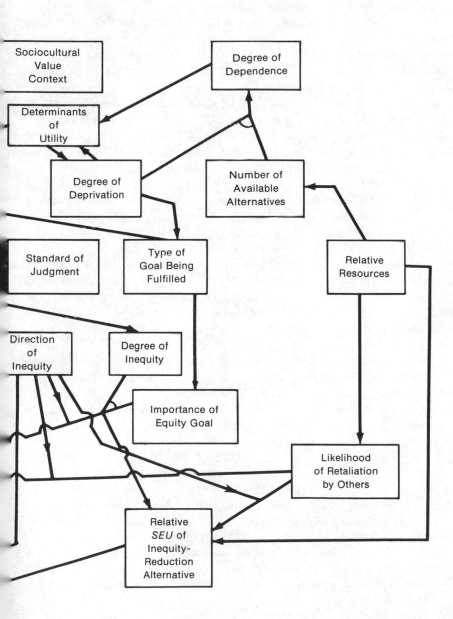

which includes the factors influencing the reactions to that estimation. The equity estimation itself is influenced by three of the seven basic variables we discussed: the basis, the criteria, and the standard of judgment. The standard specifies the relationship between particular criteria that must hold for an exchange to be judged equitable. The standard and the criteria are applied by the actor to himself or herself and to whatever basis of judgment he or she has chosen. We suggested that the choice of the basis of judgment will be influenced primarily by the type of exchange in which the actor is involved and the degree of role similarity between the actor and either a specific or a generalized other.

A number of factors determine the criteria and their values that are used in the equity estimation. We have noted that the crucial issue concerns whether social characteristics are considered as criteria. Whether they are is primarily a function of the type of goal being fulfilled in the exchange, the extent to which the exchange is regularized, the primacy of the exchange, the degree of difference between the actors' social characteristics, and the sociocultural value context in which the exchange takes place. If used, the values of these investments are derived from the actor's personal experiences or from his or her perceptions of generalized others' relative outcomes. The input and outcome criteria are estimated in terms of utilities received and forgone by the actor and of vicarious estimates of the utilities received and forgone by the other actor in the exchange. The model indicates that the actor's degree of dependence is an important factor influencing the estimations of relative rewards and costs associated with the two actors' outcomes and inputs respectively. Actors in situations of high dependence are more likely to receive smaller relative rewards and to incur larger relative costs than actors in low dependence situations.

The actor's equity estimation is divided into three dimensions: type, direction, and degree. The last two of these, plus the importance of the equity goal, are the primary influences on the emotional response of the actor. Generally, the greater the degree of inequity and the more important the equity goal, the more intense will be the emotional response. However, we have noted that this effect will vary slightly, depending upon the direction of the inequity experienced. Several other factors will also influence the emotional response. First, perceived intentionality of the inequity and perceived responsibility for the inequity will affect the emotional response regardless of the direction of inequity. Victims are likely to feel angrier if both these conditions hold and beneficiaries are more likely to feel guilty. They are each more likely to perceive intentionality and responsibility in direct exchanges than in indirect ones. Second, the effect of the likelihood of retaliation by the other actor on the emotional response will only hold for beneficiaries, thus the model indicates an effect of direction of inequity on this relationship. Third, personality characteristics and subjective expected inequity are also included in the model as influences on the actor's emotional response.

Whether the actor enacts an inequity reduction response will depend basically upon the relative subjective expected utility of that action alternative. This in turn will depend largely upon the degree of inequity and the importance of the equity goal—the greater their magnitudes, the greater the relative subjective expected utility of the inequity reduction alternative, all other things being equal. However, the subjective expected utility of this alternative will also be affected by the likelihood of retaliation by the other actor. Victims face potential retaliation from beneficiaries if they act to reduce inequity, whereas beneficiaries confront the possibility of retaliation from victims if they fail to reduce it. Thus the model also shows an interaction effect of the direction of inequity upon the effect of the likelihood of retaliation on the relative subjective expected utility of the inequity reduction alternative.

Lastly, several factors influence the type of inequity reduction response an actor makes. We show their effects directly upon the response and not upon the relative *SEU* of an alternative, although the latter may be more appropriate. These factors include the type of inequity, the direction of inequity, the perceived intentionality of inequity, and the perceived responsibility for inequity.

Many of the examples we have presented in this chapter have referred to interpersonal equity judgments, such as those made by parents and children, husbands and wives, teachers and students, and so forth. But we have also sprinkled throughout the chapter sufficient examples involving intergroup exchanges to reveal that similar processes operate at the macro level. Most of these examples have been drawn from the area of race relations, both from the contemporary period and from the period of American slavery. Other examples have been drawn from employer–employee exchanges. Equity/distributive justice judgments at the group level cannot help but be more complex than those at the individual micro level. But it is essential that they be analyzed because of their momentous role in intergroup relations in general. We hope that the framework we have presented in this chapter will lead to more meaningful analyses of this aspect of intergroup processes.

NOTES

1. It should be pointed out that Homans's latest version of the rule of distributive justice is not necessarily identical with his former two rules. We will show the difference between the 1961 and 1974 rules later in the chapter.
2. S* is a status situation in which status values and relevance relations have been defined.
3. Austin and Walster (1975) suggest a third type of equity comparison, which they refer to as Equity with the World. It refers to all the exchanges in which an actor is participating at a particular time. According to them, actors may permit inequities in exchanges with specific actors in order to attain overall equity, or Equity with the World. We will not discuss this type of equity comparison in this chapter.
4. Anderson et al. (1969) suggest the term *source* be used to refer to the party that allocates outcomes.

5. Although some writers (Morgan and Sawyer 1967; Shapiro 1975) regard equality and proportionality as different standards, we concur with Walster and Walster (1975) that they are really the same. This can be shown by taking the Walsters' approach and noting that apparent differences between the two are due to the inputs that are considered, e.g., if humanity is the only relevant input, then all humans should receive equal outcomes. It can also be shown by emphasizing, as we do, the equalities of outcome–input ratios. Thus if $O_A/O_B = I_A/I_B$, A's and B's outcome and input ratios are equal and each party's outcomes are proportional to his or her inputs.

6. See Lawler (1967) for a discussion of the role of secrecy in equity judgments.

7. Walster et al. (1978) claim that it will be easier to make equity judgments in casual exchanges than in intimate ones. Although this may be true, we still feel they will more likely be made in more regularized exchanges.

8. Several equity theorists (Weick and Nesset 1968; Donnenworth and Törnblom 1975; Pritchard 1969) have argued that the basic comparison involved in an equity situation is a self-comparison, without reference to another party, whether a specific or generalized other. For example, Weick and Nesset define own equity as a balanced input–outcome ratio. But if inputs are equal to costs and outcomes equal to rewards as we have suggested, then own equity is actually a reward–cost ratio and involves judgments regarding one's own profits irrespective of those of others. Pritchard claims that making a comparison with another party will increase whatever dissatisfaction may result from an actor's comparison between his or her situation and what he or she thinks the situation should be. We acknowledge that actors make such comparisons, but we do not consider a self-comparison the basic comparison in an equity/distributive justice situation. We feel that such situations necessarily involve a comparison with some other.

9. The status-value literature provides evidence that in task situations similar social characteristics are ignored and only dissimilar ones are taken into account (cf. Berger et al. 1972; Zelditch et al. 1970).

10. Pritchard (1969), Cook (1970), and Cook and Parcel (1977) all claim that one of the problems of equity/distributive justice theory is the difficulty of distinguishing inputs from outcomes. We do not see this problem as being that great if a clear specification is made of the action given and received by the actors and the components of both rewards and costs are kept straight, i.e., positive and negative utilities both received and forgone.

11. It might appear that the outcome of an exchange is best conceptualized as the profit received from the exchange rather than just the rewards. However, regarding rewards or profit as the outcome makes little difference. If rewards are proportional to costs, then profit will also be proportional to costs.

12. $U(B_i)$ refers to the utility of B's action for A, as in our previous chapters, e.g., $p(B_i) \times U(B_i)$.

13. Simpson (1972) also advocates the inclusion of both kinds of characteristics.

14. We have not discussed the possibility that participants in an exchange communicate with each other regarding the relevance of particular criteria, especially investments, in a given exchange.

15. Marx's description of the changes accompanying the transition to pure communism can also be seen as a case of a change in the criteria included in a distribution rule. In the stage of pure communism equity will be present when the distribution rule—from each according to his ability, to each according to his needs—is fulfilled. In prior phases of communism outcomes will still be allocated on the basis of inputs, which will be proportional to abilities, so that outcomes will be allocated unequally.

16. Legitimate and illegitimate distribution rules will be discussed more fully in chapters 10 and 11, dealing with discrimination.

17. Using profits rather than rewards here makes no difference in the conclusions.

18. Obviously one could approach this from the opposite direction and say that the type of inequity refers to the component on which there is an *equality*. That is, reward inequity exists when actors' costs and investments are unequal, but their rewards are equal. We believe it is simpler to start from a premise of equality than one of inequality.

19. See Törnblom (1977) for a much more extensive treatment of types of inequity.

20. According to Walster and Walster (1975), Leventhal has argued the same point and has suggested that there are sex differences in this regard. Weick and Nesset's (1968) finding that individuals chose situations on the basis of the other actor's input–outcome ratio rather than their own indicates that other's equity may also constitute a goal for an actor, just as other's utility may constitute a goal, and that other's equity may even be a more important goal than own equity.

21. According to Cook (personal communication), this is because the maximization of utility and the reduction of inequity are confounded for victims but not for beneficiaries.

22. Walster et al. (1978) propose that victims' responses will be determined by expectations and hope. If they experience negative inequity unexpectedly they are more likely to be angry and to demand compensation than if the experience was anticipated. They will also be more likely to demand compensation if they have some hope that their demands will be met. Hope and expectations are both easily interpreted in subjective probability terms.

23. Walster et al. (1978) suggest that the beneficiary's response to retaliation by a victim will depend upon the timing and magnitude of the victim's action, so it is likely that victims will take these factors into account in estimating the subjective expected utility of retaliation.

24. The "Beetle Bailey" phenomenon differs slightly from the "dull thud"

phenomenon discussed earlier. The former emphasizes the savings in costs, the latter the reduction in perceived rewards for the other party.

25. It is extremely interesting that the inequity resolution studies in work situations have not tested the possibility of victims' increasing their rewards by seeking higher wages (Goodman and Friedman 1971). No doubt this is also due to the problem of separating inequity reduction from maximization.

26. The "Beetle Bailey" and the "dull thud" responses both involve decreasing the quality of one's responses. The former involves saving costs while doing the same amount of work with lesser intensity, and hence less quality. The latter involves diminishing the other's rewards by lessening the quality of one's response.

27. Genovese (1976) has described how even the slaves in the American South were able to improve their situation by inducing the slave owners to grant them additional rewards—holidays, plots of land, and so forth.

28. Alexander and Simpson (1971) recommend that distributive injustice be considered a special kind of cost to be subtracted from an actor's profit. This corresponds to our discussion in terms of negative utility.

29. Walster et al. (1973) suggest that beneficiaries' psychological distress will also be influenced by the extent to which they have internalized strict ethical standards and by the extent to which positive inequity threatens their self-esteem.

30. Laboratory studies of beneficiaries' responses appear ill-equipped to reflect real-world situations in at least two respects. First, the possible forms of retaliation by victims are much less severe than those often available in the real world, so that a realistic fear of retaliation cannot be created. Second, it is conceivable that in the laboratory situation beneficiaries reduce inequity because they do not want to receive disapproval from their exchange partners, or the experimenters. These influences, of course, operate in the real world, but in many real world situations the disapproval of third parties or of the other may be of little relevance to beneficiaries, and they will be free to charge what the traffic will bear.

31. This last possibility suggests that beneficiaries may occasionally voluntarily victimize themselves as part of an overall maximization strategy. By announcing to the victim that they have put themselves in the victim position, they may soften up the victim for later inequitable exchanges.

32. Throughout this discussion we will deal with the responses of individuals who perceive themselves as beneficiaries. This is a different case than the one in which individuals do not perceive themselves as beneficiaries but are so accused by their exchange partners who perceive themselves as victims. These individuals are also likely to attempt to justify their situations, and they may even compensate because of a fear of retaliation. It is also conceivable that the process may go in the opposite direction; that is, individuals who do not perceive themselves as beneficiaries arrive at that perception

as a result of the accusations of their exchange partners. We suspect that such individuals may very well respond by overcompensating the other party as a result of their newly found sense of guilt.

33. Rewards and costs in this equation will be estimated in terms of subjective expected utilities. Investment estimates will be derived from the investment ratios we described earlier.

CHAPTER 7

Contextual Effects:
Theories and Processes

OUR PREVIOUS DISCUSSIONS of subjective expected utilities and direct exchanges between two parties have emphasized a number of complexities that
cannot readily be carried over to multiparty interactions without further simplifications. It is of course an empirical question just how actors go about this
simplification process, and we have noted that our aim as social scientists is to
introduce theoretical simplifications that in some way correspond to those made
by the actors themselves. Otherwise, we run the risk either of overintellectualiz-
ing and overcomplicating our interpretations, on the one hand, or of grossly
oversimplifying them, on the other.

In the present chapter our concern will remain with the individual actor, but
we shall examine this actor in a much more complex context than that implied
by our relatively simple exchange formulation involving a single additional actor.
This will be done by making the fundamental assumption that our actor will
attempt to simplify this context by lumping together various other actors and
by assuming a high degree of homogeneity or similarity among them, so that
they will be assumed to act in similar ways, if not in concert. There will also be
numerous other contextual variables that define the rules of behavior, that
determine which objective characteristics or properties of the actors become
resources affecting the probabilities of outcomes, and that influence the working
causal theories of the actors.

Thus although the contexts themselves may be highly complex, we assume
that each actor is forced to simplify them so that they make sense in terms of
providing guidelines for action. Specifically, they must be linked in some way
with the actor's utilities and subjective probabilities. In terms of the way the
theorist looks at it, these contextual effects will be used as explanatory variables
in the micro-level theories.

All of this may be taken as obvious. Our task, however, is to find *systematic*

288

ways of proceeding, so that we can build up step by step, adding a few complexities at a time in such a manner that we are well aware of the simplifying assumptions that are being made at each stage. Furthermore, the kinds of simplification
we make in our theoretical models must be reasonably comparable to those that
are imposed upon us by our empirical data. Otherwise the linkages between
theory and research would become highly indirect and obscure. This would
mean that the theories could never be rejected and that the pieces of knowledge
produced by particular research projects would be extremely difficult to integrate into any coherent body of knowledge. Thus although our problem is
obvious and well known, its resolution is exceedingly difficult.

Our previous focus on individual behaviors, utilities, and subjective probabilities can properly be called a psychological orientation, and indeed we have
found that very few of the studies and findings previously described have
received much attention in the sociological literature. A strictly sociological
perspective, in contrast, involves *groups* as analytic units. Many of the group
properties may involve summarizing measures over their individual members.
These summarizing measures need not be confined to simple ones such as means,
medians, proportions, or even weighted averages. Some, such as homogeneity,
consensus, or concentration of power, obviously involve the notion of dispersion, and perhaps a few also involve crude notions of skewness.

So-called global variables constitute a residual category of group properties
that are not thought to involve any summarizing measures or that are merely
recorded as present or absent. Examples include the nature of a political system,
the presence or absence of monetary exchanges, or the existence of regulations
of a particular kind. In this chapter we shall not be concerned with distinctions
among different types of group properties, except insofar as they may have
differing impacts on individual behavior. The essential point is that all such
group properties pertain to a different kind of analytic unit, namely, groups,
and thus must be treated as conceptually distinct from all individual-level variables.

How do we move back and forth between the two levels, which we have
referred to as the micro and macro levels respectively? Our verbal theories are
often sufficiently fluid (and vague) that movement between the two levels
appears to be a simple matter. Both individuals and groups are said to "aggress"
against other individuals or groups. Whites "discriminate" against blacks, both as
individuals and as groups. Whenever one is confronted with a set of numerical
data, however, such data must pertain to either individuals or groups of individuals. There will be a certain "N," or number of "cases," whether these cases
refer to persons, families, census tracts, communities, or nations. Presumably, we
have every right to expect that our theories will clearly specify the nature of
these units and their boundaries. Yet in the case of groups we recognize that this
may not be a simple matter and that our units as operationally defined may not
coincide with those whose boundaries have been delineated in terms of theoretical criteria.

In brief, it appears that in *empirical* analyses we may move between the two levels in two ways. First, as already implied, we may use macro-level variables in micro-level equations. For instance, in studying the behavior of a person we may use explanatory variables such as the average level of prejudice in his or her environment, the norms or expectations that prevail, the nature of the obstacles faced, or the behavior levels of peers or other significant persons. Second, we may use aggregated individual scores in a macro model. Thus in comparing communities or nations we may introduce such variables as median income levels, literacy rates, frequency of violent acts, or percentages of persons having specified traits.

We must also recognize that our data and our theories may be on different levels. For example, we may be interested in testing a micro-level theory about suicides or voting behavior but may only have available the rates for various units such as census tracts or precincts. In such instances we wish to infer what the disaggregated data would look like when only the aggregated data are available. In contrast, our interest may be in a macro-level theory, where the units are groups rather than persons, but our data may all involve individual-level characteristics such as those that may have been obtained from a social survey. In both instances our data are at the wrong level, and our misspecifications may be conceived either in terms of measurement errors or as involving errors of aggregation or disaggregation.

It would seem intuitively obvious that we cannot really handle these measurement or aggregation–disaggregation problems unless we have adequate theories at *both* levels and unless these theories are consistent in some sense (Hannan 1971: 18–23). In this chapter we shall assume that our theoretical interest is on the micro level and that we are given data at both the micro and macro levels. We shall turn, then, to the first type of problem mentioned above: that of finding ways to incorporate macro-level variables into micro-level equations appropriate for the study of persons as units of analysis. Following current usage, we shall refer to these as contextual-effects models.

In our efforts to relate contextual-effects models to our *SEU* and exchange formulations we shall assume that actors attempt to simplify their worlds by aggregating or grouping other actors and then using labels, stereotypes, and assumptions about their motivations and behaviors so as to treat them similarly. In particular, there will be sets of actors who are deemed similar to oneself, and whom we shall refer to as peers. There will also be sets of actors who are superordinate to the actor in terms of prestige or power, perhaps in some authority structure. There may also be subordinates with respect to prestige, power, or authority. Finally there will be different kinds of third party that may stand in several different kinds of relationship to the actor and other relevant parties: as parties that make and enforce the rules for interaction, as potential coalition partners, as parties that may gain or lose something as a result of the exchange, or as common enemies.

We also assume that actors consider a number of contextual factors that are treated as givens, or limits imposed by the system, at least over the short run.

Although behaviors may be oriented to modifying these conditions at a later time, we make the simplifying assumption that in most instances our actors take them to be exogenous and not subject to immediate modification by their own behaviors. For short-run models they are therefore assumed to be constants in any one setting, and their effects must then be inferred by means of comparative analyses.

Unfortunately, the kinds of context that have been studied or illustrated in the empirical literature on contextual effects represent only a relatively small fraction of the total contextual effects we ordinarily believe to be operative. Typically, empirical studies have focused on measures taken on the actor's peers or within some bounded unit such as a school or census tract. As we shall see shortly, one common practice is to insert group means or proportions for the independent variables in the micro equation, under the assumption that the actor is influenced by the typical behaviors or attitudes of persons who are taken to be similar. The usual assumption is that these peers are sufficiently numerous that their average behaviors or attitudes are not significantly influenced by those of any single actor and therefore that feedback or reciprocal causation can be ignored.

These formulations typically ignore means for *other* groups or aggregates, however, as, for example, those that may be attempting to control the behaviors of the actor and his or her peers. If the actor belongs to a deviant subgroup, we presume that his or her behavior will not only be influenced by other members of the peer group but also by the *difference* between levels of variables characteristic of the deviant and nondeviant groups respectively. If we are concerned about the behavior of the *i*th actor in the *j*th group, this may be influenced not only by the means of the *j*th group, but also by levels of other groups as well. In principle, then, contextual analyses can become quite complicated, even though in practice they have been confined to relatively simple causal models containing at most one or two individual-level variables and one or two contextual variables.

The kinds of contextual variable that usually appear in empirical studies are therefore very indirect indicators of what we may refer to as the true contextual variables. This generally implies that the magnitudes of the true contextual effects will be underestimated by these relatively simplistic models. This is especially likely to the degree that the method of grouping or aggregating used by the investigator, such as using members who live in the same census tract or community, does not coincide very closely with the context as defined by the actor, such as one's close friends, work associates, club members, or one's reference group. It also implies that it will be difficult to specify very precisely the theoretical links between the research operations and appropriate theoretical constructs for representing the true contextual effects. This in turn means that it will usually be hard to predict in advance the functional forms of relationships involving group means or other very simple indicators of contextual effects. This problem, as well as other types of complication, will be discussed after we briefly summarize some of the empirical literature on contextual effects.

SOME SIMPLE CONTEXTUAL-EFFECTS MODELS

We begin by assuming that we may legitimately focus upon a single behavioral dimension, such as degree of aggressive or discriminatory behavior. If there are other behavioral dimensions that must be treated simultaneously, we shall make the simplifying assumption that the actor's consideration of these other dimensions enters into the calculation of the utility functions. Thus if the actor's behavior simultaneously involves *both* aggression (defined in terms of an intent to injure) *and* exploitation (defined in terms of obtaining a highly favorable rate of exchange), then we may analyze the behavior by referring to it as aggression (or exploitation), with one of the utilities for this aggression involving a favorable rate of exchange. Thus we proceed by assuming that the behavior can be defined along a single dimension without complications arising from the possibility that a single form of behavior may have several different consequences or that several behaviors occur simultaneously.

Given this assumption, we take the behavior level Y as a sum of a series of terms each of which involves a product of a utility U_i and a subjective probability p_i. Hence $Y = \Sigma p_i U_i$, where the equation is taken to be exact under the assumption that all utilities and subjective probabilities are known and perfectly measured. We then make the fundamental assumption that *all* contextual variables C_i must operate through one or more of the U_i or p_i, as illustrated in the model of figure 7.1. The contextual variables refer to both the past and present and may or may not be intercorrelated. The behavior Y may possibly feed back to influence these C_i. The usual assumption made in virtually all *data* analyses on the micro level, however, is that the behaviors are strictly dependent, i.e., that there are no such feedbacks. This simplifying assumption then justifies one in working with a single equation rather than with a set of simultaneous equations in which certain of the C_i are dependent upon Y.

The side arrows in figure 7.1 leading into the U_i and p_i indicate that there are other omitted contextual variables that may affect these utilities and subjective probabilities. There are no side arrows coming into Y, however, indicating that in this particular model there are assumed to be *only* two utilities affecting this kind of behavior. The model obviously then implies that if all the U_i and p_i could be simultaneously controlled, there would be no association between the contextual variables and the behavior. Therefore if we had perfect measures of all relevant utilities and subjective probabilities, there would be no need to introduce any contextual variables, either contemporary ones or those involving past environmental influences (see Hauser 1974).

Why, then, do we find it desirable to introduce contextual variables? First, we may wish to locate the causes of the U_i and p_i, and this, of course, was our major focus of attention in the previous chapters. But secondly we must admit that in virtually all situations involving any degree of complexity it will be impossible to measure all such relevant U_i and p_i. Furthermore, we may not wish to have to assume that we have identified all the relevant utilities and may perhaps wish to test the adequacy of our model by introducing additional contextual variables to see whether or not the partials disappear. Thus, suppose in figure 7.1 that there were a fifth contextual variable, C_5, affecting a third utility, U_3, that could not be measured. Simultaneous controls for U_1, p_1, U_2, and p_2 would then not reduce the association between Y and C_5 to zero, and if we wished to retain the essential features of the model, we would need to postulate the existence of some additional U_i to account for this discrepancy. Thus, our second reason for introducing additional C_i is to evaluate the adequacy of the model and to make it possible to elaborate on it by postulating and eventually measuring additional U_i and their corresponding p_i.

In traditional survey research the focus is often primarily on attitudes rather than behaviors. Let us suppose, however, that we have obtained measures of behaviors as well. A major practical problem we would face is that of identifying and measuring a sufficient number of the C_i to obtain a reasonably high level of explained variance. Furthermore, without an adequate theory we would hardly know where to begin. Conventional survey research practice is to use a more or less standard set of "background variables" such as occupation, education, religious preference, age, sex, race, place of birth, and so forth. These are often plugged into the equation for Y in an atheoretical fashion or are sometimes used in conjunction with attitudinal variables to help specify the relationships between attitudes and behaviors. Obviously, this general practice must be motivated by some set of underlying theoretical assumptions. It is our belief that these implicit theories are often of the form implied by figure 7.1. At least we are willing to assume that this kind of model represents a sufficiently adequate representation of reality to be used as a good approximation.

Figure 7.1

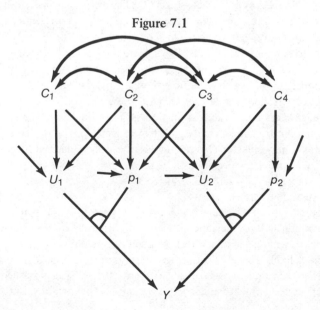

If this is the case, and if the relevant utilities can be reduced to a reasonable number, then we will have a systematic way of proceeding to build up the model and identifying the appropriate C_i. Having specified the relevant outcomes, O_i, of the behavior in question, and ideally having obtained reasonably direct measures of the actor's utilities and subjective probabilities, we would then make a theoretical search among the contextual effects thought to affect them. This would be essentially the reverse of current practice, where a more or less standard set of contextual variables are automatically introduced into almost all survey analyses.

Admittedly, however, this kind of theoretical process will usually be an extremely difficult one, especially in complex settings. Many contextual variables operate in subtle ways. Undoubtedly, then, such a strictly theoretical approach to locating contextual variables would produce upward of several hundred variables, most of which could be measured only with a tremendous expenditure of resources. Furthermore, it might be expected that many contextual variables affect nearly every U_i and p_i. Without empirical information as to the magnitudes of these effects it might be extremely difficult to eliminate parameters on a priori grounds.

The usual approach to contextual effects appears to involve a reasonable compromise strategy. This is to select a respondent's immediate peer or reference groups, obtain measures of average levels for these groups, and then insert these into the equation(s) used to explain the individual's behavior. This may be done either by asking the respondent what his or her friends (spouse, parents, or siblings) think or do, or by asking the respondent to list these individuals and then obtaining independent measures based on the actual responses of these listed individuals (Rigsby and McDill 1972). The former procedure is obviously open to the bias of positively correlated measurement errors, since respondents seem likely to believe that their friends or reference-group members think and act similarly to themselves. In actuality, then, we are really tapping the respondents' *perceptions* of the levels of these variables, which may, of course, be what is actually most important in affecting their behaviors. The latter procedure, on the other hand, provides a reality check on these perceptions but is obviously a much more expensive research operation in most instances. We shall for the time being assume that the perceived (or measured) values and true values coincide, so that we may sidestep this particular question. Presumably, psychological theories of perceptual distortion may be invoked to account for these discrepancies. Also there may be ideological factors at work that operate to create and perpetuate such distortions.

One further remark is necessary before we examine some specific contextual-effects models. It is presumed that the boundaries of the true context are clearly defined, whereas actually this will seldom be the case. Thus one's circle of friends is unlikely to be closed, and furthermore one's past friends are likely to have an impact that lasts into the present. If one is using a geographically based criterion to delineate the context, such as the neighborhood or census tract, then obviously the boundaries of this arbitrary unit will not coincide with the boundaries of the true context, if the latter notion could ever be pinned down theoretically in precise terms. This implies that one's assessment of the contextual effects is likely to depend upon the size of the units used (Valkonen 1969). It also means that it may be sensible to think in terms of "nested" contexts, such as neighborhoods within sections of a city. We shall return to these matters later. For the moment we shall assume that there are no such boundary problems and that there is a single unit or group within which the context is being defined.

The empirically based literature on contextual effects has moved from Durkheim (1951) through Stouffer and Lazarsfeld and their associates to a series of articles by Blau (1960), Davis, Spaeth, and Huson (1961), Boudon (1963), Tannenbaum and Bachman (1964), Campbell and Alexander (1965), and Sewell and Armer (1966) to a more recent series of methodological papers by Alker (1969), Valkonen (1969), Hauser (1970, 1971, 1974), Farkas (1974), Przeworski (1974), Prysby (1976), and Sprague (1976). We shall summarize the main features of the models suggested by these authors in order to relate them in the next section to our own discussion of utilities and subjective probabilities. We shall also discuss several ways in which these relatively simple models may need to be elaborated.

Models Involving Group Means

Let us suppose we wish to explain Y_{ij}, the behavior of the ith individual in the jth group or context. We may use a number of individual-level independent variables, which may be either internal states or possessions or properties such as education, occupation, or income. For simplicity we shall confine our attention to a single such variable, X. We now imagine that the behavior Y_{ij} may be influenced not only by X_{ij} but by $\bar{X}_j$ or $\bar{Y}_j$ (or both) representing the group means on the independent variable and dependent variable respectively. In the former instance we presume that individuals' behaviors are affected by the *characteristics* of the average person in their group, whereas in the latter instance we are taking the individuals' behavior as a function of the average behavior level (e.g., voting percentage, discrimination level) in the group (see Przeworski 1974). Let us confine our attention to four very simple models, as follows:

(1) $$Y_{ij} = a + b_1 X_{ij} + b_2 \bar{X}_j + e_{ij};$$

(2) $$Y_{ij} = a + b_1 X_{ij} + b_2 \bar{Y}_j + e_{ij};$$

(3)
$$Y_{ij} = a + b_j X_{ij} + e_{ij}, \qquad \text{where } b_j = c + d\bar{X}_j + u_j;$$
$$= A + B_1 X_{ij} + B_2 X_{ij}\bar{X}_j + (e_{ij} + u_j);$$

(4)
$$Y_{ij} = a + b_j X_{ij} + e_{ij}, \qquad \text{where } b_j = c + d\bar{Y}_j + u_j;$$
$$= A + B_1 X_{ij} + B_2 X_{ij}\bar{Y}_j + (e_{ij} + u_j).$$

These four simple types of model may, of course, be combined, for example, by writing an expanded version that uses all of the terms of equations (1)-(4). Let us assume, however, that we may bypass this degree of complexity by focusing on each of the models separately. We note that equations (1) and (2) are additive and differ only in that equation (1) contains a contextual-effects term involving $\bar{X}_j$, whereas equation (2) involves the group mean $\bar{Y}_j$ representing the average behavior level in the actor's group. One feature of these additive models worth noting is that if data are available only on the aggregated level, then the coefficients b_1 and b_2 will be confounded (see Valkonen 1969 and Przeworski 1974). Thus if we were given only the group means in the case of equation (1) we would have to use the aggregated equation

(5) $$\bar{Y}_j = A + B\bar{X}_j + E_j = a + (b_1 + b_2)\bar{X}_j + \bar{e}_j.$$

If one used the macro-level coefficient B to estimate the individual-level coefficient b_1 for equation (1), this estimate would be biased to the degree that b_2 departed from zero. The aggregated equation (5) will be "consistent" with the micro equation (1) only if $b_2 = 0$, which means that there cannot be any contextual effects in the micro equation (see Hannan 1971:21-24, 96-97). A similar result holds for the additive model represented by equation (2); the coefficients b_1 and b_2 cannot be separately estimated from aggregated data.

The type of equation represented by (3) was implied in discussions by Blau (1960), Davis, Spaeth, and Huson (1961), and Boudon (1963) and has also been discussed by Valkonen (1969), Przeworski (1974), and Sprague (1976). Equation (4) is an analogue to (3), with $\bar{Y}_j$ replacing $\bar{X}_j$. The essential feature of these two models is that the individual-level behavior is taken as a function of the individual-level characteristic X_{ij}, but the *slope* of this (linear) relationship is itself a function of a contextual variable represented by the group mean on either X or Y. Thus the behavior becomes a multiplicative function of the individual-level· variable and the group mean. Przeworski (1974) has pointed out that this kind of nonadditive model can in principle be identified from the aggregated data alone. For example, if we had only the group means and used equation (3), then if we summed over all individuals in each group and then divided by their respective sizes N_j to obtain expressions involving only the group means, we would get the aggregated equation

(6) $$\bar{Y}_j = A + B_1\bar{X}_j + B_2\bar{X}_j^2 + E_j,$$

which is a parabola. Provided that the first- and second-degree terms in $\bar{X}_j$ are not too highly linearly correlated, the coefficients B_1 and B_2 can be estimated by ordinary least squares, and thus the individual- and contextual-effects parameters can be distinguished. Practically, however, this may be difficult owing to specification errors in the model or measurement errors in the variables. For instance, if X_{ij} is measured with random error, the value of $\bar{X}_j$ may be a much better measure of the true contextual effects than X_{ij} is of the individual's true score.

Models Involving Homogeneity Measures

If it is expected that the contextual effects may involve not only average levels of X or Y but also their relative dispersions, it may be realistic to introduce further terms involving standard deviations or variances. There are, of course, a number of possibilities that would need to be evaluated in terms of empirical data and that might be suggested by certain theoretical considerations of the type we shall discuss in the next section. We might simply tack on terms involving the standard deviations or variances in X or Y. Alternatively, we could take the slope coefficient for X_{ij} as a function of the standard deviation or variance in either X or Y in a fashion analogous to equations (3) and (4). Or we could take the coefficient b_2 in either (1) or (2) as a function of the standard deviation or variance in either X or Y. Conceivably, for example, we might modify equation (1) by taking b_2 as a function of the standard deviation in Y rather than X. Ideally, it would be helpful to find theoretical rationales for each of the alternative possibilities. Practically speaking, however, the best we can probably hope for are some theoretical suggestions or hints at appropriate models combined with a series of exploratory empirical analyses. Of course, it may turn out that introducing terms involving variances or standard deviations will add so little to the explanatory power of the model that such possible complications will not be worth the extra effort.

Deviancy Effects

Blau (1960), Davis, Spaeth, and Huson (1961), and Firebaugh (1978) also have suggested that it may be desirable to take into consideration the degree to which the individual deviates from the group mean. Presumably, we would want to standardize the degree of deviance in some fashion, perhaps by representing it in terms of the number of standard deviations above or below the group mean. The direction of the deviance might or might not be important. If direction were irrelevant, one could use terms such as $(X_{ij} - \bar{X}_j)^2$ or $|X_{ij} - \bar{X}_j|$ or the comparable expressions in Y. If it were expected that a deviancy effect would occur only in instances of extreme departures from group means, then the former squared term would be more appropriate, whereas the absolute value expression would seem more reasonable if moderate departures from group means were also expected to have important effects.

Finally, if deviancy effects were expected to occur only where deviance is in one direction, one might use a nonlinear equation of the form

$$Y_{ij} = a + b_1 X_{ij} + b_2(X_{ij} - \bar{X}_j) + e_{ij}, \qquad \text{for all } X_{ij} > \bar{X}_j,$$

and

$$Y_{ij} = a + b_1 X_{ij} + e_{ij}, \qquad \text{for all } X_{ij} \leqslant \bar{X}_j.$$

The complications encountered in models of this type are similar to those for status-inconsistency effects, as discussed in Blalock (1967). It may be anticipated that the empirical magnitudes of the deviancy coefficients may turn out to be so small that the introduction of such complications is not justified. It will be difficult to decide this kind of question, of course, until it has been empirically investigated using a number of different data sets. Where micro-level data are available and the contextual units sufficiently numerous, however, the additional work involved in introducing such terms on an exploratory basis would not be too great.

Groups and Subgroups

Eulau (1969:14–16; 1974) has emphasized that groups are often nested in such a fashion that some larger group may provide the context for subgroups within it, as, for example, committees within a legislative body, departments within a complex organization, or neighborhoods within a city. In principle there may be several such layers, but we shall confine our attention to only two. Suppose that we are dealing with the ith individual in the jth subgroup of the kth group. Then Y_{ijk} may be a function not only of the subgroup mean $\bar{X}_{jk}$ (or $\bar{Y}_{jk}$) but also the mean of the larger group k as well. The extension of equation (1) would then be

$$(7) \qquad Y_{ijk} = a + b_1 X_{ijk} + b_2 \bar{X}_{jk} + b_3 \bar{X}_k + e_{ijk},$$

and similar equations could be written for extensions of equations (2), (3), and (4). If we had available only aggregated data based on the subgroups (say, census tracts), we would confound together the coefficients b_1 and b_2, but the coefficient b_3, representing the separate effect of the larger group (say, city), could be estimated. If, however, we only had data aggregated over the larger groups, all three coefficients would be confounded on the macro level.

As will be discussed later in this chapter, such nested groups might also be used to infer what we might call group deviancy effects as measured by the difference $\bar{Y}_{jk} - \bar{Y}_k$. For instance, an individual belonging to a very deviant subgroup might be expected to respond differently from an individual belonging to a much more typical subgroup. Both total group norms and subgroup norms might be distinguished and predicted to have differing kinds of effect on individual behavior. Conceivably, an interactive model exemplified by equation (4) might be appropriate for deviance from subgroup norms, whereas the additive model of equation (2) might hold in the case of deviance from the overall group norm. The number of theoretical possibilities is obviously large, especially if we also consider the relative homogeneities of groups and subgroups.

CAUSAL MECHANISMS THROUGH WHICH CONTEXTUAL EFFECTS OPERATE

We have indicated that our working assumption will be that all contextual effects operate through one or more utilities or subjective probabilities. This implies a theoretical strategy of allowing for contextual variables in micro equations as an expedient in helping to clarify the causal mechanisms in order to locate additional utilities that might be included in a more completely specified model. Thus the addition of contextual-effects terms serves as a form of insurance to enable us to detect imperfectly specified models. In fact, of course, since our equations will always contain specification errors, this implies that some attention should be given to contextual effects and how they are presumed to operate. In addition, since we will also wish to explain why the utilities and subjective probabilities take on specific values, we may need the contextual variables as exogenous variables in a more complete causal system.

Stated in this very general way, we suspect that there will be very little disagreement among sociologists that contexts affect the ways in which we think and behave. Yet contextual analysis, as discussed in terms of actual data analyses, is not without its critics, and we must therefore presume that, at the very least, there are certain semantic issues at stake. Precisely what do we mean by a contextual effect, as distinct from a noncontextual effect? How are contextual effects to be recognized empirically and how is their relative importance to be evaluated? These questions are not as easily answered as might be supposed. We must keep in mind that individual- and group-level measures are likely to be highly intercorrelated and therefore easily confounded, that there will be other artifacts such as measurement errors that may affect our inferences, and that the nature of the contextual unit will usually be difficult to pin down. Therefore any given interpretation of the data is likely to be open to challenge on very legitimate grounds. To the degree that the measures of the contextual effects are highly indirect, the ambiguities will become even more problematic.

Hauser (1974) has taken the position that contextual variables must have "independent effects" over and above those of the individual-level variables in order for one to infer that they have any importance. In the case of an additive model, as represented in equations (1) and (2), this has a simple meaning. It implies that $b_2 \neq 0$ and therefore that there will be an increment to the explained variance when the contextual variable is added. A single criterion for assessing the importance of the contextual variable then becomes the added explained variance.

In the case of an imperfectly specified individual-level model, however, where certain of the independent variables have been inadvertently omitted, any contextual variable that is correlated with these omitted variables will also add to the explained variance, a fact that has led Hauser (1974) to criticize contextual models as being misleading unless a large number of individual-level variables have been introduced simultaneously. Obviously, the importance of a contextual variable—or any other independent variable, for that matter—is always relative to the specific set of variables that have been included and must always be evaluated in conjunction with a theoretical model. Thus $\bar{X}_j$ may be judged important in one study but not in another, depending upon which other variables have been included, as well as the relative variances of $\bar{X}_j$ and these other variables.

In the case of nonadditive models in which the contextual variable interacts with individual-level variables there is no such simple way of assessing importance. In the case of equation (3), for example, we might say that $\bar{X}_j$ is important to the degree that it has a large impact on the slope coefficient b_j, either as measured in terms of its correlation with b_j or in terms of the unstandardized slope d. For nonlinear models linking the contextual variable to b_j the assessment of importance would be more difficult. Furthermore, it should be recognized that if the correctly specified model is nonadditive, as in equation (3), but if we used the incorrectly specified equation (1), then we would sometimes infer an independent effect of the contextual variable.

Yet the concern with assessing the importance of contextual effects is a legitimate one from a pragmatic point of view, since it addresses the question of whether or not there is likely to be a sufficient benefit in view of the added complexity. Our own position is that most of the measures of contextual effects that are usually available to the investigator will be very crude indicators of the true contextual effects. Therefore we should not expect them to make a major contribution, as measured by added explained variance. If they indeed do seem to add explanatory power, however, this should be taken as a signal that a more thorough and detailed analysis is warranted. We should then need to specify more precisely how they operate and attempt to measure a larger proportion of the variables in the more complex model. If, however, we find that the indicators of the contextual effects do not explain much added variance, we should recognize that a further search can be expected to have limited value. Provided that contextual-effects terms (such as group means and variances) can be rather simply added to our equations, we are therefore suggesting that more or less routine efforts be made to include them, just as we should ordinarily test for nonlinearities and nonadditive joint effects whenever we utilize multiple regression techniques.

Social Norms and Status

Many explanations of contextual effects, such as our own brief discussion in chapter 5, tend to emphasize the importance of group norms and possible sanctions involving the granting and withholding of status. Where the individual-level variable refers to membership in some group or category, and where the contextual variable is the proportion of other members in the area, the argument tends to be essentially as follows: if a person is a member of a given group (say, a Catholic), then the proportion of persons who are also members of this same group is an indicator of the degree to which the individual is exposed to members of this group (e.g., other Catholics) and is subject to their influence, both through persuasion and sanctions.

Thus we may expect that Catholics who live in areas where the percentage of Catholics is high will be more subject to Catholic norms (say, regarding suicide or divorce) than are those Catholics who live in predominantly Protestant areas. In effect, the proportion of in-group members becomes an indicator of the importance of or dependence upon group membership to the individual. Presumably, if we included more direct measures of this importance as additional individual-level variables in the equation, we might predict a weakening of the contextual effect, as measured by the coefficient of the $\bar{X}$ term in the additive model, or by the d coefficient in equation (3).

There are also contextual-effects explanations involving individual-level variables that are attitudes, either those that are intended to tap utilities (preferences, values) or expectancies involving subjective probabilities. These latter types of model are simpler to interpret in terms of our own orientation, and so we shall consider them first. The group-membership-type model can then be more easily discussed once we have distinguished among several versions of these attitudinal models.

Let us begin by assuming that X represents some attitude that is closely linked to a utility, as for example a social-distance score tapping, say, a majority individual's preference (utility) for avoiding members of some specific minority group. We shall assume that Y represents a form of behavior that is thought to facilitate outcomes consistent with this preference. Suppose Y represents the degree of resistance to the entrance of a minority family into one's residential neighborhood, or perhaps of a minority worker into one's union or profession. The presumption is that if the $\bar{X}_j$ for the group is high, then other members also place a high value on avoiding the minority and will tend to reward resistance behavior with high status, while punishing those who deviate from this pattern. In this way status considerations (or other possible sanctions) enter into the interpretation, as does the importance of the group to the individual, his or her vulnerability to sanctions, and other related variables.

Let us assume a very simplified model in which the actor has two utilities and two corresponding subjective probabilities, as follows:

U_1 = utility attached to an outcome that is thought to be directly affected by behavior Y;

U_2 = utility attached to receiving higher status in the group (or to avoiding negative sanctions);

p_1 = subjective probability of achieving the outcome to which U_1 is attached, given behavior Y (for simplicity assuming the outcome would not otherwise occur);

p_2 = subjective probability of increasing one's status (or avoiding negative sanctions) if behavior Y occurs.

We then may write

$$(8) \qquad Y_{ij} = a + p_1 U_1 + p_2 U_2 + e_{ij},$$

where a is some constant representing the effects of all unknown $p_i U_i$ terms that have a nonzero aggregate effect on Y, and where e is a disturbance term with expected value zero, and which is assumed to be uncorrelated with U_1, U_2, p_1, and p_2. This model, of course, oversimplifies matters considerably by taking the outcomes to be discrete rather than continuous and by assuming away all other outcomes and utilities, treating them as either constants or as having effects that in no way complicate the relationship.

Let us first assume that our individual-level independent variable directly taps U_1 with no measurement error, so that we may set $X = U_1$. The group mean $\bar{X}_j$ then refers to the average utility value for the jth group, and if we were willing to assume that all members count or can be weighted equally in terms of their influence on the group norm (or if we *define* the norm to be the simple arithmetic mean of the X's), then we may take $\bar{X}_j$ as an indicator of the norm. If we further assume that sanctions will be related to this norm in such a way that departures from the norm (in one or both directions) will be negatively sanctioned (say, by reducing status), and if the individual member becomes aware of this fact, then we may take $\bar{X}_j$ as a cause indicator of p_2. If p_2 is a linear function of $\bar{X}_j$ and if we assume U_2 to be approximately constant across individuals (or that it varies independently of other variables), then it would seem appropriate to apply equation (1) to this situation.

The probability of gaining (or losing) status is thus a function of the group mean $\bar{X}_j$, which is taken as an indicator of a norm relating to behavior Y. The importance attached to this contextual-effects term would be measured by the coefficient of $\bar{X}_j$, which should be some function of U_2, which we have taken to be unmeasured. Thus if we knew the utility attached to receiving higher status—which may be a function of the individual's present status, as well as the attachment to or dependence upon the group in question—we could make some further predictions about the magnitudes of contextual effects. For example, we could predict that the greater the utility attached to achieving status, and the greater the utility of group membership to the individual, the greater the impact of the contextual-effects term.

In a sense we may say that the individual is in an exchange relationship with the group, exchanging a degree of conformity to group norms for status or other possible positive or negative sanctions. The greater the average utility attached to obtaining the outcome(s) under consideration, the greater the slope connecting the behavior Y to these positive or negative sanctions. But since the sanctions themselves are not directly measured we take both their magnitudes and probabilities to be (linear) functions of $\bar{X}_j$. Thus $p_2 U_2$ is represented by $\bar{X}_j$ in the equation of type (1). We also expect that our arguments developed in chapter 5 on exchange can be applied, with suitable modifications, to this type of contextual-effects model.

Blau (1960) refers to the influence of networks of communication on individual behavior. One possibility discussed by Blau is that persons who are influential in the group, and who occupy central positions in the network of communications, may be less subject to status loss or other sanctions if they deviate from group norms. Therefore the contextual effects for these individuals may be less pronounced than for those who have lower status, or who have yet to prove themselves to other members. We suspect, however, that this will depend upon the utility attached to the outcome by most group members. Where the outcome is extremely important, a much higher degree of conformity may be expected of leaders than followers, as, for example, the norm that the captain is the last to abandon the ship, or that the general leads the troops into battle. The major point, of course, is that both the utility attached to status (or other sanctions) *and* the probability of sanctions actually being applied may be functions of the position one occupies in the group. This suggests, then, treating the coefficient b_2 of the contextual effects term in equation (1) as though it were itself a variable to be explained by other variables in the theoretical system.

Turning to a second possibility, we shall again assume that X taps a utility directly but that the group mean $\bar{X}_j$ affects the subjective probability of the desired outcome, given the behavior. One mechanism through which this may occur is that the individual who realizes that there are many persons with similar X levels may believe, "I am not alone. If I act, others will do likewise, and together we may achieve our objectives." Of course, there may be the opposite tendency toward overconfidence reflected in the belief that "since there are so many others like me, others will see to it that the outcome occurs, even without my acting." In either case, however, p_1 will be a function of $\bar{X}_j$. If this function can be approximated by the linear equation $p_1 = c + d\bar{X}_j$, then we shall have the result

$$Y_{ij} = a + p_1 U_1 + p_2 U_2 + e_{ij}$$
$$= a + (c + d\bar{X}_j)X_{ij} + p_2 U_2 + e_{ij},$$

which, of course, implies a nonadditive joint effect of X_{ij} and $\bar{X}_j$ of the type represented by equation (3).

Notice that in this case status and sanctions do not enter into the picture, although in realistic situations we might anticipate that the $p_2 U_2$ term may also be a function of $\bar{X}_j$, so that the combination of equations (1) and (3) obtains. The general point is that the magnitude of the interaction effect, as measured by d in the above equation (or in the equivalent equation (3)), depends upon the degree to which the average group level $\bar{X}_j$ affects the subjective probability that behavior Y will affect the outcome. Does the fact that other actors in the context are similar to oneself affect the subjective probability of achieving the outcome by means of the behavior in question? If the answer is yes, we would be led to search for the factors that affect this relationship.

Let us next consider the case where the measured independent variable taps a subjective probability rather than a utility. A reasonably pure variable of this type would be an attitudinal variable such as "political efficacy," where the respondent is asked a series of questions getting at his or her beliefs regarding the chances of affecting policies by means of the vote or other courses of action. Or the actor's "fatalism" or "optimism" may be measured either in general or with respect to specific kinds of event, such as the likelihood of war, unemployment, and so forth.

Other types of attitudinal question seem to tap a mixture of utilities and subjective probabilities, as, for example, questions involving certain minority stereotypes. If a white respondent is asked to respond to the statement "Blacks are in general less ambitious than whites," it is not clear what, exactly, its connection is with either utilities or subjective probabilities. Therefore we may anticipate that such a question may be rather difficult to link theoretically with the respondent's behaviors. On the one hand, endorsement may imply that the respondent believes that blacks should be kept out of predominantly white schools because their admission will lower the probability of his or her own children receiving a good education. On the other, it may imply that the respondent attaches a high value to minimizing interracial contacts in the school setting. In effect, the utility attached to one outcome (e.g., avoiding contact in schools) is based upon a causal theory that this outcome will affect the probability of another outcome (e.g., the respondent's children receiving a good education). Presumably, a careful specification of the outcome with which we are concerned would help one select the appropriate model.

Assuming, then, that X_{ij} measures p_1 reasonably directly, it is possible that $\bar{X}_j$ will serve as an indicator of p_2, or the sanctions anticipated as a result of the behavior Y, thus leading one to predict an additive model as in equation (1). The argument is that the average level of the subjective probability in the group measures the general level of confidence that, through concerted action, the outcome can be achieved through behavior Y. If this level of confidence is extremely low, we might predict that a laissez-faire atmosphere will prevail. In the case of a desired outcome, the high level of pessimism could be expected to produce a consensus that one's behavior level is irrelevant and therefore not worth sanctioning.

One more possibility that we may mention briefly before closing this section is that X_{ij} may measure p_1, but $\bar{X}_j$ may be taken as an indicator of variables that may affect U_1, once more giving rise to a multiplicative model as represented by equation (3). Here the average level of pessimism may affect the utility itself. If, for example, an individual is surrounded by others who believe that it is virtually impossible to achieve the desired outcome, the prevailing feeling of hopelessness may induce group members to find alternative objectives, or it may encourage them to value what may be taken as escape mechanisms, such as the use of alcohol and other drugs, athletic outlets, religious mysticism, and so forth. In contrast, if the average subjective probability rises, so may the value attached to the outcome itself. The so-called phenomenon of rising expectations of American blacks during the 1960s may be a case in point. Here, our previous discussion on the causal connections between subjective probabilities and utilities is again relevant.

Models Involving the Average Behavior Level

In all of the above models we have utilized the average value of the *independent* variables as a measure of the contextual effect. Yet we pointed out earlier, and provided equations (2) and (4) as illustrative models, that contextual effects may also be represented in terms of average levels of the dependent variable as well (Przeworski 1974). That is, Y_{ij} representing the behavior of the ith individual in the jth group may be influenced by $\bar{Y}_j$ representing the typical behavior in his or her own group. This is not tautological if we are referring to behaviors that are repeated, and if we specify that we are really saying that it is *past* levels of other group members that influence the actor's current behavior. Strictly speaking, we should subtract out the actor's own (past) behavior score from this mean, although if the group is reasonably large we may assume that the effects of this single actor's contribution to the overall mean are negligible. If we lack time-series data, we may take the contemporary value of $\bar{Y}_j$ as an indicator of past values, so that it is reasonable to utilize equations of type (2) or (4) whenever: (1) the group is at least moderately large; (2) behaviors are repeated and observable, so that the actor will have an estimate of the past levels of $\bar{Y}_j$; and (3) the levels of $\bar{Y}_j$ within the group are reasonably stable over time. In fact, if these conditions hold it seems very plausible to assume that the actor will be in a much better position to assess the group's $\bar{Y}_j$ level than the $\bar{X}_j$ levels for most of the kinds of independent variables we are likely to study.

This distinction between the use of $\bar{Y}_j$ and $\bar{X}_j$ levels may be largely academic, however. If the particular independent variable X is moderately correlated with Y, then the correlation between $\bar{X}_j$ and $\bar{Y}_j$ is likely to be extremely high if the groups are even reasonably large. Thus it may be nearly impossible to distinguish empirically between equations (1) and (2) or between equations (3) and (4). If we are dealing with several independent variables, and if we include separate contextual-effects terms for the different $\bar{X}$'s, then the multiple correlation between these $\bar{X}$ terms and $\bar{Y}_j$ will likely be extremely high. Therefore our ability to distinguish between contextual effects involving $\bar{Y}_j$ and those that use means of the independent variables will depend upon our ability to measure all variables with a high degree of accuracy and on the adequacy of our theory and model specification. Nevertheless, for theoretical reasons it seems advisable to call the reader's attention to this possibility of using group means on the dependent variable as perhaps a more valid way of tapping group norms.

There is another empirical difficulty that applies to both the use of $\bar{X}$- and $\bar{Y}$-type models but which is perhaps more obvious in the case of the behavioral measure of contextual effects. If the groups are very homogeneous, then the differences between the Y_{ij} and $\bar{Y}_j$ terms will ordinarily be very small as compared with the overall variation in Y_{ij} across all individuals. Therefore the correlations between individual scores and their respective group means are likely to be very high. In the case where we are using X_{ij} and $\bar{X}_j$ as two *independent* variables, this will produce multicollinearity problems. If X_{ij} is measured with random error, then this particular source of error in the $\bar{X}_j$ terms will be reduced through aggregation, meaning that the $\bar{X}_j$ will receive credit for the work of X_{ij} (Gordon 1968). We would require very large samples and good measurement to disentangle their separate effects.

If we are using $\bar{Y}_j$ as an independent variable in the equation for Y_{ij}, we are likely to find that this contextual-effects term dominates all of the other independent variables. This pattern will be especially likely to the extent that the groups are internally homogeneous with respect to Y. Random measurement errors in Y_{ij} will be absorbed into the error term, meaning that none of the independent variables can account for this portion of the variation. Since grouping will reduce the relative magnitude of the random errors in $\bar{Y}_j$, however, we may again expect that this contextual-effects term will dominate the remaining imperfectly measured independent variables. Hauser (1974) has cautioned users of contextual-effects models about this type of artifact, among others. Clearly, if it turns out that models of this type appear to have greater explanatory power than individual-level models, such possible artifacts will need to be systematically investigated. Studies using simulated data, or data constructed on the basis of several different levels of aggregation (e.g., both blocks and census tracts), would seem necessary unless analytic solutions can be obtained for reasonably general models.

CONTEXTS INVOLVING MULTIPLE GROUPS

In our introductory remarks we noted that contexts may be highly complex and certainly need not be confined to peer-group influences. We also noted that groups may be nested, either hierarchically or in terms of increasingly inclusive territorial units. Many groups also have fuzzy boundaries and overlapping memberships, so that what is a context for one individual may not coincide exactly with the appropriate context for another member of the same group. Such considerations imply a bewildering array of possibilities, only a few of which can be discussed in this section. Furthermore, they necessitate a consideration of alternative strategies for conceptualizing such multiple contexts.

We would suggest that the investigator first consider whether it is realistic to conceive of the contexts in terms of a series of nested groups, i.e., groups, subgroups, subsubgroups, and so forth. One may then construct elaborations on the basic models of equations (1)-(4) in a straightforward way. Practically, however, there must be reasonably large differences among the subgroups of a given group in order to distinguish their separate effects. That is, if we are concerned with the behavior Y_{ijk} of the ith individual in the jth subgroup of the kth group, then the $\bar{X}_{jk}$ (or $\bar{Y}_{jk}$) must differ substantially among themselves, so that $\bar{X}_{jk}$ and $\bar{X}_k$ are not too highly correlated. In other words, if the larger group is composed of a number of subgroups that are nearly alike, there will be no point in attempting to distinguish among them. Presumably, the most appropriate situation for this type of analysis is one in which there are relatively large group differences, but where each group is itself composed of rather distinct subgroups. Of course, if the subgroups are *too* homogeneous internally, it will then be difficult to distinguish the subgroup effects from the individual ones (e.g., X_{ijk} and $\bar{X}_{jk}$ will be too highly correlated).

Another possibility that seems very plausible in the case of many territorially based aggregates is that one's context is not easily delineated precisely but that it involves a gradation of influences that diminish in magnitude as the distance from the actor is increased. Thus we anticipate that an actor may be much more influenced by the characteristics and behaviors of his or her immediate neighbors, less so by those who live several blocks away, still less so by those who live in the same community, and negligibly by those who live in adjacent communities. This presupposes an association between proximity of residence and social interaction, as well as a causal linkage between such interactions and contextual influences. Presumably, the spatial criteria are only being used as convenient indicators of these interactions and presumed influence patterns. Clearly, however, this linkage between spatial proximity and interactions is itself a variable and may depend upon such factors as the age, sex, occupation, life style, and interests of the actors, as well as such factors as the availability of transportation and other means of communication (e.g., telephone, mail, or mass media).

In these instances, then, the territorial boundaries must be considered arbitrary or modifiable.[1] Unfortunately, one will rarely have an opportunity to use completely flexible boundary criteria unless the data are available for the individuals and unless precise spatial locations are known. We are often in the following kind of practical situation. No micro-level data are given at all, but aggregated data are given for some reasonably small territorial unit, such as the city block or census tract. This means that for an additive model, such as that implied by equation (1), the individual and contextual effects at this level of aggregation will be confounded. But one may gain at least some insights by seeing whether or not the parameter estimates are affected if one deliberately forms larger macro units by combining the smaller ones into increasingly larger ones. Let us examine what might be expected to happen if we were to carry out such an operation, under the assumption that the magnitudes of the contextual effects diminish as we move to larger and larger macro units.

Let us suppose that the true contextual effect can be represented by equation (1) and that the correct contextual unit has been used. Thus the correctly specified equation is equation (1):

$$Y_{ij} = a + b_1 X_{ij} + b_2 \bar{X}_j + e_{ij}.$$

But if the correct contextual unit must be approximated by some geographic unit (such as the city block or census tract) the incorrect micro-level equation would be represented by

(9) $$Y_{ij} = a' + b_1' X_{ij} + b_2' \bar{X}_j' + e_{ij}'.$$

If we are given only the aggregated or macro-level data, however, we have noted that the two coefficients b_1 and b_2 in the correctly specified equation will be confounded since the aggregated equation involving the means is equation (5):

$$\bar{Y}_j = a + (b_1 + b_2)\bar{X}_j + \bar{e}_j.$$

Now assume that we successively shift the level of aggregation to larger and larger geographic units. If we were given census-tract data, we might combine pairs of adjacent tracts so as to form new units of approximately double the original size. We might then recombine the tracts into sets of four, eight, sixteen, . . . , tracts each. Presumably, since we assume that the individual's true context involves a smaller area than at least some of these constructed macro units, the estimates of the contextual effects will attenuate as we move to increasingly larger units. This will generally be true empirically because of the tendency of the larger territorial units to be relatively more heterogeneous with respect to whatever variables are being measured by the X variable. Hence the estimates b_2' of the true b_2 will approach zero, and we may assume that the coefficient $(b_1' + b_2')$ in the (incorrectly specified) macro equation

$$(10) \qquad \bar{Y}_j = a' + (b_1' + b_2')\bar{X}_j' + \bar{e}_j'$$

will approach the individual-level coefficient b_1.

The suggested strategy, then, is to form various groupings of the original aggregates, to display the respective coefficients of $\bar{X}_j$ and see whether or not they appear to be approaching a limit in a systematic fashion, and then to base our estimate of b_1 on this limit. Presumably, the maximum estimate of $b_1 + b_2$ (assuming both coefficients are positive) would give insights into the approximate size of the territorial unit that best represents the true contextual effects in this particular instance. Admittedly, this kind of strategy would provide only very weak tests of the underlying reasoning, but it would at least serve to yield insights as to what happens when the sizes of the macro units are shifted. More generally, our recommendation would be to aggregate one's data at several different levels to see how this affects one's estimates of the structural parameters. This depends, of course, on the availability of data based on reasonably small geographic units such as blocks, precincts, census tracts, or counties.

Comparisons Involving both Group and Subgroup Means

Let us now examine in somewhat greater detail a third type of situation involving multiple groups. Suppose it is reasonable to assume there is a single larger group composed of a number of subgroups such that members of each subgroup think primarily in terms of only two groups, their own subgroup and the larger group as a whole. This implies that there will be two means that are relevant, the $\bar{X}_{jk}$ (or $\bar{Y}_{jk}$) for the specific subgroup of which the individual is a member, and the overall group mean $\bar{X}_k$ (or $\bar{Y}_k$). The latter may be defined as setting the group norm, from which the subgroup in question may deviate to varying degrees, or as expressing a comparison level, if we are dealing with properties or possessions such as income or occupational levels. This model seems reasonably appropriate for situations in which we are studying mutually isolated deviant groups or minorities that tend to perceive themselves as very distinct from other minorities. In effect, then, this type of model rules out comparisons among subgroups and deals only with situations in which it is reasonable to assume that each minority or deviant group can be dealt with in isolation from the others.

An individual member of the minority group (which we shall refer to as subgroup j) is then influenced not only by $\bar{X}_{jk}$ (or $\bar{Y}_{jk}$) but also the overall group mean. We assume that there are both subgroup norms and sanctions and also those imposed by the larger group and that the utilities and subjective probabilities relevant to these two groups may vary in magnitude from one individual to the next. If we make no assumptions about these individual-level coefficients whatsoever, we will of course have far too many unknowns. Given sufficient information, however, we may divide each subgroup into sets of individuals for whom the U_i and p_i will be nearly identical. Let us assume, for simplicity, that this has been done and that the coefficients within each subgroup are identical. We shall consider three apparently different equations, all of which involve extensions of the additive equation (1). These are as follows:[2]

$$(11) \quad Y_{ijk} = a + b_1 X_{ijk} + b_2(X_{ijk} - \bar{X}_{jk}) + b_3(X_{ijk} - \bar{X}_k) + e_{ijk};$$

$$(12) \quad Y_{ijk} = a' + b_1' X_{ijk} + b_2'(X_{ijk} - \bar{X}_{jk}) + b_3'(\bar{X}_{jk} - \bar{X}_k) + e_{ijk}';$$

$$(13) \quad Y_{ijk} = a^* + b_1^* X_{ijk} + b_2^*(X_{ijk} - \bar{X}_k) + b_3^*(\bar{X}_{jk} - \bar{X}_k) + e_{ijk}^*.$$

In equation (11) the individual's behavior level is influenced by three factors: (1) his or her own X level; (2) the individual's deviance (in terms of the X level) from the subgroup mean; and (3) the individual's deviance from the overall group mean. Presumably, the individual assesses himself or herself in terms of the two separate groups, without making a direct comparison between the two group averages. In equations (12) and (13), in contrast, the individual makes a comparison of his or her own level with the mean for one or the other group— the subgroup in the case of equation (12) and the total group in the case of equation (13). A comparison is also made in these latter two equations between the means of the subgroup and total group. It is as though the actor is in effect saying, "I am a member of a subgroup that differs from the overall average, and this difference is important to me." Perhaps the individual is interested in bringing the subgroup mean closer to that of the overall group, as we presume that many members of minority groups are interested in doing if they wish to raise the average income level of minority members, or have an assimilationist or integrationist orientation. It is entirely possible, however, that the individual is motivated to *increase* the average difference between the subgroup and average group member. Thus the signs of the various coefficients need not all be the same.

One would naturally raise the question as to whether in this simple additive type of model the equations (11), (12), and (13) are all observationally equivalent. Put another way, if we were given some empirical data would we be in a position to distinguish among them without imposing any additional a priori assumptions? If we rewrite each of the equations by grouping the coefficients of X_{ijk}, $\bar{X}_{jk}$, and $\bar{X}_k$ we get

(11) $\quad Y_{ijk} = a + (b_1 + b_2 + b_3)X_{ijk} - b_2\bar{X}_{jk} - b_3\bar{X}_k + e_{ijk}$;

(12) $\quad Y_{ijk} = a' + (b_1' + b_2')X_{ijk} + (b_3' - b_2')\bar{X}_{jk} - b_3'\bar{X}_k + e_{ijk}'$;

(13) $\quad Y_{ijk} = a^* + (b_1^* + b_2^*)X_{ijk} + b_3^*\bar{X}_{jk} - (b_2^* + b_3^*)\bar{X}_k + e_{ijk}^*$;

which are obviously all of the form

(14) $\qquad\qquad Y_{ijk} = A + B_1 X_{ijk} + B_2\bar{X}_{jk} + B_3\bar{X}_k + E_{ijk}$.

Thus if we were to obtain the ordinary least-squares estimates of A and the B_i we would not be able to tell from these coefficients how to decompose them into the structural parameters—unless, of course, we were willing to assume a priori that two of the three equations could be eliminated. Obviously, these particular three equations do not exhaust the list of possibilities, which is to say that there may be several alternative processes all of which are capable of producing the same empirical results.

It will perhaps be possible to specify some of the signs of the coefficients, in which case one or more of the alternatives may be rejected as not being consistent with the data. For example, if all of the b's were assumed to be positive, and if B_2 were found to be positive, one would have to conclude that (11) should be eliminated, and that furthermore if (12) were true this would imply that $b_3' > b_2'$ and that $|B_2|$ should be less than $|B_3|$.

Further refinements in the theory might suggest modifications implying nonlinearities, as, for example, the possibility that the *direction* of deviance may not matter, in which case certain squared terms could replace one or more of the expressions in parentheses. Of course, tests of these alternative formulations would depend upon one's finding not only multiple subgroups but also a number of larger groups having very different mean values. Otherwise, the variable $\bar{X}_k$ might have to be replaced by a fixed standard, in which case the problem would have become trivialized.

Mechanisms through Which Group and Subgroup Means Produce Changes in Behaviors

Of greater interest than these particular equations are the general mechanisms through which multiple-group contextual effects may be presumed to operate. In the next major section we shall look specifically at the phenomenon of inequality, and we shall see that this provides one such mechanism. In the remainder of this section we shall focus primarily on norms, sanctions, and the relative homogeneity of the subgroup and larger total group.

Let us assume a reasonably simplified model in which the forces or pressures to change an individual's behavior are a function of the deviations from the average levels for both the subgroup and the total group. We shall confine our attention to a model involving only the *behavioral* levels, Y, $\bar{Y}_{jk}$ and $\bar{Y}_k$, where for convenience we shall drop the ijk subscript from the individual-level behavior with the understanding that we are concerned with the behavior of the ith individual in the *j*th subgroup. We shall further assume that the *rate of change* in Y, dY/dt, is proportional to these two forces. Thus dY/dt will be some function of $(Y - \bar{Y}_{jk})$ and $(Y - \bar{Y}_k)$, as well as other individual-level variables that we may wish to specify in particular contexts.

There are, of course, many possible functions that might be used, but let us consider illustratively only the very simple linear differential equation

$$(15) \qquad dY/dt = a + b_1(Y - \bar{Y}_{jk}) + b_2(Y - \bar{Y}_k).$$

This equation says that the rate of change in Y will be an additive function of (1) some constant, representing the effects of numerous exogenous variables (including possibly a number of personality variables) that remain fixed over the period of study; (2) a constant b_1 times the degree to which the momentary behavior level departs from the subgroup mean; and (3) a second constant, b_2, times the degree to which the momentary behavior departs from the total group mean. We shall later discuss some variables that may affect the magnitudes of the slope coefficients b_1 and b_2.

It can easily be shown that the necessary condition for stability of this very simple equation is that $b_1 + b_2 < 0$ and that the greater the departure of $b_1 + b_2$ from zero in the negative direction, the more rapidly the behavior approaches the equilibrium level. We may rewrite the differential equation as

$$dY/dt = a + (b_1 + b_2)Y - b_1\bar{Y}_{jk} - b_2\bar{Y}_k.$$

If the necessary condition for stability is met—and, of course, it may not be—then we may find the equilibrium level by setting $dY/dt = 0$ (indicating that the rate of change is zero) and solving for the equilibrium level of Y, which we shall label Y_e.[3] We get

$$(16) \qquad Y_e = \frac{-a}{b_1 + b_2} + \frac{b_1}{b_1 + b_2}\bar{Y}_{jk} + \frac{b_2}{b_1 + b_2}\bar{Y}_k.$$

If the constant term $a = 0$ we see that the equilibrium level Y_e would be just a weighted average of $\bar{Y}_{jk}$ and $\bar{Y}_k$, indicating that if both b_1 and b_2 were negative we would expect the individual's behavior to settle down somewhere in between the levels represented by the two groups. The greater the absolute value of b_1 relative to that of b_2, the closer the behavior level would be to the subgroup mean $\bar{Y}_{jk}$, so that we may interpret b_1 and b_2 as weights representing the relative magnitudes of the two forces pulling the behavior level toward their respective means. Ordinarily we expect both b_1 and b_2 to be negative. As can easily be seen, in the case of b_1 this would imply that if Y falls below $\bar{Y}_{jk}$, the term $(Y - \bar{Y}_{jk})$ will be negative, so that a negative value of b_1 implies that the contribution to dY/dt will then be positive, meaning that there will be a tendency for the behavior level to increase. But if Y were to go above the mean $\bar{Y}_{jk}$ the term $(Y - \bar{Y}_{jk})$ would become positive, and hence the product $b_1(Y - \bar{Y}_{jk})$ would be negative, and this would tend to pull the behavior level downward toward $\bar{Y}_{jk}$. If there were no forces operating from the total group, b_2 would be zero, and if a were also zero the equilibrium level would be at $\bar{Y}_{jk}$. If the same held for all subgroup members, the Y levels would all be identical and we would have complete subgroup homogeneity.

For a person who is not at all influenced by the subgroup, b_1 would be zero, and a zero value of the constant term a would imply that the equilibrium level would be at $\bar{Y}_k$. Of course, the possibility that a will not always be zero for all actors means that certain persons' behavior levels will be lower than either $\bar{Y}_{jk}$ or $\bar{Y}_k$, whereas those of other actors may be higher. By taking a as a constant, however, we assure ourselves that the stability condition depends *only* on b_1 and b_2. If both of these are negative, then not only is stability assured but also both coefficients $b_1/(b_1 + b_2)$ and $b_2/(b_1 + b_2)$ are positive so that if $a = 0$ the equilibrium level falls between the two group means, as previously indicated. Suppose, however, that b_2 is slightly positive, although smaller numerically than b_1. Since $b_1 + b_2 < 0$ the coefficient of the $\bar{Y}_k$ term now becomes negative, so that if, say, $\bar{Y}_{jk} < \bar{Y}_k$ and $a = 0$, the behavior will stabilize *below* $\bar{Y}_{jk}$.[4] This is the case where the individual has a "negative reaction" to total group pressures, so that efforts to produce conformity merely create greater deviancy.

There are, of course, other, more complex alternative models that could be postulated, including those that use the squared deviancy terms $(Y - \bar{Y}_{jk})^2$ and $(Y - \bar{Y}_k)^2$ or those that imply forces in operation only when the deviancy is in one particular direction. We shall consider a few illustrations of such more complex alternatives in connection with macro-level models in the final chapter. Let us turn our attention to the b coefficients, however, and to factors that may affect their relative magnitudes—and therefore both the stability conditions and the equilibrium levels. Obviously, any factors that operate to decrease the sum $b_1 + b_2$ will aid stability.

We shall discuss three kinds of factor influencing the absolute and relative magnitudes of b_1 and b_2, namely: (1) the distance between $\bar{Y}_{jk}$ and $\bar{Y}_k$ relative to the subgroup and group standard deviations; (2) the importance of the behavior Y to the members of the total group and the subgroup j; and (3) the ability of the group and subgroup to apply sanctions to the individual concerned.

Considering first the difference between $\bar{Y}_{jk}$ and $\bar{Y}_k$ relative to the homogeneity of the two groups, we would generally expect that the greater the difference $\bar{Y}_{jk} - \bar{Y}_k$, the greater the stress placed on the individual, who is subject to cross-pressures. Clearly, it will be impossible to conform to both norms, and the greater the difference the more difficult it will be to resolve the stress by any particular form of behavior. Moreover, if $\bar{Y}_{jk}$ and $\bar{Y}_k$ are very close then the *relative* magnitudes of b_1 and b_2 will make very little difference as to the equilibrium level Y_e, although their *sum* as compared with the constant a (or other factors appearing in the equation) will, of course, remain important. In effect, the two group norms will be mutually reinforcive in the sense that an individual who is only very loosely attached to the total group but strongly attached to the subgroup will behave in much the same way as someone who is strongly attached to the total group but only weakly so to the subgroup.

The farther apart the two group means, however, the more likely that the individual will be tempted to modify his or her utilities or subjective probabilities in some way. One possibility is to detach oneself from an allegiance to one or the other group, as, for example, in the case of the minority-group member who attempts to "pass" or to cut off his or her contacts with other minority-group members or, in the opposite case, of the subgroup member who denounces the larger group in favor of loyalty to the subgroup. In terms of utilities, for example, the actor may attempt to satisfy status goals by obtaining recognition as a minority leader and by minimizing the importance attached to rewards emanating from the larger group.

Another possible resolution for the individual caught in this situation is to work toward bringing the two group means (or norms) closer together and, perhaps, to achieve recognition for this effort as a kind of "integrative" leader. We would predict that the subjective probability of achieving this kind of objective will depend, among other things, on the absolute and relative sizes of the two groups, as well as the amount of overt conflict. If the two groups are large, the probability of achieving a substantial shift in either level will be lower than in the case of smaller groups, and therefore we would predict that an "individualistic" resolution is more likely to be attempted by members of such larger groups.

If the absolute size of the subgroup is large, there will more likely be greater protection of anonymity from negative sanctions attempted by the larger group. This implies that as the size of a deviant subgroup increases, it becomes more and more difficult for the total group to apply sanctions to the individual subgroup members, which may in turn necessitate the use of different types of control technique. We imply that, other things being equal, an increase in size of the subgroup will tend to have the effect of increasing the magnitude of b_1 relative to b_2 (i.e., making $b_1 < b_2$ where both are negative).

As a general rule, we also expect that the subgroup will be more homogeneous than the total group with respect to the behavior Y. This will, of course, depend on the importance of the behavior to the two kinds of group member, a matter to which we shall return below. The farther apart the two means, the more homogeneous we expect the deviant subgroup to become, and also the more *motivated* its members will be to apply sanctions to keep its members in line. Assuming that the sanctioning power of a group or subgroup is inversely related to its diversity, this implies that the magnitude of b_1 relative to b_2 will be increased as the difference $\bar{Y}_{jk} - \bar{Y}_k$ increases.

This reasoning depends on the assumption that the remainder of the total group is itself relatively homogeneous. But it is also possible that there are a number of diverse subgroups whose average behavior levels are strung out along a continuum. If so, or if the subgroup boundaries are not really distinct, the individual may simply shift attachments to an adjacent subgroup and derive satisfactions from conforming to its somewhat different level of behavior. This possibility would presumably also inhibit any given subgroup from applying too extreme pressures on its members. Thus an important factor that may affect the relationship between $\bar{Y}_{jk} - \bar{Y}_k$ and the individual's behavior level is the permeability or mobility that is possible between subgroups.

In the case of minority groups, for example, there appears to be a very great difference between societies in which, say, a factor like color is defined along a continuum with fine gradations being distinguished (as in Brazil or certain Caribbean areas) and those such as the United States where there is a sharp distinction between blacks and whites. Where the continuum definition applies, color becomes one among several status criteria that are blended together, so that one may in effect substitute income for color with the result that subgroup boundaries are fuzzy and modifiable. In the United States, one of the fundamental psychological problems facing blacks is that of assessing the degree to which rigid racial boundaries really exist. Translated in terms of subjective probabilities, it is often difficult for blacks to assess the true probability that conformity to the total group norm will also bring about acceptance or improved status. If so, we would expect a tendency to vacillate between behaviors oriented toward conformity to the total group norms and those that deviate substantially from these norms.

We are basically assuming that the actor in this kind of situation has two utilities: U_1 to receive high status and recognition in the subgroup, and U_2 to receive the same in the larger group as a whole. The behavior level selected will, of course, not only depend upon U_1 and U_2 but it will also be affected by p_1 and p_2. If p_2 is very low, then the $p_1 U_1$ term of equation (8) will dominate, and the magnitude of b_1 will be much greater than b_2 in equation (15). The objective probability corresponding to p_2 may be exceedingly difficult to evaluate empirically, however, owing to the fact that the behavior is not repeated or that the patterning of responses to the behavior may be highly erratic. In such instances we expect that ideological considerations will play an important role in affecting the relative magnitudes of p_1 and p_2. There may be one ideology that says to blacks, "You can't possibly make it into the larger white society, so forget it!" whereas another says, "If you'll only conform, we'll let you in."

The second and rather obvious factor influencing the sizes of b_1 and b_2 is the importance of the behavior to the subgroup and total group. In general, we would expect that the previously discussed patterns will be intensified to the degree that the behavior is thought to be important by the members of the respective groups. One point seems worth mentioning in this connection. Certain types of behavior may be of relatively minor importance in the total group and yet have symbolic importance to subgroup members, perhaps in that they reinforce subgroup loyalties as in the case of rituals, distinctive dress or mannerisms, or art forms readily identified with the subgroup (e.g., music, dances, or literature).

It may well be the case that these "deviant" or merely different forms of behavior will actually be encouraged by members of the larger group so as to ensure the loyalty to the total group. Should these types of behavior be used by the subgroup in such a fashion as to emphasize subgroup loyalties in a *conflict* situation, however, the response of the larger-group members may alter sharply. Therefore the degree of conflict may have an important bearing on both the sign and magnitude of b_2 for these forms of behavior. When the level of conflict is low, they may be defined as "quaint" and indicative of "tolerance" by members of the larger group, whereas they may become focal points of derision, rigid stereotyping, and anger in situations in which conflict becomes pronounced, where subgroup boundaries become much more distinct, and where the behaviors in question take on important symbolic meanings to members of the opposing groups.

By the same token, as the level of conflict lessens, it is often these same forms of behavior that have the symbolic function of showing that tension is in fact really being reduced. For instance we find that the reduction in East-West tensions has resulted in so-called cultural exchanges of artists, athletes and scholars. "Afro" hair styles, originally perceived as threatening and as a symbol of "black power" by many whites, may become overemphasized in advertisements and artistic forms of behavior precisely because they emphasize a degree of tolerance for diversity or symbolic deviance that may not exist for more important forms of behavior. It is as if to say that the members of the total group are saying to subgroup members: "We'll actively encourage you to be deviant in unimportant matters in exchange for your conformity on essential ones."

Finally, the relative resources of the total group and subgroup will, of course, affect the behavior level of the individual subgroup member. We shall be specifically concerned with power and resources in chapter 8. Here it is sufficient to point out that individuals will have certain very important utilities attached to such outcomes as survival, avoiding extreme risks or unpleasant circumstances, the safety of close friends and relatives, keeping their employment, and so forth. The subgroup and total group members will differ in their ability and willingness to apply these sanctions, and there is little need to go into this matter in detail in the present context. One point is worth mentioning, however. The size and internal organization of the subgroup may have considerable impact in terms of protecting its members from negative sanctions attempted by members of the larger group.

This ability to protect subgroup members will also be a function of the importance of the subgroup to the functioning of the total group. If the subgroup, as a whole, is highly important to the larger group, and if it is in a position to shield its deviant members, say, as a consequence of their anonymity, then the larger group may have to rely totally on positive inducements for conformity. If the subgroup is relatively unimportant, however, it seems more likely that negative sanctions will be applied to the subgroup *as a whole* unless it permits its individual deviants to be sanctioned. Under such circumstances—where in effect the subgroup is in a weak power position—members of the subgroup are posed with a serious dilemma. Either they must fail to protect their individual members or they can expect sanctions applied to their membership as a whole. In such circumstances, the resulting organizational strains may further decrease the ability of the subgroup to apply positive or negative sanctions of its own. There is likely to be ambivalence concerning the alternative strategies of appealing to subgroup solidarity versus permitting individual members to act primarily as individuals, subject primarily to the positive and negative sanctions of the larger group.

Situations of this type frequently arise in minority-group relations where the subgroup (here, a minority) has marginal importance to the larger group and yet cannot be cast aside completely. Its members are then likely to be perceived primarily as nuisances to suffer "benign neglect." This thesis has been developed by Willhelm (1971), who claims that blacks in the United States are no longer really needed as a cheap source of labor because of the increasing automation of work that previously was done by unskilled labor. His argument essentially boils down to the thesis that blacks are likely to be merely shunted aside to swell the ranks of the unemployed and that in reality their urban ghettos constitute a kind of "reservation" in many ways similar to those inhabited by American Indians.

The behaviors of members of subgroups of this type are likely to be ignored as long as they do no harm to members of the larger group. Hence high crime rates, drug addiction, or other forms of deviance that affect only the minority community may be totally neglected or defined to be a "problem" that the minority itself must solve. If they spill over to the dominant-group community, however, the sanctions may be severe. Such a subgroup may be forced to call itself to the attention of the larger group through dramatic actions and thereby risk severe sanctions. The result may be an alternation between periods of extreme neglect but relative tranquility and those involving crises that seem inexplicable to members of the larger group. This is in contrast with subgroups that are sufficiently powerful to exert a more sustained pressure and a more systematic control over the behaviors of their own members.

CONTEXTUAL EFFECTS OF INEQUALITIES

A closely related subject is that of comparisons actors make that involve inequality of various types, a topic that will also be of concern to us when we discuss the measurement of discrimination. In brief, sociologists commonly assume that many of the most important social goals of actors revolve about the comparisons they make between themselves and others, as well as among various groups and categories of persons. In chapter 2 one of the important motivational factors invoked in our discussion of utilities was the size of the gap between the actor's current level of goal fulfillment, on the one hand, and some desired level, on the other. We also discussed the phenomenon of discounting the importance of goals that must be achieved at some distant point in the future, as well as satiation phenomena. All of these seem related to the comparisons one makes among various actors' levels of achievements, possessions, or relative statuses. In short, inequalities of many kinds form important contexts for the individual actor. So do the belief systems that may serve to explain these inequalities or that may encourage perceptual distortions either to exaggerate or to minimize their magnitudes and importance. There are also beliefs relating to one's chances of *changing* these inequalities, as, for example, through either individual mobility or group action.

Again, it is extremely difficult to pin down the nature of the context within which each individual is acting, to say nothing of measuring contextual influences with imperfect indicators such as group or subgroup averages. Perhaps the strategy of thinking in terms of nested groups could be applied to certain kinds of ideological influences, as well as group and subgroup comparisons. Such crude indicators would undoubtedly have to be supplemented by questions and observations directed to the individuals themselves. For instance, we might assume that all Americans are subject to certain ideological influences that affect their perceptions and interpretations of inequalities in ways that differ from those of Russians, Chinese, or Mexicans. But there might also be certain regional variations in these ideologies, or perhaps certain class or ethnic differences that could be differentiated from common impacts emanating from the larger society.

Putting aside this highly complex problem of delineating ideological contexts—which, to the writers' knowledge, has yet to be explored really systematically—let us return to the much simpler situation where the actor is in a position to observe certain rather obvious group and individual differences in objective factors such as occupations, incomes, possessions, educational achievement levels, or other factors commonly associated with status comparisons. For simplicity let us once more assume that we are dealing with the *i*th actor in the *j*th subgroup of some larger group.

The first kind of empirical question that must be answered is: What are the substantive comparisons the actor is making? Secondarily, we may also ask what *kinds* of comparison are being made (e.g., differences versus ratios). We shall discuss this latter kind of question in more detail in chapter 11, when we focus specifically on the measurement of discrimination. Let us here assume that the comparisons involve simple differences between the actor's own levels and the means of both the subgroup and the larger group. We shall confine our attention to a single variable, X_{ijk}, and the corresponding means $\bar{X}_{jk}$ and $\bar{X}_k$, and we shall assume that there are positive utilities attached to increases in X_{ijk}.

The common assumption among sociologists seems to be that it is not so much absolute levels of the X_{ijk} that are important as it is relative levels. One possibility is that the actor is making comparisons with his or her own earlier levels or perhaps between these earlier levels and those of other actors. In principle, this could be routinely handled provided that the previous levels were known to the observer and provided that it were possible to model the actor's mental processes accurately in terms of time periods. That is, one would need to know whether the actor compares only with the immediate past, with several past time periods, or possibly the most recent rates of *change* with earlier ones (e.g., the most recent pay increase with those received earlier). Such comparisons could presumably be studied reasonably easily at the micro level and would be facilitated by the fact that the previous levels will usually be known to the actor concerned.

Much more difficult is the problem of developing models appropriate for handling comparisons with *other* actors, although in principle these could be developed given sufficient data. Two specific kinds of difficulty can be mentioned briefly, since they are not new to our discussion. The first concerns the fuzziness of group boundaries and their noncomparability across actors. If we know that people tend to compare themselves with their immediate peers, for example, we still don't know precisely who is being compared: one's neighbors, others in the same occupation, one's most intimate friends and relatives, or some other reference group. It seems highly unlikely that most actors in complex situations can make very precise comparisons, given this shading of one group into another and the possibility of shifting comparison groups according to the nature of the variable under consideration.

The second problem is that of the ignorance on the part of both the actor and the investigator of the true levels for the comparison groups. There is considerable room for perceptual distortion, not only of the levels themselves but also of-the investments that are presumed to be causally related to these levels. Therefore we presume that the actor must make a number of simplifications and that the comparisons will in most instances be very inexact. One consequence, however, is likely to be that whenever any kind of exact information *is* known (say, the salary levels of one's work associates), very minor differences may be seized upon as indicators of other more important but less observable ones. For example, salary differences of a few dollars may be taken to indicate one's relative standing with the employer or even one's overall prestige in the group. There also may be a utility attached to finding out exactly where one stands, with the consequence that a pattern of elections or contests may emerge so as to facilitate this placement process—as well as to motivate the actors to improve their relative status positions.

Assuming that we are dealing with a variable X that is reasonably easy for the actors to measure, and therefore to use to make comparisons, we may construct alternative models by attempting to delineate sets of relatively homogeneous comparison groups or categories. By this we mean that the actors *think* of these groups or categories as sufficiently homogeneous that they tend to compare themselves with the averages of these groups, rather than using some more sophisticated comparison process involving, say, the standard deviations or other measures of dispersion.

Let us once more use an additive model and terms involving comparisons among the individual, subgroup, and total group levels as follows:

$$Y_{ijk} = a + b_1(X_{ijk} - \bar{X}_{jk}) + b_2(X_{ijk} - \bar{X}_k) + b_3(\bar{X}_{jk} - \bar{X}_k)$$

(17) $$+ e_{ijk}$$

$$= a + (b_1 + b_2)X_{ijk} + (b_3 - b_1)\bar{X}_{jk} - (b_2 + b_3)\bar{X}_k + e_{ijk}.$$

We again encounter an identification problem, since this particular formulation could not be distinguished empirically from any other additive model expressible in the form

$$Y_{ijk} = A + B_1 X_{ijk} + B_2 \bar{X}_{jk} + B_3 \bar{X}_k + E_{ijk}.$$

For example, the individual may be influenced by the *absolute* level of X_{ijk} plus the difference between $\bar{X}_{jk}$ and $\bar{X}_k$ or perhaps the absolute level of $\bar{X}_{jk}$ together with the difference between X_{ijk} and $\bar{X}_k$. Had we used nonlinear terms, such as those involving squared difference terms, there would have been slight differences among the alternative models that, in principle, might have been used to distinguish among them. But given the crudeness of the data and the inevitable specification errors in delineating the true context, it seems unwise to dwell upon these potential distinctions. Let us therefore assume that the above structural-equation model is essentially correct and see what kinds of qualitative implications we can draw from it.

The coefficient b_1 taps the importance attached to the individual's comparison with his or her own subgroup members or peers. We presume that most individuals will attach a positive utility to improving their relative status in their own subgroup and that this utility will generally tend to be greater than that attached to gaining ground relative to the overall mean $\bar{X}_k$. Let us assume that we are dealing with a low-status subgroup, say a disadvantaged minority, so that $\bar{X}_{jk} < \bar{X}_k$. Of course, an individual may gain ground relative to *both* groups by improving his or her own absolute level X_{ijk} more rapidly than do the average members. If we assume that changes in both $\bar{X}_{jk}$ and $\bar{X}_k$ are minimal, the sum of the coefficients b_1 and b_2, therefore, represents the importance attached to absolute changes in the individual level X_{ijk}.

In many situations we may also suppose that there is some positive utility attached to improving the relative position of the minority or subgroup average, as compared with that of the total group mean. Thus we presume that the actor is motivated to act so as to decrease the difference $\bar{X}_{jk} - \bar{X}_k$, assuming that $\bar{X}_{jk} < \bar{X}_k$, which may be accomplished by lowering $\bar{X}_k$ or raising $\bar{X}_{jk}$, or both. But lowering $\bar{X}_k$ will have the additional benefit of raising the individual's relative position in the total group, whereas raising $\bar{X}_{jk}$ (say, by helping other members of one's own subgroup) will have the opposite effect of *lowering* the actor's relative position in his or her own subgroup. This would suggest, then, that minority-group members will be more motivated to act to reduce the overall average level than to increase their own subgroup average. It would imply an interest in harming the majority rather than helping the minority improve its average absolute position.

We must remember that subjective probabilities also enter the picture, however, and that as a general rule we would expect that actors will perceive that they have a much better chance of affecting their own levels than either of the two group means. But this may also depend upon the relative and absolute sizes of the two groups as well as their relative resources. Where the overall (majority) group is extremely large and powerful, the minority actor may believe that there is virtually no possibility of affecting $\bar{X}_k$. It still remains, however, that $\bar{X}_{jk}$ might be affected, especially where the actor is thinking in terms of a relatively small subgroup rather than the entire minority membership. That is, the actor may be making comparisons with his or her immediate neighbors or work associates, in which case it *may* be possible to improve his or her own relative position by lowering the $\bar{X}_{jk}$ rather than increasing X_{ijk}. Rather weak and loosely organized minorities are thus faced with an important dilemma or problem, if we can accept the implications of this model. Since their members are motivated to improve their own individual relative positions, how can they be inhibited from acting in such a way that they work against the interests of their peers or other minority-group members in a kind of struggle for survival?

One possibility is to attempt to persuade minority individuals to compare themselves with the majority, so that the difference between X_{ijk} and $\bar{X}_k$ becomes much more salient than that between X_{ijk} and $\bar{X}_{jk}$. In effect, this would increase the absolute value of b_2 relative to that of b_1 in equation (17). This might not affect the sum $b_1 + b_2$, so that the individual's motivation to achieve would not be altered, but it would affect the relative magnitudes of the coefficients of the $\bar{X}_{jk}$ and $\bar{X}_k$ terms. Put negatively, it would tend to divert the individual's "selfish" motivations toward lowering the overall mean rather than that of the peer or minority group. "Don't fight your brother, fight the 'man'!" would become the slogan.

Another tactic relying more on positive inducements is to attempt to reward those subgroup members who actively work to improve the subgroup mean. This may be accomplished by stressing *other* utilities, such as that attached to receiving recognition within the subgroup or minority community. From the perspective of the actor this would have the effect of increasing the subjective probability p_2 of achieving a second desired outcome (e.g., increasing status within the subgroup) if one diverts a certain portion of his or her energies toward raising $\bar{X}_{jk}$. Somehow, the subgroup must raise the incentive level to a high enough level that the product $p_2 U_2$ (for subgroup status) is large relative to the $p_1 U_1$ term associated with individual achievement. The dilemma, of course, is that if too great a premium is placed on achieving subgroup status through this means, this may detract from the average level of the effort to raise the individual X_{ijk} levels.

We see this organizational dilemma in the case of predominantly lower-class minorities. Should the emphasis be placed on individual mobility, perhaps at the expense of one's immediate peers, or on working for the subgroup, perhaps at the expense of the X_{ijk} and thus the subgroup mean $\bar{X}_{jk}$? Those who prefer the first alternative are likely to attempt to raise the subjective probability associated with individual effort, while deflating that linked to group action. The reverse strategy will be appropriate for those who wish somehow or another to raise $\bar{X}_{jk}$ through group action. We may anticipate that ideologies of minority groups will almost of necessity have to cope with this dilemma in capitalistic systems, or any others in which a high premium is placed on individual achievement.

From the standpoint of mobility aspirations and expectations of the individual subgroup member, the magnitude of $\bar{X}_{jk} - \bar{X}_k$ may also affect the subjective probability that behavior oriented to raising X_{ijk} will actually succeed in achieving this outcome. If, for example, there is a large gap between the average subgroup member and total group average so that the minority actor is led to believe that forces are at work to affect his or her own "life chances," then the expectancy level may be lowered roughly in proportion to $\bar{X}_{jk} - \bar{X}_k$. It is, of course, possible that aspiration levels will also be reduced. If both p_1 and U_1 are taken as functions of this difference, then the overall effect may be proportional to $(\bar{X}_{jk} - \bar{X}_k)^2$ since we are assuming the intensity of behavior to be a multiplicative function of subjective probabilities and utilities.

If this model did apply at least to individuals who are members of low-status subgroups or minorities for which $\bar{X}_{jk} < \bar{X}_k$, and if we wrote the equation in the form

$$Y_{ijk} = a - b(\bar{X}_{jk} - \bar{X}_k)^2 , \qquad \text{with } a > 0 \text{ and } b > 0,$$

we would obtain a parabola that opens downward, as indicated in figure 7.2. Since we are concerned only with that portion of the parabola that lies to the left of the dotted vertical line at $\bar{X}_k$, this implies a monotonic increasing function with a decreasing slope. This suggests that the behavior level will drop off sharply if the gap between $\bar{X}_{jk}$ and $\bar{X}_k$ becomes very large. But it also implies that, for subgroups that have initially large gaps, a change that diminishes this gap will have a kind of double-barreled incentive value, raising both the subjective probabilities and also the utilities attached to achieving the outcome, here conceived as raising the individual's X value.

Perhaps this question of comparing $\bar{X}_{jk}$ and $\bar{X}_k$ levels may also be related to the phenomenon of discounting the utilities attached to outcomes in the remote future. As implied by our earlier discussion, discounting may in part be due to the difficulty of assessing subjective probabilities for very remote outcomes. In effect, there are so many potential contingencies and unknowns in the picture that the actor essentially gives up trying to estimate a probability and selects a near zero value. Or perhaps the outcome itself drops from the list of outcomes being actively considered merely because of the need to simplify and to give priority to those outcomes and probabilities that *can* be estimated reasonably well. At least in the case of behaviors oriented to achieving long-range goals, we

Figure 7.2

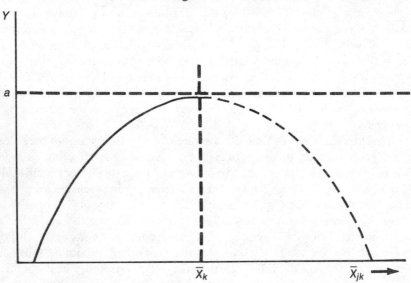

can very well imagine a process in which a minority-group member, perceiving a large gap between $\bar{X}_{jk}$ and $\bar{X}_{k}$, takes the position that the odds are so much against him or her that the investment (say, in higher education) isn't worth the effort. More generally, we are suggesting that levels of inequality may, under some circumstances, affect not only subjective probabilities but also discount rates for future outcomes.

SUMMARY

In this chapter we have identified several issues relating to cross-level or micro-macro analyses involving what have been termed contextual effects. First, we have been concerned with the *forms* that contextual-effect equations may take and the nature of the causal mechanisms that underlie these equations. We have suggested that it may prove useful to specify the utilities and subjective probabilities that serve as intervening variables between the contextual factors and the resulting behaviors. Whenever an individual-level variable X_{ij} operates through a utility, whereas the contextual effect operates through the corresponding subjective probability, or vice versa, this would suggest an interactive type of contextual-effect model rather than an additive one.

We have also been interested in situations in which there may be multiple contexts, either because of blurred or overlapping boundaries between groups or because of nested groups or the existence of several groups with which the individual may make comparisons. It has also been noted that several alternative explanatory models may all yield the same empirical results and that contextual and individual effects are often so highly intercorrelated that their effects may be hopelessly confounded. In both such instances, careful theoretical specifications involving nonlinearities may be needed if weak tests of alternative explanations are to be made.

In discussing some of the mechanisms that may be responsible for contextual effects we have also anticipated certain issues that will be treated in later chapters. For example, we have introduced the idea of control of the individual's behavior through group norms and sanctions, indicating that the effectiveness of these sanctions may depend upon the individual's attachment to the group, his or her resources or position in the group, the degree of homogeneity and consensus, and the relative size and power of the subgroup to which the individual belongs as compared with those of the total group. Furthermore, we have invoked the idea that an individual may make various kinds of comparison and that inequality of several kinds may be relevant to these comparisons. In subsequent chapters of this book we shall deal with questions of power and inequality in considerably more detail. In these subsequent discussions, however, we shall have relatively little to say about how these variables impact on the *individual's* behavior in terms of the exact nature of the contextual-effects models that they imply. It is hoped, however, that the discussion in the present chapter has at least provided certain clues as to how a number of these macro-level variables impact on individual behaviors.

NOTES

1. For an extensive discussion of methodological issues relating to modifiable areal units, see Duncan, Cuzzort, and Duncan (1961). See also Valkonen (1969) and Hannan (1971).
2. A similar set of equations could, of course, be written for *any* two kinds of group being compared, regardless of whether the one were nested within the other.
3. Algebraic equations, such as (1)–(4), of course presuppose that $dY/dt = 0$ or, in other words, that the equilibrium conditions have been met. For further discussion of this point see Blalock (1969), chapter 5.
4. This can be seen as follows. Since the coefficient $b_2/(b_1 + b_2) < 0$ and $\bar{Y}_{jk} < \bar{Y}_k$ it follows that

$$Y_e = \frac{b_1}{b_1 + b_2}\bar{Y}_{jk} + \frac{b_2}{b_1 + b_2}\bar{Y}_k < \frac{b_1}{b_1 + b_2}\bar{Y}_{jk}$$

$$+ \frac{b_2}{b_1 + b_2}\bar{Y}_{jk} = \frac{b_1 + b_2}{b_1 + b_2}\bar{Y}_{jk} = \bar{Y}_{jk}.$$

Thus $Y_e < \bar{Y}_{jk}$.

CHAPTER 8

Social Power I:
Its Nature and Sources

THERE HAVE BEEN numerous attempts to develop reasonably general theoretical frameworks for the analysis of social power, and it is also indisputable that power is an important ingredient of nearly all social relationships. Yet there has been relatively little headway in linking up our rather abstract theoretical analyses of social power with empirical research. It is equally obvious that practical decision makers also have considerable difficulties in dealing with and accurately assessing power in actual political situations. The examples of the Vietnam War and interracial confrontations in the United States are not isolated instances, by any means. Not only is it exceedingly difficult to assess the actual resources of one's opponent but it is even more of a problem to appraise motivational factors, to evaluate the relative efficiencies of alternative means, or to anticipate the behaviors of third parties to any dispute. In most situations of interest to both the social scientist and the actual participants, there are likely to be so many unknowns or unmeasured variables, as well as uncontrolled extraneous factors, that a truly systematic approach to the study of power has seemed out of the question.

One of the basic problems in connection with power and related concepts has been encountered in previous chapters, namely, the fact that the measurement of power must of necessity be indirect. There must also be a rather large number of unmeasured intervening variables in any reasonably complete theory of power. We shall discuss the definition of power in more detail in the following section. For the present it is sufficient to emphasize a point made by Kadushin (1968), among others, that power (as a potential) is a disposition concept that can be indirectly measured only under certain specified conditions. Furthermore, the isolation of a given actor's power requires replications under carefully controlled conditions plus certain a priori untestable assumptions concerning the operation of other forces (Blalock 1961).

324

James March (1966), after discussing a number of complications in the measurement of power, reaches the pessimistic conclusion that it may be advisable to do away with the concept altogether, except in rather simple situations of a very specialized nature. In fact, March warns us against the temptation of becoming overly obsessed with the need for endless conceptual clarifications and measurement efforts. The implication seems to be that the problems with the study of power are much more serious and difficult than previously recognized and that they cannot be resolved by further efforts at clarification and measurement.

We must add two further temptations to the list in an effort to redirect the social scientist's interest in power to what we hope will prove to be a more realistic effort. The first of these is the temptation, in the face of a difficult task, to avoid using the concept at all and then later discovering that it has reappeared in the literature under a slightly different name or label. Many disposition concepts seem to have had this kind of history in the social sciences, as illustrated by the assortment of terms that have been used to refer to those internal states that are presumed to serve as driving or motivating forces for human behavior: instincts, drives, needs, motives, goals, and the like. If our theories cannot seem to get along without such concepts, there may be a good reason for this fact. It would make little sense to replace one with another merely because the first has been severely criticized and discredited.

The second temptation is that of retaining the concept in some form but then confining one's attention to such extremely simple social situations that the theory loses its potential for generalizability. In the specific case of power, there may be certain situations in which power as a potential and power in action can be rather simply equated, and where there is no problem of inferring the amount of power exerted by measuring its effects. But as soon as we then wish to move from these extremely simple situations to more complex ones, the problem of external validity seems insoluble. One is therefore tempted to lower one's aspiration levels by avoiding complexities, without ever asking the fundamental question of whether the simplicity is a necessary precondition for the measurement and conceptualization, or whether a relaxation of this condition can in principle be accomplished in a systematic fashion. Some sophisticated discussions of the measurement of power, such as that of Shapley and Shubik (1954), appear to involve severe restrictions. Others, such as those of Dahl (1957) and Nagel (1975), are in principle much more generalizable though operationally less precise.

Recall that the general orientation and working assumption stated in our introductory chapter was that we must somehow or another come to grips with a very complex reality by constructing models that contain a large number of variables that cannot be measured in any given study. Furthermore, we have argued that actors themselves must find ways of simplifying this reality and that our theories must also take these simplifying assumptions into consideration. Ideally, then, we need theories and data concerning how these simplifications are made, as well as statements concerning the conditions under which simplifications of a given type will be used. We shall return to this particular subject in the following chapter when we deal with the working theories of actors. For the present we merely emphasize the desirability of developing frameworks that allow for considerable complexity, with the expectation that different kinds of simplification will be made in special cases.

With respect to measurement and conceptualization, we must again expect to encounter the possibility that certain approaches that are appropriate for very simple situations may not lend themselves to generalization in more complex situations. In particular, approaches to the conceptualization and measurement of power that ignore subjective variables and the conditions that affect the transformation from power as a potential to power in its kinetic or action form can be expected to encounter major obstacles when applied to these highly complex situations. Our objective in presenting a power framework will be at least to allow for a reasonable degree of complexity, even at the expense of introducing a large proportion of unmeasured variables. Specific simplifications may then be made in an explicit fashion to reduce the number of unknowns to manageable proportions so that rejectable theories can be stated as special cases.

As we proceed to discuss a number of social processes it will become necessary to make a few remarks near the beginning of each chapter concerning their interrelationships. Perhaps the most important point to emphasize is that most every concrete instance of interaction will simultaneously involve several analytically distinct social processes. In particular, considerations of power will enter into all exchange relationships, if only to affect the rates of exchange and the dependency levels of each party. Similarly, when we come to discuss allocation and approach-withdrawal processes we shall also need to take the relative powers of the several parties into consideration. Allocation processes will be conceptualized in terms of indirect exchange, and we shall also examine the rewards and costs of intergroup contacts in terms of exchange as well as power. Thus it would be very misleading if one were to claim a general priority of one process over the others, though in any given instance one particular process may be dominant over the others.

We have already noted the obvious point that in exchange processes the focus of attention is on mutual gain achieved through the exchange of positive utilities, implying a basically cooperative arrangement between the parties. We gave virtually no attention to the phenomenon of the exchange of negative utilities, which we referred to as conflict. Sometimes the notions of power and conflict are used almost interchangeably to refer to a very broad range of interaction patterns in which the parties are acting primarily as opponents or adversaries. Our own discussion will in principle allow for a much broader conceptualization of power in terms of the achievement of objectives or the overcoming of resistance, which may be accomplished by a variety of means that include the exchange of positive utilities as well as negative ones. In other words, the power framework we shall develop will be sufficiently broad to cover not only conflict situations—as we have defined them—but other kinds of more subtle power contest as well.

As we shall discuss in the next section, power may be defined very broadly in terms of the achievement of objectives, the accomplishment of work (as in physics), or the overcoming of resistance. Our focus of attention will be more narrow, however, in that we shall assume that there are two or more parties with opposing interests, so that for the most part the achievement of A's objectives will be at B's expense, and vice versa. This type of situation is often referred to as one in which A and B are in competition, but we have chosen not to make extensive use of this concept. Instead, we have absorbed both of the notions of conflict and competition under our discussions of other processes. In our discussion of allocation processes, for instance, we shall be concerned with situations in which an allocator, A, makes decisions that may favor one of two competing parties, B and C, as, for example, one of two candidates for a job opening or promotion. In such an allocation process there may be efforts by one or more of the parties to exert power over the others. Such efforts may result in conflict. But they also may not. Therefore it seems wise to keep the ideas of power and conflict as distinct as possible, even though in many concrete instances they will be found together.

These very general observations imply that it is essential to pay careful attention to the goals, utilities, and subjective probabilities of the separate parties. In a cooperative exchange relationship the focus is usually on common goals or the gains accruing to each party from the exchange relationship. Even in a situation in which two actors, A and B, pool their resources to achieve a common end, and even where the tangible rewards are divided equitably between them, we can expect that there will be *some* divergence of interests, if only because one of the parties is likely to receive relatively more of the credit for having achieved the success or perhaps a greater share of other types of intangible reward. There may also be a rivalry between them to control their joint decision-making apparatus.

In most types of coalition situation there is likely to be a kind of "uneasy peace" between coalition partners faced by a common opponent. Whether the situation is best analyzed in terms of exchange to the mutual benefit of both parties or as one involving a power contest between them is therefore likely to depend, among other things, upon one's assessment of the utilities attached to the different types of goal involved. There will ordinarily be elements of both a cooperative exchange and a power contest in any concrete interaction pattern one wishes to analyze.

THE CONCEPTUALIZATION OF POWER, RESOURCES, AND MOBILIZATION

In both physics and the social sciences there is a duality in the conceptualization of power as both a potential and as applied (kinetic power). In physics, power is operationally defined as work actually accomplished per unit of time, a definition that implies the necessity of isolating the effects of the operation of a particular force (say, that of an engine) from other forces that may also be operating. Thus we use an "effect measure" and make the working assumption that the other causes of the work accomplished have either been explicitly taken into consideration or may be safely ignored. Through careful replications these alternative causes may be inferred and reasonably plausible assumptions made about their behaviors (Blalock 1961). Thus even in physics the measurement of kinetic power is indirect and dependent upon the plausibility of one's causal theory linking "work accomplished" to the actions of the particular force in question.

Assuming this isolation of forces has been accomplished, it then becomes possible to develop and test rather precise theories linking power in action to power as a potential. For instance, a body weighing 1000 kilograms poised 100 meters above the surface of the earth can be expected to do a specified amount of work in driving a spike a certain distance through a resistance of known magnitude. This is because there are well-established laws predicting how the falling body will behave in the presence of the earth's gravitational force. In short, there is no doubt that the weight will "realize its potential" and will "conform" to the law of gravity. Similarly, by knowing the mechanical properties of a machine or how an electrical engine has been constructed, one can predict very accurately how it will behave because of the existence of universal laws as well as the possibility of assuming the interchangeability of machines or engines constructed with (nearly) identical properties.

These operations enable the physicist or engineer to attach empirical meaning to notions such as "full capacity" or "potential." Futhermore, they also permit the measurement of efficiency by taking the ratio of output to input energy, even in instances where the input and output energies are in different units. It is thus a *combination* of tight theories of behavior and the ability to replicate under highly controlled conditions that permit the relatively easy translation back and forth between the notions of potential and kinetic power. In more complex situations, where careful measurement and replications would be more difficult, it is then *assumed* that the properties of the machine and operative laws hold as in the simpler situations.

It is important to note that the basic concepts (time, distance, and mass) are defined and ordinarily measured in the same ways in the simple and more complex situations. If the measurement operations must be altered, there is an established mathematical function that may be used to translate from one measurement procedure to the other. Thus the meanings of the basic concepts do not shift according to the nature of the situation, even though more complex situations may require the use of additional variables or correction factors. For example, if one encounters air resistance or friction from imperfectly smooth surfaces, these additional forces are accounted for by adding terms to the equations, but there is no fundamental reconceptualization required by the added complexity.

Social power is not so easily handled. Sometimes we attempt to measure power potential directly by identifying what we call resources, or the sources of power in action. But this requires a theory concerning just how these resources become sources of kinetic power. Even more problematic is the question of predicting the degree to which resources will actually be put to use or the direction in which they will be applied, to say nothing of measuring the degree to which a party is acting to "full capacity." Sometimes we equate particular possessions (e.g., money), positions (e.g., offices held), or assumed psychic states (e.g., abilities or skills) with the resources themselves, but it should be readily apparent that the connection is not always a simple one. Is money automatically a resource? Clearly not unless it is desired by actors who are to be influenced, unless it can be exchanged for services, and unless the rules of the game permit such an exchange.

We have these difficulties in the social realm in linking potential power with kinetic power because we lack definitive theories that enable accurate predictions of behaviors. And we lack these theories in part because of the fact that actors must make decisions on the basis of unknown factors, because we are rarely in a position to replicate our research under standardized conditions, and because there are many other variables that affect the relationships we would find even in the most careful of studies.

Furthermore, in power confrontations where the stakes are high, the actors will generally behave so as to create as many unknowns as possible for their opponents. They are apt to try to distort other parties' perceptions of their true resources, to disguise their true motivations, and to create the illusion that they are both willing and able to apply considerable force. In short, they may bluff. By the same token they are likely to oversimplify the motivation of the other party. The social scientist studying power confrontations in realistic settings must somehow or another take all of these subjective factors and unknowns into consideration, if only to decide how to simplify the analysis.

Our effort to cope with this fundamental problem will involve essentially the same strategy as used in the previous chapters, namely, to introduce a large number of intervening variables between the objective characteristics (O_i) that serve as the bases for power as a potential and the final outcomes of power as actually exercised.[1] We shall focus on the specific nature of these variables and their complex interrelationships in the remaining sections of this chapter and the next. Here it is sufficient to point out that many of these will involve subjective factors that can be treated either as totally unmeasured or as indirectly measured and therefore requiring additional auxiliary assumptions. Utilities and subjective probabilities will again play a very important role in the basic models, although we shall find it necessary to translate these concepts into terminology that is more compatible with that used in the power literature.

In particular, we shall be concerned with how these subjective variables affect the relationship between objective properties and resources (the actual power potential), and how they also affect the degree and efficiency with which these resources are mobilized to yield power as actually exerted. Our primary concern will be with spelling out a framework of concepts and assumed interrelationships that is sufficiently complex to handle a variety of situations in which power is an important factor and yet which is capable of being simplified in those special cases in which certain of these complexities can be ignored.

The Scope of the Term "Social Power"

Before turning to our main discussion we need to mention two somewhat interrelated topics, namely, the scope or breadth of the concept of power and the kinds of actor to which we wish the theory to apply. At the risk of gross oversimplification of a very extensive literature, it is possible with respect to scope to identify two very distinct kinds of conception of power, the first of which is more general than the second. First, power may be defined in terms of the achievement of goals, the overcoming of resistance, or a control over outcomes. This kind of conceptualization seems closest to the general definition in physics, namely, work accomplished per unit of time, and is most compatible with analyses in which there are either a very large number of actors and no relatively permanent coalitions or where the issue of concern is not one in which the primary obstacles are the actions of other parties.

The second kind of conceptualization of power, which may be taken as a special case of the broader one, focuses on the control of one party by another. For example, it may be said that actor A has power over actor B when A can change the course of B's actions, or when A can sanction B, and so forth. This second type of definition of power seems more prevalent in the small-groups literature and in particular when the focus of attention is on the dyad or triad. It is also prevalent in the race and ethnic relations field, where notions such as control, dominance, exploitation, colonialism, and discrimination are common. Of course, if we assume that A's goal is to control or dominate B, and that the resistance to be overcome stems primarily from B or other specific actors, then we may treat this somewhat more narrow conception of power as a special case of the former, more general, one. It should be noted that this question of scope is theoretically independent of that of power as potential versus power as exercised. Thus one may define power as the *ability* to achieve objectives or to control another actor, or as the actual *exercise* of these potentials.

Gamson (1968, chap. 1) has made the point that the conceptualization of power in terms of the achievement of desired outcomes seems more compatible with a focus on system properties and system maintenance, whereas the conceptualization of power as control by one party over another is more compatible with a conflict orientation. Schermerhorn (1970) makes much the same point in connection with race relations theories. In effect, one is likely to ask different sets of questions and pose different problems when one focuses rather generally on the achievement of goals or desired outcomes, as contrasted with a power confrontation between parties A and B. In the former instance one is more likely to be concerned with system maintenance, cooperation, and control of deviance, whereas in the second case attention may be focused on questions involving competition for scarce resources, how the total pie is to be sliced, and the relative powers of the two parties. It is well to keep this possible difference in orientations in mind and to note that a relatively limited conception of power also tends to narrow the scope of substantive coverage.

Although we shall not exploit the idea further, it could be that the notion of achieving the other party's compliance is sufficiently inclusive to combine the ideas of achieving objectives and controlling others' behaviors. We might then distinguish between specific compliance and general compliance. Specific compliance would be linked to the notion of the achievement of particular goals, whereas general compliance would imply the control of one party by another over a range of settings and behaviors. When we speak of dominant and subordinate groups or parties we have in mind that the compliance of the latter party is of a generalized rather than specific or delimited nature.

Our own power framework focuses on the relationship between two parties, A and B, though allowing for the actions of third parties, C_i. Thus it deals primarily with dyads and triads, power confrontations, and, by implication, dominance. In this sense it is more restrictive than one that conceives of power in more general terms, such as the achievement of goals or the control over outcomes. We must therefore give at least some attention to the problem of extending our own framework to cover the more general approach to power, and in doing so we need to introduce some very important notes of caution against the temptation to see power always in terms of conflicts of interests between rival parties.

Let us consider several concrete examples. There are obviously a large number of human objectives that are not opposed in principle until questions arise as to the means by which they are to be achieved and scarce resources allocated among objectives. Suppose, for example, the objective is that of finding a cure for cancer, or even more specifically setting up a major cancer institute and treatment center. We presume that there will be only minimal opposition to these objectives. In the case of finding a cure, the major obstacle would appear to be that of a lack of knowledge, and one's "opponent" would be "Nature."

In fact, we rarely use the term *power* in such instances, though in a very general sense it would be appropriate to say that we lack a cure because we lack the power, if this is not indeed a tautological statement. Setting up a major cancer institute would be one means of achieving this objective, but this would require the allocation of funds and medical staff. At this point opposition might be expected to arise as actors debated the cost effectiveness of this and many alternative plans of action. Those who proposed and sponsored the institute might then very well become involved in a contest of power concerning this specific means of achieving a broader goal about which there was a high degree of consensus.

Taking a somewhat less clear-cut example, let us suppose hypothetically that most white Americans generally approve of the goal of raising black educational levels and opportunities, at least to the extent of giving lip service to this objective. We may find that certain subsets of individuals oppose very specific means of achieving this very general objective, however. Some may oppose busing to achieve school integration. There may be an overlapping set of individuals who disapprove a second means, let us say allocating supplementary funds to ghetto schools.[2]

We see from these simple illustrations that it will be difficult to separate means and goals, and also that the alignment of actors may differ according to the means being considered. It would certainly be a mistake to identify only two parties, such as "blacks" versus "whites." In the case of special funding for ghetto schools, for example, one might find opposition coming from a sizable portion of black and white integrationists, as well as those who oppose the use of any additional funds for black education. Furthermore, it might be difficult to distinguish empirically between those who really oppose the general goal (e.g., improving black educational levels) and those who happen to oppose all of the specific means that have been seriously proposed.

The more general point is that the choice of the way in which the analyst delineates the parties or actors to any given dispute must depend upon the issues being considered. In instances where there are several means to a particular general goal, one may find differing alignments according to which particular means is being considered (e.g., busing versus funds for ghetto schools). Thus our choice of actors is dependent not only upon the reasonably general goals that are at stake but upon the means as well, a fact that greatly complicates any effort to develop a systematic theory of power. Another implication is that although the resistance to certain very general goals may be nonhuman or at least very diffuse, it may be much easier to identify and analyze this opposition whenever concrete means are being considered and implemented.

Turning to the advisability of using a rather restrictive definition of power in terms of actor A's ability to control or affect B's behavior, we must recognize that control or dominance per se may be a goal having a very low utility value for either A or B. For example, A may wish to achieve certain objectives by means that B opposes. Although A may wish to remove B's opposition, and in this limited sense control B's behavior, it does not follow that A wishes to affect B's behavior in any other ways. That is, B may be considered merely as an opponent on this particular issue, and the "control" that A wishes to employ may be only very partial and limited to this single issue. Of course, if the conflict is intense and protracted, we anticipate that there will be secondary goals that may become increasingly important to A or B. These include the desire to injure the other party, to punish it for its opposition, or to make sure that there is no such opposition in the future.

The implication is that if we define power primarily in terms of control or dominance, we may implicitly redirect the analysis by giving primary attention to goals that actually have much lower utilities than others that are more instrumental in achieving some more generalized objectives. Such a focus on control and dominance, we suspect, may be one of the biases that is almost inherent in

the so-called conflict school of thought. In effect, the desire to control, dominate, or exploit others becomes a kind of master motive or goal that is a priori
assumed to have a much higher utility than more mundane objectives. In the
example of white opposition to busing, such factors as the fear of violence, a
concern for a lowering of academic standards, class prejudices, and so forth may
be interpreted as mere rationalizations that disguise the "true" motivation
to dominate, control, exploit, or aggress against the minority. In actuality, of
course, a combination of goals is much more likely.

In the case of actors that are very loosely organized—as, for example,
"whites" in contemporary U.S. race relations—it seems to make sense, then, to
break down complex power confrontations into simpler ones for which the
actors can be more easily identified. If we do this, however, we must anticipate
finding that certain of the "actors" may be simultaneously engaged in several
power contests with different or overlapping sets of opponents. For instance,
if we take party B to be blacks in a particular urban setting, and if we look at
busing as one among several possible means of achieving better education for
blacks, then the opposing party (A_1) of (predominantly) whites may consist of a
very different set of persons than those (A_2) who oppose a second means, say,
that of allocating additional funds to ghetto schools. The actors A_1 and A_2 may
or may not coordinate their actions, but from the standpoint of B this may
make little difference. It may appear as though "whites" seek to dominate or
control blacks in this instance, since in effect they jointly oppose the two means
of achieving B's objectives that B believes most viable. Yet it may very well be
the case that dominance or control is not an important goal to the members of
either A_1 or A_2, nor need there be any conspiracy between them to keep B
subordinated.

It may be a characteristic of very weak parties in general that virtually all of
their alternatives may be blocked by rather small subgroups within a much
more powerful "group," without the latter constituting an organized group in
the sociological sense of the term. One implication of this fact is that although
particular power confrontations may most easily be analyzed by delimiting the
focus and the boundaries of the active parties, there must also be an effort to
aggregate these single confrontations if we wish to obtain a more complete
picture of the power relationships among the much more loosely organized
larger groupings. In the present chapter we shall not be able to give further
attention to this kind of problem, and indeed it seems premature to attempt to
do so.

In the discussion that follows we shall take an intermediate position with
respect to the scope of situations that might be analyzed in terms of the proposed power framework. We shall not limit the term *power* to the notion of control or dominance and shall focus instead on the achievement of goals or the
control of "outcomes." But we shall presume that the situations under discussion are confined to those in which the opposition or resistance to these goals
comes at least in part from human actors who may be organized or coordinated

to varying degrees. In many instances we admit that this will require a focus on objectives that themselves may be merely means to much more general goals (e.g., good health, happiness, welfare, or equality of opportunity) that in principle are not opposed by readily identified parties.

We also admit that certain of the obstacles or resistances may stem from nonhuman sources, such as those that require substantial expenditures of resources (e.g., building dams or hospitals) or technical knowledge (e.g., finding a cure for cancer or learning how to raise attainment levels of black children). These impersonal resistances can be treated either as exogenous variables or as constants that may be added to either side of the power equation; that is, they may favor either party A or party B. In any particular analysis of power these impersonal obstacles or facilitators would need to be taken into consideration, but we shall henceforth neglect them in discussing our general framework.

Before concluding this section we need to discuss very briefly the time factor, which is explicitly included in physicists' definition of power (equals work/time) but which is generally neglected in social scientists' definitions. Other things being equal, if we compared the power exerted by A_1 against B with that of A_2 against B, we would want to say that if A_1 pushed B a given distance in less time than it took A_2 to do so, then A_1 would be exerting more power than A_2. We might even try to measure power in terms of a ratio scale, so that if it took A_1 only half as long as A_2 to do the same work, then we could say that A_1 was exerting twice the power of A_2.

"Sociological time"—if we thought this a relevant concept—may be a nonlinear function of physical time. For example, it may not make much difference whether something can be achieved in one week or three. Certainly, however, time *is* a relevant factor in many power confrontations. If A has advantages over B and can stall off B's efforts to modify the situation over a considerable length of time, perhaps even several centuries, we would take this as an indication that A is exerting much more power than if A were to make concessions to B over a much shorter period. Furthermore, since resources and motivation levels can be expected to shift over time, the time factor becomes a crucial one in affecting the strategies or means used by each party. For one party the issues may be much more immediate and pressing, whereas the other may be in a better position to operate from a longer time perspective. For instance, the former party may feel a need to achieve compliance from the other party very quickly out of a concern that at some future time the other party's resources will have increased to the point where compliance would be impossible to achieve. Or the former party's resources may be expended at a more rapid rate than those of the second party, with the same result.

Somehow or another, we must find ways of dealing with the time factor. Because of the complexities involved, however, we choose not to make it an explicit part of the definition of power. Instead, we shall make the working assumption that if we are comparing several power confrontations the time factor is approximately constant. That is, if we were in a position to study busing controversies in several cities in an attempt to assess the levels of the relevant power variables, we would assume that the time periods were comparable. If this were not the case, we would have to bring in these time differentials as an additional complicating factor. In the discussion that follows, we shall occasionally refer to past or future levels of certain variables and to the time perspectives of the actors, but we shall omit any consideration of the absolute passage of time or the speed with which events occur.

Identifying the Major Parties in a Power Contest

In the discussion that follows it will be assumed that the major parties or actors have been identified. In fact, we shall focus primarily on just two parties, A and B, with possible third parties being labeled C_i but not really brought explicitly into our models—as would become necessary if we were to extend the discussion to an analysis of coalition formation. All of the variables we shall introduce will be attached to either A or B, and for this reason it is essential that the actors be carefully delineated. Yet, as we have just implied, this is not always a simple task, and for this reason students of power are likely to resort to very different tactics or approaches in their discussion of the subject.

As one extreme, one may choose to analyze only very simple direct interactions between two persons in a carefully controlled situation, or perhaps to extend the discussion to the simple triad. Here the actor may be equated with the individual and there are no boundary problems at issue. Furthermore, a number of the variables that we shall discuss below and that really pertain to groups as actors (e.g., coordination, consensus, or leadership) can safely be ignored. Nevertheless we believe that basically the same variables may be used in connection with both individuals and corporate groups as actors, except that for the latter it becomes necessary to use (weighted) average levels or some other kind of summarizing measure appropriate to the group. Where the decision-making processes in a corporate group are highly centralized, as, for example, in the case of nations at war, it does not seem at all unreasonable to think primarily in terms of the beliefs, goals, utilities, and subjective probabilities of the decision makers as being properties of the entire group, provided that we also introduce additional variables to take care of problems of coordination, dissensus, conflicting interests and rivalries, defections and social control, and the like.

At the other extreme are situations involving very loosely organized aggregates, or groups and individuals that are in only very indirect contact. An individual American's consumption patterns affect individuals in the Fiji Islands, but it would hardly be worthwhile for the student of power to pay attention to this kind of relationship. To do so would be to include almost all instances of indirect causation under the rubric of social power, thus leading to a hopelessly complex theoretical analysis. But if other Americans and their behaviors were *aggregated,* and those of the Fiji Islanders and their neighbors were similarly, we might admit that these aggregated consequences of consumer behavior in the United States are extremely important to residents of underdeveloped and developing nations. There is certainly the potential for a power confrontation, even though neither party is particularly aware of the causal connections between their aggregated behaviors. Perhaps one party will become organized and aware of the relationship, whereas the other will not. At what point would we want to refer to this as a power confrontation or power contest?

Clearly, there are several continua here, one being the degree of *awareness* of the causal relationship by members of each party and another being the degree to which they become *organized* in order to modify this relationship. Therefore, there cannot be any single and distinct point at which one may say, "Beyond this point a power contest exists." The choice of whether or not to analyze the situation as one involving a power relationship is, therefore, one that a social scientist must make partly on the basis of convenience and the expected utility of the approach in yielding insightful conclusions. Where the actors are only remotely in interaction and mutually unaware of each other's existence there would seem to be little point in attempting to utilize most of the kinds of variables discussed in this chapter and the next.

In many situations there will be several reasonably well organized antagonists plus a large number of spectators and potentially interested third parties that are much more difficult to specify. In such instances the temptation may be to equate the boundaries of the protagonists with readily observable indicators. Thus whites and blacks in the United States may be taken as parties A and B, whereas a more accurate specification of the power confrontation would place some whites on the side of the majority of blacks, a few blacks on the side of the majority of whites, and a substantial minority of both groups as virtually neutral bystanders.

There is a special danger of oversimplification of group boundaries by two seemingly different kinds of analyst. The first consists of those who wish to use quantitative indicators such as group size, median incomes, occupational distributions, and so forth. Lacking any way to separate out the characteristics of those whites who may be siding with blacks rather than other whites, the data analyst may take the group boundaries as coinciding with racial definitions. Thus the percentage of the minority becomes a measure of the proportion of persons who are assumed to compose, say, party B, with the remainder going into party A.

The second kind of distortion is likely to be produced by social analysts who have an ideological bias in favor of oversimplifying the nature of the power contest. All whites are thought to be in alliance against all blacks, all employers against all employees, all capitalist nations against all socialist countries, and so forth. Of course, the actors themselves may *perceive* the power contest in exactly these same terms, in which case this becomes an interesting datum in itself. If the actual situation is much more complex, however, anyone who has used the much simpler two-party model may find it necessary to explain the behaviors of neutrals in terms of deviant behaviors, defections, betrayals, inconsistencies, or similar notions.

If groups cannot be defined in terms of simple racial, religious, or even national boundaries without doing injustice to the actual situation, how can they be defined? One way would be to examine the behaviors of different sets of individuals and group the individuals according to the consequences of these behaviors. Those who acted in such a way as to benefit party A would be considered either as members of A or as in a coalition with A. The problem here is that one needs a causal theory as to the consequences of the behaviors in question. Furthermore, actors may fail to anticipate correctly the consequences of their actions. Black separatists' behaviors may play into the hands of white segregationists, though one's assessment of the degree to which this is the case may depend, among other things, upon whether one is looking at immediate or long-range consequences.

Members of party A may be convinced that they are behaving in the interest of party B members and may attempt to persuade the latter that this is the case. So-called paternalistic relationships often involve asymmetric power relationships in which members of both parties are convinced that the existing system is to their mutual advantage. This may in fact be true in the short run but not the long run. The problem is that one must decide on the basis of incomplete information whether or not the two parties have compatible or incompatible interests. The situation may be a mixed one, so that from one standpoint the relationship can be taken as a dominance relationship involving mutually antagonistic interests, whereas by stressing a different set of consequences one might see the situation as involving a symbiotic relationship of mutual benefit to the two parties.

Given all of the complexities that are likely to be encountered in real-life power contests, one may always decide to confine one's attention to the much simpler kinds of situations that can be created in small-group experiments or simulation studies. But to the degree that complexities create complications for the actors as well as the analyst, we cannot expect to generalize readily from these simpler situations to the more complex ones. At least some careful delineations of parties in these more complex situations need to be attempted. How can we go about doing this? Obviously, if we cannot distinguish the party boundaries we are not going to be able to obtain accurate measures of the properties, resources, goals, expectancies, and other variables that pertain to these parties. Therefore the delineation of party boundaries is a necessary precondition for measurement.[3]

First, it seems preferable to begin by applying two kinds of criteria more or less simultaneously to assess their mutual goodness of fit and to utilize information about imperfect fits to delineate subparties that may later be taken as distinct third parties. The first type of criterion involves the social labels for group membership that are being used by the actors, together with their self-identifications. If the actors perceive that the struggle is between blacks and whites, Protestants and Catholics, or management and labor, then these labels may be used as a first approximation to the party boundaries. As a general rule, we expect that the more intense the conflict, and the longer it has been going on, the easier it will be for individuals to identify their allegiances or to label themselves as neutrals or members of distinct third parties. But where the power contest is much less obvious and direct, and where criss-crossing allegiances exist, these labels may be highly misleading. Some persons may identify the contest as being between blacks and whites, others between liberals and conservatives, and still others as being essentially a class contest.

The use of labels provides a relatively straightforward way of defining party boundaries but, as we have already implied, cannot always be trusted. This is especially true whenever the issues have been given highly oversimplified ideological interpretations that encourage the participants to see the opponent as much more homogeneous than actually is the case. Therefore, we would suggest that a second criterion be invoked, namely, the stated goals of the various actors. Some whites and some blacks may say that they are working toward integration, whereas others of both groups may prefer segregation. If they are actually acting on the basis of these stated goals—which is, of course, an empirical question—then it may make much more sense to group the actors into the two parties "integrationist" and "segregationist" than into the parties "black" versus "white."

If there is a poor fit between the labels and goal-oriented delineations, this is likely to indicate a degree of complexity that needs to be explicitly recognized. We may anticipate cleavages between white and black integrationists, and—most certainly—between white and black segregationists. It is indeed likely that in such instances there will be cleavages along lines defined by *other* goals. Though united by a preference for a separation of the races, black separatists may prefer that this be voluntary and equal status, whereas white segregationists may be thinking in terms of compulsory separation based on white dominance. A three- or even four-cornered power contest may be anticipated, with coalitions forming and breaking up according to the issue at hand.

Having decided on the major party breakdowns on the basis of a combination of labels and stated goals, one may then look for internal subdivisions within each party that are defined on the basis of secondary goals or labels. There will be class differences within a racially defined group, differences that involve choices of means that are incompatible with the goals of one segment but not those of another, and so forth. The subparties of A might be explicitly designated as $A_1, A_2, \ldots, A_k$, and similarly for B, with the anticipation that at some stage one or more of these subparties may split off and join a third party, C_i, or possibly even the opposition party. Differences among the subparties will, of course, also affect the degree of consensus, division of labor, efficiency of mobilization, and a number of other variables in the model. Insofar as the goals and means of the subparties have different utilities and subjective probabilities, it will be advantageous to note this fact rather than to aggregate the nonhomogeneous elements to obtain a single overall score.

Finally, decisions will have to be made about the boundaries of third parties. Some of these can be delineated in much the same fashion as *A* and *B,* but others will consist primarily of aggregates or categories of individuals rather than organized groups. Some of these may be pulled into either *A* or *B* as individual members, whereas others may coalesce to form organized third parties. The immediate concern of the analyst, and probably *A* and *B* as well, will undoubtedly be organized C_i that are perceived to be more powerful than either party or that have sufficient resources that, should they join either party, could be used to affect the outcome of the power contest. Such third parties are likely to be readily identified. Of course, certain third parties that may safely be ignored during one phase of a power contest may come to play crucial roles at other stages, so that one should not expect a static analysis of fixed C_i to be entirely adequate. In fact, a considerable portion of the energies of the active parties may be directed toward *creating* third parties out of loosely knit aggregates that are thought to have sufficient resources to influence the outcome.

AN OVERVIEW OF THE GENERAL MODEL

It is easiest to begin with two actors, *A* and *B,* and to talk about the power that *A* has in affecting *B*'s behavior, and vice versa. But, as already suggested, a more complete theory must allow for other actors, $C_1, C_2, \ldots, C_k$, as well. A relatively simplified extension of the two-actor model would involve taking these other actors as exogenous agents; that is, one could assume that the behaviors of the C_i may influence the outcome of the *A* versus *B* confrontation and therefore *A* and *B* would need to take these other actors into account. If the C_i are truly exogenous actors, however, *A* and *B* will not be able to modify their behaviors.

It is obviously more reasonable to assume that in most situations the behaviors of *A* and *B* will be partly directed toward *influencing* the remaining parties to join them as coalition partners, to remain neutral, or to supply them with needed resources in exchange for less important ones. In short, the behaviors and expected behaviors of these other parties must be brought into the theory in such a way as to permit them to be partly *dependent* variables as well as exogenous (independent) factors. And, of course, these other parties will have their own changeable resources, motivations, and expectancies regarding outcomes. Any general theory must indicate how these additional parties are to be handled, and it must also allow for subjective factors and unknowns in explaining their behavior as well. Our own models will be much more limited in scope and will therefore be primarily useful for handling the two-party case.

Facing uncertainties regarding the resources and motivation of one's opponent(s), a rational actor would make predictions on the basis of past performance and resources. In fact, one very rational approach would be to assume that previous behavior will continue but that it will be modified in specific ways according to changes in relative resources or perceived motivations. The point is that actors are likely to base their behaviors and expectations on past encounters, so that an adequate theory must somehow or another take these past data into account. But the extent to which the past is used as a guide will also depend upon subjective as well as objective factors, and in particular on the degree to which actors perceive the present situation as similar to past ones (cue similarity, as discussed in chapter 3). The actors may also vary in the degree to which they rely on the immediate past (say, only the last encounter) as compared with a series of more distant encounters. In effect, we should ideally build in a "decay factor" to allow for differing time perspectives of the several actors. Again, our discussion will omit any consideration of these dynamic features.

In the discussion that follows we shall assume a certain kind of symmetry in the model, though not necessarily in the structural parameters (numerical values) of the model. It will be assumed that the *processes* are the same for all actors, so that the same sets of variables may be used to characterize all actors. Furthermore, our assumption will be that the equations for each actor are the same with respect to (1) the independent variables used to explain the dependent variable in question and (2) the general *form* of the equations (e.g., linear, logarithmic, multiplicative joint effects). But *A* may have many more resources than *B, B* may have more at stake in the relationship, *A* and *B* may differ in the degree to which they base expectancies on past behavior, and so forth.

This obviously means that in any given application the theory must allow for asymmetry in connection with the relative powers of all parties. The symmetrical feature of the general *model,* however, permits a highly important kind of simplification. For instance, in the case of the two-actor model involving only *A* and *B,* we may focus attention on only one of the two actors, with our general argument applying equally well to the other party. It is an important empirical question whether or not this kind of simplification is realistic in the case of power confrontations in which there is a gross inequality of resources or a major difference in other variables. For example, it may turn out that a different set of *variables* (not just coefficients) must be used to explain the behavior of a minority or other subordinate party from those used to explain the behavior of the dominant party.

Since no effort will be made in the present chapter to specify exact forms of functional relationships, specific lags, and so forth, there is little to be gained by writing down a set of (simultaneous) equations to represent the behavior of each party. The above remarks imply, however, that if this were to be done we would need to allow for asymmetry with respect to the coefficients of each actor. For example, *A*'s resources might have a different impact on *B*'s behavior than *B*'s resources have on *A*'s behavior, though we would predict that there would be *some* impact in each case, and the direction of this impact might be the same in both instances.

In presenting a reasonably general model our objective is to provide a conceptual framework that is broad enough to apply to a wide range of specific kinds of power-conflict situations and yet specific enough to imply a set of variables that can be measured in unidimensional terms. Ideally, the theory must also specify the assumed relationships among these variables to the extent of stating all causal linkages, functional forms, directions of associations, and relative magnitudes of the structural parameters. Unfortunately, the more general the model, the more difficult the latter task, since it is extremely unlikely that all or even most specific applications will be sufficiently similar to permit such a high degree of specification.

The initial model, as given in figure 8.1, really consists of a number of blocks or sets of variables that are, as yet, unspecified. Discussions of these individual blocks will follow the presentation and brief discussion of the general model. In particular, it is impossible in the general case to indicate the numerous exogenous, or independent, variables that will affect each of the blocks of variables in question. Our explicit model is a static one, except for the fact that certain of the variables are taken as functions of past outcomes of previous power confrontations.[4]

In figure 8.1 the focus of attention is on actor A, with a similar set of variables (omitted from the diagram) being appropriate for actor B and for at least some of the C_i. We use the subscripts A, B, and C_i to refer to the characteristics of these actors. In figure 9.1, in the next chapter, we shall introduce presuperscripts to refer to the perceptions or expectations of the respective actors. Thus R_A refers to the resources of actor A. The symbols $^A R_A$ and $^B R_A$ will later be used to refer to the perceptions of A of its own resources and to B's perceptions of A's resources.

Let us now provide a brief overview of the model, at the same time explaining the symbols that have been introduced. First notice that the horizontal dashed lines separate past values of variables, labeled with the postsuperscript $t - 1$, from present values without superscripts, and from future values, designated with the postsuperscript $t + 1$. The variables are labeled as follows:

O_A, O_B, O_{C_i} = Objective properties, positions, or personal characteristics of actors A, B, and C_i;

G_A, G_B, G_{C_i} = Goals of actors, with attached utilities U;

R_A, R_B, R_{C_i} = Resources (power potential) of actors;

T_A, T_B, T_{C_i} = Theories (perceptions, expectations) of actors concerning O's, G's, and R's;

D_A, D_B, D_{C_i} = Degree of mobilization of each actor;

E_A, E_B, E_{C_i} = Efficiency of mobilization of each actor;

S_A, S_B, S_{C_i} = Secrecy of each actor;

K_A, K_B, K_{C_i} = Knowledge level of each actor;

L_A, L_B, L_{C_i} = Leadership and coordination of each actor;

M_A, M_B, M_{C_i} = Means used by each actor;

P_A, P_B, P_{C_i} = Power (kinetic) actually exerted by each actor;

Y_j = Outcomes of power contest.

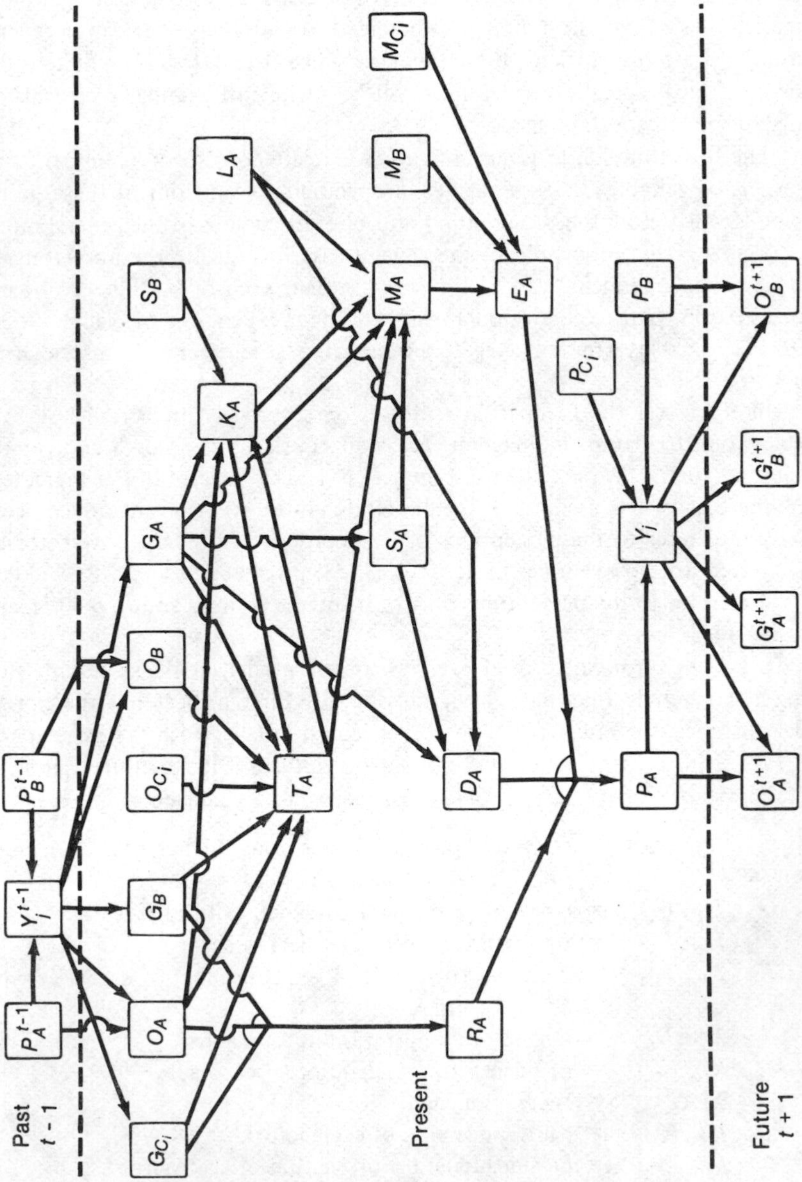

Figure 8.1. General Power Model for Power Exerted by Actor A

The model distinguishes between the actual or objective possessions and properties, O, of an actor and its resources, R, which are also a function of the motivational structures of the other parties. Thus financial assets of one party are included among its objective properties, as are official positions held, voting rights, and the ability to inflict physical harm on the opponent. But unless one also knows something about the utilities and subjective probabilities of the other parties these objective properties cannot be assumed to be automatically transformed into resources, as we have already noted in the case of money. Thus voting rights may mean nothing if an election can be rigged, if the other party does not care about the outcome of the election, or if the votes concerned are not needed to assure victory. The occupancy of a position in an authority structure is also not a resource unless there are at least some persons who are motivated to carry out one's orders. In many analyses of social power—especially those on the macro level—these objective properties are *equated* with resources on the assumption that the causal linkage between the two is not problematic. In some situations this may be a reasonable kind of assumption to make, but we must at least allow for the possibility that it is not.

In order to account for the fact that the degree and efficiency with which the resources are actually mobilized depend upon the actors' assessments of the situation, we introduce the block of variables T_A to represent actor A's perceptions and expectations as to how the other parties will behave. This block will be discussed in the next chapter. Here it is sufficient to note that each actor may not accurately perceive even its own resources since, even if A knows its own O's, it will lack complete information about how the others will react to these O's. For example, A does not know whether a third party, C, can be "bought," whether votes will be honestly counted, or whether its orders will be carried out. Furthermore, A's decisions as to what portion of its own resources to expend will depend upon A's expectations as to the proportion of B's resources that will be utilized and the means that B will employ. These perceptions of A will be influenced by numerous exogenous variables as well as A's own goals and the objective properties of A, B, and other parties, $C_{i.}$. They will also be affected by A's knowledge, K_A, which, in turn, will be affected by secrecy and deceptiveness, S_B, employed by B.

By degree of mobilization D we mean the proportion of an actor's resources that are actually mobilized in the power confrontation. Thus D will vary between zero and unity for each type of resource, R. To measure D, then, we would need to have an accurate measure of each resource. As an approximation one often simply equates resources with objective properties and may then utilize the proportion of these properties that are mobilized. For example, D_A might be measured (with some slippage, to be sure) as the proportion of A's total financial capital expended, as the proportion of eligible voters voting as specified, or by a fraction of one's total free time devoted to the issue in question. This would imply that the total power exerted, P, would be a product of $D \times R$.

But power exerted is not necessarily equal to power produced (output), because of possible inefficiency of the operation. We have already noted that in physics efficiency may be conceptualized as the ratio of output to input. In the case of social power, efficiency cannot be so simply conceptualized and measured, not only because of theoretical ambiguities but also because of the impossibility of replicating under standardized conditions so as to compare relative efficiencies. Nevertheless, it is clearly recognized that certain courses of action, or means, M, may be more efficient than others in the sense of achieving a higher power output for the same expenditure of resources. If we imagine an upper limit to efficiency of 1.0, with actual efficiency varying from zero to unity, then we may conceptualize the total effective power applied as a multiplicative function of $D \times E \times R$.

The model implies that the actor's perceptions and expectations, T, affect degree of mobilization, D, and also the means, M, utilized. These latter means are also affected by leadership and organization, L, by the actor's own goals, G (and utilities, U), the secrecy, S, of both A and B, and the degree to which the actor possesses accurate knowledge of the objective properties, goals, perceptions–expectations, and means of the other parties. Finally, the outcomes, Y_j, of the power confrontation are taken as a function of the actual power applied by each of the actors plus, of course, any exogenous factors that may also directly influence these outcomes. These outcomes, together with the actual expenditure of resources by the several parties, will then affect the levels of the O's as well as the motivational states and goals of the actors at the next point in time, here denoted by $t + 1$.

It should be noted that the model does not explicitly take into consideration the remote past and relies primarily on the use of present values of each variable to account for power exerted. As implied above, this does not deny the importance of "historical" factors that may affect such variables as present objective characteristics, goals, expectations, and mobilization. For example, past grievances may very well affect the motivational structure of one or more actors. Lacking reliable knowledge of the opponent's current characteristics, an actor may make a completely rational decision to estimate these characteristics on the basis of known past behaviors or properties. But, of course, the several actors may not all rely to the same extent on knowledge of past events. The defeated party, for example, may be affected to a much greater extent than the victor by the immediate past, and may also utilize a longer memory factor in its decision processes.

The model suggests that whenever possible the investigator should attempt to measure present states (goals, perceptions, grievances, etc.) rather than to infer these states on the basis of past values of measured values. It might be possible to bypass the measurement of one party's goals by making assumptions about how these goals are affected by past events, but this would introduce specification errors into the theory unless these assumptions proved to be exactly correct. As we turn our attention to a number of the specific blocks or sets of variables we shall have a few additional comments concerning the impact of past events on current levels of variables.

RESOURCES AND OBJECTIVE PROPERTIES

Since there are many variables that intervene between power in its potential form and power as actually exercised, it seems wise to use a completely different term to refer to power potential, so that there will be minimal confusion when discussing power in its kinetic form. Since the term *resources* is commonly used to refer to the sources of power, we shall follow this convention. But, as we have previously noted, actor A's resources or sources of power will depend upon the goals, utilities, and subjective probabilities of actor B, and perhaps those of other actors as well. Cartwright (1959) refers to these subjective factors as the "motive base" of the resource. Thus resources must also be distinguished from any objective properties, positions, or characteristics that A may have. These objective properties, O_i, will be assumed *not* to depend upon other actors' motive bases. They will be taken as objective, in the sense that they can be identified by an outside observer who is totally unaware of other parties' motivational states.

The objective properties may be orderable according to criteria other than power, as, for example, prestige. They may even have an attached metric, as in the case of money or the acreage of a parcel of land. They may or may not be divisible or exchangeable, and they may be possessed for a fixed period of time (as, for example, an elective office) or for an indefinite period. We may look upon the *conversion* of objective properties into resources as a problem of measurement, through which we might ideally assign a numerical value to each objective position or unit of property in accord with the amount of kinetic power it was capable of producing. For example, one might develop a numerical scoring system to assess the amount of resources available to a president, as compared with a vice-president or lesser official. Likewise, one might attach a metric to money as a resource, and this metric might or might not be a linear function of dollars or other monetary unit.

This measurement or conversion process, we argue, will necessarily involve assumptions about the motivational states of other actors. We shall discuss this measurement problem in more detail below. Here it is sufficient to emphasize the distinction between the O_i, which do not depend upon these motivational states, and the R_i, which do. If we look upon the conversion of the O_i to the R_i as a process of assigning numerical values to different levels of these O_i, then we must recognize that the metrics involved are likely to vary according to the type of power being considered, the situational factors that may affect these motivational states, and, of course, the motivational states themselves. Such a measurement process will indeed be complex.

Before we can come to grips with resources themselves we must ideally specify the goals involved, the alternative paths that may be used to achieve these goals, and the utilities and subjective probabilities of the actors.[5] It is thus not surprising that it is extremely difficult to say very much in general about these resources, or even to develop a reasonable list of such resources. Our own discussion of power is, as noted, limited to those objectives that lead to a power confrontation between two actors or parties, A and B, while allowing for the existence of third parties, C_i. If we further restrict ourselves to that type of power that we refer to as control, by which we mean one actor's affecting the alternative behaviors of the second actor, it becomes much simpler to develop a meaningful classification of resources.

It should specifically be noted that other lists will become necessary if we shift to a broader conceptualization of power, such as that of the achievement of objectives or the control over outcomes. For example, Clark (1968), in discussing community power, and Coleman (1971), in discussing minority resources, consider very different lists of resources. The ones we shall discuss, however, are commonly cited in the literature on control and have been adopted by Gamson (1968), among others. They also closely resemble a list of "bases of power" discussed by French and Raven (1959).

Without loss of generality we may focus on the resources that A needs to influence the behavior of B, recognizing that the roles of A and B can easily be reversed and that any of the third parties, C_i, can also be placed in the role of B. Basically, A may affect B's behavior by influencing either B's utilities or subjective probabilities. Certain of these utilities will be relatively fixed, at least over the duration of the power contest being analyzed. These will be the utilities attached to basic goals, as contrasted with those goals that are merely intermediate objectives, and whose utilities are likely to be functions of B's subjective probabilities. For example, if B believes that obtaining additional knowledge will be instrumental in achieving a more important goal, and if A can convince B that this is not the case, A may in effect modify B's utility attached to obtaining this knowledge by altering the subjective probability of achieving the more important goal through this means. In the discussion that follows, we shall ignore these instrumental goals by assuming that the utilities attached to them will be functions of subjective probabilities. If so, we may then simplify the picture by assuming that A's actions will affect only B's subjective and objective probabilities, at least in the short run.

The basic distinction that is often made, and that we shall follow, is between courses of action by A that involve either positive or negative sanctions and those that involve persuasion.[6] We shall define three general types of behavior as follows:

Rewarding behaviors are those courses of action by A that actually increase the true probabilities of B's obtaining those goals to which positive utilities have been attached or that decrease the true probabilities of B's obtaining goals to which negative utilities have been attached.

Punishing behaviors are those courses of action by A that actually decrease the true probabilities of B's obtaining those goals to which positive utilities have been attached or that increase the true probabilities of B's obtaining goals to which negative utilities have been attached.

Persuading behaviors are those courses of action by A that change B's *subjective* probabilities, in either direction, but that do not directly affect the true probabilities of obtaining goals to which either positive or negative utilities have been attached.

A number of comments about these definitions are necessary. First, it should be noted that all three definitions omit any reference to what A *intends* by the actions, since there may be miscalculations of A's own resources or B's motivational states. For example, A may intend to punish B but may actually engage in rewarding behaviors because of a lack of understanding of B's goals and relative utilities. Or an attempt at persuasion may actually be accompanied by either positive or negative sanctions that are neither recognized nor intended by A. Of course, the distinctions among rewarding, punishing, and persuading are often difficult to employ operationally because of the investigator's inability to distinguish empirically between true and subjective probabilities.

Threatening or bluffing behavior, in particular, is often exceedingly difficult to classify. For example, certain veiled threats may be implicit in persuasion attempts whenever A is obviously in a position to sanction B. If, for instance, an employer tells an employee that it will be "in your best interests" to carry out a certain act, it could be that no sanctions at all are intended, but neither B nor an outside observer would be in a position to verify this unless B actually does not follow the "suggestion." Therefore we cannot distinguish true persuasion from rewarding or punishing behavior unless we are in a position to observe a large number of replications. We can, however, attempt to assess both A's and B's *perceptions* of these processes.

We have been assuming all along that it is B's *subjective* probabilities that affect B's behaviors, with these subjective probabilities being partly determined by past "objective probabilities" or, more accurately, past relative frequencies. Thus B's behaviors can never be determined by the sanctions themselves, since the latter are applied only after the behavior in question. Therefore, in order for A to influence B's behaviors there must be a communication of A's intent, either in the form of an actual statement of what A's courses of action will be, contingent upon B's future action, or by B's inferring this intent on the basis of past behavioral sequences. In this sense one might argue that previous sanctioning behavior constitutes a form of persuasion, as we have defined this term above. This is why we have introduced the phrase "but that do not directly affect the true probabilities."

Persuasion involves only a change in B's subjective states but not in the objective situation. Thus a bluff would constitute a form of persuasion, but if A actually carried through and applied either a positive or negative sanction, then this latter act would *not* be classified as persuasion. This usage of the term *persuasion* is therefore somewhat broader than the usage that restricts the term to attempts to change B's beliefs or utilities by altering only B's causal theories. We shall use the term *convincing behavior* to refer to those forms of persuasion that involve only B's interpretations of causal theories. Thus if A can convince B that B's reasoning is faulty, or that certain of B's assumptions are incorrect, without any threats or promises of sanctions being involved, we shall consider this to be a special form of persuasion that we shall refer to as A's having convinced B to alter its behavior.

As Blau (1964a) has noted, it is not always a simple matter to decide whether a given behavior is rewarding or punishing. Where B has become used to a certain level of rewarding behavior by A, as, for example, an annual raise by an employer or regular compliments for performing certain services, the withdrawal of these rewards may in effect constitute a form of punishment. The crucial element, here, is the *direction* of change in the probability rather than the absolute level. Thus if A lowers the probability of a desired outcome, this constitutes a form of punishment.

This implies that under certain circumstances it may be extremely difficult for A to continue to reward B indefinitely. In particular, if the probability levels become very high it may be extremely costly to push them higher, as, for example, through increasingly frequent rewards. It also implies that even though the same objective properties, such as money, may be used both to reward or to punish, the actual resource units (if these could be measured accurately) may not be the same in both directions; that is, it may take more money to reward than to punish B by a given amount because the utility curves for money may have different forms for gains and losses.

Authority, Legitimate Power, Referent Power, and Expert Power

We must also briefly discuss the notions of authority, legitimate power, referent power, and expert power, the latter three terms being those of French and Raven (1959). The concept of authority is an important one in sociological theory and, as one might expect, has been defined in a number of ways. Gamson's (1968:21–22) definition places an emphasis on the right to make what he called binding decisions and seems especially useful in discussing hierarchical decision-making structures in which rights to make decisions may be delegated under certain conditions and reclaimed under others. We shall say nothing more about this usage of the term, referring the reader to Gamson's excellent discussion of the subject.

Perhaps a more common usage is that which takes A's authority over B as involving the notion that B accepts A's right to ask and expect certain behaviors on the part of B, or at least that *other* actors, C_i, accept this right and can be counted on to enforce these expectations. French and Raven consider authority as a special case of what they call legitimate power, pointing out that legitimacy need not depend upon one's position in an organizational structure. For example, A may have legitimate power with respect to B if B has made a commitment to A, perhaps as a result of a previous favor provided by A. In this case, the legitimacy may be an embodiment of a trusting relationship resulting from previous social exchanges.

According to French and Raven, the essential defining characteristic of legitimate power is B's *acceptance* of A's right to expect B to behave in particular ways. This acceptance is conditional, however, on A's following certain agreed upon rules and on the confinement of A's requests to a specified domain of behaviors. If A exceeds these conditions, French and Raven argue, this is likely to decrease A's attractiveness to B, and hence A's "referent power" over B—as discussed below.

This notion of legitimate power, or what we would have to call a resource dependent upon legitimacy, becomes much more complicated whenever there are more than two parties involved. The notion of authority (as a type of legitimate resource) usually has the popular connotation that the authority's power rests on the acceptance by numerous other parties, C_i, of A's rights to affect B's behavior regardless of whether B accepts this legitimacy. If so, A's power over B may be indirect. A may invoke legitimacy with respect to these C_i, who in turn may use positive or (more usually) negative sanctions to attempt to control B. Or, possibly, A may be able to persuade B that these sanctions will be applied by the C_i unless B obeys or acts as A directs.

Thus so-called legitimate power, or resources based on legitimacy, may be utilized in such a way that rewarding, punishing, or persuading behaviors are combined in complex ways. Where B actually accepts the legitimacy of A's influence, we presume that B attaches a positive utility to the goal of conforming to A's requests, as long as these do not exceed the agreed upon rules or limits. If so, then if B fails or is unable to behave in the fashion requested by A, there will be self-imposed sanctions by B. To the degree that B succeeds there will be gratification. In effect, then, whenever B accepts the legitimacy of A's requests, there will automatically be a form of rewarding or punishing behavior involved, even where this is not intended or even recognized by A. Put another way, we might say that there will be intrinsic rewards (or punishments) attached to B's behaviors. Of course, there may be extrinsic rewards (or punishments) as well, as, for example, an increase in pay, a future promotion, or some return of a favor.

If B does not accept the legitimacy of A's requests, but if other C_i do and are willing to employ sanctions against B, then A cannot rely on this particular goal of B's, or on self-imposed sanctions, but will in general find it necessary to rely more heavily on extrinsic rewards and punishments. This point is closely related to discussions by Etzioni (1961) and Gamson (1968) of the relationship between forms of control and the motivational orientation of subordinate actors. Both of these authors argue that certain types of control are compatible with specific kinds of orientation and that influence attempts that do not "fit" with these orientations will either be less likely to succeed or may ultimately affect the nature of these orientations. For example, where lower participants or sub-ordinates are basically trustful of authorities, efforts to convince the subor-dinates will be more effective than the application of either rewards or punishments.

Implicit in these discussions is the notion that B's acceptance of A's author-ity may be based on combinations of very different motivations—a basic trust in A, an attachment or identification with A, or a concern that other C_i will enforce A's orders. As analytic concepts, the notions of authority and legitimacy are therefore too broad for our purposes.

French and Raven also use the concept of referent power as a type of resource of A's that is dependent upon B's identification, or feeling of oneness, with A. Although we are not at all certain what the authors mean by identifica-tion, their discussion clearly implies that B wants to do as A asks, just to please A, and regardless of whether or not A will apply sanctions or even whether A can observe or verify B's behavior. A special case of referent power, we pre-sume, would be so-called charismatic leadership as discussed by Weber (1947). If we wanted to treat certain objective individual characteristics as indicating personal charisma, however, we would need to consider a charismatic relation-ship to be a joint function of both actors A and B, and in particular of B's motivational states.

French and Raven also suggest the hypothesis that, in general, referent power will entail a broader scope or range of behaviors than will legitimate power. Pre-sumably, A's ability to modify B's behavior will not be as limited by rules and expectations of reciprocity in the case of referent power, although we should be careful not to overestimate the scope of behaviors that may be affected by this type of resource. B's attachment to A is likely to be weakened if A's demands or behaviors fall outside of certain limits, although such limits may be much less specifically defined than in the case of legitimate power.

Also, we assume that a certain degree of observability or accountability may be necessary even in the case of referent power, though perhaps to a lesser degree than in the case of legitimate power. A's referent power as a resource obviously depends upon B's knowing what A expects and therefore requires at least one-way communication. It may in addition be true in the case of referent power, as French and Raven suggest, that B will continue to behave as A desires even after A's presence has been removed. This is likely since A may be in a position actually to change B's goals and utilities whenever B identifies with A, whereas this will be much more difficult if legitimacy alone is involved.

In many kinds of empirical situation we are likely to find the two kinds of resource combined, and this seems especially likely whenever A is able to rely much more heavily on rewards than on punishments. We would predict that legitimacy combined with rewarding and convincing behaviors will tend to increase B's identification with A and hence A's referent power over B. Con-versely, punishing behavior, persuasion involving bluffs or threats, or demands that overstep the bounds of legitimacy will tend to decrease A's referent power.

Likewise, if A uses legitimate power to get other parties, C_i, to apply negative sanctions to B, this should also decrease A's referent power over B unless B is unaware of A's influence over these third parties.

Finally, we need to say a few words about what French and Raven refer to as expert power. Expertise may be used in at least two different ways. First, A may use superior knowledge or information to persuade B to change B's subjective probabilities or utilities attached to instrumental goals. For example, social scientists' studies may convince blacks that forced busing is not an effective way to achieve quality education. But second, A's knowledge may be used to improve the efficiency and degree of A's own mobilization efforts, as, for example, through superior military technology, or to help A to predict B's behavior more accurately.

We do not regard this second type of expert knowledge as a resource, in our sense of the term, since it is not dependent upon B's motivational states. Rather, it is an objective property, O, that is used to affect the degree of mobilization, D, and the efficiency of mobilization, E, on the A side of the ledger. This second kind of knowledge will also have indirect impacts on B. For example, improvement in A's technological knowledge or efficiency may make it easier and less costly for A to apply specific sanctions. Expert knowledge of B's motivation and objective properties may facilitate A's defense against B's efforts to apply certain kinds of sanctions.

Defensive Resources

We also need to consider the fact that to the degree that A can either modify its own utilities so as to become less dependent on B or can find alternative sources of supply, this will have much the same net effect as controlling B's behavior by working on B's side of the ledger.[7] For the lack of a better term, we might refer to this set of alternatives as a defensive strategy on the part of A.

If A can either give up entirely or at least reduce the utilities attached to those goals that are subject to B's control, this will have the effect of reducing B's resources in relation to A. For example, if A comes to attach less importance to survival goals, or at least has a substantial proportion of its members who are willing to make extreme sacrifices, then B's threats or actual use of violence will become less important as a control mechanism. Here we are not concerned with a resource of A per se, although it may be necessary to use certain resources internally to produce this change in utilities. For example, if a group can motivate some of its members to take substantial risks by offering them high honor or more tangible rewards, it may be possible to compensate in this way for B's numerical or technical superiorities.

A may also use a portion of its objective properties more directly to protect itself from B. Perhaps it may make certain lines of action by B extremely costly, so that for all practical purposes they become ruled out as realistic alternatives. Thus the possession of mountainous territories (an objective property), combined with fortifications and the training of a citizen army in defensive warfare, has been effective in preserving Swiss independence in the presence of much more powerful neighboring countries.

As Emerson (1962) suggests, another defensive strategy A may use is to cultivate alternative sources of supply so as to reduce dependence upon B. One such alternative, of course, is to produce a sufficiently large stockpile of food, weapons, and other necessities that A can remain invulnerable to B's efforts to cut off such supplies. Still another possibility is to form coalitions with various third parties capable of replenishing A's stockpile of objective properties so that in order to cut off this supply B will have to risk bringing these C_i actively into the contest on the side of A. Coalitions with neutrals may thus be used to cut off certain alternative courses of action open to B and thereby reduce B's efficiency of mobilization.

More generally, the levels of A's objective properties may affect B's courses of action by altering B's subjective probabilities of achieving success. In this sense we refer to them as defensive resources, but we do not wish to imply that this makes them secondary or less important than the other types of resource more frequently discussed in the literature. In effect they are resources that enable A to *block* actions by B or to exercise a kind of veto power. They are akin to those implied by Bachrach and Baratz (1963) in their discussion of "nondecisions" and the factors that prevent certain types of issue from ever arising in power confrontations.

The Conversion of Objective Properties into Resources

As implied numerous times in the above discussion, objective properties may be used in different ways, with varying costs and degrees of efficiency. This in turn suggests several additional complications for our analysis. First, we must recognize that certain kinds of objective property are more easily converted into resources than are others, with the "conversion factor" depending, however, on a number of additional variables that need to be taken into consideration. We may look upon such a conversion factor as providing a metric in terms of which actual resources might ideally be measured. For example, money in dollars may be used in many different ways to achieve objectives. Some of these may be defined as legitimate, in which case we presume that services may be bought more cheaply than in the case of illegitimate usages, where there may be a greater risk factor involved. Thus one may achieve results by legitimate efforts to influence public officials, by attempting to buy them off, or even possibly through assassination. The last means may be the most efficient, in some instances, but also much more risky if one is caught. The price paid to the agent, both for the act and later cover-up, may be very high but can be evaluated against the costs of the remaining alternative courses of action.

Second, since these conversion factors will not be constant from one situation to the next we see that the measurement of resources becomes dependent upon our theory concerning the many kinds of variable that may influence the conversion of objective properties into resources. In particular, the measurement of

A's resources depends upon our theories about B's motivational structure, as well as those of other C_i, and this in turn depends upon B's perception not only of B's own objective properties but of A's motivational structure.

Thus it appears as though the measurement of A's resources is dependent upon the very theory the verification of which the measurement is intended to facilitate! As we have previously indicated, this problem is not peculiar to the measurement of resources, but in this instance we must expect to encounter a very complex measurement model or auxiliary theory. For this reason, there is little one can say about this measurement process on a highly general level. However, if we are concerned with a kind of objective property, such as money, that is useful to a wide variety of actors because of its exchangeability for many different services, it may prove to be relatively easier to be more specific.

Let us assume, then, that we are dealing with some objective property, O_i, to which a metric has already been attached, as, for example, a monetary unit. We shall also represent a single "conditioning variable" by the letter X, with the understanding that in more complex models there may very well be several such X's that need to be brought into the picture. We can distinguish several simple alternative models, as follows.

Model 1: X is either present or absent. When X is present, R_i is a monotonic function of O_i, but when X is absent, $R_i = 0$. As a very simple case R_i might be equated with O_i when X is present. For example, party A's resources are equated with A's wealth so long as this wealth can legitimately be used to affect B's behavior or to obtain a more general goal. Where the rules of the game do not permit the use of wealth as an instrument of influence (and therefore X is set equal to zero, or defined as "absent"), the value of wealth as a resource is taken to be zero.

Model 2: The conversion of O_i into R_i depends upon the level of X, which is continuous or at least capable of taking on more than two values. As a simple special case R_i might be a multiplicative function of X and O_i, $R_i = kXO_i$, or perhaps a power function of the form $R_i = kX^a O_i^b$. For example, the cost in monetary units of influencing B by a certain means may depend upon the *degree* of legitimacy involved (as represented by the level of X) or perhaps according to the wages demanded by those actors whose services are being purchased. Such wages, in turn, may depend upon their degree of loyalty to A or the risks involved.

Model 3: R_i is some nonlinear (usually monotonic) function of O_i, with the parameters dependent upon the level of X. O_i subject to satiation processes (e.g., money, food, honorific titles) are obvious illustrations. As a further example, suppose O_i represents the total number of votes that A can deliver to influence the behavior of B. If this number is very small and obviously insufficient to enable B to win an election, the slope relating O_i to R_i may be virtually horizontal at the lower levels. Similarly, once B's victory can be assured, further increases in the level of O_i may not produce more than negligible increases in R_i. But in the intermediate ranges the slope relating the two variables may be more steep, as indicated in figure 8.2. Other factors, represented here by the single variable X, may affect the slope values at different points on the curve, such as the points of inflection.

Model 4: A single R_i may be a joint function of several O_j. In particular, one or more O_j (such as knowledge) may be *necessary* in order for another O_i to be convertable into a resource. This kind of model is similar to models 1 and 2 except that here the conditioning variable, previously labeled X, is itself another objective property of A. Another possibility is that any one of several O_j may be *sufficient* to provide actor A with the resource in question. If the O_j are each dichotomous and defined to be unity when present and zero when absent, and if R_i is also dichotomous, the first of these possibilities could be represented by the equation $R_i = O_1 O_2 O_3 \ldots O_k$ and the second by the equation $R_i = 1 - (1 - O_1)(1 - O_2) \ldots (1 - O_k)$.

The first type of submodel involving a series of necessary O_j seems appropriate whenever A's course of action involves a series of stages, each of which is a necessary precondition for the next, with each of these requiring a different type of objective property (e.g., money, legal authority, or legislative approval). The second kind of submodel would be appropriate whenever A can influence B by a number of alternative means, any one of which is sufficient, with each means involving a different O_j.

POOLING, EXPENDING, AND REPLENISHING RESOURCES

A number of important theoretical questions revolve around such notions as the pooling or sharing of resources, the rates at which resources are exhausted or replenished, and the extent to which they can be detached or separated from various types of actor. In order to begin to analyze such questions it seems essential to make a number of conceptual distinctions. Actually, most of these will involve objective properties, O_i, rather than resources per se, but we shall rather loosely refer to them all under the generic label of pooling of resources.

Figure 8.2. Resources (R_i) as a Monotonic Nonlinear Function of Objective Properties (O_i)

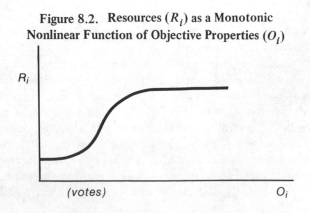

The general problems with which we shall be concerned in this section are those of how objective properties fit together or can be combined, how they are gained or lost, and what their connection is to the actors that may "possess" them in some sense.

If we are to make any sense out of the term *degree of mobilization* of resources we must somehow or another find a way of saying what we mean by the notion of total resources. This seems simple enough when we are concerned with a very straightforward kind of O_i such as money, but is by no means clear when we also include notions such as referent power, legitimate power, or expert power. In what sense can these be combined or depleted? Clearly, we are a long way from attaining any operational procedures for such a combining operation, since to do so would require both units of measurement and a set of rules for converting from one unit to another. The best we can do in this brief discussion is to introduce a number of distinctions that may help to clarify some of the issues that may be involved. We begin with the concepts of divisibility, detachability, and interchangeability.

Divisibility. By the ease of divisibility of an O_i we shall mean the degree to which a total O_i can be subdivided into smaller units of equal magnitude. We refer to this as ease, or degree, of divisibility because we recognize that in some instances such a subdivision can only be accomplished with effort and therefore at a cost. We have many examples of easily divisible properties such as money, weapons (e.g., spears, guns, airplanes), or number of votes. Other kinds of O_i, such as land, are in principle divisible, although it may be much more difficult to arrive at units that can be equated in terms of their resource value. Thus, although the acre or other areal unit may constitute a unit in physical space, we recognize that some land is more valuable per acre than other land and that the value attached to this land need not be in monetary units.

The essential idea involved in the notion of divisibility is that the units may be aggregated or combined in a straightforward additive way to give a total figure that adequately represents the O_i in question. For example, dollars can be added to yield a total financial resource figure, and it makes no difference whether the dollars come from many small donors or two or three larger ones. Similarly, votes are counted and a decision reached that does not depend upon the source of these votes. One person's vote or dollar is as good as another's. Likewise, guns or airplanes (of specified types) are assumed to be equivalent and may be combined additively to produce a single figure to represent the total O_i as a sum of its components. In contrast, there are certain kinds of O_i that obviously cannot be subdivided in this fashion without altering their fundamental quality. For example, a complex weapons system may be made totally useless if one of its components is destroyed or subtracted.

In discussing divisibility we must be careful not to confuse this question of the additivity of smaller units with the possibility that there may be a nonlinear relationship between the magnitude of the O_i and some outcome variable. For example, it may be that it takes only a certain amount of money or number of votes to achieve a given purpose, so that the addition of further funds or votes may have a negligible impact on this outcome. Likewise, the possession of an extremely large nuclear arsenal or other type of weapons system may permit overkill, but beyond a certain point there are only marginal gains from additional weapons. Nevertheless, we would still want to consider these types of O_i as divisible.

Detachability. Objective properties also differ with respect to the ease or degree to which they can be detached from particular parties. This will depend upon the rules under which the actors are operating and the degree to which these rules are enforced by outside third parties. Whereas money can rather easily be detached from a given actor, votes cannot, at least in the American political system. In other words, an individual can contribute a certain sum of money to a political campaign, in which case the dollars become completely detached from this actor and placed in an overall pool controlled by a different set of actors. But votes cannot be bought or sold, at least in the literal sense of the term. Each voter is entitled to a single vote and must appear in person at the voting booth. A failure to do so may, of course, affect the ultimate outcome, but there is no sense in which this vote can be detached from the actor. In effect, getting an actor's vote requires his or her behavioral cooperation.

Whenever O_i can be detached from one actor and given to another there will in general be less need for overall coordination, except, of course, to persuade the actor to part with the O_i in question. But if the O_i cannot be detached, so that the actor's physical presence is also required to use the O_i, we can anticipate that there will be additional problems of coordination, timing, and the necessity of expending supplementary resources to assure the necessary cooperation. A case in point is manpower as a resource. Since physical labor or military force that is dependent on the sheer number of militia cannot be divorced from the individual actors, coordination efforts will necessarily have to involve the actual behaviors of these individuals vis-à-vis another party or in relation to a specific task. If so, the total resources will be roughly proportional to numbers, although the efficiency with which these resources can be mobilized is likely to decrease with size. Whether or not the actual power applied ($= D \times E \times R$) will increase with numbers will then depend upon the functions that relate size to total resources, on the one hand, and efficiency, on the other.

Interchangeability with Respect to Use. By this cumbersome phrase we refer to the fact that any given O_i may be a very important resource in the hands of some actors but virtually useless if possessed by other actors who may lack the skills, technical knowledge, or experience to use it. Money, we presume, can be used by anyone provided that experts are available who can be bought. Certain kinds of weapon can be used with minimal training, whereas others require detailed technical knowledge before they can be used as actual resources.

We must distinguish this interchangeability notion from that of detachability. Although weapons may easily be exchanged or stolen, it does not follow that the new owners will be able to use them efficiently. Thus interchangeability refers not to the O_i themselves, but to the *actors* who will put them to use.

Where these actors are also interchangeable, a given O_i in one actor's hands is equivalent to that same O_i in another actor's hands in the sense that they are capable of using it in exactly the same way.

Here we are obviously introducing the idea of knowledge, training, or expertise as a characteristic of the actor that interacts with the objective characteristics of the O_i in question. Under ordinary circumstances, this knowledge is not detachable in the sense that it must necessarily go along with a given actor. But it can be transmitted, by which we mean that it can be learned by other actors, though presumably at some cost. Likewise, it can be withheld or communicated in such a fashion that it can be used only under very limited circumstances. We also need to take note of the possibility that actors may wish to invent or discover new O_i about which they have a monopoly of knowledge, so that they may use this as an advantage over their competitors.

Generalizability. By the degree of generalizability of an objective property we mean the number and diversity of types of alternative courses of action (means) that can be facilitated by the O_i in question. Where these courses of action require the services of other actors (such as laborers, mercenaries, police, or assassins) generalizability may be measured in terms of the numbers of different kinds of service that can be obtained in exchange for this property. As is frequently noted (see, for example, Clark 1968:64), money is an extremely generalizable property in market economies, although its use for certain illegitimate purposes may be regulated with varying degrees of effectiveness. French and Raven (1959) argue that referent power is also likely to be highly generalizable, perhaps more so than legitimate power. The combination of high generalizability, detachability, and interchangeability that characterizes money makes this type of property especially important whenever flexibility in the choice of means is needed. Other types of O_i may require the actor to make a greater commitment to a smaller number of alternatives.

Indispensability. There are certain conditions under which one or more O_i will be necessary, though perhaps not sufficient, in achieving a given objective or in affecting the behavior of another party. This means that there are no other O_i that may be substituted for them, so that an actor may be blocked from achieving success unless these particular O_i are possessed. We have already noted that this kind of situation seems especially likely whenever the course of action requires that certain steps be carried out in sequence, with success at any one stage being a precondition for success in the following stage. For example, a project may have to clear a series of legislative hurdles, then legal challenges, and finally require major funding. A lack of the necessary resources at any one stage would mean failure, so that an opponent will have effective veto power if the project can be held up at any single point in the process. Here the notion of a simple pooling of resources (in the sense of adding O_i) would be misleading. Instead, we would have to think of the O_i as being combined multiplicatively, at least in the sense that a zero value for any one O_i will imply a zero value for the total resource level. There is no way in which the supply of other objective properties can compensate for the lack of any one of them.

A property such as knowledge can be thought of as operating in this multiplicative fashion, provided that it makes sense to think of zero knowledge as making effective action impossible. It will be rare for actors to approach this level of zero knowledge in most kinds of power confrontation, but if we think of power more generically the notion makes a good deal more sense. If, for example, actor A's goal is to prolong his or her life to an age of 150 years, one may say that the actor lacks the power to do so because of a lack of knowledge. In effect, knowledge affects efficiency of action, and if we take efficiency to be near zero, then the effective power applied will also be near zero, regardless of the degree of mobilization or the total resource base. It is immaterial whether we treat knowledge as a factor that affects efficiency or as a resource that combines with other resources multiplicatively. It will have exactly the same implications in terms of the actual power applied.

Expendability. Objective properties also differ with respect to the rates at which they are depleted or depreciated in the course of being used, with this expendability rate being a function of the actor's knowledge and care as to their use. Where the properties are divisible this rate of expendability is relatively easy to calculate as compared with, say, the expendability of one's authority or other type of legitimate power that may depend upon obligations incurred through social exchange. As Blau (1964a) has stressed, social exchange is characterized by considerable ambiguity and lack of precision, so that an actor's obligations (and therefore a second actor's legitimate power) are very difficult to assess. Therefore not only does expendability vary by degree but also by ease of assessment, so that perceived expendability may depart considerably from the true expendability rate. Also, of course, the *quality* of an O_i (say, a weapons system) may slowly deteriorate but to an unknown degree.

Nevertheless, actors must be concerned about the possible depletion or deterioration of their own and other parties' O_i and are therefore likely to "test" these O_i periodically as a means of making this assessment. Where assessment is difficult but yet where rapid expendability is anticipated, we would expect that such periodic tests will be both more frequent and more varied in nature. Also, the less obvious the linkage between the objective properties, O_i, and actual resources, R_i, the more necessary it becomes to conduct such tests. For instance, it is entirely possible that although the levels of certain O_i have not changed, the motivational base linking them to the R_i will have altered considerably, as in the case of the authority of an officeholder or the charisma of a demagogue.

In connection with the notion of expendability we should also consider a certain type of O_i, namely, the authority to grant honorific titles, special prizes, medals, or other forms of intangible rewards. Such authority is not expended in the sense that it is depleted. We recognize that the rewards involved may be cheapened through overuse, however, so that they certainly do not constitute an inexhaustible property. Their rate of expendability may be extremely difficult to calculate and under certain circumstances may be near zero during a relatively short period of time. In a sense some such rewards may be saved and then allocated during a brief period of crisis, as, for example, the awarding of medals of honor for bravery during wartime.

Replenishment Rate. Although the replenishment or appreciation of O_i in one sense represents the opposite process from that of their expendability or depletion rate, it is nevertheless useful under some circumstances to keep the two ideas distinct. For one thing, they may occur at very different rates. For another, the causes or sources of the two phenomena may be very different. The O_i are generally expended as a result of the mobilization of resources directed toward a particular objective, whereas the need to replenish them may require other courses of action and an allocation of other kinds of resource to this task. Furthermore, these two processes may be predictable to different degrees. In some instances a highly regular expenditure rate can be anticipated, perhaps owing to the necessity of taking care of cyclical biological needs (e.g., food consumption). But the source of supply of these O_i may be relatively less under the actor's control, so that not only the rate of replenishment but also the certainty of this rate may also be at issue.

We therefore recognize that an actor's control over the source of supply (e.g., food, means of production, jobs, or land) may become just as important as the present level of the O_i in question. We would obviously expect that the importance of source control, as compared with absolute level, will increase with the expected duration of the confrontation and therefore will affect the actor's strategy or choices among alternative courses of action. In particular, we would expect that the less control an actor has over this source the more likely that it will employ means that give it the initiative with respect to timing, and in particular the more likely that it will employ offensive rather than defensive strategies. Also, the less the control over sources of supply, the more necessary it will be for the actor to rely on coalition partners. As we shall note in the next chapter when we discuss alternative courses of action, this will create a number of dilemmas for the actor, especially in instances where these third parties may be alienated by offensive strategies or other means used to reduce the duration of the confrontation.

These and possibly other dimensions that refer to the ways in which resources may be combined or divided, augmented or depleted, and shared or exchanged obviously pertain much more directly to actual objective properties O_i than to resources, as we have used these two terms. Yet we have also argued that in most instances the O_i cannot be directly converted into resources unless one makes certain assumptions about actors' motivations. This in turn implies a degree of complexity that actors themselves will not be able to handle in their day-to-day decisions. It is no wonder, then, that there is a strong tendency to equate resources and objective properties.

This will create fewer problems for the actors concerned than the social scientist because of the fact that the former are usually concerned with very specific situations in which these simplifications are often realistic. The social scientist, in contrast, must attempt to develop theories appropriate to a diversity of situations for which these motivational factors, and hence the relationships between the R_i and the O_i, cannot be assumed constant. In the following chapter we shall consider a series of additional variables that can be expected to introduce still further complexities for the student of social power.

NOTES

1. In order to use symbols that are easily recalled we shall continue to represent basic variables by the first letter of the word to which they correspond. Unfortunately, in some instances this will require a change of notation from that which we have previously used. In this chapter and the next, the letter O will represent "objective properties," rather than outcomes, and the letter P will represent "power exerted," rather than a subjective probability.
2. Other potential means may never be seriously proposed because there would be such widespread opposition that their (subjective) probabilities of being implemented would be virtually zero. Bachrach and Baratz (1963) have emphasized this point in connection with their critique of the "issue-oriented" approach advocated by Dahl (1961) and others.
3. This is, of course, similar to other kinds of boundary problem, such as those of delimiting racial or spatial boundaries, in that the fundamental difficulty is that of converting continuous variables into discrete categories.
4. In the diagram of figure 8.1 we have continued to use the visual device of representing nonadditive joint effects by arrows coming from G_{C_i}, O_A, and G_B that intersect before they reach R_A, rather than as all being separately directed toward R_A. The same feature appears below and to the right in connection with the arrows from R_A, D_A, and E_A to the total power exerted by A, namely, P_A. Whenever we predict a *multiplicative* type of non-additive joint effect between two variables this will be indicated by an arc drawn between the two variables concerned. If two independent variables (such as G_B and G_{C_i}) each have multiplicative relationships with a third independent variable (such as O_A) we indicate this by two nonconnecting arcs. This implies that there is no specified type of (nonadditive or additive) joint relationship between the two outside independent variables (e.g., G_B and G_{C_i}). If we wish to indicate that all *three* independent variables have a multiplicative joint effect on a dependent variable, we indicate this by a single arc. We shall discuss one such situation below in connection with the joint effects of R_A, D_A, and E_A on P_A.
5. Unfortunately, since we cannot discuss everything at once, a detailed consideration of these goals and alternative means will have to be postponed until the next chapter.
6. Our list of more specific means, in the following chapter, will crosscut this very simple distinction between rewards, punishments, and persuasion.
7. This strategy will also be discussed in the following chapter and is related to our subsequent treatment of insulating mechanisms in connection with approach–withdrawal processes (see also Emerson 1962).

CHAPTER 9

Social Power II: Degree and Efficiency of Mobilization

THE GENERAL PURPOSE of this chapter is to discuss the question of how and under what conditions power as a potential is translated into power in its kinetic form; that is, we shall be concerned with the actual mobilization of resources, both with respect to the degree of mobilization and also the choices among alternative courses of action that affect the efficiency with which power is actually applied to affect outcomes.

We have implied in many different ways that the study of objective properties and resources, alone, will not be sufficient to enable one to understand the nature of power contests. Put another way, the possession of resources may be a necessary condition for the application of power, but it is certainly not a sufficient one as well. In order to predict how these resources will actually be mobilized it is also necessary to bring into the picture a large number of variables that relate specifically to goals and utilities, to ideological and normative constraints on alternative courses of action, to the knowledge and working assumptions of the several actors, and to the actual and expected behaviors of various third parties.

The chapter begins with an attempt to delineate a number of reasonably general goal and ideological dimensions. We then turn to a consideration of actors' working causal theories and to the block of variables that pertains to knowledge and secrecy. Finally, we shall consider a number of general dimensions along which alternative courses of actions may be analyzed as well as some factors that relate to possible constraints or incompatibilities among these means.

OUTCOMES AS COMPARED TO GOAL DIMENSIONS

We have already noted that many discussions of power are in terms of outcomes rather than goals or objectives. Our own earlier discussion of the *SEU* model

361

clearly places the emphasis on goals, although we have often referred to utilities attached to outcomes. How are the two notions related, and what are the implications for our analysis of social power? In brief, the concept of outcome is reasonably close to the operational level in the sense that most types of outcome are observable or at least recognizable. Outcomes are also likely to be very complex and multidimensional, however, as our earlier discussion of utilities has implied. Actors may desire certain outcomes for many different reasons, and there may also be outcomes about which actors are ambivalent because they desire certain features but are opposed to others.

Thus even though many kinds of real-world outcome are observable, it does not follow that we can develop *explanatory* models or theories without breaking these outcomes down into components. It will then be necessary to invoke actors' goals, objectives, preferences, utilities, or similar notions. Furthermore, we do not see any effective way to construct theories without assessing the dimensionality question. The same argument applies to any type of complex behavior, of course. For example, if we observe that an actor has made a certain choice (say, selecting one occupation in preference to another) we are then faced with the problem of explaining this choice in terms of specific dimensions such as prestige, amount of pay, job security, or enjoyment of the work.

In the discussion that follows we shall therefore focus primarily on the goals of a given actor, say, actor A. We must also take into consideration the possibility that the goals of actors B and C_i may stand in a certain kind of relationship to those of actor A. We admit, however, that the actors are more likely to be thinking in terms of overall outcomes rather than unidimensional goals. We have also been assuming that they crudely assess each outcome in terms of the subjective probability that it will satisfy the relevant goals. Thus the actors themselves may be directing their attention to the (possibly complex) outcomes, and therefore, at least to this extent, we must also deal with such outcomes.

In a general formulation such as this one it does not seem possible to say anything very specific about such outcomes, primarily because they are most likely to be highly concrete and therefore not easily amenable to theoretical analysis. In brief, we are claiming that although an analysis in terms of outcomes may make a good deal of sense in any *specific* power analysis, whenever we wish to generalize the argument or provide theoretical interpretations it becomes essential to dimensionalize the notion of outcomes in terms of goals. It may be that very concrete discussions of power of the type that have characterized the literature on community power have suffered precisely because the outcomes or issues being discussed have rarely been treated in any such general fashion.

Because many kinds of outcome are highly complex and multidimensional and can be described and perceived according to different perspectives, both the observer and the actors themselves are confronted with a number of possible complications that are less likely to arise in simpler situations in which outcomes can be linked in a one-to-one fashion with particular goals. Before concentrating on a number of reasonably generalizable goal dimensions, it will therefore be advisable to note very briefly a few of the theoretical problems that this complexity poses for the analyst.

First, when we consider parties C_i that may at any given point in time be taking a neutral stance with regard to an issue or potential outcome, we must recognize that this neutrality may derive either from true indifference or apathy, on the one hand, or from ambivalence, on the other. The term *indifference*, we believe, usually has the connotation that the actor really does not care about the outcome because it is not expected to have any consequences for goals to which high utilities have been attached. The outcome in question is simply irrelevant. *Apathy* has the connotation that, although the actor may attach a reasonably high utility to goals affected by the outcome, the subjective probability of the outcome is not thought to be affected one way or another by any action the actor may take on the matter. In either case, the actor is presumed to be immobilized by a very low level of either a utility value or a subjective probability.

In contrast, *ambivalence* generally has the connotation that in some respects the actor strongly desires the outcome but that in other respects a strong negative utility is attached to it. Presumably, this ambivalence results from the multidimensionality of the outcome or the fact that it has simultaneous consequences for two or more goals. Obviously it may make a considerable difference whether the primary motivation is one of indifference or ambivalence. In the latter case, for example, it may be possible to modify the outcome somewhat (as, for example, by amending a proposed law) so as to reduce this ambivalence. In short, the tactics used by either party to a dispute in attempting to modify the behaviors of third parties may very well depend on their assessments of the goal structures of these C_i as they relate to complex types of outcome.

Since outcomes may often be packaged in different ways, it may also be possible by slight modifications in the package to induce an actor either to join one party or to remain neutral. Consider an actor, C, that basically sides with A in a dispute with B; that is, if A's preferred outcome actually occurs, this will be to C's advantage as well. Why should C enter the dispute if C is reasonably certain that A will win? By supporting A it is likely that C will incur certain costs, perhaps in terms of depleted resources or increased antagonism between B and C. Knowing this, however, A may attempt to modify the outcome slightly by finding ways to reward C over and above the gains that C would obtain if their mutually desired outcome should occur as a result of A's action alone. Of course, we may also expect B to attempt to modify the outcome so as to make it to C's disadvantage to join forces with A.

The analyst may handle this kind of situation by conceptual redefinition of the outcome; that is, the outcome as first described might be labeled Y and the second or modified outcome as Y'. For instance, the first type of outcome may involve a victory by nation A over nation B, with certain spoils of this victory being turned over to A. If C is induced to join the battle with the promise that it may share in these spoils, the new outcome can merely be described in much the same terms, except that C also receives a share of the spoils as well as the security or satisfaction it derives from B's defeat. Alternatively, the analyst may conceive of there having been two distinct outcomes, namely, the defeat of B and the collection of spoils by either A or the A-C coalition. We see in this illustration the kind of conceptual difficulty one is likely to encounter as long as outcomes have multidimensional characteristics.

There are many situations in which one needs to take into consideration that outcomes will not be discrete or easily confined to a single point in time. Furthermore the several parties may not define outcomes in the same way; that is, what is an outcome for A may be of no real interest to B. In the process of working toward the desired outcome (say, a profitable cotton crop), A may behave in such a way as to affect a different set of outcomes for B (say, slavery or economic subjugation). In this instance the outcome for B may be a direct result of a particular course of action by A; if A were to use a different means, B's outcome would be quite different. If A is using B to achieve A's goals in such a way that B's outcomes are adversely affected in the process, we often refer to the relationship as an exploitative one, and this may indeed produce a power confrontation between A and B. But from the perspective of another actor (say a competitor of A's that is following a different course of action) the A-B relationship might even be looked upon as a kind of antagonistic coalition or partnership.

It must also be realized that the basic relationship between such an A and B may change, with no alteration in the objective situation, merely because B's utilities have changed. For example, A may be using B's labor in exchange for a given level of objective properties (e.g., money, land, or crops). Whether or not B defines this relationship as exploitative in the sense of involving an unfair rate of exchange may depend on B's utilities for these objective properties as compared with the costs involved in providing A with these services. Thus the objective outcomes for B might not change, whereas the utilities associated with these outcomes might shift to such a degree that there could even be a reshuffling of the coalition patterns among A, B, and C.

The above rather general remarks imply that although outcomes may sometimes be rather easily describable, it does not follow that unique *measures* can be attached to these outcomes because of the multidimensionality involved. In particular, it becomes necessary to consider "outcomes for A" separately from "outcomes for B," since the patterning of goals among the actors may be very different. We expect that whenever outcomes are not discrete events but more or less continuous processes it will be extremely difficult to attach any kind of measures to such outcomes unless the utilities of the several actors can be assessed. As we have already indicated, it seems necessary to identify approximately unidimensional goals or objectives in order to estimate such utilities. Thus we see the importance of assessing utilities and also, by implication, subjective probabilities in analyses of social power.

SOME GOAL DIMENSIONS RELEVANT TO POWER CONFRONTATIONS

Unfortunately, it is no simple matter to produce a list of goals that are broadly enough conceived to apply to most if not all power confrontations, as well as to both of the major parties, A and B, and to third parties, C_i, considered as potential coalition partners. Yet if this is not done, and if goals are defined too specifically, it becomes almost impossible to link them theoretically to the remaining variables in the system and thereby contribute to our general knowledge about power confrontations. The types of goal listed and briefly discussed in this section should therefore be considered very tentatively as an initial effort to produce a reasonably complete list appropriate to a diversity of situations.

At least some of the goal types discussed in this section are basically residual categories that allow for this diversity. For example, our first three types of goal—those over which the parties are in basic agreement, those over which there is disagreement or competition, and those that are irrelevant to the immediate power confrontation—are essentially of this nature. In some instances the investigator may be in a position to identify one or two really major goals in each category, but there may be other situations in which, say, the irrelevant goals are extremely numerous. Hopefully, however, it will be possible to come up with a rough estimate of an overall utility attached to such inclusive goal categories so that one can say something meaningful about the importance of goals that are irrelevant to the confrontation, as compared with goals in one of the other categories. If we fail to include these irrelevant goals, we run the risk of ignoring their importance altogether and thereby perhaps underestimating the problems that the party faces in connection with mobilization.

G_1. Goals Desired by Both Parties A and B

In almost any power confrontation there will be certain goals that are shared by both A and B.[1] If the analysis of power is divorced from other aspects of the total relationship, or if the analyst is focusing primarily on the process of conflict, there may be a temptation to underestimate the utilities attached to goals of this type. In a few types of situation in which there has been extreme and prolonged conflict it may be that G_1-type goals are, in fact, of relatively minor significance. In more ordinary situations, however, it is likely that A and B will not only share a number of important values but may find themselves on the same side in other confrontations of at least equal importance to the one being analyzed. Furthermore, under most conditions the parties will have a mutual interest in seeing to it that the level of conflict does not become too costly and that certain rules are enforced.

This implies that a conflict strategy usually presupposes that one's opponent is either unwilling or unable to dish out more negative sanctions than it receives. We suspect, then, that conflict per se will generally be distasteful unless it is thought to be accompanied by benefits of some kind. This is virtually true by definition, if we mean by conflict the mutual exchange of negative sanctions or punishments. In effect, if there are mutually desired goals that are hindered by the power confrontation, this will contribute to the "fatigue" of both parties, in the sense that this term was used by Richardson (1960). These goals thus become an important mechanism for conflict regulation, and any factors that increase the utilities attached to G_1 goals can be expected to dampen or reduce the level of conflict.

G_2. Goals Opposed by the Other Party or Over Which There is Direct Competition

These are the types of goal that are most often emphasized by students of power and conflict. Since the relative utilities attached to goals are subject to change and manipulation, it is likely that mobilization efforts and ideological systems will also be focused heavily on G_2-type goals, either to stress their importance vis-à-vis other types of goal or to increase the subjective probabilities of attaining them.

Also, to the degree that these goals are compatible or consistent with certain other goals that are deemed illegitimate, we may expect a displaced emphasis on G_2-type goals. For example, if most members of party A are in competition with party B (say, for land) and *also* wish to injure or dominate that party, it becomes convenient to place a very great emphasis on the competition or opposition involved, and to argue that extreme measures must be used to eliminate the competitor or at least turn it into a permanent subordinate party. Likewise, members of the subordinate or weaker group may wish to legitimate their aggressive tendencies by placing a premium on G_2-type goals and the necessity of using almost any available means to achieve these ends. It is no wonder, then, that G_2-type goals are likely to be perceived as important, both for the analyst and by the members of the respective parties.

G_3. Goals That Are Irrelevant to the Confrontation but That Compete for Scarce Resources with G_1 and G_2 Goals

As noted, this type of goal almost constitutes a residual category for goals that are not of types G_1 and G_2. But we especially have in mind those goals that actually detract from the party's efforts because their fulfillment requires basically the same kinds of resource (or O_i) as do G_2-type goals. For example, consumer goals that compete with a military budget or a minority's "escapist" goals that hinder its mobilization are obvious illustrations of goals of this type. Seen from the perspective of the power analyst or leader who is trying to mobilize resources, these types of goal are dysfunctional in terms of the immediate power confrontation.

In general, the more important the G_3 goals relative to those in category G_2, the lower we expect both the degree and efficiency of mobilization to be. G_3-type goals will also contribute to Richardson's "fatigue coefficient," the more so if the O_i they require are easily depleted and only replenished with great difficulty. Therefore it becomes necessary in a prolonged confrontation to develop ideological mechanisms that stress the need for "sacrifice" of G_3 goals, or to encourage the belief that they can only be satisfied if G_2 goals are also achieved, i.e., that they are luxuries dependent upon the satisfaction of the more basic G_2 goals. If, for example, party A is a nation engaged in an unpopular war or a war the purpose of which is not easily understood, it may become necessary to overplay the seriousness of the threat posed by the other party in order to divert scarce O_i into the war effort. In doing so, it becomes relatively easier to weaken the positions of those who place a greater premium on "irrelevant" goals by, in effect, claiming that these latter persons are naïve, selfish and unwilling to sacrifice, in league with the opposition, or perhaps even all three.

By the same token, A's G_3 goals provide a leverage for the other party. If B can succeed in persuading members of party A that the G_2 goals are of lesser importance, or that they can be achieved only at the cost of hindering important G_3 goals, then it may weaken party A's mobilization efforts. Whenever one party (say, party A) is seriously divided internally concerning the importance of certain G_3 goals, we may anticipate that the other party will attempt to exploit this difference by appealing to those who attach a high utility to these G_3 goals. One way of doing this, of course, is to create an ideological system that links achieving these G_3 goals to giving up the G_2 goals in question. For example, an appeal may be made to an internal minority (say, blacks in the United States) to reject an external expansionist policy (say, in Africa or Asia) because such a policy will only detract from efforts to achieve equality at home.

An interesting and very important set of problems centers on changes over time in the relative utilities attached to G_2 and G_3 goals (and, of course, G_1 goals as well) and the factors that affect these changes. Presumably, any factors that increase the subjective probabilities of achieving G_2 goals, or that give rise to optimism that these goals can be achieved more easily or more rapidly than previously expected, will also produce at least a temporary decrease in the utilities attached to G_3 goals. At least they will increase the willingness to defer the achievement of these latter goals. If the confrontation drags on for a much longer period than had originally been anticipated, however, and if at least some G_3 goals have had to be deferred, we may anticipate that these latter goals will increase in importance, i.e., the gap between goal achievement and degree of goal fulfillment will be increased. This, in turn, would seem to imply accelerating fatigue unless some means can be found to increase the subjective probabilities of achieving the G_2 goals or to increase the utilities attached to them, perhaps by exaggerating the consequences of a defeat by the opposing party.

Where the relative SEU's attached to G_2 and G_3 goals cannot be modified to favor the former, an alternative will be to reduce the SEU's attached to G_1 goals, or even to convince the party's members that there are, in fact, no goals that the two parties share in common, and that beliefs to the contrary are either misguided or deliberately fostered by members of the opposition. That is, efforts may be made to convince members that the opposition group really do not share the G_1 goals. For instance, in wartime it is convenient to believe that enemy soldiers are in basic ways nonhuman, "savage," or "fiendish," rather than fathers, husbands, farmers, or ordinary citizens with basically the same kinds of fear and loyalty that characterize members of one's own group.

In general, we anticipate that the more prolonged and bitter a conflict situation, the lower the utilities attached to G_1 goals as compared with G_2 goals, but the relative subjective probabilities of these two types of goal can be expected to depend on many other factors. Although G_1 and G_3 goals both operate in the same fashion to dampen the degree of conflict involved, and perhaps also reduce the duration of the confrontation, this does not imply that they are expected to be positively associated. Indeed, reductions in the SEU's attached to the one type of goal may be accompanied by increases in the other, both because they may be oppositely related to the duration of the confrontation and because they both compete with G_2 goals.

The relative mix of G_1 and G_3 goals, however, may determine whether the orientation toward the opposition is one that is partly ambivalent (i.e., love–hate) or one of basic indifference. If both G_1 and G_2 goals are very important to the actor, we may expect the emotional reaction to be one of ambivalence, as exemplified by a love–hate relationship between two parties. Large utilities attached to G_3 goals as compared with G_1 and G_2 goals can be expected to produce a high degree of indifference to the opposition. Such G_3 goals may be especially characteristic of members of a very strong dominant group that is dealing with a weak and unimportant minority, as, for example, in the case of whites and American Indians in contemporary U.S. society.

G_4. Goals That Can Be Blocked by the Other Party

Although goals of type G_4 may involve some overlap with goals of types G_1' and G_3, we have in mind here those goals that *are* relevant to the power confrontation but that constitute sources of vulnerability for the party (A) with which we are concerned. We exclude, however, type G_2 goals over which the parties are in direct competition. Whereas G_3 goals are basically irrelevant to the confrontation except for the fact that they compete with G_2 goals, goals of type G_4 are those that are subject to the control of party B in the sense that B can by direct action alter the probability of achieving them, or can affect the subjective probability of their attainment by threatening such action. The blockage need not be complete as long as A's access is made significantly more costly or risky through B's action. Goals that A can achieve through exchange relationships with B are clearly instances of G_4-type goals.

Obviously, the greater the utilities that A attaches to G_4 goals, and the greater A's dependence on B in supplying these goals, the weaker A's position will be in relation to B. As noted by Emerson (1962) and Blau (1964a), A may improve its position in this respect either by decreasing the utilities attached to G_4 goals or by finding alternative sources of supply, which will have the effect of reducing B's ability to affect the probability of attaining the goals in question. Where the G_4 goals depend on the possession of certain O_i we can expect that increases in utilities attached to these G_4 will imply a need to stock-pile these O_i and to see to it that they can be replenished (See G_{11} below). If utilities for G_4 goals cannot be reduced, or alternative sources of supply found, it may be necessary to lower the utilities attached to G_2 goals, thereby avoiding a confrontation with the other party.

G_5 . Goals Involving Biological Survival

This class of goal could be considered as subtypes of G_4 or possibly G_3 goals, but it seems wise to separate them from other goals because of their basic and virtually constant nature; that is, except under unusual conditions actors will attach extremely high utilities to G_5 goals, so much so in fact that in most kinds of confrontation they are not really at issue. Since the use of physical force or the withholding of the means of survival are ultimate sanctions, a control over the O_i that can actually be used to apply these extreme sanctions gives the possessor an extremely important weapon in any power confrontation.

Of course, it is for this very reason that most types of potential confrontation, except for those between the "big powers" themselves, are carefully regulated by third parties that are capable of applying these extreme sanctions if necessary. Being extreme, however, they must be used sparingly to be effective. This generally implies that they will be reserved for confrontations involving goals to which very high utilities have been attached and that can only be satisfied by a small number of means that are incompatible with the goals of other parties. Thus, although the utilities attached to G_5 goals are ordinarily extremely high, the subjective probabilities of their being achieved are also very high except under unusual circumstances. Under such circumstances we expect G_5 goals to dominate all others, however, so that parties that are dependent upon other parties for their satisfaction are in a highly vulnerable position. If so, it is obviously to their interests to see to it that these kinds of sanction cannot be employed except at a very great cost.

If there are certain members of, say, party A to whom survival goals are much less important than others, this affords a major opportunity for this party to apply important sanctions to the opposition party, B, provided that it can be assured that the remaining members of A will not be threatened. This is clearly the situation with respect to guerrilla warfare and terrorism, which depend very heavily upon the willingness of the dominant party (here B) to absorb threats to its own members without retaliating on the remaining members of A. This, in turn, depends upon at least the pretense that the majority of members of the weaker party (A) do not condone or support this kind of activity and that their own behaviors cannot significantly affect the probability of its occurring. Therefore, to be successful, terrorist activities either have to be attributed to a third party that cannot be controlled by A or must depend upon some other inhibitory mechanism to prevent B from retaliating on innocent victims.

One such mechanism is the presence of powerful third parties that may be expected to step in on the side of A if B were to overreact. Another mechanism would be the basic indifference of members of party B to the power confrontation, as a result of a preponderance of G_3 goals. Here, the weaker party is able to threaten survival goals of members of the stronger party, so that the latter is willing to end the confrontation by giving up its G_2 goals or otherwise modifying its behavior. The risk is that indifference may be turned into alarm, hatred, and a desire to aggress against or otherwise punish the entire membership of the weaker party. Where both parties are of approximately the same strength, we may find splinter groups from both parties engaging in such action, with the possible result that there is an accelerating movement toward conflicts involving ever increasing numbers from each party.

G_6. Desire to Injure, Aggress, or Retaliate against the Other Party

This goal has already been mentioned by implication in the above discussion but is clearly distinct from that of survival or self-protection. It may be, of course, that under certain circumstances the utilities attached to G_5 and G_6 goals may be inversely related, perhaps because the desire to aggress may increase one's willingness to take risks to one's personal safety. We also expect that the utilities attached to G_6 goals will be decreased to the degree that the party perceives that G_1 common goals predominate over G_2 goals involving clashes of interest.

The strength of the desire to injure the other party will also depend upon the history of previous conflicts and the outcomes of these power confrontations. Richardson (1960) refers in his arms-race models to grievance terms that he takes to be constants and that we presume will affect the utilities attached to G_6 goals. Ordinarily, we expect that subordinate groups that perceive a high degree of exploitation in their relationships with the dominant party will also attach high utilities to aggression or retaliation. Their actual behaviors, however, are likely to be inhibited both by low subjective probabilities of achieving success by this means and by a fear of retaliation.

Given such high utilities but low subjective probabilities, we would also expect exploratory acts of aggression in order to test whether the anticipated retaliation actually occurs and whether the use of this means results in concessions by the dominant party. If the subjective probability of success increases without an accompanying increase in sanctions by the dominant group, this can be expected to lead to successive increases in aggression. Such increases will be inhibited, however, to the degree that the subordinate party anticipates a delayed but vigorous reaction (the so-called backlash). If members of the subordinate group are in disagreement with respect to choices among means, this may also imply that those who place a stronger emphasis on short-run effects will tend to prefer aggressive tactics, whereas those who think more in terms of long-range consequences are likely to be more inhibited by a fear of a delayed response.

Where members of the dominant party attach high utilities to G_2 or G_6 goals, we expect that responses to subordinate-group aggression are likely to be immediate and to involve a reciprocation of aggression, rather than some more subtle response. Where dominant-group members are relatively indifferent, mobilization of a response will tend to be more difficult and therefore delayed. If there is a subgroup of dominant-group members to whom the confrontation is highly important, or if certain of their members have in effect been designated as persons who will respond immediately, and in kind, then we may expect that aggression by the one side will be accompanied by aggression by the other.

This kind of instant retaliation phenomenon in the presence of a largely indifferent dominant group appears to have characterized relationships between militant blacks and police in American urban ghettos during the late 1960s. In effect, police violence against young urban black males was tolerated by the general white populace as a kind of control mechanism to prevent an escalation of urban guerrilla tactics. Whether or not such retaliation results in an accelerating conflict, as in Northern Ireland, or a dampening effect, will depend upon the actions of third parties and their abilities and willingness to control the behaviors of the active participants.

G_7. Desire to Maintain Dominance over Other Party or to Increase or Reduce Dominance

Occasionally there may be an interest in dominance for its own sake, but it is also likely that dominance over another party will be desired partly because it is instrumental in attaining other goals, such as that of reducing the opposition or the competitive position of the other party, facilitating aggression, or protecting one's own members from injury. In the case of subordinate parties, however, we expect the goal of achieving freedom from domination to be relatively more important in its own right, as well as being instrumental to the achievement of these same types of goal.

By dominance we shall mean the *actual* control over the behavior of another party, in the sense of affecting choices among alternative courses of action, such that the dominant party can almost dictate the subordinate party's behaviors. Such a high degree of control usually requires the actual periodic use of negative sanctions as well as the observation of the other party's behavior. Where the control is only potential but never exercised, we do not ordinarily use the term *dominance*. Presumably, any party with substantial resources *may* choose to dominate a weaker one. For instance, right-handed persons could obviously dominate left-handed persons were they to focus their attention in this direction, but since they do not we would not refer to them as a dominant group or even as a dominant category.

In theory, it would be possible for one party to control the behavior of another without the actual use or even threats of negative sanctions. We believe, however, that sociological usage implies that there must also be at least some application of negative sanctions. One possible reason may be that it is difficult to imagine a case in which A can control B's behaviors through rewards alone, if only because changes in B's levels of expectations are likely to be such that even continual rewards may come to be defined as punitive unless they are either increased at an accelerating rate or accompanied by increases in the recipient's autonomy. Furthermore, if the rewards are in the form of gifts of objective properties, there will be a point at which these O_i become so depleted that further rewarding behavior will be too costly.

G_8 . Desire to Avoid Using Negative Sanctions

It may be that A attaches a high utility to influencing B either by means of rewards or by convincing B to modify its behavior by altering its utilities or subjective probabilities. To the degree that there are strong bonds of mutual attraction, or at least that A is attracted to B, we expect that the utility attached to G_8 will also be high. The greater the utilities attached to G_1-type goals, the greater the desire to avoid applying negative sanctions whenever feasible. Thus, if A attaches high utilities to G_1- and G_2-type goals simultaneously, we would expect that A will attempt to influence B by positive inducements rather than negative ones. In contrast, the utilities attached to the goals of injuring the other party and avoiding having to use negative sanctions should be inversely related. The stronger the utility attached to G_8 goals, the more restricted the actor's choice of means, and this will of course weaken its power or degree of dominance over the other party. We would therefore generally expect to find the utilities attached to G_7 and G_8 goals to be negatively related. Likewise, G_6 and G_8 will be inversely related, though there will be a number of instances where there is little or no utility attached to injuring one's opponent and yet the utility attached to G_8 may be either high or low on grounds of expediency. Assuming that dominance is ordinarily instrumental to achieving survival goals, we would also expect the utilities attached to G_5 and G_8 to be inversely related. Given that we are assuming the former to be almost universally high, however, this prediction would make more sense if turned into the following proposition: to the degree that B actually threatens A's survival, we expect A's utility attached to G_8 to be low. Thus G_8, which is closely linked with choices among alternative means, to be discussed below, is also likely to be correlated with other goal dimensions, but yet is distinct from each of them.

G_9 . Desire to Increase Affective Bonds between A and B

We expect the utilities attached to this type of goal to be positively related to those for G_8 goals. Nevertheless, the two types of goal are analytically distinct. One party may wish to avoid using negative sanctions, perhaps as a matter of principle or as an expediency, while attaching a very low priority to increasing the affective bonds with the other party. This particular combination of motives may be relatively more characteristic of very strong and highly prestigious parties that do not need to apply negative sanctions but that also do not care to increase ties with an extremely weak party. Even here, one would expect that such a party will at least wish to foster an asymmetric attachment in the form of increasing the weaker party's loyalty and respect, while at the same time maintaining a status gap between the two. In the case of more equal parties, however, we can expect that the motivations between G_8 and G_9 goals will be so closely intertwined that, in the interests of simplicity, they may be treated as involving a single dimension.

G_{10} . Desire to Increase Degree or Efficiency of Mobilization

We are referring to the utility level of this goal based on reasons that are extraneous to the immediate confrontation itself. Obviously a party engaged in a power contest will attempt to increase its own mobilization levels relative to those of its opponent, but there may be additional factors that influence the importance of these goals. In particular, the leadership of one party may wish to increase mobilization, or win a victory over the other party, primarily to consolidate its own internal position, or perhaps to distract the attention of other segments from failures, private gains, or other objectives that would weaken internal control. It is commonly argued that political leaders must often find external scapegoats in order to retain their positions. The need for mobilizing forces against a common enemy is thus only in part a realistic one. Mobilization may become an end in its own right, or a means that is consciously employed by some elements of one party in order to keep others of their own group under control.

G_{11} . Desire to Conserve or Increase Resources or Objective Properties

Finally we must take into consideration the time perspective of each party and in particular the goal G_{11} of preserving resources and objective properties for future encounters. For A, party B may not be the real enemy. Both A and B may be aware of the possibility that certain of the C_i may be holding back, waiting for A and B to exhaust themselves. One of the two parties may perceive the struggle as being a very extended one, with the necessity of preserving scarce resources under the assumption that the other party will either deplete its supply of objective properties or lose its motivation to prolong the contest. The goal G_{11} is, of course, compatible with the objective of improving the *efficiency* of mobilization but may be negatively related to the goal of increasing the *degree* of mobilization. This would apply not only to objective properties, such as money, natural resources, and military weapons, but also to resources that depend upon the good will of certain of the C_i. In order to retain the latter, for example, it may be necessary to appear to use only relatively humane methods and not to apply overwhelming force against a weak opponent.

Although we have hinted at a number of interrelationships that may exist among these goal dimensions, it seems premature to attempt to formalize these speculations in terms of a causal diagram or set of diagrams. In the first place, we suspect that interrelationships among goal dimensions are likely to be very much dependent on exogenous variables, and in particular upon the actors' resources that help to determine the extent to which there are constraints on alternative courses of action. Such constraints on means will be discussed toward the end of the chapter. Also, it is difficult to say very much about the direction of causation between a pair of goals unless one is dealing with a very specific situation and unless the temporal sequences are reasonably clear-cut. Thus in some situations it may be clear that the fact that B can block one of A's important goals may cause A to wish to injure B, but under other circumstances the causal relationship might even be reversed or nonexistent.

In any specific setting, however, it may make sense to attempt to assess goal incompatibilities in much the same way that we shall do in the case of constraints among means. It is not necessary that two goals be completely incompatible, in the sense that the achievement of G_i absolutely prevents the attainment of G_j. Incompatibility varies by degree and seems best conceived in terms of probabilities, either objectively or subjectively defined. We may say that G_i and G_j are mutually incompatible to the *degree* that $P(G_i|G_j) < P(G_i)$ and $P(G_j|G_i) < P(G_j)$, where $P(G_i|G_j)$ refers to the probability of achieving G_i given that G_j has been achieved, and similarly for $P(G_j|G_i)$. Conceivably, G_i may be incompatible with G_j and yet the reverse may not occur. This would mean that the achievement of one goal may not hinder a second, whereas in the reverse case achievement of the second will reduce the probability of achieving the first. As implied by our previous remarks, these various probabilities will in general be functions of the actors' relative resources and other factors, some of which will be considered in the remainder of this chapter.

IDEOLOGIES AS EXOGENOUS AND ENDOGENOUS VARIABLES

It is probably unwise for the student of relatively micro-level power confrontations to become overly engrossed with the impacts of ideologies, except possibly as they may interact with other variables to affect the relative magnitudes of structural parameters. In the case of macro-level confrontations that have rather long durations or that have been repeated a number of times, however, we may expect that certain kinds of ideological variable will need to be treated as endogenous and subject to change during the period of study. Therefore we cannot afford to ignore them altogether by merely assuming that they can be adequately handled in terms of utilities and subjective probabilities.

The notion of ideology is extremely slippery, in part because it is usually unclear just how general a set of beliefs or shared values must be in order to be considered as constituting an ideology. There will be a number of beliefs and stereotypes that pertain to one's opponent and to the use of specific courses of action. If the confrontation is a very micro one, as, for example, one between a husband and wife pair or two rival employees, we would hardly refer to such beliefs as constituting an ideology, even if they are shared by several actors. If the parties are two warring nations engaged in a prolonged conflict, however, we tend to refer to the relevant belief systems as constituting an ideology. In spite of this ambiguity, it does appear that there is at least a reasonable consensus among social scientists that certain kinds of very macro-level shared beliefs, commonly held values, and working theories serve to motivate, constrain, or otherwise influence actors to follow certain courses of action rather than others, to evaluate their situations in accord with certain common definitions, and to select among a number of different possible explanatory systems.

With these remarks in mind, we can turn very briefly to several possible ideological dimensions that seem to have reasonably general relevance to power confrontations and in particular to goals and expectations. We are thinking, in all instances, of rather pervasive sets of beliefs that create a central tendency in the directions implied, so that they tend to influence specific belief or value systems that pertain to more limited confrontations; that is, they create a general atmosphere that affects the ways in which actors value and perceive their immediate situations.

I_1 . Degree of Simplicity of Belief Systems

Although it is one of the general functions of ideological systems to provide reasonably simplified working theories that can be used to confront immediate and highly specific situations, such ideologies obviously differ among themselves with respect to the degree of simplicity they admit. Some, for example, tend to posit a single overarching explanatory process, such as the will of God, economic determinism, or the forces of good and evil in human beings. Others may specify certain conditions under which such simple explanatory systems would not be appropriate and may admit to internal inconsistencies and permit exceptions to behavioral regulations.

In general, extremely simplistic ideologies would seem to have the advantages of facilitating decision making, doing away with the need for detailed knowledge and contingency plans, and offering justifications for extreme courses of action. They often stress a small number of goals to which extremely high utilities are attached. Presumably, they also tend to produce subjective probabilities that are close to either zero or unity, enabling the actor to do away with uncertainties. They have the disadvantage of inducing the actor to make premature and incorrect decisions, however, thereby lowering the efficiency of the mobilization effort in this respect. To the degree that nearly all members share the ideology, such simplistic belief systems may help to increase the overall degree of mobilization and improve coordination. But if members have been successfully exposed to competing ideologies, the very reverse may occur, namely, severe internal dissension with respect to utilities, strategies, and the general assessment of the opposing party.

I_2 . Degree to Which Other Party Is Blamed for the Confrontation

Generally, though not necessarily, we would expect that extremely simplistic ideological systems will operate to place the blame on whatever other party is currently being opposed. Where there are numerous opposing parties, such ideologies are likely to stress a single explanatory connection among them, as for example a conspiracy or a common causal agent such as the devil, capitalism or communism, or perhaps a common racial characteristic. There may also be instances where simplistic ideologies do not place the blame on the other party, however, and therefore it seems wise at least to allow for the possibility that the two dimensions are distinct. In general, the placement of blame on the other party will tend to facilitate mobilization and may also justify certain courses of action that may be expedient for other reasons. For example, if dominant-group settlers perceive indigenous peoples as being savages who are responsible for massacres of innocent women and children, then almost any form of retaliation may be justified. Such retaliation, of course, also has the function of eliminating them as competitors for the best available land.

I_3 . Degree of Punitiveness or Justification for Aggression

As already implied, we expect this third ideological dimension to be highly correlated with the previous two in that highly simplistic ideologies permit one to place the blame on the other party and therefore are also likely to justify extreme sanctions against it. But we can also imagine cases of rather simplistic ideologies that are nonpunitive and that even entail a high degree of self-blame. Certain rather idealistic belief systems characteristic of religious sects may be of this nature and may in fact encourage such groups to avoid power confrontations. On the one hand, their members may be primarily concerned with living up to a small number of absolute principles. On the other, they may tend to blame themselves for failures and to eschew violence. Such parties could easily be victimized by less scrupulous groups not bound by rigid ethical principles. Knowing this, their members may deliberately segregate themselves and develop noncompetitive, symbiotic relationships with other parties in their environment. Such groups will generally escape the attention of the student of power. If their territory or possessions were to become valued by other parties, however, or if their "peculiar" patterns were to become irksome or sources of guilt among these other parties, we may anticipate that they are likely to be expelled or persecuted.

Thus, in general, we expect that the combination of ideological simplicity and intrapunitiveness is much more likely to characterize weak and semi-isolated parties than dominant ones. Intrapunitiveness in a subordinate party may also be fostered more or less deliberately by dominant parties, as, for example, through religious ideologies that place a heavy emphasis on guilt, shame, fatalism, and a promise of future rewards in exchange for a renunciation of aggression or hatred. An ideology may also stress that the other party is to blame but that aggression against this other party must be inhibited, either because there is an unobservable third party (e.g., a deity) that will ultimately punish them or because there are real-world third parties that can be induced by means of this strategy to enter the contest on the side of the weaker party. This is obviously the basic strategy motivated by the ideology of nonviolent resistance movements such as those of Gandhi or Martin Luther King.

I_4 . Degree of Fatalism

By *fatalism* we mean the belief that objective probabilities cannot easily be altered by one's behaviors. Although, in principle, fatalism may involve a basic optimism that everything will work out well in the long run, we generally associate this term with a much more pessimistic outlook to the effect that the objective probabilities of desired outcomes are extremely low and that they cannot be increased, regardless of the action one may take. Such a fatalistic belief system may or may not be realistic. It is often quite realistic in the case of a very weak or powerless party under the domination of a very strong one.

Ordinarily, a fatalistic orientation will tend to lower both the degree and efficiency of mobilization. A dominant party faced by a numerically much larger subordinate group (as, for example, in South Africa or Rhodesia) obviously has a vested interest in preserving a fatalistic ideology among the latter members. To a lesser degree, however, *any* party in a power confrontation will tend to favor a fatalistic orientation on the part of its opposition, while striving to overcome such an ideology among its own members. Fatalism may be compatible with either I_1 or I_2, but we expect it to be negatively associated with degree of punitiveness toward the opposition, as well as the remaining two ideological dimensions discussed below.

The relationship between ideological simplicity and fatalism is a potentially interesting one. Highly simplistic ideologies may be either fatalistic or exactly the opposite. In general, we would expect that ideological complexity would inhibit fatalism, but we can at least imagine situations in which members exposed to an extremely complex ideological system might be inhibited from taking action by this very complexity. In effect, they might see good reasons for just about every possible action or inaction, so that decision making would become virtually impossible. Over a long period, one could imagine a fatalistic orientation emerging as a consequence of such indecisiveness.

I_5 . Degree of Urgency Expressed

Ideologies obviously differ with respect to time perspectives and the degree to which patience is counseled. Urgency presumably calls for action rather than inaction and a priority system that permits the use of means that promise quick effects even at the cost of efficiency or the violation of normative rules. We would also generally expect that urgency will be positively associated with simplicity, blame of the other party, and punitiveness. A sense of crisis is also functional in achieving rapid mobilization, unless the crises become so common that fatigue sets in.

Where the predominant ideology stresses the need for quick action, rapid progress, or immediate victories, however, a party may become demoralized and consequently demobilized if its opposition can successfully block its actions. Therefore veto power becomes a very important asset for any party faced with an opponent adhering to such an ideology. This has important implications in terms of the nature of the resources needed to achieve the appropriate outcomes, as well as choices among alternative courses of action. We would generally expect a party characterized by such a sense of urgency to employ offensive strategies and be less concerned with the depletion of its resources, whereas a party with a longer time perspective may be much more willing to use defensive tactics and attempt to exhaust its opponent.

I_6 . Degree to Which Conformity, Centralization of Control, and High Mobilization Are Believed Necessary

We have grouped together here a number of possibly distinct kinds of belief that may form a kind of authoritarian syndrome. In general, we would predict this dimension to be positively related to I_5 , a sense of urgency, and negatively to fatalism.[2] We would also expect this kind of ideological dimension to be facilitated by simplicity, though we hesitate to go so far as to argue that simplicity is a necessary precondition. Obviously, an emphasis on conformity and centralization support rapid mobilization and a certain degree of efficiency with respect to coordination problems. However, it may inhibit efficiency in instances where conformity and centralization tend to rule out certain courses of action requiring flexibility and decentralized decision making.

Presumably, ideological dimensions such as these affect not only the utilities attached to certain goals but the subjective probabilities of attaining these goals via a given course of action. They also affect actors' working theories of social causation as well as their specific expectations and perceptions of other actors' behavior. On the very general level at which we are discussing the subject of power, however, we do not believe it makes much sense to insert them into our causal diagrams. Were we to do so, we would use them as exogenous variables for most kinds of rather limited power confrontation, and this might seem to give them a greater importance than is actually warranted. It will often be possible to handle them implicitly through the device of assuming the goals, working theories, and normative regulations to be predetermined in a given analysis. But if one is attempting to make comparisons across a wide range of different settings, then most certainly these and other ideological dimensions will need to be taken into account.

WORKING THEORIES

It has been emphasized that an actor's mobilization efforts will depend directly on its working theory, or perceptions and expectations, rather than on the objective state of affairs per se. By *perceptions* we shall mean the actors' *estimates* of the present actual values of objective properties, motivational characteristics, and resources of each party. By *expectations* we mean subjective probabilities that certain events will occur in the future, as, for example, expectations that the other party will employ certain means or will be able to mobilize to a given degree. Thus the essential difference between the two kinds of concept is that perceptions refer to present levels, whereas expectations refer to future levels or behaviors. The model of A's working theory, T_A, given in figure 9.1, takes A's expectations and perceptions (designated by the presuperscript A) as functions of two kinds of variable: the actual values themselves and also A's perceptions of immediately past values of the same variables. This model of T_A obviously involves a number of gross simplifications, some of which we shall discuss in the remainder of this section.

In general, A's perceptions and expectations will be based not only on past experiences with B (and the other parties as well) but also on a number of variables in A's goal–ideological block discussed previously. These latter connections have not been indicated in the diagram and may be difficult to specify very concretely in a very general model. One would anticipate that A will tend to project motivation from itself to B, as, for example, goals to injure the other party. To the degree that A relies on an extremely simplistic ideological theory, as, for example, the belief in a monolithic Communist conspiracy, there may also be a tendency to oversimplify B's motivational structure. For instance, A may believe that B will be so dedicated and obsessed by the confrontation that it will mobilize all of its resources, or that B is so homogeneous and monolithic that its efficiency will be almost unity. A fatalistic ideology may tend to produce consistently low estimates of one's own resources and mobilization potential and high estimates of one's opponent's capabilities.

The model also presupposes that A will utilize in its working theory basically the same kind of model as given in figure 8.1 of the previous chapter. To the extent that this model is, in fact, correct, this would imply a very rational kind of decision-making process. It implies that A assesses its own resources by relating its own objective properties to the motivational structure of the other parties. Perhaps, however, A equates its O's with resources by ignoring these motivational states, or by merely assuming that O's can automatically be transformed into R's. This will not invalidate the general model, since in any given instance one may simply equate certain of the variables (e.g., O_A, ^AO_A, and ^AR_A), while taking certain of the other possible causal connections to have zero values. There may be other respects in which the model is invalid, however, as, for example, if A introduces a host of other considerations into its working theory that we have ignored. Thus it becomes an important empirical problem to study the nature of these perceptions and expectations to infer just how they are developed and the additional kinds of variable that need to be introduced into the model. Small-group experiments seem ideally suited for this purpose.

In general terms, the T_A submodel takes the degree of A's mobilization, D_A, and also A's choice among means, M_A, as a function of A's perception of its own resources, ^AR_A, and its expectation as to the amount of power, ^AP_B, that B will actually apply. We shall later consider other factors that influence D_A and M_A but here confine our attention to these two particular sources as aspects of T_A. A's perceptions of its own resources are, in turn, a function of three other perceptions: of its own O's and of the goals of B and C_i. Similarly,

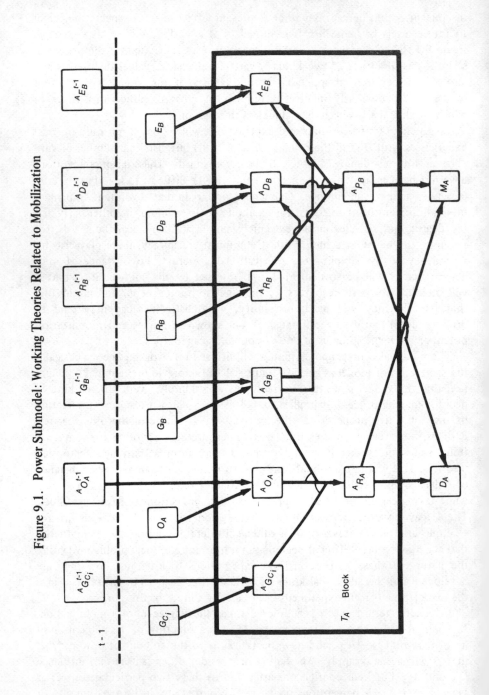

Figure 9.1. Power Submodel: Working Theories Related to Mobilization

A's expectation of the power that will be applied by B, namely, ^AP_B, is a multiplicative function of A's perception of B's resources and A's expectations as to the proportion of these that will be mobilized and the efficiency (considering B's means) with which this will be done. If A simply ignores B's efficiency, we assume that this is equivalent to assuming an efficiency of unity. These six variables involving A's perceptions and expectations are each, in turn, functions of the actual or true levels and A's perceptions of past levels.

The degree of knowledge, K_A, that A possesses has not been explicitly introduced into the diagram because of the complications it would create visually. However, we anticipate that K_A will affect the relative *slopes* (and probably correlations) relating both the true present values and the perceived past values to the perceived present values. Recognizing that K_A may differ according to each variable being considered, we, in general, expect that the greater the actual knowledge of present values the greater weight A will give to these true values. However, the less faith A has in this knowledge (whether it is actually true or not), the less reliance will be placed upon it. If A and B have been in previous power contests, or if A has been in a contest with an opponent perceived to be highly similar to B, or if A has witnessed a contest between B and an opponent deemed similar to A, then it will be rational (in the absence of other information) to rely heavily on this knowledge of past performance. Also, the more *consistent* this past performance has been, the more sense it makes to extrapolate from the past to the future. In other words, the greater the K_A (as perceived by A), the closer the slopes connecting perceived values to true ones will come to unity, and the greater the reliance on these present values. The poorer A's knowledge of present states, the greater the reliance on past levels. Hence K_A should, in each instance, interact statistically with present levels and perceived past levels in affecting perceived present levels.

This again assumes a rational model on the part of the actor. Modifications may prove necessary in instances where ideological factors produce strong emotional responses. For instance, a party that has been consistently defeated in the past, has high grievances, and has come to expect certain behavior on the part of the dominant party may place a much greater emphasis on past behavior than might otherwise seem justified. Even if it possesses factual knowledge about present values, such a party might not trust this knowledge, being afraid of being deliberately misled. Therefore it is not actual knowledge that is as relevant as perceived knowledge. Likewise, the actor's knowledge may be faulty and therefore less reliable than past information, but this knowledge may be taken as accurate and form the basis of policy. To the degree that deliberate deception and secrecy have characterized past relationships it is to be expected that both parties will not trust present efforts by the other side to convey the true state of affairs.

A possible feedback of these perceptions and expectations on knowledge-seeking behavior is also not included in the diagram. For example, if A believes that B has been remarkably consistent in the past and that B's O's have not changed, then A will presumably be much less motivated to invest resources to obtain more knowledge about B. Thus consistency in the past may reduce efforts to obtain special information about the present, thereby emphasizing all the more the reliance on past events. Presumably, inconsistent past behavior or radical shifts in the relative distributions of O's will motivate A to obtain up-to-date information so as to rely more heavily on present values.

Also not taken into consideration explicitly is the role of third parties as suppliers of objective information and the degree to which these sources are really trusted by A and B. For instance A may believe that B is deliberately deceiving C in order to pass along incorrect information to A. Another factor in determining the relative weights given to past events and present information is the degree to which A perceives that the *setting* has changed, namely, that the levels of certain exogenous variables and the interests of third parties have shifted.

Working theories also contain assumptions about the nature of the *outcomes*, Y_j, that will result under various conditions. This includes assumptions about whether or not the other party (or third parties C_i) can be trusted to keep its word. If A yields to B, to what extent will B remove many of A's properties and positions, which are the sources of the R_A? How will B's future utilities and subjective probabilities be affected by different strategies employed by A? For example will B seek revenge if A employs one strategy but not another? These matters, of course, go beyond present perceptions, but since they involve expectations as to future behaviors we can anticipate that they are likely to be included in A's working theory. A more complete formulation of the T_A block would need to include such expectations. Again, these are very likely to be affected by previous events, so that a reasonable approximation may be to take certain of A's perceptions and expectations as functions of other outcome variables for previous time periods.

KNOWLEDGE, OBSERVABILITY, AND SECRECY

The exercise of power by A over B requires at least some knowledge by A of B's behavior. This is due to the fact that any sanctions applied by A must be *contingent* on B's behavior or responses. It would perhaps be more correct to say that A must *believe* it knows what B's behavior is, and B must believe that A knows this response. These conditions, of course, imply that there must be at least some degree of observability of B's behavior so that A may verify it and act accordingly. We may generalize the notion of observability beyond its usual connotation that A must actually witness B's behavior. For A may also obtain knowledge if there are certain C_i that are in a position to observe B's behavior, and if these C_i accurately report such behavior to A, and if A actually believes such reports. Also, of course, B will observe its own behavior and may provide a report to A, which A may or may not believe. We shall include all of these possibilities under the general notion of observability, recognizing that observability may vary by degree and that the knowledge A obtains may be more or less accurate and also believed to varying degrees.

Observability also depends on the clarity of the criteria being used to classify or report the nature of B's behavior. For example, A may actually witness this behavior directly but may not be able to interpret it accurately because of certain ambiguities. Perhaps parties A and B may have thought that they had reached agreement on certain rules, the breaking of which by B would bring about sanctions by A. But it may turn out that the rules had not been defined as clearly as had been thought, and that B's behavior might or might not be defined as in violation of the rules, depending upon one's interpretation. International conflicts have involved notorious examples of such situations, where each party may claim that it is the other side that has broken the rules. Both may be correct in the view of a neutral observer simply because of ambiguities in the criteria being used to judge the behaviors concerned.

With these preliminary remarks in mind, we provide a simple model in figure 9.2 to explain the degree of knowledge, K_A, by A of B's behavior. Our symbols (constrained, since we have already used up many of the letters of the alphabet) are as follows:

$^\sigma G_B$ = dispersion in relative utilities of goals among B's members;

F_A, F_{C_i} = Favorableness of the objective situation to observation by A or C_i of B's behaviors and characteristics;

U_A, U_{C_i} = Understandability or clarity of criteria to A and to C_i;

W_A, W_{C_i} = Witnessability or actual ability of A and C_i to record, classify, and assess B's behavior and characteristics;

$^A V_{C_i}$ = Veracity, degree to which A trusts the report by C_i of B's behavior and characteristics.

The remaining symbols are as previously explained: R_B = B's resources; S_B = secrecy by B; G_B = B's goals; T_A = A's perceptions and expectations; M_A = means used by A; E_A = A's efficiency; and $^A R_B$ = A's perception of B's resources.

According to the model, B's degree of secrecy, S_B, is taken as a function of B's resources, R_B, and goals, G_B, and also the diversity of B's goals, $^\sigma G_B$. Diversity is expected to inhibit secrecy through several mechanisms. First, a disagreement on the relative importance of goals may force a higher degree of openness of discussion, some of which will inhibit secrecy. Also, if there is a low degree of consensus among B's members it may be easier for A to find informants or espionage agents from among these members. Secrecy of B is then assumed to interact with F and U variables to affect W_A and W_{C_i}.[3] The argument is that the latter causes of the W's, which refer to the actual observability of A and C_i respectively, will depend not only on the objective nature of the opportunities, F_A and F_{C_i}, that A and C_i have, but also on the degree to which B is able to employ secrecy. S_B and F_A interact in the sense that the higher the

Figure 9.2. **Power Submodel: Knowledge Block**

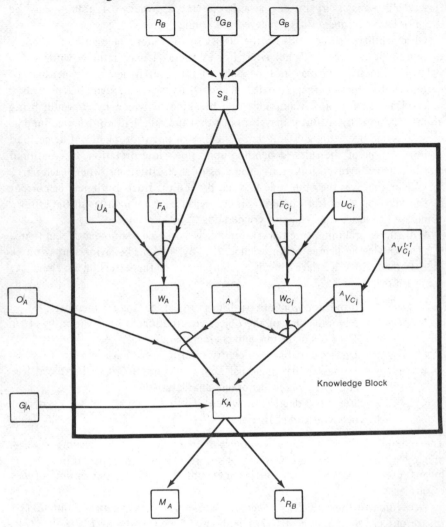

degree of objective favorableness, the less possible it will be for B to employ secrecy.

In other words, the importance of secrecy as a mechanism varies according to the nature of the objective situation; some things are easier to hide than others. As we have already implied, however, W_A depends not only on these two variables but also on U_A, or the clarity of the criteria used in defining the nature of the objective properties or behavior of B. Some situations will be inherently more clear-cut or easier to define than others, leading us to expect that the importance of clarity will depend upon the nature of the objective situation, F_A. Therefore both S_B and U_A are predicted to interact with F_A in affecting the level of W_A. The same argument holds for the comparable variables having C_i as a subscript.

But K_A depends not only on A's goals, G_A, and on W_A and W_{C_i} but also on T_A, O_A, and $^A V_{C_i}$. Actor A must expend certain O_A to interpret the information received, and this interpretation will also be affected by T_A, or the set of A's perceptions and expectations. Here is where expertise comes into play. It may be necessary to set aside a certain portion of the total O_A for a staff of advisors whose primary function is to process intelligence reports and eventually utilize them in assigning relative weights to various alternative means, M_A. The model implies interactions among the three variables, O_A, W_A, and T_A. Some W_A will be sufficiently straightforward that they may be translated into knowledge without much perceptual distortion or expenditure of O_A. But other kinds of W_A may be more subject to interpretation that depends significantly on T_A. In the case of information supplied by C_i we add one more variable that may interact with W_{C_i}, namely, the degree to which A trusts C_i. This current level of trust, $^A V_{C_i}$, is taken as a function of past levels of trust, which also depend upon the previous actions of C_i. Presumably, if C_i has supplied what is perceived to be accurate information in the past, this level of trust will be high.

ALTERNATIVE MEANS AND THEIR INTERRELATIONSHIPS

Although it is difficult in a general discussion such as this to say very much about the nature of the specific goals that may be at stake in a power confrontation between A and B, we can be a bit more definite about rather general types of means or courses of action that may be employed. Certain of these means may be treated as instrumental goals that have become important in their own right. We would generally expect that this will tend to occur whenever the confrontation is a prolonged one, whenever it recurs at frequent intervals, or whenever the issues involve goals that have extremely high utilities attached to them. Thus, as we have already noted in chapter 2, the distinction between means and ends is not always easy to draw. In particular, certain means may become goals in their own right because they are presumed to be highly generalizable to a number of diverse types of ends. For instance, if an actor's working causal theory postulates that the attainment of a college education or a specified office will enable one to obtain not only prestige and security but also the opportunity to influence the behavior of others, then these means are likely to become goals to which a high utility is attached.

We encounter here an ambiguity that, at least in part, seems to derive from linguistic usage. It is not clear whether by the term *means* we imply some intermediate goal or state of affairs such as the possession of an A.B. degree or the occupancy of a position, or whether we are referring to some course of action, such as acquiring knowledge, which also happens to involve certain states of affairs. Perhaps it would be wise to substitute terms such as *state of affairs* or *course of action* for the single word *means*, but in the interest of simplicity we shall not do so. Our emphasis, however, will be on the courses of action usage, with the recognition that many courses of action may involve states of affairs that may be used to *indicate* that these courses have been followed. For instance, we commonly substitute formal positions, reputations, years of schooling completed, and other relatively easily measured indicators for what we take to be courses of action that the actor has followed in the past or is likely to follow in the future. To the degree that our theory is formulated in terms of courses of action or processes, however, we should be alerted to possible slippages whenever these "state" indicators are used.

As has frequently been noted, means or courses of action will in general be constrained in many ways. In fact some students of power (e.g., Abramson, Cutler, Kautz, and Mendelson 1958) develop the notion of power around such constraints. In effect, A's power or control over B is closely linked with A's ability to limit or constrain B's alternative courses of action. We shall not follow this usage for several reasons, the first being that alternative courses are seldom completely blocked in some absolute sense but rather are made more or less costly or more or less inefficient. Second, it is not the *number* of alternative paths that is crucial but rather their efficiency or effectiveness. Thus A may be able to constrain B to a single line of action, but this means may be sufficient to overcome A and may, in fact, be precisely the line of action that B would prefer to use. Third, alternatives will be influenced by many factors in addition to A's behaviors, so that we need to consider these other sources of constraints as part of the total picture.

Nevertheless a focus on alternative paths and the constraints that exist among them seems to be an important tool in analyses of social power. As a general rule we expect that the weaker B's resources, the fewer the alternative courses of action that will be feasible and the more incompatibilities that will exist among them. Thus dilemmas of strategy can be expected to be much more severe for a weak or subordinate party than for a strong or superordinate one, and we shall return to a brief discussion of certain of these dilemmas toward the end of the chapter. Before doing so, however, we need to take up the prior question of delineating a reasonably general set of alternative courses of action that may be appropriate under a wide variety of types of power confrontation.

Our aim in this section is to list a series of ten courses of action each of which stands a reasonable chance of being represented in terms of a single dimension, or at least a relatively small number of dimensions, so that comparisons of power confrontations of diverse types can be made. As will be obvious from the brief discussions of each action course, certain of these means will be closely interrelated in that they will be either highly compatible or else nearly incompatible. By *compatible* we shall mean that if actor A follows one course of action this will not decrease the objective probability that a second course will lead to success in attaining a given goal.

If we use S to refer to a success and the symbols M_i to refer to these various means, this says that if M_i and M_j are compatible, then $P(S|M_i + M_j) \geqslant P(S|M_i)$ and also that $P(S|M_i + M_j) \geqslant P(S|M_j)$.[4] It is theoretically possible for the first inequality to hold without the second, or vice versa, in which case we would have a situation in which one means reinforces a second, but where the use of the second lowers the effectiveness of the first. In the interest of simplicity, however, we shall ignore this possibility. Similarly, we shall say that two means are incompatible if the joint use of the two means *lowers* the probability of success for either means taken alone.

Notice that these definitions say nothing about the *costs* entailed by using both means at once. In general we would presume that the use of several means at once will tend to increase costs and deplete resources more rapidly than the use of either alone. But this may not apply to certain of the means listed below. Clearly, compatibility and incompatibility will vary by degrees and will depend upon the circumstances, so that we wish to avoid the implication that a particular pair or set of means are universally compatible or incompatible. We will therefore need a number of theories that specify the conditions under which two or more means are mutually compatible or incompatible.

M_1. Degree to Which A Attempts to Increase B's Overall Dependence on A

Keeping in mind that A may or may not care about B's overall dependence as long as A is able to attain whatever objective is in question, it may nevertheless facilitate A's goals if B can be made generally dependent on A. We shall use the notion of dependence here in a rather restricted sense to mean A's ability to control the access to goals that B may desire.[5] To the degree that A can reduce the (objective) probabilities of B's attaining these goals, regardless of the course of action B may take, then we shall say that B is dependent on A. In particular, in the case of exchange situations we noted that if A is the only supplier of a valued good or service, or if A can control the behaviors of alternative sources of supply, then B becomes dependent upon A.

As Emerson (1962) has noted, this dependence may be reduced by one or more of four specific alternative courses of action, two of which involve B's side of the equation. B's dependence may be reduced by giving up or attaching lower utilities to those goals that are controlled by A, or by finding alternative sources of supply On the other side, B's net dependence on A may also be decreased if there are increases in A's utilities attached to goals controlled by B, or if A's alternative sources of supply are either cut off or begin to demand a higher rate of exchange for these goods or services. The argument of Thibaut and Kelley (1959) to the effect that B's dependence on A is a function of what they symbolize as "CL_{alt}" seems to be essentially the same point. Actor B's "CL_{alt}" represents the comparison level between the expected benefits in an exchange relationship with A and those that would be anticipated if B were to break off the relationship in favor of some alternative. The less favorable B's expected alternatives, the more dependent B is on A. Therefore one means that A may use to increase this dependence is to attempt to reduce these alternative opportunities.

M_2. Degree to Which A Attempts to Reduce B's Degree of Mobilization

M_1 essentially involves efforts to reduce B's resources or resource supply. A second course of action, M_2, is to attempt to reduce B's mobilization effort, either by trying to get B to modify its goals or relative utilities or by altering B's subjective probabilities. If B can be persuaded that there is little to be gained by opposing A, or that the costs will be too great relative to the expected gain, then B's effort may be reduced. Perhaps this can be accomplished by helping B find alternative goals or means that do not conflict with A's objectives. To the degree that A's behavior is perceived by B as threatening, then B's motivation to oppose A may be decreased by convincing B that the threat is not real, as, for example, by disguising one's real intent, by convincing B that the real threat is elsewhere, or by causing B to underestimate A's actual resources. Other efforts may be directed at convincing B that opposition is hopeless or that it will result in extreme punishments.

As a first approximation we would predict that the relationship between these first two courses of action against B will be a function of the degree of B's dependence on A. If B's dependence on A is initially low, then efforts to increase this dependence will be expected to *increase* B's mobilization, thereby imposing a constraint on the joint use of these two means. But once B's dependence becomes high, then it may be possible for A to employ the two strategies simultaneously by convincing B that opposition will result in very high costs and/or have a very low probability of succeeding. If the trend is in the opposite direction of decreasing dependence of B upon A, then this implies that A may find it increasingly difficult to employ both strategies simultaneously and, in particular, may need to find alternatives to approaches that have previously been used to keep B's mobilization at a low level. In effect, we assume that if B's dependence on A is even moderately high, B will attach a high utility to reducing this dependence but may be immobilized by the threats of retaliation or by a very low subjective probability of success. As this dependence is decreased, the subjective probability of B's success can be expected to increase and to be less influenced by threats or other actions of A.

M_3. Degree to Which A Concentrates the Application of Power (Applies Pressure)

In physics, the notion of pressure refers to force/area, or force per unit of area. Thus for a constant force the smaller the area to which it is applied, the greater the pressure on this area. If, for example, a force can be applied to a very small area, this may produce a puncture of a surface much more efficiently than would the same force applied to a much larger area. The notion of pressure as used in the social sciences or ordinary language seems to have a similar though less precise connotation. The basic idea is that an actor may achieve objectives by applying a force in a concentrated fashion, as, for example, by applying pressure on certain gatekeepers of discrimination.

Such a strategy would seem especially effective whenever a breakthrough in a limited area can have a catalytic effect in other areas, as, for example, the hiring of the first minority member in a particular occupation or the setting of a legal precedent. As a general rule, these gains in a very limited area must be held for a sufficient period in order for the catalytic effect to take place. The strategy will also tend to be more effective to the degree that actor A can locate certain key points of vulnerability in B's defense, just as pressure applied to the weakest area of a surface will be more effective in breaking through this surface than the same pressure applied to stronger areas. This observation is, of course, obvious in the case of offensive military strategies that aim to find the enemy's most vulnerable points. The effectiveness of this concentration of pressure at a small number of points depends upon the ability of B to close the gap, or fix the puncture, before too much damage has been done.

We would predict that to the degree that B's resources are highly concentrated and dependent upon the actions of a very small segment of its total membership (e.g., gatekeepers or key decision makers), this will increase the efficiency of those courses of action by A that involve the application of pressure on these concentrated resources. In contrast, where B's exertion of power is a result of highly diffuse acts by many uncoordinated individuals, the application of pressure to a few of these individuals will have much less impact. For instance, if a minority cannot locate specific gatekeepers of discrimination (as, for example, those who can be held responsible for racial segregation), it becomes much more difficult to apply pressure in an effective way.

There is also the danger that pressure applied to relatively innocent individuals (as defined by members of party B or by third parties, C_i) may create martyrs, so that immediate gains won by applying pressure at these points may be wiped out or even turned into losses if this results in an increase in B's mobilization or alliances between B and these third parties. Although the term *pressure resources* was used by Blalock (1967b) in a slightly different sense to refer to resources that a minority may use to punish members of a majority or dominant group, the argument in that connection was essentially similar. The application of pressure may work in order to achieve token breakthroughs, but consolidation is likely to require other kinds of resource that can compensate for the likely increase in the other party's mobilization efforts.

M_4. Degree to Which A Relies on Secrecy or Deception

If A can make it difficult for B to predict its future behavior, this is likely to decrease the efficiency of B's mobilization effort, though not necessarily the degree of mobilization. In particular, B will find it much more difficult to plan a sequence of responses (and to develop the necessary resources for these responses) or to plan a suitable defensive strategy against A. Therefore, other things being equal, it is to A's advantage to apply a mixed strategy and to shield its decision-making process from observation. Secrecy and deception also have their disadvantages, however, especially where they are not permissible under the rules that regulate the power confrontation. A's past deception may be used by B to convince its members that a higher degree of mobilization is necessary against an enemy that cannot be trusted. It may encourage B to employ an offensive strategy (e.g., the preemptive strike), and it may also convince third parties that they should enter the contest on the side of B.

Where the secrecy must be employed against members of its own group, this may also weaken both the degree and efficiency of A's own mobilization effort, if only through the necessity of devoting a certain proportion of its scarce resources to protecting these secrets. We would expect that such internal secrecy and deception will be necessary to the degree that A's membership is heterogeneous with respect to variables that are directly relevant to the power confrontation, and in particular where it is thought that there will be a sizable number of A's members who are sympathetic to B. Where such internal secrecy and deception is discovered, it may very well increase the fissures and cause a sizable segment of A's membership to become either neutral or openly allied with B, thereby creating an even greater need for further secrecy and deception.

Thus we would expect that the use of this strategy will have the greatest payoff in instances where the duration of the power confrontation is short and where the party A is highly homogeneous with respect to the motivation to win the power confrontation regardless of the means used. Also, we would expect secrecy and deception to be most feasible whenever there is a high concentration of decision-making power within A's leadership structure. We also expect secrecy and deception to be minimized by the presence of powerful third parties that are committed to the regulation of this means and that make it very clear to both parties to the confrontation that they will, in effect, form a coalition with whichever party appears to be the victim of such secrecy or deception.

M_5. Degree to Which A Follows a Consistent Strategy over Time

This dimension is, of course, closely linked with M_4 but seems analytically distinct from it. Clearly, if a consistent policy is followed the element of surprise is removed unless the policy is consistently that of deception and secrecy. Much inconsistency in A's behavior may be primarily a consequence of confusion, poor coordination, a lack of knowledge and planning, or changing circumstances, however, so that it would be inappropriate to equate this with secrecy or deception. Presumably, highly consistent behavior is to A's advantage in that it is likely to make it much easier for A to accumulate the necessary resources, to justify its courses of action to its own members and to third parties, and to train its members to use its resources efficiently. Consistency also improves communication with B, in effect announcing exactly what A's course of behavior will be in response to any future action by B.

We generally expect that consistency will be relatively more characteristic of strong parties than weaker ones for several reasons: (1) there is less need to rely on deception if "brute strength" can be applied; (2) consistency makes

B's responses more subject to *A*'s control since misunderstandings are less likely; and (3) a stronger party is less likely to be vulnerable to minor changes in circumstances, internal disorganization, and disagreements over strategy.

M_6. Degree to Which *A* Adheres to Rules That Regulate the Power Confrontation

In general, we would expect adherence to any rules that are perceived to be to one's advantage and a tendency to disobey those that are to one's opponent's advantage. Degree of adherence will also depend upon the expected costs of deviance, both in terms of sanctions that may be applied by third parties that are serving in enforcing capacities (e.g., judges, referees, or other neutral actors) and also in terms of the reactions of members of one's own party and the opposition. Adherence to rules will usually require a reasonably high degree of consistency of behavior and a relative absence of secrecy and deception except where these rules permit such deception.

Where rules are perceived as differentially enforced by regulators who are not believed to be totally neutral, we may expect one or more of several responses. If the regulators and those who make the rules are thought to be under the control of the other party (here *B*), appeals may be made to still other parties to replace these parties or to modify their behaviors. If this course of action is perceived to have a low probability of succeeding, rule violations may be deliberately perpetrated in order to challenge the legitimacy of the system. Such a tactic is likely to be risky, however. On the one hand, it may help to mobilize one's own members and certain third parties by making the inequities explicit. On the other hand, to the degree that these parties define the situation to be fair and cannot be convinced that the rules are being differentially enforced, the tactic may reduce *A*'s efficiency of mobilization by creating dissension within its ranks, and it may also reduce support from among potential allies.

Where *A* perceives that support for the rules is substantial among all parties but where *A* believes they are being differentially enforced in *B*'s favor, another tactic may be to induce *B* to violate these rules through some provocative behavior, as, for example, nonviolent resistance. One possibility in this connection is to violate rules that are deemed relatively unimportant in order to induce *B* to violate much more important regulations, thereby engendering greater sympathy among neutral parties and those who are enforcing these rules. Such a tactic is likely to be especially characteristic of extremely weak parties whenever they perceive that there are a sufficient number of potential allies that can be shocked out of their previous neutrality by extreme behaviors perpetrated by their more powerful opponent.

It should be noted that under most circumstances rule violations by *A* are likely to produce additional violations by *B*, which in turn provide incentives to *A* to increase the degree of rule violations. If unchecked, this dynamic process may result in an accumulation of violations that ends in an explosion or radical alteration of the situation. Accelerating border violations between nations, acts of terrorism, and armaments races are obvious illustrations of this kind of unstable process. There appear to be only two kinds of mechanisms capable of dampening such processes, namely, the intervention of more powerful third parties and the increasing fatigue of the parties A and B. In the latter case, assuming negligible regulation by third parties, a linear-type system of differential equations (Richardson 1960) implies that the *product* of the fatigue coefficients of A and B must be large, meaning that the fatigue of a single party will not be sufficient to curb the accelerating violations if the fatigue of the other party is close to zero. Although this notion of fatigue is a very general one, we presume that it will ordinarily be a function of both resource depletion and factors that affect motivation to continue the pattern in question.

In the present case, the fatigue factor would involve the costs entailed by accelerating rule violations by both sides, with the resulting need to reestablish regulatory mechanisms. To this end, previously neutral third parties may actually be sought out by both A and B, in which case both must be willing either to turn over power to the third party (as in binding arbitration) or to abide by a revised set of regulations that are negotiated with C's assistance. Where C is relatively weak as compared with A and B, so that a coalition with C will not really affect the outcome of the power contest, stability is most likely to be achieved to the degree that there are *other* parties that will, in effect, accept C's judgments and indicate their willingness to join a coalition with whichever party abides most closely to the rules. The observability of the behaviors in question and the clarity of the rules become crucial factors since there must be some means by which these other parties can assess the degree of rule violation.

M_7. Degree to Which A Seeks to Modify the Rules

This dimension is obviously empirically related to the previous one, though they are analytically distinct since we may imagine instances where party A adheres to rules while attempting to get them modified or, conversely, where it violates the rules while opposing their modification. This implies, then, that if A finds certain rules to its disadvantage, rule violation or rule modification can be seen as possible alternatives. Where A has a strong interest in preserving the legitimacy of the relationship, but where certain rules are to its disadvantage, we would expect it to attempt rule modification whenever feasible. In particular, where rules can be modified in such a way that they appear to be strictly neutral but yet actually favor A, we expect A to encourage these modifications while simultaneously placing a strong emphasis on legitimacy and the obligation of both parties to abide by these rules.

Since rules will affect the degree to which one's objective properties, O_i, can be transformed into resources, we would generally expect that each actor will favor those rules that give the advantage to those O_i that it possesses to a greater degree than its opponent. For example, a football team that has a strong passing attack relative to its running game will favor rules that give the advantage to passing as compared with running. Persons who occupy certain offices will favor rule changes that legitimize the power of these offices and that restrain the behavior of those who do not occupy them. Members of a legislative body will favor rule changes that increase their power relative to the executive, and so forth. Similarly, if A finds it desirable to employ secrecy as a strategy it will tend to favor rule changes that inhibit the other party from obtaining information or that in other ways legitimize this secrecy.

M_8. Degree to Which A Relies on Punishments and Threats

A's courses of action will usually involve a combination of positive and negative sanctions, as well as persuasion through threats and efforts to convince B. To the degree that the mix of these approaches involves primarily punishments and threats of negative sanctions, we may generally expect B to reciprocate in kind. We have previously defined the degree of conflict as the degree to which there are exchanges of negative sanctions on both sides. Presumably, A will rely primarily on the use of negative sanctions to the degree that A perceives this approach will be advantageous, whether in terms of achieving immediate compliance by B, in increasing B's overall dependence on A, or in persuading B not to attempt retaliation in spite of B's motivation to do so.

As Thibaut and Kelley (1959), among others, have noted, the use of negative sanctions by A is likely to increase A's problems of surveillance. Furthermore, the application of punishments will generally tend to weaken legitimate power and referent power, according to French and Raven (1959), so that there will be costs in efficiency to A as well as the risk of retaliation. As a general rule we would expect that the application or threat of negative sanctions will increase B's *utilities* attached to retaliation, and to injuring A, but not necessarily the subjective probability of achieving tangible gains through this means. If A is considerably more powerful than B, the use of repeated negative sanctions may literally "whip B into line," and this may be an effective means of obtaining compliance provided that B's behaviors are easily observed. Where negative sanctions can be made roughly commensurate with the seriousness of B's departures from A's expectations, this form of control may remain highly efficient as long as the difference in power is considerable and the sanctions not too severe. Many forms of political control of weak satellite nations and exploitative economic systems such as slavery and peonage seem to be based primarily on this form of control.

However, if B's behavior becomes more difficult to monitor, and if the responsibility for acts of sabotage or aggression cannot be pinned on any single subordinate party, we anticipate that B's high utility attached to revenge or to A's injury will begin to result in retaliation that makes this means of control much less effective. If A should begin to shift the mix of courses of action away from the use of negative sanctions and toward positive inducements, it does not necessarily follow that B's motivation to apply negative sanctions will be reduced. In fact, the change in A's behaviors may be taken as a sign of weakness, with the result that B's subjective probabilities of achieving success through this means may sharply increase, so that the degree of conflict may rise rather dramatically over a very short period of time.

If there is a substantial lag period between the onset of this increased conflict and a severe reaction on the part of A (the so-called backlash), we may anticipate the acceleration of conflict in much the same fashion that armaments races among nations have been described. Whether or not the system will eventually stabilize prior to a major reaction on the part of the dominant party, A, will depend upon the magnitude of the forces that operate to produce fatigue in both parties, as compared with those that affect the sensitivities of each party to (negative) sanctions on the part of the other. If the utilities that A attaches to dominance or control of B are rather low, as, for example, where slavery or other forms of economic exploitation are no longer profitable, then we may expect that conflict will subside relatively quickly. In contrast, where control of B is deemed essential to A's survival or prosperity, we may anticipate that the use of retaliatory tactics by B is likely to lead after a brief period of confusion and exploratory responses to an extreme show of force on the part of A and a return to a point closer to the earlier level of stability in which B's retaliatory responses are limited to desperation moves or more subtle forms of sabotage or noncooperation.

In these illustrations we are suggesting that a heavy reliance on negative sanctions will generally be incompatible with the second course of action, M_2, discussed above, namely, the effort to reduce B's degree and efficiency of mobilization. But this generalization must be qualified, as implied above, by the observation that if A is much more powerful than B, and if A attaches a very high utility to the control of B and is in a position to monitor B's actions, then the actual use of punishment on a regularized or symbolic basis may serve to keep B's subjective probabilities so low that retaliation is out of the question. For instance, the frequent lynchings of blacks in the South immediately after the Reconstruction era and the extreme show of force by the Russians in the case of abortive uprisings in Hungary and Czechoslovakia undoubtedly served to emphasize that their threats of punishments were no idle bluffs. But since these means were also costly to these dominant parties in other ways—especially in the need to improve surveillance and to cope with various forms of noncooperation and reduced efficiency of production—they appear to have been dependent on A's continued motivation to control B's behavior even at considerable cost.

M_9. Degree to Which A Attempts to Appeal to Third Parties
There will, of course, be several kinds of third party to which A and B may appeal, though we may safely neglect those third parties that are substantially weaker than A and B and also those that are thought to be so remote from the

dispute that the probability of their taking part is thought to be extremely low. One very important kind of third party that cannot be neglected by either party, however, is the neutral party that is sufficiently strong to influence the outcome either way, but that in effect serves as a regulatory agent by virtue of the fact that it can be expected to enter the dispute on the side of the aggrieved party. Appeals to this type of third party will be weakened by rule violations, resorts to secrecy and deception (unless permitted by the rules), and the overuse of negative or punitive sanctions.

There is another type of third party whose behaviors may be much more difficult to predict but that nevertheless may play an important role in the power confrontation. This is the party that stands in much the same relationship to A as does B, but that may also be in competition with B for A's favorable treatment. For example, if A is a dominant group and B a minority, the party C may be a second minority that may have slightly greater (or less) power or status than B. There may be several such C_i arranged in a hierarchy of power, with the question arising concerning the likelihood of their forming coalitions with various partners. Caplow (1968) shows that under certain rather plausible conditions, "conservative" coalitions that do not disturb the hierarchical arrangement can be expected.

In the case of only three parties, with B and C being subordinate to A, Gamson (1961) and Caplow (1968) both predict that the B-C coalition is relatively more likely to occur whenever the combined power of B and C is greater than that of A, as compared with the situation where A is stronger than B and C combined. But the correctness of this argument depends upon a number of other factors. These may include imperfect or incorrect information about the resources of each party or the willingness to mobilize and expend these resources, the existence of common values or ideologies, a concern about future power as compared with present capabilities, and common or opposing interests (see Blalock 1967b).

Presumably party A will attempt to convince C that a coalition with B will be more costly to itself than either neutrality or a coalition with A, and B will attempt to persuade C that the opposite is the case. In many instances C is likely to gain from the A–B confrontation (Simmel 1902) unless it elects to enter the contest on what turns out to be the losing side, or unless—having won—it finds itself at the mercy of its coalition partner (Caplow 1968). In particular, this means that the kinds of appeal that A and B can make to C will depend upon whether or not the confrontation is a recurring one, or one that is likely to be repeated with C in the role of either A or B. Other things being equal, a punitive course of action by either A or B is likely to repel C to the degree that C perceives this to have been due to factors that are expected to operate similarly with respect to itself. Thus if both B and C are being dominated by A, and if A uses undue force to control B, it is likely that C will expect that A will apply the same means to itself if it were to behave similarly to B. If B is able to retaliate successfully, this may induce C to join forces with B. But if B's efforts are met with extreme punitive action on the part of A, and if this appears to subdue B almost completely, we expect that C will be very hesitant to join with B in a future coalition.

We see here that timing may be very important. If A is able to apply extreme sanctions to B while C remains an observer, no B–C coalition may form. But if there is a "near coalition" such that A believes it imperative to punish C as well as B, this may, of course, drive the two subordinate parties closer together. A may also attempt a mixed strategy, making different appeals to the two other parties with the hope that it may induce one or the other to join with it in a coalition or at least keep B and C in a position of rivalry. We expect this kind of strategy to be most successful whenever B and C are only slightly unequal in power (or status), whenever there are other important differences (e.g., cultural or occupational) between these subordinate parties, and whenever there has been a history of competition, conflict, or mistrust between them. In each of these kinds of situation, members of B and C can be expected to attach high utilities to goals that involve the "besting" of the other party, or to what Gamson (1961) calls "nonutilitarian preferences."

M_{10}. Degree to Which A Relies on Offensive Rather Than Defensive Strategies

The notions of offense and defense are, of course, obvious in the case of many sports events and also military tactics, though the distinction may be much less clear in many other kinds of power confrontation. Nevertheless, we recognize that A either may lie back and wait for B to take the initiative, and then counter this initiative once B has made the commitment, or may take this initiative itself. A defensive strategy would generally seem to have the advantage of requiring fewer resources, or at least involving a lower expenditure of resources. As Abramson et al. (1958) point out, once commitments have been made by an actor, certain alternative lines of action may effectively be closed off.

In contrast, an offensive strategy has the advantage of catching the opponent by surprise, possibly winning a quicker (and less costly) victory, and permitting the actor to decide upon matters of timing. We ordinarily anticipate that an offensive strategy is highly compatible with secrecy and deception, a lack of consistency of behavior over time (thus reducing predictability), the application of pressure concentrated at the opponent's most vulnerable points, a willingness to violate rules should this be convenient, a lack of need to rely heavily on coalition partners, and the willingness to apply negative sanctions whenever necessary. We would also expect that an offensive course of action will be relatively more likely whenever A attaches a high utility to B's injury, whereas a defensive strategy seems more compatible with a motivation to avoid contact with the other party.

We have already noted that actors may differ in their time perspectives, including both the length of their memories and the degree of patience they have in achieving their goals. To the degree that actor A wishes or needs to accomplish these objectives very rapidly, we expect a preference for an offensive strategy (thus taking the initiative from the opponent), violations of those rules that would have the effect of eliminating those courses of action that might give speedier results, and secrecy and deception in instances where a more deliberate and open policy would permit delaying actions on the part of B. However, as already implied, many of these same tactics are likely to alienate third parties, whose divergent interests from those of A might require coordination efforts and negotiations that could only take place over a longer period of time.

Whether or not A attempts a blitzkrieg attack on B is also likely to depend upon A's working theory of B's motivational structure, and in particular the degree to which the use of such tactics would result either in the consolidation of B's members or in demoralization and internal conflict. Also, the pace of A's actions will presumably depend upon the relative capabilities of the two parties for replacing depleted resources. Whichever party perceives itself to be the less capable of a long-term effort to replenish these resources can be expected to be more strongly motivated to bring the confrontation to a rapid conclusion. In contrast, a party that believes itself capable of replenishing its resources without undue cost, and therefore in a position to wear the other side down from sheer exhaustion, can be expected to prefer delaying actions, a defensive strategy, and continual negotiations.

EFFICIENCY OF MOBILIZATION AND CONSTRAINTS ON MEANS

In the general power model given in figure 8.1 of the previous chapter we took the efficiency of mobilization as a function of the means M_i, which are, of course, themselves functions of other variables in the theoretical system. In particular, these other variables may affect the actors' beliefs about the relative efficiency of different means as well as impose restraints on the use of these means, either individually or in combination. In the present section we shall take a closer look at the problem of assessing relative efficiency as well as the nature of different kinds of constraint that may be in operation. Again, since the model is extremely general we cannot begin to assess the kinds of exogenous factor that may, in turn, affect relative efficiencies or the degree to which the several kinds of constraint may be applicable in any given setting.

Turning first to the notion of efficiency itself, we can provide a deceptively simple definition of efficiency as being the ratio of outputs to total inputs. This definition obviously derives from a similar notion in physics, where, say, the efficiency of an engine is defined as output divided by input. But in the case of definitions of efficiency in physics there are well-known conversion factors that make it possible to translate from one form of energy to another, so that, for example, one may translate mechanical energy into electrical, or electrical energy into heat energy. This makes it possible to express the output and input measures in terms of the same units so as to arrive at an efficiency measure that varies between zero and unity. Since it is also possible to standardize operations (such as the way a machine is constructed) and to replicate experiments, it is then possible to make reasonably precise statements concerning the relative efficiencies of two or more types of device under specified conditions.

We have already noted that out*comes* may be multidimensional and complex, whereas we are implying the need for converting out*puts* into a single dimension. Another distinction between these two notions seems advisable, though we shall not explore its implications further. An out*put* is associated with what an actor actually *does*. If we refer back to the general power model presented in figure 8.1 of the previous chapter, we note that we can make the following distinctions:

$$\text{Input} = \text{Degree of Mobilization} \times \text{Resources } (D \times R);$$
$$\text{Output} = \text{Efficiency} \times \text{Degree of Mobilization} \times \text{Resources}$$
$$(E \times D \times R),$$
$$= \text{Power actually applied by actor;}$$

and therefore

$$\text{Efficiency} = \text{Output/Input.}$$

Outcomes, in contrast, are functions of the outputs of *several* parties as well as possible exogenous factors, some of which may be nonhuman in nature. In particular, these other parties may *react* to the output of the actor with which we are concerned, so as either to reinforce or to partly negate it. As a result the net outcome may be quite different from what would have occurred had there been no such reactive force.

An actor will often be much more concerned with this total or net outcome rather than with his or her own output per se, and therefore may want to take the reactive forces into account. The notion of efficacy may be used to refer to these total out*comes* in relation to the actor's input, perhaps being defined as the ratio of outcomes to inputs. This indeed seems to be what is implied by the concept of political efficacy, namely, the idea of the total or net impact (say, on the outcome of an election) of an actor's behavior. Given the formidable difficulties of measuring either efficiency or efficacy, however, the distinction between the two concepts may not prove to be very useful unless, of course, the actors themselves make this distinction and actually behave in terms of it.

Obviously we cannot hope to achieve any very precise measurement of efficiency of mobilization of resources in the case of social power, and yet we commonly recognize that not all courses of action are equally effective in achieving one's objectives. That is, a fixed sum of money can be spent in various ways, and it is both theoretically meaningful and highly practical to ask what combination of expenditures will have the greatest probability of achieving success, or the greatest expected yield. Put differently, one may ask what amounts to the same question: what combination can achieve a fixed objective with the smallest total outlay of funds? If all inputs can be expressed in terms of monetary units, and all outputs in terms of some other common unit, then one may relatively easily assess various alternative courses of action and select from among them that which maximizes the relative efficiency. Indeed, this mode of thinking is an almost essential ingredient of economic theory in providing the behavioral underpinnings for economic analysis. It has also been implicit in our earlier discussion of maximization of subjective expected utilities, although we did not at that time make explicit use of the notion of efficiency per se.

One danger in using such a very simple notion of efficiency and in attempting to express all inputs and outputs in common units is that, in doing so, we run the risk of omitting many kinds of input and output for which a metric is unavailable. Or we may lump them together into a single residual category of intangibles, or unknowns, which we then proceed to neglect because of our inability to specify their nature with any precision.

From here it is but a simple further step to assume that *actors* are also willing to neglect them and that they are of negligible importance to either the numerator or denominator of the fraction representing the notion of efficiency. Thus the "psychic costs" (including effects on health) to one's employees, or the ill will created by a company's pollution of the environment or unsatisfactory hiring or retirement policies, are the kinds of factor that are extremely difficult to include in one's efficiency calculations, but this does not mean that they have negligible effects on either inputs or outputs (or outcomes). Similarly, if party *A* applies extreme negative sanctions to party *B* this may have impacts on third parties or in terms of *B*'s future responses.

Somehow or other these intangible inputs and outputs need to be included in our assessments of efficiency. Additionally, the notion of efficiency needs to encompass both positive and negative total impacts. Needless to say, however, this requires a reasonably complete causal theory that makes it possible to provide a virtually complete listing and assessment of both inputs and outputs. Obviously, then, it will be difficult to be very precise about efficiency except in cases where the situation is an extremely simple one. Yet it is clear that the actors must make *some* assessment of efficiency, if only to ignore it by assuming that all alternative courses are equally efficient. Thus at the very least we shall need to be concerned with actors' beliefs about relative efficiency, as well as the ideological factors and past experiences that may have affected these beliefs. Furthermore, in many kinds of situation it will be necessary to distinguish between short-term consequences and longer-range ones, thereby introducing the additional complication that there may be several assessments of relative efficiency depending on the temporal perspective being used.

We have observed not only that outcomes may be multidimensional but also that actors *A* and *B* may attach different weights or utilities to these outcomes. In particular, we must be careful not to equate *A*'s control over *B* with *A*'s outcomes. For example, if *A* is a slave owner whose primary goal is to produce a cash crop at minimum cost, the control over *B* may be important as a means to achieve this objective. There will be other factors that also affect the crop production and profit level, however, so that even with complete control over B's behavior A may not be able to achieve the desired outcome. Yet for B the primary objective may be that of achieving a reduction in this control or perhaps a reduction in the proportion of negative sanctions. Such a reduction in A's control may come about through the operation of exogenous factors that affect A's most important outcomes and, perhaps, the efficiency of using a control over B in order to achieve these outcomes. Here we also see the possible need for several measures of efficiency (or efficacy), one for each outcome dimension that is at issue. A course of action that is highly efficient in achieving one outcome (e.g., control over one's slaves) may be much less efficient in achieving another outcome (e.g., producing a cash crop at a substantial profit).

Our discussion in the previous section pointed to at least certain kinds of compatibility and incompatibility among different courses of action, with the implicit recognition that these interrelationships may either increase or decrease the efficiency of using any particular combination of means in a given instance. In the discussion that follows we shall list a further set of factors that may affect efficiency by imposing certain constraints on the use of single means or the joint or sequential use of several means in combination. In the short run many of these constraining factors may be taken as exogenous, but since they are also to some degree subject to control by either A or B, or both, we also need to entertain the possibility that in long-run power confrontations they will need to be treated as endogenous as well.

Constraints on Particular Means

1. *Depletion of Resources.* The use of objective properties such as money, manpower, weapons, land, or industrial outputs in a power confrontation will all be counted as part of A's input. The rate at which these resources (really O_i) are being depleted, relative to their total supply and in terms of the expected duration of the power contest, may affect the degree to which they can continue to be utilized and thus the efficiency of the operation. To the degree that A *anticipates* that this rate of depletion is excessive, given the time period involved and A's alternative needs for these O_i, it may become necessary to change courses of action or to devote additional energy and resources to the problem of finding ways of replenishing them at a more rapid rate.

Therefore the constraints imposed by resource depletion will generally be greater for weaker parties than stronger ones and also for parties that are engaged in many simultaneous confrontations rather than a single one. The greater A's need to continue the course of action over a very long period, the greater this particular kind of constraint and the greater the corresponding need to assure itself that a steady source of replenishment can be found, either by developing its own capabilities or by relying on coalition partners. Also, where A perceives that B is likely to have a serious problem of resource depletion we would anticipate that A will rely on efforts to weaken coalitions between B and the C_i, to rely heavily on defensive strategies that require B to expend a high degree of effort at the risk of lowered efficiency, and to attempt to prolong the confrontation to take advantage of the exhaustion of B's supply of O_i.

2. *Lack of Time.* Certain courses of action require more time than others, especially where there are problems of coordination or there is a need to gain greater knowledge or to accumulate O_i. Therefore if action must be taken very rapidly this may have to be at the cost of lowered efficiency because a good many courses of action may have to be eliminated. Sometimes temporal constraints may be imposed by the rules of the game or by conditions imposed by third parties or other aspects of the environment. In other instances the temporal constraints may be primarily functions of the motivational states of the parties A and B themselves, in which case they may be modifiable by changes in utilities or subjective probabilities. For instance, A may initially wish to control B's behavior very rapidly but may come to realize that this cannot be accomplished without a considerable cost, in which case a shift in time perspective may occur in order to permit the use of less costly or risky courses of action. Thus we should not look upon temporal constraints in absolute terms but rather as factors that themselves can be modified at some cost or change in priorities.

3. *Moral, Normative, or Legal Constraints.* Many courses of action are effectively ruled out because they are considered unethical, inappropriate, or actually illegal. In such instances we would say that their implementation would involve additional outcomes entailing costs to the actor, in the form of either self-imposed sanctions, such as guilt, or the fear of punishments from other parties, including the supernatural. Here we recognize the importance of ideologies, not only in connection with the emphasis on normative constraints but also in terms of the degree to which they are ambiguous in permitting deviations under a wide variety of circumstances. In general, the more ambiguous the ideological system and the greater A's autonomy in interpreting the ideology, the fewer the constraints on A's behaviors.

Whenever certain of the C_i are in a position to interpret the ideology with some "authority," as, for example, a priesthood or judicial body, the more necessary it becomes for A to form a coalition with these parties so as to modify these normative constraints. This would seem especially necessary whenever the degree of consensus within A is low, so that there is a risk of alienating a sizable segment of A's members if the means being used are denounced by an authoritative body as incompatible with the normative constraints. To the degree that A's members uniformly attach very high utility values to goals directly relevant to the confrontation, however, we expect that the constraining effects of normative or ideological systems will be minimal, given the flexibility and ambiguities that usually characterize such systems. If the power confrontation is a prolonged one it may also become possible to modify the ideology in question, or at least to find loopholes that in effect define the desired course of action to be legitimate under special circumstances.

4. *Lack of Consensus on Means.* Whenever the members of A do not agree

on legitimate or desirable courses of action we may expect that certain extreme courses will have to be ruled out, or at least that they cannot be sustained over a long period. There is more likely to be a "least-common-denominator" phenomenon involving a search for those courses of action that satisfy all important segments, even at the expense of greater efficiency. Or, if there is an internal struggle within A to control policy, we are likely to see major vacillations in choices of means, as one or the other faction gains temporary control. As we shall discuss below, such vacillations are more likely to characterize weak parties than stronger ones, if only because the probabilities of success will be lower in the case of weaker parties. Having tried one course of action and failed, a weak party's leadership is likely to be successfully challenged whenever a high degree of dissensus exists. Any means that requires speedy action is also likely to be constrained by a lack of consensus unless there is a high internal concentration of power. We would therefore expect that a lack of consensus will tend to favor defensive strategies over offensive ones and also (as previously noted) to make it much more difficult to rely on secrecy and deception.

5. *Lack of Knowledge and Failure to Consider Certain Alternatives.* As we noted in chapter 4 in connection with our discussion of satisficing strategies, certain courses of action may be eliminated either because they never occur to the actor or because they would be dependent upon a degree of knowledge that is not available or that would be too costly to obtain. This lack of knowledge may involve either a lack of expertise in the use of the means in question (e.g., lack of training or the inability to construct a particular weapon or means of defense) or a lack of information as to the probability that the means will actually be effective. Where the duration of the power confrontation is expected to be short, it simply may not be feasible to attempt to improve this knowledge base. Therefore a lack of knowledge is likely to be a more important constraining factor in short-range confrontations than in those that are expected to be more prolonged.

Since obtaining knowledge generally requires the allocation of scarce O_i from other more immediate uses, the knowledge constraint is likely to be a more severe one for weaker parties than stronger ones. Where there are surveillance costs involved, these costs may have the effect of constraining parties to means that encourage self-surveillance and trust on the part of the other actor, as, for example, a preference for utilizing rewards over punishments and a reliance on referent power and convincing behavior. Finally, whenever the duration of a confrontation is expected to be long, it becomes necessary to distinguish between short-run and long-run consequences of a given course of action, and in general the latter will be more difficult to assess. To the degree that an actor is primarily concerned with long-term consequences, it therefore becomes more important to employ those means that are believed to be most easily assessed in terms of their consequences. Other things being equal, this is likely to favor those means that have successfully been used in the past, in constrast with those that are relatively untried.

6. *Reduced Flexibility Due to Committed Resources.* There are many circumstances under which it may be necessary for A to commit itself to a course of action and to invest resources in this course so as to improve efficiency. This is especially likely whenever a definite sequence of actions is needed, so that once committed to action a, the actor must follow this by action b, and so forth. Abramson et al. (1958), in discussing how one actor's power is restricted whenever certain alternative courses of action are closed, seem to imply that commitments have the consequence of reducing an actor's power, since they may foreclose certain alternative lines of actions. This is obviously not necessarily the case, however, since the course of action selected may be a highly efficient one and since a commitment of resources to this course may make it still more efficient relative to others.

Whether such commitments actually reduce A's net power, as applied, will depend on many other factors, including the stability of the environment or circumstances under which the power confrontation occurs, the degree to which surprise and deception are needed, the proportion of A's resources that are expended by the commitment, and the degree to which coalition partners can be induced to compensate for the commitment. Other things being equal, we would expect A to avoid a high degree of commitment to a given course of action whenever the situation appears to be highly changeable or ambiguous, whenever it is difficult to evaluate the efficiencies of alternative means, whenever A wishes to rely primarily on an offensive strategy and on deception, and whenever A's total supply of resources is small as compared with B's.

It should be noted that in many circumstances the A versus B confrontation may be secondary as compared with other objectives for either party. If so, one party may have committed its resources to such a degree that its alternatives with respect to the other party are very much limited. This does not necessarily mean that this will be to the second party's advantage, however. Suppose, for example, that party A consists of plantation owners and B of slaves. The owners obviously have a major commitment to a particular form of economy and to a system of economic and political control over the slaves. Should there be major downward shifts in the price of the crop being produced, this may force the plantation owners to extract increasing amounts of work from their slaves in order to compete successfully in the world economy. If so, the courses of action of both parties may be constricted, but this does not necessarily imply that B will gain at the expense of A. In fact if A's alternative courses of action were widened, perhaps to include the cultivation of other kinds of crop, this could very well result in the weakening of A's control over B because of A's decreased dependence upon B to produce a single item for a highly specialized market.

Constraints on Combinations of Means

We should note briefly that there may be constraints on the joint operation of certain combinations of means, as well as on the individual means. First, there may be logical incompatibilities in the sense that it is impossible to do both something and its opposite. We suspect that such logical constraints are much more rare than one might expect, unless we define our courses of action in such a way that polar opposites are treated as separate alternatives. Thus it is impossible both to kill and not to kill one's opponent. But where courses of action may vary by degree, as we believe is most often the case, it is possible to select a single course of action somewhere in between two extreme alternatives. For example, one may injure one's opponent to varying degrees without going to the extreme of killing. One may likewise alternate between two apparently opposite courses of action, such as rewarding and punishing or convincing and threatening. In fact, under certain conditions such a mixed strategy between supposedly incompatible means may be an advantageous one. Under others, as, for example, where a trusting relationship between A and B is essential, such a mixed strategy may be a very ineffective one. In this case the incompatibility may be a genuine constraint on A's behavior.

Perhaps a more common type of joint constraint is one in which several possible courses of action all require the same depletable resources, so that resources expended on one means cannot be used for another. Here it is obvious that the degree of constraint will depend upon the total supply of resources or O_i that can be allocated to the confrontation at issue, and, of course, on the rate of depletion relative to the actor's anticipated duration of the confrontation. Therefore, relatively powerful actors and actors that anticipate a very speedy victory will be less constrained than those actors that have fewer total resources to commit or those that foresee a prolonged contest. Again, the actors may not be confronted with an "either/or" situation, since it will often be possible to select intermediate or moderate levels for each of several courses of action. There will nevertheless be a constraint on the total expenditure of resources, implying that increases along one dimension will have to be accompanied by decreases along another.

There is also the possibility that one course of action will have an effect on B or C_i that may be partly negated or even exactly canceled out by a second course of action, so that if one segment of A is behaving in one fashion toward B, whereas a second segment is behaving so as to negate the effects of the first segment, the net impact may be very slight. This type of incompatibility appears to be reasonably common, at least in the minds of those who are concerned that a diversity of means or extremely loose coordination among members is likely to have this kind of effect. For example, if certain members of A are trying to give B the impression that force will be met with an even greater counterforce, whereas other members of A convey the impression that they do not wish to apply force, or that they are eager to compromise, the net effect may be to convince B that A will be immobilized.

There are circumstances under which an apparently inconsistent policy may really not be so at all, however. Consider the following possibility: Course of action 1 will have the effect of increasing A's own mobilization effort but is also likely to increase B's as well. Course 2 is expected to reduce B's mobilization effort, however. Perhaps course 1 involves an appeal to in-group loyalties by blaming one's adverse circumstances on one's enemy. Such an appeal may also heighten the fears of members of the opposing party, but if it is simultaneously accompanied by a second course of action that reduces these fears, then the two courses of action are compatible in the sense that their joint application will increase in-group mobilization without having any major effect on the mobilization of the other party. If the second course of action also reduced in-group mobilization, then the two courses of action would have opposite effects on *both* dimensions or outcomes and would be largely incompatible.

Finally, we may just mention a few additional possibilities. Conceivably, rules or moral principles may operate to place restraints on the *joint* use of certain means, whereas they do not constrain the use of either means singly. It is rather difficult to find really good illustrations of this possibility. It is also conceivable that there may be certain practical reasons why it may be difficult to combine several distinct means, perhaps because of problems of coordination, timing, or a lack of technical knowledge. Factional disputes may result in compromises that in effect rule out certain combinations of means while permitting others for which the resulting package can be "sold" to a maximum number of participants, thereby achieving a higher degree of mobilization than would have been possible with a different combination.

Dilemmas Faced by Weak Parties

As implied several times in our previous discussion, constraints are likely to be more severe in the case of parties that have limited resources and little control over the rules that regulate their interactions with stronger parties. Not only will certain alternative means be effectively cut off, either because of a severe depletion of resources or a fear of punitive action by stronger parties, but relatively weak parties will often face situations in which the objective probabilities of success are very low. In the case of weak parties that are also subordinate or dominated groups such as minorities or small nations, this low probability of success is also likely to be accompanied by goals to which there have been attached extremely high utilities. In particular, the goals of achieving independence from dominance and gaining revenge through aggression are likely to be very important in such instances, even where they may not be overtly expressed because of a fear of suppression.

This combination of high utilities and low objective and subjective probabilities is apt to generate a high degree of dissensus over means, as well as vacillation in policy. Whenever a particular strategy seems to result in tangible gains, there is likely to be an immediate shift to this strategy. But this may be followed by disillusionment once it is realized that the gains are more limited than previously realized, that they are difficult to consolidate, or that the means in question may also have had indirect consequences that are not so favorable. Changes in leadership and ideological underpinnings are also likely to occur with shifts in strategy, with the net result that overall coordination of policy is made all the more difficult.

Because of these very high utility values, slight changes in subjective probabilities are likely to have important implications for choices among means. Since there will inevitably be ambiguities involved in assessing the impacts of these alternative courses of action, however, these subjective probabilities are unlikely to be anchored in terms of objective probabilities or relative frequencies of success. Therefore the impact of ideological systems may be considerable in the case of subordinate groups. Dominant groups that are in secure positions vis-à-vis these weaker groups are more likely to be characterized by a relative indifference to alternative strategies or belief systems pertaining to the confrontation *unless* these impinge rather directly on certain of their immediate interests. We have, for instance, the familiar thesis advanced by Myrdal (1944) that white Americans are largely indifferent to and conveniently ignorant of the state of most American blacks.

One of the major dilemmas faced by a weak group is that of whether or not to attempt to resolve the confrontation by disappearing as a distinct party or by retreating or surrendering. In the case of racial and ethnic minorities there are basically two kinds of solution of this nature, but unfortunately for the subordinate group neither can be achieved without the cooperation of the dominant party. The first is to attempt to integrate or to become as much as possible like the dominant group, so that its members may pass into the latter group. If this strategy is followed it obviously becomes difficult to stress the group's uniqueness, to call for in-group loyalty and sacrifice, or to attempt to mobilize members for a power confrontation.

The second way a subordinate group may attempt to avoid the power confrontation is through retreat. In effect, the strategy is to ask to be left alone and either to isolate itself in an area that is undesirable to the dominant party or to rely heavily on a defensive strategy that depends on making it too costly for the dominant group to attempt to invade the territory in question. These alternative strategies of approach and withdrawal, which will be discussed in later chapters, appear to be virtually incompatible, though, of course, it is conceivable that some members of the subordinate group could achieve one solution, while others achieved the opposite one. Perhaps there can be approach in some respects and withdrawal in the others. More likely, there will be vacillation between the two depending on the circumstances and policies of the dominant group, as illustrated in the case of black–white relationships in the United States (Wilson 1973). Regardless, there will be a major dilemma of strategy for members of the subordinate group, with the result that disagreements and confusion are likely to occur.

A second kind of dilemma confronting relatively weak groups concerns the extent to which reliance should be placed on coalitions with several different kinds of third party, where such third parties exist. Any coalition will presumably increase the total number of resources available, though possibly increasing problems of coordination and mobilization. But there will be the added problem of assessing costs in terms of loss of autonomy and the possibility that one's coalition partner may merely switch places with one's present opponent. Three kinds of potential coalition partner are: (1) parties that are rivals or approximate equals with the dominant party; (2) parties that stand in essentially the same relationship to the superordinate party as does the subordinate party in question (e.g., other minorities or small nations); and (3) members of the dominant party who may defect from it or at least support the subordinate group.

The first kind of coalition partner is presumably powerful enough to be of substantial help, but there is the risk that it may merely replace the dominant group and even oppress the subordinate group to a greater degree. Parties that are in a similar position to the subordinate group are more likely to have common interests but are also likely to be in a competitive relationship with it. In particular they may wish to avoid a confrontation with the dominant group and may see themselves in a more favorable position to achieve their objectives by other means. They may also fear subordination to another minority or may believe that their interests are fundamentally incompatible with those of the other subordinate parties. Therefore the dominant party may be in a position to play one group off against another, especially if there are major differences among them or if there are time lags between the implementation of their similar strategies. For instance, one subordinate group may have already undergone a highly militant phase and achieved certain gains as a result. It may stand to lose these gains if it were to ally itself with a somewhat less powerful subordinate party.

Attempts to break off members of the dominant group also have their advantages and disadvantages, the latter including the necessity of eliminating certain extreme courses of action that would alienate these potential allies. In general, the greater the diversity of one's coalition partners, the greater the restrictions placed on alternative means and the greater the risk that the coalitions can be only very loosely coordinated. An exception to this general observation may occur, however, if the coalition partners have available to them complementary types of resources that permit a greater diversity of action alternatives.

Finally, there will be dilemmas revolving around the problem of raising one's own degree and efficiency of mobilization relative to those of the opponent. A subordinate party is often weak because of a relatively low level of resources, at least those that can be mobilized on a short-term basis. Therefore, it must rely on a higher level of mobilization than its opponent. As we have just indicated, a weak party that is also in a subordinate relationship can be expected to attach high utilities to goals that involve a reduction in this subordination or dependence. A stronger party, in contrast, may be largely indifferent or at least have a low level of mobilization unless aroused. The problem for the subordinate party, then, is to find ways of achieving steady gains, thereby raising the subjective probabilities of its members, while at the same time not arousing the stronger group to a higher level of mobilization.

One way to achieve this is to attempt to create dissension within the dominant group, perhaps by splitting off a sizable segment that is sympathetic to the subordinate group. For example, the nonviolent protest movement among predominantly southern blacks in the 1960s seemed to be oriented to this objective, in part through the device of enticing extremist reactions that would create sympathy among those whites who were less directly involved in the immediate issues. In order to raise the subjective probabilities of subordinate group members sufficiently to increase mobilization efforts, however, it may be necessary to produce tangible gains at an accelerating or at least steady rate. These gains may, of course, raise the anxiety level of the dominant group sufficiently to increase its own mobilization levels and thereby counteract the increases within the subordinate party.

If the subordinate party can work on objectives that have high priority to itself but low priority to the dominant group, it may be possible to raise the one level of mobilization without increasing the other. This principle was noted by Myrdal (1944) in his discussion of his famous "rank-order-of-discriminations hypothesis." In effect, Myrdal argued that objectives that are most important to blacks are apt to be least important to whites, so that their preferences are roughly in reverse order. Even if this were strictly true, however, it is clear that somewhere in the black hierarchy we would reach a point where the white utilities attached to a given form of discrimination would be sufficiently high that efforts to achieve further gains would be likely to arouse a stiff opposition and even possibly a backlash that had the effect of undoing the results of previous actions.

In brief, if a subordinate group is attempting to achieve objectives that are strongly opposed by members of the dominant group, then it becomes extremely difficult to find ways of increasing mobilization in the subordinate group without also arousing an even stronger opposition within the party that has the advantage of greater resources. At this point the weaker group faces a dilemma of choosing between a strategy aimed at increasing its own mobilization or one of attempting to reduce that of the dominant group.

CONCLUDING REMARKS

Perhaps it is wise, at this point, to return to some observations made in our introductory chapter. We have encountered in our discussion of power an extremely large number of variables that will obviously be very difficult to measure. Yet we believe that these variables, and others, are important ones in all but the simplest forms of power confrontations. Therefore if they are totally ignored one's account will to that extent be incomplete, if not actually misleading. Admittedly, however, a single investigator with limited time and resources cannot possibly hope to deal with all this complexity without becoming almost totally discouraged in the process.

What, then, are the implications? First, we have strongly advocated the desirability of stating one's assumptions as explicitly as possible. These will often take the form of assertions to the effect that certain variables are assumed to be constants in a given setting or that certain coefficients are assumed to be approximately zero. The former kind of assumption (constancy) may then motivate other investigators to compare the situation being analyzed with others for which the factors treated as constant either vary or have constant values at other levels. The second (zero coefficient) type of assumption may motivate others to examine very different situations with a view to determining the conditions under which a given variable or set of variables may safely be neglected. In either case, the explicit statement of such simplifying assumptions serves as a challenge to other investigators to make specific kinds of comparisons.

Second, even in situations where measurement must be very imprecise, we believe some sort of crude measurement is preferable to neglecting the variables altogether. One can do better than the simple dichotomy "present" versus "absent," so that three or four levels of each important variable can be distinguished. If such measurement efforts are accompanied by reasonably thorough discussions of the procedures being used, so that crude replications become possible, then a cumulative process may be set in motion. What this implies is that extreme perfectionism with respect to measurement procedures can be inhibitive of any efforts to measure the most difficult variables. From here it is an easy step to neglecting them altogether and to a kind of convenient ignorance of their importance. In addition, we recommend that the investigator make a qualitative statement concerning the approximate levels of any variables that must be treated as constants in the particular setting being described.

Third, this degree of complexity obviously calls for a much more closely coordinated division of labor and consensus on measurement operations than is yet in evidence in the social sciences. Clearly, if every investigator goes about a study of power—or of any other complex social process—with the idea that he or she will develop totally unique instruments that seem best suited to that particular setting, then cumulation will be extremely slow. It will be almost impossible to disentangle substantive disputes from methodological ones. In short, complexity in the phenomena we are trying to study virtually dictates that the scale of the research be large, and this in turn requires a reasonable degree of consensus on concepts, dimensionalized variables, and measurement operations. This does not imply that modifications can never be made, but only that this process of gradual improvement and refinement needs to be conducted in a rational and coordinated fashion.

NOTES

1. By *shared goals* we do *not* mean similar goals involving scarce resources, such that the attainment of A's goal reduces the probability of B's also achieving the goal. Thus if A and B both want the same job or piece of land we would

consider this to be a G_2-type goal, rather than a G_1 goal. But if A and B *both* desire that A receive the job, this would constitute a shared goal of type G_1. A possible distinction that we have not been able to exploit in this chapter is between G_1 goals that are divisible (e.g., money or land) and those that are not. We are treating both as instances of shared goals.

2. A certain kind of optimistic fatalism, as exemplified by Communist beliefs in the inevitability of historical processes, may enable an ideological emphasis on conformity and centralization to coexist with a more long-range time perspective.

3. The reader should keep in mind that the U's in this diagram refer to understandability or clarity of criteria and *not* to utilities, which have been absorbed into the notion of goals G_i.

4. Note that we are here referring to a *single* goal, while assessing the compatibility of several alternative means. It is also possible that the particular means used to achieve, say, G_1 will reduce the probability of achieving a second goal, say G_2. If this holds true for all courses of action open to actor A, then the *goals* G_1 and G_2 will also be incompatible for actor A. More generally, if actor A wishes to achieve several goals simultaneously, this will restrict the choices among alternative courses of action. (Blalock 1967*b*:40.)

5. Although the notion of dependence is not quite the same as that of dominance, as discussed above in connection with G_7, it may turn out that the distinction between them will have little practical value in most empirical applications. In theory, however, actor B may be highly dependent on A without A's dominating B in the sense of *actually* controlling B's behaviors. Also recall that in our earlier discussion of dependence in the chapter on exchange processes we emphasized that dependence is a function not only of the control of alternative sources of supply but *also* of the actor's expected utilities for various outcomes affected by these sources of supply.

PART THREE

Allocation and Approach–Withdrawal Processes

CHAPTER 10

Allocation I: Allocation Processes and Discrimination

ONE OF THE CENTRAL PREMISES of this book is that actors attempt to achieve valued outcomes through their actions. In part 1 we presented a detailed model of the manner in which they estimate the subjective expected utilities of their potential actions and choose those actions that they believe will bring them the outcomes they desire. The exchange and power processes described in the previous section represent two common ways in which actors acting on the basis of their subjective expected utilities attempt to achieve these outcomes. In this and the succeeding two chapters we analyze discrimination, another common process characterizing the achievement of valued outcomes in intergroup relations.

In the case of exchange processes outcomes are achieved through the development of relationships between actors with complementary interests. Actor *A* receives from actor *B* an outcome that *A* values, and *A* gives to *B* in return an outcome that *B* values. Consequently exchange processes involve the *mutual* achievement of valued outcomes by parties to the exchange and tend to create bonds of interdependence between the parties. These processes therefore may be seen as underlying many consensual models of society.

Power processes are typically characterized by opposing interests of the actors involved. Actor *A* receives from actor *B* an outcome that *A* values, but this constitutes an action that *B* would prefer not to enact. Or actor *A* prevents *B* from attaining a goal that *B* desires. In such processes the dependence of one party upon the other promotes the *unilateral* rather than the mutual achievement of desired outcomes, as the dependent party has less power than the independent party to avoid complying with the latter's desires. Thus these processes may be seen to provide the basis for conflict theories of society. Conflict, it will be remembered, we have defined as the exchange of negative utilities.

413

Despite these outward differences between the two types of process, they do not represent mutually exclusive categories. For one thing, both of them are characterized by a normative component. In exchange situations normative boundaries primarily involve the consequences of the exchange. In our discussion of equity and distributive justice we analyzed the comparisons of inputs, outcomes, and social characteristics made by participants to an exchange. Apparent inequalities in what each party to the exchange receives in comparison to his or her contribution precipitate the sense of a normative violation. Power confrontations are also bounded to some degree by normative agreements, but these agreements generally refer to the manner in which outcomes are achieved rather than to the ultimate outcomes. Actors exerting power over others may be sanctioned by concerned third parties for going outside the bounds of fair play in the pursuit of their objectives.

Probably more important is the tendency of exchange situations to contain elements of power situations and vice versa. An inequality of resources between the parties to an exchange will very likely influence the rate of exchange that is established. Parties with greater resources may set the terms of the exchange or may be willing to invest a greater proportion of their objective properties or resources in order to obtain a desired outcome. Furthermore, even though we have characterized an exchange as yielding a mutual achievement of desired outcomes, it is possible that the parties involved will have conflicting interests regarding outcomes external to the exchange.

Similarly, power situations may involve an exchange of positive utilities, with the more powerful party achieving compliance by "bribing" the other party through promises of positive–utility outcomes, contingent upon enactment of the desired action. This pattern will be most probable in situations in which the difference in resources between the two parties is relatively great, so that the actor with greater resources will have little to lose by the additional expenditure of resources. In a situation of this type, then, there will be a tendency toward the mutual achievement of desired outcomes.

Although we have phrased our discussion to this point in terms of the achievement of desired outcomes, we should note that it is also applicable to gaining access to the *means* for attaining desired outcomes, or what might be called performance rights. In part 1 we noted a general problem characteristic of means–goals analyses, namely, the difficulty of differentiating between means and goals, given the sequencing of behaviors and outcomes. What may appear to be a goal at one point in time (e.g., gaining admittance to college) may be seen at a later point in time as actually having been a means to another goal (e.g., obtaining a high-status occupation). Thus whether a particular desired outcome is labeled a goal or a means depends partly upon the time at which one makes the judgment. Nevertheless, it seems necessary to make this distinction in some cases, especially those involving power. A power contest may very well be focused on gaining access to the resources on which actual power is based. Thus, attaining money has little use as an end in itself. Instead it has use as a resource for attaining other outcomes that may provide utility. Participants in a power confrontation therefore may either be striving to achieve (or prevent) outcomes that only one of them desires, or they may be striving for the resources to achieve (or prevent) these and other outcomes at some future time.

EXCHANGE, POWER, AND THE DISTRIBUTION OF VALUED OUTCOMES

A somewhat less obvious consequence of exchange and power processes, in addition to the mutual or unilateral achievement of outcomes (or means), is the distribution of valued outcomes among actors. One might anticipate that exchange processes would yield relatively egalitarian distributions of these outcomes while power processes would yield skewed distributions, but this is not necessarily the case. Power contests may be initiated by those possessing fewer resources for the express purpose of reducing inequalities. Through superior mobilization of their resources and/or the formation of coalitions with third parties they may achieve this result. Conversely, depending upon the utilities of the actors involved and the value of the social "commodities" that are being traded, exchange processes may lead toward a maldistribution of valued outcomes.

Therefore an analysis of the impact of exchange and power processes upon the distribution of valued outcomes (and means) among actors is of equal importance to the analysis of the dynamics of such processes. The resultant distribution of outcomes and means will constitute a major determinant of subsequent exchanges and power confrontations. It will influence the supply of commodities available for exchange, the rates of exchange, and the power resources available to actors. This effect can be seen at the level of the individual actor also. As we pointed out in part 1, actors' perceived resources will constitute one of the determinants of their subjective probabilities and may thereby affect their utilities. This fact complicated our behavioral model, but it indicates more clearly the effect of the distribution of outcomes at one point in time on behaviors at a subsequent point in time. So even though we have not emphasized the distributive consequences of exchange and power processes in our prior discussions these consequences should be recognized.

THE ALLOCATION OF VALUED OUTCOMES

Exchange and power processes constitute relatively unstructured mechanisms for the distribution of valued outcomes among actors. In fact, their effects on this distribution may be considered largely unintended consequences of actors' pursuit of desired outcomes, or in most cases at least secondary in importance to the achievement of outcomes for the actors involved. But they are not the only social processes affecting the distribution of outcomes. Processes that are relatively more structured or formalized are also present in a variety of situations. The greater structure of these processes may be represented by referring to them as mechanisms for the *allocation* of desired outcomes among actors. This term implies that the distribution of outcomes and means is the primary function of these processes rather than being secondary in importance, as in the case of exchange and power processes.

These relatively formalized processes for the allocation of valued outcomes become more and more important as societal complexity increases. In very simple societies exchange and power processes may completely determine the distribution of valued outcomes among societal members. Those with greater physical strength or more ingenuity in forming exchange relationships may amass a greater proportion of valued outcomes than those lacking these characteristics, but the discrepancy may not be sufficient to produce dissatisfaction among those who are less well off. At a slightly higher level of complexity the allocation of certain valuable outcomes may come under the aegis of a leader, such as the headman of a tribe, or a small elite. In a highly complex society a variety of "gatekeepers" will very likely be established to allocate the manifold outcomes and means, some of which may be necessary for continued societal functioning, sought by members of that society.

These allocation processes have several characteristic features. First, they involve an identifiable allocator. This role may be filled by actors having direct control over the outcomes to be allocated, for example, a business owner who allocates jobs. Or the role may be delegated to other actors by those who do have direct control over the outcomes, as in the case of a corporation with a personnel office. The allocative role may also have a specific or a diffuse locus. When identifiable actors fill the role, as in the two examples just cited, the locus is specific. In a complex society there will also be diffuse loci of allocation, such as the legal system, controlling valued outcomes or means. Within that system, however, there will also be specific allocators, such as judges and law enforcement officers.

Second, there will be two or more actors desiring the outcomes and/or means being allocated who represent "applicants," or "candidates," for them. These actors may be seen as presenting a variety of characteristics to the allocator that constitute qualifications for the receipt of the outcomes/means. The allocator takes these characteristics into account in decisions regarding how the outcomes/means will be allocated.

Third, the outcomes being allocated are generally, although not necessarily, subject to the constraints of scarcity, so that not all who are seeking the outcomes/means obtain them. The outcomes/means may be either continuous or discrete, with receiving a job an example of the former and being allocated a certain salary an example of the latter.

Fourth, the allocation of outcomes is based upon some standard, or distribution rule, that varies in explicitness in different situations. It may be advertised by the allocator before or after the allocation is made, or it may be inferred by the recipients and nonrecipients of the outcomes/means, or by interested third parties, after the allocation is completed.

These four characteristics therefore indicate that allocation processes are formally identical to the indirect-exchange situations described in chapter 5. This is shown by figure 10.1, which represents an allocator, *A,* and two candidates, *B* and *C. B* and *C* are each involved in a direct exchange with *A*—qualifications in exchange for the outcome—and in an indirect exchange with each other. Furthermore, we have noted that exchange situations are likely to be subjected to equity/distributive justice judgments. If an exchange is judged to be inequitable or unjust it precipitates the sense of moral indignation characteristic of a normative violation rather than the disappointment resulting merely from unrealized expectations. Allocation processes are also likely to involve such judgments, particularly on the part of those candidates who do not receive the desired outcome.

There are also significant similarities between allocation processes and power situations. First, the applicants and the allocator represent two parties with different resources, with the allocator in control of outcomes/means that are desired by the applicants. The applicants therefore are dependent upon the allocator for obtaining the outcome, but the allocator may also be dependent upon them to a degree. The degree of dependence of the allocator will depend upon the number of applicants relative to the number of outcomes to be allocated and upon the value of the applicants' characteristics to the allocator. Second, the achievement of outcomes will be unilateral when a comparison is made between the allocator and nonrecipients, although it may be considered mutual for the allocator and recipients.

Third, control of allocation processes may be one of the major means by which members of one group maintain their position of superior power over another group. To the extent that the former control important allocative roles or are able to specify the distribution rule for the allocation process they have the capability to allocate valued outcomes/means to themselves and to prevent members of another group from gaining access to them. By contrast, the more dependent a subordinate group is upon a dominant group for the allocation of desired outcomes/means, the less able they will be to challenge the existent distribution rules or their application.

So allocation processes constitute a major mechanism in complex societies for manipulation of the distribution of valued outcomes. They should be re-

Figure 10.1. Model of Allocation Processes

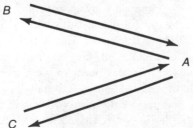

garded as one of the major determinants of the distribution of power and privilege in such societies.

Discriminatory Allocations

It is to processes of this type that the term *discrimination* is most often applied. Some allocations of outcomes/means are claimed to be discriminatory; others are regarded as nondiscriminatory. Characteristically the former judgment is accompanied by expressions of moral indignation. The implication is that certain outcomes/means have been allocated in an unfair manner, but the precise basis for the conviction that a moral violation has occurred is not always clear. We believe that considering discrimination within the context of allocation processes will help to clarify its nature.

First, discriminatory situations can generally be viewed as involving the four characteristics of allocation processes described previously. Specific allocators, such as employers, teachers, and policemen, may be charged with discriminatory behavior, with the last of these accused of allocating punishments unfairly. Or the allegation of discrimination may be directed at a diffuse allocator. The economic system of a society may be criticized for discriminating against non-whites and women. In addition, the charge is made only when more than one actor is striving for a particular outcome/means and when there is an unequal allocation. And the charge of discriminatory behavior is usually directed at the distribution rule that is perceived to be operative in the situation.

A situation involving discrimination, therefore, can be viewed as a special case of the more general class of equity/distributive justice situations described previously. Like equity/distributive justice situations, cases involving discrimination involve a comparison of outcomes with some other factor, which one would expect to be either the inputs of the actors involved or their social characteristics. Because a discrimination situation represents a case of *indirect* exchange, such comparisons will be made between the applicants rather than between an applicant and the allocator. Like equity/distributive justice situations also, discrimination situations evoke convictions that a normative violation has occurred. The only major difference between the two situations appears to be that in one case an unsatisfactory allocation of outcomes is labeled as discriminatory while in the other case it is considered inequitable or unjust.

But discrimination situations, like allocation processes in general, also bear a strong resemblance to power processes. Discrimination represents a major means whereby members of a dominant group can maintain their power position by allocating valued outcomes disproportionately to their own group. The proponents of the "vicious circle" model of discrimination have vividly described the implications of discrimination for the maintenance of power differences between racial groups. From this point of view, a discriminatory allocation of outcomes at one point in time handicaps those who are its victims in subsequent allocations, simply because a future allocation will be dependent upon a prior allocation. For example, if one is to receive a college degree he or she must previously have been admitted to college. Thus the effects of discriminatory allocations may cumulate and increase the power differences between groups. There is also a growing body of research attempting to determine which members of the dominant white group in the United States specifically benefit from racial discrimination (cf. Reich 1972; Glenn 1966; Szymanski 1976).

In the case of race relations in this country there have been countervailing processes that have prevented the vicious circle from reaching the point where less powerful groups are completely excluded from desired outcomes/means. We shall not discuss these in detail here but simply note that they have included attempts to reallocate outcomes and to change distribution rules. The dominant white group has also not had complete control over the allocation of outcomes and means. One of the consequences of the physical separation of racial groups has been the duplication of institutions, so that minority-group members have had control over certain selected allocation processes. Also the "applicants" for desired outcomes have consisted predominantly of minority-group members in some cases. These have often involved roles that have had low utility for dominant-group members, for example, various service occupations. This fact, plus the necessity of filling some of these roles in a complex industrial society, has resulted in their being disproportionately allocated to minority-group members.

We have shown that the concept of discrimination applies to situations that may be considered special cases of more general indirect-exchange situations and that a judgment of discrimination can be considered comparable to a judgment of inequity regarding an allocation of outcomes. But we have not specified what distinguishes discriminatory allocations from nondiscriminatory ones. To deal with this problem we turn to the area in which the concept has received the fullest attention: the field of minority-group relations. Because discrimination has occupied a prominent place in theories in that area there have been numerous attempts to conceptualize it. Many of these conceptualizations have not been very precise, however, and conceptual consensus has not been attained. These conceptual inadequacies have in turn hindered attempts to measure the degree of discrimination accurately, and we consider that topic in the following chapter.

Elements of a Conceptualization of Discrimination

It is possible to abstract several conceptual elements from the variety of existing definitions of discrimination. These elements are generally found in combination, for reasons we shall note, and some of them receive greater emphasis than others. We have isolated six such elements or common themes, three of which have been emphasized most often.

Differential Treatment. The modal element in discrimination conceptualizations is differential treatment or, in terms of our above discussion, an unequal allocation of outcomes/means. Generally one thinks in terms of rewarding outcomes being allocated, but it is possible for punishments to be alloted unequally also. In that case the victim of discrimination will be the recipient of the outcome being allocated rather than the nonrecipient.

Since a discrimination situation may be considered a special case of equity/ distributive justice situations, a simple inequality of outcomes is not sufficient to define discriminatory behavior. In chapter 6 we observed that an inequality of outcomes will be considered inequitable if it is disproportional to the inputs plus the values of the social characteristics of the actors participating in an exchange. In a discrimination situation an inequality of outcomes also represents the starting point for making a judgment as to whether the allocation of outcomes is discriminatory, and it is necessary to include additional elements in one's conceptualization.

Criterion. The most prevalent means of specifying conceptually the nature of a discriminatory allocation of outcomes is the inclusion of a second element, which we call the criterion element. The rationale for inclusion of this element is that an allocation of outcomes is based upon the characteristics of the applicants for those outcomes. These characteristics, therefore, constitute the criteria used by allocators in deciding how to allocate outcomes among applicants. The allocation is considered to be discriminatory when some characteristics are the criteria for allocation and nondiscriminatory when other characteristics are the criteria. Or, in equity terms, the allocation is considered discriminatory when certain characteristics constitute at least a partial distribution rule.

What characteristics of applicants make an allocation discriminatory by virtue of their being used as the criteria for allocation? This question has been answered conceptually in two ways. The first way involves the specification of characteristics that automatically make an allocation discriminatory when they are used as criteria. An explicit statement of this is found in Vander Zanden's (1972:26) definition: "overt action in which members of a group are accorded unfavorable treatment on the basis of their religious, ethnic, or racial membership." According to this definition an unequal allocation of outcomes is discriminatory if it is based upon the criterion of religion, ethnicity, or race.

This apparently clear and simple definition conceals much complexity, however, because of the variety of ways in which differential treatment in the form of an unequal allocation of outcomes may be based upon a specific characteristic, such as race. Tables 10.1 through 10.10 illustrate the varied relationships that may be present between differential treatment and a criterion variable. In each case it may be inferred that the differential treatment is "based upon" the criterion, but in some cases the basis is more direct and more obvious than in others.

In these tables we assume two racial groups represented by A and B in the column headed R. An allocation of outcomes is symbolized in the columns, T_i, with an entry of 1 representing reception of an outcome and an entry of 0 representing nonreception of that outcome. Thus the first row in table 10.1 indicates that a member of group A did not receive an outcome. The columns, C_i, in some of the tables indicate whether applicants for outcomes possess another *nonracial* criterion characteristic, such as a high school diploma. An entry of 1 there represents possession and an entry of 0 nonpossession of that characteristic. For each of the tables we have also included the equations representing the relationship between T_i, the treatment; R, the racial criterion; and C_i, the nonracial criterion. For the sake of simplicity we have assumed a frequency of 1 for each row in each table. In real situations, of course, frequencies among rows would vary. We have also represented the C_i and T_i as dichotomous; in actuality they are both likely to be continuous variables. R is assumed to equal 0 for group A and 1 for group B.

Tables 10.1 and 10.2 show the simplest relationship between race and the allocation of outcomes. In table 10.1 T equals R, so that applicants from group B receive the outcome and actors from group A do not. In Table 10.2, which we call the reverse discrimination model, the allocation of outcomes is the opposite, as $T = 1 - R$. In both of these cases it is indisputable that the allocation of outcomes is based upon the racial criterion, and both can be considered as cases of discriminatory behavior. How one labels the discriminatory behavior depends upon the identity of the two groups. Normally reverse discrimination refers to cases in which subordinate-group members instead of dominant-group members are allocated positive outcomes. But it is obvious that in either case the allocation of outcomes is based directly on the racial criterion. In equity terms, race constitutes the distribution rule.

	Table 10.1 Discrimination Model $T = R$			Table 10.2 Reverse Discrimination Model $T = 1 - R$	
R		T		R	T
A		0		A	1
B		1		B	0

Table 10.3, the nondiscrimination model, represents the allocation of outcomes on the basis of a nonracial criterion, with T equal to C. If C represents a high school diploma, then allocation of outcomes on this basis would normally not be regarded as discriminatory, although there is no logical reason to prevent one from regarding it as an example of educational discrimination.

Table 10.3
Nondiscrimination Model
$T = C$

C	T
A	0
B	1

Table 10.4 indicates the pattern of allocation of outcomes when a combination of criterion characteristics is considered. Column T_1 shows the allocation pattern when race is the criterion for differential treatment; column T_2 shows the pattern when the nonracial characteristic is the criterion. Thus with this pattern of outcomes it would be easy to determine the criterion on which the treatment was based.

Table 10.4
Comparison of Discrimination and Nondiscrimination Models

R	C	T_1	T_2
A	0	0	0
B	0	1	0
A	1	0	1
B	1	1	1

But in table 10.5 we introduce a significant complication that will appear to varying degrees in empirical situations. In this case the correlation between R and C is perfect and positive. Or in terms of our above example, only members of group B possess high school diplomas, and consequently only members of that group receive the outcome. The problem, of course, is to determine which of the characteristics, R or C, constitutes the criterion of differential treatment. This is impossible to determine because $T = R = C$.

Table 10.5
Identification Problem
$T = R = C$

R	C	T_1	T_2
A	0	0	0
B	1	1	1

So in tables 10.1 through 10.4 determination of the criterion for differential treatment, or the distribution rule, is simple, and one can easily make judgments about discrimination, if discrimination is defined as differential treatment on the basis of the racial criterion. But when the characteristics of outcome applicants are highly correlated, as in table 10.5, one cannot judge which of the characteristics has served as the criterion.

Assessing the significance of characteristics as criteria is also complicated by the possibility of *indirect* relationships between characteristics and outcomes. In the above examples, allocations of outcomes have been based directly on race or a nonracial characteristic. In tables 10.6 through 10.10 we represent situations in which differential treatment is indirectly based upon the characteristic of race.

In Table 10.6 we see the first of these possibilities, involving the application of different criteria to members of the two racial groups. The indirect influence of race is shown by the equation. The allocation of outcomes is directly based on nonracial criteria, i.e., $T = C_i$, but these criteria are influenced by race, i.e., $i = R + 1$. Members of group A are subjected to criterion C_1, and criterion C_2 is applied to members of group B. If T represents an employment offer, then C_1 may represent a high school diploma and C_2 previous job experience.

The T column shows the allocation of outcomes that results from this indirect influence of the racial criterion. Which of these outcomes is most likely to be regarded as evidence of racial discrimination? Since we have indicated that judgments of discrimination, like equity judgments, are based on comparisons made among the applicants for outcomes, it is probable that individuals #4 and #5 will consider themselves to have been victims of discrimination. Each of them can point to an actor of the other racial group who has received T as a result of possessing a given C_i. Actor #4 can be compared to actor #6 and actor #5 to actor #3. But the fact that an equal number of members of both racial groups will not receive the outcome may make it seem as if the allocation of outcomes was not based on race. This example therefore shows that an equality of outcomes is not prima facie evidence of discrimination *not* being present, assuming that an allocation decision based indirectly on the racial criterion is discriminatory.

Table 10.6
Application of Different Criteria
to Different Groups
$$T = C_i, \text{where } i = R + 1$$

#	R	C_1	C_2	T
1	A	0	0	0
2	B	0	0	0
3	A	1	0	1
4	A	0	1	0
5	B	1	0	0
6	B	0	1	1
7	A	1	1	1
8	B	1	1	1

Table 10.7 represents a possibly more common case in which members of one group are required to fulfill more criteria than members of the other group. The equation $T = \prod_{i=1}^{k} C_i$, where $k = 2 - R$, indicates that those from group A are scrutinized on both C_1 and C_2, while those from group B are judged on only C_1. Or members from group A are required to have both a high school diploma and previous job experience whereas those from group B need have only the diploma to obtain a job.

Table 10.7
Application of More Criteria
to One Group

$$T = \Pi_{i=1}^{k} C_i, \text{ where } k = 2 - R$$

#	R	C_1	C_2	T
1	A	0	0	0
2	B	0	0	0
3	A	1	0	0
4	A	0	1	0
5	B	1	0	1
6	B	0	1	0
7	A	1	1	1
8	B	1	1	1

If this model represents the manner in which characteristics have been used as the criteria for allocating outcomes, then there will be somewhat more evidence of discrimination than with the previous model. An applicant from only one of the groups, #3 from group A, can discover another actor from the other group, #5, who received the outcome that #3 did not receive, although both possessed the same combination of characteristics. The outcomes will also be disproportionately allocated to members of group B. One actor from each group (#4 and #6) may claim that he or she possessed a characteristic that should have qualified him or her for receiving T, but neither will be able to find another applicant who received T while only possessing that same characteristic.

Table 10.8 reveals a common variation on the situation represented by table 10.7. This table depicts a situation in which members of one of the racial groups are required to possess a higher level of a given criterion than are members of the other racial category in order to receive T. The same equation may be used for this table as was used for table 10.7, but it is necessary to restrict the possible values of C_1 and C_2. If we let C_1 represent possession of a high school diploma and C_2 possession of a college diploma, then if $C_1 = 0$, C_2 must also

Table 10.8
Application of Different Levels of
Same Criterion to Different Groups

#	R	C_1	C_2	T
1	A	0	0	0
2	A	1	0	0
3	A	1	1	1
4	B	0	0	0
5	B	1	0	1
6	B	1	1	1

equal zero. If $C_1 = 1$, then C_2 may equal either zero or 1. And, as before, members of group A must possess both C_1 and C_2 whereas members of the other group need have only C_1. The similarity to the situation represented by table 10.7 is obvious. But because of the restriction on possible values for C_2, depending upon the value of C_1, this situation does not yield the somewhat ambiguous cases of actors #4 and #6 in the previous table. We have only the one more clear-cut victim of discrimination, actor #2.

The above three cases, in which differential treatment is indirectly based on race, share the characteristic of being double-standard situations. Differential treatment is based upon the differential application of nonracial criteria rather than upon the direct application of the racial criterion as in the previous models. But the differential application of the nonracial criteria is itself based upon the racial criterion. These three cases, therefore, might be referred to as differential treatment on the basis of race "once removed." It appears desirable to include these cases as examples of discrimination, rather than simply limiting the term to cases in which differential treatment is directly based on the racial criterion. To do so conceptually it will be necessary to take into account both direct and indirect influences of the racial characteristic on differential treatment.

Table 10.9 represents the interesting case of a combination of direct and indirect influences of the racial characteristic on differential treatment. The direct influence is shown by the fact that both members of group B receive T regardless of whether or not they possess C. The indirect influence is present in the fact that members of group A need to have C in order to get T, while members of group B do not. So in this case race—specifically, membership in racial group B—constitutes a sufficient condition for receiving T, but not a necessary condition. Possession of C by a member of group A can compensate for the incorrect value on the racial criterion. A realistic example would be that of a white job applicant receiving employment on the basis of race and a black applicant also being required to possess a high school diploma. Therefore, this case can also be seen as a special case of the situation in which more criteria are applied to one group than to the other. A single criterion is used for group B and two criteria are applied to group A. And in this case actor #1 would likely be judged a victim of discrimination in comparison with actor #2.

Table 10.9
Race as a Sufficient Condition

$$T = R + C_i, \text{ where } i = 1 - R$$

#	R	C	T
1	A	0	0
2	B	0	1
3	A	1	1
4	B	1	1

Finally, table 10.10 depicts the case in which there is a combined influence, or a multiplicative effect, of race and a nonracial characteristic on differential treatment. In table 10.1 and 10.2 race constitutes both a necessary and a sufficient condition for receiving an outcome. In table 10.10 race constitutes a necessary condition for receiving an outcome, but not a sufficient condition. An actor must not only belong to group B in order to receive T, but must also possess C. However, possessing C cannot compensate for the incorrect racial value for a member of group A. The discriminatory nature of the allocation is most apparent in the comparison of actors #3 and #4.

Table 10.10
Race as a Necessary Condition
$$T = R \times C$$

#	R	C	T
1	A	0	0
2	B	0	0
3	A	1	0
4	B	1	1

These examples reveal the variety of ways in which a specific characteristic, in this instance race, can constitute the criterion for an unequal allocation of outcomes. Conceptually it appears most satisfactory to define differential treatment in the form of an unequal allocation of outcomes as discriminatory when it is either *directly* or *indirectly* based on a characteristic such as race. Empirically, however, it may be difficult to determine the characteristics that actually served as the criteria for an unequal allocation of outcomes.

The second way in which the criteria that make an allocation of outcomes discriminatory have been specified has emphasized the relevance of criteria for receiving outcomes. Thus an allocation on the basis of race is considered discriminatory when race is regarded as an irrelevant criterion. Antonovsky's (1960:81) definition—"the effective injurious treatment of persons on grounds rationally irrelevant to the situation"—exemplifies this orientation. Pascal and Rapping (1972:120) describe discrimination as a "discrepancy in treatment between candidates who are identical in all 'relevant' characteristics." The obvious problem with this conceptual strategy is determining which characteristics are relevant criteria for the allocation of particular outcomes or means.

One might argue that a characteristic that was a necessary condition for receiving an outcome or being given access to a means would constitute a relevant criterion. But how is this determination to be made? The difficulty is compounded when continuous rather than discrete outcomes or characteristics are involved. In such cases it may be claimed that race may not be a necessary characteristic for a minimal level of performance, but that it is necessary for a satisfactory level. For example, it may be asserted that it is not necessary for a ghetto policeman to be black, or that a salesman serving a predominantly white clientele be white, but that allocating these jobs on the basis of race is necessary for effective performance. Resorting to a distinction between ascribed and achieved characteristics does not solve this problem because the issue is whether or not ascribed characteristics are ever relevant. So any attempt to conceptualize discrimination in terms of irrelevant criteria is likely to lead to disagreements between advocates of different viewpoints regarding the relevance of these criteria.

Consequences. The third element in current discrimination conceptualizations also attempts to resolve the problem of distinguishing discriminatory and nondiscriminatory allocations of outcomes by referring to the effects of the allocation upon those who are nonrecipients. We refer to this as the consequences element. Burkey's (1971:1-2) definition—"differential treatment by members of a dominant social category which functions to deny or restrict the choices of members of a subordinate social category"—is one of the clearest examples of this approach.

This approach is also problematic because of the difficulty of conceptually denoting the most significant effects of an unequal allocation of outcomes. Burkey's strategy of specifying particular effects—the denial or restriction of choices—may be criticized for not sufficiently encompassing consequences that are discriminatory. The implication, of course, is that an unequal allocation disadvantages one group and favors another group, but, as in the case of the relevance of a criterion, there will likely be differing views regarding the extent to which failure to receive outcomes or means actually constitutes a disadvantage. An extreme example is the apartheid ideology of South Africa, which claims that the provision of separate geographical areas for nonwhites actually is advantageous for them.

In some cases the determination of the degree of disadvantage poses no great problems. Access to education is an important means to a variety of goals. The availability of money is a major determinant of "life chances." It is difficult to see how South African nonwhites benefit from apartheid. But in other cases the situation is less clear. Do restrictions on intermarriage between dominant- and minority-group members disadvantage the latter? Are women disadvantaged if they are not allowed to participate on athletic teams with males?

A partial resolution of this dilemma may be achieved by concentrating on the patterning of outcome and means allocations over time. If favorable outcomes are allocated alternatively between groups, then this pattern will likely be considered less discriminatory than if they are consistently allocated to one group. Thus *systematic* disadvantage, or a consistent failure to allocate apparently favorable outcomes to one group, will be the mark of discriminatory behavior. Still this does not specify which outcomes are favorable or unfavorable and hence is not completely satisfactory.

Goal Conflict. This problem may be approached from a different angle by taking into account a fourth element in current conceptualizations of discrimination, which we refer to as the goal-conflict element. It has been suggested that an unequal allocation of outcomes must conflict with the goals of nonrecipients for it to be considered discriminatory. Allport (1954:50), for example, states that discrimination "comes about only when we deny to individuals or groups of people equality of treatment *which they may wish*" (emphasis added). Thus we might conclude that an unequal allocation of outcomes disadvantages nonrecipients if it conflicts with their goals.

This approach creates several additional problems, however. First, basing a conceptualization solely on this element, without taking into consideration the characteristics of applicants, may lead to erroneous inferences. Any applicant failing to receive a desired outcome as the result of an allocation process may be assumed to have had his or her goals thwarted and to be disadvantaged as a result. But if nonrecipients concluded that their qualifications were less adequate than those of persons who were allocated the outcomes, they would be unlikely to see themselves as victims of discrimination.

Second, it also does not adequately handle actors with atypical goals. One of the claims made by opponents of the Equal Rights Amendment has been that its passage will lead to sexually integrated restrooms and locker rooms. And indeed a member of either sex could claim that access to such facilities normally reserved for the opposite sex constituted an important goal, so that restrictions on access constituted discrimination. In this case it would be necessary to point out that an equal *disadvantage* is present in the situation, since both men and women are restricted from access to the opposite sex's facilities. But in case only one sex were so restricted then the situation would be discriminatory. In other words, the allocation of rights in this former case is equally restrictive for the sexes. The same argument would apply to the case of females on male athletic teams, and in fact in recent years males have been given legal support to participate on female athletic teams.

Third, it is also possible that individuals will not appear to desire outcomes or means that outside observers would agree are important. Thus employers may claim that they have not discriminated against minority-group members because few or none of them presented themselves as applicants for the jobs being allocated. In this case one might argue that these minority-group members are being disadvantaged by not being allocated jobs, and hence they are victims of discrimination. Or one might assert that their failure to apply indicates that the outcome is not an important goal to them so that they have not been discriminated against.

We will analyze this issue in more detail in chapter 12 in our discussion of eligibility pools. Conceptually it appears preferable to restrict the concept of discrimination to cases in which exclusion does conflict with goals. But empirically it is probable that a failure to apply for an outcome cannot be taken at face value as evidence of the unimportance of that outcome. It has repeatedly been argued that one of the effects of discrimination is the molding of expectations of its victims. Thus in terms of the subjective expected utility model, the utility of a particular outcome may be quite high, but the subjective probability of attaining that outcome (receiving the job upon application for it) may be so low that the subjective expected utility of presenting oneself as a candidate is lower than the subjective expected utilities of other alternatives.

The disturbing empirical implication of inclusion of the goal-conflict element in a conceptualization of discrimination is that the goals of subordinate-group members would have to be measured in order to estimate the degree of discrimination. Inclusion of the fifth element in the existing conceptualizations of discrimination carries a similar implication.

Intentionality. This conceptual element complements the goal-conflict element in that it emphasizes the goals of those responsible for allocating outcomes. We call it the intentionality element. Those who include this element suggest that allocations are discriminatory if they are *intended* to disadvantage nonrecipients but nondiscriminatory if they fulfill other goals. For example, Mitchell (1968:58) includes intentionality in his definition—"the use, by a superordinate group, of its superior power to impose customary or legal restrictions and deprivations upon a subordinate group in order to maintain a situation of privilege and inequality." Newman (1973:199) makes intentions and consequences substitutable—"the intent and/or effect of differential treatment is to create a disadvantage of some sort."

Empirically, of course, including this element in one's conceptualization of discrimination would necessitate an investigation of the goals of allocators. This would be difficult in situations in which there were normative standards against the overt expression of discriminatory intentions. But such an investigation appears to be the only means to determine whether discrimination has occurred in cases where the racial characteristic is highly correlated with other characteristics, as we illustrated previously in table 10.5.

Thus two employers having quite different intentions may allocate jobs to applicants in an identical manner. For example, one of them may desire to disadvantage minority-group members whereas the other may be solely interested in obtaining a satisfactory work force. If race is very highly correlated with another characteristic that the latter employer deems important for satisfactory performance on the job, so that he or she perceives minority-group members to lack that characteristic, then he or she will also allocate the majority of jobs to members of the dominant group. Furthermore the former employer may disguise his or her intentions if he or she is aware of the high correlation, while the latter may be accused of discrimination. Intuitively it seems that the former's actions should be regarded as more discriminatory than the latter's, but this could only be determined by a fairly comprehensive analysis of their utilities and subjective probabilities. If that were impossible, one might observe the two employers' allocations over time. If one's choices systematically disadvantaged one group and favored another, and if the racial characteristic were more consistently correlated with the allocation of outcomes than a variety of nonracial characteristics were, then an inference of intention to disadvantage would be somewhat more plausible.

Normative Conflict. The last element included in current discrimination definitions is that of normative conflict. In this case the argument is that an unequal allocation of outcomes on the basis of certain criteria is discriminatory if it conflicts with a dominant normative standard. Yinger (1965:27) highlights this element when he says, "Differential treatment solely on the grounds of race, religion, national origin, ethnic group, class, age or sex is a violation of the dominant American value system and legal structure and is therefore discrimination." Brown (1973) extends this argument by pointing out that discrimination, like many sociological concepts, is value relational, and hence it must always be defined in terms of some standard, which he suggests is usually a social policy. Thus discrimination is similar to the concept of deviance in this respect.

The difficulty created by this element is that it makes discrimination situation specific. If an allocation of outcomes is discriminatory when it conflicts with a dominant normative standard, then one must determine what that standard is empirically or specify it conceptually. Comparisons of quite different situations would require determining the dominant normative standard in each situation. If one assumes that historically there has been greater normative support for discrimination in the southern United States than in the North, then two past allocations of outcomes with the same degree of inequality and the same relationship between criterion characteristics and outcomes would have had differing degrees of discrimination in these two areas.

In a heterogeneous society such as the United States there are likely to be conflicting normative standards, so that it is difficult to ascertain a dominant one. The legal system has formally specified equality of citizenship rights but this norm has obviously not been consistently upheld. "Equality of opportunity but inequality of results" comes closest to a dominant normative standard for the allocation of economic outcomes or means in this society. But given the prevailing degree of disparity in qualifications and resources among different classes and different racial and ethnic groups, inequality of opportunity and inequality of results may just as well be considered the dominant standard.

So just as it has proven impossible for the Supreme Court to specify absolute standards delineating pornographic literature, it is also impossible to specify an absolute normative standard, or an absolute distribution rule, applicable to all cases in which outcomes or means are allocated. The disagreements that we noted earlier in connection with the relevance of criteria for allocations are likely to occur whenever diverse normative standards are present.

We therefore believe that it is preferable *not* to define discrimination in terms of prevailing normative standards. This does not mean, however, that normative standards are insignificant for the analysis of discriminatory behavior. As we shall indicate shortly, they are more satisfactorily included in causal models of the conditions under which discrimination occurs and the responses that it precipitates than in the definition of discrimination itself.

Summary of Existing Conceptualizations of Discrimination

Thus a variety of solutions have been offered for the problem of distinguishing discriminatory allocations of outcomes from nondiscriminatory ones. Two or more of the six elements we have described can be found in some combination in virtually all current conceptualizations of discrimination. Another of Yinger's definitions (1968:449)—"the persistent application of criteria that are arbitrary, irrelevant or unfair by dominant standards, with the result that some persons receive an undue advantage and others, although equally qualified, suffer an unjustified penalty"—is unique in including four of the elements—differential treatment, criterion, normative conflict, and consequences—and possibly a fifth—intentionality—if we regard persistence as evidence of an intention to disadvantage.

Inclusion of some of these elements in a conceptualization of discrimination promises significant complications for measurement of the degree of discrimination. First, we have noted the difficulty of determining the criteria on the basis of which outcomes are allocated when these criteria are highly correlated. Second, determining the extent to which unequal allocations are disadvantageous is also problematic. Third, the goal-conflict and intentionality elements necessitate measurement of the utilities of nonrecipients of outcomes and the utilities and subjective probabilities of outcome allocators, and we have noted the problems that will involve. Fourth, attempting to measure dominant normative standards, particularly across situations, will also be difficult.

One way to distinguish discriminatory from nondiscriminatory allocations and to avoid these empirical problems would be simply to attribute any inequalities between groups to discrimination, on the grounds that both past and present discrimination have been, and are, so pervasive that they are virtually the sole causes of inequalities. We object to this conceptual strategy for two reasons. First, it presents discrimination as an equality rather than an equity/distributive justice concept. As we have shown in our discussion earlier in this chapter, we believe it is preferable to conceptualize discrimination as a special case of equity situations. From our perspective discrimination occurs when outcomes are allocated on the basis of a particular distribution rule. Inequalities of outcomes are not sufficient to define either inequities or discrimination. Rather they must be related to inputs and/or characteristics of the applicants for the outcomes being allocated.

Second, we believe this approach also makes discrimination too broad a concept. Conceptually we believe that discrimination should refer to actions taken by one group toward another group, generally by a dominant group toward a subordinate group. Inequalities of outcomes at one point in time will be partly attributable to discrimination in the outcome allocation, but they are likely also partly attributable to at least three other influences. Discriminatory actions in the past by members of the dominant group may have denied minority-group members outcomes that constituted means for receiving outcomes in the present. Second, members of the subordinate group may not have applied for the outcomes being allocated in the present, either because their utilities for those outcomes were very low or because they saw little likelihood of receiving the outcomes even if they did apply. And third, subordinate-group members may not have sought important outcomes in the past to the same degree that dominant-group members did.

The major empirical problem therefore will be the disentanglement of these four influences—past and present discrimination and past and present actions by minority-group members—on observed inequalities and the determination of their relative significance. It may very well be that current and past discrimination will account for most of the observed disparities empirically. But this should be an empirical conclusion and not one necessitated by a definition of discrimination solely in terms of inequalities.

A "Compromise" Conceptualization of Discrimination

One can follow two rather different strategies for the conceptualization of discrimination. The first is to define it very narrowly, including most or all of the conceptual elements we have described. Thus with this approach discrimination might be defined as: differential treatment (revealed in an unequal allocation of outcomes) by members of one group (usually a dominant group) toward members of another group on the basis of certain criteria (such as social characteristics of the target group) that has systematic disadvantageous consequences for members of the target group, that also conflicts with the goals of that group, that is intended by the perpetrator to have disadvantageous consequences, and that conflicts not only with the goals of the victim group but also with major societal norms. This type of conceptualization, although including all of the elements we have considered, makes discrimination a very specific type of behavior, possibly found only in unusual situations.

Empirically this type of conceptualization would create major problems, unless one were willing to make numerous assumptions. It would undoubtedly necessitate leaving a number of elements unmeasured, although it is conceivable that more satisfactory results could be achieved in measuring them than have been attained heretofore.

The second strategy involves a more general definition of discrimination, such as differential treatment of members of one group by members of another group on the basis, either directly or indirectly, of the social characteristics of the latter group. The other conceptual elements—consequences, goal conflict, intentionality, and normative conflict—will not be explicitly included in the definition but will be handled elsewhere in the theoretical model. Measurement problems with this approach will be less severe than with the first approach, but it will still be difficult in some cases to determine the criteria on the basis of which outcomes are allocated. And if the other elements are still taken into account in the overall causal model, we have simply removed the problem of measuring them for the time being.

We believe that the second strategy is the more practical from an empirical standpoint, although it is not completely satisfactory conceptually. It does have the major virtue of restricting the concept of discrimination to a quite specific type of behavior. As we shall presently see, determining the criteria for the allocation of outcomes is fraught with enough difficulties that compounding these problems by including conceptual elements that can be measured only very imperfectly does not seem the most sensible way to proceed.

Therefore we shall define discrimination as "the allocation of outcomes and means on the direct or indirect basis of the social characteristics of 'applicants' for those outcomes and means." This conceptualization may refer either to general or to specific allocators, and it also allows for different types of discrimination, depending upon the social characteristics that constitute the bases for allocations. Thus one may refer not only to racial and sexual discrimination but also to class, status, religious, and age discrimination. Theoretically any social characteristic may serve as the basis for an allocation of outcomes or means, but some will be much more common than others and will affect significantly larger numbers of people.

We have said that discrimination refers to a type of equity situation. Our conceptualization now specifies that it is a type in which outcomes and means are allocated on the basis of the social characteristics of the applicants. Discrimination therefore constitutes the application of *a specific type of distribution rule*. From this perspective, discrimination is *not* inherently inequitable, but it will be *perceived* as equitable or inequitable under certain conditions. We will refer to *equitable* discrimination as *legitimate* discrimination and to *inequitable* discrimination as *illegitimate* discrimination. Both modifiers, of course, refer to actors' perceptions.

These two connotations of the term *discrimination* have often been commented upon. On the one hand, one may be praised for being discriminating while, on the other hand, one may also be condemned for discriminating. For example, someone may commend another for being discriminating in his or her choice of friends. The person paying this compliment is essentially saying that the characteristics that constitute the other's criteria for the allocation of friendships are legitimate ones from his or her point of view. Or, to put it differently, the other person is utilizing a legitimate distribution rule to allocate friendships among "applicants."

Similarly a condemnation of discrimination exemplifies a judgment that the allocation of outcomes or means on the basis of particular characteristics, such as race or sex, represents the application of an illegitimate distribution rule. And those who regard these characteristics as irrelevant for the allocation of specific outcomes and means will regard any allocation based upon these characteristics as illegitimate. The pervasiveness of this distribution rule in the allocation of rights and outcomes in the past, with its disadvantageous consequences for racial and ethnic groups, has led many to consider discrimination an inherently illegitimate distribution rule. Here we have presented it as an inherently neutral distribution rule that will be judged to have varying degrees of legitimacy by parties to, and observers of, a specific allocation situation. Their differing perceptions of the legitimacy of the distribution rule in that situation, we antici- pate, will be a major factor determining both whether the distribution rule is applied and reactions to its application.

Conceptually, therefore, discrimination refers to the application of a type of distribution rule. Theoretically one's major interests will be in the conditions under which this distribution rule is most likely to be applied and the conditions that influence responses to its application. Empirically the objective will be to determine whether it is actually the operative distribution rule in a situation. Determining the influence of discrimination upon an observed inequality of out- comes will also involve assessing the degree to which the inequality is attribut- able to past and current applications of that distribution rule.

THE LEGITIMACY OF DISCRIMINATION

Because allowances have rarely been made in models of discrimination for the possibility that beliefs about the legitimacy of discrimination may vary among the parties involved in an ostensibly discriminatory situation, in this section we will discuss some of the major implications of including these beliefs as signifi- cant intervening variables. Our discussion will be partially guided by discussions in the equity/distributive justice literature regarding actors' responses to inequit- able or unjust exchanges.

Beliefs regarding the legitimacy of discrimination will necessarily be situation specific. Since discrimination involves the allocation of outcomes/means on the direct or indirect basis of specific criteria, there are a number of types of dis- crimination. Certain types, such as racial, religious, or sexual, have, of course, been most pronounced, but the concept may apply to other types, such as age, class, and physical. Therefore a judgment about the legitimacy of discrimination will always apply to the use of a *specific* criterion as the basis for the allocation of a *specific* outcome or means. Actors may regard allocation on the basis of a criterion as legitimate in one allocative situation but illegitimate in a different situation.

The legitimacy of discrimination will constitute an important variable at two places within a discrimination model. First, it will primarily affect allocators by influencing their likelihood of behaving discriminatorily. (The other major factor affecting this likelihood will be the utility of discrimination for them, which we discuss at length in chapter 12.) Generally the greater the legitimacy of allocat- ing outcomes or means on the basis of certain criteria in |particular situations from an allocator's perspective, the greater the likelihood that he or she will discriminate, i.e., allocate on the basis of those criteria. In some situations, however, allocators may be confronted with varying perceptions of legitimacy by other actors who are relevant to them. Consequently they may find themselves in cross-pressure situations that will make the occurrences of discrimination less predictable.

Second, discrimination models often pay little attention to the *reactions* of the parties involved in a discriminatory situation. It is usually assumed that nonrecipients of outcomes will be angry and that recipients will be pleased with an allocation. The reactions of potentially significant third parties to the allocation are also generally ignored. But the reactions of actors from each of these categories will be significant and their reactions will be influenced partly by their beliefs concerning the legitimacy of a specific type of discrimination in a specific allocation. Generally we expect that those who believe discrimination to be legitimate in a situation will have more positive reactions, regardless of whether they are recipients or nonrecipients, than those who view it as illegitimate. But if nonrecipients judge the discrimination to be illegitimate, then we expect them to be angry and possibly to attempt to reverse the outcome of the allocation. Likewise recipients of outcomes may not be wholly satisfied with receiving them if they are perceived to be the consequence of illegitimate discrimination. Interested third parties will be more likely to attempt to exert influence over the allocation procedure if they believe it involves illegitimate discrimination and if intervention has positive utility for them.

Reactions to discriminatory situations on the part of recipients, nonrecipients, and third parties will not be influenced solely by their judgments regarding the legitimacy of discrimination. Equally important will be their perception that discrimination has in fact been involved in the allocation process. We suggest a variable that we label *clarity of the situation* to take into account the very real possibility that a judgment that discrimination has occurred will not always be straightforward. Earlier in this chapter we discussed at length the difficulties involved in trying to develop a satisfactory definition of discrimination. In the next two chapters we discuss the hazards encountered in attempting to verify the existence of discrimination empirically. Therefore it is not surprising that participants in a possibly discriminatory situation will face problems similar to those confronted by the methodologist attempting to measure discrimination. The participants' views regarding the legitimacy of discrimination will only have their full impact upon their responses to the situation if they are simultaneously convinced that the situation is a discriminatory one.

A third important variable influencing reactions will be simply the utilities of the outcomes or means being allocated. The influence of the prior two variables—legitimacy and clarity—will be compounded by these utilities. The higher the stakes involved, i.e., the greater the utilities of the outcomes/means, the more intense the reaction that one will expect to occur, provided that the other factors are consistent with each other. Thus we expect the reaction of a nonrecipient to be most intense if he or she unequivocally determines that discrimination has occurred in the allocation of an outcome or means that has very high utility to him or her. The reactions of recipients in such situations are somewhat more difficult to predict and we will deal with them presently. The major significance of including the influence of these three factors upon the reactions of recipients, nonrecipients, and third parties is that this scheme allows for greater complexity, and hence is more realistic, than simply assuming satisfaction on the part of recipients and dissatisfaction on the part of nonrecipients.

Ultimately the ability of the groups of actors involved in an allegedly discriminatory situation to influence the allocation, either to reverse it or to reinforce it, will depend upon their relative power. In this regard nonrecipients will be at a disadvantage in most cases, because prior allocations will likely have deprived them of the resources needed to mount an offensive against the allocator. Their primary recourse will be to powerful third parties whom they can convince that the allocation involves illegitimate discrimination and whom they can motivate to intercede on their behalf. This, of course, has been the tack taken by both blacks and women who have appealed to the federal government for legal assistance in recent years. As this powerful third party has gradually swung around to the point of view that discrimination is illegitimate, it has used its constitutional powers to overturn allocations and to modify allocation procedures.

Since allocators in discriminatory situations are likely to award outcomes/ means to members of their own social category as a method of retaining power over other social categories, one would expect coalitions to form between allocators and recipients in order to retain the existing system of privilege. The combined power of these coalitions has been greatest when the allocators have technically been servants of the recipient group. The system of southern school segregation was maintained for a number of years, for example, by government officials in allocative roles who systematically denied nonwhites entry to white educational facilities. One chink in their armor turned out to be members of the dominant group who slowly began to perceive such discrimination as illegitimate. Nevertheless, it took the combined strength of black demonstrators and the military force of the federal government to change the allocative system in the 1950s and 1960s. This result was in turn enhanced by events that helped to clarify the situation for another amorphous group of third parties, northern whites. The mass media accounts of this period, showing blacks being turned away from southern educational institutions by state governors backed up by angry mobs, made clear rather quickly to this group the reality of the discrimination that was occurring. Thus changes in the clarity of the situation, combined with northern whites' views of the illegitimacy of the discrimination, brought about pressures upon the federal government that undoubtedly played a significant role in strengthening the determination of branches, such as the Justice Department and Congress, to revise the existing system for allocating educational opportunities.

Thus the reactions of the parties involved in a discriminatory situation may become quite complicated and may not be easily predictable simply from an observer's inference that a given amount of discrimination is present. We shall next look more closely at the principal categories into which actors can be divided, the major factors determining their perceptions of the legitimacy of discrimination, and their probable behaviors given their perceptions. We shall find that some of the elements of a conceptualization of discrimination that we discussed earlier in this chapter and then discarded will prove significant in this context.

Allocators and the Legitimacy of Discrimination

Our interest in the significance of the legitimacy of discrimination for allocators is twofold. First, given that they will be more likely to allocate outcomes or means on a discriminatory basis the more legitimate they perceive discrimination to be, we will be concerned with the major factors influencing their attitudes regarding legitimacy. Second, we will also be interested in those situations in which they are most likely to face cross-pressures that will modify the influence of their attitudes concerning legitimacy.

Determinants of Allocators' Attitudes Concerning Discrimination. Working from the outside in, so to speak, from the parameters characterizing an entire society to those that reflect the specific allocator, the prevailing opinions within a society regarding the legitimacy of a specific type of discrimination without reference to specific situations will undoubtedly be a first major factor influencing the perceptions of allocators regarding the legitimacy of discrimination in these specific situations. Thus if the dominant normative standard upholds racial discrimination as legitimate, we do not expect allocators to deviate from that standard. Earlier we noted the suggestion that allocations be considered discriminatory only if they conflict with dominant normative standards and the complications involved in incorporating that idea in a discrimination conceptualization. When we take into account the influence of the legitimacy of discrimination upon allocators, we see more clearly the disadvantage of including that element in one's conceptualization. If one were to include it, then one would be confronted with a paradox in situations in which racial discrimination was the dominant normative standard, such as occurred historically in the American South. The existence of this normative standard would simultaneously increase the likelihood of racial discrimination through its influence upon allocators' perceptions of legitimacy and also define away the existence of such discrimination. As has been repeatedly pointed out, the presence of widespread "patterned evasions" in the South after the federal government had declared racial discrimination illegitimate (i.e., in the form of school segregation) documents the true normative standard operative in that situation.

A second and perhaps more influential variable for allocators' perceptions of legitimacy will be the views of those in more immediate contact with them regarding legitimacy or illegitimacy. The two most important sets of actors here will be those who are in either superior or laterally equal positions to a specific allocator. Thus if allocators in positions such as personnel officers in organizations perceive that both their superiors and their fellow personnel officers consider discrimination to be legitimate in the allocation of outcomes such as jobs, then their own views regarding the legitimacy of discrimination will undoubtedly reveal this influence.

It should be noted that there is a very real possibility of slippage between the actual views of an allocator's superiors and peers regarding the legitimacy of discrimination and that allocator's perceptions of their views. Conceivably allocators' perceptions can err in either direction in this regard, but given the historical prevalence of certain types of discrimination, such as racial and sexual, it is probable that most allocators will perceive greater legitimacy for these types of discrimination on the part of their superiors and fellow allocators than may actually exist at a given point in time. To the extent that existing patterns of allocation have been legitimated over time by their very existence, we anticipate that allocators will be more likely to err on the conservative side, i.e., to perceive the legitimacy of discrimination as being actually greater than it is.

Third, we cannot ignore the personal prejudices and stereotypes of allocators as influences on their beliefs regarding the legitimacy of discrimination. If, as a consequence of their stereotypes and their level of prejudice, they perceive members of certain groups as lacking characteristics that they regard as important prerequisites for the outcomes/means being allocated, then this perceptual data will not only increase the likelihood of their discriminating against members of those groups, but it will also strengthen their perceptions regarding the legitimacy of discrimination in that situation. Thus, from an allocator's perspective, if a black applicant by virtue of being black lacks characteristics conducive to satisfactory performance on a job, it will be *illegitimate* for him or her *not* to allocate jobs on the basis of race, that is, not discriminate. In chapter 12 we discuss the factors determining the utility of bias, or discrimination, in a specific situation. If members of a group, such as blacks, are stereotypically perceived to lack certain necessary characteristics for an outcome or means, then discrimination on the basis of race will have greater utility for an allocator than nondiscrimination. Here we are suggesting that this course of action will have additional support through the effect of these perceptions upon allocators' beliefs about the legitimacy of discrimination in a situation.

A study by Quinn, Kahn, Tabor, and Gordon (1968) of discrimination in the hiring of Jews to executive positions has revealed the influence of all of these factors upon the actions of allocators. Although this study did not consider specifically the allocators' views regarding the legitimacy of discrimination, many of their findings can be translated into those terms. The study found three sets of factors particularly important in determining the likelihood that managers would discriminate against Jews in the selection of executives. First, they were more likely to discriminate if they perceived significant third-party pressures favoring discrimination, such as from superiors and potential customers or business associates with whom an executive might come into contact. These pressures can be interpreted as partly affecting the utility of discrimination for managers; nondiscrimination was perceived by them as bringing consequences with negative utility, namely, sanctions from these other parties. But it can also be interpreted as partly affecting the managers' perceptions of the legitimacy of discrimination. If their superiors and outsiders to the company expected discrimination, then surely they also regarded discrimination as legitimate, and hence it is likely that the managers were influenced by their beliefs.

Second, the researchers found that the managers' own attitudes regarding Jews had a significant independent effect upon their likelihood of discriminating. These attitudes included, on the one hand, strong expressions of anti-Semitism, which undoubtedly influenced their perceptions of the legitimacy of discrimination against Jews. On the other hand, they also included their stereotypes regarding Jews. In the terms of the researchers, those managers who perceived Jews as lacking *nonability* criteria that they believed essential to adequate performance of the executive role were more likely to discriminate against Jews. (The researchers note that, in the case of blacks, those managers who believed that blacks lacked essential *ability* criteria, rather than nonability criteria, would be most likely to discriminate.) These perceptions of the characteristics possessed by Jews were a direct result of the managers' stereotypes regarding Jews. Thus it can be inferred that discrimination had both utility and legitimacy for the managers possessing these stereotypes.

A third major factor singled out in this study was the perception of managers that their companies were actually only paying lip service to the standard of nondiscrimination. In other words, if managers perceived that their companies formally gave support to equal employment opportunities, but that this support was only a formality and actual practices deviated sharply from that norm, then they were more likely to discriminate. This factor can be seen as clearly influencing the managers' perceptions of the legitimacy of discrimination. If their superiors were only going through the motions of supporting nondiscrimination, then the logical inference was that they believed discrimination to be legitimate. Therefore it is not surprising that the managers themselves also perceived discrimination as legitimate. It is also likely that there was a reciprocal influence here between managers' perceptions and a company's hypocrisy. Those managers who perceived discrimination as legitimate very likely also perceived their companies as paying lip service to nondiscrimination.

A last factor that we anticipate will be a major influence upon allocators' perceptions of the legitimacy of discrimination will be the utilities of the outcomes/means that they are responsible for allocating. However, it is likely that the influence of this factor will depend upon some or all of the other factors we have discussed. Specifically, if the other factors are conducive to discrimination's being perceived as legitimate by an allocator, then their influence will be accentuated by the utility of the outcomes/means that are being allocated. Just as the stakes may be high for applicants they may also be high for allocators. Thus discrimination may not be seen as legitimate or utilitarian if relatively insignificant outcomes/means are to be allocated. But if an outcome/means is being allocated that is of great importance for continued operation of the allocator's organization or that offers significant opportunities for members of disliked groups to increase their power, then it is probable not only that discrimination will have high utility but that it will also have high legitimacy. The rationale may be on the order of: it would be illegitimate to offer or entrust that high-utility outcome/means to members of *that* group.

So we anticipate at least four major factors influencing allocators' perceptions of the legitimacy of a specific type of discrimination in specific situations. The most general influence will be the prevailing standards regarding the legitimacy of that type of discrimination. In addition, allocators will be influenced by their perceptions of the extent to which their superiors and peers regard that type of discrimination in the situation as legitimate, by their own prejudices and stereotypes, and by the utilities of the outcomes/means to be allocated.

Cross-pressures Confronting Allocators. Under what conditions are allocators most likely to face cross-pressures that may complicate their formulations of well-developed beliefs regarding the legitimacy of discrimination and what will be the implications of these cross-pressures for the likelihood that they will discriminate?

The most obvious instance of such cross-pressures will arise in situations when the four influences discussed above are not consistent. These inconsistencies may appear in a variety of combinations. For example, while the dominant normative standard may present racial discrimination as legitimate, and an allocator's superiors and peers may be perceived by him or her to have attitudes supporting the dominant standard, the allocator may be personally inclined to regard it as illegitimate. In this case one or the other of two of Merton's (1949:100–101) classic four consequences is possible—the nonprejudiced nondiscriminator or the nonprejudiced discriminator. Whether the allocator discriminates will depend partly upon the relative strength of his or her views regarding legitimacy as compared to the strength of the other two influences. But it will also depend upon the utility of what is being allocated. Depending upon the allocator's strength of convictions regarding legitimacy, he or she may solve the dilemma by following his or her predilection if the outcomes/means being allocated are of low utility but following the guidance of the other influences in cases involving high-utility outcomes or means.

One of the other two cases described by Merton—the prejudiced nondiscriminator—may result from a different combination of cross-pressures. In this case we anticipate that the allocator's own beliefs legitimate discrimination, but that he or she is more strongly influenced by one or more of the other three factors. Thus the allocator's superiors and peers may regard discrimination as illegitimate and/or the outcomes/means being allocated may have little utility.

We should make it clear that we are not suggesting that the legitimacy of discrimination perceived by allocators is the sole factor influencing whether or not they actually discriminate. Instead, as figure 10.2 indicates, the utility of discrimination from an allocator's perspective will be equally important. Although we are primarily interested in the influence of the legitimacy of discrimination in this context, it is the combined influence of these two factors that determines the likelihood of discrimination. The major factors influencing the utility of discrimination, or bias, will be discussed at length in chapter 12.

**Figure 10.2. Determinants of the Likelihood of
Allocator Discrimination**

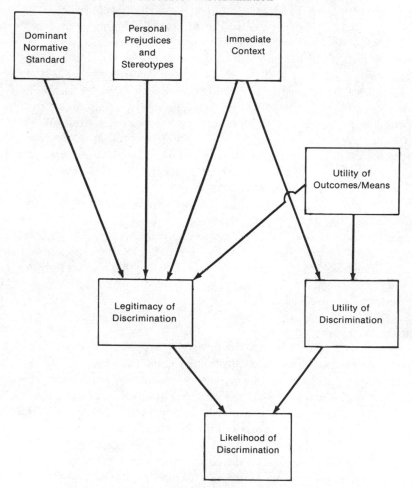

Here we simply note that two factors—an allocator's immediate context (i.e.,
beliefs of superiors and peers) and the utility of the outcomes/means being allocated—affect both the legitimacy and the utility of discrimination. The other
two factors—the dominant normative standard and an allocator's own attitudes—
primarily affect only the legitimacy of discrimination.

Because the likelihood of discrimination is a function of the legitimacy and
the utility of discrimination from the allocator's perspective, a disparity between
these two influences may also create cross-pressures for the allocator. The first
cross-pressure situation will occur when the legitimacy of a specific type of discrimination is high in a situation but its utility is low. For example, a racially

prejudiced allocator may be located in an organization in which racial discrimination is legitimate in an area of the country where the dominant normative standards support racial discrimination, and a high-utility outcome may be the object of the allocation process. The utility of discrimination may be low in this situation, however, because a powerful third party, such as the federal government, has threatened dire consequences for the organization if it detects discrimination in its allocations of outcomes. Another possibility is that the legitimacy of discrimination may be high for the allocator because of his or her very strong prejudices against members of a minority group. But the utility of discrimination may be low in this situation because the allocator's superiors have forcefully given their support to nondiscriminatory allocations and threatened allocators not following that norm with dismissal. In this case one would expect a low probability of discrimination by the allocator, but also a significant degree of emotional stress for him or her.

The opposite cross-pressure situation—low legitimacy but high utility of discrimination—may result in equally intense emotional stress for a nonprejudiced allocator. Opting for a discriminatory allocation in this situation may cause such an allocator to experience a strong guilt reaction. However, ignoring the utility of discrimination and not discriminating in accord with his or her feelings regarding-legitimacy may result in negative consequences for the organization and loss of position for the allocator.

Responses to Discrimination

As indicated above, the responses stimulated by an allocation that appears to be discriminatory will be a function of three variables: the clarity of the situation, the legitimacy of that type of discrimination in that allocative situation, and the utility of the outcomes/means being allocated. The responses of actors in three categories—nonrecipients, recipients, and interested third parties—will be of greatest import for that and subsequent allocations.

Nonrecipient Responses. The reaction of nonrecipients to their failure to be awarded an outcome/means for which they have more or less formally applied has naturally received the greatest attention. In most cases it is only as a result of their reactions that allocations have been questioned and ensuing allocations modified. Recipients presumably will be satisfied with the results of the allocation, and third parties may not take note of possible discrimination unless it is called to their attention by the aggravated party.

Overt reactions may, of course, not be forthcoming on the part of nonrecipients. Their lack of response may be attributable to a variety of factors. They may not perceive that they have been victims of discrimination, they may regard the discrimination as legitimate, or they may believe any reaction to the situation to be hopeless and even harmful because it will decrease the probability of being awarded favorable outcomes/means in subsequent allocations. Explanations such as the last have generally been advanced to account for the relative docility of blacks in the United States prior to the upsurge of the civil rights movement. Since nonrecipients are most likely to provide the initial impetus for changes in the allocation process, an analysis of the factors influencing their responses is of major importance for a dynamic view of discrimination.

A first important issue is determining what factors will make nonrecipients most likely to infer that a particular allocation has been discriminatory. It is at this point that the clarity of the situation becomes crucial. As is the case in the empirical measurement of discrimination, the clarity of an allocative situation will be diminished to the extent that outward characteristics of the nonrecipients, such as race or sex, are highly correlated with other less ascribed characteristics, such as amount of education. Simply put, nonrecipients will face an identification problem identical to that the researcher confronts. They will be unable to determine whether an allocation was based upon a characteristic such as race or upon some other characteristic highly correlated with race.

Secondly, clarity of the situation will be increased to the extent that the distribution rule governing the allocation has been formally stated by allocators, or to the extent that the criteria of allocation are explicit rather than implicit. A nonrecipient may still be suspicious of discrimination in cases of a high relationship among characteristics, even though another characteristic has been formally presented as the explicit criterion of allocation according to the distribution rule.

In such cases nonrecipients are therefore likely to be influenced by other characteristics of the situation, and they may make inferences about the presence of discrimination on that basis. For example, a history of previous discrimination on the part of certain allocators or in the allocation of certain outcomes/ means may be perceived as ample justification for the conclusion that discrimination has also been present in the current situation. Another possibility is that nonrecipients will make inferences regarding the intentions of the allocator. (We noted above that some have suggested intentionality as a component in conceptualizations of discrimination.) If nonrecipients assume that an allocator has made an allocation so as intentionally to disadvantage them, then they are likely to infer that discrimination has occurred, even though they may not be able to find concrete evidence that the allocation was based on a characteristic such as race.

It is probably more likely that nonrecipients, especially those who have been striving to attain a particular outcome/means over a long period of time, will conclude that discrimination has occurred whenever there is an inequality of outcomes between them and members of another group. Little consideration may be given by nonrecipients to the relevant base of comparison for judgments of discrimination, an issue we explore in chapter 12. The possibility of erroneous perceptions is obviously present here, as it is in all cases involving perceptions. However, we do not wish to stress the possibility of discrimination's being perceived where it does not exist so strongly that we overlook the very real possibility that nonrecipients may fail to perceive that they have been victimized by discrimination. Thus allocators may claim that other characteristics have served as the criteria of allocation when in fact they have made an allocation on the basis of characteristics that the nonrecipients regarded as illegitimate.

Outlining the factors influencing nonrecipients' perceptions of the legitimacy of discrimination in a particular situation is a somewhat simpler task. A major factor here will be the extent to which discrimination conflicts with major goals held by the nonrecipients. Looking at the issue of the legitimacy of discrimination independently of the issue of its actual occurrence in a given situation, we can make the following generalization: the more that discrimination conflicts with or blocks the major goals of nonrecipients, the less legitimate they will perceive discrimination to be. Or to put it slightly differently, the greater the utility of outcomes/means that are being allocated, the greater will be the illegitimacy for nonrecipients of discrimination in the allocation of those outcomes/means. Thus in such situations, if an allocation is judged to have been discriminatory by nonrecipients, we expect their dissatisfaction to be relatively great.

Nonrecipients' beliefs regarding the legitimacy of discrimination will also be influenced by the dominant normative standards of a society, albeit by their group's interpretation of those standards. If they perceive that the dominant standards hold a type of discrimination to be illegitimate, then they too will be more likely to perceive it as illegitimate. This suggests that blacks in the southern United States historically may have been confronted by a perceptual dilemma. On the one hand, they were no doubt aware of the formal standards of equality expressed in documents such as the Declaration of Independence. But, on the other hand, they were daily confronted by a dominant group that displayed to them in an infinite number of ways the fact that the operative normative standard upheld the legitimacy of racial discrimination. Given this situation, it is possible that some did not react to discrimination because they viewed it as legitimate. However, the dominant normative standard within the black group may also have neutralized the impact of everyday experience, so that beliefs that racial discrimination was illegitimate remained widespread.

It should be realized that nonrecipients may also view discrimination in their own favor as legitimate in some situations (in which case it would probably be labeled reverse discrimination) and they will react negatively when this legitimate discrimination does not occur. This judgment regarding the appropriateness of discrimination will be determined by nonrecipients' views regarding the relevance of a characteristic, such as race, for receiving outcomes/means, a point we discussed earlier in this chapter.

The focus has typically been upon nonrecipients' views regarding the illegitimacy of discrimination, with one of the supports for this view being the conviction among nonrecipients that a characteristic like race is not relevant for receiving most or all outcomes/means. But in some instances nonrecipients may regard race as a relevant characteristic and hence regard racial discrimination as legitimate. Perhaps one of the best examples of this is the conviction of many blacks in American urban areas that the police officers patrolling their communities should be black. In this situation race is regarded as a relevant characteristic for obtaining employment as a policeman, and those holding this point of view will regard discrimination on that basis as legitimate. Similarly some have argued for the legitimacy of black university students' establishing fraternities and sororities primarily on the basis of race.

Thus the relevance of a characteristic constitutes another factor influencing beliefs in regard to the legitimacy of discrimination. If a characteristic is considered relevant for receiving an outcome/means by members of a group, then allocation on the basis of that characteristic (i.e., discrimination) will be regarded as legitimate by them.

These two factors—beliefs regarding the legitimacy of a specific type of discrimination in a specific situation and the perceived occurrence of that type of discrimination in that situation—will have a multiplicative effect upon the reaction of nonrecipients to an allocation. Nonrecipients will be dissatisfied (a negative reaction) when they conclude with a high degree of certainty either that illegitimate discrimination has occurred (a negative times a positive) or that legitimate discrimination has not occurred (a positive times a negative). They will be satisfied (a positive reaction) either when illegitimate discrimination does not occur (a negative times a negative) or when legitimate discrimination occurs (a positive times a positive.).[1] Their degree of satisfaction will be approximately zero, therefore, when either of these factors is approximately zero. This will occur either if the situation is so unclear that they cannot determine whether discrimination has taken place or if they lack an opinion regarding the legitimacy of a particular type of discrimination.

The third major factor that will influence the reactions of nonrecipients to an allocation is the utility of the outcome/means being allocated. We have previously suggested an indirect influence of utility upon their reactions through its influence upon legitimacy; now we are suggesting an additional influence. The major additional effect of utility will be to determine the *intensity* of the satisfaction or dissatisfaction of nonrecipients. Hence utility will interact with the combined effect of legitimacy and perceived occurrence to affect the degree of satisfaction. In other words, the satisfaction or dissatisfaction felt by nonrecipients as a result of the influence of legitimacy and perceived occurrence will be weighted by the utility of the outcome/means. If the utility is very high, then the degree of nonrecipient satisfaction or dissatisfaction will be particularly strong. But if the utility is relatively low, then recipient attitudes will be close to neutrality. Conversely, if the combination of legitimacy and perceived occurrence yields neutral attitudes because either of the factors is close to zero, then nonrecipient attitudes will be neutral regardless of the utility of the outcome/means being allocated.

The possible relationships between these determinants and the degree of nonrecipient satisfaction with an allocation are presented in figure 10.3. Generally the greater the degree of nonrecipient dissatisfaction with an allocation, the more likely they will be to attempt to change it or subsequent allocations. The greater they perceive their power to be, the more likely they will be to

Figure 10.3.   Determinants of Recipient and Nonrecipient Responses to Discrimination

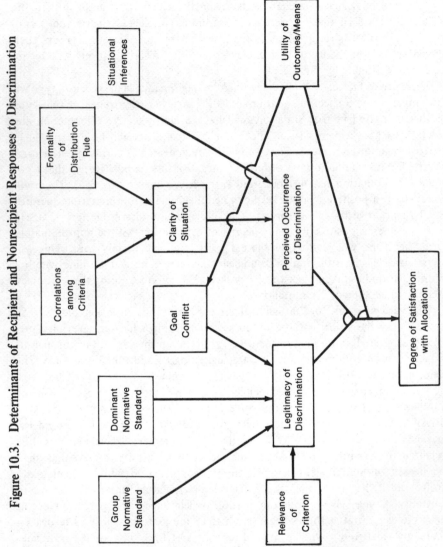

initiate such attempts on their own. The less they perceive their relative power, the more likely they will be to seek out sympathetic third parties and to try to persuade them of the fact that an illegitimate type of discrimination has occurred or that a legitimate type has not occurred in that situation.

Recipient Responses. Very little thought appears to have been given to the reactions of the recipients of outcomes/means in discriminatory allocations. They are presumably pleased, although they may attempt to rationalize receiving something as a result of discrimination if they have doubts about its legitimacy. Recipients' beliefs regarding the legitimacy of a particular type of discrimination in a specific situation will be determined by the factors we described in our analysis of nonrecipient responses; that is, they will be more likely to regard it as legitimate if it does not conflict with dominant normative standards or with standards of their subcultures, if it does not conflict with important goals of theirs, and if they perceive that the characteristics on the basis of which the outcomes/means were allocated are relevant for their reception. Since recipients of outcomes/means are generally the beneficiaries of discrimination, it is generally assumed that they are as satisfied with the outcome as nonrecipients are dissatisfied with it. But this view may be oversimplified. We have previously noted that the equity/distributive justice literature indicates that beneficiaries of inequitable exchanges may not be satisfied with their position and may suffer negative emotional reactions. They may also take steps to make the exchange more equitable. We expect the same to be true of discrimination situations.

We shall concentrate directly upon the conditions under which recipients' satisfaction will vary. The extremes of satisfaction and dissatisfaction will be attained under high-utility conditions. Recipient satisfaction will be greatest in one of two very different cases. The first, in which discrimination is believed to be legitimate by the recipient and is perceived to have occurred, is exemplified by the white supremacist's belief that race is a proper basis for the allocation of outcomes. The other case—illegitimate discrimination perceived not to have occurred—represents the opposite extreme, the recipient offended by discrimination who is convinced that outcomes/means have been allocated to him or her on the basis of criteria he or she does not regard as discriminatory. These may, of course, be regarded as the identical case, but keeping them distinct allows us to show the wide variety of recipients that may have similar responses for different reasons. As was the case with nonrecipients, recipients' attitudes will be most neutral if they cannot determine whether discrimination has occurred, if the utilities of outcomes/means are low, or if they have no strong beliefs regarding legitimacy.

The two cases of recipient dissatisfaction are also informative. The first, resulting from the nonoccurence of legitimate discrimination, may appear an impossibility. The most satisfactory example that comes to mind is that of an extremely prejudiced individual who regards discrimination (say, on the basis of race) as legitimate and who is forced to submit his or her credentials in competition with members of another racial group that he or she perceives as inferior, and who is chosen on the basis of a nonracial criterion. Consequently there is dissatisfaction because the right outcome has been received for the wrong reasons.

The second type of dissatisfied recipient is particularly interesting. This recipient has been rewarded by receiving a high-utility outcome, but he or she has received it through an allocation that he or she regards as illegitimate. According to equity/distributive justice theory, persons in this situation— the beneficiaries of inequitable exchanges—should experience guilt as a result. We are not aware that this question has been systematically explored in regard to discrimination, although Myrdal, in *An American Dilemma* (1944), suggested that most white Americans feel at least some guilt because of the discrepancy between their professions of equality to all and their treatment of minority-group members.

Each of the hypothetical individuals we have described is likely to make a characteristic response to the accusations that discrimination has occurred that may be leveled against them by nonrecipients or third parties. The two for whom discrimination is legitimate are likely to form a coalition with the allocator to ensure that the allocation is not changed, although the recipient who is nevertheless dissatisfied because the allocation was not discriminatory will be placed in a bind if he or she has received something with high utility. Conceivably he or she may be willing to relinquish what has been allocated and may seek to receive the same outcomes/means from a different allocator.

One would expect the recipient who is certain that the allocation decision was not the result of discrimination to attempt to convince dissatisfied nonrecipients of that fact, possibly by pointing out to them the criteria he or she possessed and they did not. This leaves our potentially guilty recipient. Again the equity/distributive justice literature suggests some possible overt responses, as we noted in chapter 6. One may relinquish or attempt to share what has been allocated, a difficult step if it has high utility. It is more probable, at least in equity/distributive justice terms, that one will attempt to increase one's *input* to balance off the inequitable *outcome* that has been received. We have noted that according to the equity literature inequity occurs when two parties' input/outcome ratios are not equal; hence the two major alternatives for the beneficiary are decreasing outcomes or increasing inputs. In the discrimination context this increase in input would likely be accomplished by the recipient's calling to his or her own and the nonrecipient's attention the manifold other positive characteristics that he or she possessed.

Thus the potential responses of recipients in discriminatory situations are somewhat more complex than might be imagined. Those who are basically satisfied will generally attempt to preserve the allocation system or point out its correctness. Those who are basically dissatisfied may go so far as to give up what they have been allocated, but we expect it is more likely that they will attempt to assuage their feelings by less drastic modifications of the allocation system.

Third-party Responses.   Potentially influential third parties will be of interest to nonrecipients and of concern to recipients in a discrimination situation. They, too, will make judgments regarding whether or not discrimination has occurred and will have views regarding the legitimacy of discrimination in specific situations. But the crucial question in regard to them involves the conditions under which they are likely to take action, either to lend support to an allocation or to attempt to nullify it.

The model we have used for recipient and nonrecipient responses may be partially applied to third parties; that is, they will be most likely to take action to change the allocation system the greater their dissatisfaction with it, and they will be most likely to be dissatisfied if they are certain either that illegitimate discrimination has occurred or that legitimate discrimination has not occurred. They will be more likely to take action in support of the allocative system the more satisfied they are with it, and their degree of satisfaction will be greatest when they perceive that legitimate discrimination has occurred or illegitimate discrimination has not occurred.

However, utility plays a somewhat different role for third parties than for recipients or nonrecipients because third parties do not receive direct utility from the outcome or means being allocated. The important consideration for them is the amount of utility they stand to gain or lose by action or failure to act. And this determination will be largely influenced by the relative power of recipients and nonrecipients. If nonrecipients are relatively weak, then third parties have little to gain by taking action in support of them, such as reversing the allocation or changing the allocation procedure. But if nonrecipients are relatively strong, or have benefits to offer the third party in exchange for third-party support, then action on their behalf becomes more likely.

The sequence of actions of the federal government in regard to blacks in the United States in the two decades immediately after World War II is instructive. The general trend was from the course of piecemeal actions taken during World War II, such as President Roosevelt's appointment of a Fair Employment Practices Commission in response to a threatened march on the nation's capital by blacks, to a full-scale assault on discrimination through the series of civil rights bills enacted in the 1960s. How does one explain this change in the stance of this very significant third party?

It was no doubt partly the result of increased dissatisfaction with existent allocative mechanisms that stemmed from a growing conviction that racial discrimination was illegitimate and an increased awareness of its pervasiveness in the South. But equally if not more important was the change in the utility of action on behalf of nonrecipient blacks for the federal government. The political strength of blacks had increased sharply as a result of their extensive migration to northern urban areas, and President Kennedy's election in 1960 was widely attributed to the black vote. Furthermore, as Wilson (1973:132) has pointed out, the termination of colonialism elsewhere in the world put the practices of racial discrimination in a bad light internationally. In addition, Wilson suggests that many of the actions taken by the federal government did not impose severe utility losses upon southern whites. And, as we noted previously, the government was also facing pressures from its northern white constituency.

So, for a variety of reasons, the utilities shifted in favor of governmental action in support of black victims of racial discrimination. Beliefs regarding the legitimacy of discrimination and perceptions regarding its occurrence played parts in the transition, but it appears that in this case the positive utilities to be gained from action were the overriding factor.

CONCLUDING REMARKS

In this chapter we have traversed a broad area, from a discussion of the difficulties of defining discrimination through an analysis of the significance of the legitimacy of discrimination for allocators, recipients, and nonrecipients, to some observations regarding the conditions that predispose third parties to act to change discriminatory allocation mechanisms. The significance of allocation mechanisms in a society remains a vital issue that we have barely touched upon in this context. Nor have we explored all the ramifications of discriminatory allocations. For example, we were only able to raise peripherally the important question of which portions of a dominant group benefit from discrimination against a minority group. Yet these omissions underscore the great complexity of the phenomenon of discrimination, which is quite often subjected to a less precise and systematic analysis than is required. In the following two chapters we continue this exploration.

NOTE

1. Either of these two sets of possibilities is reducible to one possibility. For example the nonoccurrence of illegitimate discrimination can be regarded as identical to the occurrence of legitimate discrimination since they both basically involve the judgment that a legitimate criterion has been used as the basis for allocation. We have kept the two possibilities separate in each case, however, because they are likely to apply to quite different empirical cases, as we shall show shortly.

CHAPTER 11

Allocation II: The Measurement of Discrimination and Inequalities

THE CONCEPTUALIZATION of discrimination that we have proposed specifies a deceptively simple requirement for the measurement of discrimination, namely, determining the degree to which a given allocation of outcomes is based, directly or indirectly, on a social characteristic. The measurement of racial discrimination therefore will require determining the extent to which an allocation of outcomes is based upon race. As we shall see, this may be a difficult task, and there may be slippage between true discrimination and measures of discrimination.

Under very rare circumstances one can imagine the possibility of reasonably direct measures of discrimination. If, for example, an employer, realty agency, or voluntary organization openly excludes blacks from consideration or admits to penalizing them through a point system of some kind, then it is clearly discriminating on the basis of race. Similarly, if a law school places blacks or white women in a separate pool of candidates and then accepts them on the basis of a lower predicted grade-point average than is required for white males, then it is openly discriminating against the latter category. Less explicit policies can on occasion be uncovered surreptitiously if the investigating team is in a position to find informants or place a spy within the organization concerned. Or perhaps an objective observer watching the selection process as it actually takes place will be in a position to count instances of discriminatory behaviors as they occur.

The more usual situation, at least in societies where the official norms do not condone discriminatory treatment, is that the actual acts are not observed as they take place. Nor are there written rules that refer directly to a minority and indicate that it should be discriminated against. As we have already noted, the processes involved are apt to be much more subtle than this, and the investigator must *infer* discrimination on the basis of frequency counts of one kind or another. This is the case for several reasons. First, if discrimination is intentional

451

it is likely to be disguised, and records are not likely to be kept of differential treatment. Second, many decision criteria are only vaguely defined and are therefore difficult to pin down. A particular person may be rejected not because he or she is black but because the interviewer formed a negative impression and was able to invoke other criteria as the supposed basis for the decision.

Third, decisions are usually made about *individual* cases rather than about blacks or women as a group. Since no two individuals are identical and, in fact, will inevitably differ with respect to a number of characteristics, if one were to confine one's attention to a single pair of cases (say, one white and the other black), it would be exceedingly difficult to establish that the decision was based on category or group membership rather than a number of other characteristics on which the individuals differed. An employer, for example, could practically always single out a particular characteristic on which the pair differed and then claim that the decision was based on this characteristic. Such a possibility is especially likely whenever the supposedly relevant characteristics (e.g., personality, potential, drive, or interest) are vague and difficult to measure.

For all of these reasons, discrimination is usually inferred or measured on the basis of a *set* of *outcomes* in the form of inequalities in frequency distributions. As we have noted, in the most simple and naive model, the working assumption is that since discrimination is likely to result in inequalities, then whenever we find such inequalities we may infer that discrimination has taken place. In the less naive model it is recognized that there may be other causes of the inequalities, so that the refined estimate or measure of discrimination will involve controls for these other variables.

This type of approach can be represented by the model in figure 11.1. An inequality of outcomes, I, is assumed to be caused by discrimination, D, and by another control or criterion variable, C. D may represent discrimination by an employer in the hiring process and I may be an index comparing the proportions of blacks and whites (from some pool) that have actually been hired within a specified period of time. Let the control variable C be years of formal education, the presumption being that it will be necessary to control for educational levels of the black and white pool members since educational qualification is an obvious criterion for employment. Or let us suppose we are trying to infer salary discrimination against women (D) on the basis of income inequalities (I) controlled for years of service (C).

Figure 11.1. Model of Discrimination

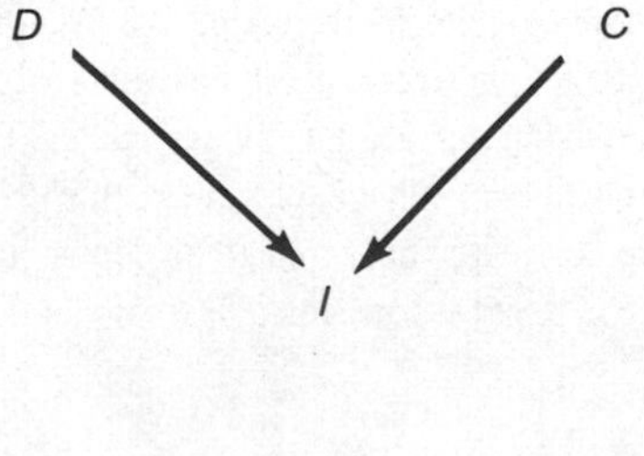

The usual procedure in such situations is to compare the inequalities before and after controlling. If the inequalities persist, even with multiple controls, discrimination is inferred and is measured by the degree of "standardized" inequality remaining after the controls have been introduced. Thus discrimination is inferred on the basis of what may be termed a *residualizing operation*. The argument is that if all of the remaining causes of inequality have been controlled, the remaining inequalities must be due to discrimination.

In the case of racial discrimination, defined as the unequal allocation of outcomes on the basis of race, an R, representing race, can be substituted for the D in figure 11.1, and discrimination will be inferred from the presence of a nonzero influence of R on I when C is controlled. In the case of salary discrimination against women, a nonzero influence of sex on income while controlling for years of service would lead to an inference of discrimination. Thus this model illustrates that true discrimination, D, is measured indirectly in terms of the influence of some variable, such as R, on an outcome after all other influences on that outcome have been taken into account. The outcome may be a continuous variable, such as level of income, or a discrete variable, such as an employment offer. The influence of R on I represents the standardized inequality resulting from the imposition of controls. This model may also be extended to include multiple controls, as represented by the equation

$$I = b_R R + b_1 C_1 + b_2 C_2 + \cdots + b_k C_k \, ,$$

which indicates that discrimination would be inferred from a nonzero partial correlation between I and R.

The adequacy of the residual approach of course depends upon the adequacy of the underlying causal model *and* on the degree to which the control variables have been perfectly measured. Logically, as Wohlstetter and Coleman (1972) have pointed out, it is a procedure that could also support biological explanations of differences between racial groups.

In our section on eligibility pools in the following chapter we shall discuss certain difficulties with the approach and point out that the measure will always require assumptions about the pools of eligible individuals and the mechanisms by which individuals move from one type of pool to another. In the next three sections we shall concentrate on complications of a number of other kinds involving the presumed relationships between the control variable(s), which we shall label C_i, and discrimination, D, which is being measured indirectly by an inequality, I, that has been standardized for C.

MAJOR TYPES OF DISCRIMINATION STUDIES

The residual approach is the basis for two major types of discrimination studies—quasi-experimental studies and statistical analyses. The quasi-experimental studies have involved the confrontation of dominant-group actors, either personally or via written credentials, by minority-group members applying for various rewards or performance rights. These applicants are matched, either actually or hypothetically (in the case of written applications), on other criteria assumed to be relevant in the selection process. The degree of discrimination is inferred from the difference between (or the ratio of) the number of selectees from each racial group, so that discrimination equals $Y_D - Y_M$ or Y_M/Y_D, where Y_D and Y_M represent the number of dominant and minority selectees respectively. The number of original applicants from each group is equal and all relevant criteria are assumed to be taken into account.

Examples of recent research using either an experimental or a quasi-experimental strategy include Gaertner's study (1973) of the willingness of Liberal and Conservative party members in New York City to help anonymous phone callers of different races and sexes and Sturdivant and Hanselman's study (1971) of merchants' treatment of customers of different races. The English study reported in Daniel (1968) used situation tests of this type to determine the degree of discrimination against nonwhite immigrants in housing, employment, and automotive services. Boyanowsky and Allen's study (1973) of willingness to agree with black allies is an example of a recent laboratory experiment.

The statistical analyses of discrimination can be subdivided into two types. The type most obviously similar to the quasi-experimental studies matches dominant- and minority-group members by means of cross-tabulations on variables assumed to be relevant to whatever dependent variable is being considered. Differences between (or ratios of) group values are compared for matched subgroups. Thus discrimination is again measured in terms of $Y_D - Y_M$ or Y_M/Y_D.

These cross-tabular studies can be further subdivided into two types depending upon the way in which the dependent variable for minority-group members is derived. The first of these we call the O-O type because both the dominant- and minority-group values are *observed* directly from aggregate data. The other subtype we call the O-E type because the comparison is between *observed* dominant- and *expected* minority-group values. These expected values are obtained by setting the minority distribution on other criterion variables equal to the dominant-group distribution. This procedure therefore controls differences in frequency distributions on the criterion variables between the racial groups. With this approach discrimination equals $Y_{M'}/Y_D$ or $Y_D - Y_{M'}$, where $Y_{M'}$ represents the expected minority-group value. Gwartney and McCaffree (1971) have compared black and white employment and income ratios in different occupational classifications by calculating expected black-white ratios based on the criterion variables of regional location and quantity of education within occupational classifications. Gwartney (1970) has used the criterion variables of quantity of education, level of scholastic achievement, region, age, and city size to calculate similar expected values for blacks. Other examples of O-E studies include those by O'Neill (1970), on the effect of discrimination on earnings, and by Johnson and Marple (1973), on the incomes of black professional basketball players and their representation on teams. Examples of O-O-type studies include the study of tax assessments by Hendon (1968) and the studies of income differences by Rasmussen (1971) and Katzman (1968).

The second major type of statistical analysis utilizes multiple regression techniques and most clearly exemplifies the $I = R + C_k$ model. These analyses are conducted in one of two ways. The most common procedure inserts race as a dummy variable, and its influence (and hence the degree of discrimination) is ascertained by comparing the beta for race with the betas for the other independent variables. Among studies using this technique are Welch's study (1967) of the marginal product of education, Gwartney's study (1970) of income and earnings differences, Gilman's study (1965) of unemployment, Kain and Quigley's study (1972) of home ownership, and King and Mieszkowski's study (1973) of housing rentals.

The alternative use of multiple regression techniques involves the estimation of separate regression equations for the groups being studied. This mode of analysis of course eliminates the racial variable from the regression equation. It makes possible a comparison of the influence of the other independent variables on a given inequality. If these independent variables have differential payoff for the racial groups, differences in slopes between the two equations can be taken as a measure of discrimination. This approach therefore measures discrimination in the form of an allocation of outcomes *indirectly* on the basis of race, as we illustrated in tables 10.6 through 10.10 in chapter 10. There we indicated the possibility of an interaction between race and a criterion variable. The presence of different unstandardized slopes between racial groups would imply the existence of such an interaction. Thus this is the only one of the current methods for measuring discrimination that allows for an indirect effect (in the sense discussed in chapter 10) of a discriminatory variable on an inequality.

At least two researchers have combined this approach with the O-E approach. Schiller (1971), in his limited study of occupational and educational differences, ran separate equations for blacks and whites and then used the white slopes and the black means to estimate expected values for his dependent variables, which he then compared with observed values. Lapham (1971) proceeded somewhat differently in her study of housing rentals—calculating separate equations and then using the difference between the white and black slopes plus the black and white means, rather than the slopes from one group and the means from the other, to derive expected values. And Blinder (1973) has used this measure *plus* the difference between the residuals of his two equations (i.e., the u_i terms) as a measure of discrimination.

ASSUMPTIONS OF THE RESIDUAL APPROACH

Each of these methodological derivatives of the residual approach rests on three very important assumptions: (1) that *all* other causes have been controlled simultaneously; (2) that each of the control variables has been perfectly measured; and (3) that the form of the equation (usually linear) has been correctly specified. Unfortunately if one or more of these assumptions is not met, the measure of discrimination will be biased, usually but not always away from zero. Also, the less careful one is about the controlling operation the greater the biases are likely to be. Thus anyone wanting to "prove" discrimination may be able to do so by merely claiming that he or she could not obtain the proper data for the relevant controls, or that there was not a sufficient number of cases to use simultaneous controls. This is certainly not a good position to be in, from the scientific standpoint, since it may well create a vested interest in low-quality research on the part of those who may wish to obtain high estimates of the extent of discrimination. Let us comment on each of the three above necessary assumptions.

Suppose there are three or four factors that affect inequalities (say, in hiring or in income distributions) in addition to discrimination. These may include differences in quantity, type, or quality of education, amount of previous experience or years in the labor force, certain personality characteristics, and perhaps some motivational factors that affect a worker's effort on the job. It is much more likely that the so-called objective factors will be measurable than the subjective ones. Perhaps the only two controls that are made possible because of the lack of available data will be "years of formal schooling" and "number of years of experience." This possibility is represented in figure 11.2, where C_3 and C_4 represent unmeasured criterion variables.

Let us also suppose that simultaneous controls are made (assuming an additive model) for C_1 and C_2 and that inequalities remain. What can one conclude? *If* the remaining causes were all highly correlated with these two control variables, which is unlikely, and *if* the control variables have been perfectly measured, then our inability to control for the others will not cause a serious bias. If the variables that are omitted are not correlated with the control variables or with D, then we can assume that their influence will be randomly distributed, with no resulting bias. But these intercorrelations among the control variables will, of course, be unknown whenever certain of them cannot be measured. Furthermore, we expect that, in different situations and for different employers, these intercorrelations among possible control variables will not all be the same. Therefore the *degree* of bias will be both variable and unknown.

Cross-tabular techniques for measuring discrimination are the least able to cope with the problem of omitted criterion variables because of the small num-

Figure 11.2. Model for Discrimination with Unmeasured Criterion Variables

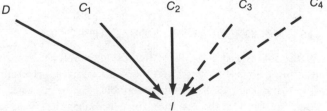

ber of variables that are usually simultaneously controlled. This methodology is also the most susceptible to the possibility of investigators' producing almost whatever degree of discrimination they may want to find. Armed with knowledge of the distribution of racial groups on variables in the real world, they may choose their matching variables or subgroups so as to derive high or low estimates of discrimination. This is the device used by Banfield (1968) to show the irrelevance of race for income differences. His conclusion was based on the very restricted subgroups of black and white northern families with heads under thirty-five years of age and both husband and wife working. Selection of different subgroups would have revealed a much greater degree of estimated discrimination in all probability.

Multiple regression enables the investigator to handle more variables than does the cross-tabular technique, while the quasi-experimental method permits the investigator to select control variables that are not correlated with race as a result of the design used. So either of these methodologies is preferable for meeting this assumption.

Next, suppose that all relevant causes of inequality have been identified and introduced as controls, but that some have been imperfectly measured. One very common practice among sociologists whenever controls are numerous is to use only a very small number of control categories, sometimes only two for each variable. Thus, someone wanting to control simultaneously for "education" and "experience" may use only three levels of education and two of experience, yielding a combination of six subcategories. It may be thought that such crude categorization is necessary whenever control variables are numerous, though this is, of course, not the case.

It may not be recognized that substantial measurement errors are introduced by such extremely crude categorization. It may also not be recognized that random measurement errors in control variables have the effect of lessening the reductions in the case of a spurious causation model. In other words, in instances where perfectly measured control variables would have lowered a correlation to zero, control variables measured with random error will *not* reduce the partial to zero. The magnitude of the bias (away from zero) will increase with the extent of the random measurement error variance in the control variable(s) as compared with the variance in the true scores. These facts are well known to methodologists but not necessarily to those who are constructing the "measures" of discrimination. Once more, the person wishing to "prove" discrimination may have a vested interest in low-quality research, in this instance the crude measurement of control variables.

The above refers only to strictly random measurement errors, such as might be obtained through coding, punching, and random response errors. When measurement errors in control variables are *systematic* the distortions may be much more serious, and the directions will obviously depend upon the nature of these errors. Consider "education" of blacks and whites in the United States. If one looks at employment inequalities adjusted for "years of formal schooling" does this constitute a proper control for education? The answer depends upon what one means by education and just what the employer is looking for when this criterion is being used in the selection process. If a high school diploma is nothing more than a "union card," and if quality of schooling is unimportant, then years of formal schooling will be the appropriate measure. But if "knowledge," "ability," or "persistence" are also criterion variables, the employer may also legitimately be interested in such things as grades received, type of program, quality of the school, and teachers' recommendations.

If any of these latter variables were actually used in the employer's decision process, but if the investigator uses only "years of formal schooling" as the control, there will of course be measurement error. Whether or not this is biased or systematic will depend upon the circumstances, such as the relative quality of the schools attended by blacks and whites, or possible differences in courses taken or performance levels. Certainly, one cannot argue in the same breath that blacks attend inferior schools and receive inferior educations, on the one hand, and that "years of formal schooling" constitutes an unbiased measure of education, on the other. Ideally, if the data were available, corrections for quality would have to be built into the measure of education before it was used as a control variable. For example, if it were ascertained that there is a three-year differential in performance levels in a certain locale, then black college graduates would have to be compared with whites having a single year of college, and so forth. Actually, the situation would generally be more complex than this because many employers would be combining the "union-card" aspects of education with a crude indicator of quality rather than merely using just the one criterion.

The problem of measurement error resulting from crude categorization will also be most severe with cross-tabular techniques for measuring discrimination. It should be a less severe problem if multiple regression techniques are used. The quasi-experimental methods permit the most precise matching of applicants on variables other than race, especially in studies that use identical written applications, such as that by Walster, Cleary, and Clifford (1971) on college admissions practices. With this approach any systematic error in measurement of a control variable such as education should be equal for both racial groups.

Finally, most standardization procedures, as, for example, the use of partial correlations, presume additive effects of discrimination and the several control variables; that is, discrimination is assumed to have the same effect on inequality levels, regardless of the levels of the remaining causes. In particular, a given level of discrimination is presumed to have the same effect for all minorities, regardless of the minority reactions or adaptive mechanisms and regardless of the alternative opportunities that may or may not be open to them. To the extent that this assumption is not met, a simple statistical control across the board will result in estimates of discrimination that are too high in some instances but too low in others. Such statistical interactions could, of course, be investigated empirically if one had available the direct measure of discrimination as well as measures for the control variables. But when the former variable must be taken as an *unknown* that is measured only indirectly, the additivity assumption becomes untestable, at least in any direct sense of the term. Thus again, our measure of discrimination depends upon the nature of the *theoretical* assumptions one is willing to make about how the causes of inequality fit together.

This is a particularly crucial assumption because, as we noted in our previous discussion, discrimination may involve precisely such an interaction. Specifically, the differential application of criterion variables to members of different racial groups, which is characteristic of double-standard situations, involves an interaction between the racial variable and a criterion variable. Hence, in such a situation, measurement of discrimination in terms of the direct effect of race on an outcome, while controlling for the criterion variable, cannot possibly provide an accurate estimate of discrimination. In such cases discrimination should be measured in terms of an interaction term, such as $R \times C_i$. The problem, of course, will be in determining what interaction term should be used. Calculating separate regression equations for different racial or ethnic groups may give some clues in this regard, but without knowledge of what is occurring at the micro level, where the acts of differential treatment that lead to the observed consequences are taking place, it will be difficult to know. One strictly empirical possibility would be to estimate discrimination initially by means of an equation containing both direct and indirect influences of R, and then to reestimate with an equation from which terms with insignificant slopes have been eliminated.

CORRELATIONS BETWEEN CONTROL VARIABLES AND DISCRIMINATION

In discussing these three crucial assumptions required by the residualizing strategy of measuring discrimination in terms of standardized inequalities we have been assuming that the control variables are either totally uncorrelated with discrimination or spuriously related to it for reasons that are not attributable to the actor or actors who are supposedly discriminating. But there are a number of other possible models linking true (but unmeasured) discrimination to the control variables, and unfortunately they do not all have the same implications for the indirect measurement of discrimination. In such cases it will not be clear whether the control variables should actually be controlled. In the discussion of several such possibilities that follows we shall assume that there is a single control variable, C, that is perfectly measured. Obviously, in reality there will be several such C_i and not all of these may be related to D by the same mechanisms. Therefore for *each* control variable to be considered, one must postulate a theory concerning its causal connection to the unmeasured variable, D.

1. *Control Variable an Effect of Discrimination.* Suppose we assume that the model of figure 11.3 is correct, in which discrimination, D, affects inequalities, I, directly and also indirectly through the control variable, C. As an example of this possibility an employer who wished to discriminate against blacks in the

Figure 11.3. Measurement Model for Discrimination with Control Variable an Effect of Discrimination

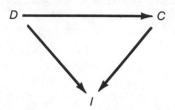

hiring process (a direct effect of discrimination on inequalities) might also accomplish the same thing if it were possible to control the educational processes (C) to such a degree that nearly all black candidates were less qualified than their white competitors. If this were possible, then it would enable the employer to use strictly nonracial educational criteria while still refusing to hire blacks in anywhere near their proportions in the local population. Thus the inequalities are achieved by a combination of direct discrimination in hiring plus indirect discrimination through a manipulation of the educational system. If we wanted to measure discrimination using a degree of inequality we would *not* want to control for educational inequalities in this instance unless we were only interested in the magnitude of the *direct* path, or the discrimination that actually takes place in the hiring process. The total degree of discrimination, which is presumably what we wish to measure, would be given by the combination of the direct and indirect paths.

The same principle obviously applies to multiple indirect paths. If the hypothetical employer were able to prevent blacks from making applications for employment through a combination of tactics such as controlling the educational system, threatening those blacks who actually applied for positions, passing discriminatory legislation, or other devices, it might be totally unnecessary to use discriminatory screening procedures once the candidates had applied for specific openings.[1] Nevertheless, we would want to consider this to be an instance of discrimination. Were we to control out all the intervening C_i we might indeed find that the inequalities between the races disappeared. But where the control variables appear as intervening variables in a model such as this, the disappearance of a partial association (here measured as an inequality between the races) merely means that we have located all or nearly all of the important mechanisms through which the discrimination has been accomplished. Therefore our measure should not control out these mechanisms.

This kind of model suggests that standardization should not be applied. But it is likely that the situation is nowhere near this simple. The employer may have only a very partial control over the educational and political systems, or perhaps over one but not the other. If so, C is a function not only of D but of other variables as well, with the latter variables being correlated with D for various reasons. One such model is diagramed in figure 11.4, where the extraneous

Figure 11.4.   Model of Discrimination with Control Variable a Partial Effect of Discrimination

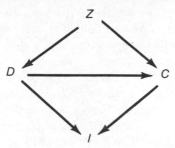

variable, Z, is a common cause of both D and C. Perhaps Z represents a general climate of prejudice in the area that affects both the policies of the employer, and therefore D, and also the educational system, and therefore C. In this case D remains a cause of C, but the correlation between D and C is also partly spurious. If we have correctly specified the model, and *if* all variables were perfectly measured, we could measure the contributions of each direct path and estimate the total impact of D on I while taking out the effects of Z.

Unfortunately, however, we will be in the situation where D has not been directly measured and therefore must be treated as an unknown. Also it is likely that variables such as Z will likewise be unknown or unmeasured, or at least imperfectly measured. There will simply be too many unknowns in the system to yield any kind of meaningful estimate of the effects of D on I. This, in turn, will mean that we will not know how to standardize I so as to obtain a measure of D. If we were willing to assume negligible effects of Z on the relationship between C and D, then we should leave C uncontrolled. But if Z disturbs this relationship then we will not be able to adjust the measure properly without having previously measured the very variable (D) that we are attempting to measure! The model is what is called underidentified, which means that it is empirically hopeless without imposing additional assumptions.

Several different issues involving this kind of model seem worthy of brief consideration. The first is the case of the overqualified minority that, without discrimination, would attain more than its proportional share of the positions being allocated. Before World War II, and even afterward, quotas were placed on the admission of Jewish students to many colleges and universities. Even after such overt discrimination ceased, a correlate of ethnic status—geographic residence—was often used to prevent large numbers of Jewish students from New York City and other eastern cities from entering certain of the prestige schools in that region. It is possible to imagine similar quotas being applied to blacks in professional sports, where their actual numbers are far greater than would be expected if strictly chance factors were operative.

In both of these illustrations, the exact mechanisms for the minority overrepresentation may be unclear, but they obviously involve the fact that the minority subculture has been able to adopt a compensatory mechanism that motivates and socializes so that they have competitive advantages in these particular respects. It might be that if there were no discrimination elsewhere in the system this competitive advantage would be lost and the percentages would be equalized under a completely nondiscriminatory setup. But on a short-run basis, and looking at this single part of the total picture, the presumed effects of Z on the minority behavior, C, are such that zero discrimination, D, would result in inequalities *favoring* the minority. If we therefore found *no* inequalities we might infer the existence of D through a system of quotas that limited the minority percentage to that in the larger population. In this case, then, we would want to control for C (say, the performance levels of Jewish and gentile students on standardized exams) in any attempt to measure D on the basis of I.

Another interesting possibility is that discrimination, D, affects the minority behavior, C, through rather subtle processes for which the discriminator is not held morally responsible. As implied in our earlier discussion, sometimes discrimination may interact with certain minority characteristics. Some minorities, when faced with apparent discrimination, may in effect give up or turn to compensatory activities. Younger generations may lose motivation to obtain the necessary training to compete successfully with members of the dominant group. A second minority may develop mechanisms for coping with discrimination by, in effect, redoubling its efforts and becoming overtrained. Thus D affects C through processes that may be unknown to the discriminating actor and by no means under his or her control. Should these indirect effects on inequalities be lumped in with the direct ones in our measure of discrimination? One's answer may depend upon the use to which the measure is being put. If one is primarily concerned with assessing the objective direct and indirect effects of discrimination, and basing a measure on the resulting inequalities, then one should not control for C. If one were using the measure to assess a particular employer's responsibility for the inequality, however, only the direct path should be counted, in which case a control for C should be made. Our theoretical assumptions concerning the causal linkage between C and D are seen to be crucial in making this decision.

What do these models imply for the measurement of *racial* discrimination, measured in terms of the influence of race on an inequality of outcomes? The residual approach necessitates controlling those variables that are assumed to affect the outcome and that are correlated with race so that their influence does not bias the estimate of discrimination. But we have just suggested that if we assume that the values of these variables for different racial groups are partly affected by discrimination, then we would not want to remove their influence by controlling. It is also desirable to keep four different influences on an inequality of outcomes separate—present discrimination, past discrimination, and the present and past differential desires of, and actions taken by, racial or other minority groups.

The critical question therefore is: what accounts for the assumed correlation between race and a potential control variable? If it can be assumed that the correlation is due solely to discrimination, then it is clear that one would not control for this variable. The influence of present discrimination (say, in hiring) could be derived from the influence of R on I, and the influence of past discrimination on C, in the educational process, for example, could be inferred directly from differences between racial groups on that variable. Total discrimination then would consist of the sum of the influences of R on I and of C on I.

But as we have noted this is not a very realistic assumption. It is far more probable that a correlation between race and a potential control variable is only partly the result of discrimination. It may also be partly due to the differences in desired outcomes and motivations that we have said we want to separate out from the influence of discrimination. Therefore, if this is one's assumption, then one would want to control for these factors so as to derive an accurate estimate of the influence of R on C. And this assumption ties in with the residual procedure for measuring the discrimination in regard to C, namely, controlling all determinants of C that are assumed to be correlated with R. It should be realized, however, that to measure the influence of R on C accurately, it will be necessary to meet the three assumptions we have previously discussed, namely, that all causes of C have been taken into account, that the control variables are perfectly measured, and that there is no interaction between them and R.

This situation is exemplified in figure 11.5, in which the X_i represent the other causes of C. The measurement of total discrimination in this situation therefore would be given by the sum of the direct influence of R on I plus R's influence on C times the influence of C on I.

But an alternative assumption is that the X_i have themselves been partly influenced by past discrimination. For example, the overqualified and the

Figure 11.5. Model for Measurement of Present and Past Racial Discrimination

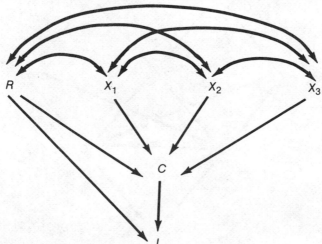

discouraged minorities may have made different responses to discrimination. Therefore an influence of R on the X_i should be included in the model, and if one wishes to include this form of past discrimination in the estimate of total discrimination, then it will be necessary to locate variables that are causes of the X_i along with discrimination, as shown in figure 11.6, in which exogenous Z's have been included.

Obviously one could get caught in an infinite regression with this approach. It could be claimed that the Z's are not truly exogenous and are also partly influenced by discrimination, for example. Therefore one may decide to attempt to measure only present discrimination (the influence of R on I) and one type of past discrimination (the influence of R on C). But one should realize that in so doing the estimate of discrimination may not account for total discrimination.

One possible way out of this dilemma is to posit an exogenous variable as the determinant of both the influence of R on C and of the value of C, as we did with prejudice as represented in figure 11.4. But the measurement implications of this model are not quite what they may seem. A theoretical influence of prejudice on discrimination empirically implies an interaction between prejudice and the racial variable in their effect on C, as shown in figure 11.7. Since the measurement of racial discrimination involves measuring the extent of the influence of R on I, specifying prejudice, Z, as a cause of discrimination necessarily implies that the influence of R on I will differ with different levels of prejudice. Thus the assumptions one makes about the causes of the correlations between race and other variables will determine the appropriate means for measuring racial discrimination.

Figure 11.6.   Model for Measurement of Present and Two Types of Past Racial Discrimination

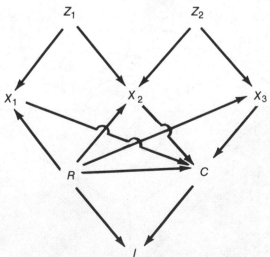

Figure 11.7. Model for Measurement of Racial Discrimination with Exogenous Cause

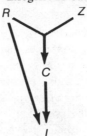

2. *Control Variable as Possible Cause of Discrimination.* It is also possible for a potential control variable to have an effect on discrimination. Suppose, for example, that a minority group engages in behaviors, *C*, that involve performance criteria. Perhaps a high percentage of them are inefficient workers, create morale problems for other workers, or make unusual demands of one kind or another. If so, this may serve to increase an employer's prejudice and tendencies to discrimination. Therefore there will be an influence from the control variable to discrimination.

To some extent this involves the question of whether a given form of discrimination is defined as legitimate or not. If the behaviors involved are not easily measured at the time a worker is hired, is it legitimate to use indicators of such behaviors in much the same way that one uses grades in high school or college to predict later performance on the job? Would we say that an employer is illegitimately discriminating against poor students? Probably not, because the criterion being used is at least a *performance* criterion, even though it may not be highly predictive of very different job performance levels. Suppose an employer inquires as to whether or not a potential employee is a troublemaker, and suppose it turns out that evaluations of this and possibly other behavioral criteria are correlated with race. May the employer use such criteria as bases for hiring decisions without its being considered illegitimate discrimination?

This type of situation is very likely to provoke disputes regarding the legitimacy of discrimination. But it also has serious implications for the measurement of discrimination. Taking the example of racial discrimination, this possibility suggests that a perceived correlation between race and a criterion variable on the part of one who is allocating outcomes will affect the extent to which an allocation of outcomes is influenced by race. Or in terms of our models, a perceived correlation between *R* and *C*, if *C* has an important influence on *I*, will affect the influence of *R* on *I*. The greater the correlation between *R* and *C*, the greater the influence of *R* on *I*. This influence may work in either direction for a given racial group, since members of the group may be perceived to have positive or negative characteristics to a disproportionate extent.

Therefore, if we can assume that perceptions of the characteristics of different racial or ethnic groups are accurate (which may not be a safe assumption), then we would expect that the greater the actual correlation between R and C, the greater the influence of R on I. But, as we have repeatedly observed, the greater the correlation between R and C, the greater will be the collinearity problem involved in determining which of the two has the greater influence on I. At the extreme, in which all members of one racial group possess C and all members of another racial group do not possess it, it will be impossible to determine whether R or C is responsible for receiving a given outcome if that outcome is only allocated to members of one of the groups.

Thus in this case it would not be possible to determine whether in fact there was an influence of this type from the control variable to discrimination simply by looking at sets of outcomes and the characteristics of applicants for those outcomes. The only feasible alternative appears to be micro-level studies in which one studies the goals and working theories of those who are allocating outcomes.

3. *More Complex Models.* Since there are likely to be several variables in the position of C, this will necessitate the construction of models connecting each of these potential control variables to D and to each other. For example, C_1 may be a cause of C_2, which in turn feeds back to affect D through some subtle means. Not only this, but the *inequalities* of several kinds may affect each other, and also feed back to influence D and some of the C's. In our usual model we have supposed that it is discrimination that causes the inequalities rather than vice versa. But, especially in the case of long-run situations, the mere existence of inequalities between groups may be one of the causes of prejudice and therefore discrimination. Ideally, we might be able to specify the time lags involved, as, for example, from one generation to the next. But in macro-level models, where discrete changes may be much more rare than continuous ones, it may be virtually impossible to specify such lags. And without a direct measure of D it becomes impossible to estimate D through the use of I without making numerous simplifications, which take us back to some of the models previously considered.

We have also noted previously that discrimination may exist in the form of an interaction between a variable, such as race, and a criterion variable. Such interactions may coexist with the effects of past discrimination on the criterion variable. The implication is clear. This form of indirect measurement requires very simple causal models. Unless one is willing to assume such models, the measurement of discrimination therefore becomes hopeless. We must either make no pretense at measurement, or we must state that our measurement has been based on a specified set of assumptions.

Our assertions therefore may take the following form. One may legitimately say, "I *found* certain inequalities," or, "I found certain inequalities that were modified in the following ways when controls were introduced for X, Y, and Z." One may then add assertions of the following nature: "*If* one is also willing to assume a certain specified causal model, *then* these standardized or unstandardized inequalities may lead us to *infer* discrimination of a certain degree or magnitude." It then becomes clear that discrimination is being treated as an unmeasured variable and that inferences about discrimination must presuppose certain theoretical assumptions that should be specified.

This scientific fact of life is, of course, due to the way discrimination has been defined, namely, in terms of a causal connection between differential treatment and a social characteristic, such as categorical or group membership. Because the causal connection is included in the definition but yet cannot be established directly through empirical means, the measurement of discrimination must be indirect in the sense that the linkage between the "true score" or the theoretical construct, on the one hand, and the indicator, on the other, is also a causal one that cannot be established solely by empirical means. In other words, "true discrimination" causes a relationship between a variable, such as race, and an inequality of outcomes to appear empirically, but this relationship cannot be separated accurately from the influence of other variables on that inequality.

INEQUALITIES

In the present section our concern is not with inequalities as indicators or indirect measures of discrimination but as variables that are important in their own right. Usually inequalities are taken as dependent variables, but it should be pointed out that they may also become major independent variables for actors who base their decisions upon them or at least upon their perceptions of such inequalities. In an important sense, to be discussed below, the measurement of inequalities should depend upon our assumptions about the roles they play in relation to other variables in the theoretical system, and in particular how these inequalities are "measured" and evaluated by different kinds of actors whose behaviors may be partly determined by the inequalities. We shall once more find that measurement decisions depend upon one's theoretical assumptions linking the variables that appear in the theory—the so-called true values—and the empirical indices that are usually available to the investigator. We shall first look at the problem of the measurement of inequality and then turn to the question of inequality as an independent variable. We shall see that the two problems are not as distinct as might be imagined.

The Measurement of Inequalities

The notion of inequality implies a comparison of at least two quantities with each other, rather than with some absolute standard. In the simplest case of just two groups or individuals, which is the only case we shall consider, the obvious way to compare two scores is to use either a difference or a ratio of some kind. One could, of course, use much more complex functions, such as a difference raised to any positive power, a ratio of two quantities raised to different powers, or perhaps ratios of differences. Since the main points we wish to raise can be discussed in terms of simple differences or ratios, however, and since the quality of our data rarely warrants any more sophisticated measures, there is no point in extending the argument to such more complex measures.

Suppose we have two groups or individuals for which there are numerical scores of some kind. These might be either measures of central tendency, such as means or medians, or they might be proportions or percentages (which are, of course, special cases of means). For example, we might want to compare the median incomes of blacks or whites or perhaps the relative percentages who are unemployed or who have professional status. Conceivably, we might also want to refer to inequalities with respect to dispersion. We cannot think of important substantive applications of such a notion, however, nor does it correspond very well to the usual layman's notion of inequality.[2]

A rather obvious point that we need mention only briefly, since it will be discussed in more detail in the following chapter, is that it is always necessary to specify the population, or "pool," to which a given measure applies. Does it refer to all blacks and whites in the United States, all black and white males over eighteen who are included in the Bureau of the Census definition of "labor force," or some other specified category of individuals? Furthermore, it must be recognized that several different comparisons involving the same conceptual variable may be necessary whenever the two groups are not homogeneous. For instance, a comparison of black and white median incomes tells us about persons who are in the middle range of the respective income distributions but not about either extreme. One might also want to compare blacks and whites in the bottom and top deciles of their respective distributions, since it is entirely possible that a comparison of medians alone could be misleading if extrapolated to either of these extremes. In the discussion that follows we shall assume that we have already resolved such questions of the populations or subpopulations being compared so that we may focus on the measures themselves.

Let us designate the measure characterizing group (individual) number 1 by X_1', and the corresponding measure for group (individual) 2 by X_2'. The primes are used in recognition of the possibility that the measured scores may not coincide with the true ones, which we shall designate as X_1 and X_2 respectively. It will be our contention that the choice between a difference and a ratio measure should depend, at least in part, on the assumptions we are willing to make about the equations linking these measured and true scores. The use of ratios, of course, presupposes that a zero point has been established and that the denominator of the ratio is not zero or too close to zero. A ratio measure of inequalities will cancel out common factors of proportionality, whereas a difference will not.

It would be a simple matter if we could rely solely on such mathematical properties of the respective measures, but as can be seen from this very simple comparison we shall need to make some a priori assumptions about the linkage between true and measured values before this can be done. One might like in addition to rely on *statistical* properties of the two kinds of measure, and in particular how the two components X_1' and X_2' each contribute to the explained variance. Difference measures obviously lend themselves immediately to use with the linear regression model. But since we may readily convert a ratio to a difference by the simple device of working with logarithms, this particular kind of difference in their respective properties does not seem important unless, of course, the denominator of the ratio is approaching zero.

Before looking at the algebra let us briefly consider several illustrations of the kind of problem we are likely to encounter. One very common measure of inequality between blacks and whites is the ratio of black median incomes to those of whites. Here there is no danger of the denominator's approaching zero, and it is usually presumed that since income is a ratio scale there is no problem with the zero point. But if income is to be taken as an indicator of "purchasing power" or of "level of living," the matter is not so obvious. Recorded income may not include farm produce consumed at home, miscellaneous sources of funds, or perhaps certain welfare payments. Some families must pay rent out of pocket, whereas others may have housing provided in connection with their work. Presumably, a really satisfactory measure of "real income" or "purchasing power" would make proper adjustments for all such factors, whereas "reported income" may be quite different from this figure.[3]

As a second kind of example consider "percentage of the labor force that is unemployed." It is well recognized that the official unemployment figures underestimate true unemployment rates since persons who have merely given up trying to find a job are not counted. Thus the true zero point does not correspond to what would be reported as "zero unemployment," but unfortunately we do not know exactly how the true and reported figures compare. Nor are they likely to be identical for all segments of the population. It is also possible that "unemployment rates" are being used in a theoretical model as an indicator of some other variable, as, for example, "perceived unemployment rate" or "subjective probability of becoming unemployed," or even as a measure of degree of "economic threat." The first two of these theoretical variables at least have a conceptual zero point that might be estimated by asking people something about their perceptions or interpretations of unemployment figures. Thus it is an empirical question whether or not the zero points for these internal states correspond with the zero points as measured in terms of the census data.

A similar problem exists with the notion of education as measured in terms of years of formal schooling. Is a person who has not entered the first grade (in the United States) to be considered as having had "zero education"? Or is education dated from birth or some other point? There is at least some evidence from the scaling literature to support the thesis that, at least when education is used as an index of prestige or status, the zero point is *not* entry into the first grade but much closer to age zero (Hamblin 1974). Similarly, if income is used as a prestige indicator the effective zero point may not be zero income but a figure that is above this absolute minimum figure.

Not only is the zero point problematic, but so is the "scale factor," or the slope connecting true values with measured ones. If income is being used as a measure of "purchasing power," and if one is studying changes in inequalities over time, one would want to make adjustments for changes in the value of the dollar. If, for example, one were to report a *difference* between the median incomes of blacks and whites of $600 in 1960 and $800 in 1970, does this imply that blacks are losing ground in relative terms? Not if $600 bought the same amount of goods in 1960 as $800 did in 1970. But this, of course, implies that the variable of theoretical interest is "purchasing power," rather than "income in dollars." It also presupposes that the factors that convert dollars into units of purchasing power are the same for blacks and whites, an assumption that has been questioned (Levitan, Johnston, and Taggart 1975).

Let us assume a very simple linear relationship between the true values and their indicators, since nonlinearities would introduce further complicatons that would take us beyond the points that are immediately at issue. We shall also assume that there is no stochastic or random-error component to the measurement error, as would occur as a result of response or interviewer errors, coding or punching errors, or other minor sources. At least we assume that such errors are negligible as compared with the magnitudes of either the true or measured scores. Otherwise, they might create zero or near zero values in indicators where the true values were non-negligible. We therefore may write the following equations:

$$X_1' = a_1 + b_1 X_1$$

and

$$X_2' = a_2 + b_2 X_2,$$

from which we see that the expressions for the ratios and differences become, respectively,

$$X_1'/X_2' = (a_1 + b_1 X_1)/(a_2 + b_2 X_2)$$

and

$$X_2' - X_1' = (a_2 - a_1) + (b_2 X_2 - b_1 X_1).$$

Without loss of generality we may take X_2' to be greater than or equal to X_1' in absolute value, so that the ratio of the two measured values (though not necessarily the two true values) will always be less than or equal to unity in absolute value.

We may now look at a number of special cases and the simplifications they imply. *If* we are willing to assume that the zero points of the true and measured values coincide, so that $a_1 = a_2 = 0$, and if we are also willing to assume that the two slopes, b_1 and b_2, are equal to each other, but not necessarily to unity, then the ratio X_1'/X_2' becomes identical to the ratio of the true values X_1/X_2. The difference measure $X_2' - X_1'$, however, becomes equal to $b(X_2 - X_1)$, where b represents the common value of the two slopes. It is presumably this kind of assumption that is used to motivate the use of a ratio of median incomes rather than a difference. The presumption is that the zero points for measured income are the same as those for "true incomes," "purchasing power," or whatever other conceptual variable is being tapped. The assumption of equal slopes, in this instance, implies that the conversion factor that changes measured income into, say, "purchasing power" is the same for both blacks and whites. If this were not the case, then $b_1 \neq b_2$ and the ratio of X'_1/X'_2 would be X_1/X_2 times the (usually unknown) factor b_1/b_2.

As a second special case suppose that the two intercepts, a_1 and a_2, are not zero but are equal to each other. Perhaps "education" starts with birth, rather than with entry into first grade. Suppose, also, that $b_1 = b_2 = 1$ so that there is no error in the scale factor. Under these conditions our ratio and difference measures become, respectively,

$$X'_1/X'_2 = (a + X_1)/(a + X_2)$$

and

$$X'_2 - X'_1 = X_2 - X_1,$$

where we have let a represent the common intercept value. In this instance we would prefer the difference measure, at least in terms of the criterion that it accurately represents the inequality measure for the true scores. In the case of the ratio measure, if the intercept value a were considerably larger than either X_1 or X_2 it would dominate both numerator and denominator, with the result that the ratio would be close to unity regardless of X_1 and X_2.

Of course, these two simple special cases *are* special, and we would more generally anticipate intermediate situations. Where the slope and intercept values are known, corrections can obviously be introduced. But we are here supposing that the true values of X_1 and X_2 are unknown, in which case it will be necessary to make some a priori assumptions about these quantities. If we are willing to assume that the intercepts are approximately zero, and the slopes approximately equal to each other but not to unity, then the ratio measure would be preferred on these grounds—though not necessarily on substantive ones to be discussed below. But if there is considerably more doubt about the intercepts, or true zero points, than about the departures of the slopes from unity, then a difference measure is to be preferred. Obviously, then, the decision must depend upon the nature of the theoretical or substantive variable that is being tapped by the measure.

Inequalities as Independent Variables

There are, however, other considerations that must be examined before one decides on a choice of the type of measure to be used, and this leads us to the question of why one would want to measure inequalities in the first place. We have already discussed one important reason: inequalities are indicators of discrimination levels. They may also be important as independent variables that affect the "life chances" of members of the several groups. Regardless of the reasons for income inequalities between blacks and whites, for example, these certainly have consequences in terms of life styles, health, educational opportunities, self-images, and the nature of intergroup relations. If so, then are such inequalities more appropriately measured by ratios or by differences? As we might anticipate by now, the answer will depend upon the nature of the variables being linked to these inequalities. Given our incomplete knowledge, we shall therefore find it necessary, in any given situation, to make certain untested a priori assumptions in order to justify our decisions about which measures to use.

Let us suppose we are dealing with some kind of a percentage, such as the percentage of the labor force that is unemployed, the percentage of illiterates, the percentage having professional status, or the percentage of families with incomes over $5000. Suppose, also, that there is absolutely no measurement error involved, so that we need not be concerned with problems of the type that we have just raised in connection with intercepts and scale factors. Should we compare the percentages for blacks and whites by taking a difference or by using a ratio? Our answer may depend upon the presumed *consequences* of the particular kind of inequality for the persons concerned. Let us suppose that in community I (or at time 1) only 1 percent of the black labor force are professionals, whereas in community II (or at time 2) 3 percent of the black labor force are in this category. Suppose that the comparable figures for whites are 5 and 10 percent respectively. Which community (or time period) has the greater inequality?

It is clear that we may make two different first-order comparisons, depending upon which direction we wish to go in computing ratios or differences. It will be an empirical question, however, to determine what kinds of comparison are most frequently made by different actors in real situations. Thus we may either compare blacks with whites in the same community, or compare blacks with blacks (or whites with whites) across the two communities. Of course, cross-community, cross-race comparisons are also possible theoretically but seem unlikely to correspond to comparisons that are likely to be made in real-life situations. We may then make second-order comparisons by taking either differences of differences or ratios of ratios.[4] The results for our simple hypothetical example are shown in Table 11.1.

Table 11.1

	Community I	Community II	Ratio I/II	Difference II − I
Blacks	1%	3%	1/3	2%
Whites	5%	10%	1/2	5%
Ratio B/W	1/5	3/10	2/3	—
Difference $W − B$	4%	7%	—	3%

Whites and blacks are both better off in community II than in community I, but our decision as to which one has the greater inequality depends upon whether we select the ratio or the difference measure. From the lower right-hand subcell we see that the ratio of ratios figure of 2/3 indicates less inequality in community II than community I, whereas the difference of differences figure of 3 percent favors community I. We might, of course, make similar comparisons for the two groups at two points in time within a single community. Once more, our conclusions as to whether or not blacks were gaining on whites would depend upon the choice of ratio or difference measure.

With such gain scores it would be advantageous to have a number of different points in time so that one might be able to pass some sort of best-fitting curve through the points in order to project them a short distance into the future or to theorize about the processes that may have generated these curves. Several such possible curves are diagramed in figure 11.8. In the context of the present discussion our concern would be how we would compare the heights of these two curves at any particular point on the horizontal or temporal axis. Would we take the *difference* between their two heights or the *ratio* of these heights? Whenever the Y levels or heights are large, the ratios will be close to unity, even though the differences may be just as great as those that are obtained at much lower levels. Needless to say, the determination of a zero point is an important matter in the case of ratio comparisons.

Thus far our only real concern has been with the mathematical properties of differences and ratios, though we have implied that lying behind such considerations may be matters of substantive importance having to do with the role that inequalities play in our theories and in the experiences and behaviors of the actors who are the subject of these theories. We must therefore return to the question with which this section began. How do inequalities appear as independent variables in our theories? We shall consider two important kinds of impact they may have, admitting that there may well be others. The first very general kind of mechanism is through their influence on motivational and organizational variables: on minority morale, expected opportunities, symbolic gains, leadership goals, and so forth. The second mechanism involves the actual impact of inequalities on the real "life chances" of individuals through much more direct channels, as, for example, the effects of persons' incomes on their abilities to pay rent, buy adequate food and clothing, pay for medical or dental expenses, or send their children to college.

Effects through Motivational Variables.   There has apparently been virtually no systematic research on precisely how minority individuals are motivated by examples of success stories involving members of their own group, but there can be no doubt that such influences are real. A change from no black major league baseball players to one (Jackie Robinson) was undoubtedly an important symbolic factor to numerous black ghetto youths, in much the same way that Joe Louis was to the previous generation. We may surmise that the addition of a

Figure 11.8

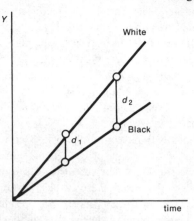

(a) Constant ratio, increasing difference

$$d_2 > d_1$$

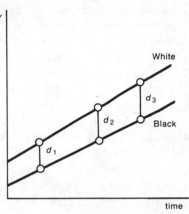

(b) Constant difference, increasing ratio

$$d_1 = d_2 = d_3$$

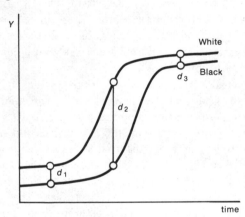

(c) Approach to common upper limit, with changes in both ratios and differences

$$d_2 > d_1, d_3$$

second black to the ranks of the major leagues was relatively less important than the first, a third less so than the second, and so forth; that is, a constant increment of blacks does not result in a constant increment in motivation in situations where the symbolic nature of the advance is a crucial feature of the process. The net addition of even fifty black players to the major leagues might have less total impact upon this motivation than the single change from 0 to 1.

This implied nonlinear relationship would seem to argue in favor of a ratio-type measure rather than a difference measure. In our hypothetical example, the difference between 1 and 3 percent of the black labor force in professional occupations might have a much greater impact on motivation, visibility, and minority morale than a greater difference involving larger percentages. Let us suppose that communities I and II both contain 10 percent blacks and 90 percent whites. In community I the ratio of black to white professionals would be 1:45, whereas it would be 1:30 in community II. This might make black professionals in community II noticeably more visible than those in community I, even though the difference in the total numbers of black and white professionals would be much greater in community II. If both communities contained 100,000 persons in the labor force, community I would contain 100 black professionals and 4500 white professionals, whereas the figures for community II would be 300 and 9000 respectively.

Obviously, we do not have sufficient empirical knowledge to assess how people will respond to such figures, say, in terms of evaluating their own chances of occupational success. Do black children, for example, focus primarily on a relatively small number of symbolic success stories or on what they perceive to be the average experiences of persons in their immediate environment? This undoubtedly depends upon the nature of the occupation, the opportunities for visibility, and how all of this relates to the immediate experiences of the child. A first in some area of athletics, entertainment, or politics is likely to have an important symbolic impact, whereas the first black actuary or President of the American Statistical Association would hardly be noticed. We do not know much about how subjective probabilities are affected by actual frequencies in these instances. The chances of a given boy ever becoming a star basketball player are rather remote, for both blacks and whites, but the subjective probabilities would not be expected to coincide with these realistic odds.

We thus would expect on the basis of anecdotal evidence and common sense— but not solid empirical data—that ratio measures of inequality would come closer than difference measures to approximating the perceptions of minority actors in such instances. In a similar way, ratio measures may also be better approximations to the ways that majority-group individuals may evaluate inequalities at the opposite end of the scale, namely, the "failures," such as welfare recipients, criminals, and school dropouts. In other words, it may be the *ratios* of their own members to those of the minority that they tend to utilize in forming their judgments and in acting upon these evaluations. Such a conjecture is, of course, subject to empirical test.

We are concerned here with how the actors themselves may perceive and in effect "measure" inequalities. We do not imply that they attempt to obtain precise measures or that there is a conscious distinction between difference-type measures and ratios. It may in fact turn out that many persons do not think in terms of variations in degree of inequality, believing simply that inequalities exist. Nor may they distinguish between inequalities and their presumed causes, among which is discrimination. We can envisage a rather large-scale program of research aimed at learning more about precisely how these objective inequalities are transformed into beliefs and how they may affect motivational levels. At an early stage of this research it would be important to find out, perhaps through magnitude estimation techniques, what the functional forms of the relationships are between psychological assessments of the degree of inequality, on the one hand, and both difference and ratio measures, on the other.[5]

Subjects might be asked to supply magnitudes based on comparisons of the type given for our hypothetical communities, with these magnitudes then being plotted against both ratios and differences to see whether or not the one or the other type of measure provides uniformly better predictors of these subjective measures. If the situation is at all complex, such a series of studies would never-theless provide insights as to the conditions under which either type might be more appropriate. Our hunch in this connection is that for symbolic situations, in which minorities are grossly underrepresented in important social positions, the ratio type may turn out to be preferable, whereas for more average situations the difference measure may be superior.

Direct Effects on Life Chances. In one sense it may be claimed that motiva-tional and attitudinal variables always intervene between situational stimuli and behavioral responses. But in many instances the impact is much more direct than in the situations previously under consideration. One's income must be used to purchase food, pay the rent, clothe one's family, and so forth. The fact that, say, a black athlete or entertainer may have reached an annual salary of $500,000 may have symbolic value for one's children, but it is one's own income that affects the immediate situation. Here it appears that difference measures are likely to be much more appropriate, except when adjustments must be made for differences in slope coefficients as already noted. It is frequently pointed out that an increase of $1000 means much more to a family with an income of $3000 than to one with an income of $30,000, but the meaning of this state-ment needs to be examined for its implications. One possibility is that income taxes will absorb a larger proportion of the difference for the higher-income family than the lower, but this is generally not what is implied. Another is that income is merely being used as an indicator of status, and that an increment of $1000 could not even be detected in the case of the family with high income, presumably because the difference would probably go into savings or into some nonvisible addition to the family household. A third interpretation for this statement would be that, at low income levels, a very high proportion of the budget must go into necessities, so that an increment of $1000 would make a basic difference in diet, type of housing, and other essentials. It would give the family a greater psychological and physiological boost. But in any of these instances, would one want to take the position that a ratio would provide a better measure of the change? This would imply that a change from $3000 to $4000 is equivalent in some sense to a change from $30,000 to $40,000.

We are encountering some of the same problems as before, and the answers must depend upon both the nature of the conceptual variables being measured and our assumptions or possible data linking the two. We are in this section thinking in terms of income inequalities as affecting levels of living rather than one's happiness, psychological satisfaction, or status in the larger community. The answers to our questions, then, would have to depend upon the uses to which the income is put. Here it seems sensible (in the absence of data to the contrary) to argue that a dollar is a dollar, so to speak, and that an increment of $1000 will pay for the same additional amounts of food, fuel, rent, or medical bills, regardless of the uses to which the remaining income is put. To be sure, the *utilities* of the family members will depend upon the degree to which certain needs have or have not been satisfied, and this will be a function of the absolute levels of incomes. But this gets into motivational factors, for which we have admitted that ratio-type measures may be more appropriate. We are here talking about the services that may be purchased or the differences in services that are available to families with different income levels.

When our comparisons involve proportions or percentages an analogous type of argument holds. Suppose, for example, that the percentage of blacks who are unemployed is 2 percent, whereas only 1 percent of whites are unemployed. The ratio of black to white unemployment is therefore 2:1, a figure that has remained approximately stable for the U.S. male labor force for several decades. Now suppose these unemployment rates rise to 4 percent and 2 percent, or even to 20 percent and 10 percent. Would we want to say that the same inequalities held? If the inequality rate were being used in a macro-level model for the U.S. economy, it might for some purposes make good sense to use the ratio measure and thus in this instance show stability. But if we were interested in the *numbers* of persons affected, the impact of the change would be much greater on the average for blacks than for whites. This can be seen if we push the example to the extreme in which *all* blacks are unemployed but only half of the whites. The problem with a ratio measure may also be seen, in this instance, by asking how the ratios of *employed* members of the respective groups would look. In the first instance the ratio of black to white employed would be 98/99. Where the unemployed figures were 10 and 5 percent respectively, the employed ratio would become 90/95, whereas in the extreme situation the ratio would become 0/50.

The "index of dissimilarity," which is used as a measure of both segregation and inequality, is a generalization of a difference-type measure where there are multiple categories.[6] This measure is readily interpretable in terms of the number of persons who would have to exchange positions in order for equality to be achieved. This kind of interpretation gives a practical measure to the inequality notion that emphasizes the number of persons being affected. A difference of proportions (or percentages) is thus readily transformed into a difference in numbers. Where these sheer numbers are important, a difference measure therefore seems more appropriate than a ratio measure. For instance, in the above unemployment illustration it would presumably take much less effort to equalize unemployment rates of 1 and 2 percent than rates of 10 and 20 percent, even though the ratios are the same. Furthermore, the latter situation would undoubtedly be described by black leaders as much more serious.

In the absence of reliable empirical knowledge as to precisely how inequalities affect other variables, and how they are perceived by different actors, one may always play it safe by using several different measures, including both simple differences and ratios. In many situations it may not make much difference which kind of measure is used, in which case it might be argued that the whole issue is a moot one, at least from the empirical standpoint. Nevertheless, we believe it important to attempt to supply the theoretical underpinnings for such research, if only to stimulate further thought on the matter. In the present context, we can only comment on the single aspect involving the ways that persons, particularly members of minority groups, tend to make comparisons based on objective inequalities.

Given the fact that accurate data are generally unavailable to most individuals, such comparisons must of necessity be crude and imprecise. A person may know a considerable amount about his or her own level and may also be in a position to evaluate reasonably well the levels of those with whom there is immediate contact. Most certainly, group means will ordinarily be unavailable and so comparisons with those who are rather remote must be made on the basis of very incomplete information, as, for example, impressions formed on the basis of images conveyed through the mass media. We also suspect that members of one group will tend to view persons in other groups as much more homogeneous than is actually the case. Nor will individuals be in a position to compare levels across communities. For example, if we are examining the perceptions by blacks of white median income levels in different cities, occupations, or educational or age groupings, we would expect these perceptions to show much less variation than the true values. Thus, for minorities, the majority-group levels may be perceived to be approximately constant even where this is far from the actual case. Even so, it makes sense to attempt to formulate the theoretical problem on the basis of the assumption that better information may become available to actors.

Absolute versus Relative Levels

Ever since the notion of relative deprivation was used to account for apparently anomalous findings about the attitudes of American soldiers during World War II (Stouffer et al. 1949), sociologists have continually emphasized that many if not most comparisons that people make are relative rather than absolute. Of course, in one sense there can be no such thing as an absolute comparison without reference to some kind of standard. In chapter 6, for example, we discussed the impossibility of developing absolute standards of equity and exploitation. What seems to be at issue, however, is the nature of such standards. Is there some *constant* level with which one compares oneself, as, for example, a level of "zero food consumption," "zero income," or "no education"? We presume that such comparisons are rarely made. More likely is the possibility that comparisons are made with one's own levels in the immediate past, so that the standard may be a continuously changing one that does not necessarily involve comparisons with other specific individuals or types of individual.

Although the sociological literature tends to downgrade comparisons of these types in relation to considerations of relative status, we do not neglect them altogether. In fact, the idea of an absolute standard—if it has any meaning at all—may entail precisely this notion. This implies that each individual has his or her own standard for comparison that depends, at least in part, on the levels to which he or she has become accustomed to experiencing. The basic question one would ask, when applying such an absolute standard, is "Am *I* improving or not, regardless of what is happening to those around me?" It is in this sense that we shall use the notion of absolute standard.[7] In the context of a regression equation it implies that we may insert as an independent variable the present *level* or score of the individual concerned. Since the zero point will depend upon certain past levels in a complex and unknown way, there will be an intercept term in the equation for each individual that will not really be a constant across individuals. In a careful empirical analysis one would want to account for these possibly differing intercept terms, which will be taken as a single constant in our own very sketchy initial formulation.

Let us return to the type of model we discussed in chapter 7 in connection with contextual effects involving nested groups, though with a primary focus on the notion of how actors may compare themselves with others. Once more, simplifications will be necessary in the absence of detailed knowledge from each individual actor as to the nature of the comparisons that he or she is making. Let us suppose that we are concerned with explaining a certain type of minority behavior, Y (say, rebellion), or perhaps some expressed attitude, such as dissatisfaction with the status quo. The individual's level on some independent variable (say, income) will be designated as X. The group means for the "in-group" (here, the minority) and "out-group" (here, the dominant group) will be designated by $\bar{X}_1$ and $\bar{X}_2$ respectively. Of course, there may be more than two groups with which the individual is making comparisons, and there may also be more than a single independent variable used in predicting Y. The principles under discussion are readily generalized, however, so that we may confine our attention to this very simple kind of explanatory model.

We may first note that certain questions cannot easily be answered empirically because of identification problems (of the types encountered in chapter 7) involving too many unknowns for solution. It is important in these instances to recognize the existence of such problems so as to reformulate one's theory in such a way that it may be tested by empirical means. Our experience with the status-inconsistency and mobility literatures should be instructive in this regard (Blalock 1967a). If one wishes to separate out the effects of two (or more) status *levels* from those of status inconsistency, it turns out that unless one has formulated very specific nonlinear models, or has modified the theory in some other way, one cannot separate out the inconsistency effects from the so-called main effects of the status variables. This is because status inconsistency is generally measured as a *difference* between two status levels and thus is an exact linear function of the other two variables. In the linear regression model this linear functional dependence among supposedly independent variables invalidates the assumptions required by ordinary least squares (or any other estimating device), making estimation impossible without modifying either the linearity of the model or the exact linear functional relationship among the independent variables.

We shall encounter exactly the same problem in the case of inequality if we use a difference measure of inequality and if we also introduce the two absolute levels in the prediction equation. Suppose, for example, that we wanted to separate out the effects of (1) an individual's own absolute level X; (2) the absolute level for a comparison group $\bar{X}$ (say, that of the average white); and (3) the inequality between the two absolute levels, as measured by the difference $X - \bar{X}$. Psychologically, it is at least conceivable that a person looks at his or her own level, that of another party, and *also* the difference between the two. Supposing that the comparison is being made between the level of the single actor and a group mean, $\bar{X}$, this would imply the equation

$$Y = a + bX + c\bar{X} + d(X - \bar{X})$$
$$= a + (b+d)X + (c-d)\bar{X}.$$

If we tried to estimate the four quantities, a, b, c, and d, from a regression equation in which Y is taken as a linear function of just two quantities, X and $\bar{X}$, we would have one too many unknowns, and no solution could be found. In other words, we could not unconfound the *difference* coefficient d from the coefficients b and c representing the main effects of the two levels. In substantive terms, we could not evaluate the degree to which the actor was motivated by looking at an actual difference directly, as compared with an examination of the two absolute levels separately.

If the actor were using a ratio measure of inequality, then the last term would become $d(X/\bar{X})$, in which case the model would imply a nonlinear relationship between Y and the two independent variables, X and $\bar{X}$. With really good data one might be able to test the explanatory power of such a model against that of a linear equation and might then be in a position to estimate the separate parameters. Practically, however, we would not expect much payoff as a result of subtle alterations in our models because of collinearity 'and the substantial measurement errors in all variables as well as the magnitude of the unexplained variances usually resulting from such very simple models.

This kind of formulation, which allows for main effects of absolute levels of both the actor and others as well as differences (or ratios) among these levels, may for all practical purposes be untestable. But *some* absolute levels and inequality measures may be considered simultaneously as long as we are willing to make assumptions to the effect that others have zero or negligible effects. In the above very simple example, we might assume that an individual is influenced by his or her own absolute level plus an inequality level of some kind, with the main effects of the absolute level of the comparison group being zero. In the above equations this would imply the assumption that $c = 0$, in which case we may now solve for the remaining parameters, a, b, and d, through the usual estimating procedures.

In more complex setups there will be a number of different sets of theoretical assumptions that may (or may not) imply somewhat different empirical predictions. Rather than merely taking an atheoretical stance and letting the empirical data speak for themselves without attempting to predict values in advance, we would advocate attempts to state explicit theoretical models to see what these may imply. Let us illustrate in terms of the same kind of example but with the added complication that the actor (a minority member) may compare his or her own absolute level with that of the average level for the in-group, $\bar{X}_1$ (say, blacks), and also that of another group, $\bar{X}_2$ (say, whites). Psychologically, the individual may be motivated by (1) his or her own level as compared with whatever standard has been developed; (2) the average status level of in-group members; and (3) the average status level of out-group members. Let us contrast the implications of several possible ways that comparisons might be made. We can compare the implications of each of these possibilities for the coefficients of the empirical equation

$$Y = A + BX + C\bar{X}_1 + D\bar{X}_2$$

that might be estimated from the data without any resort to an underlying theoretical explanation of the comparison processes that could be at work.

For our first model suppose that the individual always uses relative comparisons among the three scores. That is, comparisons may involve (1) self and average member of the in-group; (2) self and average member of the out-group; and (3) average member of the in-group with average member of the out-group. For example, a minority member may be dissatisfied not only because he or she compares poorly with members of the in-group and out-group but also because the in-group compares unfavorably with the out-group. Thus a black doctor may be very satisfied on the first two counts but not the third. This model implies that there are no main effects of the absolute levels themselves but only the comparisons.

The theoretical equation would be as follows:

$$Y = a + b(X - \bar{X}_1) + c(X - \bar{X}_2) + d(\bar{X}_2 - \bar{X}_1),$$

which may be rewritten as

$$Y = a + (b + c)X - (b + d)\bar{X}_1 + (d - c)\bar{X}_2,$$

from which we see that

$$A = a, \quad B = b + c, \quad C = -b - d, \quad \text{and} \quad D = d - c.$$

If we add the coefficients B, C, and D we get

$$B + C + D = b + c - b - d + d - c = 0.$$

Thus this particular formulation implies that when we estimate the three regression coefficients their sum should be approximately zero, except, of course, for sampling and measurement errors. If this prediction is not supported by the data we may reject the underlying theory and then proceed to modify it.

Two very simple alternative models with trivial implications are that the individual makes no comparisons involving the in-group, in which case C should be zero, or the out-group, in which case D should be zero. Another possibility is that one's own absolute level is used along with the difference between the in-group and out-group average levels. In this case what is called the structural equation representing the underlying causal process becomes

$$Y = a + bX + c(\bar{X}_2 - \bar{X}_1),$$

which, of course, implies that the coefficients C and D of $\bar{X}_1$ and $\bar{X}_2$ are predicted to be approximately equal in magnitude but opposite in sign.

Finally, we need to note that a number of alternative structural models will not give specific predictions apart from the signs of the coefficients, nor will they be empirically distinguishable. Consider the following two possibilities. First, an individual may be influenced by (1) his or her own absolute level; (2) the difference between the individual's level and the average in-group level; and (3) the difference between the individual's level and the average out-group level. If so, the structural equation would be

$$Y = a + bX + c(X - \bar{X}_1) + d(X - \bar{X}_2)$$
$$= a + (b + c + d)X - c\bar{X}_1 - d\bar{X}_2,$$

from which we have

$$A = a, \quad B = b + c + d, \quad C = -c, \quad \text{and} \quad D = -d.$$

Here $B + C + D = b$, or the coefficient representing the main effect of the individual's absolute level, but we do not have any specific predictions about the magnitudes of B, C, and D, other than that C and D should not be zero.

As a second alternative suppose that the behavior in question is a function of (1) the individual's absolute level; (2) the individual's departure from the in-group mean, and (3) the difference between the in-group and out-group means. The structural equation would be

$$Y = a + bX + c(X - \bar{X}_1) + d(\bar{X}_2 - \bar{X}_1)$$
$$= a + (b + c)X - (c + d)\bar{X}_1 + d\bar{X}_2,$$

and therefore

$$A = a, \quad B = b + c, \quad C = -c - d, \quad \text{and} \quad D = d.$$

Once more $B + C + D = b$, or the effect of the individual's absolute level. But merely from the values of A, B, C, and D as estimated from the data we cannot distinguish this situation from the previous alternative. Both, however, are distinguished from the first example discussed, where the sum $B + C + D$ was predicted to be zero. Of course if $b = 0$, then all three formulations predict the same result.

There is not a whole lot to be gained by exploring the implications of a large number of alternative comparison processes unless and until better data become available. Our principal point is that when it does become feasible to conduct such studies it will be important to construct theoretical models that link up the comparisons that persons make on the basis of whatever evidence is available to them with the inequality measures we may construct on the basis of quantitative data available to us. Presumably, these theories can be based in part on self-reports of respondents who are asked a series of questions about how they believe they make such comparisons. Not all theories will yield predictions that are empirically distinguishable, but at least some may imply rejectable conclusions. But one important consequence of focusing theoretical attention on perceptions of inequalities and precisely how comparisons are made may be that sociologists may come to treat objective inequalities as independent as well as dependent variables in their theories of social causation.

NOTES

1. In the next chapter, when we discuss sequential pools through which actors must pass to become eligible for entry into a final pool, we shall encounter a very similar type of question.
2. Where internal dispersion seems relevant to an explanation of group differences (e.g., in cohesiveness or leadership patterns) such inequality measures might prove useful. Coalitions between members of different groups might also be explainable in terms of inequalities in dispersion, but we shall not explore such possibilities further in the present work.
3. Also, it may be that the conceptual variable of interest includes the actor's wealth or total assets as well as income. The essential point is that the linkage between the true and measured values for *both* parties needs to be specified or assumed prior to one's choice of inequality measure.
4. Of course we might also take differences between ratios, or ratios of differences, in which case the direction in which the first comparison is computed will make a difference in the score obtained.
5. Since these techniques are based on the assumption that equal stimulus ratios yield equal subjective response ratios (Stevens 1959), ratio measures of inequality would appear more appropriate.
6. This index will be discussed in greater detail in chapter 13.
7. A similar problem arises with the measurement of utilities, namely, determining what constitutes zero utility for an individual. One solution to this problem, as we noted in chapter 2, has been to regard one's current position as zero utility and to measure the utilities of other outcomes in comparison to it.

CHAPTER 12

Allocation III: Eligibility Pools and Candidate Selection Processes

IN THE PREVIOUS CHAPTER we have emphasized a number of complications that arise in the measurement of discrimination, which is a micro-level process, whenever the measures must be based on aggregated data that are resultants of rather complicated decision processes involving three or more parties. This discussion illustrated several general points that we have tried to bring out in our treatment of other topics as well. First, there is a need for micro-level theories even where the analysis is intended to be on the macro level, one reason being that such micro theories are often required to provide the underpinnings for measurement decisions at the macro level. Second, when one has available only aggregated data on the macro level, and when one wishes to infer what the micro-level processes have been that have produced these macro-level results, there is a great danger of imposing overly simplistic assumptions either because of data limitations or because of one's intellectual biases. Third, it is clear that situations vary considerably with respect to their complexity, so that an auxiliary measurement theory that is appropriate in one setting may be very inadequate in another. For all these reasons we have stressed that complex causal models of these processes need to be constructed so that one's assumptions are made as explicit as possible.

In connection with allocation processes we have not yet really addressed a number of important kinds of question, only two of which can be considered in the present chapter. The first of these concerns the problem of determining how it is that only certain individuals actually enter the pool of candidates from which the allocator ultimately selects a small number of winners, whereas many others who are potentially qualified may either select themselves out or never become aware of the opportunity to enter the pool. The second question, which we shall consider in more detail, is that of the nature of the factors that may affect the allocator's decision processes, given the composition of the pool of eligible candidates.

There are a number of additional processes that we shall not be able to consider, both because of their inherent complexity and our space limitations. Early socialization and later schooling opportunities will obviously affect pool entry in many ways, not only in terms of the achievement of the necessary technical skills but also in terms of more subtle factors such as aspirations and expectations, the ability to compete in threatening situations, the learning of appropriate behaviors (e.g., middle-class norms of politeness and proper verbal responses), and so forth. Also, if a candidate happens to be selected for a given position, it does not automatically follow that he or she will accept the offer or remain in the position for more than a short period of time. This may be due partly to characteristics of the candidate and partly to the behaviors of other actors in the candidate's environment. A more complete and detailed theory would be needed to take these and other complications into consideration.

In the following section we shall be concerned with the problem of who becomes eligible for candidacy in the selection process. For sake of simplicity we shall assume we are dealing with situations in which candidates actually apply for a position or entry into a program of some kind. Even in such relatively simple kinds of situation there are a number of important factors to consider: the allocator must make the positions and candidate qualifications known to some population, potential candidates must be in a position to learn of the openings and must take the necessary steps to apply for them; and, of course, they must have obtained the proper qualifications through a series of previous steps. Clearly, pool entry is not a random process. The basic question is "To what degree and in what respects should our measures and analyses of discrimination include a careful consideration of the nature of these pools and the processes through which individuals either enter or are excluded from them?"

ELIGIBILITY POOLS

Whenever one wishes to obtain an actual index of inequality, one must face the problem of exactly who is being compared. For example, if one is counting the *numbers* of minority- and dominant-group individuals who are accepted for certain positions, admitted to college, awarded loans, elected to offices, appointed to jury panels, given prison sentences, and so forth, it becomes essential to divide these figures by the appropriate *denominators* so as to obtain comparable rates. This then raises the question of the nature of the "eligible" population, or pool, from which these persons should be considered to have been drawn.

Suppose one is comparing the numbers of blacks and whites employed in a certain capacity (say, as assembly-line workers) within a plant located in a particular metropolitan area. Perhaps 5 percent of these workers are black. Should this be compared with the percentage of blacks in the United States? the state? the metropolitan area? a ten-mile radius? only those with a high-school diploma, between certain ages, who live within a ten-mile radius? The conclusions one reaches about equal opportunities or discrimination will depend upon the nature of the denominator used.

We may begin by noting that eligibility pools ordinarily have spatial boundaries that are somewhat flexible, though perhaps overly rigidly defined in legal terms. They are also defined in terms of attributes that are thought to be relevant for the purpose at hand. For instance, employees will generally be selected from within a certain geographic territory, although in certain instances they may be encouraged to migrate from other regions. Eligibility requirements may be rigidly set in accord with territorial boundaries, as, for example, states or local political units. Sometimes attributes are defined in terms of certain minimum or maximum levels, as, for example, the requirement that one must have a college degree, or an income no higher than $5000. As with territorial boundaries as well, the eligibility criteria for personal attributes may also be flexible and vaguely defined. One should be "intelligent," "efficient," "attractive," or have "experience." Such nonrigid criteria have obvious advantages in terms of flexibility and in permitting weighting schemes that make it possible for high scores on one dimension to compensate for low ones on another. They make it very difficult to pinpoint the precise nature of the pools from which the individuals are being selected, however.

Given these complexities, we suggest a threefold distinction among explicit pools, qualified pools, and potential pools. By explicit pools we shall mean actual *lists* of individuals who have been considered in the process of making decisions. Examples of such lists would be persons who actually have applied at a personnel office, students making formal application to a college, persons actively considered for bank loans, or persons registering for welfare or other public benefits. Pruned from such lists, however, would be all individuals who do not meet rigidly defined eligibility requirements: nonresidents, persons under the minimum specified age or having more than a maximum specified income, and so forth. In other words, the explicit pool consists of all eligible individuals whose names or other identifications actually appear on an explicit list from which candidates are being selected.

The qualified pool, in contrast, consists of the explicit pool *plus* all individuals who would have been eligible to enter the explicit pool but who may not have done so out of preference, ignorance, policy, or for any other reason. Whereas members of the explicit pool can be identified operationally in terms of lists of candidates, the other members of qualified pools will in general be much more difficult to locate. Nevertheless, given sufficient resources we can imagine such individuals being identified explicitly in terms of a listing of some kind. In practice it is much more common to make an estimate of the approximate size of the qualified pool on the basis of crude indicators such as the percentage of the minority that was in the area at the time of the most recent census survey, perhaps modified by an estimate of its age and educational distribution. To the degree that one's qualifications can only be assessed through elaborate testing procedures, interviews, or recommendations, such approximations can, of course, be subject to considerable error. In contrast with potential pools (discussed below), however, qualified pools can at least in principle be obtained without resort to theoretical assumptions, provided that sufficient resources are expended to obtain the necessary empirical information.

Finally, we introduce the notion of a potential pool to cover not only individuals belonging to the qualified pool but also those who *might* become qualified under certain specified circumstances. Some potential pools merely require modification of physical or spatial parameters, as, for example, the improvement of transportation to the locale of the work setting, migration, or a redefinition of boundary qualifications. Others may require a certain type of training, a period of experience, modifications in home environments, or simple aging. It is presumed that persons in the potential pool could, with a reasonable expenditure of resources or the passage of time, be brought into the explicit and qualified pools.

Obviously, a number of theoretical causal assumptions are necessary to define the boundaries of such potential pools. Exactly which individuals have the potential qualifications to do college-level work, become successful lawyers, vote intelligently, pay back mortgage loans, or become good neighbors? Answers will depend upon the assumptions one makes as to the variables that influence each of these behaviors as well as the likelihood of a particular individual's achieving the necessary scores on these independent variables.

Assuming that the boundaries of these three types of nested pools can be defined by common agreement, it will then become necessary to decide which type of pool is to be used in the (indirect) measure of discrimination, since the relative compositions of the pools may differ considerably in terms of group or category memberships. Among those actually applying for a job or being actively considered, only 3 percent may be black. The qualified pool may contain 6 percent black, and perhaps it may be argued that blacks and whites have the same potential, so that the potential pool contains the same percentage of blacks as exist in the United States. Suppose an employer in Waterloo, Iowa, actually hires blacks in proportion to the numbers in the explicit pool. Does this constitute discrimination? Should this employer have expended more resources to tap the larger qualified pool, say, by extensive advertising and visitations within the minority community? Should the entire U.S. population have been searched, migration encouraged, and extensive training programs instituted so as to make the boundaries of the potential and explicit pools more nearly identical?

It is here where one's measure of discrimination is likely to be influenced by one's ideological biases and theoretical assumptions about causal processes relating to the several pools. Looked at methodologically, however, we can translate these theoretical and ideological questions into considerations concerning the pool boundaries. We therefore turn to a series of questions about such pools, their interrelationships, and the processes of moving from one kind of pool to another.

Hierarchical Pools

One of the first complications that must be considered is the obvious fact that, in reality, there will seldom be a single pool that is relevant to any particular individual at a given point in time. Very commonly there will be multiple pools with overlapping boundaries and with hierarchical properties. Two obvious examples are the cases of occupational pools in industrial societies and of multiple organizations (e.g., colleges) all competing for the same kinds of personnel. Before generalizing the argument, let us first consider these two types of illustration in somewhat more detail.

Occupational structures in complex societies involve a division of labor that is by no means clear-cut and obvious. This implies that the pools for a particular occupation will necessarily overlap those for another, in the sense that some of the same individuals will be eligible for both pools. There are many kinds of job for which college graduates or even M.D.'s are eligible, and these will ordinarily vary according to prestige, required ability level, pay scales, and other relevant features. We may imagine three organizations, *A, B,* and *C* all bidding for the same kinds of individual (say, Ph.D.'s in physics). If *A* is generally more attractive than *B,* which in turn is more attractive than *C,* then we may imagine that the *qualified* pools may be represented in a nested fashion as in figure 12.1.

Certain individuals may believe that they are employable only by *C* and therefore may not apply to either *A* or *B,* regardless of whether or not they really fall within the boundaries of the qualified pools of these other organizations. Such individuals will appear in the explicit pool of *C,* but not of *A* or *B,* regardless of their true qualifications, unless these latter organizations make a special effort to recruit from their more inclusive potential pools. If hiring decisions are made in sequence, then those individuals who are turned down by *A* are likely to enter the explicit pool of *B* and perhaps of *C* as well. This, in turn, will affect the fates of those individuals who do not fall within *A*'s qualified pool.

Thus the pools of one employer are affected by decisions made by others. If decisions are made simultaneously, or in random order, then many individuals may apply to all three employers and make their decisions on the basis of their

Figure 12.1. Nested Qualified Pools of a Hierarchical Nature

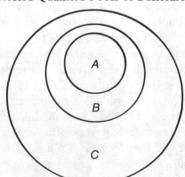

fate in the acceptance structure. Presumably, persons selected by *A* will also be selected by *B* and *C* (with error, to be sure), and most of these individuals will then decide in favor of *A*. Those refused by *A* but selected by *B* and *C* will tend to select *B*, and so on down the line in this very simplified type of model.

One obvious implication is that anyone wanting to assess discriminatory hiring policies on the basis of frequency distributions would need to base a judgment not on the proportions of candidates *actually employed* but on the proportions of offers that were made, assuming these offers are made in good faith. In a market situation favoring dominant-group members over a minority, we would presume that *A* will have the smallest percentage of minority employees and *C* the greatest, even where all three have made offers to exactly the same percentage of minority members.[1] The reason, of course, is that minority members who have been refused by *A* on discriminatory grounds will become members of *B*'s explicit pool. Presumably, these persons will be slightly more qualified than the other candidates in *B*'s explicit pool, but will "bump" some of the relatively less qualified minority candidates from *B*'s list down to *C*'s. The reverse kind of situation will, of course, hold in situations where there is pressure to hire minority workers. The most prestigious institutions will have least difficulty in filling their quotas, and lesser institutions will suffer higher refusal rates from these persons.

Exactly the same kind of process will occur in the case of educational institutions competing for students, athletic teams competing for players, or social clubs competing for members.[2] The most sought-after categories of individuals, regardless of the reasons, will tend to be found in the organizations enjoying the highest status or success and offering the greatest rewards. This will be true even though their decision behaviors are based on identical criteria. This assumes a certain overlap in the qualified pools and therefore a vertical movement from one explicit pool to another in accord with outcomes (both real and expected) at the different levels. In general, we expect this flow to be downward, with rejects in higher explicit pools becoming members of lower ones.

Given such a process, we have argued above that any inferences about discrimination should be based on percentages of offers made rather than on the relative numbers of individuals who actually join—unless, of course, all individuals who are accepted agree to join. The distinction between offers and acceptances becomes most crucial for organizations that are relatively far down the hierarchy, since we presume that offers made by prestigious institutions are much more likely to be accepted than are those made by organizations at lower levels.

But what if these processes are clearly recognized and acted upon by the latter kinds of organization? Knowing that their acceptance rates are apt to be higher for less desirable applicants than for more desirable ones, it is possible that they may adjust their own decisions accordingly. One possibility, for example, is that they may deliberately cater to minorities or other disadvantaged groups and thus take advantage of discriminatory policies of others in order to obtain a relatively higher level of quality than would otherwise be possible. Probably more common, however, is the possibility that such lower status organizations may make relatively too few offers to minority candidates, knowing that a higher proportion of these individuals will ultimately accept. This would constitute discrimination by our definition of the term but would not be discovered through an examination of the actual frequencies of those who accept the offers. Thus a business or educational institution that can demonstrate that it has its proper quota of minority members may be discriminating to a greater extent than one that does not, simply because of their relative positions in the prestige hierarchies.

Sequential Pools

In the case of hierarchical pools we have considered the possibility that there may be a number of qualified pools all appropriate to the *same* individuals at a single point in time. This provides at least some individuals with choices as to which explicit pools they wish to enter and which positions they wish to accept if offered. We shall now consider a somewhat related possibility that could possibly be confused with hierarchically arranged pools. We refer to sequential pools characterized by the fact that the same individual may pass from one pool to another sequentially as he or she ages or acquires (or loses) certain specified skills or other qualifications. As already noted, an obvious example of this kind of situation is that of an educational system through which a candidate graduates from one level to the next. Seniority systems often operate in a similar fashion. Or there may be a set of hierarchically arranged positions or offices that are occupied as a result of a set of sequential steps through which one is promoted or elected to successively higher offices within the institution. Sequential pools obviously have a number of features in common with hierarchical pools, most notably the likelihood that the stages will be hierarchically arranged. If A represents the highest level, B the next highest, C the third highest, and so forth, then individuals who are members of A will have also been members of B and C; individuals who are presently in B will have been in C but will not necessarily all reach A, and so forth. Usually, we expect dropouts along the way, and the probability of entry to each higher level will be a function of a number of variables, possibly including ascribed characteristics.[3]

If one is willing to use an extremely simplistic set of assumptions, one may infer discrimination against a minority (or other group) on the basis of the relative frequency distributions at the various levels. But this presupposes either strict equality within the respective levels or at least that the criteria used in selecting into the higher levels are completely uncorrelated with minority status. Not all members of one pool may be considered as true candidates for the next higher pool, of course. Therefore it is advisable to retain our earlier distinction among explicit, qualified, and potential pools. In the sequential setup, however, we assume that a *necessary* condition for being considered in the explicit pool at a higher level is that one be an actual member of the next lower pool. Thus one must have been admitted to college before being admitted to law school. One must have served as vice-president before being selected as president, and so forth. To the degree that these requirements are not strictly met—and that exceptions are therefore permitted—the situation deviates from the pure case of sequential pools.

The degree to which a given instance fits this model of sequential pools will depend upon the definition of the pool boundaries. For example, college and university faculty generally move sequentially through the ranks of assistant, associate, and full professor. But this does not mean that the associate professors at any given institution will be drawn only from the pool of assistant professors at that same institution. If the pool were much more broadly defined, however, to include assistant professors at comparable institutions, then the sequential-pool model would be closely approximated. Similarly, a large corporation may select its officers or departmental heads from among a list of candidates in branch offices across the country, rather than always promoting through the ranks within each particular branch. If the entire organization is considered as the basis for defining the pools, then the setup would be sequential, whereas if single branches are examined separately, this model might not be deemed appropriate.

This boundary question may be relevant for measuring or inferring discrimination in that the more broadly defined the pools, the greater the flexibility in the system, and also the greater the opportunity to practice discrimination. Thus if a black is next in line for promotion in his or her department, it would be possible to give the job to a relatively senior person in another department or branch office without appearing to discriminate. Where branches or other organizational units are geographically dispersed, or whenever the qualifications of persons coming from different units are difficult to compare for any reason, it will ordinarily be harder to infer discrimination than in instances where the qualifications of the different candidates are well known and easy to compare.

In the case of sequential pools as well as hierarchical ones, our inferences about discrimination will depend upon our assumptions concerning the causal mechanisms through which persons move through the sequence, and in particular on the degree to which we assume that the allocator actually controls or is responsible for the entry from one level to the next. Where we are concerned with promotions within a single organization, we commonly assume that such movement is controlled by a single source. Actually, of course, top management may not be at all well informed as to what really goes on at lower levels—official policy notwithstanding. For instance, blacks may not be promoted from the very lowest levels, thereby blocking their eligibility at much higher levels. If so, however, *responsibility* for such practices is generally assigned to those who have the official authority to make policy and enforce it. In effect, we are willing to simplify the causal model sufficiently to assign total responsibility all along the line to a given set of actors.

Thus if we are also willing to assume equality of qualification by race, and if the initial pool contains 12 percent blacks, then if the second pool contains 6 percent blacks, the next four, the next two, and the final only 1 percent, our measure could be decomposed into components as follows:

$$\text{Total discrimination score} = \frac{1}{12} = \frac{6}{12} \times \frac{4}{6} \times \frac{2}{4} \times \frac{1}{2},$$

where the score at each stage is taken as a simple ratio of the minority percentage in the higher pool to the minority percentage in the next lower pool.[4] Such a decomposition shows the relative disadvantage of the minority at each stage of the process, with the overall disadvantage score indicating the minority disadvantage in terms of moving from the bottom to the very top level.

It is often the case that responsibility for the movement from one pool to the next cannot be so simply assigned because of a complex division of labor, the very imperfect control by actors at one level of selection processes at lower levels, and the behavior of the minority itself. Consider the following hypothetical figures. Suppose the American Sociological Association contains only 2 percent black members but that 6 percent of its officers and standing committee personnel are black. Suppose, also, that 12 percent of the U.S. adult population is black, 6 percent of the college graduates who major in sociology are black, and 3 percent of sociologists with either M.A. or Ph.D. degrees are black. Are sociologists discriminating against blacks, or possibly against whites?

Even if we were to make the very simple assumption of complete equality of qualifications within each of these pools, our answer will depend upon our assumptions about the responsibility of sociologists for the various sets of figures. If sociologists only have control over policies once an individual has entered their professional organization, then one should compare the figure of 6 percent black officers and committee members with their smaller percentage in the organization, concluding that whites are disadvantaged by a ratio of 3 to 1. But presumably, not all M.A.'s and Ph.D.'s in sociology become members, and if responsibility for this fact were totally assigned to the white members, then one should compare the figure of 6 percent blacks with that of 3 percent in the M.A. and Ph.D. pool, with the result that blacks would now be favored by a ratio of 2 to 1.

Sociologists, as faculty members, are also *partly* responsible for whether or not their undergraduate majors go on to graduate school and thus become eligible for membership. If total responsibility could be assigned to them, then the 6 percent officers and committee members should be compared with the 6 percent of undergraduate majors, indicating precise equality (and presumably no discrimination). Finally, if sociologists should be held responsible for the fact that the percentage of blacks majoring in sociology is only half that of whites, then the 6 percent numerator should be divided by 12 percent, implying that (white) sociologists are in fact discriminating against blacks within their professional organization. The decomposition of the total score in this instance would be

$$\text{Total discrimination score} = \frac{1}{2} = \frac{6}{12} \times \frac{3}{6} \times \frac{2}{3} \times \frac{6}{2},$$

where in this instance we would infer discrimination against blacks in each of the first three chronological stages and reverse discrimination in the final stage.

This set of calculations, which is based on the same procedure as in the first example, would undoubtedly be rejected as unreasonable because sociologists simply do not control the processes associated with entry into college and have only minor control over what happens between entry and graduation. In contrast, they do have a higher degree of control over entry into graduate school and graduate training, though certainly not complete control. The problem here is one of diminishing control and responsibility as the pools broaden at the lower end. It might be said that the *association*, as an entity, is discriminating against its white members insofar as the association itself has no say about entry into any of the lower pools. But *sociologists* play a dual role as members *and* as faculty involved in the training process. Therefore in the latter role they might be held partly responsible for the presumed discrimination between time of entry into college and entry into the association.

Ideally, we would want to be able to attach a weight as a measure of this responsibility and to use such weights at all levels to arrive at an overall discrimination measure. The simplest weights, of course, are 1s and zeros. In both of the above hypothetical examples we have used weights for unity for all levels. In contrast we might have used weights of zero for all levels below the top, indicating the association's responsibility for only this single level.[5] The general point is that one needs a causal theory assigning weights to the several parties before a measure of discrimination can be derived in this manner. Only when all or none of the responsibility at a given level can be assigned to the supposed discriminator can we expect to obtain a simple measure, even where we assume complete equality within each pool level.

Pool Boundaries and Minority Characteristics

We have noted at several points that inequalities result in part from minority characteristics and behaviors as well as from actual discrimination. In fact, discrimination and minority characteristics may have nonadditive joint effects on inequality, which is to say that not all minorities react in the same ways to discrimination. In the present context it is also possible that minority characteristics and behaviors may be related to those of the dominant group in ways that are dependent upon the nature of pool boundaries or the manner in which individuals may pass from one pool to another. One obvious possibility is that the percentage of minority members in a higher-level pool in a hierarchical or sequential setup may affect the relative numbers of those who are motivated to achieve the characteristics necessary to enter pools at intermediate levels. The degree to which this occurs, however, may depend upon elements in the minority subculture that make it possible for successful individuals to serve as role models for younger persons. If so, should the differences in pool entry levels be attributed solely to discrimination? If, for example, large corporations have very few black executives, to what degree are these organizations and their leaders responsible for the failure of young blacks to graduate from high school or college?

Since this kind of question is basically similar to those we have just discussed, in the sense that measurement decisions would require one to attach weights to the several actors in accord with one's causal assumptions, let us turn to several other kinds of question that also relate to pool boundaries and minority characteristics but that involve somewhat different kinds of issue. Suppose we were to ask how the percentage of a minority might be affected by the level at which minimum (or maximum) qualifications have been set. Assume that there are a number of colleges of varying prestige and excellence and that they set different cutoff points on some standardized entrance examination. Perhaps the mean for white applicants to each college is 500 and the standard deviation is 100. The mean for blacks might be 400 and the standard deviation also 100. This correlation between C and R (as discussed in chapter 11) might be due to any number of factors—test biases, poorer preparation of black students, or whatever. Regardless of the reasons, if each college applied the same kind of standard for entrance but applied different cutoff points, the relative percentages of white and black students accepted would differ in spite of the fact that discrimination (in the sense of differential treatment because of race) is the same at all of these institutions.

If there were equal numbers of black and white applicants at all institutions and if college A used a minimum cutoff-point score of 600, college B a score of 500, and college C one of 400, then for normally distributed scores the ratios of whites to blacks accepted by the three schools would be approximately 8:1, 3:1, and 5:3 respectively. Assuming that identical percentages of students accepted the offers extended by these three schools, the pools of entering freshmen at the schools would contain very different percentages of minority students. The relative percentages ultimately completing their degrees might likewise be affected by the levels of performance set by the respective faculties, assuming, of course, that scores on the entrance exam are a reasonable predictor of success after entry and that the relationship between minority membership and later performance is the same as that between minority membership and the original test scores. These latter scores may have been equally biased at all three schools. The essential point is that the ratios of white to black students will be affected by the *levels* of the cutoff points selected, regardless of the reasons for the differential scores.

Would we want to argue that school A is more discriminatory than school C simply because of the higher cutpoints used by A? If the screening examination and cutoff-point selection had been deliberately used to discriminate against blacks, the answer would be yes. If it were a criterion that had been found useful in predicting college success, many would say no. And if it were both a predictive criterion and also a shield against admitting too many minority students, the answer would presumably be somewhere in between. Assuming all three schools have used the same testing procedure and criteria but have merely been able to apply different cutoff points, how do we then measure the relative degrees of discrimination?

Pools will also vary in the degree to which members are *homogeneous* with respect to certain criteria. If an extremely high cutoff point has been used in the case of one criterion (test scores, for example), then the pool that is selected—and within which there will be competition to enter the next higher pool in the case of sequential pools—is likely to be very homogeneous with respect to that particular criterion. This, in turn, will mean that scores on this criterion will not predict as well as will those on other criteria on which the pool is much more heterogeneous. Thus if a pool is carefully screened for ability level (as measured by an aptitude test) but not for motivation level, then we can anticipate that motivation will become a better predictor than ability in terms of successful entry into the next higher pool.

To the degree that minority membership is highly correlated with those relevant criteria that also vary to a considerable degree within the pool, then we may anticipate that minority status will be correlated with success as well. But perhaps those criteria most highly associated with minority membership in the general population will have been in effect controlled through the pool entry process, in which case minority membership will not be highly related to later success among those admitted to the pool. In our hypothetical example, the relatively small percentage of minority students admitted into college *A* may be approximately equal to the white students on test performance (and related variables). Perhaps they may even be more highly motivated than those whites who have also been selected, in which case they can be expected to have a higher success rate. Or motivational levels and other relevant factors may be uncorrelated with race at this high level, in which case we would expect nearly equal success rates. The point is that all of these different kinds of resultant (expressed in the form of inequalities) could have occurred either in the presence or in the absence of discrimination. One simply cannot tell without further information or assumptions.

It is often the case that the objective requirements for pool membership are such as to imply a high degree of homogeneity with respect to the criteria that are really the most relevant for entry and later performance. Thus many occupations require rather uniform performance levels involving a certain minimum skill level, but without affording the individual much of an opportunity to perform at higher levels. So-called technician roles are an obvious example. A TV repairman, dental hygienist, plumber, or stenographer must perform at an adequate level, but truly outstanding work in these occupations would be much more difficult to recognize than in the case of surgeons, lawyers, scientists, or artists and writers. Similarly, residential neighborhoods are often homogeneous with respect to type and cost of homes. Many social clubs and other voluntary organizations in effect deliberately select from homogeneous pools with respect to status, age, sex, and occupation.

Whether or not we would expect to encounter a high degree of discrimination in connection with movement into such pools will depend, among other things, on the size of the potential pool relative to the number of actual openings and on the attractiveness of the occupation, neighborhood, organization, or other kind of grouping as compared with that of its competitors. If the potential pool is very large and yet the openings are attractive, we expect to encounter a high degree of discrimination or a selection on the basis of criteria that are largely irrelevant for entry into the qualified and explicit pools.

One way of accomplishing this, where specialized training is required in order to enter the qualified pool, is by restricting the access to this training through a tightly controlled apprenticeship program of some kind. Such access may be limited by applying ascriptive criteria (e.g., race and sex), by relying on a network of primary-group ties through which only the friends of present members are recommended for entry, or by universalistic criteria, such as drawing lots or operating on a first-come, first-served basis. In other instances there may be "gatekeepers," such as realtors or personnel officials, who may use more informal methods of discouraging potential applicants. Or the openings may be kept secret except to selected potential applicants. Whether or not minority discrimination is actually intended in such instances will again be difficult to ascertain, especially when the mechanisms for selection into the qualified and explicit pools are left deliberately vague.

If required performance levels are homogeneous and reasonably demanding but the position involves low pay or status, there may be very small qualified and explicit pools simply because the position is not sufficiently attractive to induce persons to invest their resources in the necessary training. In such instances, individuals with the fewest alternatives are the most likely to desire and actually obtain this training. Many so-called female occupations are of this type. They require reasonably high skill levels but tend to be low paying, so that persons with better alternatives cannot afford to enter them. If one were to attempt to measure discrimination in such occupations by counting the relative numbers of different types of occupant, one might be led to the inference that in fields such as nursing and elementary school teaching there is discrimination against men. It is only because we are willing to make certain assumptions about the mechanisms through which women are self-selected into these occupations that we rule out this kind of possibility.

SOME MODELS RELATING DISCRIMINATION TO ORGANIZATIONAL GOALS AND SELECTION CRITERIA

We have discussed in some detail a number of complications in the measurement of discrimination and have noted that in any reasonably complex decision process involving several parties there are a number of behaviors that may result in inequalities, only some of which are commonly considered to involve discrimination. We have not, however, attempted to diagram these processes in an overall model, nor have we discussed the important question of the interrelationship between an actor's goals and the ultimate specification of criteria in terms of which other actors are evaluated and allocated rewards or punishments. These processes are, of course, far too complex to be treated in one or two summary models, and therefore the present discussion must be delimited.

We shall assume first that we are dealing with an actor (which may be either a single individual or an organization) that has no responsibility for the pool composition. This means that the characteristics of applicants must be taken as predetermined or as givens, though we recognize that the actor's allocation decisions may affect pool compositions at a *later* point in time. We shall also assume that external constraints on the allocator are givens. These constraints may either favor a minority or serve to reward the allocator for discriminating against it. We also take as given the allocator's utilities and subjective probabilities, beliefs concerning minority characteristics, and working theory concerning the best way to achieve organizational goals. Our focus of attention in this section will be on the relationship between such goals and the criteria that the allocator actually selects for evaluating the performance levels or the "potential" of alternative candidates.

Ideally, then, we need a specification of the *goals* of the organization or other actor, the *means* by which these can be achieved, and the working theory as to the relationship between these ends and the criteria used to assess individuals' qualifications. Turning first to goals, it must be recognized that not all goals will be explicitly stated for public consumption. Indeed, certain goals may relate directly to the minority or other category or group. An employer or realtor may have the goal of maintaining a racially homogeneous working force or neighborhood but may attempt to disguise this goal through a series of rationalizations. One law schools may have only the goal of turning out students capable of doing well on the state bar examination and in later law practice. A second may explicitly set a goal of turning out a fixed number of minority lawyers or of encouraging its students to specialize in defending minority members or in handling civil rights cases.

Thus certain goals may be directly relevant to the minority or other category of concern, whereas others may be such as to affect it only indirectly. If the latter happen to result in unequal treatments for reasons that are extraneous to the goals of the organization in question, should the policies involved be considered discriminatory? If, for example, a law school decides, on the basis of the best available evidence, to use a combination of grade-point average and a standardized aptitude test to select among applicants, can it be charged with discriminatory practices if minorities happen to do poorly on this standardized test? Is it discriminatory if a football coach selects players on the basis of speed, weight, physical strength, passing ability, and so forth even if such criteria "discriminate" against women, older men, or persons with IQ's above 150? Should the goals of the coach be oriented solely to winning games, or should consideration be given to the handicapped? Is a law school discriminating when it uses a test that favors any group over another? Answers to such questions depend, in part, upon what are considered to be legitimate goals of the organization in question. To this extent, we become involved with normative questions if we permit ourselves to challenge goals on the basis of their relevance to the minority or other category of person being considered.[6]

It is also usually the case that the relationship between means and ends is problematic in the sense that there will be disagreements over the relative efficiency of alternative sets of means. An employer may work out a division of labor that seems most efficient to achieve certain objectives and may then attempt to specify roles and qualifications that will most effectively do the job. But perhaps a different kind of division of labor, or another set of qualifications, would be relatively more advantageous to a particular group or category. If the first set is used, is the employer discriminating against that group? For instance, if it were true that certain kinds of police work and skill (e.g., vaulting over six-foot fences) are either too dangerous or difficult for women, does this justify excluding women from candidacy? It might have been possible, for example, to redesign the role of policeperson so that only a certain portion of the staff is assigned duties requiring such physical skills. Suppose it could be shown that doing so, however, resulted in a certain loss in efficiency. Could it then be claimed that a police department using the first criteria is discriminating against women?

It is rarely true that any single attribute is *necessary* for adequate performance. There are persons who score low on aptitude tests who do better work in related areas than those who score high. Not every policeperson needs to be able to vault a six-foot fence, nor are college grades a perfect predictor of performance in law school. Does this then mean that such imperfect criteria should be rejected if they "discriminate" against certain kinds of persons? The answer one gives to this kind of question will once more partly determine the measure of discrimination used. If an employer or other screening agent uses a multitude of measuring instruments in a rational fashion (e.g., a regression equation) so as to maximize predictions about performance, we would not ordinarily argue that this is discriminatory unless the goals themselves involved the group in question, or unless the criteria selected were deliberately used to handicap the group. But how can one tell whether or not this is the case?

In the previous chapter we noted that if one of the unstated goals is to exclude the group in question, a very convenient device for doing so is to locate screening criteria that are highly correlated with group memberships and then to give these criteria major weights in the selection process. Another possibility is to use vague criteria, or criteria that cannot be easily assessed, and then to pretend that these were the real criteria being used rather than group membership. In the job interview, for example, the personnel officer can attempt to evaluate "personality," "attractiveness," "potential," "interest," "sensitivity," or similarly vague characteristics. A person is then rejected, not because he or she is black or Jewish but because he or she does not have the appropriate personality or because a competitor seemed to have a greater potential. Are "personality" and "potential" legitimate criteria for selection? Presumably, but this all depends upon the nature of the tasks under consideration. The problem is also obviously that of determining whether or not the measurement of these nebulous traits has been influenced by the individual's group membership characteristics.

Thus we see that anyone who wishes to claim that there has been discrimination may base a charge in connection with a number of different points in the total selection process. There may have been discrimination in determining the nature of the initial pool of candidates, in the selection among organizational goals, in the choice of means to achieve these goals, in the criteria used to select among applicants, or in the misuse of these criteria through biased measurement procedures. Such a charge will involve a combination of normative assumptions about appropriate behaviors as well as theoretical assumptions about the causal connections at various points along the chain. A social scientist attempting to measure the *degree* of discrimination involved will, of course, encounter analogous problems of assigning weights to arrive at a single summary measure. It is no wonder, then, that grossly oversimplified models and assumptions are generally used. But this does not mean that these can be justified on scientific grounds unless, of course, the situation being studied is indeed this simple and clear cut. Usually, it is not.

With these general observations in mind, let us consider the summary model given in figure 12.2, in which variables pertaining to the allocator are given to the left of the vertical dashed line and those applying to the recipients have been placed to the right of this line. As previously noted, the allocator's level of prejudice, certain exogenous norms and outside pressures, and the pool characteristics are taken as predetermined. Both prejudice levels and exogenous influences are presumed to affect the allocator's goals as well as the working theory linking these goals to allocation criteria. It is important to recognize, however, that in some situations neither prejudice nor outside constraints will have any real bearing on these allocation decisions. Our task, of course, is to attempt to spell out the *conditions* under which these exogenous variables will, in fact, have a major impact on such decisions. Certain of these conditions will be examined below in connection with the model of figure 12.3, but they are not represented in the model with which we are presently concerned.

In figure 12.2 the assumption is that goals and priorities interact with variables in the actor's working theory to affect the actual criteria used in the allocation process; that is, the utilities that are attached to the goals of the organization will be multiplied by subjective probabilities that themselves are functions of variables in the actor's working theory. These will generally take the form of beliefs to the effect that certain means will work better than others, either in terms of yielding a greater level of output or as involving lower costs, or

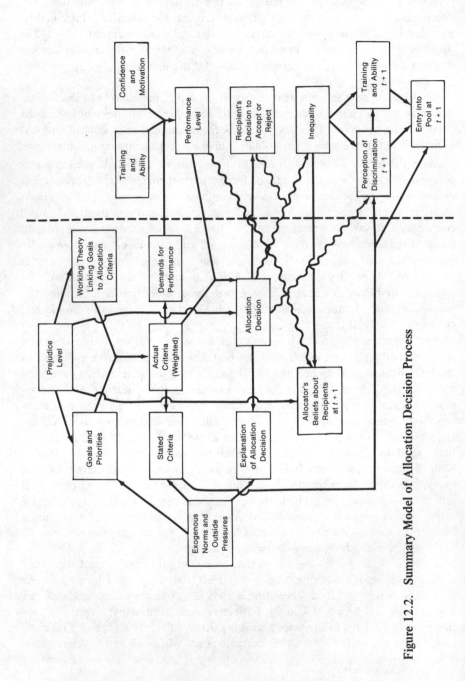

Figure 12.2.   Summary Model of Allocation Decision Process

a combination of the two. In the ideal case, the actor then uses this working theory to arrive at a set of weights assigned to the criteria for allocation, with this weighting scheme being of especial importance in the case of multidimensional performance criteria. But the *true* criteria and their respective weights may, of course, not be the same as the *stated* criteria, since the latter will also be influenced by exogenous norms or pressures. Thus the allocator may actually give considerable weight to an applicant's sex or race in terms of the actual criteria being used in a selection process, but the announced or stated criteria may either neglect these characteristics altogether or substitute correlates for them.

The model assumes that these true characteristics, and their weights, will affect the "demands for performance" that the allocator places on the candidates, perhaps in the form of a series of tests, information about past performance, responses to interview questions, or observable behaviors in a social setting, such as a luncheon meeting with potential work colleagues. The candidate's performance is, of course, affected by previous training and ability and also the candidate's level of confidence and motivation. These candidate characteristics are assumed to interact with the allocator's criteria to affect the actual performance level; that is, we must at least allow for the possibility that the relationship between training, ability, and confidence, on the one hand, and the allocator's demands, on the other, may be fairly complex. In particular, in the case of discrimination we must include the possibility that the allocator deliberately may make demands that, say, undermine the self-confidence of minority candidates or that in other ways place them at a competitive disadvantage. These possibilities are merely allowed for schematically in the diagram by suggesting a nonadditive relationship among all three variables.[7] A more detailed model would be needed to specify an additional set of variables that might affect these interrelationships.

We have also implied a nonadditive relationship between performance level and the allocator's criteria, as these variables jointly affect the final allocation decision. We have in mind the likelihood that the actual criteria will be multidimensional and that the weights attached to different types of performance are unlikely to be either precise or explicit. In many instances, then, an allocator will be faced with a decision in which candidate A is stronger with respect to certain characteristics or actual performances, whereas B is stronger with respect to another set. If so, the ultimate decision may be influenced by extraneous factors, such as the allocator's prejudice level, a concern about repercussions of the decision, or even an effort to balance out the present decision with previous ones.

In theory, it is possible to argue that such extraneous factors have already been considered in determining the real weights assigned to the actual criteria. It is possible, however, that the weights may shift between the time of the performance and the final evaluation. We have in mind the case of the evaluator who, perhaps subconsciously, invariably finds "reasons" for rejecting a minority applicant regardless of performance levels. This may be done either by shifting weights ex post facto or by invoking the importance of some highly intangible characteristic such as "personality" or "potential." This allocation decision must, in many instances, be explained to the candidates themselves or perhaps to some third party. Such an explanation will depend not only on the facts of the decision but also on exogenously determined norms and outside pressures. Once more we anticipate that rationalizations for an action may very well involve the use of weights other than the true ones or criteria that are either extremely vague or that entail information such as confidential reports that are unavailable to these third parties.

After an allocation decision has been made, the recipient of an offer must decide whether or not to accept. In many cases we may assume an automatic positive response. In our discussion of eligibility pools we pointed out, however, that under certain circumstances where the candidate has made multiple applications this decision cannot be considered irrelevant either to one's explanations of inequality or to a measure of discrimination. In effect, there are at least two parties to the transaction, and a neglect of the behavior of one can lead to incorrect inferences concerning the behaviors of the other. Our model does not deal with another kind of complication, however, namely, the possibility that the recipient's decision may be affected by the *manner* in which an allocator's decision has been made or the results communicated. For example, the allocator may simultaneously accept an applicant and try to discourage him or her from accepting, perhaps by pointing to competitors' advantages, indicating that chances for promotion are not favorable, that the community reaction will be hostile, or that future work associates may be uncooperative. A more complete model would incorporate variables that may affect this kind of impact on the recipient's decision-making process.

We have drawn in four wavy arrows to represent causal connections that involve an aggregation process. One of these goes from performance level to the allocator's later beliefs regarding recipient characteristics. The idea is that if candidates with given characteristics consistently perform well or poorly on a particular task, this aggregate result will have an impact on the allocator's beliefs and therefore on his or her decisions regarding *other* applicants with similar characteristics. These aggregated performance levels will also be subject to memory distortions and other possible biasing factors related to the allocator's belief system and other exogenous influences. The second wavy arrow has been drawn between the recipient's decision to accept and any aggregate measure of inequality that one might wish to construct; that is, we presume that the recipient's decision represents the final step in the process and therefore that these decisions, when aggregated, will determine the percentages of applicants of various types who ultimately are counted as having been enrolled, employed, promoted, or whatever. The third and fourth wavy arrows lead from the allocation decision to inequality and to later perceptions of discrimination.

Finally, this measure of inequality—or a more crudely constructed estimate of inequality made by others—may affect later values of several variables, including the allocator's future beliefs, other actors' perceptions of discrimination and other actors' willingness to obtain the necessary training to make them eligible for entry into a future pool. This says, of course, that the variables that we treated as exogenous are not really so, particularly if we want to construct a long-run model and if the allocator is sufficiently important and the number of decisions sufficiently numerous as to have a major impact on these aggregated levels.

Opportunities and Motivation for Bias

Although we cannot elaborate on the basic model of figure 12.2 in any great detail, we can supplement our earlier discussions of the measurement of discrimination and inequality· by focusing briefly on certain factors that may be expected to affect the allocator's opportunities and motivation for introducing biases in the selection process. In the model of figures 12.3A and B we have taken the actual selection bias as a multiplicative function of the opportunity for bias and the utility for bias. In effect, the opportunity factor can be thought of as representing a probability term perhaps best described as a probability of being able to introduce biases without this being detected and sanctioned. In some cases the allocator may also be unaware of these biases. In others the process may be such as to make it difficult or impossible for an outside observer to detect or verify the presence of such biases. We shall first focus our attention on the "opportunity" variables, which are represented in the left-hand portion of the diagram of figure 12.3A. We then turn to a discussion of factors that influence the utility or motivation for bias, some of which also may affect the opportunity factor as well.

The allocator's goals are not explicitly represented in the diagram, since the relationship of goals to criteria involves an additional set of complications that we cannot consider in this abbreviated discussion. As a general rule, we would expect that such factors as goal clarity, the simplicity of their relationship to specific means, the mutual consistency or compatibility among goals, the ease with which progress toward goals can be measured or assessed, and the degree to which priorities have been made explicit will all influence the clarity and simplicity of the criteria to evaluate candidates or recipients of rewards or punishments.

Also of possible interest may be the question of whether or not these goals refer directly to the actors being evaluated or whether these actors will merely be serving as means to these ends. For example, we presume that a college or professional school considering applicants will have, as goals, the training of these applicants themselves, rather than merely using them as employees who are assigned tasks designed to increase the efficiency of production. Where applicants are being used primarily as means, for example, an employer may prefer to hire certain minorities that are willing to work for lower wages or that appear to represent a relatively docile labor force. Factors such as these may be

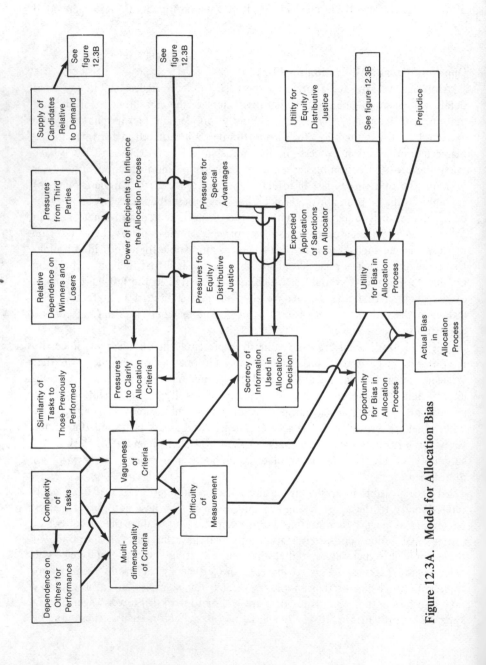

Figure 12.3A. Model for Allocation Bias

Figure 12.3B. Model for Allocation Bias (continued)

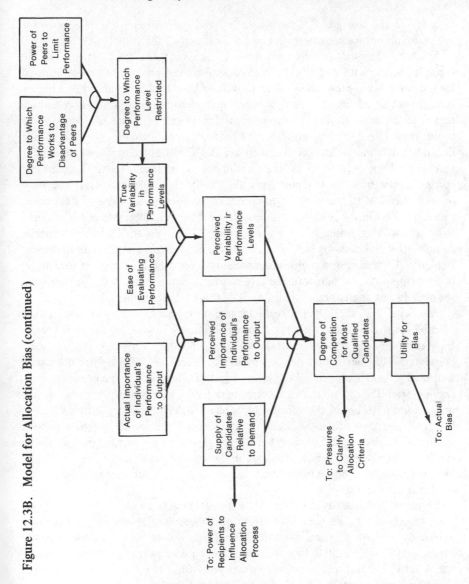

included in the true goals of the allocation and therefore have implications for the evaluation process, but yet may not appear among the stated goals.

Whatever the goals, which we assume to be givens, the model begins (at the top left corner) with certain characteristics of the tasks that are to be performed by the candidates, presumably after they have been hired, promoted to a higher level, or admitted into a training program, residential neighborhood, voluntary organization, or whatever. The three major dimensions of these tasks that appear in our model are (1) task complexity; (2) the degree to which task performance depends upon the cooperation of others; and (3) the degree to which similar tasks have been performed by the candidates in the recent past. There are, of course, many other task dimensions that could be delineated, but we have limited ourselves to these three because of our interest in focusing on the opportunity for bias in the selection process. These three task dimensions are assumed to affect two dimensions relating specifically to the evaluator's selection criteria, namely, the vagueness or lack of clarity of these criteria and their multidimensionality. Vagueness and multidimensionality affect the difficulty of measuring or assessing potential performance levels, which in turn affects the opportunity for bias. Let us briefly elaborate on each of these relationships.

Whenever the task to be performed is highly complex, we may anticipate that even where it is possible to break it down explicitly into a number of subtasks, the skills required will be multidimensional and only very imperfectly inter-correlated. This means that persons placed in these roles will perform unequally well in the various aspects of the overall task. If there is a single product forthcoming from the effort, the evaluation may have to be based primarily on this product rather than on the various component behaviors that produced it. But how can one then evaluate a candidate's potential *before* he or she has been admitted or hired and therefore before the product has been produced? If the candidate produced a similar product under conditions that are also judged to have been similar to those under consideration, this product may be used to help resolve the difficulty.

Thus task complexity and similarity to previous tasks may interact in their joint effects on the vagueness of selection processes. For example, it may be extremely difficult to assess the "potential" of a quarterback in football, or the "team play" of an athlete in any sport that requires a large number of coordinated activities. But a professional sports team finds it relatively easy to select among competing candidates through the simple device of watching them play in college competition. In contrast, the promotion of an employee into a position requiring "executive abilities" may be based on much less adequate information because the candidates may never have performed any tasks similar to those deemed necessary in their new role.

Similarly, if the role demands a high degree of cooperation from others in the environment, then the criteria for selection should ideally involve an assessment of the degree to which this cooperation will be forthcoming. We assume that the greater the complexity of the task, the more such cooperation will be needed, and so we have drawn in an arrow leading from task complexity to dependence on others for cooperation. This relationship itself will depend upon a number of other factors. There may be certain highly complex tasks involving manipulations of things or ideas, rather than other actors, for which such cooperation is not required. We often refer to these kinds of task as "technical" ones and generally expect that it will be easier to assess such technical skills than others precisely because we do not need to assess simultaneously the impacts of behaviors of third parties. Where such third parties, as, for example, one's work associates, are prejudiced against a minority, it becomes possible for them to hamper a minority candidate's performance to the degree that he or she is dependent upon them for cooperation.

All three of these task characteristics are presumed to affect vagueness, with the joint effects of task complexity and similarity to previous tasks being non-additive. Complexity and dependence on others are assumed to affect multi-dimensionality of criteria. The two criterion dimensions—multidimensionality and vagueness—are taken as determinants of measurement difficulty. The existence of multidimensional criteria, of course, necessitates the assignments of weights to the criteria, and we assume that in most instances this will be exceedingly difficult to achieve in a rational way. As a result, we expect that the reliability across allocators will be relatively low, even in instances where they may agree on scores for the separate dimensions. In particular, some allocators are likely to place a relatively high emphasis on performance measures, whereas others may tend to stress motivational factors more heavily. Vagueness necessitates the substitution of judgmental criteria for objective ones, again tending to reduce interallocator reliability.

In many kinds of allocation decision some of the most important criteria for selection are likely to involve either rather vague operational criteria or weighting schemes that remain implicit and often unknown to the allocators themselves. This is especially likely whenever it is necessary to base such decisions on relatively scanty information or on long-run predictions as to future development of an actor's potential. Therefore it must not be thought that a failure to operationalize such criteria or their weights is, ipso facto, an indicator of a preference to hide the decision-making process from view or to introduce deliberate biases. Nevertheless, one suspects that the greater the utility attached to avoiding such biases, and the greater the pressure that is placed on the evaluator to make such criteria and weights explicit, the less vague these criteria will be. For this reason, we have drawn in arrows from pressures to clarify criteria to vagueness and from the evaluator's utility for bias to vagueness. In effect, then, the more important it is for the evaluator to avoid bias, the greater the expenditure of resources to clarify criteria and to reduce this vagueness. Thus the utility for bias indirectly affects the opportunity for bias, presumably with a time lag necessary for refining the measurement task.

Utility for Bias or Discrimination

The difficulty of measurement, along with the allocator's ability to keep the decision-making process secret from relevant parties, is assumed to affect the opportunity for bias, and therefore actual bias or discriminatory behavior. But the *motivation* for bias also must be present for there to be actual bias, if we assume that strictly random errors of judgment will tend to equalize over the long run. Of course, the utility or motivation for bias need not be explicitly recognized and may, in fact, be deeply embedded in the subconscious. Presumably, such factors as the allocator's level of prejudice and incorrect working theories may contribute to these hidden biases, but we shall treat such factors as exogenous to the model. Our focus in this section will be on two somewhat related sets of causes of the utility for bias, namely, those stemming from the actions and interests of the recipients and their coalition partners, on the one hand, and those relating to performance characteristics that necessitate making careful judgments, on the other. We shall first consider how the power positions and actions of the recipients may affect these utilities, as indicated by the set of variables located toward the right side of figure 12.3A.

Relative Power of Recipients. Candidates for a position will differ with respect to the degree of power they can mobilize to affect the allocator's decisions. We have indicated three exogenous variables that may affect this power: (1) the supply of candidates of a given type, relative to the demand; (2) pressure that may be imposed by third parties, including those who are in a coalition with one or another set of candidates; and (3) the relative dependence of the allocator on the future behaviors of the winners and losers in the allocation process.

If there is a substantial oversupply of other potential candidates, who cannot be controlled by the candidates under immediate consideration, then the latter candidates will be in a weak position to insist upon partial control over the allocation process. In effect, each candidate under such circumstances is likely to be placed in the position of having to compete primarily in terms of whatever characteristics the allocator may demand, since it is likely that rival candidates can rather easily be found who simultaneously are equally qualified and who are willing to play a more docile role in connection with efforts to influence the allocation process.

If, however, there are powerful third parties that can be brought into the picture, either to enforce the application of universalistic criteria or to insist on quotas or other mechanisms for affecting the distribution of outcomes, then we would anticipate efforts of at least certain candidates to enlist the support of these third parties as coalition partners. A numerically large group of candidates may, of course, exert political pressure or the threat of violence either to reduce the supply of its major competitors or to pressure the allocator to use criteria or weights that discriminate against these competitors. This implies, then, that the second kind of "exogenous" variable listed above may, under certain circumstances, be taken as endogenous. In particular, the supply–demand situation may indirectly affect these actions by third parties precisely because a segment of the potential recipients bring pressure to bear on these third parties. The point to underscore in this connection is that the allocator is seldom exempt from outside influences, including those affected by the recipients themselves.

The third factor we have listed involves the degree to which the recipients and nonrecipients of an allocation process may, through their anticipated subsequent behaviors, influence the allocator. Consider two extreme kinds of situation. In the first, the allocator selects a certain number of winners, and the losers then drop completely out of the picture. For instance, a college or an employer may admit or hire some applicants, with those being rejected simply going elsewhere or in no way challenging the decision. In contrast, consider the common case of promotion decisions in which those who are not promoted remain as employees and therefore must continue to be motivated to perform at satisfactory levels. In this latter instance, the allocator not only must be concerned about selecting the best candidates for higher positions but also must find ways of compensating the losers, perhaps encouraging them to apply again for promotion. Therefore these losers have considerably more latent power than those who simply drop out of the system, and they are therefore in a much better position to press for a clarification of criteria and for information concerning their relative performance on these criteria.

We have drawn in arrows from each of these three exogenous variables to a variable labeled power of recipients to influence the allocation process. This variable, in turn, is assumed to influence three others: (1) pressures to clarify allocation criteria, thereby reducing vagueness; (2) pressures for equity/distributive justice; and (3) pressures for special advantages. We have already commented on the first of these three mechanisms. Where candidates are rather similar in terms of ascribed characteristics, or where the latter cannot be easily used as a basis for selection, we would expect that the greater the recipients' power, the greater the pressure placed on the allocator to apply criteria consistent with notions of distributive justice or equity. However, where certain potential recipients are much more powerful than others, and also rather easily identified by ascriptive characteristics such as race, sex, or age, we may anticipate pressures for special advantages based on these criteria, though perhaps suitably disguised or rationalized in terms of correlated characteristics that are seemingly more relevant to the tasks being performed.

Both of these latter two types of pressure, we argue, operate through two mechanisms as indicated by the arrows. First, they may operate to affect the secrecy of the allocation process, which in turn affects the opportunity for bias, either positively or negatively, as the case may be. Second, the recipients may attempt to apply direct sanctions on the allocator. The *expected* level of sanctions will depend not only on past sanctioning behaviors but also on the degree to which these recipients have knowledge about the workings of the allocation process. Therefore we have drawn in an additional arrow from secrecy to expected sanctions. This expected level of sanctions is then taken as a direct cause of the allocator's utility for bias.

In connection with secrecy, we are arguing that secrecy reduces the recipients' ability to apply sanctions on the allocator, at least to the extent that the justification for such sanctions depends upon demonstrating exactly what has taken place during this allocation process. We must remember, however, that secrecy *may* work in favor of equity/distributive justice if such secrecy helps to reduce pressures from those who may be demanding a bias in their own favor. Pressures toward "open" decision-making processes may, under certain circumstances, inhibit free discussion and subject the allocator to sanctions applied by the most powerful groups of recipients, or by those recipients who are most willing to apply pressure in their own behalf. This is to say that degree of secrecy interacts with type of pressure to affect the actual bias in the allocation process. In our diagram, secrecy thus operates both through the opportunity for bias dimension and (indirectly) on the utility for bias. The pressure variables operate directly on secrecy and on the utility for bias through the mechanism of expected sanctions. Therefore the direction of the relationship between degree of secrecy and degree of bias is not necessarily a positive one.

Performance Characteristics and Utility for Bias.   Obviously, certain characteristics of the task itself may affect the allocator's utility for bias. As a general rule we would expect that whenever performance levels are highly variable, easily evaluated, and highly important to the total output levels of interest, it becomes of great importance to the allocator to locate the candidates with the optimal combination of characteristics. If performance levels are relatively uniform and not terribly important to the overall output, however, then candidates may be more or less interchangeable, so that considerations of efficiency may dictate that screening considerations are far less important than turnover rates, pay scales, relationships with outside parties, or other "extraneous" variables. For example, where workers' outputs are relatively constant after a relatively short training period, but where pay scales are expected to be determined on the basis of seniority, it may be to an employer's advantage to encourage relatively high turnover rates or to favor candidates, such as young women, who may be expected to drop out of the labor force after a relatively brief period of time.

In an earlier discussion of the success of blacks in entering professional sports in large numbers, one of the authors (Blalock 1967b) noted that there are a large number of characteristics of this occupation that favored the entry of minorities, once the initial barrier had been broken. The fact that an athlete's performance obviously works not only to the advantage of the employer but also of one's teammates tends to inhibit control mechanisms that restrict the athlete's level of productivity. Also, in at least some sports, an athlete's performance is not as heavily dependent on the cooperation of his or her work associates as may often be the case in other occupations. This, of course, varies by type of sport, but it is often the case that efforts by one's teammates to hamper one's performance level would be highly visible to coaches and fans. In effect, each athlete must get ahead by means of his or her own performance level, given the high degree of competition for starting positions. This implies that it is difficult to place road-blocks in the path of one's competitors. Also, training is available to a large number of candidates rather than being highly restricted as in the case of a tightly controlled apprenticeship program.

Given these facts, the degree of performance variability is considerable. Also, performance is highly visible and relatively easy to measure in terms of standardized criteria such as batting and pitching records, points scored, passes caught, yards gained, and similar measures. As we noted previously, it is also rather simple in the case of professional sports to predict to future performance because of the opportunity to observe the candidates in similar roles. Finally, there is considerable competition among employers for the best talent, with the outcomes for these employers being very much dependent on getting a highly accurate reading on performance potential. In short, the utility for avoiding bias in the selection procedure would be expected to be extremely high.

These considerations suggest a model that has been diagramed in figure 12.3B, which is actually a continuation of figure 12.3A, but which has been separated from it so as to reduce the confusion resulting from a diagram with too many variables. Notice that the ultimate dependent variable in the model of figure 12.3B is utility for bias, which interacts with opportunity for bias to affect the actual degree of bias in the allocation procedure. The immediately prior variable, degree of competition for the most qualified candidates, is itself a function of three variables: (1) supply of candidates relative to demand, which also appeared as an exogenous variable in figure 12.3A; (2) perceived importance of the individual's contribution to output; and (3) perceived variability in performance levels. Actually, a fourth variable, namely, the importance of the output to the allocator, could also be introduced into the model, but we shall here merely assume that the output in question (e.g., winning games) is in fact of considerable importance.

The second and third of these causes of degree of competition for qualified candidates are both affected by the ease of evaluating performance. This variable refers to evaluating performance *after* the selection process has occurred, as, for example, a baseball player's batting average or pitching record. This "ease of evaluation" variable is assumed to interact with the true variability in performance in affecting perceived variability, and also with the actual importance of performance to the total output in affecting the perceived importance. The idea is that if the allocator can accurately assess true performance levels, it becomes easier to assess both the true variability in these levels and the actual importance of performance to the overall product. Although ease in evaluating actual performance is not to be equated with the ease of measuring a candidate's *potential* for performance, we have already suggested that whenever candidates have had previous experience with highly similar tasks, these two evaluation procedures may also be virtually identical. For example, a major league baseball team may assess an athlete's potential with a high degree of accuracy by watching him perform for a minor league team.

The overall implication of figure 12.3B, then, is that in very competitive situations in which performance levels are highly variable and easily measured, the allocator will generally be motivated to select the best-qualified candidates and to improve the efficiency of any measuring instruments designed to predict to this performance. This assumes, of course, that the allocator strongly desires a high performance level and is also unable to persuade competitors to restrict the availability pool in some artificial fashion. Thus, as long as all major league teams excluded black baseball players from the competition, no single team was handicapped by a decision to restrict its membership to whites. But as soon as the Brooklyn Dodgers admitted Jackie Robinson to their team, and the competitive advantage became obvious because of his high visibility as an outstanding performer, there was an almost immediate rush to tap the pool of black athletes. Had Robinson's teammates been able and motivated to restrict his performance to any significant extent, however, or had it been almost impossible to compare performance levels in precise terms, we assume that the motivation to retain racial bias would have been much greater. Although not in our diagram, in this case it was also true that there were interested third parties, namely, the fans, who could also rather easily evaluate performance levels and who could apply financial incentives in support of the goal of having a winning team.

Finally, at the extreme upper right of figure 12.3B we have added three variables that operate to affect the true variability in performance. The argument is that if an actor's performance works to the disadvantage of his or her peers, then they will be motivated to restrict this performance. Similarly, if they lack the power to limit an actor's performance level—even when motivated to do so— there will be little or no restriction of performance due to this source. Since the first of these exogenous variables relates to utilities, whereas the second affects subjective probabilities, we anticipate a multiplicative joint effect on the degree of restrictions placed on performance level through this source.

CONCLUDING REMARKS

With the exception of quasi-experimental studies such as those we discussed in the previous chapter, micro-level models and studies of discrimination appear to have lost favor among sociologists in recent years. The trend has been toward increased reliance upon statistical analyses of discrimination based on aggregated macro-level data. By the micro level we mean models and studies that focus either on the allocators of outcomes or on the recipients and that analyze allocators as decision makers, influenced like all decision makers by utilities and subjective probabilities. The model of candidate selection processes presented above exemplifies this micro-level approach.

Our discussion in the previous two chapters has outlined a number of very severe problems that result when one attempts to infer discrimination from aggregated data. Micro-level studies will not be problem free, but we believe that the knowledge gained from them may help to clarify macro-level analyses.

This clarification may occur in several ways. First, micro-level studies may provide information regarding additional variables that should be used as control variables in macro-level studies. Second, such studies may also yield information about interactions among control variables and between them and characteristics, such as race, that are typically the focus of discrimination studies. Such interactions should be specified in macro-level models so as to yield less biased estimates of discrimination. Third, such studies are the only means of assessing the part played by the perceptions of applicants that are held by allocators. Their perceptions of the degree of correlation between race or sex and certain control variables, for example, may be an important intervening variable explaining the manner in which these control variables are applied as decision criteria.

Fourth, such studies can also provide information regarding eligibility pools. In order to have this result they would have to take into account the applicants for the outcomes and the part that self-selection plays in the transition from one pool to another. Fifth, micro-level studies may also provide insights regarding the contextual effects, such as perceived pressures from superiors or anticipated negative reactions from third parties, that affect allocators. Sixth, information about the goals of allocators and their views of the manner in which the application of certain criteria relate to these goals may also be gained from studies focused at the micro level.

Seventh, we have suggested that perceptions will be significant at two other points in models of discrimination. On the one hand, the perceived legitimacy of discrimination in a specific situation on the part of allocators will be a major variable influencing the likelihood of their discriminating in that situation. On the other hand, perceived legitimacy *and* the perceived occurrence of discrimination in a situation will combine to influence the responses of recipients, nonrecipients, and third parties. Data regarding these perceptions can only be gained from micro-level studies.

Lastly, micro-level studies conducted in different settings and using different criteria may also be helpful in determining whether the same measurement model is appropriate for different types of discrimination and different situations. Should sexual discrimination, for example, be measured with models using the same variables that are used in the measurement of racial discrimination? Should discrimination in the allocation of incomes be regarded as identical to discrimination in the allocation of jobs? Or should discrimination in different kinds of employment situation, for example, professional as compared to unskilled, be measured using the same model? Micro-level models will be most likely to provide data for questions such as these.

NOTES

1. This assumes an oversupply of candidates in all three qualified pools. Actually, in practice we may find that *A* makes relatively fewer offers to minor-

ity members than C because of its greater ability to attract dominant-group members. We are also assuming, here, that the utilities for joining A, B, and C are identically distributed across the dominant and subordinate groups.

2. We are here assuming that if, say, an athletic team needs only a certain number of players for each position, the candidates for these positions are considered to constitute (nearly) distinct pools (e.g., quarterbacks are not in competition with running backs).

3. Although we have not exploited the idea of vacancy chains (White 1970) in the present context, there is an obvious parallel between this notion of sequential pools and that of chains of openings in a hierarchical organization. In terms of mobility opportunities, the basic idea developed in White's work is that vacancies created near the top of an organization will produce successive vacancies further down the line as positions are filled by candidates who, in turn, vacate still other positions.

4. This product-type measure of discrimination can be interpreted in terms of a series, each of which is an odds ratio representing the relative proportion of minority- and dominant-group members who are promoted or who actually move to the next stage. As we shall see in our next illustration, one or more of these odds ratios may be greater than unity, indicating that the minority is actually favored at a given stage.

5. In order to avoid an overall discrimination score of zero, in this instance, we would need to devise a weighting scheme with the property that, as the responsibility weight approached zero, the fraction corresponding to the relevant stage would approach unity, so that the term would have a negligible impact on the overall product. This suggests using exponents as weights.

6. As noted in our earlier discussion of possible definitions of discrimination, we would take issue with Brown (1973), who seems to believe that normative questions must necessarily be entangled with the concept of discrimination and a number of other basic social science concepts.

7. Arcs have not been included in this diagram because we do not wish to imply that these suggested nonadditive joint effects are necessarily multiplicative ones.

CHAPTER 13

Approach and Withdrawal I: Segregation, Integration, and Related Concepts

WE HAVE EXAMINED a number of relatively general social processes under the headings of exchange, equity, social power, and allocation and distribution. It is clear that although such processes may be analytically distinct, almost every concrete instance of social interaction will involve features of each of these rather general processes. This is undoubtedly why it is possible for the social analyst to focus primarily on only one of these processes and to claim that its ubiquitous nature indicates that it can be taken as *the* fundamental factor in social interaction. In the remaining chapters we shall examine still another highly general social process, namely, that of approach and withdrawal. Given our interest in applying the analysis to problems in the field of racial and ethnic relations, we shall concentrate rather heavily on the concepts of segregation and integration, but obviously this somewhat narrowed focus is not incompatible with the position we have taken in previous chapters. Any reasonably complete theory of race and ethnic relations will have to be a special case of a more general theory of intergroup relations, and it will also have to encompass a wide variety of social processes on both the micro and macro levels of analysis.

Obviously, all social interactions will involve varying degrees of spatial and social distances among the participants. Two exchange partners, for example, may engage in so-called silent exchange involving a total absence of physical contact, or at the opposite extreme they may elaborate upon their exchange relationship in such a way that the exchange almost necessarily involves a high degree of intimacy and extensive personal contacts. Dominant parties may interact frequently with their subordinates, though usually in such a fashion that it is clearly understood where the power lies, or they may effectively insulate themselves from contacts with subordinates by dealing through intermediaries. And, of course, many persons who are social equals but who do not share a common cultural heritage or who, for whatever reasons, prefer not to

515

interact with each other may sort themselves spatially and organizationally so as to minimize contacts. Also, persons who are not necessarily mutually attracted to each other may find themselves in rather extensive interaction merely because they are individually attracted to the same locations or forced to use the same facilities. All of this is to say that one may analyze the processes of approach and withdrawal, or segregation and desegregation, as being distinct from, although undoubtedly correlated with, the several processes we have previously discussed.

These approach-withdrawal processes are also highly complex and therefore create the same kinds of measurement and conceptualization problem as those we have had to face in connection with exchange, power, and allocation processes. Certain individual behaviors, such as spatial movements and the construction of barriers preventing the movements of others, are easy to observe and aggregate. But since behaviors and motivations cannot be simply linked in a one-one fashion, we shall again encounter measurement and conceptualization problems whenever the theoretical construct involves a presumed or postulated internal state, such as the desire to avoid another party or an attraction to that party. For example, although we may record instances of whites moving from a city to its suburbs and their replacement by blacks, we cannot assume that the "retreat" to the white suburbs constitutes avoidance behavior, if by this term we mean behavior motivated by a utility to reduce contact.

Spatial proximity and interaction cannot be equated. We cannot assume that a movement of blacks into a predominantly white neighborhood or school district constitutes integration, if by this term we mean a high degree of intimate or equal-status contact between members of two groups. Integration could, in principle, be measured through detailed observation. In most macro-level studies, however, data on interaction patterns may have to be replaced by information about spatial locations and group memberships, and this will of course require assumptions about the relationship between spatial location and interaction patterns of different types.

We may therefore anticipate that there will be substantial data gaps in the study of approach-withdrawal processes, as well as for the other processes we have previously discussed. Furthermore, the nature of these gaps will depend upon the data-collection instruments, the theoretical orientation of the social scientist, and the level of the analysis. On the one hand, it appears as though macro-comparative analyses tend either to lack the fine-grained details that enable one to link up specific interaction patterns with spatial locations, or they tend to be focused rather narrowly on one or two specific kinds of process, such as residential segregation. On the other hand, micro-level analyses oriented to the study of individual differences in interaction patterns tend to neglect contextual variables or, at most, involve comparisons of only two or three contexts of a highly specific nature.

Before attempting to provide a set of variables and possible models that we hope will prove useful in integrating these several distinct approaches, we shall first characterize very briefly three distinct race-relations literatures that deal rather directly with this central topic but that appear to contain very few cross-references or even common terminology. These are (1) the social psychological literature on the relationship between prejudice and intergroup contact; (2) the comparative literature on racial and cultural pluralism; and (3) the demographic and ecological literature on residential segregation. Each of these bodies of literature is extensive and difficult to summarize, even in an entire book. Our purpose is therefore the very limited one of merely orienting the reader who is unfamiliar with the field of race and ethnic relations.

THREE APPROACHES TO THE STUDY OF
CONTACT AND SEGREGATION

Prejudice and Intergroup Contacts

There have literally been hundreds of studies relating individual prejudice to interracial or interethnic contact of various kinds, and, of course, the notion of social-distance prejudice implies a negative utility attached to cross-group contact. The reader is referred to Allport (1954) and Ehrlich (1973) for excellent summary treatments of this body of literature. In general, social psychologists have found rather modest positive associations between the extent of contacts with members of another group and favorable orientations to them. But these relationships are nowhere nearly as strong as one might expect, and the general conclusion seems to be that it is only the rather intimate and voluntary types of contact that predict well to individual prejudices. Furthermore, it seems apparent that market-oriented or other impersonal intergroup contacts have little impact in reducing prejudices, whereas sharply competitive or threatening contact may actually increase them. In the United States there has been a rather dramatic decrease in expressions of prejudice since World War II, but this decrease seems most marked in connection with stereotypes and willingness to grant minorities equal access to opportunities, legal equality, and freedom of movement. The decline in prejudice seems much less pronounced in connection with highly personal relationships or contacts that are "close to home" in the sense that they are likely to impact directly on the respondent.

There are, however, ambiguities with respect to direction of causation in most studies that show an association between attitude and contact. It is difficult to tell whether it is primarily those with low initial levels of prejudice (or other personality characteristics favorable to attitude change) who have self-selected themselves into contact situations, or whether the contacts themselves have actually reduced the prejudices. The detailed relationships between spatial location and interaction patterns do not seem to have been systematically investigated by sociologists. Perhaps the classic early study of this question was Deutsch and Collins's investigation (1951) of the presumed effects of segregated and integrated housing patterns on attitudes and interracial contacts, in which the authors provided evidence favoring the position that spatial proximity (under these circumstances) had at least a moderately strong impact on visitation and other forms of neighboring patterns. The work of Robin Williams (1964) and his associates shows that the relationships between contacts, attitudes, and behaviors are highly complex and that in unstructured or ambiguous situations behaviors are at least as likely to depend upon cues provided by other actors as an individual's own level of prejudice.

The overwhelming majority of these social psychological studies of which we are aware have involved situations in the United States subsequent to World War II and have also been limited to relatively flexible and unstructured contact situations in which individual choices have not been highly constrained. With the possible exception of studies conducted in the rural South (which have not been numerous), most of the settings have been what we might characterize as permissive, though discouraging of intergroup contacts. The predominant pattern has been one in which individual decisions result in a general sifting of persons toward members of their own group and away from those who differ in terms of modal culture patterns, religion, race, age, and socioeconomic status. Such a social setting is, of course, in marked contrast to that found in extreme pluralist societies characterized by truly major cultural differences, a multitude of distinct languages and dialects, relatively self-sufficient subsistence economies, and a high degree of political control of one group by another.

Macro-level Studies of Pluralism

For the most part, the literature on so-called comparative race relations has been written by social scientists with backgrounds in anthropology and social history, or by sociologists whose training has been nonquantitative in nature. Much of this literature is highly descriptive and/or historical in nature and has not contained detailed quantitative information about individual interaction patterns or spatial locations. Unfortunately, this difference in scholarly orientation has been confounded by the fact that the societal settings of the contact situations described in these works have generally been extremely different from those studied by American social psychologists and other race relations specialists.

As a general rule, the macro-level studies of pluralism have been conducted in colonial or neocolonial areas of Africa, Southeast Asia, and Latin America and the Caribbean area. As noted above, these societies have usually been characterized by extreme internal differences in culture, language, and socioeconomic backgrounds, as well as dominance patterns.[1] Some scholars, such as Furnivall (1948) and Smith (1965), go so far as to *define* pluralistic societies as being those that are controlled by a numerical minority of the population (generally whites, of course) and that are characterized by a high degree of economic exploitation of the numerical majority. We agree with van den Berghe (1969) that it seems unwise to make minority rule a defining characteristic of such pluralistic societies. The fact remains, however, that the societies being studied are vastly different from the United States and other "developed" Western nations.

The notion of spatial segregation does not appear to play a crucial role in the explicit theories of cultural and racial pluralism, but this is undoubtedly because it is taken for granted. One also gains the distinct impression from this literature that cross-group contacts are kept to the bare minimum necessary for economic exchanges and that it is almost the essence of pluralistic societies that the cross-group contacts are those of strangers.[2] With the exception of highly urban contacts, we are also given the impression that there can be very few individual choices relating to these interactions. It may be that the constraints operating against cross-group contacts are so pronounced, and the contacts themselves so highly regulated, that micro-level analyses of individual preferences and behaviors are not needed. Nevertheless, such constraints cannot be taken as givens over the long run and may be expected either to diminish under pressures of urbanization or possibly to increase in the presence of intergroup power struggles. Unfortunately, at least in terms of our own reading of this literature, there appear to have been very few efforts to link these macro-level and rather general discussions of pluralism with either the social psychological literature on prejudice and contacts or with the ecological literature on residential segregation.

As a general rule, this comparative race relations literature seems highly useful in pointing to the wide range of possibilities that exist throughout the world, including some that involve much more extreme separation and cultural diversity than that found in the United States. But it does not appear to be the kind of systematic literature needed in the process of theory construction and contains relatively few theoretical propositions interrelating well-defined variables. In effect, it serves to remind us that generalizations based on U.S. studies must be highly tentative, and it also provides a few general frameworks for analyzing social change. But many of these discussions on the macro-comparative level are weak precisely where we would expect, namely, in their failure to relate to micro-level assumptions about individual attitudes and behaviors and in their lack of comparability in terms of both focus and data-collection techniques.

Ecological Studies of Residential Segregation

Macro-level analyses of residential segregation are also comparative, though using units smaller than nation-states. For the most part, data-availability problems have restricted these studies to metropolitan areas of the United States and Canada. These studies tend to be highly quantitative, methodologically sound, and analytic in the sense that attempts are made to distinguish among closely interrelated concepts, careful attention is given to problems of measurement, and interrelationships with other variables are hypothesized, tested, and evaluated. In general, however, they have been sharply restricted in scope and closely tied to the availability of quantitative data. Earlier studies in this field tended to be relatively more descriptive and historical in nature, with less attention being given to problems of intercity comparability. In general, the earlier studies documented both the extent and nature of residential segregation in urban areas but contained relatively little information as to its correlates or systematic theory as to its causes. Certain of these earlier studies, notably Wirth's classic study (1928) of Jewish ghettos in medieval Europe and Chicago prior to 1930 and studies by Woofter (1928), Johnson (1943), and Weaver (1948) of black-white segregation, apparently provided the stimulus for comparative work of a more quantitative nature.

Detailed studies of residential trends in Chicago by Duncan and Duncan (1957) and in ten major cities by Lieberson (1963) have been supplemented by comparative studies of residential segregation in U.S. cities by Taeuber and Taeuber (1965) and others. These ecological studies have provided careful discussions of the measurement of residential segregation and the problem of choosing among spatial units, matters that will be of concern to us later in the chapter. In effect, they have served to point up the fact that even a relatively simple concept such as that of residential segregation is multidimensional and rather easily confounded with closely related concepts.

These studies have also provided valuable trend data based on procedures that can be replicated over time with relatively few conceptual ambiguities. They have also provided correlational data, and some over-time data as well, yielding information as to possible causal relationships between spatial location and other macro-level variables pertaining to urban areas. Overall, however, they have not provided many clues as to the linkages between residential segregation and micro-level processes, such as changes in individual attitudes and behaviors, interaction patterns of various types, or the micro-level mechanisms that may operate to inhibit or encourage intergroup contacts. This shortcoming seems to stem from the basic data gap and a lack of information that would make contextual-effects models a useful tool. Almost without exception, these ecological studies have been confined to census-type data involving rather simple information concerning such things as family income, native versus foreign-born ancestry, race, and (in some instances) native language.

The general findings of these segregation studies are, of course, complex and therefore cannot be summarized in any simple fashion. In very broad terms, relationships between both racial and ethnic residential segregation and various socioeconomic indicators have been surprisingly weak. In the case of white-nonwhite segregation, index of dissimilarity scores for block data have been uniformly high over the past three decades and only very weakly related to indicators of economic inequalities. There have been some slight changes, such as a dip in segregation scores outside the South during the 1950-1960 decade but a rise in segregation during this same decade within the South. These slight changes in segregation scores have been interpreted by the Taeubers as being partly explainable in terms of changes in the housing market and differences in location patterns owing to historical factors. For instance, they argue that a pattern of "piling up" noted by the Duncans in Chicago prior to 1950 appears to have been primarily due to the combination of a housing shortage and the large influx of blacks during the war period.

Similarly, the early pattern of black–white settlements in some southern cities, such as Charleston and New Orleans, produced rather low segregation scores that are currently increasing to the levels of other cities in this region. Generally speaking, there is a tendency for southern cities to be somewhat more segregated than those located elsewhere, especially those in the Far West. But the overall levels are so uniformly high and basically unchanging that it is difficult to find variables that can explain the variations among them. In the case of ethnic minorities, Lieberson (1963) and others (Darroch and Marston 1971; Kantrowitz 1973; and Guest and Weed 1976) have found slowly decreasing levels of residential segregation, but, especially in the case of so-called newer immigrant minorities, there is still a much higher level of segregation than would be expected on grounds of income, education, or occupation.

In view of the relatively restricted goals of these segregation studies, as well as the tendency of the authors to stick very closely to their data, it is perhaps not surprising that there are virtually no cross-references between this highly quantitative and largely American body of literature and the previously mentioned cross-cultural literature on pluralism. Perhaps the closest connection between the two consists of a relatively small body of literature on pluralism within the United States, as exemplified by the work of Kennedy (1944), Gordon (1964), Glazer and Moynihan (1970), and others who have discussed the so-called melting-pot theory of assimilation into American society.

Like the cross-cultural literature, much of this assimilation literature tends to be historical-descriptive and nonquantitative in nature. Although this permits the use of a wider range of variables in explanatory systems, it also appears to make this literature more vulnerable to theoretical disputes that are not susceptible to empirical falsification. In particular, it is very easy to find evidence either to support or to refute the general thesis that cultural pluralism exists in the United States and that efforts to modify the degree of pluralism in either direction should or should not be made. We generally agree, however, with van den Berghe (1967:135–36), who points out that whatever cultural pluralism exists today in the United States is of an extremely mild or bland form. This will make it difficult to locate explanatory variables to account for such a truncated distribution. If so, we must ultimately look to cross-cultural studies to provide our major explanatory variables.

This brief overview of the literature suggests that we need to combine important features of each of the three types of study that we have characterized. First, we must obtain micro-level data on individuals, tapping both attitudes and approach–withdrawal behaviors. Second, we will have to make cross-cultural comparisons at this micro level. Third, our measures will need to be *standardized* across studies, as exemplified by the careful work of students of residential segregation. And finally, it will be necessary to compare results across a number of different types of interaction, ranging from the casual to the intimate.

ISOLATION, INSULATION, AND AVOIDANCE

A distinction that is not commonly made within the social science literature, but which we nevertheless believe to be important in terms of our subsequent discussion, is that between isolation and insulation. We shall say that a system is isolated if it is not subjected in any manner to outside environmental forces. Therefore, for a completely isolated system it becomes plausible to assume that outside forces can safely be neglected, as may be done when one is studying the gross movements of the planets within the solar system. In contrast, by insulation we shall mean the degree to which a system is *protected* from outside disturbing forces, when present. A well-insulated thermodynamic system, for example, is one for which one may safely ignore changes in outside heat levels because insulating materials prevent heat transference across the boundaries of the system, from inside to outside, or vice versa.

In the case of human groups, an isolated group would be one that is completely out of contact with other groups, whereas a well-insulated one is capable of resisting their impacts even if present. This distinction is important because, even though both types of group are not influenced by outside events, the *mechanisms* that produce this result may be very different. In the case of the isolated group there simply are no others in the immediate environment, whereas a well-insulated group may not be influenced by outside forces precisely because it was deemed necessary in the past to build up defensive mechanisms of a protective nature. Thus an isolated group is more likely to be separated from others by large distances, major natural barriers, or perhaps because the territory occupied is not at all attractive to outsiders in terms of the expected costs of migrating to it or exploiting its resources. An isolated group that is suddenly discovered, or whose territory becomes valuable to others, may lack insulating mechanisms precisely because it has in the past been able to rely on this isolation. In contrast, a group that wishes to insulate itself in spite of proximity to others must find ways of erecting barriers to compensate for the presence of these potentially disturbing environmental forces.

This distinction between isolation and insulation relates closely to the means that are used by whatever group or society is being considered, as well as to the degree of success that it achieves in resisting environmental impacts. As a general rule, we would expect that isolation will be a function of spatial separation and that, if ample space is available, a group that wishes to isolate itself from others will tend to withdraw from territory that is jointly occupied, provided that the movement is not too costly. If the withdrawing group is weaker than its neighbors we can expect that it will retreat to the least desirable land, thereby hoping to isolate itself through this means. A stronger group occupying territory that is desired by several groups, however, is more likely to insulate itself by erecting protective barriers against their invasion. This may literally be accomplished by constructing fortifications or by other means that have the effect of making entry by outsiders extremely costly.[3]

Where land is scarce relative to demand, and where there are no gross differences in quality so that all territory is desired by a reasonably large proportion of the total population, we may anticipate that groups wishing to insulate themselves from others will stake out territorial claims roughly in proportion to their relative power positions, since isolation will be virtually impossible. But if a functional division of labor requires continual contact, and if other processes that reduce segregation are also at work, we may expect these insulating mechanisms to break down. The essential point is that isolating and insulating mechanisms will depend upon the nature of the circumstances and will require different kinds of behavior on the part of the relevant actors. As a general rule, we expect that insulating behavior will require a more active orientation, both in terms of keeping members of other groups at a reasonable distance and also in terms of preventing the group's own members from becoming absorbed or influenced by these other groups. Behaviors of certain small religious sects, such as the Amish and Hutterites, illustrate this latter type of insulating mechanism.

Although we may anticipate a strong relationship between isolation and the physical distance separating two or more groups, it would be a mistake to conclude that measures of spatial separation, or segregation, will always be appropriate as indicators of isolation. We can certainly imagine situations in which there may be physical proximity and yet a high degree of isolation. This may be true, for example, when members of the two groups mutually have no interest in interactions beyond the bare minimum necessary for strangers who live close to one another. Also, if members of group A know that members of B will erect barriers to contact, or that contact will prove costly for other reasons, then this may produce a situation approximating that of a high degree of isolation in which members of group B will be left alone to pursue their own interests without interference. In general, however, we presume that such instances of high isolation coupled with proximity will tend to be unstable and of rather short duration, given almost inevitable disputes over the occupancy of space, the distribution of goods and services, and political competition. It nevertheless seems advisable to keep the ideas of insulation, isolation, and spatial separation as conceptually distinct.

Turning next to concepts that specifically refer to behaviors and interactions, we shall again encounter the problem of definitions of behaviors that contain references to, or assumptions about, motivations or other postulated internal states. The notion of avoidance or avoidance behavior is obviously important in connection with approach and withdrawal behaviors. In ordinary usage, the term *avoidance* usually has the connotation that the actor is moving away from someone or something with the *intent* of reducing contact. When we speak of someone as deliberately avoiding another person or perhaps some activity, such as work, we practically always have in mind that the behavior in question is not coincidental.

For instance, if we are not at home when friends visit because we happen to be out shopping or visiting someone else, this is not considered to be avoidance behavior. But if this repeatedly occurs in spite of the fact that we are also frequently at home on other occasions, the inference may be made that there is an intent to reduce or minimize contact. Often, avoidance involves spatial movement away from other actors, but the term is also used to refer to instances in which barriers to contact are intentionally erected. Thus if someone's office door is always locked or if knocks go unanswered, one may infer avoidance behavior in spite of the fact that there may be no physical movement. But if the knock is not heard, or if the actor cannot be interrupted in spite of a willingness to engage in contact, we do not ordinarily characterize the behavior in question as avoidance behavior.

Therefore the measurement of avoidance requires either a knowledge of the actor's intent or an inference about internal states, as well as an observation of the behavior. This will, of course, create the same kinds of measurement problem as those that arise in connection with concepts such as aggression and discrimination. We shall use the terms *avoidance* and *avoidance behavior* as generic terms to refer to the broad class of behaviors oriented toward a reduction of contacts with other persons, groups, or objects. Our more specific theoretical models, however, will distinguish between internal states, such as motivations or avoidance utilities, and behaviors that can be defined without direct reference to these internal states.

In principle it is certainly possible to observe actors moving toward or away from each other and even to measure the magnitudes of spatial distances and rates of changes in these distances, where appropriate. More generally, actors may approach or withdraw from each other not only by means of spatial movements but also by increasing or decreasing interactions that may not require spatial proximity. For example, one may cut off correspondence or reduce the frequency or duration of telephone contacts with other actors. We shall use the term *approach* to refer either to movements toward another actor in spatial terms or to increases in interactions that do not require physical proximity. We shall refer to movements in the opposite direction as withdrawal. There will be no assumption that these movements are necessarily motivated by a desire either to increase contacts with or to avoid the other party, though we may, of course, predict approach or withdrawal behaviors to occur if these motivations are present, provided that other conditions are also met.

We shall refer to another class of insulating mechanisms under the broad heading *regulating behaviors*. These behaviors will include the erection of physical barriers between parties, the limitation of contacts to those that occur only under specified conditions (e.g., formal appointments) or at specific times and locations, and the regulation of contacts by means of specified rituals or role expectations. Although all of these forms of regulation may have the effect of restricting contacts, we again do not need to assume that avoidance is actually intended. If, however, we are willing to assume an avoidance motivation, combined with factors that make withdrawal inconvenient or costly, we may, of course, predict that efforts will be made to regulate those contacts that cannot be prevented by other means. Specifically, in the case of contacts between super-ordinate and subordinate groups we are familiar with various patterns of etiquette that emphasize the asymmetric nature of the contacts. Thus, members of a minority may be expected to employ deference behaviors, to initiate contacts only in such a way that their lower status is clearly emphasized (e.g., by entering via the back door), and to avoid engaging in highly personal forms of interaction that would imply status equality.

We shall have more to say about these approach–withdrawal and regulating behaviors in the following chapter. Here we merely wish to emphasize that the models in which they will appear are basically concerned with *interaction* patterns rather than spatial separation per se. This is likewise true of virtually all of the social psychological literature, mentioned earlier, that deals with the relationship between prejudice and contact. This is in contrast with the ecological literature on residential segregation, which has focused almost exclusively on *spatial* locations. This difference in focus is undoubtedly partially explained on the basis of data-availability problems, particularly in the case of macro-level comparative studies for which detailed information about interactions would be extremely expensive and virtually impossible to obtain. But it implies that we may anticipate a degree of slippage when we attempt to move back and forth between notions of spatial separation and those that focus more directly on interaction patterns or their absence.

In the next sections we shall turn our attention to the concept of segregation, which has generally been defined in spatial terms, and that of integration, which we shall define in terms of interaction patterns. When we hear assertions to the effect that desegregation does not imply "genuine" integration, we may infer that the latter term implies something different from the former. Unfortunately, the notion of integration has not been given a consistent or precise meaning in the social science literature, and therefore its relation to segregation has also not been pinned down. We shall see, however, that part of the methodological discussion of indices of residential segregation has involved the question of the optimal or ideal spatial units that should be employed, and in our judgment this particular question is likely to be closely linked to the problem of specifying the relationship between spatial location and interaction patterns. Therefore, the methodological problem of measuring residential segregation—to which we now turn—seems intimately bound to that of studying or inferring patterns of interaction.

SEGREGATION

We shall define the segregation between two or more groups as the degree to which they are physically separated, either in terms of location in space or by organizational membership. The concept of segregation will be distinguished from that of integration, which will be defined in the next section in terms of patterns of interaction between two or more groups. We will note, however, that for practical reasons it may become necessary to use segregation scores as indicators of interaction patterns, so that empirically it is often difficult to disentangle the two ideas. Nevertheless, as implied earlier, it seems wise to retain a conceptual distinction between them.

Methodological discussions of segregation have focused almost entirely on residential segregation, as measured in large American cities. But the basic issues encountered may readily be generalized to other forms of segregation. For example, in the case of organizational segregation we often deal with nested units and subunits that may be handled in exactly the same fashion as census tracts and city blocks. In the case of school segregation we have school districts, schools, classrooms, and seating patterns within classes. In complex organizations we may have branches, departments, sections of departments, and spatial locations within these sections. In contrast to city blocks or census tracts, however, many of these organizational units have clear-cut boundaries that correspond reasonably well to formal and informal interaction patterns and the division of labor. It may therefore be relatively more easy to sidestep at least some of the methodological problems that arise in connection with residential segregation. We shall confine our methodological discussion to the problem of measuring residential segregation, with the hope that few important complications would be introduced if we were to apply the same kinds of argument to units with more clear-cut boundaries.

The literature on the measurement of residential segregation contains discussions of two distinct kinds of question. The first is that of the choice of an appropriate numerical index of segregation and the second that of appropriate units and subunits to which these measures can be applied. The first issue was debated rather extensively in the late 1940s and early 1950s but, in our opinion, has now been satisfactorily resolved, thanks to the work of Duncan and Duncan (1955). As can be imagined, there are any number of possible measures of residential segregation, all of which take on the value of zero when there is a uniform distribution throughout the units and a value of unity (or 100) whenever there is complete segregation. But the several measures that were used in the earlier comparative studies (see Hornseth 1947; Jahn et al. 1947; Williams 1948; Jahn 1950; Cowgill and Cowgill 1951; and Bell 1954) tended to give different empirical results, and in particular some were much more highly correlated with minority percentage than others.

The Duncans, however, showed that certain of these measures contained a built-in relationship with minority percentage and that, of the indices then in use, two—the Gini index and the index of dissimilarity—possessed more desirable properties. Of these two, the Gini index seems to come closest to having the ideal conceptual properties but is more difficult to calculate than the index of dissimilarity. Fortunately, as the Duncans demonstrate, the two measures will almost inevitably be highly correlated, with the result that the index of dissimilarity has become the single index in common use today.[4]

The index of dissimilarity also has the advantage of being familiar to many readers and is in rather widespread use in connection with measures of inequality of various types. It does not use information regarding the *ordering* of categories (here city blocks or census tracts), however, and is therefore insensitive to rearrangements of these units.[5] In the case of residential segregation it is calculated in the following way. We first obtain the proportion of the minority population that is contained in each block (tract) and do the same for the proportion of majority-group members. For each block (tract) we take the absolute value of this difference and then add over all such units. The index of dissimilarity (D) is then given by

$$D = \tfrac{1}{2}\Sigma |(B_i/B) - (W_i/W)|,$$

where B_i and B respectively represent the number of minority members (say, blacks) in the ith block and the total population, and W_i and W represent the comparable figures for the majority group (say, whites).

The index of dissimilarity can be interpreted either as a measure of the number of persons from one population who would have to be moved in order to achieve a uniform distribution (i.e., exactly the same proportions of minority members in each block) or as the maximum difference between the so-called segregation curve and a diagonal representing the perfectly uniform distribution. For more extensive discussions of this and other measures of residential segregation, the reader is referred to the previously mentioned paper by Duncan and Duncan (1955) and to the methodological appendix in Taeuber and Taeuber (1965) as well as the references cited in note 4.

Since neither the index of dissimilarity nor any of the related measures discussed by Duncan and Duncan really make use of the *location* of the blocks or census tracts, this implies that other measures must be constructed if location is deemed relevant to one's purposes. For example, if distance from the central business district is of concern, a centrality index may be obtained by drawing concentric circles surrounding this section of the city and counting the proportion of members of each group who are in each zone. Also, once the geographic boundaries of the units (e.g., tracts) have been set, the index of dissimilarity does not take into consideration the proximity of these units to each other. *If* the units are treated as givens, this property of the measure may be considered irrelevant, but, as we shall see below, if the boundaries are taken as problematic, then the sensitivity of the measure to boundary alterations becomes a matter of concern.

In the discussion that follows we shall presume that the index of dissimilarity can safely be used as an appropriate measure of residential segregation, once the problem of unit boundaries has been resolved. But we shall want to focus on the second question—that of choice of the appropriate unit—which has also been carefully discussed in the residential segregation literature. Our own discussion derives from earlier ones by the Cowgills (1951), the Duncans (1955),

Lieberson (1963), and the Taeubers (1965) but differs from them slightly in our emphasis on the need to relate one's choice of unit boundaries to the presumed relationship between spatial location and patterns of interaction.

The problem is not a trivial one empirically in view of the findings that, for example, white–nonwhite segregation scores are uniformly high and only very weakly correlated with scores on other variables. This suggests that "artifactual" differences in scores produced by slight boundary modifications might account for a substantial proportion of the empirical variance in segregation scores, either across cities or over time. Given the fact that segregation scores based on the larger tract units are consistently lower than those based on block data, and that the Taeubers found intercorrelations between block and tract data to be in the neighborhood of .70, which is not especially high, we may conclude that the choice of units problem cannot be ignored.

More generally, serious methodological problems are likely to occur whenever geographic proximity is related to variables of theoretical interest in ways that are either highly complex or poorly understood.[6] As we have already suggested, investigators who are constrained to use aggregated data that are available only for arbitrary geographic units will be faced by a number of important dilemmas that they may tend to suppress through the simple device of employing strictly operational criteria while neglecting to construct explicit auxiliary measurement theories. When this is done, however, it becomes impossible to pin down the notion of a true value or to assess the degree of measurement error. But at least in the absence of an adequate measurement theory it will still be possible to employ alternative measures (in this instance based on different boundary definitions) and to study their empirical interrelationships. We shall return to this point after examining a few of the specific issues encountered in connection with the measurement of residential segregation.

Choice of Unit Boundaries

Since measures of segregation involve internal spatial distributions, one would naturally expect that the choice of unit boundaries will affect the magnitude of the index of dissimilarity or any other measure of segregation. Interaction scores will also be affected by the choice of units and subunits. Yet in any practical piece of research the investigator will not be in a position to define the unit boundaries in accord with ideal conditions, even assuming that these could be specified. Measures of residential segregation commonly make use of block statistics, although data for census tracts are also used when block data are unavailable. But exactly why is it that we have come to prefer block statistics over census tracts? And why should we stop with blocks as the smallest subunits? The answers might seem obvious on pragmatic grounds, but the mere fact that one may be limited by the availability of data does not imply that one is therefore justified in plunging ahead without a careful examination of the theoretical and conceptual issues involved.

The rationale for using relatively small units, such as city blocks, apparently is that one is willing to assume that *within* these smaller units there is either no spatial segregation, or there is random interaction, or both. Otherwise, one would want to select a still smaller subunit. The argument against the use of a larger subunit, such as census tracts, is that such a unit may itself be internally segregated. Perhaps blacks will be located mainly in one corner of the tract in an area adjacent to a primarily black corner of a second tract. This kind of arrangement could conceivably result in the kind of pattern indicated in figure 13.1. If one used the four tracts as subunits, one might reach the conclusion that no segregation exists, whereas blacks are actually concentrated in a single central zone represented by the shaded area in figure 13.1.

The problem, of course, is that exactly the same patterns *could* occur in the case of blocks as subunits. In fact we could simply modify figure 13.1 so that the four larger squares referred to blocks instead of tracts, with black families being concentrated in the corners of these blocks in such a way as to constitute a segregated section within the four-block area. It is presumably because we are willing to assume that such within-block patterns will be rare that we prefer blocks to census tracts as the smallest subunits. Obviously, however, this is a matter that should be resolved empirically whenever feasible. It could be done in the case of census tracts by measuring the degree of segregation within tracts, using the blocks as smaller units.

If we found negligible segregation within tracts it would then be appropriate to use these larger areas as the ultimate subunits. But because within-block data are not available, one would either have to select a sample of blocks and collect separate data on the within-block spatial distributions or to make the a priori assumption that within-block segregation is negligible. Presumably, this is the implicit assumption being made whenever one decides to use blocks as the ultimate subunit. Interestingly enough, if one were to select households as the ultimate subunit, even those spatial (block) units that appeared to be relatively unsegregated would have very high segregation scores, since—at least with respect to blacks and whites in the United States—the extremely low intermarriage rate implies almost completely segregated households.

Figure 13.1. Ghetto, Concealed by Choice of Census-tract Subunits

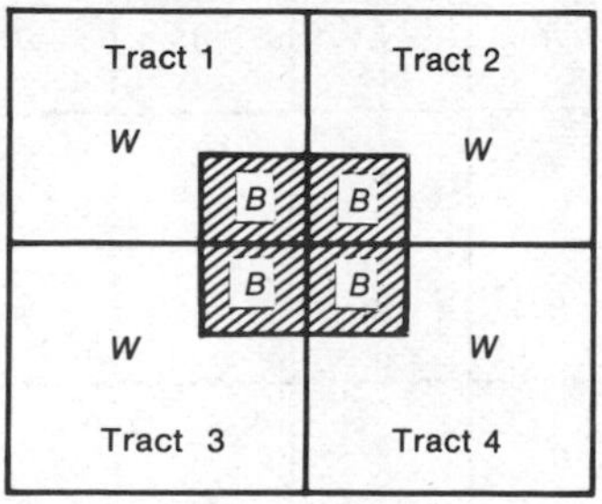

These rather extreme examples illustrate the major point that any measure of segregation will be affected by one's choice of subunits. This fact is obvious, of course. Less apparent is the matter of the *degree* to which segregation scores are highly sensitive to differences in the units selected. Among other things, this will depend upon the *locations* of the segregated pockets within a larger territory, the *shapes* of the subunits, the outside *boundaries* of the larger unit (e.g., central city or SMSA), and possible differences in *sizes* of the subunits. We can see some of the issues involved by examining the extreme forms of a checkerboard pattern (figure 13.2) and a concentric circle pattern (figure 13.3).

In the checkerboard pattern in which alternate subunits contain either all black or all white families, if our subunit boundaries happened to coincide exactly with these completely segregated subunits, then our measure of segregation would reach an upper limit of unity. If, however, our subunits were each composed of two adjacent blocks of all-white or all-black areas, then in the extreme case the measure might be reduced to zero. Theoretically the segregation measure could also reach zero even where the subunits were no larger than these segregated areas, provided that the boundaries were carefully selected so as to bisect each of the segregated areas. Thus a checkerboard-type pattern is highly sensitive to one's choice of subunit boundaries. Obviously, no city's spatial distribution will ever conform to this extreme pattern, but to the degree that a minority's distribution is approximated by this pattern and involves a large number of relatively small racial islands, we may expect that the segregation score for that city will be hypersensitive to one's choice of subunit boundaries.

To illustrate the problem of the shape of the subunits, consider the ideal-type concentric zone model of figure 13.3, where we imagine that the inner circle is 100 percent black, the next circle 80 percent black, and so on, until we reach the outermost circle, which contains no blacks. If our subunits were to consist of pie-shaped sectors, as represented by I, II, and III at the top of the figure, then each sector would contain approximately the same percentage of blacks, and our measure of segregation would be near zero. Of course, if we knew of the concentric zone patterns we would not be so foolish as to use pie-shaped

Figure 13.2. Checkerboard Pattern of Segregation

B	W	B	W
W	B	W	B
B	W	B	W
W	B	W	B

Figure 13.3. Gradient of Partial Black–White Segregation Concealed by Using Center-to-Periphery Wedge-shaped Subunits

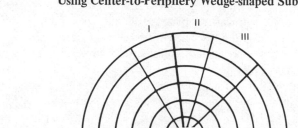

sectors as subunits. But why? Because we would see that *within* each of the sectors there is a high degree of segregation, with blacks being concentrated toward the center and whites toward the periphery. We would thus be invoking the principle that the subunits must be selected in such a way that we are willing to assume no segregation within them.

Pie-shaped sectors represent an extreme possibility. Bar-shaped subunits might produce similar results to the degree that they were pointed toward the center of the city. Likewise we might imagine a series of concentric ovals with bar-shaped subunits. The measure of segregation might then depend upon the direction of the bars in relation to the major and minor axes of the ellipses. Presumably, one advantage of square-shaped blocks over large census tracts is that the former have more regular shapes than the latter. But it is possible that some cities have more nearly square-shaped blocks than others and that certain elongated blocks in some cities may be internally segregated. To our knowledge, such matters have not been seriously studied by sociologists. One suspects that the effects on segregation measures are minimal, but it is just possible that they are not.

The relative *numbers* of highly segregated and mixed subunits, however, will obviously affect the measures of segregation, and these in turn will depend upon the outer limits of the larger unit. In the bottom half of figure 13.3 we have illustrated the possibility that the outermost concentric circle may have been divided up into many more subunits than the intermediate or mixed zones. If the central zone also contains a very large number of subunits, then the city will appear to be much more highly segregated than a city for which the intermediate zones are most numerous. Of course, no social scientist would knowingly rig the data in such a fashion, but there are several ways that such a difference could come about inadvertently.

Suppose, for example, that the outermost zone is a very large one and that it is completely segregated. The number of blocks into which this very large zone is subdivided may then have a major impact on the numerical value of the measure of segregation. Let us also suppose that this outermost zone is nowhere near as densely populated as the intermediate and central zones. How should blocks in these outermost areas be defined? If a distance unit were used, perhaps a single wealthy estate will contain as much territory as several innercity blocks. If so, we would certainly want to use a much larger physical boundary for the block. This brings up the matter of blocks of very different-sized populations, a question that will concern us below. The main point is that if one blindly uses a census definition of "block," and if this assures one that there will thus be a certain degree of uniformity from city to city with respect to this physical definition, this does not automatically imply that the choice-of-units problem has been resolved theoretically.

The difficulty becomes especially apparent when we recognize that the outer limits of the territory for which block data are available (ordinarily the boundaries of a politically defined unit) will not coincide with the sociological boundaries in the case of very large metropolitan areas. Many residences will spill out into the countryside, up the sides of mountains, or around lakes. If so, the boundaries of blocks become very hard to define. To the degree that the suburbs are highly segregated, the more such smaller units there are within the boundaries of the larger unit, the greater the segregation score will be.

If block statistics are available only for central cities, whereas the larger metropolitan area is the proper sociological unit of analysis, then the happenstance of political boundaries may have a major impact on the measured segregation score. One city might have a relatively small central city that contains a very high percentage of minority members, with mixed zones extending out to the city limits. A second city might conceivably have exactly the same patterning of minority and majority residents except that the city boundaries extend far out into the all-white suburbs. This latter city would then have relatively more enumerated blocks containing no minority members and a higher segregation score. In terms of figure 13.3 the first city's boundaries might extend only to the zone containing 20 percent blacks, whereas the boundaries of the second might extend beyond the outermost circle. An investigator who merely plugged block data into a segregation index would not be able to correct the measure for such a difference.

Obviously, social scientists must work with fallible data and subunits and boundaries that are defined by someone else. Since we cannot go inside of city blocks to measure their internal segregation, and since we cannot obtain block statistics outside of certain boundaries, what can we do as a practical expedient? One must stop somewhere and make simplifying assumptions. This has been our thesis in all of the chapters in this book, and it also applies to measures of segregation. If we are dealing with the smallest subunits for which data are available, we may need to make the untested assumption that these subunits are internally unsegregated. If our subunits are themselves decomposable with available data, we may, of course, test this particular assumption. Or it may be possible to obtain the necessary resources to select a sample of the subunits for intensive analysis. Likewise, one may be able to obtain supplementary information beyond the bounds of the larger units for which subunit (e.g., block) data are readily available. But these procedures will be costly, and there is, of course, no guarantee that patterns will hold up from one city to the next or across time periods.

A much less expensive, though less satisfactory, alternative is to conduct a series of methodological studies with existing data by seeing what happens to index scores when one modifies subunit boundaries or extends or contracts the boundaries of a larger unit. Suppose, for example, that block data are only available out to the edges of the central city, as defined by its political boundaries. One may then combine blocks in various ways to see whether two- or four-block subunits give basically the same results as single-block subunits. Of course, one might expect a slight overall reduction in index scores as units are increased in size. But perhaps the *relative* reductions will be greater in some cities than in others. For example, reductions may be greatest for cities with large minority percentages, older cities, or cities whose boundaries are constrained by physical barriers. If so, then generalizations that purport to show regional differences or relationships with minority percentage are suspect.

One may also modify artificially the "outer limits" of a city by subtracting blocks that are closest to its official boundaries, or by taking out blocks that are not close to a major artery or some other physical boundary. If these boundary modifications produce major changes in relative segregation scores, we will have indirect evidence that generalizations based on presently available data are suspect. If, on the contrary, the segregation scores remain stable in spite of these boundary and subunit modifications, then there is at least indirect evidence that the kinds of issue raised in the present section have little practical significance.[7]

Segregation versus Integration and the Choice of Units

We have implied at several points that one important reason for obtaining measures of residential or other types of segregation may be that one wants to use these as indicators of the degree of integration or approximately equal-status interaction that occurs across group lines. For instance, we may assume that residents of a city block are in interaction with each other, at least if the block is not too large. But we also recognize that many kinds of interaction among neighbors are extremely minimal and that they vary with the age and sex of the actors. Very young children and their mothers may interact much more frequently and intensively with their immediate neighbors than older children or fathers. Adult companions may easily be selected from well outside the block or neighborhood, but the degree to which this occurs will depend upon such things as the availability of public transportation, the daily schedules of the residents, and the economic position of each family.

If an index of segregation is to be used as an indirect measure of integration rather than simply as a measure of physical separation, then the choice of sub-unit should depend upon one's theory as to the relationship between whatever form of interaction may be of interest and the spatial distribution of the parties who are engaged in this interaction. This will usually be difficult because the frequency of interaction may vary inversely with some *continuous* function of distance, so that any physical boundaries that are drawn will be arbitrary.

A city block is defined by the Census Bureau in such a way that persons on opposite sides of the same street are placed in different blocks. Such boundaries (as indicators of interaction) will be unrealistic in all instances where the streets are narrow and the traffic is light. Across-the-street neighbors would indeed be much more likely to interact in most neighborhoods than persons on the same block but at opposite corners. Of course, we are likely to be "saved" in this instance because of the likelihood that two adjacent city blocks will have nearly identical degrees of internal segregation, although we can again produce our checkerboard example to illustrate the extreme case. If the small squares in figure 13.2 represented city blocks, we would have a situation in which black and white families faced each other across city streets. In this case, the black–white interactions might be relatively frequent, perhaps much more so than the interactions that would occur between members of the same race who lived back to back in the same block.

There may be certain very simple situations in which interaction patterns and spatial layouts coincide so as to enable one to use the latter as excellent indica-tors of the former. If we were to observe a school cafeteria and note that all tables contained either all-black or all-white groupings of students, then even though the layout of the tables formed a checkerboard pattern, we might be willing to assume that a measure of segregation based on the tables as subunits provides an excellent measure of integration. This is because we might be willing to assume that persons interact only with others at their own table and pay negligible attention to what is going on at other tables. If, however, there were considerable cross-table interaction (or interblock interaction), then we would want to use a different subunit for our measure of segregation.

We noted in the case of suburban versus innercity blocks that blocks defined in spatial terms may contain very unequal numbers of persons. This is presum-ably irrelevant so long as we are talking about *segregation*, which we are defining in spatial terms. A park may be totally segregated even though one portion is densely crowded whereas another is not. But if residential or other kinds of spatial pattern are being used as indicators of *interaction* patterns, then it would seem much more appropriate to select subunits that contain approximately equal numbers of persons. This would be based on the assumption that each individual will interact only with a limited number of persons and that this num-ber is only weakly related to population density.

Thus if a block contains a huge apartment complex, individuals within this block may interact primarily with persons who live on the same floor or who use the same entrance. In a less densely populated area, however, it is assumed that persons will interact with persons who are spatially farther removed, and who may be several city blocks away. But this obviously again depends upon the nature or kind of interaction under consideration and is a matter that must be determined empirically.

We suspect that the effects on measures of segregation would be pronounced, in this instance, because a minority such as blacks tends to be concentrated in densely populated blocks, whereas the all-white counterparts in the suburbs will often be the least densely populated. A shift in the definition of "block" so as to place approximately the same numbers of persons in each subunit would therefore tend to increase the number of blocks within the ghetto and decrease the number in the suburbs. The effect on the index of dissimilarity would therefore likely be a function of the percentage of the minority in the metropolitan area.

In sum, then, if we are going to use a segregation index as a measure of integration, communication, or any other form of interaction, another kind of consideration must enter into our selection of subunits. Unless we are willing merely to assume a relationship between spatial and interactional distributions we shall find it necessary in this instance to collect at least some interactional data in order to validate the selection of subunits. We cannot simply combine smaller subunits in different ways to see how the results may differ because we still do not know how any of these subunits may relate to interactional patterns. Furthermore, since different kinds of interaction may have different spatial patternings—as we have already implied in the case of neighborhood interactions—what may be an ideal spatial subunit to measure one kind of interaction may be much less desirable as a measure of a second kind. Until we know considerably more about the relationship between the two than we do at present, we at least must become properly cautious and must learn to state our assumptions as explicitly as possible.

MEASURES OF INTEGRATION AND EXPOSURE

It is sometimes suggested that desegregation does not imply "true" integration. Presumably, then, *integration* must mean something slightly different from the polar opposite of segregation, which we have defined in terms of internal spatial or organizational distributions. The usual connotation given to the notion of integration is that there must not only be physical proximity among races, ethnic groups, or other categories being considered, but that there must be reasonably intimate interaction as well. But the kind of interaction that occurs between superordinates and subordinates is also not implicitly included in the layman's usage of the term. We would not say, for example, that the armed services are integrated if all of the commissioned and noncommissioned officers are white and all of the privates and seamen black, even where there is a high degree of interaction across ranks. The usual connotation of integration seems to involve what we might think of as a random mixture in the sense that the super-ordinate–subordinate relationships that occur along with more or less equal-status contacts are not predominantly one-sided from the standpoint of the groups whose integration is being measured. For example, blacks would be just as likely as whites to be in superordinate positions.

If we are to adopt a theoretical definition of integration that is compatible with this popular usage we must therefore focus on reasonably intimate inter-actions that are either equal status or, where inequalities do exist, are not systematically related to the relevant characteristics of the individuals being compared. For example, it may generally be true that younger members of a group consistently defer to older ones, but if age and race are unrelated then this age grading will not systematically affect the status relationships among blacks and whites who are in interaction. We may possibly encounter some slippery problems whenever inequalities are correlated with race, ethnicity, sex, or what-ever other criterion is being considered. This is much the same problem encoun-tered in our discussion of discrimination and inequality. For example, is a basketball team integrated if all of the first-string members happen to be black and all of the second-string white? Is an organization in which all of the leader-ship roles fall to white males integrated so long as there is sufficient interaction across race or sex lines? We shall here presuppose that such issues can be side-stepped and that it is possible to decide, first, just what behaviors constitute instances of interaction and, second, which ones of these are either equal status or involve status differences that are irrelevant to race, ethnicity, or whatever other characteristics are being used to define group memberships.

We may then say that the degree of integration is proportional to the degree to which these approximately equal-status and reasonably intimate interactions approach a distribution that one would expect on the basis of chance; that is, the greater the integration, the more nearly the cross-group interactions approxi-mate the within-group interactions, taking their relative sizes into consideration. In theory, we can imagine situations in which cross-group interactions are relatively more frequent than within-group ones, in which case we might refer to artificially high integration scores or some such term. In very small samples, we would, of course, expect to encounter situations in which there might be slightly more cross-group interactions than would be expected by chance, but in our theoretical conceptualization we are thinking in terms of large numbers of indi-viduals or repeated interactions, so that we need not be concerned with this possibility. The implication for the behavior of our empirical results, however, is that we may from time to time expect to encounter some instances in which our integration measure may go above unity if we construct this measure in such a way that unity represents a completely uniform mixture.

Before turning to actual possible measures of integration based on frequency counts of interacting pairs let us point to an obvious practical difficulty that in many instances will necessitate the substitution of an inverse measure of segregation for such a measure of integration. Suppose one is studying school desegregation and attempting to distinguish empirically between a desegregated school and an integrated one. As we are using the term, desegregation refers to spatial distributions within certain specified units. If our larger units are school systems or districts and our subunits schools, then our segregation measure will be obtained by counting the numbers of students of a given type within each school. If our large units are schools, and the smaller ones are classrooms, then we will take frequency counts within these classes. Or we might move to spatial distributions within the classrooms by studying seating arrangements.

But how would we study integration in a practical way? It would certainly not be feasible to study all possible interaction pairs. We might select out certain locations in which we assumed that interactions would be more or less voluntary and equal status. For instance, we might study seating patterns within a school cafeteria or the locations of children on the playground during unsupervised recess periods. Even here it might be difficult to ascertain just which pairs of persons were in interaction. We might assume that persons sitting at the same table are in interaction, or that boys or girls playing in a certain corner of a playground are in interaction.

Thus, as a shortcut to actually observing interaction patterns in detail, we could take spatial distributions as an *indicator* of equal-status interactions. As a practical expedient we therefore might use certain kinds of spatial distributions (e.g., assignment to schools or to classrooms) as measures of desegregation, whereas other kinds of spatial distribution were being used as indirect measures of integration in the sense of equal-status interaction patterns. It is no wonder that it is easy to confuse the two concepts in practice. Some authors who distinguish between "desegregation" and "genuine integration" may be using the latter term to refer to actual interaction counts, whereas others may be referring to spatial patternings for activities considered to involve such interactions. At issue, then, may be the choice of one's spatial units as well as the distinction between spatial distributions and interaction patterns.

Having pointed to this practical difficulty in measuring integration through frequency counts of actual interactions, let us ask how integration might be measured under more ideal conditions. What properties do we want our measure to have? First, we do not want it to be confounded with the relative sizes of the two groups. It may, of course, turn out empirically that both relative and absolute sizes may be correlated with degree of integration, but we do not want this to be a built-in artifact of our measure of integration. We also want our measure to take on a value of zero whenever there is no cross-group interaction and to have a value of unity when cross-group and intragroup interactions are of equal proportions once one takes into consideration the relative numbers involved. In addition we want our measure to allow for the possibility that the intragroup interactions may not be the same for both groups. This means that we will need to use not only the numbers of *possible* interactions, which are easily determined from the group sizes, but also the *actual* interactions that occur within

Table 13.1 Some Hypothetical Interaction Patterns within and across Two Groups

Subtable I
$N_1 = 5$ $N_2 = 15$

| | Types of Pairs | | | |
	(G_1, G_1)	(G_2, G_2)	(G_1, G_2)	Total
Possible Pairs (P)	10	105	75	190
Actual Pairs (A) in Interaction	6	42	15	63
A/P	.60	.40	.20	
$P - A$	4	63	60	

Subtable II
$N_1 = 10$ $N_2 = 10$

| | Types of Pairs | | | |
	(G_1, G_1)	(G_2, G_2)	(G_1, G_2)	Total
Possible Pairs (P)	45	45	100	190
Actual Pairs (A) in Interaction	27	18	20	65
A/P	.60	.40	.20	
$P - A$	18	27	80	

Subtable III
$N_1 = 15$ $N_2 = 5$

	(G_1, G_1)	(G_2, G_2)	(G_1, G_2)	Total
Possible Pairs (P)	105	10	75	190
Actual Pairs (A) in Interaction	63	4	15	82
A/P	.60	.40	.20	
$P - A$	42	6	60	

Subtable IV
$N_1 = 5$ $N_2 = 15$

	(G_1, G_1)	(G_2, G_2)	(G_1, G_2)	Total
Possible Pairs (P)	10	105	75	190
Actual Pairs (A) in Interaction	5	52	15	72
A/P	.50	.50	.20	
$P - A$	5	53	60	

and across the groups. Some possibilities for two groups, G_1 and G_2, with N_1 and N_2 individuals respectively are displayed in table 13.1.

Focus first on subtables I, II, and III, which are distinguished on the basis of the relative sizes of the two groups, G_1 and G_2. In all three subtables 60 percent of the possible (G_1, G_1) pairs are actually in mutual interaction, whereas only 40 percent of the (G_2, G_2) pairs are in interaction. These figures contrast with those in subtable IV, in which half of both sets of intragroup pairs are in mutual interaction. In all four subtables we see that 20 percent of the possible cross-group pairs (G_1, G_2) are actually in interaction. Do we want our measure to be invariant across all four subtables? At least in terms of the *ratios A/P* of the actual to the possible interactions, the first three subtables are identical, although they differ with respect to the relative sizes of the two groups. But subtable IV differs from the others in that the two groups display equal intragroup percentages which, however, have the same arithmetic mean (i.e., .50) as that of the first three subtables. Additionally we note that because of the differing numbers of pairs across the subtables, the *differences P − A* are not comparable. For this reason we shall reject the use of difference-type comparisons and consider only ratio-type measures.

If we use as the numerator the ratio of actual to possible cross-group interactions (which is .20 in all four subtables), the question arises as to which figure we should select for the denominator. If we wanted a *symmetric* measure we might select the arithmetic mean of the A/P ratios for the intragroup interactions of the two separate groups. For subtables I, II, and III this would be $1/2(.60 + .40) = .50$, which is, of course, exactly the same as the figure that would be obtained from subtable IV. Thus, for a symmetric measure of integration, we would obtain the same figure of $.20/.50 = .40$ for all four subtables. This measure is symmetric in the sense that the ratio of actual to possible cross-group interactions is being compared to an average figure for the two separate groups rather than with either of them separately.

We also might want to look at the matter from the perspective of either one group or the other, in effect comparing the relative number of cross-group interactions with its own internal interaction pattern. For the hypothetical data of subtables I, II, and III the first group, G_1, is relatively more active than G_2 in the sense that a higher percentage of its members are in mutual interaction than is true for G_2. In subtable II, where the two groups are of equal size, there are 27 pairs in actual interaction within G_1, whereas in G_2 there are only 18. Relatively speaking, then, the members of G_2 are engaged in a higher proportion of cross-group interactions than are the members of G_1. We may construct two very simple asymmetric measures by using as denominators the figures .60 and .40 representing the A/P ratios of the respective groups. Our asymmetric measures of integration for subtables I, II, and III would thus be $.20/.60 = .33$ for G_1 and $.20/.40 = .50$ for G_2. For subtable IV the asymmetric measure would, of course, give the same result (i.e., $.20/.50 = .40$) for both groups.

In addition one might want to construct asymmetric measures of the degree of *exposure* to the other group, as measured by the number of cross-group contacts as compared with the total number of interactions that members of the two groups may have. Such a measure of exposure will, of course, be a function of the relative sizes of the two groups. For example, suppose the total population contains many more whites than blacks and that the number of *WW* interactions is much greater than the number of *BB* interactions. If we fix the total number of cross-race interactions, then it will obviously be the case that the average white member will experience a relatively smaller number of cross-race interactions than will the average black.

To measure the average exposure level of whites we could take the ratio of the *actual* number of *BW* interactions to the total number of *BW* + *WW* interactions. Similarly, the black exposure rate could be measured as the ratio of *BW* to *BW* + *BB*. If blacks were G_1 and whites G_2 for the above data, then for subtable I the black and white exposure rates would be 15/21 and 15/57 respectively. For subtable III, in which blacks outnumber whites by three to one, the black and white exposure rates would be 15/78 and 15/19 respectively.

If we define exposure in this way, exposure becomes a joint function of relative size and the number of actual cross-category interactions. In effect, if exposure to another group is responsible for certain consequences to the individual, we are saying that the consequences of integration depend upon the relative sizes of the two groups, quite apart from any status, power, or cultural differences that may also be brought into the picture. The degree of integration has more important consequences for a small minority simply because the minority members will, on the average, experience relatively more cross-group interactions than will majority members.

This point will be developed further in the next chapter, where we consider costs of cross-group contacts to minority members as a function of minority-group size.

Let us summarize briefly. We have a symmetric measure of integration, two asymmetric measures of integration, and two asymmetric measures of exposure. To construct these measures we may proceed as follows:

1. We first calculate the numbers of *possible* pairs of three types:

$$P_{11} = N_1(N_1 - 1)/2 \quad \text{possible pairs within } G_1;$$

$$P_{22} = N_2(N_2 - 1)/2 \quad \text{possible pairs within } G_2;$$

$$P_{12} = N_1 N_2 \quad \text{possible cross-group pairs.}$$

As a check, the sum $P_{11} + P_{22} + P_{12}$ must equal $N(N - 1)/2$, where $N = N_1 + N_2$.

2. We then observe the corresponding *actual* numbers of pairs in interaction. Let us label these A_{11}, A_{22}, and A_{12}, respectively.

3. We may then calculate the following measures:

Symmetric measure of integration, I_s:

$$I_s = \frac{A_{12}/P_{12}}{\frac{1}{2}[(A_{11}/P_{11}) + (A_{22}/P_{22})]} = \frac{A_{12}/P_{12}}{\frac{1}{2}\left[\frac{A_{11}P_{22} + A_{22}P_{11}}{P_{11}P_{22}}\right]}$$

$$= \frac{2A_{12}P_{11}P_{22}}{P_{12}(A_{11}P_{22} + A_{22}P_{11})};$$

Asymmetric measures of integration, I_1 and I_2 :

$$I_1 = \frac{A_{12}/P_{12}}{A_{11}/P_{11}} = \frac{A_{12}P_{11}}{A_{11}P_{12}} \quad \text{and} \quad I_2 = \frac{A_{12}/P_{12}}{A_{22}/P_{22}} = \frac{A_{12}P_{22}}{A_{22}P_{12}};$$

Asymmetric measures of exposure, E_1 and E_2 :

$$E_1 = \frac{A_{12}}{A_{11} + A_{12}} \quad \text{and} \quad E_2 = \frac{A_{12}}{A_{22} + A_{12}}.$$

As a final note of caution we should call the reader's attention to the facts that these measures not only depend upon the definition of the group boundaries, the nature of the behavioral acts that are included under the definition of interaction, and the types of interaction that are to be considered approximately equal status, but they are also insensitive to *which* individuals are engaged in the various types of interaction. For instance, a single black may be responsible for all of the black–white interactions. Or perhaps there are a few blacks and a few whites who account for all of the cross-group interactions, with the remaining members of both groups refusing to interact with members of the other race. Or there may be several interracial subgroups that do not interact with each other.

Additional measures would need to be constructed if such patternings of the interactions were deemed relevant for the investigation at hand. One possibility would be to construct a score for each individual member of G_1 and similarly for the individuals in G_2. One could then measure the dispersion in these scores to determine the extent to which a few individuals were accounting for most of the cross-group interactions. The measures we have presented above refer only to group totals, rather than to individual differences within or between groups.

CONCLUDING REMARKS

We have already noted that spatial location and interaction patterns are likely to be highly intercorrelated, and it is perhaps for this reason that there are few if any systematic discussions of these interrelationships. At least in the literature on race and ethnic relations, as we have suggested, there is a tendency to deal empirically with either the one concept or the other, but not both simultaneously. The focus of attention in the present chapter has been on the necessity of making conceptual distinctions between these two types of variable. In the next chapter our basic concern will be with delineating a number of variables that directly or indirectly affect the frequency and duration of intergroup contacts.

Most of these variables obviously will also be linked in some way with segregation, with the general relationship being that of mutual reinforcement between the two kinds of factor; that is, proximity facilitates interactions, and preferences for interaction partners will, in turn, affect actors' locational preferences. But we also recognize that these interrelationships will not be perfect and that other factors may affect the nature and extent of the associations between spatial locations and interaction patterns of differing types. Therefore it becomes important to specify what some of the relevant kinds of interaction may be and how they are linked to spatial locations.

There are, of course, a number of exogenous factors that will affect locational patterns, quite apart from considerations of interaction partners. Land is not only scarce, but it is also highly variable in quality and desirability as well as being a resource for outcomes to which high utilities are attached. In particular, land is important as an economic resource—so much so that some form of competition for the most advantageous locations seems to be one of the few universals that characterize not only human interaction patterns but also those of many other life forms as well.

If "territoriality" claims are not universals among all animal species, this may only be because in some instances space may be sufficiently plentiful and approximately equal in quality that occupancy of a particular location does not confer any special advantages to those individuals who can maintain control over it. At least among humans, however, we may assume that spatial locations confer important economic, political, and social advantages (or disadvantages) on their occupants. We may usually assume that these advantages will be sufficient that the competition for desirable land will involve utilities that are substantial as compared with those for specific interaction partners. This is because the number of potential interaction partners is generally much greater than the number with whom any given actor may actually interact. Furthermore, in many kinds of situation these partners are virtually interchangeable, giving the actor considerable flexibility of choice among these partners.

These considerations suggest that in many if not most situations the competition for space will be both causally prior to and also more important than one's choice of specific interaction partners. But we must introduce a number of qualifications to this broad assertion. First, the utility patterns of actors will not be identical and will be influenced not only by their specific interaction partners but also by ethnic or other subgroup norms. Some groups may develop cultural patterns that are much more suitable to one type of spatial location than another, and they may also come to attach symbolic or sentimental significance to particular territories that may yield very few economic advantages.

Therefore we may expect a certain amount of sifting to occur, through which groups of people develop preferences for locations that are not as strongly desired by their competitors. In this way the amount of direct competition for space may be reduced. In general, however, we expect that the most powerful groups and individuals will tend to hold the most desirable locations, with the distribution of territory being approximately proportionate to their relative exercised powers. Over time, weaker parties that have been relegated to the least desirable locations may develop adaptive mechanisms that enable them to exploit their territory much more effectively than their more powerful neighbors. If they become too successful, however, they may find themselves again in competition with encroachers or perhaps forced to pay a portion of their surplus products in tribute.

In any given instance involving either intergroup or interindividual relations, we must ask whether the most important question at stake really involves the issue of competition over spatial locations, or whether it is rather more a matter of utilities concerning interaction patterns. In some instances groups may attach such significance to their autonomy and the need for isolation from outside influences that they are willing to make considerable territorial sacrifices so as to gain or retain this isolation. As a general rule, we suspect that such "retreat" reactions are far more likely to characterize extremely weak groups than powerful ones, and we have already suggested that powerful groups will be in a much better position to erect barriers against outsiders who would wish to dispute their territorial claims. In effect, weak groups desiring isolation must rely on low utilities on the part of others for both cross-group interactions and for the territory they occupy. The result is that they tend to become social outcasts or are forced to locate in extremely undesirable locations.

NOTES

1. Most of these societies fit rather closely to the pattern of what van den Berghe (1967:27–34) refers to as "paternalistic," as contrasted with what he calls the "competitive" type race relations situation that is more characteristic of industrialized societies. Van den Berghe lists segregation as a characteristic of competitive but not paternalistic societies, but it is our own impression, in reading the literature, that spatial separation is also prevalent in such pluralistic societies in spite of the absence of quantitative data establishing this fact.

2. This emphasis on contacts among strangers is commonly made in connection with so-called middleman minorities. See, for example, Hilda Kuper (1969). Bonacich (1973) stresses the "sojourner" status of this type of minority. It is our qualitative impression, on reading the literature on pluralistic socie-

ties, that cross-group contacts in these settings are, in general, highly impersonal and basically those of strangers, but perhaps to no greater degree than those that occur in an American metropolitan area.

3. It may also insulate itself by controlling either the rules that regulate contact or the allocation process (e.g., by reserving certain occupations for itself).

4. More recently the index of dissimilarity has been criticized by Cortese, Falk, and Cohen (1976), Falk, Cortese, and Cohen (1978), and Winship (1978); it has been defended by Taeuber and Taeuber (1976).

5. It can be shown that the index of dissimilarity is just Goodman and Kruskal's lambda b standardized so as to equate the sizes of the two groups; see Goodman and Kruskal (1954). For a measure that does use the ordering among categories or spatial units, see Lieberson (1976).

6. These methodological problems are especially serious whenever one wishes to develop and test cross-level theories of the type with which we are concerned. It can be shown that the criterion for aggregation (here, spatial proximity) must be related in relatively simple ways to the other variables in the causal system, and this is rarely the case in practice. See Blalock (1971) and Hannan (1971).

7. The Taeubers (1965:238-42) discuss comparable boundary manipulations in connection with territorial annexations that occurred in the case of 24 cities between 1950 and 1960. For these very limited boundary changes they found negligible modifications in segregation scores.

CHAPTER 14

Approach and Withdrawal II: Some Models of Intergroup Interaction

IT HAS BEEN NOTED that studies of residential segregation show that even if economic inequalities were to disappear there is no evidence to indicate that residential segregation would also be eliminated. This conclusion is not at all surprising to students of race relations, particularly those who emphasize the deep-seated nature of prejudice or racism or those who have studied the history of racial and ethnic conflicts throughout the world. Obviously, there are many noneconomic factors at work, but it is not sufficient merely to point to this fact or to attribute the residual or adjusted segregation scores to some global variables such as prejudice, discrimination, or cultural differences. It becomes necessary to specify as clearly as one can just what the underlying mechanisms are that produce residential segregation levels that are far in excess of those that would be predicted on the basis of economic factors alone.

In this and the concluding chapter we shall be concerned with such mechanisms, examined from two very different points of view. In the present chapter our focus will be on micro-level processes and the decisions that actors make regarding intragroup and cross-group interactions. Such contacts will be influenced by the degree of segregation through a number of mechanisms that we shall attempt to identify and make explicit through causal models. Although space limitations prohibit us from examining the reverse mechanisms in detail, we assume that these interaction patterns, in turn, affect residential segregation at a somewhat later point in time; that is, there is a causal flow from residential segregation to the nature of interaction patterns and back to segregation. This comes as no great surprise, of course, but it does not follow from this that we do not need to pay close attention to the specific mechanisms through which this linkage between spatial proximity and interaction patterns occurs. As we have previously argued, this is precisely where one of the major gaps in the literature lies.

545

After having constructed a reasonably general model of these processes, we shall focus in the remainder of this chapter on the rewards and costs of cross-group contacts from the perspective of the individual actor. Macro or contextual variables will enter the picture as factors that may affect the shapes and levels of the reward and cost functions, with allowance being made for the possibility that under certain circumstances actors who cannot adjust their behaviors to these reward and cost levels may act in a concerted way to alter them; that is, in reasonably complete and realistic theories we must also treat these contextual variables as endogenous rather than as exogenous variables, or givens. Our own more limited models, however, merely hint at this possibility.

The next and concluding chapter on dynamic formulations will also focus on segregation processes, though from a more macro perspective. One of the major emphases will be on how a phenomenon such as segregation persists through time because of the fact that it functions in certain ways for different sets of actors, who, in turn, exert power either to increase or to decrease the existing levels. Once more, it is not sufficient to point this out in a general way. It becomes essential that one attempt to identify the relevant actors or parties concerned, theorize how each is affected by the existing degree of segregation (or other contextual variable), and how that party will react. If one can also assess the degree of power that each party will then exert, as well as the most likely courses of action it will pursue, one can then attempt to make reasonably specific predictions concerning rates of overall change in the levels of a macro variable such as degree of residential segregation.

SOME VARIABLES RELEVANT TO CROSS-GROUP INTERACTION

Interaction patterns can be classified in many different ways that are dependent on the substantive problem one is studying, as well as the kinds of setting in which these interactions take place. For example, in the field of race and ethnic relations one could classify urban contacts in terms of the places in which they occur: in restaurants, parks, department stores, on the job, and so forth. One then might obtain frequency counts of either numbers of participants or actual cross-group interactions in these settings and, hopefully, relate them to the degree of residential segregation in the area. Molotch (1969) has, in fact, obtained some very interesting results in this fashion, and more research of this nature needs to be conducted. Our own aim is to work toward the development of a reasonably general theory involving a set of variables of a more abstract nature. Needless to say, the list of such variables that we shall discuss in the present section presents a host of measurement problems that we shall have to sidestep in the interests of brevity.

Whenever we examine a pair, triad, or larger set of interaction partners it is evident that there are several different kinds of score that we may compute.

First, we may obtain some measure of central tendency, such as the mean or median, to represent an average level for the group in question. When we do so we in effect treat the members symmetrically and assume that their interaction can be adequately represented by a score that does not make distinctions among the interaction partners. For instance, we may refer to the "level of intimacy" or the "amount of conflict" that characterizes the interaction, thereby ignoring any differences in levels that may exist among the members.

Clearly, then, we may also need a second kind of measure to tap these differences. Where there are a number of actors involved, a standard deviation can be computed. Where there are only two, a simple difference or inequality score may be used. Thus one member of a pair may be much more dependent on the interaction than the partner, or perhaps the first actor may be more constrained than the second in terms of regulations that affect his or her responses. In the discussion that follows it will usually be clear from the context whether we are referring to a measure of central tendency or of inequality or dispersion. Conceivably, there may also be situations in which one might want to characterize interaction patterns in terms of some measure of skewness, but we shall ignore this possibility in the present context.

Frequency of Contacts

Interactions obviously vary in terms of the frequency with which they occur. By *frequency* we shall mean the total number of times (in some specified time period) in which a given pair or set of actors is engaged in interaction, regardless of the duration of each encounter. It will also be useful to have a related term to refer to the frequency with which similar interactions occur at the macro or contextual level, and it seems advisable to keep these two ideas distinct. For instance, a black and white couple may interact with a given degree of frequency in the context of either frequent or rare biracial interactions in the local community.

We shall use the term *prevalence* to refer to the contextual variable representing the *proportion* of other actors in the context who engage in some amount of the interaction in question, and the term *total frequency* to refer to the total number of interactions of this type that occur in this context. Thus if we are referring to a black-white couple in interaction, the contextual variable for the white partner might be the prevalence of other whites who engage in this activity, and similarly for the black partner. But it may also be the case that the total frequency of interactions—regardless of which individuals are taking part— is more relevant in explaining this couple's interactions. In other words, it is possible that under some conditions the contextual variable should be conceptualized in terms of the numbers of individuals who engage in the interaction, whereas under others it may be more reasonable to refer to the number of interactions that are occurring. Usually, of course, the two will be highly correlated.

Duration of Contacts

Here we are referring to the length of time that elapses between the onset and completion of each particular interaction. Obviously, a set of actors who are mutually attracted may partially compensate for a relatively low frequency of interaction by simply increasing the duration of each encounter. This may in a way counteract the distance factor, since actors who find it inconvenient to interact frequently—perhaps because they are spatially segregated—may increase the total amount of contact in this way. Thus for many purposes the relevant variable may be the total amount of contact, defined to be the sum of the durations of each separate contact. A refined theory might be capable of handling all three concepts—frequency, average duration, and total contact—but we have been unable to take advantage of this distinction in the discussion that follows.

Since frequency of contact seems more closely linked to segregation than does duration, we shall henceforth refer primarily to frequency and assume that the duration of each contact is either irrelevant or very closely correlated with other variables, such as degree of intimacy. Where either of these assumptions seems unreasonable, however, it may become necessary to retain this distinction between frequency and duration of contact. A comparable distinction might also be made in connection with contextual variables, as, for example, between total frequency and average duration.

Intimacy

The notion of intimacy is often discussed in connection with interracial contacts in general and intermarriage in particular. Undoubtedly it is multidimensional in character and is commonly given a number of different connotations that include sexual attraction, mutual loyalty and supportiveness, the exchange of very private communications, prolonged and diffuse contacts, and at least a degree of exclusiveness that implies that no actor can be really intimate with more than a few persons at any given time. In spite of this complexity we infer that the meaning of the term is reasonably clear and that, given the present state of our knowledge, it would be difficult to make specific predictions pertaining to these separate dimensions or connotations of the term.

It may prove useful to distinguish between heterosexual intimacy and unisexual intimacy, given their different implications regarding intermarriage and caste endogamy. In theory it is possible to have extremely intimate contacts between groups that are confined to a single sex, while retaining very strict taboos against cross-sex, cross-group interactions. In the discussion that follows, however, we shall ignore this possibility by assuming that the intercorrelations between single-sex and cross-sex degrees of intimacy will be extremely high when applied to cross-group interactions. But to do so, we shall have to exclude what might be termed cross-sex exploitative contacts from the category of intimate ones. Specifically, sexual encounters between dominant-group males and subordinate-group females will be excepted from our discussion, unless these might also be considered intimate on nonsexual grounds.

The concept of diffuseness and the analytic dimension of specificity–diffuseness, as proposed by Parsons (1951:65–66), seems relatively close to the notion of intimacy, although one can certainly imagine situations under which the two would not be perfectly correlated. In general, interactions that are highly specific in nature are assumed not to be intimate. But it is again conceivable that there may develop a strong mutual attraction, a willingness to share private thoughts, and high supportiveness among partners whose interactions are confined to a very specific type. The assumption would be that, under such circumstances, the two would extend their interactions to include a much wider range of settings and activities. But this might depend upon the nature of the constraints placed upon them. In the case of interracial contacts, for example, it is quite possible for a highly specific type of interaction pattern to be accompanied by a degree of intimacy that cannot be permitted to spill over into a more diffuse kind of relationship. This suggests that in a more refined theoretical discussion it may be worthwhile to retain the distinction between intimacy and diffuseness, and perhaps other related dimensions as well. For simplicity, however, we shall confine our attention to intimacy.

Degree to Which Equal Status Is Implied

There are some kinds of contact situation that imply that the partners are of approximately the same status, so that the probability of interactions of these types is markedly reduced whenever the individuals have very different statuses. "Social" interactions are often of this type, if all participants must have at least some minimum status level in order to become eligible for inclusion. A number of honorary societies, functional groups (e.g., decision-making boards), and voluntary organizations also contain members of approximately equal status. Of course, there will be many contacts involving persons whose statuses are approximately equal by coincidence, and this is why we have added the notion that equality of status is implied by the contact. It is not necessary that this near equality be required, in some functional sense, as long as it is merely expected.

In contact situations of these types an actor's status may be judged in terms of his or her partner's status, so that contact with those who have considerably lower status than oneself may result in a reduction in one's own status; that is, there will be an expected status loss *if* the contact is observed by certain relevant parties. For instance, if one must be careful about whom to invite to one's party, or as an overnight guest, we would presume that considerations of status differentials are likely to be involved. Under ordinary circumstances we might measure expected status equality indirectly in terms of some measure of status dispersion that actually occurs in contacts of a given type, although this kind of measure may very well give different results from one that is based on actors' *perceptions* of the degree to which status equality is implied in the contact.

Implied status equality and intimacy are often confounded in theoretical discussions, and, of course, we expect them to be reasonably highly intercorrelated in many instances. But there are a number of forms of contact, such as cocktail parties, involving expectations of equal status but yet relatively low degrees of intimacy. Many residents of certain neighborhoods have very minimal contacts with each other and yet are perceived as having approximately equal statuses. Thus if middle-class whites object to the entry of a black family into their neighborhood, they may be primarily concerned about the status implications, about potential intimacy, both, or neither. Intimacy also occurs across sexes and age levels in spite of the fact that there may be very clear status differentials among the actors. Of course, this all depends upon how one defines status and what status dimensions are involved. If members of a family take their statuses from that of the breadwinner, then by definition all members of the family have the same status. But if one refers primarily to occupational status, the statuses of husbands and wives may obviously differ.

The familiar Bogardus social-distance scale (1928) seems to tap not only degree of intimacy but also implied status equality as well. At the one extreme of refusal to admit the minority to one's country, there is obviously no contact at all permitted. At the opposite pole of admitting the group to kinship through intermarriage, we have the combination of extreme intimacy and implied status equality. But there are a number of items at intermediate levels that seem to tap one or both of these dimensions in such a fashion that a unidimensional ordering of close items might not be expected. Admitting the minority into one's neighborhood presumably implies status equality and at least the risk of intimacy. Admitting its members into one's own occupation implies status equality but certainly not intimacy.

It is also possible that the scale taps still another dimension, namely, the threat of economic competition. Admitting minority members to one's occupation implies a willingness to compete on equal terms, thereby risking one's source of livelihood. Numerous studies have shown, however, that in spite of possible multidimensionality, these social-distance scales not only "scale" in the Guttman sense, but the ordering of items holds up remarkably well across sections of the country, age, sex, and SES levels, and also different minorities (Simpson and Yinger 1972). This suggests, then, that intimacy and implied status equality may be difficult to distinguish in practice.

Visibility of Contact

The probability of an individual's interaction with another person being detected obviously varies according to the nature of the situation and the duration and frequency of contacts, as well as any distinguishing characteristics between the two groups being represented. Even if, say, a black–white pair is observed, it does not follow that the particular individuals concerned can be identified and the information accurately conveyed to other relevant parties. Under conditions of extreme anonymity, as, for example, contacts that occur in urban settings that are remote from one's friends and neighbors, even though an interaction is technically "visible" the actors may never be held accountable for their behaviors. We shall use the term *degree of visibility* to refer to the probability of an individual's interactions with another party actually becoming known to relevant third parties who are in a position to sanction the actor(s) concerned. Thus the concept is asymmetric in the sense that degree of visibility for one partner (say, a white) may not be the same as that for another party (say, a black). Of course, this implies that their respective degrees of visibility will depend upon the nature of the setting in which the interaction occurs.

Legitimacy of Contact

It does not follow, however, that merely because a contact is visible to significant others or one's reference group it will actually be sanctioned either positively or negatively. Therefore it seems wise to distinguish visibility from another variable, namely, the degree to which the particular kind of interaction is approved by this set of persons. We shall use the term *legitimacy* to refer to the degree to which this contact is approved or accepted by the actor's reference group. Thus, the legitimacy of a contact may also be asymmetric in that it may be approved by one set of actors (say, middle-class blacks) but not by another (say, middle-class whites). This notion of legitimacy is not quite the same as that of "normal" or even "expected" behavior in that certain contacts may be rare and even unexpected but still approved or even admired precisely because they are rare.

As a general rule we would expect that visibility and legitimacy will combine multiplicatively in terms of their impact on sanctioning behaviors. An interaction must *both* be observed *and* be legitimate (illegitimate) in order to be rewarded (punished). Both of these variables of course involve relationships with third parties, and in fact their measurement depends on the nature and positioning of these third parties. This is also true with respect to the next variables we shall discuss, namely, the degree to which interactions are predictable and/or regulated.

Degrees of Predictability and Regulation

The degree to which an actor entering into a contact situation can accurately predict the behaviors of other parties is obviously an important factor affecting the actor's willingness to engage in such interaction. We assume that there will ordinarily be a tendency to avoid ambiguous situations in which the subjective probabilities of the responses to one's behaviors are very difficult to estimate (Langley 1977; Langley and Barth 1978). Especially if the interaction is highly intense, intimate, or expected to be of prolonged duration it is essential that each actor be able to predict with a high degree of accuracy how the other will respond. In the case of interactions that have a high total frequency and that cannot be avoided without incurring considerable cost, we therefore expect that the contacts will be regulated by interested third parties so as to increase this predictability.

In situations involving contacts between parties having very unequal statuses or power, but where the contacts might otherwise be expected to lead to increasing intimacy or status equalization, we generally find these interactions to be culturally regulated so as to preserve the inequality and also to make it very clear to both parties that certain forms of behavior are definitely proscribed, whereas others are prescribed and highly ritualized. The "etiquette" of southern race relations (Doyle 1937)—which is rapidly breaking down—is an obvious illustration. Here the elaborate pattern of expectations concerning terms of address, the demeanor of blacks when conversing with whites, the restrictions placed on the types of possible interaction and the locations in which they could occur, and the general pattern of deference behavior were obviously aimed at emphasizing the status inequality involved in black–white interactions.

Along with this "etiquette" were a host of socialization techniques designed to prevent the possibility of intimacy between the two groups. The entire system operated to produce a very clear set of expectations on both sides as to how and under what conditions the interactions must take place. Exceptions, of course, occurred, but they were sanctioned whenever possible and furthermore were surrounded with feelings of discomfort and suspicion. A white who appeared too friendly, or who flouted the traditional rules, could never really be trusted as sincere. A black who violated the rules could never be sure whether or not extreme sanctions would be applied if he or she stepped too far beyond the bounds of acceptable behavior.

Under circumstances where there is a high degree of mutual dependence between the parties, and where interactions are necessary to carry out exchanges, there will also be a set of regulations that place restrictions on the behaviors of the dominant party and that limit the degree to which the weaker party can be exploited in any given encounter. These regulatory mechanisms, which are protections against the arbitrary abuse of power, of course indicate that the weaker party has at least some power or ability to withhold needed services. We would generally expect increasing symmetry with respect to the degree and nature of each party's regulations as we approach equality of power. But we would also expect that the number of regulations applied to both parties will decrease as the necessity for direct contact diminishes and as the contacts become increasingly voluntary.

Degree to Which Interaction Is Intrinsically Rewarding or Costly

By intrinsic rewards or costs we shall mean those rewards or costs that are direct results of the interaction itself, rather than outcomes that occur indirectly as a result of actions by third parties or for any other reasons. We normally think of intrinsic rewards or costs as stemming from the process of interaction itself, and as being consummatory rather than instrumental in nature. But we shall extend the notion to include certain kinds of instrumental reward, provided that they are obtained directly from the exchange relationship and not from third parties. The reason we do not want to equate "intrinsic" with "consummatory" rewards is that there are many kinds of outcome that involve both consummatory and instrumental rewards simultaneously. Furthermore the consummatory–instrumental distinction depends upon the later actions of the party that is the recipient of the reward or cost. The distinction that we find most useful for present purposes is that between intrinsic rewards or costs and extrinsic ones that are only indirect outcomes of the interaction process. In this section we may then focus on the behavior of the potential interaction partner.

Either party may reduce the utility derived by the other through the simple device of making the interaction unpleasant, uncomfortable, unpredictable, embarrassing, or inconvenient, thereby affecting the degree to which the second actor obtains intrinsic rewards from the interaction process itself. The party with the higher status may snub or patronize the lower status party, whereas the latter may offend the former by committing embarrassing or offensive acts such as creating disturbances, engaging in deviant behaviors, refusing to conform to norms concerning aesthetic qualities (e.g., failing to keep up one's property in a neighborhood), or using insulting remarks or gestures.

Some members of a group may attempt to improve relations with a second group, whereas others may insist on offensive behaviors. Such a "group ambivalence" will, of course, make it much more difficult for members of the second group to predict the consequences of attempts they may make to increase contacts with the first group. Sometimes they will be accepted, whereas on other occasions they will be rudely rejected. Therefore, in the aggregate, the total number of intergroup contacts are likely to be reduced as a result of the strains produced.

This type of insulating mechanism can easily be used not only by high-status or powerful groups but by subordinate parties as well. Given the fact that it does not require actual retreat from a spatial location, or even expensive physical barriers or tight controls over points of entry, this form of insulation is often remarkably successful in preventing voluntary interactions between members of different groups. To the degree that the groups are perceived to be extremely different with respect to culture, interests, and informal interaction patterns, there will ordinarily be sufficient strains to interaction that a few additional purposeful insults or unpredictable behaviors may be sufficient to keep unnecessary contacts to a bare minimum. If so, the mere anticipation of discomfort or the expectation of embarrassment may maintain this very low level of contact, even where no deliberate efforts to block interaction are occurring. Under these conditions, however, once a few successful encounters do occur we would expect interactions to increase at an accelerating rate as the level of mutual understanding and tolerance for differences rises. Whether this kind of accelerating contact occurs, or whether the low level of contact is maintained more or less deliberately, will depend upon the level of conflict and mutual fear that exists, as well as on the degree to which the two groups are in direct competition for scarce resources.

Degree to Which Interaction Is Extrinsically Rewarding or Costly

We shall later construct a causal model in which the frequency and duration of contacts are taken as direct consequences of expected intrinsic and extrinsic rewards and costs, both of which interact with the degree to which the contact is voluntary to both parties. In one sense, extrinsic rewards and costs may be considered as a kind of residual category covering all rewards and costs that are not direct consequences of the interaction itself.

In the case of cross-group contacts we may anticipate that many of these extrinsic outcomes will involve primarily the cost side of the ledger. In particular, there will be costs incurred as a result of the sheer inconvenience of meeting—travel costs, time consumed, the need to preserve secrecy, and so forth. Presumably, the greater the spatial segregation between the two groups, the greater the average level of such costs. Included among the extrinsic rewards and costs are the sanctions imposed by third parties. In the case of cross-group contacts we would generally anticipate that such sanctions will tend to involve relatively more costs than rewards to the interacting partners, with the degree of cost in turn depending upon such factors as the amount of overt hostility and conflict between the two groups, the legitimacy of the contact, its visibility, and the vulnerability of the actors to the application of such sanctions. There will also be certain alternative opportunities forgone, such as the opportunity to interact with members of one's own group, or perhaps individuals representing other types of group. In some instances there may be certain demands from what Homans (1950) referred to as the "external system," as well as rewards that are conditional on the level of performance. For example, in the case of an interracial work force the interaction may be required by the employer, with the payoff (constituting an extrinsic reward) being conditional on the quality or quantity of the product of the team effort.

Operationally, it may be difficult to distinguish between intrinsic and extrinsic rewards and costs, but it is nevertheless theoretically useful to make the distinction. The reason is that the sources of *change* in the levels of rewards and costs will differ in the two instances. In the case of intrinsic rewards or costs, it is presumably one's interaction partner who provides the incentives for interaction, whereas in the case of extrinsic rewards or costs, these are determined by exogenous factors. For instance, a reduction in the overall degree of segregation between the two groups can be expected to decrease the extrinsic costs of interaction, regardless of the behavior of one's interaction partner. Similarly, changes in the demands of one's employer, or the nature of the work requirements, may either increase or decrease the incentives for interactions, regardless of the behaviors of one's partner.

We also recognize the possibility of statistical interactions between extrinsic rewards and costs and certain other factors. For example, if an employer requires a higher degree of cross-group interaction to receive a given payoff, then the actors become more dependent upon each other's cooperation and thus more dependent on the interaction. This may affect the relative power of the two actors, depending on which has the greater need for the extrinsic reward. It may also, of course, affect the degree to which the interaction is voluntary for each of the participants. The achievement of objectives set by an outside party may also have the indirect effect of increasing the affective ties between members of a work group, thereby reducing prejudices and increasing the intrinsic rewards of their cooperative interaction.

Amount of Conflict Expected

Certainly voluntary contacts that involve a large amount of conflict, fear, and distrust will ordinarily be avoided unless they are expected to be only short-run and instrumental to other objectives. In many instances, however, the exchange of negative sanctions is likely to be asymmetric, with one party being in a much better position to punish the other. Furthermore, the nature of the negative sanctions may differ, with one party being in a better position to employ violence than the other. If so, the party that poses the greater threat is more likely to attempt to initiate contact and to sustain it, in effect using this contact itself as a resource in the power contest. Although we ordinarily think of dominant groups as most likely to be in this initiating position, this is not necessarily the case. In particular, a subordinate party that attaches a very high utility to gaining power or achieving rapid change may attempt to harass the stronger party in this fashion, by exposing the latter's members to risks of violence in order to extract concessions. A subordinate party may also employ nonviolent resistance as a deliberate strategy to provoke violence against its own members in order to gain the sympathy of third parties.

Whichever party stands to lose the most from the exchange of these negative sanctions can be expected to have the greatest interest in finding ways to regulate such behaviors and in inducing third parties to act in this fashion. In the case of the civil rights movement of the 1960s, it was the southern blacks and their allies who welcomed the forces of "law and order" imposed by the federal government. But more recently in the urban North it is the residents of predominantly white suburbs who welcome outside assistance to help control "crime in the streets."

Degree of Dependence on Contact

Actors will, of course, vary in terms of the degree to which they are dependent upon specific others as exchange partners. This degree of dependence may be either symmetric or asymmetric in nature. As we have already seen, if actor A is highly dependent upon B, but if B can turn to other actors, $C, D, \ldots, K$, then B's power over A will be enhanced (Emerson 1962). Furthermore, A's interaction with B will be much less voluntary than B's, and we would also expect A to attempt to initiate interaction with B much more frequently than B initiates interaction with A. In general, then, degree of dependence will be highly correlated with degree of voluntariness, but it nevertheless seems wise to keep the two ideas distinct.

To the extent that a contact involves a high degree of intimacy and has occurred over a long period of time, one or probably both parties will, in effect, have rather large "sunk costs" in the relationship, which will also increase their degree of dependency on this relationship.[1] It will be costly to leave one's partner and to attempt to find a new one, and therefore dependency will increase. But it is certainly possible for two or more parties to be mutually dependent upon each other without there being a high degree of intimacy involved. In fact, a high degree of interdependence, coupled with power inequalities and conflict, is most likely to imply a very low degree of intimacy and a strong preference for alternative partnerships. Where sunk costs are high and yet the potential for conflict seems great, we would anticipate a tendency for one or both parties to regulate the interaction and to confine it to the bare minimum necessary for the exchange. Such regulation would tend to reduce the potential for intrinsic rewards from the interaction, however.

It should be noted that several parties may be dependent on the same spatial location, as, for example, a highly desirable business location. They may therefore share an interest in regulating each other's behaviors and in reducing overt conflict. In a sense, then, they are dependent upon each other for cooperation and for a minimal degree of interaction so as to achieve this end. We shall not refer to this kind of situation as involving "mutual dependence," however, unless these parties find it necessary to cooperate to defend their territory against a common enemy.

Degree to Which Interaction Is Voluntary

In popular terminology we find the phrase *voluntary segregation* being used—usually in referring to a minority's behavior—as more or less the opposite of legally enforced segregation. The implication is that the minority prefers it that way, and that if given a completely free choice it would rather naturally keep to itself. But this, of course, begs the question of why such a preference occurs or whether the withdrawal is conditional on the behavior of the dominant party. One meaning of the term would be "If we [dominant-group members] continue to behave exactly as we are now behaving, members of the other group would prefer to keep to themselves." But another meaning is "If we were to behave toward them exactly as we behave toward ourselves, they would still prefer to keep to themselves."

Thus there is usually an ambiguity as to whether an actor is "voluntarily" withdrawing from contact conditionally or unconditionally, and, of course, it may make a tremendous difference, practically and theoretically, whether or not the withdrawal behavior would be altered if the other party's behaviors were to change. One would ordinarily expect withdrawal behaviors to be conditional, and since the range of alternative behaviors of the other party will usually be extremely great, it seems most feasible to use the term *voluntary* in the first sense discussed above; that is, if one party is given a free choice of behaviors and elects not to interact with the other party—whose behaviors are taken into consideration in making this choice—then we say that the choice was a voluntary one. By *free choice* we mean that there are no positive or negative sanctions, or other costs or benefits, that are contingent on this choice, apart from the expected intrinsic gains or losses derived from the contact situation itself.

This use of the term *voluntary,* although perhaps easier to assess operationally, admittedly has the disadvantage of seeming to imply that the party in question really does not prefer contact under *any* conditions. If we wanted to retain the distinction between conditional and unconditional preferences we might use the term *preferred segregation,* or *preferred withdrawal,* if the party in question preferred spatial separation or a very low level of contact under almost all conditions. Clearly, an assumption to this effect would be highly speculative under most circumstances.

It is also necessary to understand that a contact that was voluntary under an initial set of circumstances may become much less so as the situation changes. Once a contact has occurred it may prove to be costly or inconvenient to cut it off or even to reduce the frequency of interaction. For instance, once a member has been admitted to a voluntary organization, the rules may make expulsion difficult or likely to be subject to outside constraints. In such an instance it may be much simpler to change the party's utility structure, perhaps by making membership extremely unpleasant, so that he or she voluntarily withdraws from interaction. Likewise, once an actor engages in an interaction there may be demands of the environment that make it difficult to reduce this level of interaction, so that the pattern in question may no longer be considered as primarily voluntary.

The degree to which a contact is voluntary, therefore, depends upon the utility structure of the actor concerned, since we have used the term *free choice* in such a way as to imply that there are no outside sanctions. Thus someone who is not being rewarded by the external system can be considered to be engaging in voluntary interaction, whereas someone whose withdrawal would result in externally produced costs would be considered to be an involuntary participant. This is an additional reason why the notion of voluntary interaction is difficult to pin down operationally.

Finally, we note that degree of voluntariness may be asymmetric and that one party may virtually control the conditions of contact—its initiation, frequency, duration, intimacy, location, and so forth. But it is also possible that the second party may at least veto or block the interaction at minimal cost, in which case we may wish to refer to this kind of situation as one of voluntary blocking of interaction. This may occur through the literal erection of barriers, by making the contact unpleasant or costly to the first actor, or by withdrawing to such a distance that the interaction is no longer feasible. If any of these mechanisms involves a substantial cost, however, then to this extent the interaction becomes involuntary. Clearly, voluntariness varies by degree and cannot be assessed without a knowledge of costs and gains and therefore the utility structure of the actors concerned.

Figure 14.1. Causal Model Explaining Frequency and Duration of Cross-Group Contacts

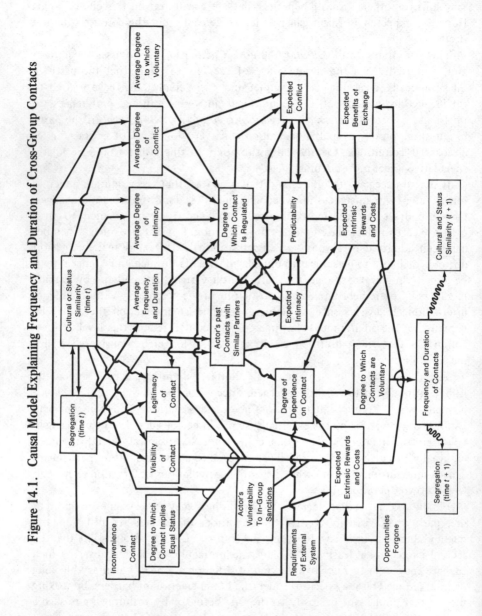

A TENTATIVE MODEL EXPLAINING CROSS-GROUP CONTACTS

We may now pull the previous discussion together in the form of a tentative model, as indicated in figure 14.1. The dependent variables in this diagram are the frequency and duration of the interaction in question, though allowance is made at the bottom of the figure for the possibility that this interaction, when aggregated over a large number of sets of individuals, may feed back at a later point in time to affect both degree of segregation and cultural or status similarity. The model is for the most part recursive and involves the existing levels of segregation and status and cultural similarities between groups as predetermined. These two types of factor, plus several additional exogenous variables, ultimately affect the three variables: (1) degree to which contacts are voluntary; (2) expected intrinsic rewards and costs; and (3) expected extrinsic rewards and costs. The latter three factors, in turn, affect the frequency and duration of contacts.

Some additional comments about the model are necessary. As was also the case with our models dealing with social power, the focus is on either of the interaction partners, with third parties playing the role of exogenous agents. Presumably, the same set of variables will be appropriate to all interaction partners, regardless of whether they belong to a dominant or subordinate group. The magnitudes of the coefficients and levels of exogenous variables can be expected to differ, however. These exogenous variables are essentially contextual factors and may be somewhat different for the two (or more) parties. We ideally want to construct a model in which the same conceptual variables appear in the equations for both actors, though perhaps in certain special cases having zero coefficients. In this rather simple model attention is focused on the *levels* of each variable rather than on inequalities or measures of dispersion for the interaction parties. Where gross inequalities exist with respect to status or other variables, however, this will affect the expected intrinsic rewards or costs of the interaction and perhaps the expected level of intimacy or conflict.

The model involves *expected* levels of such variables as degree of conflict, intimacy, and intrinsic and extrinsic rewards and costs. These expectations will depend upon the actors' previous encounters with the specific partner or with other actors defined as being similar to the partner, and upon existing beliefs or stereotypes about such partners, various personality factors, and possibly other exogenous variables that have not been included in the model. Once the interaction begins to occur, these expectations may be modified by actual experiences derived from the contact situation, with these objective experiences in turn affecting the actors' perceptions of the interaction as it is unfolding. These and other complications have not been included in the simplified model of figure 14.1.

To the degree that the interaction is voluntary for only one partner, and therefore can be cut off without incurring additional costs to this actor, the frequency and duration of the contacts will depend upon the levels of the variables for this actor. Where the interaction is voluntary for both partners and thus may be cut off by whichever actor has the least to gain from it, the frequency and duration of the interaction will be primarily determined by the coefficients and levels of exogenous variables for this (first) actor. But knowing this, the second or responding actor may adjust his or her own behavior so as to provide sufficient benefits to the first actor to maintain the second actor's desired level of contact.

This means that the power of the actor with the lesser *SEU* for maintaining the interaction will be enhanced to the degree that the other actor is, in effect, willing to make concessions in exchange for maintaining the interaction. An actor who is more or less forced into the interaction unwillingly, but who nevertheless depends on maintaining the contact, will thereby be at a disadvantage as compared with the actor who enters into it voluntarily. As was the case with respect to our earlier discussions of both exchange and power, a more complete model would therefore have to involve simultaneous relationships between the variables appropriate to each actor, with the variables for actor *A* in effect serving as predetermined factors (at any point in time) that may affect the behaviors of actor *B*.

Notice that the model of figure 14.1 implies that the voluntariness of contacts is an intervening variable between degree of dependence and frequency and duration of contacts. From the standpoint of our previous discussions of exchange and power it therefore seems unnecessary to introduce the notion of voluntariness at all, since frequency and duration are, in effect, multiplicative functions of dependence and expected rewards and costs. Because the notion of voluntary segregation is commonly used in discussions of race and ethnic relations, however, we have explicitly included it in our model to indicate where we believe it fits into the overall causal explanation of approach–withdrawal processes.

In the case of cross-group contacts the two variables, legitimacy and implied equal status, are assumed to interact multiplicatively with visibility to affect the level of expected extrinsic rewards and costs and also the degree to which the contact is regulated; that is, if the level of visibility is high, the slopes relating legitimacy and implied equal status to extrinsic costs and regulation will be steeper than if visibility is low. In the special case where the visibility is zero, and therefore the interaction cannot be detected by outside actors, neither legitimacy nor implied equal status will affect regulation or the expected extrinsic costs.

In addition, implied equality of status and the actual status similarity between the actors will interact multiplicatively to affect both regulation and the extrinsic rewards or costs. Specifically, the slope connecting implied equal status with extrinsic costs (or regulation) will be steeper in instances where the actor concerned has a substantially higher status than his or her partner, as, for example, in the case of a dominant-group member interacting with a relatively low-status minority. Looking at the matter in terms of the degree of actual

status inequality, the expected status loss to a dominant-group member interacting with a low-status minority will be greater in the case of a contact involving a high degree of implied status equality (say, an intimate social contact) than
one in which status equality is not implied (say, a casual encounter in a market
situation). These multiplicative relationships are indicated, toward the left-hand
side of the diagram, by means of arrows that converge prior to reaching their
common effects.[2]

The two macro-level variables—degree of (spatial) segregation and degree of
cultural and status similarity, the latter of which is really an entire set of variables—are assumed to affect directly a number of variables in the model. We have
already commented on their relationships with visibility, legitimacy, and inconvenience of contact. They are also assumed to affect stereotypes as well as the
actor's own past experiences in contact situations, both with the immediate
partner under consideration and also other partners perceived to be similar.
In particular, where the contact involves cross-group interactions, each actor will
bring to the situation memories of his or her own past contacts with other members of the potential partner's racial, ethnic, or other social category, as well as
expectations based on these prior contacts. A high degree of segregation, for
example, may have limited these contacts to specified types or to a highly
selective sample of out-group members.

Arrows have been drawn from segregation and cultural and status similarity
to three additional macro-level variables, namely, (1) average frequency and
duration of contacts of this type; (2) average degree of conflict; and (3) average
degree of intimacy, with these three variables in turn affecting the degree to
which the contact is regulated. These three average-level variables, plus "average
degree to which the contacts are voluntary" (which is taken as exogenous) have
been inserted into the model in order to account for the degree to which contacts are regulated. The basic idea is that not all contacts will be regulated, but
whenever cross-group contacts are reasonably frequent, difficult to avoid, and
yet potentially problematic, we may expect regulation to occur. Thus if there
has been a relatively high level of either conflict or intimacy (without benefit
of regulations), or if the contacts are becoming relatively frequent and prolonged, efforts may be made to regulate them *if* it is thought necessary or
desirable to do so. This latter qualification, of course, implies that additional
exogenous variables not included in the model will also affect the degree and
effectiveness of the regulating mechanisms. One such exogenous variable is the
power of the regulatory agents, or their ability and willingness to apply effective
sanctions to those who may deviate from expected patterns.

We have also drawn in an arrow from the visibility/legitimacy/equal-status
block of variables to degree of regulation, implying a greater degree of regulation
whenever contacts are highly visible, deemed illegitimate (unless regulated),
and implying approximately equal status under normal unregulated conditions.
An alternative possibility (not diagramed) is that similarity and status equality
interact to affect legitimacy. Thus if contact in situation *A* implies equal status

for the participants, then that contact will be legitimate if the participants are of equal status and illegitimate if they are of unequal status.

Since the model is a micro-level theory that contains certain macro variables as contextual factors, we argue that the basic explanatory mechanisms must involve subjective probabilities and utilities. Actually, utility variables are only implicit in the model. It is assumed that the actors value intimacy positively and conflict negatively and that they also anticipate both intrinsic and extrinsic rewards or costs resulting from the contacts. So as to keep the model general, we have not specified what these rewards and costs might be.

In the case of cross-group contacts it seems relatively safe to assume that most actors will attach a positive utility to remaining members in good standing of their own groups and therefore that they will be sensitive to control mechanisms aimed at reducing or regulating contacts with out-group members. But, of course, the degree to which actors attach high utilities to such in-group values will vary, as will their vulnerability to sanctions. Thus a more complete model would need to take these utilities explicitly into consideration and possibly link them to variations in degree of segregation, cultural or status similarities between groups, and perhaps also the set of variables tapping average levels of contacts between groups.

Subjective probability variables have been included in the model in the form of *expected* levels of a number of variables. Since we are admitting that each of these levels (e.g., of conflict) may vary by degree rather than merely being present or absent, we have substituted the idea of an expected value for that of a subjective probability. Exogenous to this micro-level model are whatever other variables that might affect these expectancy values. The essential point is that it is not the variables that in some sense cause each other. Rather, it is expectancies and utilities attached to these contact variables that motivate the actors to behave in certain ways. Many times when we construct causal models involving either aggregated variables or variables that refer to pairs or sets of actors, we may find ourselves leaving out these subjective or motivational types of variable. To add them to each model in a fully explicit fashion will often overcomplicate the picture and nullify the heuristic advantages of a visual diagram. Therefore we have followed the compromise route of inserting them only in the case of certain expectancy levels, though at the same time introducing the above caveat concerning the absence of utility variables.

It is perhaps advisable to comment in addition on the interrelationships in the model among contact regulation, predictability, expected conflict, and expected intimacy. In the case of potential conflict situations involving cross-group contacts between members of racial or ethnic groups, for example, we anticipate that regulations will operate to dampen this conflict both directly (e.g., through actions of the regulatory agents) and indirectly via increased predictability; that is, the regulations make it easier to predict the patterned behavior of one's partner, thereby reducing the number of potential misunderstandings and restricting the alternative courses of action of each party. Thus we have drawn in an arrow from predictability to expected conflict. But the level of expected conflict, in turn, may have a feedback on predictability. If one actor expects conflict to occur, this may encourage that actor to surprise or deceive the potential opponent or to engage in "preventive" offensive actions that reduce the level of predictability.

Likewise, in situations where the contact would ordinarily be expected to lead to more intimate relationships, regulation serves directly to inhibit such intimacy, but it may also have an indirect effect through the predictability variable. We would in general assume that predictability ordinarily reinforces intimacy, and vice versa. But the kinds of predicted behavior produced through regulations may have the opposite effect of creating stereotyped behaviors and responses. For example, regulations that constrained the relationships between white masters and their black slaves, or between potential friends who were members of different races, have served to inhibit those forms of behaviors that are conducive to intimacy while encouraging those that maintain social distance. Thus the signs of the relationship between predictability and intimacy will depend upon the nature of the circumstances. In the case of most types of intergroup contact situation with which we are concerned, however, we would expect these signs to be negative in both directions: high predictability inhibits intimacy, and high intimacy reduces predictability of this type of regulated behavior.

As already noted, our use of the term *utilities* may give the impression that we believe that actors are engaged in a very explicit and rational process of calculation, whereas this is often far from the case. Especially in situations involving a high degree of emotional intensity, a single goal, such as that of achieving revenge or inflicting injury or even death to one's enemy, may become an obsession that dominates all other objectives and that completely distorts an actor's ability to arrive at reasonable subjective probabilities. If, at the same time, such acts of aggression would lead to almost certain reprisals, the actor may be placed in an intolerable situation involving an extreme degree of internal tension and a need for unusually effective mechanisms of self-control. Accompanying this may be a corresponding tendency to displace this rage onto some relatively innocent third party, including members of one's own group.

It has been emphasized over a number of years in the psychiatric literature that this necessity of controlling one's impulses, especially when combined with a basic self-hate, has had important consequences for the personality development of minorities (see Kardiner and Ovesey 1951; and Karon 1958). More recently, certain black psychiatrists have placed an even greater emphasis on notions such as rage, hatred, and impulses toward violence (see Fanon 1963; and Grier and Cobbs 1968). A minority member feeling this inner rage, and simultaneously placed in an ambiguous situation in which it will be difficult to predict whether or not one's partner will touch a sensitive nerve or even deliberately bait one into an extreme reaction, will tend to avoid such contacts if at all possible. Likewise, a dominant-group member who suspects the minority of harboring such rage and who fears an irrational outburst without apparent provocation will also tend to avoid such interactions unless they are carefully regulated and delimited in scope, intensity, and duration.

Finally, we need to consider the relationship between the macro concept of integration and the variables considered in our simplified model. We defined integration essentially in terms of the degree of intergroup interactions of two types: those that are approximately equal status and those that are reasonably intimate. If there are a high proportion of intimate and equal-status contacts that occur across groups, relative to within-group interactions of the same type, then we say that integration is high. Notice that we deliberately excluded conflictual contacts from this definition, though it is, of course, possible that the proportions of conflictual and intimate contacts may be simultaneously high. In the present section, however, we have argued that intimacy and equality of status should be treated as distinct variables, at least on the micro level, where we are concerned with individual contact pairs. Thus the notion of integration is potentially multidimensional whenever intimacy and status equality are not highly correlated. If we wish to use the concept integration as though it were unidimensional we must therefore either explicitly recognize that it involves a summary or composite index, or we must assume a high intercorrelation among the component dimensions.

The latter assumption is subject to empirical test on both the micro and macro levels. Assuming a moderately high correlation on the micro level, however, it seems reasonable to assume that when individual pairs of interaction partners are *aggregated* this correlation will become sufficiently high that, under most circumstances, it will do no harm to combine the two dimensions. Thus although we may imagine a reasonable proportion of interaction pairs for which there is a high degree of intimacy but yet low status equality, or high status equality but low intimacy, when these become aggregated over some larger unit, such as a neighborhood or school, these aggregated intimacy and equal-status contact scores will be very highly correlated, in which case one could use either measure separately, or combined into an index, without affecting one's conclusions in any important ways. But one should always be alert for situations in which the two interaction dimensions will be only very weakly interrelated on the micro level, in which case the notion of integration may need to be redefined. Cross-sex relationships may be just such an example, though, as we noted previously, whether or not such relationships should be assumed to involve partners of equal status will depend upon precisely how the notion of status is defined.

A Note on the Concept of Similarity

In this very general model we have used "cultural and status similarities" as an exogenous variable without referring to any specific dimensions of similarity along which the groups may be compared. This is partly because the subject is beyond the scope of the present discussion but also because we are well aware of the possibility that actors may seize upon almost any kind of difference and then magnify its significance all out of proportion to what a neutral or outside observer would consider to be an important one.

Certain major kinds of cultural difference, such as language, kinship structure, legal patterns, or clashes of basic values, are not only likely to hinder communication but also to be accompanied by duplicating institutional structures. These kinds of major cultural difference are emphasized in the literature on cultural pluralism associated with British or European sociology and cultural anthropology: scholars such as the Kupers, M. G. Smith, Furnivall, and van den Berghe.[3] In present-day American society these cultural differences are much less dramatic, except in the case of a very small number of relatively isolated groups of American Indians. This has not meant, however, that the relatively small differences have been ignored in this country; in fact they can and do serve as focal points for major cleavages.

Cultural or phenotypical differences that seem relatively minor to a neutral third party may be emphasized or exaggerated whenever a natural dichotomy can be constructed. This is obviously true with respect to religious differences such as those between Christians and Jews, Protestants and Catholics, or Hindus and Muslims. In such instances one often finds a considerable concern with history, and in particular those periods of history during which major schisms between these religions may have occurred. Usually such dichotomies will also be correlated with variables that are either continuous in nature (such as income) or at least orderable by status, prestige, or power. Disputes that are in part economic or political can become drastically simplified by organizing the conflict around the dichotomized attribute. Once this occurs and the conflict becomes intense, the other sources of cleavage may then become incidental. One cannot easily identify or attack an enemy if that enemy can only be defined along a continuum such as wealth. But if one has a simple label, such as Catholic or Protestant, the battle lines can be drawn.

Furthermore, such a dichotomy makes it possible to simplify many kinds of economic transaction. The notions of a dual wage system and split labor market are, of course, dependent upon actors' abilities to label one another in a simple way and then to offer a completely separate set of wages or occupations to members of the two groups (see Bonacich 1972). Such a system could also conceivably operate with three or four distinct groups but would become unmanageable if the characteristic (such as race or color) were defined along a continuum. The essential point is that the notion of similarity is much more difficult for actors to pin down whenever a continuum is involved. Ideologies may operate to simplify this picture by attempting to draw a sharp line between groups, as, for example, between bourgeoisie and proletariat.

FACTORS AFFECTING REWARDS AND COSTS OF CROSS-GROUP INTERACTIONS

In the previous discussions of cross-group contacts we did not focus explicitly on rewards and costs except to distinguish between intrinsic and extrinsic rewards and costs. We also did not emphasize expectancies and had virtually nothing to say about utilities. In the present section the focus is much more directly on rewards and costs and therefore utilities. Although we shall not stress the fact that expectancies enter the picture, it should always be understood that we are dealing with subjective expected utilities; that is, actors will necessarily assess rewards and costs with a degree of uncertainty. Some rewards and costs are immediate and obvious, so that their subjective probabilities are approximately unity. But others will be delayed and only imperfectly associated with the relevant form of contact, so that the expectancy component will be problematic, even though our own discussion of this component will be veᵢy limited in the present section.

Basically, we shall be concerned with distinguishing analytically between expected rewards, on the one hand, and expected costs, on the other. Here we shall recombine extrinsic and intrinsic rewards or costs so as to simplify the analysis, though in a more detailed discussion it may prove worthwhile to make a fourfold distinction between intrinsic rewards, intrinsic costs, extrinsic rewards, and extrinsic costs. Our approach will be to consider hypothetical reward and cost functions related to the degree of cross-group interactions. After considering the general nonlinear forms that these reward and cost functions can be expected to take, we shall turn to a discussion of certain general implications for the study of their equilibrium-level properties. Finally, we shall indicate a few of the factors that may affect the shapes of these reward and cost functions by relating them specifically to some of the variables discussed previously.

General Forms of Reward and Cost Functions

Especially in the case of those cross-group interactions where there is at least a moderate degree of hostility or conflict of interest between two or more groups, we may anticipate that almost every cross-group encounter will involve a degree of ambivalence on the part of the actors; that is, there will tend to be certain benefits or rewards of the interaction, but there will also be costs. Of course, this assertion applies to all interaction patterns, but in the case of cross-group interactions the dilemmas created by this kind of ambivalent situation are likely to be especially intense, particularly in the case of members of subordinate groups.

Therefore it seems wise to split apart the reward and cost components and to analyze each separately, keeping in mind that the actors may or may not make this explicit distinction in their own decision-making processes. We shall for the time being assume that these rewards and costs are rather easily calculable, though we recognize that this will seldom be the case. We shall then address the question of how ideological systems serve to simplify this process, while possibly also distorting the actor's estimates of the true rewards and costs.

Consider the diagram of figure 14.2, in which an actor's cross-group interactions are expressed as a proportion of that actor's total interactions with all parties. This variable, which we shall refer to as the percentage of cross-group

**Figure 14.2.   General Forms of Functions Relating Percentage of
Cross-Group Contacts to Rewards and Costs**

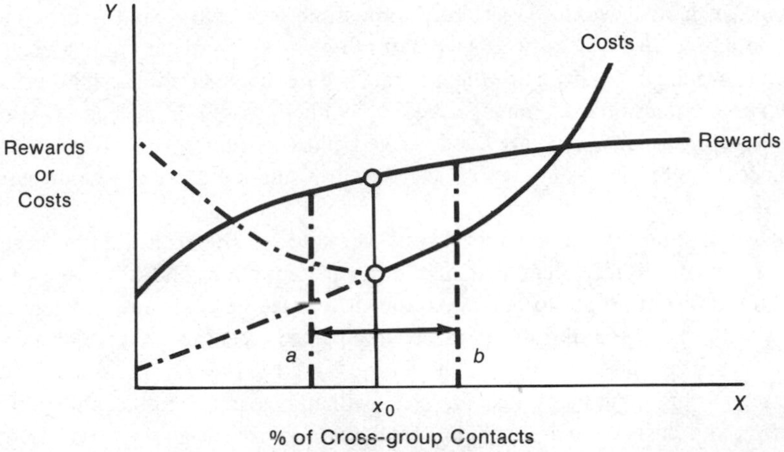

% of Cross-group Contacts

contacts, is thus standardized to take into consideration that some actors will
engage in more interactions than others. Percentage of cross-group contacts, X, is
given along the horizontal axis, with degree of reward or cost, Y, being represented by the vertical axis.

We shall assume that the general form of the reward curve will be that of an
increasing function with a decreasing slope, indicating a satiation or diminishing returns phenomenon; that is, the actor is assumed to benefit from a certain
number of cross-group contacts, perhaps because of the need to exchange goods
and services or perhaps because the nature of job demands for such interactions.
There also may be certain cultural benefits in the form of the advantages of an
exposure to persons with differing life styles, beliefs, and experiences. We
assume, however, that beyond a certain point the marginal gains derived from
increases in cross-group interactions will be subject to satiation and will therefore be insufficient to compensate for the rise in costs, so that an equilibrium
level will be reached.

Turning to the shapes of the cost functions, we shall assume that cost curves
will in general rise more steeply than reward functions. In some cases, especially
for numerical minorities and subordinate groups, there will also be costs incurred
if the proportion of cross-group contacts drops too low. In these instances the
cost functions will tend to be U-shaped, though not necessarily symmetrical.
But in other cases, especially for persons who are members of groups that are
overwhelming numerical majorities and also that hold dominant positions, the
costs incurred as a result of minimal cross-group interactions may be extremely
low, at least in terms of the perceptions of the actors concerned.[4]

Thus the white resident of rural Vermont or Idaho may not experience any
perceived loss by virtue of the fact that he or she has practically no contact

with blacks or other low-status minorities. In contrast, a white Southerner would experience costs of extreme avoidance as a result of restrictions of movement, as well as the inability to take advantage of a cheap and available labor supply. In fact, it would be virtually impossible for a white Southerner to avoid all contacts with blacks, though we naturally expect that the relative costs will depend upon the nature of the contact being considered. Certain types of intimate contact, for example, may be avoided with minimal costs, whereas others cannot. Thus we have used dashed lines in figure 14.2 to indicate two distinct possibilities as we approach the low end of the cross-group contact continuum.

If we assume that at some level of X the slope of the cost function begins to increase more rapidly than that of the reward function, and if we also assume that the actor attempts to maximize the difference between rewards and costs, there will be an equilibrium point at which the percentage of cross-group contacts stabilizes. This is indicated in figure 14.2 by the vertical line at X_0. Of course, it is highly unlikely that the actor will engage in an explicit calculation of rewards and costs or that either can be estimated with a high degree of accuracy. Therefore it is much more reasonable to suggest that there will be a *band* within which the percentage of cross-group contacts will fluctuate and within which the actor is virtually indifferent as to the level of these interactions. In the case of the U-shaped cost function, such a band might be represented by the dashed vertical lines intersecting the X axis at a and b. To the left of a, the actor begins to see that decreased cross-group interaction will be disadvantageous, and to the right of b further increases will result in a steep increase in costs. Therefore the expected range of interaction will be between a and b, assuming that this actor controls the actual degree of contact.

Such an assumption is reasonable if there are a variety of potential interaction partners, each of whom has a somewhat different ideal equilibrium point. But there also may be certain constraints operative, depending upon the average cost and reward curves for members of the other group, as well as the relative numbers in the two groups. If there are many members of the numerical majority who wish to interact with members of a tiny minority, and if the latter do not desire a high degree of interaction, the actual levels of cross-group contacts will be adjusted to a point somewhere between the optimal levels for members of the two groups. We may also expect that members of the larger group will find it necessary to offer certain concessions in exchange for the opportunity to interact with the smaller group on a more regular basis.

As an obvious example of such a phenomenon we may note the case of a small social elite in heavy demand as interaction partners and therefore in a position to extract deference behavior and other rewards from those members of the masses who are most eager to interact with them. Presumably, however, there will be a diminishing returns or satiation effect operative, so that only a certain amount of social contact with the masses will have sufficient payoff to compensate for the costs involved.

We may now consider on this very general level what can be expected to happen if these cost and reward functions shift in various ways. For instance, it is obvious that if the cost function shifts to the left, the equilibrium levels will be lowered. If the reward function tends to be relatively flat toward the upper end of the X continuum, the position of the cost function will be the primary determinant of the equilibrium level. Should the cost function become more steep, in either or both directions, this will obviously reduce the width of the indifference band represented by the difference between a and b in figure 14.2. These rather obvious points will be of interest later on when we consider some of the factors that may operate to shift the reward and cost functions.

Much less obvious, however, is the question of what can be expected to happen if the cost function is simply raised in level, or the reward function dropped, so that it becomes possible that there is *no* level of interaction for which the net rewards exceed the net costs. This possibility is diagramed in figure 14.3. In the case of cost curve A we have basically the same situation as previously discussed. If we move to cost curve B we see that there is only a narrow range within which the actor may engage in cross-group interactions and still experience a net gain. But in the case of cost curve C there is a net loss regardless of how the actor behaves!

In the case of curve A, and to a lesser extent curve B as well, we may generally expect that most actors will simply *adjust* to the situation by selecting an

Figure 14.3. Comparison of Different Levels of Cost Functions, Holding Reward Function Constant

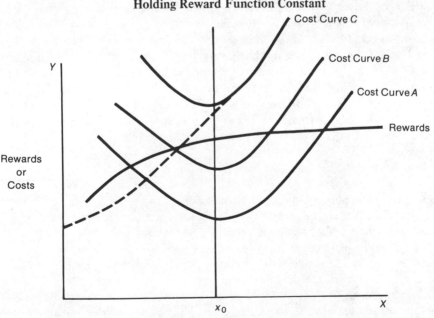

Cost Curve C

Cost Curve B

Cost Curve A

Rewards

Y

Rewards or Costs

x_0

X

% of Cross-group Contacts

appropriate level of cross-group interactions; that is, since they experience a net gain from some levels of interaction, they will tend to move *along* the curves until they find a range of interaction frequencies that are reasonably satisfactory. But in the case of curve *C* there is *no* form of adjustment that is satisfactory, though obviously some degrees of contact are more unsatisfactory than others. Regardless of the degree of interaction selected, the actor is subjected to stresses that cannot be sufficiently reduced by simply moving along the curve. We may anticipate reactions designed either to change the objective situation or to modify the actor's own motivational structure.

One possible response to this kind of intolerable dilemma, then, is to attempt to alter the objective situation so as to reduce the cost curve's level such that, at some points, it will be beneath that of the reward function. Conceivably this might be achieved at the upper end of the *X* continuum by radically altering the shape of the cost curve, or by reducing its overall level (back to that of curves *A* or *B*). But in the case of a subordinate group, such as a racial or ethnic minority, it may be much easier to modify the cost function by reducing costs at the low interaction end of the continuum.

We shall suggest below that geographic concentration, combined with a duplication of major institutions in the minority community, may function to lower the avoidance end of the cost curve for minority members, at least in terms of immediate and readily perceived costs. In the extreme, we may imagine the possibility of a completely pluralistic or dualistic system involving the virtual isolation of each group, so that the minority community provides all of the necessary services for its members, including occupational security and opportunity approximately equal to that in the majority community. If so, cost curve *C* would be modified as indicated by the dashed curve, which falls below the level of the reward curve at the very low contact end of the continuum. Of course, in real social systems we would predict that the *true* costs of such isolation (assuming these could be measured) would be much greater than the perceived costs. The dominant group would hardly be expected to permit this degree of isolation without extracting concessions from the minority, and this would have the effect of raising the true cost function.

Ideologies and Reward and Cost Functions

As noted previously, belief systems and ideologies often operate to enable an actor to simplify an overly complex reality by providing a working causal theory that eliminates certain kinds of consideration altogether, reduces uncertainties, and explains away incompatibilities among goals and behaviors. In any reasonably complex kind of interaction there will be certain obvious costs and rewards, as well as others that are linked to all sorts of contingencies and not at all directly related to the immediate contact situation. Especially in instances in which an interaction has not yet taken place, or where the actor must guess at the similarity between a potential future interaction partner and other past partners, there must be some kind of simplified working theory to enable the actor to make a reasonably quick decision. It is the *expected* rewards and costs that determine the actor's behavior, and as we have already discussed in considerable detail, these expectations may be based on a wide variety of factors. Presumably, the more complex the situation the greater the actor's need for a simplified working theory in order to make these decisions.

In the case of cross-group contacts, where we may anticipate a high degree of uncertainty and ambivalence, such ideological factors may be extremely important. But where competing ideologies are in evidence, as, for example, segregationist–separatist versus integrationist working theories, we may also anticipate a high degree of ambivalence toward these ideologies themselves, as well as tendencies to vacillate between them. Under such circumstances we may also expect that relatively slight shifts in reward and cost functions may, when aggregated, produce rather dramatic shifts in the degree to which one or the other extreme ideology gains ascendancy.[5]

For instance, as long as reasonably tangible gains could be achieved by the nonviolent civil rights movement of the 1960s, the integrationist ideology dominated black thinking in the United States. But when this movement began running into more formidable obstacles, a separatist ideology became much more popular, particularly with the younger generation of blacks. This ideology, in turn, led to a rejection of contacts with whites based on an extremely over-simplified theory of "black power." At this writing, this separatist ideology once more seems to be losing some of its popularity, but one may safely predict a vacillation between the two extremes in accord with changing circumstances.

Any careful and complex synthesis of these two fundamentally opposing ideological systems can be expected to create too great a mental burden on most actors who attempt to thread their way between them. The basic reason, of course, is that no one can engage in everyday interactions while at the same time making highly complex decisions based not only on immediate gains and rewards but also on long-run consequences that have to be based on future contingencies. For these reasons, an oversimplified world view greatly facilitates the decision-making process and in this sense is rational, even though based on incorrect premises, a neglect of complexities, and a failure to consider all but a very few outcomes and utilities. In effect, the behavior becomes rational in terms of the short-run consequences for individual actors, though dysfunctional, perhaps, for the larger group of which they are members.

Ideologies also enable actors to look to *future* outcomes as a compensation for present unpleasant ones. An essential ingredient of integrationist ideologies, for example, is the belief that even though certain pioneers who are the first to integrate a given organization or neighborhood may have to suffer temporary difficulties, as time passes and as other members of their own group come to occupy similiar positions, the long-run advantages to the group as a whole will be worth the temporary sacrifices. To the degree that such an integrationist ideology is accepted in principle and acted upon by members of either or both groups, those who make these temporary sacrifices may also receive compensatory immediate rewards in the form of recognition and notoriety or perhaps more tangible benefits such as honorific positions or leadership roles.

More generally, we see in this illustration an example of a situation in which organized efforts by corporate groups can modify individual actors' reward and cost functions by, in effect, serving as third parties to their interactions and by adding or subtracting future increments to their expected rewards or costs. They may also affect these functions by regulating the interaction patterns that occur, as we noted in the previous sections. Thus if cross-group interactions tend to be costly because of a high degree of expected conflict, these corporate actors may intervene to inhibit extreme forms of aggression or to routinize the contacts in such a way that each actor's behavior follows predictable lines.

Finally, an individual actor who is unable to alter the reward and cost functions, either through concerted action or by modifying his or her own utilities and expectations, may prefer to escape altogether from the situation.[6] This assumes, of course, that such escape is possible and that some alternative location can be found that does not involve such an intolerable situation. There will always be certain costs of moving, as well as a degree of uncertainty as to what to expect in the new situation. Again, belief systems may operate to persuade such actors that the grass *is*, in fact, greener in the other pasture and that there will be delayed rewards for those who succeed in escaping.

The Reward Function

As previously indicated, we expect that reward functions will generally tend to have relatively horizontal slopes at the moderate to high levels of the X continuum, indicating that once a given level of cross-group interaction has been reached there will be only very slight gains from further increases. But, of course, this all depends upon the nature of the contact being considered, as well as the levels of certain exogenous variables. As a general rule, the greater the dependence of the actor on the contact, the higher will be the rewards function, and also the steeper the slope will be at moderate levels of cross-group contacts. This hypothesis is represented in a diagram of figure 14.4.

If one could assume a constant cost function applicable to these two curves, we would therefore expect that the equilibrium level for the high dependence situation would be at a higher proportion of cross-group contacts, say, at X_1, than would occur in the case of the lower dependence situation, where the equilibrium level might be at X_0. But, of course, it is also likely that the cost curves would be different in these two situations, with the costs generally being higher in the high dependence situation, especially toward the lower end of the cross-group contacts continuum. Therefore it is difficult to say very much about the relative equilibrium levels without further assumptions about the levels of exogenous variables.

We may also expect that individuals' dependence on contacts with members of other groups will be a function of both their relative and absolute sizes, particularly the latter. In the case of a very small minority, not only will there

Figure 14.4. Relationships between Percentage of Cross-group Contacts and Rewards for Differing Levels of Dependence for Subordinate Groups

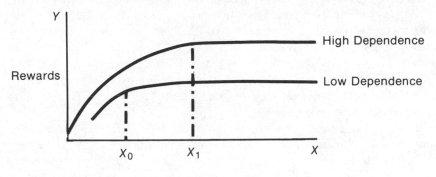

% of Cross-group Contacts

usually be economic dependence upon larger groups but, in terms of purely social contacts as well, members of such very small groups will have a limited choice of interaction partners from within their own group. Assuming a reasonable degree of heterogeneity within each group with respect to matters of taste, social standing, value orientations, and other factors that relate to one's selection of interaction partners, this implies that members of a very small group must look to outsiders if they are to find a sufficient pool of compatible associates.

This seems to be a matter of absolute size rather than percentages, given the fact that any single actor can only have a very limited number of close associates. Persons with rather unusual combinations of tastes or values will have a much more restricted range of choice than those with rather typical ones, implying the likelihood of relatively more cross-group contacts among individuals with such unique tastes. Presumably, then, both the levels and slopes (at intermediate levels) of the reward functions will be greater in the case of these deviant individuals than for more typical ones, since their dependence on members of the other group will be greater.

In the case of numerical minorities, and also subordinate groups more generally, we expect that any steps taken to increase the group's autonomy from a larger or dominant group will also tend to reduce the proportion of cross-group contacts. To the degree that such groups can find the means to service their own members through an array of separate institutions and provide alternative forms of psychic rewards, this will tend to reduce the levels of the rewards for cross-group interactions and thereby also reduce the magnitude of the gap between rewards and costs—assuming the former to be greater than the latter. If the cost functions remain unchanged in the process, we therefore expect an approximation to the situation implied by cost function C in figure 14.3.

Thus, perhaps paradoxically, moves toward greater independence of a minority may tend to raise minority discontent with the existing level of cross-group contacts. In effect, under conditions of moderate to high dependence on cross-group contacts, members of the minority may perceive at least a sufficient number of tangible gains to justify continued contact. But, with increased self-sufficiency combined with nonnegligible costs, any level of contact may appear to be more costly than it is worth. If so, it becomes necessary to reduce the cost function as well, and, as we have just indicated, it may be much easier to do so at the very low end of the X continuum. If there are very few costs of total withdrawal, such withdrawal from contact may turn out to have the most favorable net effect for the actor, with the result that the aggregate level of cross-group interaction becomes very low.

An analogous phenomenon may occur in the case of those members of a numerically large and dominant group who derive psychic benefits from contacts with members of a minority. For the most part, rewards for the average dominant-group member who engages in cross-group contact will be relatively low, so that such contacts are likely to be confined to casual ones that cannot easily be avoided without substantial cost. But for those who attempt to interact more extensively, and who derive benefits from playing leadership roles in minority-oriented social movements, any increases in the minority's self-sufficiency are likely to be associated with tendencies to reject such dominant-group members, or at least to reduce their psychic rewards. If, at the same time, there are alternative forms of behaviors that promise these dominant-group individuals similar rewards, we may expect a retreat or escape into these alternative patterns.

In the case of American white liberals, for example, there are many "causes" that seem deserving of attention, as well as faddish trends that shift the reward structure. The liberal may simply follow the fads, while still salving his or her social conscience and continuing to play leadership roles. If one looks at any single "cause" (such as that of blacks in the United States), this behavior on the part of white liberals indeed seems inconsistent, but if one aggregates together a number of such "causes," the level of activity may seem much more consistent over time. Slight changes in the reward and cost functions for any *given* activity, however, may have rather dramatic consequences for that activity because of the wide range of alternative behaviors that satisfy basically the same kinds of general goal. The situation is quite different, of course, for the minority activist for whom a single issue predominates.

Before closing this section we need to comment briefly on what may appear to be a tautology involving the notions of rewards and dependence. Is it not the case that what we mean by dependence is the same thing as the receipt of rewards in excess of costs? The problem is made especially difficult because both constructs will be exceedingly hard to measure. Even so, we believe it useful to retain the distinction precisely because of the need to make the kind of analysis hinted at in the previous paragraph. In our exchange chapter we noted that dependence is a function of both degree of goal fulfillment and the number of alternatives. There may be a number of instances in which an interaction may be highly rewarding to an actor who, nevertheless, is not dependent on it because of the existence of numerous alternatives. As long as the rewards exceed the costs by a reasonable amount, there is no need to change interaction partners, even though others are available.

We are suggesting, then, that this lack of correspondence between reward reception and dependence is likely to be more characteristic of members of a dominant group than those who are members of either a very small numerical minority or a subordinate group. More generally, the degree of correspondence between the two variables is likely to depend upon the actors' relative resources for attracting alternative partners, as well as the simple availability of such partners. It is also possible, of course, for an actor to be highly dependent on a relationship and yet to receive very low rewards, in which case in popular terminology we tend to refer to the relationship as being an exploitative one.

The Cost Function

Although we have suggested that cost functions will tend to be either U-shaped or monotonically increasing with accelerating slopes, we do not mean to imply that this will hold for *all* types of cost or all forms of interaction. Therefore it is perhaps wise to begin by noting a major kind of exception. To the degree that expected costs are based on ignorance or unrealistic fears about another group, or that initial contacts will be uncomfortable and ambiguous because the actors are simply inexperienced and likely to misunderstand the actions of the other party, we would expect the cost function to *decrease* with increasing contacts, perhaps according to the form of the curve given in figure 14.5. One mechanism that could produce this result is that high initial prejudice produces an expectation of unpleasant contacts; when they do not materialize, the prejudice level is then lowered.

The curve of figure 14.5 suggests that the initially high expected costs will drop rather rapidly as the actor gains experience with cross-group contacts, with the cost-function tending to level off as the rate of contacts increases. Presumably, if the groups are antagonistic there will always remain a certain positive level of costs because of this potential strain and uncertainty, especially whenever the actor meets a new out-group representative whose behavior cannot be predicted in advance and from whom a certain amount of initial hostility can be expected.

**Figure 14.5. Hypothesized Cost Function When Expected Costs
Are Based on Fear or Ignorance**

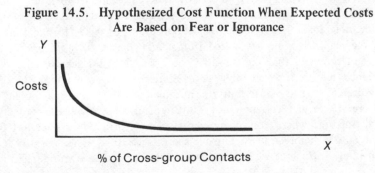

These types of cost that arise from inexperience, ambiguities, and intergroup hostilities, and that are hypothesized to diminish in accord with functions of the type exhibited in figure 14.5, may be expected to combine with other costs that rise with increasing contacts. If so, this would tend to produce the kind of U-shaped function suggested by figure 14.3. The height of the curve at the very low end of the X continuum can therefore be expected to depend upon such factors as the degree of familiarity the actors have with members of the out-group, the amount of hostility or tension between groups, and the similarities between interaction partners. We generally assume that the greater these simi-larities with respect to such things as education, occupation, religion, or general value orientations, the greater the degree of common ground upon which to base the interaction. Therefore the easier it will be to establish an ongoing rela-tionship with minimal strains.[7] Thus, on the aggregate level, the greater the similarities between groups, the lower these types of cost and the higher the equilibrium level for cross-group interactions.

The degree of residential and organizational segregation will also affect the cost functions, though perhaps differentially according to the relative sizes and average status levels of the two groups. We have already commented on the obvious fact that, for a very small numerical minority, the costs of complete avoidance may be extremely high because of the limitations placed on spatial movement, an inability to find suitable exchange partners, and the limited range of occupations that could permit such a high degree of isolation. But these costs may be reduced if such a small minority is geographically concentrated, econom-ically self-sufficient, or engaged in occupational pursuits that do not require frequent exchanges, and in other ways in a position to insulate itself from con-tact. Undoubtedly, this will also depend upon perpetuating a motivational structure and belief system that yield low-utility values attached to outcomes that depend upon interactions with the larger group. The maintenance of isola-tion or insulation may itself involve certain costs to the group as a whole in terms of the necessity of devoting a substantial proportion of its resources to this objective.

In situations where small minorities are thrown into contact with members of dominant or majority groups, there will be substantial costs to these minority members unless they engage in at least a moderate number of intergroup con-tacts. This is the basic reason why we have postulated a U-shaped cost function for such individuals. The situation is quite different, however, for most members of a large majority group, *provided that a high degree of segregation already exists*, and provided that the minority occupies only the least desirable terri-tory. Since few persons are able or even desire to move about through all occupied areas, the loss of mobility is minimal. Although outsiders might argue that there are, in fact, certain losses resulting from a narrowing of intellectual or cultural horizons when cross-group contacts are restricted, it does not follow that the actors themselves will perceive these as costs, given a set of utilities that are not likely to include such contacts as desirable in their own right. Therefore the cost functions for these individuals may approximate zero at the no-contact end of the X continuum for all forms of contact except those casual contacts that cannot easily be avoided and that, basically, involve a bare minimum of actual face-to-face interaction.

There may be certain hidden or indirect costs to such majority members, as well as to a minority that also attempts to insulate itself from contacts. In particular, it may become necessary to employ certain "gatekeepers" of segregation and to buy off the minority through processes by which a certain portion of the majority's resources are allocated to the minority community in exchange for its willingness to accept the segregated arrangement. But the larger the numerical majority, and the greater its relative resources, the smaller the average share of individual resources expended in this fashion.

Certain psychic costs, such as guilt reactions and occasional tensions produced by unexpected encounters, may in part be reduced by ideological mechanisms, such as beliefs to the effect that a segregated system is best for all parties and actually preferred by the minority. Myrdal's (1944) thesis of the "American dilemma" notwithstanding, the costs of a segregated system to the average white American are not very substantial, at least in terms of these actors' perceptions of the costs. Instead, it is the costs of *contacts* that tend to be emphasized in popular white-American ideology—things such as potential friction in integrated schools brought about by forced busing, fear of crimes of violence (presumably by blacks), and neighborhood deterioration.

In this connection it is possible to link our discussion of rewards and costs with an earlier distinction made by one of the authors (Blalock 1967b) between two types of minority resource, which were referred to as "competitive resources" and "pressure resources." The notion of pressure resources involves the idea that minorities may apply punishment power to make discriminatory behaviors costly to the dominant group. In the case of blacks in the United States, and we suspect more generally as well, pressure resources have often been successful in opening the door to initial contacts or employment opportunities as a result of legal action, boycotts or other economic pressures, or the threat of unfavorable publicity. This has made complete avoidance extremely costly to certain selected majority members. But once a token number of minority members have been hired or admitted to an organization or board of directors, these avoidance costs diminish because of the increased difficulty in proving discrimination against the actor. An equilibrium is likely to be reached at a relatively low level in terms of minority percentages or the degree of cross-group contacts.

Competitive resources, in contrast, involve the kinds of resource that make it possible for the minority actually to reward the relevant members of the dominant group. For instance a minority employee may possess certain skills that provide a competitive advantage in hiring. As a potential neighbor the minority member may be thought to have some highly desirable traits, such as gardening skills or upper-middle-class manners. If so, these individuals have something positive to exchange in return for permission to engage in interaction with the dominant-group members. In effect, they are able to reward their interaction partners rather than making it costly to avoid them.

If a minority can obtain a sufficient number of these competitive resources, the resulting equilibrium level is likely to be higher than that which would be obtained as a result of the application of pressure resources alone. In the present context we are considering only the cost functions, and the basic argument is that the use of pressure resources is likely to be successful in increasing the costs of keeping interactions at a very minimal level but is less likely to affect the cost function toward the upper end of the X continuum. This is because the maintenance of pressure requires close surveillance, the continuous threat of action, and often the cooperation of coalition partners whose motivation to apply such pressure is likely to diminish once token gains have been made.

Costs Related to Segregation and Absolute Numbers. Presumably, the factor that is most directly linked to the costs incurred by a member of a numerical minority will be the actual number of fellow members residing within some convenient territorial boundary. If so, it is neither degree of segregation nor minority percentage per se that affects these costs, but rather a joint function of the two. A highly segregated group that is also numerically very small may not be able to provide the services sufficient to reduce the costs of avoidance, but the same may be true for a much larger group that is also highly dispersed. As we have already implied, however, it may not be appropriate to use a measure of segregation based on block statistics. Such a very small unit may be inadequate for representing an actor's true interaction boundaries, though this will, of course, depend upon the actor concerned and the type of interaction involved. Leaving aside this problem, we shall assume that the variable with which we are concerned in this section adequately taps the *number* of in-group members who are located within some convenient distance.

If we compare the hypothetical cost functions for minorities that are relatively large with those for numerically smaller minorities, we would expect the two cost curves to be roughly as indicated in figure 14.6. The cost function in the case of a large minority will take on lower values at the low end of the X continuum and may even be approximately horizontal in the case of infrequent cross-group interactions. This is because of the assumed greater ability of the minority community to provide segregated facilities and specialized services and also to offer a larger proportion of job opportunities within the local area. But as we move toward the high cross-group interaction end of the continuum, the costs should rise more rapidly than in the case of the second curve representing costs for a smaller minority. This is based on the assumption that a larger minority will be in a better position to apply negative sanctions to those of its members who participate too actively with members of other groups. Also, in the case of a large minority there may be greater opposition to cross-group contacts on the part of the majority group as well.

If these assumptions are correct, we would therefore expect the two cost

Figure 14.6. Hypothetical Cost Functions for Large and Small Minorities

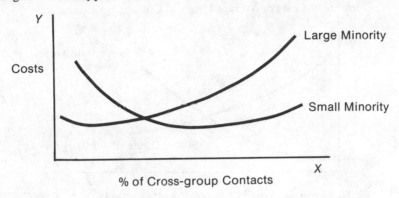

functions to intersect, given the steeper rise in costs in the case of the curve for the larger minority. We would also anticipate that the equilibrium level of cross-group contacts will be lower in the case of the larger minority.[8] To the degree that this reduced interaction resulted in increased residential segregation, this would also lead to the prediction that minority size and degree of residential segregation will be positively related.[9] This latter prediction, however, is dependent upon the proper choice of spatial units and the extension of the overall boundaries to some natural larger unit, such as the SMSA rather than the central city.

If we now look at the costs to members of the majority group, which we shall here assume to be the dominant group as well, we need to consider a somewhat different set of costs. For the time being let us ignore those dominant-group members who attach a high utility to cross-group interactions, perhaps because of a desire to exploit the minority or a feeling of guilt or wish to help it. For the most part, the remaining members of the dominant group can be assumed to attach at best rather low positive utilities to cross-group interactions, so that a failure to interact will involve very low costs. We have already noted some indirect costs of avoidance due to restrictions on movements. Holding constant the total number of minority members in some larger area, the more highly concentrated this minority is geographically, and the lower the average level of cross-group contacts, the less costly it will be for any given majority-group individual to avoid them. If a minority is more or less evenly dispersed residentially and organizationally, a majority individual can expect to encounter them regularly and almost without warning, so that complete avoidance would require an extreme restriction of movements. Therefore if we plot "flexibility of movement costs" against either the *average* level of cross-group contacts or degree of desegregation, these types of avoidance cost can be expected to increase monotonically with an increasing slope, as indicated in figure 14.7.

As we have previously suggested, there will in addition be certain status-loss costs for dominant-group individuals who engage in visible cross-group inter-

Figure 14.7.   Hypothesized Cost Functions Relating Status and Flexibility of Movement Costs to Average Levels of Cross-group Contacts

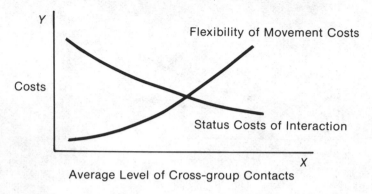

actions. These costs may be expected to *decrease* as the average level of cross-group interaction (or desegregation) increases. Presumably, the principal mechanism producing this decrease in costs will be the fact that as such contacts become more frequent they will become less noticeable and visible and also more difficult to sanction negatively. Therefore this second kind of cost function when combined with the first may produce an approximately horizontal line or perhaps a U-shaped curve with a very shallow dip.

We must remember that the X axis for these two functions is *not* the individual's level of contacts but the average level pertaining to the majority-minority groups as a whole. What this says is that to the degree that these two types of cost predominate in the mind of the majority-group actor, and are of approximately equal weight, then this actor may be relatively indifferent as to the levels of cross-group interaction (or segregation) that exist in the larger community. If this average level of interaction is increased, he or she will gain in some ways but lose in others, assuming a fixed level of personal interaction with members of the other group. But this assumes a constant utility structure for the actor concerned. Presumably, as cross-group interactions increase, the actor's own resistance to such encounters will also decrease, and of course this utility for interaction is not represented in the diagram of figure 14.7. Factors such as fear of intergroup conflict, willingness to interact with strangers, concern about property values, and the degree of overall similarity between minority and majority members will undoubtedly be of much greater significance than the two factors diagrammed in figure 14.7.

Finally, we need to consider possible complications that arise in instances where there may be more than two groups involved, and in particular where some individuals have either intermediate characteristics (such as a mixed-blood population) or inconsistent statuses. As a general rule we would expect that to the degree that such individuals experience ambivalence and guilt feelings about cross-group interactions, this will add to their costs and therefore be more likely to create situations in which costs are greater than rewards, regardless of the level of interaction that is selected. If so, such individuals will be more motivated either to press for changes in the system or to attempt to escape it altogether.[10]

Perhaps the most extreme examples of what we have in mind are so-called marginal men who find themselves between two cultures or in ambiguous situations with regard to their degree of acceptance by the dominant group.[11] For instance, the Cape Coloured of South Africa, the Eurasians of Indonesia, the Metis of Canada, and certain tiny groups of mixed bloods in the United States all have found themselves in the position of aspiring to white status, being at least partly rejected, and in turn tending to dissociate themselves from the darker "full-blooded" minorities that have lower status than themselves. The status-inconsistent minority member, such as the black doctor, is often in an analogous position.

Many contact situations for these persons are ambiguous, it being difficult to predict before an encounter whether or not there will be acceptance and a relative lack of tension involved. Furthermore, as one shifts from one type of interaction situation to another, as, for example, from one involving moderate intimacy to high intimacy, it will also be difficult to predict the degree of acceptance. Once an accepting partner has been found, such marginal or status-inconsistent persons may be especially reluctant to shift to a new partner with the attendant risk of rejection. Therefore they are more likely to become dependent on these accepting partners, with possible added strains resulting.

There is also likely to be an ambivalence concerning just how much interaction there should be with full-status minority members, with an attendant guilt feeling at having deserted or snubbed them. Such marginal or status-inconsistent individuals are especially likely to be labeled in a derogatory fashion by the groups that are both above and beneath them. The latter may tend to brand them as hypocrites or as persons who are ashamed of their minority heritage. The labels "oreo" and "banana," for example, are used to refer to blacks or Asian-Americans who are colored on the outside but white on the inside.

In effect, these marginal individuals are almost forced to make a gamble based on highly uncertain information. If they attempt to associate with the upper status groups, they may perhaps in time become accepted to a reasonable degree, in which case they may become the vanguard of an integrationist movement and receive additional rewards. But if they should fail and if separatist tendencies and ideologies predominate, they may become scapegoats against whom the latent hostility toward the upper groups is displaced. In the case of certain mixed-blood groups and middleman minorities in recently liberated colonial territories, such as Indonesia and most of black Africa, when the colonial powers have given up their control to indigenous peoples, there has in fact been a turning of tables. Those marginal peoples who have been unable to emigrate have often faced discrimination at the hands of their erstwhile social inferiors, partly because they have remained a symbol of the colonial era (see Gist and Dworkin 1972).

We may speculate that the cost functions for individuals in these marginal positions will tend to be somewhat flatter than those for minorities in less ambiguous positions. This suggests that marginal individuals will also tend to vacillate in their interaction patterns in response to very slight shifts in their acceptance rates by members of the groups that are above and beneath them. Also, in times of conflict between these other groups we expect that their dilemmas will become even more pronounced and that their cost curves will generally rise. Such individuals therefore have a vested interest in reducing this level of conflict and in serving as liaison persons and as agents who attempt to regulate such conflict.

In many situations, of course, these marginal individuals will be insufficiently powerful to serve as a major stabilizing force unless there has been a long enough period to permit their numbers to increase, either through miscegenation (in the case of mixed bloods) or upward mobility (in the case of status inconsistents). Once their numbers have increased to a point where they may become a major third force, however, their presence may then serve to inhibit the rise of future conflicts. The relatively strong position of persons of mixed ancestry in Brazil, most Caribbean areas, and Hawaii has come about partly because of the fact that, given their numbers and certain historical factors inhibiting early dichotomization by race, it would have been virtually impossible at a later date to draw sufficiently distinct lines of demarcation to exclude them from social contacts with members of the dominant group. In effect, color or race becomes defined in terms of a continuum in such instances, so that it is even difficult to identify the membership status of one's interaction partner.

Intimacy and Visibility Related to Costs. Whenever there is at least a moderate degree of hostility between groups, or a major effort by one or both groups to retain their separate identities, we would in general expect to find cross-group intimate contacts to be more costly than more casual ones. Similarly, those contacts that are relatively more visible may be expected to be more costly than those that cannot as easily be detected. These predictions are based on the assumption that negative sanctions will be applied against persons whose cross-group contacts deviate from those that are normatively accepted. A similar prediction could be made in connection with contacts implying a high degree of status equality, but we shall not elaborate on this last type of contact.

In the case of intimacy, we would predict the kinds of cost functions indicated in figure 14.8. For high-intimacy interactions, the cost function is predicted to increase monotonically with an accelerating slope, rather than taking the more U-shaped form predicted for low-intimacy contacts. At the low end of the X continuum there is no reason to expect rising costs as one approaches zero in the case of intimate contacts, since such contacts are assumed unnecessary in the conduct of one's ordinary affairs. In the case of less intimate contacts, however, as we have already indicated, nearly complete avoidance will ordinarily imply the necessity of restricted movements, fewer job opportunities, and general inconvenience, at least in the case of actors who are not in extremely

**Figure 14.8. Hypothesized Cost Functions for Contacts
Involving High or Low Intimacy**

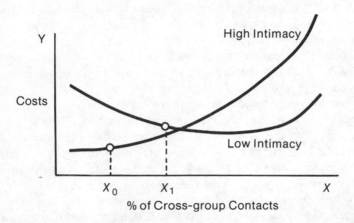

% of Cross-group Contacts

segregated settings or overwhelming numerical majorities. For higher X levels, the costs of contacts involving a low degree of intimacy would not be expected to rise as quickly as in the case of high-intimacy contacts. We would also expect the equilibrium level to be farther to the right in the case of low-intimacy contacts. This, of course, assumes that the reward functions will be relatively flat and that the cost functions will be the major determinants of these equilibrium positions (at X_0 and X_1 in figure 14.8).

In addition we would predict that the rate of increase in costs, as both degree of segregation and minority size also increase, will be steeper in the case of highly intimate contacts than less intimate ones. This implies that increases in either segregation or minority size will tend to inhibit cross-group intimacy to a greater extent than more casual contacts, which, of course, means that intimacy interacts with these two variables in affecting frequency and duration of contact. As suggested earlier, this interaction occurs through extrinsic costs, rather than on the intrinsic costs side, because of the presumed increase in negative sanctions applied to those who interact too freely with members of the other group.

With respect to visibility, we in general expect that the greater the visibility the greater the costs of cross-group contacts. As already suggested, visibility and intimacy will interact in their joint effects on frequency and duration of contact. For contacts involving a very low degree of intimacy and that can be characterized as casual, we expect a very small cost differential between low and high visibility situations. In the case of highly intimate contacts, however, visibility may make a considerable difference in terms of costs, again under the assumption that negative sanctions will be applied to those who deviate from norms that restrict such contacts.

If, however, an actor substantially increases his or her interactions with members of the other group, we then may expect that the application of these sanctions will become relatively less successful in actually inflicting costs on such an individual; that is, an individual who interacts very frequently on an intimate basis with members of the other group will be less influenced by the degree of visibility than will someone whose interactions are much less frequent. This implies a closing of the gap between the cost functions for the low- and high-visibility curves as we move toward the higher end of the X continuum. This prediction is exemplified by the curves given in figure 14.9 and implies that a concern about visibility should be most important to those who interact relatively infrequently with members of the other group.

This concludes our brief discussion of possible kinds of reward and cost functions, as illustrative of the type of analysis that may be used to supplement our previous discussion of variables that link spatial locations to interaction patterns. Such rewards and costs will obviously be very difficult to measure with any degree of accuracy, either by the actors themselves or by social scientists. Perhaps it is well to emphasize once more that it will be the *expected* and *perceived* rewards and costs that actually influence actors' behaviors, so that it may be somewhat less difficult to measure these quantities than one might imagine.

Even so, we suspect that the primary value of this type of analysis will be in the generation of hypotheses that do not directly involve either rewards or costs but that may specify predictions concerning possible nonlinear relationships or other linkages that are not intuitively obvious. If this turns out to be the case, our "tests" of theories based on rewards and costs will have to be indirect. As we have already seen on many occasions throughout this work this will also be true of most portions of any general theories.

It is as though these theories were analogous to an iceberg, with only that small portion of the iceberg visible above the surface being equated to the testable hypotheses. The structure and behavior of the entire iceberg has to be inferred on the basis of its visible portion, but in order to accomplish this, one obviously needs a theory that takes into consideration the larger unobservable

Figure 14.9. Hypothesized Cost Functions for High and Low Visibility Contacts

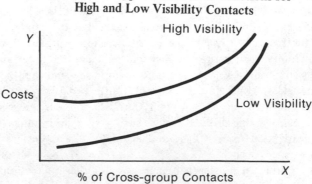

portion. Our hope, of course, is that we may find ways of bringing an increasing proportion of the total mass above the surface so as to assess the adequacies of our theories about the unobserved portions. In the case of the relationship between spatial locations and interaction patterns, we are suggesting the need for collecting additional data in attempts to measure the kinds of variables under discussion in the present chapter.

NOTES

1. The notion of sunk costs will be discussed in greater detail in the next chapter in connection with historicist types of explanation of social change. See Stinchcombe (1968:120-25).
2. We also use arcs between those pairs of variables assumed to have multiplicative joint effects. Thus both "implied equality of status" and "legitimacy" are assumed to interact with "visibility" but not with each other. "Actor's vulnerability" interacts multiplicatively with the combined effect of all three of the variables that join with it to affect "expected extrinsic rewards and costs."
3. For an important symposium relating to the works of these and other authors on the subject of pluralism, see Kuper and Smith (1969).
4. There have been several quantitative studies that have reached somewhat different conclusions regarding the *objective* economic gains and costs to whites of economic discrimination against blacks. The methodological issues encountered in even this kind of straightforward analysis are formidable. For a recent study and literature review, see Szymanski (1976).
5. Wilson (1973) discusses such shifts in the ideologies of black Americans in some detail and emphasizes their dependence upon the contemporary reactions of whites to efforts to achieve integration and/or equality.
6. Another form of escape that may not involve physical withdrawal is, of course, deviant behavior. A minority member who plays the numbers or engages in petty theft may gain psychic or tangible rewards without having to work at a low-paying job that also may involve unpleasant contacts with members of the dominant group.
7. A possible exception or additional complication may occur if increased similarity leads to more intensive competition (e.g., for jobs) between groups, thereby increasing the tension between them. Thus scarcity may interact with similarity to affect costs of contact. In a situation of scarcity, for example, if a minority is similar to the dominant group with respect to competitive resources (see below), this may make cross-group contacts less pleasant than in a situation of plenty.
8. In this case, cross-group contacts should be measured as the proportion of the *minority* member's total contacts.
9. Marshall and Jiobu (1975) argue, with some empirical support, that minority size is more closely linked to residential segregation than is minority

percentage. Notice, however, that effects of minority size, minority percentage, and city (or SMSA) size are likely to be difficult to disentangle because of the exact nonlinear functional relationship between these three variables.

10. Similar arguments have, of course, been made in connection with the behaviors of status-inconsistent persons (Lenski 1954), although the very extensive literature on this subject has led to inconclusive results.

11. The classic book on marginality is that of Stonequist (1961). For a more recent symposium on the subject, see Gist and Dworkin (1972).

PART FOUR

Dynamic Theories

CHAPTER 15

Toward the Formulation of Dynamic Models of Macro Processes

FOR THE MOST PART, we have not been concerned about time processes or what are called dynamic theories that deal with stability and instability, the specification of lags, or the patterns of change that may occur as a system either approaches stability or undergoes accelerating movements away from some initial position. Such theories generally require considerably more knowledge than is presently available, as well as good time-series data for testing and estimating purposes. Even so, it seems advisable in this concluding chapter to address a few questions concerning the nature of the steps one might take in moving toward the goal of constructing dynamic theories, particularly those that could be applied to macro-level phenomena such as residential segregation or changes in levels of inequality.

In our discussions of micro-level processes we referred to the influence of past variables, such as the NO_j/NA_i ratios and the recency and patterning of outcomes, and we argued that actors' behaviors may be expected to change, if only because of the satiation phenomenon and the need to replenish certain goals and resources. We also allowed for contextual effects in the form of aggregated levels that refer to system properties that may have resulted from past behaviors. For example, we noted that existing levels of segregation will affect actors' experiences with members of other groups. Similarly, past levels of inequality may affect the expectation levels of employers or minority applicants.

These types of argument, which we have used rather extensively in previous chapters, are basically incipient or crude forms of dynamic theories, but they do not really pin down the temporal processes in an explicit fashion. Time does not enter into them in an essential way, as required in truly dynamic theories (see Samuelson 1947:314–17). They are *suggestive* of how such theories might be constructed, however, and therefore may be used as starting points for dynamic theories. We must anticipate that a number of additional assumptions will have

589

to be introduced concerning lag periods or the forms of equations dealing with rates of change.

In situations where there are only a very small number of actors, either persons or highly unified groups with a centralized leadership, it becomes possible to analyze their interactions in terms of relatively simple stimulus–response setups. Actor A does something at time 1 that is perceived by actor B shortly afterward, perhaps at time 2 or almost instantaneously at time 1. B then responds at another time, this response being perceived and interpreted by A at a somewhat later time, and so forth. Provided that data can be collected at the appropriate time intervals, which need not be of constant duration, one can actually construct a recursive-type causal model that permits an equation-by-equation type of analysis. In nonquantitative terminology, this implies that the behaviors may be described and analyzed in sequence, with no major complications beyond the usual problems of missing variables, measurement errors, autocorrelation, and incorrectly specified models.

In such cases time may be considered as though it were discrete, the assumption being that there are finite intervals during which the values of the variables are constant, with changes in values occurring only with shifts in the (discrete) times; that is, time 1 is treated as an entirety. We ignore any changes that are going on during that period. This is, of course, never completely realistic, but it permits a very important kind of theoretical simplification in enabling us to take present levels of variables as functions of past levels. This is an intuitively appealing approach that has been very effectively used in economic theory building, that is readily translated into empirical research in which observations must necessarily be separated by finite intervals, and that has been well studied in terms of statistical estimation procedures. Most of the models with which we have been concerned have utilized this approach.

As we move to more highly aggregated data and to models in which there are a very large number of loosely coordinated actors whose behaviors do not occur simultaneously or with a high degree of regularity, this simple kind of stimulus–response formulation will not be adequate. One such situation occurs in demographic models involving birth, death, and migration rates. Although births, deaths, and geographic movements are discrete events on the micro level of the individual, it is rarely the case that they are coordinated to coincide with specific points in time; that is, birth and death rates rise and fall continuously, rather than displaying discrete jumps at particular times. Of course there are exceptions, such as wars and plagues or other natural disasters during which sharp changes can be detected. But the more usual pattern is for rather smooth curves with several rises and dips, with perhaps one or two dramatic shifts that can be attributed to specific causes. Similarly, changes in segregation and inequality levels, deviancy rates, and variables such as level of industrialization and urbanization are best described in terms of relatively smooth curves.

In these situations it makes more sense to think of time as a continuous variable. Also, for these large aggregates or groups, the variables of interest tend to be rates, averages, or proportions that can be treated as genuine ratio scales, though sometimes with fixed upper and lower bounds (as in the case of percentages). Strictly speaking, the variables are not really continuous since all populations are finite, but it is usually reasonable to make this assumption. Such *rates* on the macro level are often readily conceptualized as *probabilities* on the micro level, as, for example, when we translate death rates from different causes into probabilities or expectations on the part of individuals. The assumption needed to justify this translation is that the individuals being aggregated are homogeneous in terms of the parameter values. For example, we assume that each individual in the population has the same risk of getting cancer, of being in an auto accident, or having a stroke. When we question this assumption we attempt to regroup the individuals into more homogeneous aggregates, as, for example, age-sex-race categories of persons residing within a particular geographic territory.

All of this suggests that there will be some correspondence or parallel between micro- and macro-level dynamic theories. Although in the present chapter our primary goal is to construct dynamic theories of macro processes, we shall again find it necessary to operate with micro-level processes in which the individual actor is the focus of attention. In the case of corporate groups it will be relatively easier to construct parallel arguments than will be true for much more loosely coordinated groups and quasi groups. Since in the case of macro-level phenomena, such as segregation, there will be multiple actors having very different sets of utilities and subjective probabilities, it makes sense to try to explain the macro-level phenomenon in terms of its consequences for these diverse actors. Their behaviors may then be aggregated in some fashion to account for either the persistence of or changes in the phenomenon in question.

We shall illustrate this general process in terms of segregation by turning to a consideration of so-called historicist and functionalist explanations, both of which are concerned with the time dimension. In the final section of the chapter we shall then see how the arguments used in these types of theory may be expressed in mathematical language involving differential equations in a fashion that is similar to a dynamic analysis of motions produced by forces in a mechanical system.

HISTORICIST EXPLANATIONS

We have already mentioned two common observations about residential segregation, namely, that residential segregation rates are often much higher than those that would be expected on the basis of economic causes and that residential segregation is itself important as a cause of other types of segregation as well as cross-group interaction patterns. Both of these arguments would suggest that residential segregation cannot be adequately explained by models in which it is taken as a simple dependent variable. Therefore, any reasonably adequate theoretical explanation of residential segregation must include its consequences as well as causes in such a fashion as to allow for feedbacks of segregation upon some of the same variables that are presumed to be its causes. In other words, our explanatory models will have to involve feedbacks of segregation upon itself.

There has been considerable dispute over and misunderstanding of certain kinds of nonrecursive model that allow for such reciprocal causation, which may in part account for the tendency in empirical quantitative research to treat residential segregation as though it were a simple dependent variable. In particular, "historicist" and "functionalist" arguments have sometimes been described in such simplistic ways that the basic types of causal model they imply have been made to seem absurd. It will be our own position that important features of both the historicist and functionalist arguments can and should be combined into complex causal models and that there is nothing inherent in these two types of explanation that is incompatible with the causal modeling approach to theory construction.

In the discussion that follows we shall rely heavily on Stinchcombe's (1968) excellent treatment of the logical structure of these two approaches, both of which are oriented to explaining a given phenomenon—here, residential segregation—in terms of a combination of its causes and consequences. We shall begin with the historicist type of explanation, then turn to the functionalist approach, and finally attempt to integrate both approaches in terms of a more complete causal model. Throughout, we shall be orienting the discussion to the basic question of accounting for changes or lack of changes over time.

Of course one type of historicist explanation is simply a series of descriptive statements about how a given pattern changes over time. Ordinarily, we would not dignify such descriptive accounts by calling them explanations. Sometimes these descriptive statements, however, are accompanied by references to such notions as traditions, inertia, heritage, culture, or other terms that have a pseudo-explanatory character. It is then difficult to decide whether or not a true explanatory model is being attempted, since the precise mechanisms remain unspecified. There is presumably some implied causal theory to the effect that the level of X at time 1 affects the level of X at time 2, or perhaps the level of X at time 1 affects the rate of change in X between times 1 and 2.

In the case of residential segregation the argument would be that to explain present levels of segregation, one must examine past levels, as well as the factors that may have affected these past levels. The presumption is that past levels of segregation will persist into the future unless there are changes in some levels of some of its causes. This is certainly a plausible kind of argument, as far as it goes, and it is also a very practical guideline for *predicting* future levels of a variable in the absence of a detailed knowledge of future parameter values. Yet the explanation has a kind of tautological nature to it, given the slippery nature of concepts such as those of tradition, heritage, or inertia. If a pattern persists this can be taken as evidence for a heritage, whereas if it changes one may simply claim that the heritage or tradition bolstering the pattern is also undergoing alteration.

Behind this kind of explanation there may be two very different kinds of implicit causal argument (see Stinchcombe 1968:101ff.). The first can be stated in terms of a simple recursive model in which a phenomenon such as residential segregation is caused by a number of independent variables that themselves do not change in value over the period in question. Therefore, for this model, the problem of explaining stability or instability is pushed back one or more stages in the causal chain to that of explaining why the levels of the independent variables are or are not changing. Thus if residential segregation between blacks and whites is partly due to income inequalities between the two groups, we would not expect the degree of segregation to change unless such inequalities (and other causal variables) were to be modified. We have seen, however, that residential segregation of blacks and whites does not seem to have changed much over several decades in spite of an improvement in the ratio of black to white median incomes. It is possible that such a decreasing gap in income levels has been counterbalanced in its impact on segregation by changes in other variables such as the continued migration of blacks to large metropolitan areas. If so, we might account for the stability of residential segregation in terms of a relatively simple model involving exogenous variables that are shifting in opposite directions in terms of their impacts on segregation.

The second type of argument involves a role for the dependent variable itself in affecting its own later values. In the example under consideration, segregation at a given point in time has consequences for other variables that, in turn, affect later segregation levels. Put most simply, $Y_{t_1} \rightarrow X_{t_2} \rightarrow Y_{t_3}$. Such an explanation will obviously be unsatisfactory unless the intervening mechanism(s) symbolized by X_{t_2} can be specified theoretically. Of course, we may generally anticipate that there will be a number of intervening mechanisms X_i, with some producing positive feedbacks and others negative ones. If so, the direction of the effects of Y on itself may be ambiguous and dependent upon the relative magnitudes of the separate effects. Therefore it becomes crucial not only to specify what the intervening mechanisms are but also to theorize about the variables that will either intensify or dampen the various feedbacks in question.

If the net effect of Y on itself is positive (e.g., increases in segregation lead to further increases), then any factors that increase (decrease) segregation will have a greater impact than would be expected in the absence of such a feedback. Conversely, if the feedback of segregation on itself is negative, then the total impact of an exogenous change in either direction will be dampened. Under certain conditions, especially where nonlinearities are involved, we may expect that when the level of segregation is low the total feedback may be positive, whereas for higher levels of segregation the direction of feedback may be reversed. It is also possible—but certainly not inevitable—that changes in exogenous variables will have very little net impact on the dependent variable in question because of a tendency to resist changes in either direction. This last possibility will be discussed in somewhat greater detail when we turn our attention to functionalist-type arguments.

Stinchcombe (1968:120–25), in his discussion of historicist-type arguments, points out that one very common mechanism by which levels at time 1 affect levels at time 2 is through the mechanism of sunk costs. If a person is a doctor today, then we may predict that he or she will be a doctor tomorrow because, having invested so much in prior training and costly equipment, it would be foolish to change occupations. Similarly, a person's residence at time 1 will explain the residence at time 2 in large part because of sunk costs and investments in the local area (e.g., friends, schools, or psychological attachments). In effect, in many instances changes are costly and they also imply uncertainties that mean that subjective probabilities cannot easily be calculated. Provided that a given pattern of activity works, it is foolish to modify it unless an obviously superior alternative is available. Furthermore, we may anticipate that ideological systems will tend to provide actors with working causal theories that exaggerate the benefits of the existing system and the costs of alternative ones.

Obviously many changes *do* occur, however, and our causal theories must account for these changes as well as for stability. It is sometimes claimed that so-called functional theories cannot account for change without postulating "strains" in the system and that, basically, such theories tend to be conservative. The same might be claimed of historicist theories of the type discussed by Stinchcombe. It seems to us that arguments over the conservative nature of either or both types of explanation are useful only to the extent that they suggest specific mechanisms through which either change or stability is produced. These theories should ideally be stated in such a way that both stabilizing and change-producing mechanisms are made explicit. One may then go about the major task of specifying the conditions under which the one or the other type of mechanism is likely to predominate.

With these preliminary thoughts in mind, let us turn by way of illustration to a number of possible mechanisms by which a given level of residential segregation at time 1 may be expected to affect levels of segregation at later points in time. Several such mechanisms have been identified in the race relations literature, though, to our knowledge, little systematic attention has been given to the equally important task of specifying the variables that can be expected to affect their relative importance in terms of the magnitudes of the relevant slopes. Nor are we aware of any serious discussions of possible nonlinearities or other complications in the functional relationships.

Attachments and Investments

As already implied, one important mechanism that helps to maintain stability in residential patterns, whether segregated or desegregated, is that of investments that cannot easily be recovered if a change of location were to take place. Homeowners will tend to have a greater economic stake in a residential area than renters, though this difference should not be exaggerated. The basic stabilizing variable here would be the proportion of one's total objective properties (e.g., income) that would be lost if a movement were to occur. If someone could sell a home at a reasonable profit and purchase another residence without great sacrifice, then the sunk costs would not be too great. But certain investments of a noneconomic nature could not so easily be recovered. In particular, to the degree that one has formed sentimental attachments to the home, neighborhood, local institutions (schools, churches, voluntary organizations), and to other local residents, we may anticipate that the psychic costs of movement will be high.

Certain of these costs can be expected to diminish as the nature of the area becomes modified—as one's neighbors move away, as the character of local institutions changes, or as landmarks disappear. Therefore, in an important sense, stability feeds upon itself and changes weaken ties to the local area. In effect, the actors' utilities for remaining in the area will be altered. As we pass from one generation to the next, we expect that childhood attachments to one's neighborhood, school district, and peers will operate to produce positive utilities for remaining in the area, with these utilities decreasing as a result of any changes that tend to make the area less similar to what it was in the past.

Reduced Cross-group Interactions

To the degree that residential segregation reduces interactions between groups, or restricts them to interactions of specified types, we have already argued in connection with figure 14.1 of the previous chapter that this will increase actors' uncertainties about what to expect when interactions of unfamiliar types do occur. This is also likely to intensify fears of increased contact or feelings of embarrassment or discomfort in the presence of members of the other group. Furthermore, reduced contacts may increase the probability of "cultural drift," or the gradual formation of distinctive subcultures, and therefore the tendency for members of each group to perceive each other as strangers whose behaviors are either at variance with one's own patterns or else difficult to predict. In the case of groups with cultures that are already clearly distinct, segregation is also likely to be a mechanism that perpetuates existing cultural differences.

In most instances we anticipate that these mechanisms will result both in reducing utilities for cross-group contacts and in making it much more difficult to estimate accurately what the consequences of these contacts will be. There will, of course, be differential access to members of the other groups according to one's age, sex, and economic function, so that the overall impact of segregation on itself via this mechanism will depend upon the relative power and influence of those who have the most frequent contacts. In particular, if persons who have the least contacts tend to be most influential within the segregated community, it will be relatively more difficult to break down existing patterns. In the case of white immigrant groups in large American cities, for example, as members of the first generation begin to age and transmit power to their children, who have greater exposure to integrated environments, we would expect desegregation to occur relatively rapidly. But in cases where this first generation is able to maintain a high degree of control, perhaps through an extended family network or strong religious system, desegregation would be impeded.

Unequal Resources and Distribution of Goods and Services

As is commonly noted, segregation often facilitates the unequal allocation of goods and services and thus resources. Ordinarily, this will be to the benefit of the dominant group and detriment of a minority group, so that the consequences of segregation will be such as to increase dominant-group members' utilities for continued segregation while reducing those of the minority. If the minority's *resources* are diminished as a result of segregation, however, this may reduce its *ability* to desegregate in spite of the increased motivation to do so.

A case in point is the impact of segregation on the quality of education received by ghetto children, with this in turn lowering their occupational aspirations and expectations and their ability to compete with dominant-group members. Also, if residential segregation results in reduced occupational opportunities by virtue of the fact that minority members select only from among those occupations in proximity to their residences, then the resulting lowered income may make it less easy to buy one's way out of the ghetto. Here, residential segregation increases inequalities, which in turn help to perpetuate the segregation. Over the long run, the segregation of the parental generation leads to handicaps in the next generation, which in turn increases the probability that, as adults, the second generation will also remain segregated. Assuming that this pattern is recognized by members of the dominant group, they will have a vested interest in maintaining a system that perpetuates these inequalities.

In summary, then, to the degree that segregation produces inequalities and that this mechanism is recognized by both parties, the consequence is likely to be a vicious circle or positive feedback mechanism via the dominant group, with increased segregation leading to dominant-group gains and thus to further efforts to perpetuate segregation. From the standpoint of the minority, however, the disadvantages of segregation should increase the *motivation* to reduce segregation but, at the same time, weaken the minority's *resources* for achieving this goal. Thus, from the minority's standpoint, the direction of the feedback could be either positive or negative, depending upon the relative magnitudes of these two effects.

Development of Autonomous Institutions and Leadership

Another common observation is that segregation may produce a vested interest in perpetuating further segregation via the mechanism of strengthening a dual institutional arrangement, with an accompanying leadership that is at least partly dependent on the maintenance of segregation (Myrdal 1944; Frazier 1957). These autonomous institutions, such as churches, schools, and businesses, may also help to perpetuate cultural differences that further discourage intergroup contacts. Certain of these institutions may depend upon the total size of the minority, as well as its spatial distribution. But, keeping size constant, we would expect that the greater the spatial concentration of a group's members, the greater will be the hold of segregated institutions on them. In the case of political leaders, a geographic concentration of a minority may facilitate election to office under a system of proportional representation by district, though not necessarily in at-large elections. Segregation may also facilitate the development of a power base by affording protection and anonymity to those who would otherwise have to risk negative sanctions for challenging the status quo. A dual system of institutions may likewise provide job security and mobility opportunities for minority members unable to obtain comparable positions in integrated institutions, whether because of discrimination or other competitive handicaps.

As already implied, residential segregation helps to preserve the mutual isolation between groups, which in turn serves to perpetuate or even increase any cultural differences that may exist between them. In the causal model of figure 15.1, which follows this discussion, we shall assume that the degree of cultural distinctiveness is directly influenced by the two intervening mechanisms of limiting cross-group interactions and encouraging the development of dual institutions and leadership. We shall also allow for the possibility that the reduction of cross-group interactions and the formation of a dual institutional system operate directly on actors' utilities to increase or decrease segregation, quite apart from their impact via the preservation of cultural differences.

Segregation may conceivably operate to increase cultural differences through additional mechanisms, but if so, we are unable to specify what they are. The notion of institution is sufficiently broad (and vague) to cover a multitude of culture-preserving mechanisms, but certainly among the most important of these would be separate religious institutions, special language schools, and voluntary organizations oriented toward emphasizing cultural patterns such as folk music, arts, and a sense of historical distinctiveness. Many of these kinds of institution, of course, depend upon there being a sufficient minority population in terms of absolute numbers, as well as a reasonable degree of geographic concentration.

Costs to Dominant Group

Segregation may also result in certain costs as well as gains to the dominant group. It is easy to exaggerate the nature and extent of such costs, particularly in efforts by antisegregationists to appeal to members of the dominant group on rational grounds. Nevertheless, there may be certain economic disadvantages of residential segregation, particularly in settings in which transportation costs from home to workplace are substantial. To the extent that the minority is engaged in economic roles that require continual interaction or at least proximity with the dominant group, residential segregation can result in additional transportation costs, part of which will undoubtedly be absorbed by members of the dominant group. In areas where domestic servants are in common use, transportation costs must be included in wages paid. Employers utilizing cheap sources of labor must either locate close to this labor supply or absorb a portion of the transportation costs. During the era in which relatively cheap mass transportation was unavailable, it was reasonably common to find servants and unskilled labor either "living in" with their employers, or residing in back alleys or other proximate residences, as, for example, in Charleston and New Orleans.

Thus there will be some upper limit to the degree of residential separation, with the limit being dependent upon a combination of transportation costs (in both time and money) and the occupational division of labor. For this reason, the extreme form of segregation envisioned in the official South African doctrine of apartheid seems unworkable. In the case of more limited urban areas, however, it would seem unwise to exaggerate the extent of these restrictions in modern industrial societies where transportation costs are relatively low. Nevertheless, to the degree that minorities become occupationally desegregated in the urban labor force, in the sense that proximity is required by the division of labor, we may expect that there will be a decrease in the motivation to preserve residential segregation on the part of those dominant-group members for whom this segregation results in increased costs. We must recognize, however, that other members of the dominant group may be motivated to preserve residential segregation precisely because it helps to reduce minority competition.

Restriction of Movements

We have suggested that residential segregation restricts movements of individuals via the mechanism of transportation costs, but our earlier discussion of reward and cost functions also implied that there may be other, more indirect, mechanisms that also have the net effect of further restricting these movements. Ordinarily, the most important kinds of restriction are imposed on minority members, and so we have omitted this factor (in figure 15.1) in connection with dominant-group members. Restrictions, of course, depend upon rules and their enforcement, but at least in the United States and western Europe many facilities and locations are off limits to individuals because of private property restrictions or requirements that users must be residents of the local community. Thus, to the degree that the minority is restricted residentially to areas outside the bounds of these communities, their ability to use these services will also be restricted. Even though legally entitled to use them, they may in addition be inhibited as outsiders by informal mechanisms of control that clearly indicate that they are not welcomed. To the degree that these restrictions of movements impose hardships on a minority, we would expect these consequences of segregation to increase the minority's motivation to reduce this segregation. Thus both of these last two consequences of segregation, which involve costs to the dominant group and minority respectively, can be expected to imply negative feedbacks, with increased segregation leading to increased motivation to reduce future levels of segregation.

Summary Model

The above arguments can be summarized into a causal model, such as that given in figure 15.1. Several additional comments about this model are needed.

It can be seen that all but one of the consequences of segregation that we have just discussed have been placed in the row immediately below that of segregation at time 1. Each of these linkages with segregation is itself highly complex. For example, the entire model of figure 14.1 has, in effect, been replaced by the single arrow between "segregation at time 1" and "proportion of cross-group interactions."

The first consequence we discussed, namely, that of attachment to the neighborhood, has been separated out from the remainder and placed above them because we do not consider it to be an actual consequence of segregation, but rather a possible correlate of it; that is, one may form attachments to a neighborhood regardless of whether or not it is segregated, though it may be true that in most instances such attachments are indeed stronger in the cases of segregated residential areas. But given an existing high degree of segregation, such attachments will tend to operate to perpetuate this segregation.

Therefore if segregation is initially high, any factors that operate to increase these attachments will increase the actors' utilities for remaining in the area and, presumably, to resist efforts to reduce segregation. This will hold for both minority- and dominant-group members, and therefore we have drawn in arrows from "attachment to local neighborhood" to both the dominant-group and minority utilities to increase or decrease segregation. Conceivably, in the case of residential areas in which there is a very low degree of segregation, this factor may operate in the opposite direction, namely, to preserve this low degree of segregation. Ordinarily, however, we expect it to operate to increase the vested interest in segregation, though perhaps more so in the case of dominant-group members than the minority.

Signs of relationships have also been inserted on a tentative basis to suggest what seems to be the most plausible directions of relationships under ordinary conditions. One must recognize, however, that exogenous variables (not shown) may interact with the explicitly included variables in affecting segregation at time 2, and in some instances these interactions may produce sign reversals.

In particular, minority members may be ambivalent about the objective of preserving a distinctive culture whenever there are fairly obvious advantages to assimilation. More accurately, perhaps, *some* minority members may prefer to retain a distinct subculture, whereas others may wish to minimize cultural differences, so that the aggregated impact on utilities to reduce segregation may depend upon the relative proportions and powers of these two minority segments. A similar ambivalence may exist within the dominant group, though we would expect that the salience of the issue of cultural pluralism will be less in the case of dominant groups. If, however, the dominant group is a numerical minority and if its control over the weaker groups rests very heavily on preserving these cultural differences, we may expect a much greater emphasis on preserving segregation so as to preserve these differences. The apartheid program and ideology of the Nationalist party in South Africa is an obvious case in point.

Notice that we have also drawn in several arrows between variables located in the second row, indicating direct causal connections among them. In particular,

**Figure 15.1. Model Suggesting How Segregation at Time 1 Feeds Back
to Affect Segregation at Time 2**

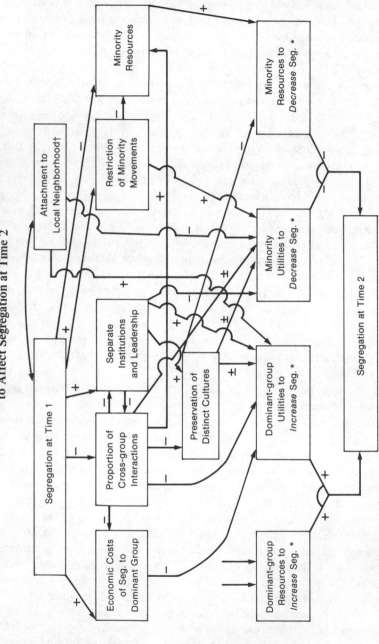

†Assumes that most neighborhoods are initially segregated.
*Dominant group and minority utilities for segregation here assumed to be in opposite directions.

we are presuming that a reduction in the proportion of cross-group interactions may have the direct effect of increasing certain kinds of economic costs to the dominant group, as well as limiting the minority's resources or objective properties. Also, the restriction of a minority's movements may have a direct impact on its resources, and we expect a reciprocal causative relationship between the degree to which there are separate minority institutions and leadership and the proportion of cross-group interactions.

We have omitted any consideration of exogenous variables—such as relative size, degree of conflict, or factors relating to the division of labor—that may affect either the level of segregation or any of the intervening variables in the model. So as to retain a symmetry in the model between the dominant-group and minority utilities and resources variables, we have inserted a box labeled "dominant-group resources to *increase* segregation." We assume that this variable will be primarily affected by exogenous variables rather than by mechanisms that operate through the level of segregation.

If one traces through the various alternative paths from "segregation at time 1" to "segregation at time 2" it will be noted that the majority of products of the signs are positive, suggesting that the net impact of segregation on itself is positive. It is possible, however, that the smaller number of paths implying a negative feedback may actually be more important in terms of magnitude, so that under certain conditions the net feedback may be negative. Also, the model as drawn does not take possible nonlinearities into consideration. As we suggested in the previous discussion of reward and cost functions, it is entirely possible that such nonlinearities may operate to help keep the level of segregation within certain bounds.

Finally, it should be noted that if we were dealing with actual aggregated data it would be virtually impossible to specify two particular points in time, t_1 and t_2, to which the argument applied; that is, the various micro-level processes would be occurring at irregular and noncorresponding intervals, so that it would be much more realistic to represent the aggregated results in terms of a continuous time model. We shall postpone our consideration of such models until after our discussion of functionalist arguments. But we can note that the mechanisms implied by the model of figure 15.1 suggest that there will be forces operating to change the level of segregation in one direction or the other. When we later consider the nature of possible equations to represent the factors that affect the rate of change in segregation levels, it will become necessary to use the type of theory implied by this or similar diagrams.

FUNCTIONALIST EXPLANATIONS

The above historicist type of explanation has a rather obvious functional flavor to it, at least in the sense that it entails the thesis that segregation feeds back to affect itself, often in such a fashion as to involve resistances to change. But the notion of functionalism, at least as it has been adopted in sociology, has a number of distinct elements to it, not all of which need to be incorporated in every causal model one wishes to construct. Therefore we shall need to discuss very briefly some of these features.

One feature of functional arguments that has occasioned considerable debate is the "teleological" type of reasoning that accounts for the persistence of a phenomenon in terms of its consequences. Actually, if one adds several explicit assumptions to the historicist model exemplified in figure 15.1, one can very easily turn the argument into one that closely resembles a functionalist argument, but without the undesirable teleological features that seem to imply that consequences can become the causes of earlier events (Buckley 1967:52). If we merely assume that functions are "manifest" (Merton 1968), in the sense of being clearly recognized by at least some major sets of actors, *and* if we also assume that these actors in fact behave in such a way as to bring about the intended consequences, then there is no need to invoke teleological arguments. In the case of residential segregation, for example, if some of its functions, or consequences, for the system are recognized, and if this recognition leads to actions that are successful in perpetuating the segregation, then the basic causal argument may be diagramed as in figure 15.2.

In effect, it is not the consequences themselves that cause the pattern in question but rather the *expected* consequences, combined with actions to bring them about. The pattern, in turn, then presumably brings about the intended consequences, thereby reinforcing the previous set of expectations. If the pattern (here, segregation) does not lead to the intended consequences, or if it has additional consequences that had not been anticipated ("latent" functions), then these facts—when filtered through the perceptions of the actors at a later point in time—may serve to modify the expectations regarding the future consequences of the pattern in question. We see in figure 15.2 the familiar features of our multiplicative models in which motivations to act are joint functions of expectations or subjective probabilities, on the one hand, and utilities, on the other.

The mere motivation to act is not sufficient, however, unless it is accompanied by the necessary power resources. *If* sufficient power is exerted to alter or preserve the pattern in the presence of possibly opposing forces, as represented by the side arrows in the center of the figure, then we may say that the *expected* consequences have affected the pattern in question. Presumably, all of this will require a noticeable lapse of time, which will also permit modifications in the actors' behaviors if the intended consequences are not in evidence or if the unintended consequences are relevant to utilities other than those being considered. Thus the expected consequences at t_1 and those at t_2 may be quite different, in which case we may anticipate changes in the actors' behaviors.

This type of functional argument allows for changes through a number of mechanisms, including the slippage between intended and actual consequences, as well as modifications in the relative power resources of actors having different utility combinations. In particular, the expectations of consequences do not in

Figure 15.2. Causal Model Exemplifying a Functionalist Argument

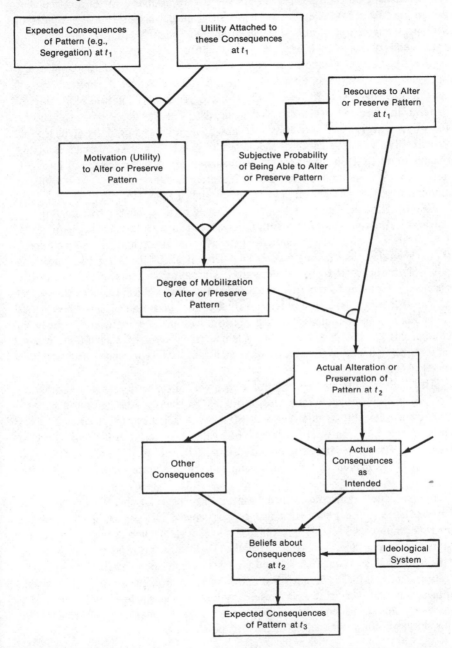

themselves bring about these consequences unless accompanied by action and the necessary resources. Thus, as also noted by Stinchcombe (1968:93ff.), power considerations enter very directly into the model, given the likelihood that there will be multiple parties attempting to alter the pattern in opposing directions. We believe that this type of causal model preserves a very important insight characteristic of functionalist arguments, namely, that patterns may be explained in terms of their expected consequences.

Certainly the distinction between manifest and latent functions implies the necessity of introducing actors' expectations into the overall explanatory system. It also suggests that other kinds of factor, such as the nature of ideological systems and the extent of knowledge, need to be considered so as to account for varying *degrees* of "manifestness" and "latency" among diverse subgroups. Presumably, it is a function of ideologies to make certain consequences highly manifest and to keep others latent or unrecognized. Since it is not our intent to develop a more complete model of these processes, however, we have omitted any consideration of such variables in the model of figure 15.2.

The functionalist and historicist models may now be meshed by inserting any particular consequence of residential segregation into the model of figure 15.2. For instance, in the case of the reduction of cross-group interactions we expect that segregation may maintain itself over time if all of the following conditions hold: (1) reduced cross-group interaction is desired by actors who (2) have the necessary resources to maintain the segregation, and who (3) believe that segregation will in fact lead to a reduction in these contacts and (4) also believe that the remaining consequences of segregation will not be sufficiently costly to counterbalance the expected gains. Clearly, the levels of each of these four factors may change over time, perhaps as a result of experiences with previous segregation.

The analyst must also realize that actors will differ with respect to combinations of utilities, expectations, and resources, so that in a disaggregated analysis of the separate actors, different sets of weights will have to be used. The net force in the direction of either increased or decreased segregation will then be a resultant of these separate forces. Any changes in the overall or total force will have to be explained in terms of changes in one or more of these component forces.

Implied, then, is the necessity of asking "For *whom* [what actors] does the pattern in question have particular consequences?" If we are dealing with a highly complex and loosely coordinated social system, such as the entire United States or even a large urban area, it makes little sense to refer to functions for "the system," as though these could be treated in some uniform fashion. In contrast, a system that is much less complex and that contains highly homogeneous actors with very similar interests may be analyzed more easily in terms of a relatively smaller number of forces that may be assumed to react to changes in a similar fashion. We shall return to this point below.

Homeostasis

There is another feature of functionalist arguments that has been characteristic of theories used to explain biological processes but that has been much more controversial and problematic in the case of social systems. We refer, of course, to the notion of stable equilibrium, or homeostasis. In the case of biological organisms it is recognized that the survival of the system is conditional on the maintenance of certain steady states, such as body temperature (Cannon 1939). Assuming this to be the case, it then makes sense to analyze the parts of the body in terms of their contributions to the maintenance of these steady states, and in particular how the body compensates for changes that may be occurring exogenously. Thus if the organism is exposed to undue external heat (or cold), one may ask how the body compensates so as to preserve a constant internal temperature. Similarly, if foreign objects are injected into the organism, it is of importance to study how the body reacts so as to neutralize this invasion from the environment. Indeed, if survival is intimately bound with the maintenance of homeostasis, a study of mechanisms for survival may almost be equated with a study of the mechanisms that produce homeostasis.

It has been observed that in the case of social systems the notion of survival is much more problematic (Homans 1950:268–72). Clearly, it cannot be assumed that survival depends upon the maintenance of certain *steady* states, though it may indeed depend upon the maintenance of certain *minimal* levels of such phenomena as birth rates, internal order, and economic productivity (see Aberle, Cohen, Davis, Levy, and Sutton 1950; and Buckley 1967:16). In particular, there may be circumstances under which survival depends upon continually *increasing* levels of certain variables, as is often argued in the case of armament technologies. There are obviously many phenomena that may vary within extremely broad limits without in any way threatening the survival of the system in question. Residential segregation would appear to be one such phenomenon.

Unless one is willing to resort to mystical reasoning, it is necessary to postulate explanatory mechanisms that produce a homeostatic situation characterized by forces that move a system back toward a stable equilibrium level whenever a disturbance in either direction occurs. A simple mathematical model representing this kind of process, whenever both time and the variables concerned are treated as continuous, is given by the equation

$$dY/dt = K(Y - Y_o),$$

where Y_o represents the equilibrium level, and where $K < 0$.[1] If Y is temporarily raised to a level above Y_o, then dY/dt will be negative, meaning that there will be a return toward equilibrium at a rate that is proportional to the magnitude of the disturbance. Similarly, if Y is reduced below Y_o, dY/dt will become positive, and Y will be increased back to Y_o. As long as $Y = Y_o$ there will be no change.

It is questionable, however, that there will necessarily be the reactive forces that operate to restore a system to equilibrium in accord with the kinds of mechanism implied by an equation of the simple form $dY/dt = K(Y - Y_o)$. As noted above, it seems much more likely that there will be combinations of forces that operate in different ways, some tending to lower the level of Y and others to increase it. If there were a single major force—such as that of a powerful centralized government—having a utility for change that was approximately zero whenever $Y = Y_o$, but that could be counted on to mobilize its resources to counteract a change in either direction, then an equation of this type might indeed be appropriate.

In such a case the major actor would remain essentially dormant unless departures from equilibrium were to occur. It would then mobilize its resources roughly in proportion to the magnitude of the disturbance and in such a fashion that the rate of return to equilibrium would be approximately proportional to this degree of disturbance. The presumption is that this reactive force would encounter roughly constant opposition, which might serve to delay the return somewhat. The counterreactive forces would not be sufficient to prevent the ultimate return to equilibrium, however.

In the case of residential segregation and many other social phenomena we can expect to find several different forces operating in each direction. The forces in one direction may possess much greater resources but be essentially dormant owing to a low utility for modifying the situation. Those pushing in the opposite direction, however, may be mobilized almost to maximum capacity, so that little or no additional reactive force could be applied in this direction. If so, a major change in the direction counter to that of these latter forces might in fact lead to their breakdown rather than a return to equilibrium. In contrast, an initial change working in the direction opposite to that of a relatively dormant force might lead to a counterreaction (e.g., the so-called backlash) that could produce a new equilibrium level that is far removed from the initial one.

Some potential forces may continue to remain dormant, however, perhaps because of adjustments in utility levels that accommodate themselves to each relatively small shift in the level of Y. In effect, this implies that Y_o need not be a constant but may be treated as a variable in its own right, subject to changes produced either by exogenous variables or by sets of factors that are themselves affected by Y (here, the level of segregation). If so, the notion of a moving equilibrium may be more appropriate. As long as the changes in Y_o keep pace with those of Y, in the sense of involving approximately the same time span, the reactive forces may never become mobilized.

If we were to analyze, say, the forces opposing desegregation into a number of components representing actors with different sets of interests, we would expect these actors to be characterized both by different reaction times and by different utility combinations. The overall or aggregated reactive force would then be a function of the coordination or degree of coupling among these separate components. Where this coupling is weak we might expect that certain kinds of reactive forces might be insufficient—at least over the short run—to counteract the changes that are occurring. Whether or not there would later be a delayed but also more substantial reaction would then depend, in part, on the ability of one set of actors to influence those who may have less immediate interests at stake but who may have the resources needed to return the system close to its initial level. More generally, any explanation of changes in highly aggregated rates will ideally need to take into account the causal interconnections among the forces operating in each direction. This, of course, requires a consideration of coalitions, efficiency and timing of mobilization, and the internal distribution of resources within such coalitions.

Let us illustrate by assuming that changes in the levels of residential segregation are likely to occur as a result of a large number of relatively small-scale shifts in different parts of a city. Thus unconnected neighborhoods on the borders of a larger segregated area may each be subjected to minority in-migrations. These may initially take the form of compositional changes in the racial or ethnic makeup of adjacent areas, plus perhaps the entry of one or two minority families into the immediate neighborhood. We may imagine that individual majority-group residents may become quite disturbed by these changes and therefore have high utilities for returning to the previous level of segregation. But although their utilities for preventing desegregation may be high, their individual resources may be insufficient to produce this return to the previous state. Some may indeed take individual actions against their new neighbors, so as to get across the message that they are not wanted. Their children may be forbidden to play with those of the new occupants, negative sanctions may be applied, and other neighbors discouraged from interacting with them. But unless there are similar reactions on the part of other majority-group residents, these sanctions may be insufficient to produce the desired result.

Such neighbors may become coordinated, however, and begin to form neighborhood protective associations or even to cooperate in acts of violence. To the degree that such organizations are already in existence, or capable of spreading their activities into adjacent communities, the reaction time may be speeded up. Also, the prior existence of such organizations or the availability of information about similar groups in other localities may affect not only the immediacy of the reaction but also its degree. In effect, each individual actor with a utility for preserving segregation will also have a subjective probability of achieving this goal through action, and this subjective probability will be affected by the knowledge that coordinated efforts have been successful elsewhere or that they are likely to be achievable in the local area.

These coordinated neighborhood controls will in turn be facilitated or hindered by the actions of others who are farther removed from the immediate context and who presumably would otherwise react much less quickly to the local changes. For example, the reactions of the local police and judicial authorities may be crucial either in protecting the rights of the new occupants or in essentially informing them that they may expect no such help. Officials in lending institutions may coordinate their behaviors with those of the local residents or, more likely, anticipate them by refusing to give financial support to minority members who wish to buy into previously segregated areas. On a still more remote level, state or federal laws affecting legal rights, applying penalties for infractions, and instituting policies relating to mortgage insurance, public housing, and zoning restrictions may either promote or hinder changes in the degree of segregation. But it is unlikely that changes in these policies will come about as a result of immediate pressures at the local level unless these pressures are all applied at approximately the same time or on a sustained basis.

Therefore if changes in racial or ethnic composition are occurring more or less continuously at the local level, but in such a fashion that the changes in one neighborhood are likely to be of little interest to persons in another area, it seems unlikely that reactions to these changes will occur at an even pace or become coordinated. Here the phenomenon of shifting expectations may be highly important. If each change is small-scale and of little concern to remote actors, and if these changes go relatively unnoticed except in their immediate areas, there may be rather steady shifts in expectation levels of remotely affected actors without there being any general reaction to the change.

To the degree that (1) the resources for resisting change are concentrated in the hands of actors who are only remotely affected, and (2) those parties most immediately affected have little influence over the behaviors of the more remote actors, we may therefore anticipate that the reactive model implying a stable equilibrium will be inadequate. In contrast, where local actors' behaviors can have major impacts on a phenomenon such as segregation, or where they are capable of exerting rapid collective pressure on the more remote actors, the model seems much more appropriate.

These remarks suggest the more general point that a "homeostatic" type of functional argument will be more appropriate under certain circumstances than others. In particular, where the social system is characterized by a centralized control mechanism capable of relatively rapid reactive behaviors, it may be sensible to attempt this line of reasoning. Corporate actors controlled by a relatively small policy-making group that is not subjected to diverse cross-pressures may indeed be found to react to disturbances in approximately this manner. But in the case of extremely heterogeneous quasi groups, such as exemplified by the white majority in the United States, the situation will indeed be much more complex. Certain types of actor may react to changes in this fashion, and may attempt to return the system to its previous levels, but it does not follow that they will have much impact on the overall rates of change.

Instead, the levels of exogenous factors that are not of this reactive type may be much more important in accounting either for change or for a high degree of stability in the system. In the case of residential segregation in the United States, we suspect that these nonreactive forces are the ones that have the greatest impact. Changes in overall tension levels, political centralization, economic conditions, or even ideological factors affecting the salience of race and ethnic relations could operate to make the reactive-type model much more appropriate under other circumstances, however. In a sense, the notion of indifferent equilibrium (Myrdal 1944:392-96) seems appropriate for describing the former kind of nonreactive situation. Such a system may not be changing in important ways, but this does not mean that, should changes begin to occur, they will necessarily be counteracted by opposing forces.

A STRATEGY FOR DEVELOPING CONTINUOUS-TIME MODELS
OF MACRO PROCESSES

Let us now return to the very simple differential equation of the form

$$dY/dt = K(Y - Y_o).$$

If $K < 0$ the level of Y will stabilize at the equilibrium value Y_o, with the rate of approach to stability depending upon the numerical magnitude of K. Thus we see that the constant, K, plays a crucial role in affecting the behavior of Y through time. It therefore becomes extremely important to learn more about this constant. By implication this suggests treating it as a possible variable that may be affected by other variables in the theoretical system. We may also need to introduce complications into the equation so as to modify its simple linear form.

Why should the rate of change in Y be a function of the level of Y? Presumably, this is in large part because there are actors in the situation who are motivated to change the value of Y to some level at which they would be satisfied. Some such actors may seek only to bring Y down to a certain point and may not care what happens below this point. Others may be dissatisfied if Y drops too low but may be indifferent when it becomes very high. Still others may seek to keep Y within limits that are defined as neither too high nor too low. Of course, these actors will have different abilities or resources with which to influence Y. Some may attempt to reduce Y but may miscalculate and actually raise it. Furthermore, these parties are likely to be in mutual interaction, with the behaviors of one influencing those of another. For instance, if a coalition partner is already acting so as to move Y to the level that another party also desires, the latter may decide not to act so as to preserve its own resources. Or it may anticipate the actions of a third party that is expected to attempt to shift the level in the opposite direction. Presumably, the actual rate of change in Y will be a function of all these forces, thus necessitating a much more complex type of differential equation.

One of the first steps, then, is to delineate a finite set of actors, who may be single individuals, corporate groups, or mere aggregates of individuals assumed to be characterized by the same set of parameter values. Let us designate these actors by the subscripts $1, 2, \ldots, k$. Next we need to make some assumptions about the nature of the functions that will be appropriate for each kind of actor, as these need not necessarily be all the same. For each actor let us assume, however, that there will be some indifference level at which the actor's activity (to change Y) will be zero.

If all actors had the same indifference levels we could use a single symbol, say, Y_o as above, and this would imply that if Y were at this level there would be no actors motivated to change it. Of course, Y might be shifted by exogenous forces, so that we cannot assume that Y would necessarily rest in a state of constant equilibrium even under these most unusual circumstances. Needless to say, we do not generally expect all actors to have the same indifference levels, nor do we expect their resources or their sensitivities to departures from indifference levels to remain constant.

Let us indicate the indifference level of actor i by Z_i, where Z_i may be affected by other variables in the system and thus also subject to change during the time period under consideration. Suppose that actor i's resources, R_i, and sensitivity, S_i, to departure from the indifference level, Z_i, are also variables and that the total power exerted by actor i is, in addition, a function of the power being exerted by other actors j and k.[2] If we represent the power exerted by i as P_i, this implies that P_i may be a reasonably complicated function not only of $Y - Z_i$ but of S_i, R_i, and P_j and P_k as well. Clearly, a number of simplifications will become necessary.

One very important kind of simplification will be that certain of these potential variables are really constants during the interval being studied. The reasonableness of such assumptions will obviously depend upon the time period of concern. Presumably, relatively short-run models will tend to be simpler but yet less realistic than long-run models that permit more of these factors to be treated as variables rather than as constants. It will also simplify the equation system if certain of the variables can be taken as instantaneous functions of others rather than as involving delayed effects that will have to be represented as additional differential equations. For example, it may be realistic in some instances to assume that if the power exerted by actor i is a function of P_j and P_k, any changes produced in P_i by these variables will be more or less instantaneous.

Finally, we may take the rate of change in Y as some function of the P_i representing the actual power being exerted by each of the parties that have been delineated. Assuming that these P_i have been given either a positive or a negative sign in accord with the direction in which the actor is attempting to move Y, it then becomes plausible to express dY/dt as a simple linear function of these P_i:

$$dY/dt = \sum_{i=1}^{k} P_i.$$

This implies that Y will not change immediately as the P_i are changed, but that there will be a kind of smooth delayed reaction. The sum of the P_i represents a resultant of forces that require time to consummate, with the *rate* of change in Y being proportionate to this aggregate of the forces in either direction.

There will be a number of different types of function linking the P_i to Y and to the other variables we have mentioned. Some possibilities are

(1) $P_i = k(Y - Y_o)$ Constant coefficient, constant indifference level, same for all actors;

(2) $P_i = k_i(Y - Y_{oi})$ Constant coefficient, constant indifference level, each differing by actor;

(3) $P_i = k_i(Y - Z_i)$ Variable indifference levels for all actors;

(4) $P_i = kR_i(Y - Z_i)$ Unequal resources among actors;

(5) $P_i = kS_iR_i(Y - Z_i)$ Unequal resources and sensitivities among actors;

(6) $P_i = kP_jS_iR_i(Y - Z_i)$ P_i also proportional to P_j;

(7) $P_i = kP_jS_iR_i(Y - Z_i), \quad Y > Z_i$ P_i exerted only if $Y > Z_i$;
       $= 0 \qquad\qquad\qquad\quad Y \leqslant Z_i$

(8) $P_i = kP_jS_iR_i(Y - Z_i)^2$ P_i insensitive to direction of deviation from Z_i.

The distinction between the k_i, which may be different for all actors, and terms involving Z_i, R_i, S_i, and P_j is that the latter are conceived to be variables that may shift their values during the period concerned, whereas the k_i and also the Y_{oi} are assumed to be fixed. Let us suppose that there are three P_i, one of which is related to the other variables in accord with equation (3), a second as in equation (6), and the third as in equation (8). This would result in a rather complex expression for dY/dt, but nevertheless one that might be solved if the necessary data were available.

If there were several simultaneous nonlinear differential equations, we might very well encounter mathematically intractable situations, in which case further simplifications would become necessary. Obviously, neither our degree of knowledge nor our measurement procedures are presently sufficient to justify such a high degree of complexity, but it has been our thesis throughout this work that it makes sense to attempt to specify as explicitly as possible the various kinds of complication that seem necessary so that simplifications can then be made on a rational basis.

One kind of extreme simplification would be to use only equations of the form (2). If the indifference levels Y_{oi} are reasonably close together, or unknown and impossible to estimate, then perhaps it will also be necessary to use a single level Y_o with the recognition that this will represent a kind of average of the actual levels of the actors concerned. If we make these very considerable simplifications then we will have:

$$dY/dt = \Sigma P_i = \Sigma k_i(Y - Y_o) = K(Y - Y_o), \qquad \text{where } K = \Sigma k_i.$$

We have implicitly assumed, in this instance, that the P_i are *not* functions of other P_j and do not shift their values (during this period) according to the levels of these other P_j. This implies that there are no additional differential equations that need to be considered simultaneously with this single equation.

Under these assumptions it is well known that the necessary condition for stability (at Y_o) is that K must be negative. This does not necessarily mean that *all* of the actors will have k_i that are negative; it merely implies that their sum must be negative. The greater the absolute value of K, the more pronounced the net reaction to departures from equilibrium, and the more rapid the return to Y_o after a disturbance. This suggests that if there are many actors behaving in opposite ways and with approximately equal force, even though K is slightly negative it may take a long time to return to Y_o after a disturbance. Presumably, during this time a considerable number of exogenous variables could also shift their levels, so that it would be difficult to decide empirically whether the endogenous equilibrating forces were being ineffective (i.e., $K \approx 0$) or whether these exogenous agents were responsible for the continued changes.

Whether or not it is reasonable to treat the several k_i coefficients as constant parameters or as variables will depend on the length of the time period involved, and in particular the speed with which the equilibrating forces operate. If K is not numerically large but less than zero, so that continuous change is being experienced, it may be much more realistic to use at least some variable indifference levels as well. Perhaps these indifference levels shift gradually over time as actors learn to adjust to, say, increasing crime rates, racial disparities, or unemployment rates. If so, we may wish to write down equations for the rates of change in these Z_i as functions of Y and other variables. This may force us to use a set of simultaneous differential equations, which will of necessity have rather simple forms if the mathematical implications are to be extracted.

Summary

We may suggest a number of concrete steps by way of summary.

1. On the theoretical level we delineate a finite number of parties, which may be single individuals, corporate groups with explicit decision-making processes and well-defined outputs, quasi groups with informal interaction patterns, or statistical aggregates for which we are willing to assume homogeneity in the structural parameters.

2. We indicate which changes are to be taken as (approximately) simultaneous, which involve delayed reactions, and which are so slow that constant parameters may be used to represent the values of these variables during the period of relevance. In the case of delayed reactions we also need to decide whether a discrete-time model involving specifiable lag periods can be used, or whether it will be more appropriate to treat variables as changing continuously over time.[3]

3. We next write an equation for each of the parties designated in the first step, recognizing that the functional forms of these equations may possibly differ for each party, as may the lag periods and structural parameters.

4. Even in instances in which our data are extremely crude and incomplete we may then try to make a series of qualitative theoretical assertions about the forms, lag periods, or parameters in each equation. For example, we may attempt to identify the conditions that will increase or decrease the length of lag periods or the values of the parameters, including those conditions that will

produce near zero values of some of these parameters, thereby simplifying the equations.

5. We then need to examine the implications of our equations for data collected at the micro level and for various levels of aggregation, noting the possibility of identification problems in which certain of the separate parameters cannot be estimated.

6. Finally, we may use this theoretical formulation as a guide to data-collection and aggregation decisions.

These suggestions may sound highly unrealistic and perfectionistic in view of the present state of our knowledge, and indeed they are intended to stretch the limits of our theorizing beyond the confines of our present data-collection capabilities. It has been our position throughout this work that we cannot begin to cope with a very complex reality unless and until we make much more serious efforts to wed our theories and knowledge of methodological principles, on the one hand, with our more delimited efforts to conduct empirical research, on the other. To the extent that attempts to do so help us to locate gaps in our knowledge and deficiencies in our data-collection efforts, we shall draw closer to the day in which our knowledge of important social processes can actually be used for practical purposes.

NOTES

1. An alternative form for the same equation is $dY/dt = a + bY$, where $a = -KY_o$ and $b = K < 0$.
2. Sensitivity, S_i, will, in turn, be some function of actor i's utilities. Here we are ignoring actors' subjective probabilities, which will presumably be linked to the R_i terms.
3. For more detailed discussions of strategies in setting up dynamic models of various types, see Baumol (1959), Blalock (1969), Coleman (1964), Land (1975), and Simon (1957).

REFERENCES

Aberle, D., A. Cohen, A. Davis, M. Levy, and F. Sutton. 1950. "The Functional Prerequisites of a Society." *Ethics* 9:100–11.

Abrahamsson, B. 1970. "Homans on Exchange: Hedonism Revived." *American Journal of Sociology* 76:273–85.

Abramson, E., H. Cutler, R. Kautz, and M. Mendelson. 1958. "Social Power and Commitment: A Theoretical Statement." *American Sociological Review* 23:15–22.

Adams, J. S. 1963. "Toward an Understanding of Inequity." *Journal of Abnormal and Social Psychology* 67:422–36.

Adams, J. S. 1965. "Inequity in Social Exchange." In L. Berkowitz, ed., *Advances in Experimental Psychology*, vol. 2, pp. 267–300. New York: Academic Press.

Alexander, C. N., and E. Q. Campbell. 1964. "Peer Influence on Adolescent Educational Aspirations and Attainments." *American Sociological Review* 29:568–75.

Alexander, C. N., and R. L. Simpson. 1971. "Balance Theory and Distributive Justice." In H. Turk and R. L. Simpson, eds., *Institutions and Social Exchange: The Sociologies of Talcott Parsons and George C. Homans*, pp. 69–81. Indianapolis: Bobbs-Merrill.

Alexander, K. L., and B. K. Eckland. 1975. "Contextual Effects in the High School Attainment Process." *American Sociological Review* 40:402–16.

Alexander, K. L., and B. K. Eckland. 1977. "High School Context and College Selectivity: Institutional Constraints in Educational Stratification." *Social Forces* 56:166–88.

Alker, H. L. 1969. "A Typology of Ecological Fallacies." In M. Dogan and S. Rokkan, eds. *Quantitative Ecological Analysis in the Social Sciences*, chap. 4. Cambridge: MIT Press.

Allport, G. W. 1954. *The Nature of Prejudice*. Cambridge: Addison-Wesley.

Anderson, B., J. Berger, M. Zelditch, and B. Cohen. 1969. "Reactions to Inequity." *Acta Sociologica* 12:1–12.

Antonovsky, A. 1960. "The Social Meaning of Discrimination." *Phylon* 21:81–95.

614

Arrow, K. 1963. *Social Choice and Individual Values.* New York: Wiley.

Atkinson, J. W. 1957. "Motivational Determinants of Risk-taking Behavior." *Psychological Review* 64:359–72.

Atkinson, J. W., and D. Birch. 1970. *The Dynamics of Action.* New York: Wiley.

Austin, W., and E. Walster. 1975. "Equity with the World: The Trans-relational Effects of Equity and Inequity." *Sociometry* 38:474–96.

Bachrach, P., and M. S. Baratz. 1963. "Decisions and Non Decisions: An Analytic Framework." *American Political Science Review* 57:632–42.

Banfield, E. 1968. *The Unheavenly City.* Boston: Little, Brown.

Barclay, S., and L. R. Beach. 1972. "Combinatorial Properties of Personal Probabilities." *Organizational Behavior and Human Performance* 8:176–83.

Bar-Hillel, M. 1973. "On the Subjective Probability of Compound Events." *Organizational Behavior and Human Performance* 9:396–406.

Baumol, W. J. 1959. *Economic Dynamics.* New York: Macmillan.

Beach, L. R., and L. D. Phillips. 1967. "Subjective Probabilities Inferred from Estimates and Bets." *Journal of Experimental Psychology* 75:354–59.

Beach, L. R., and J. A. Wise. 1969. "Subjective Probability and Decision Strategy." *Journal of Experimental Psychology* 79:133–38.

Becker, G. B., and C. G. McClintock. 1967. "Value: Behavioral Decision Theory." *Annual Review of Psychology* 18:239–86.

Becker, S. W., and S. Siegel. 1962. "Utility and Level of Aspiration." *American Journal of Psychology* 75:115–20.

Bell, W. 1954. "A Probability Model for the Measurement of Ecological Segregation." *Social Forces* 32:357–64.

Benedict, R. 1934. *Patterns of Culture.* Boston: Houghton Mifflin.

Berger, J., M. Zelditch, B. Anderson, and B. Cohen. 1972. "Structural Aspects of Distributive Justice: A Status Value Formulation." In J. Berger, B. Anderson, and M. Zelditch, eds., *Sociological Theories in Progress,* vol. 2, pp. 119–46. Boston: Houghton Mifflin.

Berger, P. 1963. *Invitation to Sociology: A Humanistic Perspective.* Garden City, N.Y.: Doubleday.

Berscheid, E., D. Boye, and E. Walster. 1968. "Retaliation as a Means of Restoring Equity." *Journal of Personality and Social Psychology* 10:370–76.

Blalock, H. M. 1961. "Theory, Measurement, and Replication in the Social Sciences." *American Journal of Sociology* 66:342–47.

Blalock, H. M. 1967a. "Status Inconsistency, Social Mobility, Status Integration, and Structural Effects." *American Sociological Review* 32:790–801.

Blalock, H. M. 1967b. *Toward a Theory of Minority Group Relations.* New York: Wiley.

Blalock, H. M. 1969. *Theory Construction: From Verbal to Mathematical Formulations.* Englewood Cliffs, N.J.: Prentice-Hall.

Blalock, H. M. 1971. "Aggregation and Measurement Error." *Social Forces* 50:151–65.

Blau, P. M. 1960. "Structural Effects." *American Sociological Review* 25:178–93.

Blau, P. M. 1964a. *Exchange and Power in Social Life.* New York: Wiley.

Blau, P. M. 1964b. "Justice in Social Exchange." *Sociological Inquiry* 34:193–206.

Blinder, A. S. 1973. "Wage Discrimination: Reduced Form and Structural Estimates." *Journal of Human Resources* 8:436–55.

Blumstein, P. W. 1973. "Subjective Probability and Normative Evaluations." *Social Forces* 52:98–107.

Blumstein, P. W., and E. A. Weinstein. 1969. "The Redress of Distributive Injustice." *American Journal of Sociology* 74:408–18.

Bogardus, E. 1928. *Immigration and Race Attitudes.* Lexington, Mass.: D.C. Heath.

Bonacich, E. 1972. "A Theory of Ethnic Antagonism: The Split Labor Market." *American Sociological Review* 37:547–59.

Bonacich, E. 1973. "A Theory of Middleman Minorities." *American Sociological Review* 38:583–94.

Boudon, R. 1963. "Propriétés individuelles et propriétés collectives: Un problème d'analyse écologique." *Revue Francaise de Sociologie* 4:275–99.

Boulding, K. 1962. "An Economist's View." *American Journal of Sociology* 67:458–61.

Boyanowsky, E. O., and V. L. Allen. 1973. "Ingroup Norms and Self-identity as Determinants of Discriminatory Behavior." *Journal of Personality and Social Psychology* 25:408–18.

Brim, O. G. 1955. "Attitude Content–Intensity and Probability Expectations." *American Sociological Review* 20:68–76.

Brown, R. 1973. *Rules and Laws in Sociology.* Chicago: Aldine.

Buckley, W. 1967. *Sociology and Modern Systems Theory.* Englewood Cliffs, N.J.: Prentice-Hall.

Burgess, R. L., and J. M. Nielsen. 1974. "An Experimental Analysis of Some Structural Determinants of Equitable and Inequitable Exchange Relations." *American Sociological Review* 39:427–43.

Burkey, R. M. 1971. *Racial Discrimination and Public Policy in the United States.* Lexington, Mass.: Heath Lexington.

Cameron, P., and J. L. Myers. 1966. "Some Personality Correlates of Risk Taking." *Journal of General Psychology* 74:51–60.

Campbell, E. Q., and C. N. Alexander. 1965. "Structural Effects and Interpersonal Relationships." *American Journal of Sociology* 72:284–89.

Cannon, W. B. 1939. *The Wisdom of the Body.* New York: Norton.

Caplow, T. 1968. *Two against One.* Englewood Cliffs, N.J.: Prentice-Hall.

Cartwright, D. 1959. "A Field Theoretical Conception of Power." In D. Cartwright, ed., *Studies in Social Power,* chap. 11. Ann Arbor: University of Michigan Press.

Clark, T. N. 1968. "The Concept of Power." In T. N. Clark, ed., *Community Structure and Decision-making: Comparative Analyses*, chap. 3. San Francisco: Chandler.

Coleman, J. S. 1964. *Introduction to Mathematical Sociology.* New York: Free Press.

Coleman, J. S. 1971. *Resources for Social Change.* New York: Wiley-Interscience.

Coleman, J. S. 1973. *The Mathematics of Collective Action.* Chicago: Aldine.

Cook, K. S. 1970. "An Extensive Review of the Sociological Literature on the Problem of Inequity." Unpublished paper, Stanford University.

Cook, K. S. 1973. "An Experimental Study of the Activation of Equity Processes." Ph.D. dissertation, Stanford University.

Cook, K. S. 1975. "Expectations, Evaluations, and Equity." *American Sociological Review* 40:372–88.

Cook, K. S., and T. L. Parcel. 1977. "Equity Theory: Directions for Future Research." *Sociological Inquiry* 47:75–88.

Coombs, C. H. 1964. *A Theory of Data.* New York: Wiley.

Coombs, C. H., and S. S. Komorita. 1958. "Measuring Utility of Money through Decisions." *American Journal of Psychology* 71:383–89.

Coombs, C. H., and D. C. Pruitt. 1960. "Components of Risk in Decision-making: Probability and Variance Preferences." *Journal of Experimental Psychology* 60:265–77.

Coombs, C. H., T. G. Bezembinder, and F. M. Goode. 1967. "Testing Expectation Theories of Decision Making without Measuring Utility or Subjective Probability." *Journal of Mathematical Psychology* 4:72–103.

Coombs, C. H., R. Dawes, and A. Tversky. 1970. *Mathematical Psychology.* Englewood Cliffs, N.J.: Prentice-Hall.

Cortese, C. F., R. F. Falk, and J. K. Cohen. 1976. "Further Considerations on the Methodological Analysis of Segregation Indices." *American Sociological Review* 41:630–37.

Cowgill, D. O., and M. S. Cowgill. 1951. "An Index of Segregation Based on Block Statistics." *American Sociological Review* 16:825–31.

Dahl, R. A. 1957. "The Concept of Power." *Behavioral Science* 2:201–15.

Dahl, R. A. 1961, *Who Governs?* New Haven: Yale University Press.

Daniel, W. W. 1968. *Racial Discrimination in England.* Baltimore: Penguin.

Darroch, A. G., and W. G. Marston. 1971. "The Social Class Basis of Ethnic Residential Segregation: The Canadian Case." *American Journal of Sociology* 77:491–510.

Davidson, D., P. Suppes, and S. Siegel. 1957. *Decision Making: An Experimental Approach.* Stanford: Stanford University Press.

Davis, J. A., J. L. Spaeth, and C. Huson. 1961. "A Technique for Analyzing the Effects of Group Composition." *American Sociological Review* 26:215–25.

Degler, C. N. 1971. *Neither Black nor White: Slavery and Race Relations in Brazil and the United States.* New York: Macmillan.

Deutsch, M. 1975. "Equity, Equality, and Need: What Determines Which Value Will Be Used as the Basis of Distributive Justice?" *Journal of Social Issues* 31:137–49.

Deutsch, M., and M. E. Collins. 1951. *Interracial Housing.* Minneapolis: University of Minnesota Press.

Donnenworth, G. V., and K. Y. Törnblom. 1975. "Reactions to Three Types of Distributive Injustice." *Human Relations* 28:407–30.

Doyle, B. W. 1937. *The Etiquette of Race Relations in the South.* Chicago: University of Chicago Press.

Duncan, O. D., R. P. Cuzzort, and B. Duncan. 1961. *Statistical Geography.* New York: Free Press.

Duncan, O. D., and B. Duncan. 1955. "A Methodological Analysis of Segregation Indexes." *American Sociological Review* 20:210–17.

Duncan, O. D., and B. Duncan. 1957. *The Negro Population of Chicago.* Chicago: University of Chicago Press.

Durkheim, E. 1951. *Suicide.* New York: Free Press.

Edwards, W. A. 1960. "Measurement of Utility and Subjective Probability." In H. Gulliksen and S. Messick, eds., *Psychological Scaling: Theory and Applications,* pp. 109–27. New York: Wiley.

Edwards, W. A. 1961. "Behavioral Decision Theory." *Annual Review of Psychology* 12:473–98.

Edwards, W. A. 1962a. "Subjective Probabilities Inferred from Decisions." *Psychological Review* 69:109–35.

Edwards, W. A. 1962b. "Utility, Subjective Probability, Their Interaction and Variance Preferences." *Journal of Conflict Resolution* 6:42–51.

Edwards, W. A. 1968. "Decision Making: I. Psychological Aspects." In D. L. Sills, ed., *International Encyclopedia of the Social Sciences,* vol. 4, pp. 34–42. New York: Macmillan and Free Press.

Ehrlich, H. 1973. *The Social Psychology of Prejudice.* New York: Wiley.

Einhorn, H. J. 1971. "Use of Nonlinear, Noncompensatory Models as a Function of Task and Amount of Information." *Organizational Behavior and Human Performance* 6:1–27.

Ekeh, P. P. 1974. *Social Exchange Theory: The Two Traditions.* Cambridge, Mass.: Harvard University Press.

Emerson, R. D. 1962. "Power–Dependence Relations." *American Sociological Review* 27:31–41.

Emerson, R. D. 1969. "Operant Psychology and Exchange Theory." In R. J. Burgess and D. Bushell, eds., *Behavioral Sociology,* pp. 379–405. New York: Columbia University Press.

Emerson, R. D. 1972a. "Exchange Theory, Part I: A Psychological Basis for Social Exchange." In J. Berger, B. Anderson, and M. Zelditch, eds., *Sociological Theories in Progress,* vol. 2, pp. 38–57. Boston: Houghton Mifflin.

Emerson, R. D. 1972b. "Exchange Theory, Part II: Exchange Relations and Network Structure." In J. Berger, B. Anderson, and M. Zelditch, eds., *Sociological Theories in Progress,* vol. 2, pp. 58–87. Boston: Houghton Mifflin.

Etzioni, A. 1961. *A Comparative Analysis of Complex Organizations.* New York: Free Press.

Eulau, H. 1969. *Micro-Macro Political Analysis: Accents of Inquiry.* Chicago: Aldine.

Eulau, H. 1974. "Some Aspects of Analysis, Measurement and Sampling in the Transformation of Micro- and Macro-level Unit Properties." Unpublished manuscript, Stanford University.

Falk, R. F., C. F. Cortese, and J. Cohen. 1978. "Utilizing Standardized Indices of Residential Segregation." *Social Forces* 57:713–16.

Fanon, F. 1963. *The Wretched of the Earth.* New York: Grove Press.

Farkas, G. 1974. "Specification, Residuals and Contextual Effects." *Sociological Methods and Research* 2:333–64.

Feldman, J. 1974. "Race, Economic Class, and the Intention to Work: Some Normative and Attitudinal Correlates." *Journal of Applied Psychology* 59:179–86.

Ferguson, C. E. 1965. "Theory of Multidimensional Utility Analysis in Relation to Multiple-goal Business Behavior: A Synthesis." *Southern Economic Journal* 32:169–75.

Firebaugh, G. 1978. "Groups as Contexts and Frog Ponds: Some Neglected Considerations." Unpublished manuscript, Vanderbilt University.

Fishburn, P. C. 1974. "Lexicographic Orders, Utilities, and Decision Rules: A Survey." *Management Science* 20:1442–71.

Fogel, R. W., and S. L. Engerman, 1974. *Time on the Cross: The Economics of American Negro Slavery.* Boston: Little, Brown.

Ford, D., G. Huber, and D. Gustafson. 1972. "Predicting Job Choices with Models That Contain Subjective Probability Judgments: An Empirical Comparison of Five Models." *Organizational Behavior and Human Performance* 7:397–416.

Frazier, E. F. 1957. *Black Bourgeoisie.* New York: Free Press.

French, J. R. P., and B. Raven. 1959. "The Bases of Social Power." In D. Cartwright, ed., *Studies in Social Power,* chap. 9. Ann Arbor: University of Michigan Press.

Furnivall, J. S. 1948. *Colonial Policy and Practice.* London: Cambridge University Press.

Gaertner, S. L. 1973. "Helping Behavior and Racial Discrimination among Liberals and Conservatives." *Journal of Personality and Social Psychology* 25:335–41.

Galanter, E. 1962. "The Direct Measurement of Utility and Subjective Probability." *American Journal of Psychology* 75:208–20.

Gamson, W. A. 1961. "A Theory of Coalition Formation." *American Sociological Review* 26:373–82.

Gamson, W. A. 1968. *Power and Discontent.* Homewood, Ill.: Dorsey Press.

Genovese, E. D. 1976. *Roll, Jordan, Roll: The World the Slaves Made.* New York: Vintage.

Georgescu-Roegen, N. 1968. "Utility." In D. L. Sills, ed., *International Encyclopedia of the Social Sciences,* vol. 16, pp. 236–67. New York: Macmillan and Free Press.

Gergen, K. 1969. *The Psychology of Behavior Exchange.* Reading, Mass.: Addison-Wesley.

Gilman, H. 1965. "Economic Discrimination and Unemployment." *American Economic Review* 55:1077–96.

Gist, N. P., and A. G. Dworkin, eds., 1972. *The Blending of Races: Marginality and Identity in World Perspective.* New York: Wiley-Interscience.

Glazer, N., and D. P. Moynihan. 1970. *Beyond the Melting Pot,* 2nd ed. Cambridge: MIT Press.

Glenn, N. D. 1966. "White Gains from Negro Subordination." *Social Problems* 14:159–78.

Goodman, L. A., and W. Kruskal. 1954. "Measures of Association for Cross Classification." *Journal of the American Statistical Association* 49:732–64.

Goodman, P. S., and A. Friedman. 1971. "An Examination of Adams' Theory of Inequity." *Administrative Science Quarterly* 16:271–88.

Gordon, M. M. 1964. *Assimilation in American Life.* New York: Oxford University Press.

Gordon, R. A. 1968. "Issues in Multiple Regression." *American Journal of Sociology* 73:592–616.

Gouldner, A. W. 1960. "The Norm of Reciprocity." *American Sociological Review* 25:161–78.

Grier, W. H., and P. M. Cobbs. 1968. *Black Rage.* New York: Basic Books.

Guest, A. M., and J. A. Weed. 1976. "Ethnic Residential Segregation: Patterns of Change." *American Journal of Sociology* 81:1088–111.

Gwartney, J. D. 1970. "Discrimination and Income Differentials." *American Economic Review* 60:396–408.

Gwartney, J. D., and K. M. McCaffree. 1971. "Variance in Discrimination among Occupations." *Southern Economic Journal* 38:141–55.

Halter, A. N., and G. W. Dean. 1971. *Decisions under Uncertainty.* Cincinnati: South-Western Publishing Co.

Hamblin, R. L. 1971. "Ratio Measurement for the Social Sciences." *Social Forces* 50:191–206.

Hamblin, R. L. 1974. "Social Attitudes: Magnitude Measurement and Theory." In H. M. Blalock, ed., *Measurement in the Social Sciences: Theories and Strategies,* chap. 3. Chicago: Aldine.

Hannan, M. T. 1971. *Aggregation and Disaggregation in Sociology.* Lexington, Mass.: Lexington.

Hauser, R. M. 1970. "Context and Consex: A Cautionary Tale." *American Journal of Sociology* 75:645–64.

Hauser, R. M. 1971. *Socioeconomic Background and Educational Performance.* Washington: American Sociological Association.

Hauser, R. M. 1974. "Contextual Analysis Revisited." *Sociological Methods and Research* 2:365–75.

Hays, W. L., and R. L. Winkler. 1971. *Statistics: Probability, Inference, and Decision.* New York: Holt, Rinehart.

Heinrich, B. A. 1971. "Direct and Indirect Methods for Measuring Utility." Ph.D. dissertation, University of Washington.

Hendon, W. S. 1968. "Discrimination against Negro Homeowners in Property Tax Assessment." *American Journal of Economics and Sociology* 27:125–32.

Higbee, K. L., and T. Lafferty. 1972. "Relationships among Risk Preferences, Importance, and Control." *Journal of Psychology* 81:249–51.

Holmstrom, V. L., and L. R. Beach. 1973. "Subjective Expected Utility and Career Preferences." *Organizational Behavior and Human Performance* 10:201–207.

Homans, G. 1950. *The Human Group.* New York: Harcourt, Brace.

Homans, G. 1961. *Social Behavior: Its Elementary Forms.* New York: Harcourt, Brace.

Homans, G. 1974. *Social Behavior: Its Elementary Forms,* rev. ed. New York: Harcourt Brace Jovanovich.

Hornseth, R. 1947. "A Note on 'The Measurement of Ecological Segregation.'" *American Sociological Review* 12:603–604.

Howell, W. C. 1972. "Compounding Uncertainty from Internal Sources." *Journal of Experimental Psychology* 95:6–13.

Hurst, P. M., and S. Siegel. 1956. "Prediction of Decision from a Higher-ordered Metric Scale of Utility." *Journal of Experimental Psychology* 52:138–44.

Irwin, L., and A. J. Lichtman. 1976. "Across the Great Divide: Inferring Individual Level Behavior from Aggregate Data." *Political Methodology* 3:411–39.

Jahn, J. A. 1950. "The Measurement of Ecological Segregation: Derivation of an Index Based on the Criterion of Reproducibility." *American Sociological Review* 15:100–104.

Jahn, J. A., C. F. Schmid, and C. Schrag. 1947. "The Measurement of Ecological Segregation." *American Sociological Review* 12:293–303.

Johnson, C. S. 1943. *Patterns of Negro Segregation.* New York: Harper.

Johnson, N. R., and D. P. Marple. 1973. "Racial Discrimination in Professional Basketball: An Empirical Test." *Sociological Focus* 6:6–18.

Jones, E. E., and C. A. Johnson. 1973. "Delay of Consequences and the Riskiness of Decision." *Journal of Personality* 41:613–37.

Kadushin, C. 1968. "Power, Influence and Social Circles: A New Methodology for Studying Opinion Makers," *American Sociological Review* 33:685–99.

Kain, J. F., and J. M. Quigley. 1972. "Housing Market Discrimination, Homeownership, and Savings Behavior." *American Economic Review* 62:263–77.

Kantrowitz, N. 1973. *Ethnic and Racial Segregation in the New York Metropolis.* New York: Praeger.

Kardiner, A., and L. Ovesey. 1951. *The Mark of Oppression.* New York: Norton.

Karon, B. P. 1958. *The Negro Personality*. New York: Springer-Verlag.

Katzman, M. T. 1968. "Discrimination, Subculture, and the Economic Performance of Negroes, Puerto Ricans, and Mexican-Americans." *American Journal of Economics and Sociology* 27:371–75.

Keeley, S. M., and M. E. Doherty. 1972. "Bayesian and Regression Modeling of Graduate Admission Policy." *Organizational Behavior and Human Performance* 8:297–323.

Kennedy, R. J. R. 1944. "Single or Triple Melting-Pot? Intermarriage Trends in New Haven, 1870–1940." *American Journal of Sociology* 49:331–39.

King, A. T., and P. Mieszkowski. 1973. "Racial Discrimination, Segregation, and the Price of Housing." *Journal of Political Economy* 81:590–606.

Koopmans, T. C. 1949. "Identification Problems in Economic Model Construction." *Econometrica* 17:125–43.

Korpi, W. 1974. "Conflict, Power and Relative Deprivation." *American Political Science Review* 68:1569–78.

Krantz, D. H., R. D. Luce, P. Suppes, and A. Tversky. 1971. *Foundations of Measurement*, vol. 1. New York: Academic Press.

Kuper, H. 1969. " 'Strangers' in Plural Societies: Asians in South Africa and Uganda." In L. Kuper and M. G. Smith, eds., *Pluralism in Africa*, chap. 8. Berkeley: University of California Press.

Kuper, L., and M. G. Smith, eds., 1969. *Pluralism in Africa*. Berkeley: University of California Press.

Land, K. C. 1975. "Comparative Statics in Sociology: Including a Mathematical Theory of Growth and Differentiation in Organizations." In H. M. Blalock, A. Aganbegian, F. M. Borodkin, R. Boudon, and V. Capecchi, eds., *Quantitative Sociology*, chap. 17. New York: Academic Press.

Lane, I. M., and L. A. Messé. 1971. "Equity and the Distribution of Rewards." *Journal of Personality and Social Psychology* 20:1–17.

Langley, C. T. 1977. "Structural Ambiguity." Ph.D. dissertation, University of Washington.

Langley, C. T., and E. A. T. Barth. 1978. "Attitude Content or Situational Ambiguity: What Is Measured by Social Distance Scales?" Unpublished paper, University of Washington.

Lapham, V. 1971. "Do Blacks Pay More for Housing?" *Journal of Political Economy* 79:1244–57.

Lawler, E. E. 1967. "Secrecy about Management Compensation: Are There Hidden Costs?" *Organizational Behavior and Human Performance* 2:182–208.

Lee, W. 1971. *Decision Theory and Human Behavior*. New York: Wiley.

Lenski, G. E. 1954. "Status Crystallization: A Non-vertical Dimension of Social Status." *American Sociological Review* 19:405–13.

Leventhal, G. S. 1976. "The Distributions of Rewards and Resources in Groups and Organizations." In L. Berkowitz and E. Walster, eds., *Advances in Experimental Social Psychology*, vol. 9, pp. 92–131. New York: Academic Press.

Levitan, S. A., W. B. Johnston, and R. Taggart. 1975. *Still a Dream: The Changing Status of Blacks since 1960*. Cambridge, Mass.: Harvard University Press.

Lieberson, S. 1963. *Ethnic Patterns in American Cities*. New York: Free Press.

Lieberson, S. 1976. "Rank-sum Comparisons between Groups." In D. R. Heise, ed., *Sociological Methodology 1976*, chap. 11. San Francisco: Jossey-Bass.

Liebow, E. 1967. *Tally's Corner*. Boston: Little, Brown.

Long, J., and P. H. Wilken. 1974. "A Fully Nonmetric Unfolding Technique: Interval Values from Ordinal Data." In H. M. Blalock, ed., *Measurement in the Social Sciences: Theories and Strategies*, chap. 2. Chicago: Aldine.

Luce, R. D. 1959. *Individual Choice Behavior*. New York: Wiley.

Luce, R. D., and P. Suppes. 1965. "Preference, Utility and Subjective Probability." In R. D. Luce, R. Bush, and E. Galanter, eds., *Handbook of Mathematical Psychology*, vol. 3, pp. 249–410. New York: Wiley.

Lupfer, M., and M. Jones. 1971. "Risk Taking as a Function of Skill and Chance Orientations." *Psychological Reports* 28:27–33.

March, J. G. 1966. "The Power of Power." In D. Easton, ed., *Varieties of Political Theories*, chap. 3. Englewood Cliffs, N.J.: Prentice-Hall.

Marshall, H., and R. Jiobu. 1975. "Residential Segregation in United States Cities." *Social Forces* 53:449–60.

Maslow, A. H. 1954. *Motivation and Personality*. New York: Harper & Row.

Mason, P. 1970. *Patterns of Dominance*. London: Oxford University Press.

Mauss, M. 1954. *The Gift*. Translated by I. Cunnison. New York: Free Press.

McCauley, C., and N. Graham. 1971. "Influence of Values in Risky Decision Making: A Formalization." *Representative Research in Social Psychology* 2:3–11.

McClelland, D. C. 1961. *The Achieving Society*. New York: Free Press.

McClelland, D. C., and D. G. Winter. 1969. *Motivating Economic Achievement*. New York: Free Press.

McClintock, C., D. Messick, D. Kuhlman, and F. Campos. 1973. "Motivational Bases of Choice in Three-choice Decomposed Games." *Journal of Experimental Social Psychology* 9:572–90.

Meeker, B. F. 1971. "Decisions and Exchange." *American Sociological Review* 36:485–95.

Merton, R. K. 1949. "Discrimination and the American Creed." In R. M. MacIver, ed., *Discrimination and National Welfare*, pp. 99–128. New York: Harper & Row.

Merton, R. K. 1968. *Social Theory and Social Structure*, rev. ed. New York: Free Press.

Messick, D. M. 1970. "Learning Probabilities of Events: A Discussion." *Acta Psychologica* 34:172–83.

Miller, G. A. 1956. "The Magical Number Seven, Plus or Minus Two: Some Limits on Our Capacity for Processing Information." *Psychological Review* 63:81–97.

Mitchell, G. D., ed. 1968. *A Dictionary of Sociology*. London: Routledge & Kegan Paul.

Mitchell, T. R., and A. Biglan. 1971. "Instrumentality Theories: Current Uses in Psychology." *Psychological Bulletin* 76:432–54.

Mitchell, T. R., and D. M. Nebeker. 1973. "Expectancy Theory Predictions of Academic Effort and Performance." *Journal of Applied Psychology* 57:61–67.

Molotch, H. 1969. "Racial Integration in a Transition Community." *American Sociological Review* 34:878–93.

Moore, B. 1966. *Social Origins of Dictatorship and Democracy.* Boston: Beacon.

Morgan, W. R., and J. Sawyer. 1967. "Bargaining, Expectations, and the Preference for Equality over Equity." *Journal of Personality and Social Psychology* 6:139–49.

Mosteller, F., and P. Nogee. 1951. "An Experimental Measurement of Utility." *Journal of Political Economy* 59:371–404.

Myrdal, G. 1944. *An American Dilemma.* New York: Harper & Row.

Nagel, J. H. 1975. *The Descriptive Analysis of Power.* New Haven: Yale University Press.

Newman, W. M. 1973. *American Pluralism: A Study of Minority Groups and Social Theory.* New York: Harper & Row.

Nielsen, J. M. 1972. "Experimental Analysis of Equitable and Inequitable Social Exchange." Ph.D. dissertation, University of Washington.

Nikolinakos, M. 1973. "Notes on an Economic Theory of Racism." *Race* 14:365–81.

Ofshe, L., and R. Ofshe. 1970. *Utility and Choice in Social Interaction.* Englewood Cliffs, N.J.: Prentice-Hall.

O'Neill, D. M. 1970. "The Effect of Discrimination on Earnings: Evidence from Military Test Score Results." *Journal of Human Resources* 5:475–86.

Parsons, T. 1949. *The Structure of Social Action.* New York: Free Press.

Parsons, T. 1951. *The Social System.* New York: Free Press.

Pascal, A. H., and L. A. Rapping. 1972. "The Economics of Racial Discrimination in Organized Baseball." In A. H. Pascal, ed., *Racial Discrimination in Economic Life,* pp. 119–56. Lexington, Mass.: Heath.

Payne, J. W. 1973. "Alternative Approaches to Decision Making under Risk: Moments versus Risk Dimensions." *Psychological Bulletin* 80:439–53.

Pepitone, A. 1971. "The Role of Justice in Interdependent Decision Making." *Journal of Experimental Social Psychology* 7:144–56.

Peterson, C. R., and L. R. Beach. 1967. "Man as an Intuitive Statistician." *Psychological Bulletin* 68:29–46.

Peterson, C. R., L. J. Ulehla, A. J. Miller, L. E. Bourne, and D. W. Stilson. 1965. "Internal Consistency of Subjective Probabilities." *Journal of Experimental Psychology* 70:526–33.

Phillips, L. D. 1970. "The 'True Probability' Problem." *Acta Psychologica* 34:254–64.

Pritchard, R. D. 1969. "Equity Theory: A Review and Critique." *Organizational Behavior and Human Performance* 4:176–211.

Pritchard, R. D., and P. J. De Leo. 1973. "Experimental Test of the Valence-

Instrumentality Relationship in Job Performance." *Journal of Applied Psychology* 57:264–70.

Pritchard, R. D., and M. S. Sanders. 1973. "The Influence of Valence, Instrumentality, and Expectancy on Effort and Performance." *Journal of Applied Psychology* 57:55–60.

Pruitt, D. G. 1962. "Pattern and Level of Risk in Gambling Decisions." *Psychological Review* 69:187–201.

Prysby, C. L. 1976. "Community Partisanship and Individual Voting Behavior: Methodological Problems of Contextual Analysis." *Political Methodology* 3:183–98.

Przeworski, A. 1974. "Contextual Models of Political Behavior." *Political Methodology* 1:27–60.

Quinn, R. P., R. L. Kahn, J. M. Tabor, and L. K. Gordon. 1968. *The Decision to Discriminate: A Study of Executive Selection*. Ann Arbor: Institute for Social Research, Survey Research Center, University of Michigan.

Rapoport, Amnon. 1968. "Choice Behavior in a Markovian Decision Task." *Journal of Mathematical Psychology* 5:163–81.

Rapoport, Anatol. 1967. "Exploiter, Leader, Hero, and Martyr." *Behavioral Science* 12:81–84.

Rapoport, A., and L. V. Jones. 1970. "Gambling Behavior in Two-outcome Multistage Betting Games." *Journal of Mathematical Psychology* 7:163–87.

Rapoport, A., and T. S. Wallster. 1972. "Individual Decision Behavior." *Annual Review of Psychology* 23:131–76.

Rapoport, A., L. V. Jones, and J. P. Kahan. 1970. "Gambling Behavior in Multiple-choice Multistage Betting Games." *Journal of Mathematical Psychology* 7:12–36.

Rasmussen, D. W. 1971. "Discrimination and the Income of Non-white Males." *American Journal of Economics and Sociology* 30:377–82.

Reich, M. 1972. "The Economics of Racism." In R. C. Edwards, M. Reich, and T. E. Weiskopf, eds., *The Capitalist System*, pp. 313–20. Englewood Cliffs, N.J.: Prentice-Hall.

Restle, F., and J. G. Greeno. 1970. *Introduction to Mathematical Psychology*. Reading, Mass.: Addison-Wesley.

Richardson, L. F. 1960. *Arms and Insecurity*. Pittsburgh: Boxwood Press.

Rigsby, L. C., and E. L. McDill. 1972. "Adolescent Peer Influence Processes: Conceptualization and Measurement." *Social Science Research* 1:305–22.

Rokeach, M. 1973. *The Nature of Human Values*. New York: Free Press.

Royden, H. L., P. Suppes, and K. Walsh. 1959. "A Model for the Experimental Measurement of the Utility of Gambling." *Behavioral Science* 4:11–18.

Ryan, W. 1976. *Blaming the Victim*. Rev. ed. New York: Random House.

Samuelson, P. A. 1947. *Foundations of Economic Analysis*. Cambridge, Mass.: Harvard University Press.

Schermerhorn, R. A. 1970. *Comparative Ethnic Relations: A Framework for Theory and Research*. New York: Random House.

Schiller, B. R. 1971. "Class Discrimination versus Racial Discrimination." *Review of Economics and Statistics* 53:263–69.

Schmitt, D. R., and G. Marwell. 1972. "Withdrawal and Reward Reallocation as Responses to Inequity." *Journal of Experimental Social Psychology* 8:207–21.

Schuman, H. 1975. "Free Will and Determinism in Public Beliefs about Race." In N. Yetman and C. Steele, eds., *Majority and Minority,* 2d ed., pp. 375–80. Boston: Allyn & Bacon.

Sewell, W. H., and J. M. Armer. 1966. "Neighborhood Context and College Plans." *American Sociological Review* 31:159–68.

Shapiro, E. G. 1975. "Effect of Expectations of Future Interaction on Reward Allocations in Dyads: Equity or Equality." *Journal of Personality and Social Psychology* 31:873–80.

Shapley, L., and M. Shubik. 1954. "A Method for Evaluating the Distribution of Power in a Committee System." *American Political Science Review* 48:787–92.

Shinn, A. M. 1971. "Measuring the Utility of Housing: Demonstrating a Methodological Approach." *Social Science Quarterly* 52:88–102.

Siegel, S. 1956. "A Method for Obtaining an Ordered Metric Scale." *Psychometrika* 21:207–16.

Siegel, S. 1957. "Level of Aspiration and Decision Making." *Psychological Review* 64:253–62.

Siegel, S. 1959. "Theoretical Models of Choice and Strategy Behavior: Stable State Behavior in the Two-choice Uncertain Outcome Situation." *Psychometrika* 24:303–16.

Siegel, S., A. E. Siegel, and J. M. Andrews. 1964. *Choice, Strategy, and Utility.* New York: McGraw-Hill.

Simmel, G. 1902. "The Number of Members as Determining the Sociological Form of the Group." *American Journal of Sociology* 8:1–46, 158–96.

Simon, H. A. 1957. *Models of Man.* New York: Wiley.

Simon, J. L. 1974. "Interpersonal Welfare Comparisons Can Be Made—And Used for Redistribution Decisions." *Kyklos* 27:63–98.

Simpson, G. P., and J. M. Yinger. 1972. *Racial and Cultural Minorities,* 4th ed. New York: Harper & Row.

Simpson, R. L. 1972. *Theories of Social Exchange.* Morristown, N.J.: General Learning Press.

Slovic, P., and S. Lichtenstein. 1968a. "Importance of Variance Preferences in Gambling Decisions." *Journal of Experimental Psychology* 78:646–54.

Slovic, P., and S. Lichtenstein. 1968b. "Relative Importance of Probabilities and Payoffs in Risk Taking." *Journal of Experimental Psychology Monograph* 78:1–18.

Slovic, P., and S. Lichtenstein. 1971. "Comparison of Bayesian and Regression Approaches to the Study of Information Processing in Judgment." *Organizational Behavior and Human Performance* 6:649–744.

Smith, M. G. 1965. *The Plural Society in the British West Indies.* Berkeley: University of California Press.

Sprague, J. 1976. "Estimating a Boudon Type Contextual Model: Some Practical and Theoretical Problems of Measurement." *Political Methodology* 3:333–53.

Stack, C. 1974. *All Our Kin.* New York: Harper & Row.

Stevens, S. S. 1959. "Measurement, Psychophysics, and Utility." In C. W. Churchman and P. Ratoosh, eds., *Measurement: Definitions and Theories,* pp. 18–63. New York: Wiley.

Stevens, S. S. 1966. "A Metric for the Social Consensus." *Science* 151:530–41.

Stinchcombe, A. L. 1968. *Constructing Social Theories.* New York: Harcourt, Brace.

Stonequist, E. V. 1961. *The Marginal Man.* New York: Russell and Russell.

Stouffer, S. A., E. A. Suchman, L. DeVinney, S. A. Starr, and R. M. Williams. 1949. *The American Soldier,* vol. 1. Princeton, N.J.: Princeton University Press.

Strauss, A. 1978. *Negotiations.* San Francisco: Jossey-Bass.

Sturdivant, F., and W. Hanselman. 1971. "Discrimination in the Marketplace: Another Dimension." *Social Science Quarterly* 52:625–30.

Suppes, P. 1970. *A Probabilistic Theory of Causality.* Amsterdam: North-Holland.

Szymanski, A. 1976. "Racial Discrimination and White Gain." *American Sociological Review* 41:407–13.

Taeuber, K. E., and A. F. Taeuber. 1965. *Negroes in Cities.* Chicago: Aldine.

Taeuber, K. E., and A. F. Taeuber. 1976. "A Practitioner's Perspective on the Index of Dissimilarity." *American Sociological Review* 41:884–89.

Tannenbaum, A. S., and J. G. Bachman. 1964. "Structural versus Individual Effects." *American Journal of Sociology* 69:585–95.

Taylor, M. 1970. "The Problem of Salience in the Theory of Collective Decision-making." *Behavioral Science* 15:415–30.

Terhune, K. W., and S. Kaufman. 1973. "The Family Size Utility Function." *Demography* 10:599–618.

Thibaut, J. W., and H. H. Kelley. 1959. *The Social Psychology of Groups.* New York: Wiley.

Thomas, K. 1973. "Situational Determinants of Equitable Behavior." *Human Relations* 26:551–66.

Törnblom, K. 1977. "Distributive Justice: Typology and Propositions." *Human Relations* 30:1–24.

Tversky, A. 1967a. "Additivity, Utility, and Subjective Probability." *Journal of Mathematical Psychology* 4:175–201.

Tversky, A. 1967b. "Utility Theory and Additivity Analysis of Risky Choices." *Journal of Experimental Psychology* 75:27–36.

Tversky, A. 1972a. "Choice by Elimination." *Journal of Mathematical Psychology* 9:341–67.

Tversky, A. 1972b. "Elimination by Aspects: A Theory of Choice." *Psychological Review* 79:281–99.

Valkonen, T. 1969. "Individual and Structural Effects in Ecological Research." In M. Dogan and S. Rokkan, eds., *Quantitative Ecological Analysis in the Social Sciences,* chap. 3. Cambridge, Mass.: MIT Press.

Valvanis, J. 1958. "The Resolution of Conflict When Utilities Interact." *Journal of Conflict Resolution* 2:156–69.

van den Berghe, P. L. 1967. *Race and Racism.* New York: Wiley.

van den Berghe, P. L. 1969. "Pluralism and the Polity: A Theoretical Exploration." In L. Kuper and M. G. Smith, eds., *Pluralism in Africa,* pp. 67–81. Berkeley: University of California Press.

Vander Zanden, J. W. 1972. *American Minority Relations.* 3d ed. New York: Ronald.

Veblen, T. 1912. *The Theory of the Leisure Class.* New York: Macmillan.

Vinokur, A. 1971a. "Cognitive and Affective Processes Influencing Risk Taking in Groups: An Expected Utility Approach." *Journal of Personality and Social Psychology* 20:472–86.

Vinokur, A. 1971b. "Review and Theoretical Analysis of the Effects of Group Processes upon Individual and Group Decisions Involving Risk." *Psychological Bulletin* 76:231–50.

Vlek, C. A. 1970. "Learning Probabilities of Events: An Analysis of the Problem and Its Relevance for the Study of Decision Making." *Acta Psychologica* 34:160–71.

von Neumann, J., and O. Morgenstern. 1944. *Theory of Games and Economic Behavior.* Princeton, N.J.: Princeton University Press.

Vroom, V. H. 1964. *Work and Motivation.* New York: Wiley.

Walster, E., and G. W. Walster. 1975. "Equity and Social Justice." *Journal of Social Issues* 31:21–43.

Walster, E., E. Berscheid, and G. W. Walster. 1973. "New Directions in Equity Research." *Journal of Personality and Social Psychology* 25:151–76.

Walster, E., T. A. Cleary, and M. M. Clifford. 1971. "The Effect of Race and Sex on College Admission." *Sociology of Education* 44:237–44.

Walster, E., G. W. Walster, and E. Berscheid. 1978. *Equity: Theory and Research.* Boston: Allyn & Bacon.

Weaver, R. C. 1948. *The Negro Ghetto.* New York: Harcourt, Brace.

Weber, M. 1947. *The Theory of Social and Economic Organization.* New York: Oxford University Press.

Weick, K. E., and B. Nesset. 1968. "Preferences among Forms of Equity." *Organizational Behavior and Human Performance* 3:400–16.

Welch, F. 1967. "Labor-market Discrimination: An Interpretation of Income Differences in the Rural South." *Journal of Political Economy* 75:225–40.

Wendt, D. 1970. "Utility and Risk." *Acta Psychologica* 34:214–28.

White, H. C. 1970. *Chains of Opportunity.* Cambridge, Mass.: Harvard University Press.

Wilken, P. H., and H. M. Blalock. 1979. "The Generalizability of Indirect Measures to Complex Situations: A Fundamental Dilemma." Unpublished paper.

Willhelm, S. M. 1971. *Who Needs the Negro?* Garden City, N.Y.: Anchor Books.

Williams, J. 1948. "Another Commentary on So-called Segregation Indices." *American Sociological Review* 13:298–303.

Williams, R. M. 1960. *American Society*. New York: Knopf.

Williams, R. M. 1964. *Strangers Next Door*. Englewood Cliffs, N.J.: Prentice-Hall.

Wilson, W. J. 1973. *Power, Racism, and Privilege*. New York: Macmillan.

Winship, C. 1978. "The Desirability of Using the Index of Dissimilarity or Any Adjustment of It for Measuring Segregation." *Social Forces* 57:717–20.

Wirth, L. 1928. *The Ghetto*. Chicago: University of Chicago Press.

Wise, J. A. 1970. "Estimates and Scaled Judgments of Subjective Probabilities." *Organizational Behavior and Human Performance* 5:85–92.

Wise, J. A., and W. P. Mockovak. 1973. "Descriptive Modeling of Subjective Probabilities." *Organizational Behavior and Human Performance* 9:292–306.

Wohlstetter, A., and S. Coleman. 1972. "Race Differences in Income." In A. H. Pascal, ed., *Racial Discrimination in Economic Life*, pp. 3–81. Lexington, Mass.: Heath.

Woofter, T. J. 1928. *Negro Problems in Cities*. Garden City, N.Y.: Doubleday.

Wyer, R. S. 1970. "Quantitative Prediction of Belief and Opinion Change: A Further Test of a Subjective Probability Model." *Journal of Personality and Social Psychology* 16:559–70.

Wyer, R. S., and L. Goldberg. 1970. "A Probabilistic Analysis of the Relationships among Beliefs and Attitudes." *Psychological Review* 77:100–120.

Yinger, J. M. 1965. *A Minority Group in American Society*. New York: McGraw-Hill.

Yinger, J. M. 1968. "Social Discrimination." In D. L. Sills, ed., *International Encyclopedia of the Social Sciences*, vol. 12, pp. 448–51. New York: Macmillan and Free Press.

Zelditch, M., J. Berger, B. Anderson, and B. Cohen. 1970. "Equitable Comparisons." *Pacific Sociological Review* 13:19–26.

NAME INDEX

Aberle, D., 605, 614
Abrahamsson, B., 176, 614
Abramson, E., 386, 396, 403, 614
Adams, J. S., 179, 225, 226, 227, 228,
   230, 237, 239, 250, 252, 253, 257,
   261, 262, 270, 614
Alexander, C. N., 23n, 253, 275, 286n,
   295, 614, 616
Alexander, K. L., 614
Alker, H. L., 295, 614
Allen, V. L., 454, 616
Allport, G. W., 428, 517, 614
Anderson, B., 223, 227, 257, 258, 272,
   283n, 614, 615, 629
Andrews, J. M., 32, 76n, 113, 626
Antonovsky, A., 426, 614
Armer, J. M., 295, 626
Arrow, K., 172n, 615
Atkinson, J. W., 29, 36, 134, 615
Austin, W., 283n, 615

Bachman, J. G., 23n, 295, 627
Bachrach, P., 352, 360n, 615
Banfield, E., 457, 615
Baratz, M. S., 352, 360n, 615
Barclay, S., 111, 113, 615
Bar-Hillel, M., 112, 113, 615
Barth, E. A. T., 551, 622
Baumol, W. J., 613n, 615
Beach, L. R., 111, 112, 113, 114, 121n,
   615, 621, 624
Becker, G. B., 32, 59, 165, 615
Becker, S. W., 50, 615
Bell, W., 526, 615
Benedict, R., 206, 615
Berger, J., 223, 227, 228, 284n, 614,
   615, 629

Berger, P., 109, 615
Berscheid, E., 224, 231, 271, 615, 628
Bezembinder, T. G., 73, 617
Biglan, A., 165, 172n, 623
Birch, D., 29, 36, 134, 615
Blalock, H. M., 6, 23n, 77n, 297, 323n,
   324, 328, 389, 395, 410n, 479, 510,
   544n, 577, 613n, 615, 629
Blau, P. M., 23n, 128, 175, 176, 183,
   194, 201, 225, 226, 228, 242, 243,
   275, 295, 296, 297, 302, 348, 358,
   368, 616
Blinder, A. S., 455, 616
Blumstein, P. W., 118, 121n, 257, 268,
   616
Bogardus, E., 550, 616
Bonacich, E., 543n, 565, 616
Boudon, R., 295, 296, 616
Boulding, K., 176, 616
Bourne, L. E., 111, 624
Boyanowsky, E. O., 454, 616
Boye, D., 271, 615
Brim, O. G., 118, 119, 616
Brown, R., 430, 514n, 616
Buckley, W., 602, 605, 616
Burgess, R. L., 242, 254, 255, 256, 274,
   616
Burkey, R. M., 427, 616

Cameron, P., 172n, 616
Campbell, E. Q., 23n, 295, 614, 616
Campos, F., 171n, 623
Cannon, W. B., 605, 616
Caplow, T., 395, 616
Cartwright, D., 345, 616
Clairmont, D. H., 43, 72
Clark, T. N., 346, 357, 617

630

Cleary, T. A., 458, 628
Clifford, M. M., 458, 628
Cobbs, P. M., 563, 620
Cohen, A., 605, 614
Cohen, B., 223, 227, 614, 615, 629
Cohen, J. K., 544n, 617, 619
Coleman, J. S., 28, 346, 613n, 617
Coleman, S., 453, 629
Collins, M. E., 517, 618
Cook, K. S., 222, 224, 227, 229, 231,
    232, 236, 238, 243, 247, 248, 253,
    255, 261, 262, 284n, 285n, 617
Coombs, C. H., 68, 71, 73, 74, 75, 96,
    113, 114, 117, 151, 154, 164, 165,
    172n, 617
Cortese, C. F., 544n, 617, 619
Cowgill, D. O., 526, 527, 617
Cowgill, M. S., 526, 527, 617
Cutler, H., 386, 614
Cuzzort, R. P., 323n, 618

Dahl, R. A., 325, 360n, 617
Daniel, W. W., 454, 617
Darroch, A. G., 521, 617
Davidson, D., 32, 68, 69, 74, 112, 617
Davis, A., 605, 614
Davis, J. A., 23n, 295, 296, 297, 617
Dawes, R., 113, 114, 151, 165, 617
Dean, G. W., 112, 114, 620
Degler, C. N., 238, 617
De Leo, P. J., 165, 624
Deutsch, M., 243, 517, 618
DeVinney, L., 627
Doherty, M. E., 114, 622
Donnenworth, G. V., 284n, 618
Doyle, B. W., 552, 618
Duncan, B., 323n, 520, 526, 527, 618
Duncan, O. D., 323n, 520, 526, 527,
    618
Durkheim, E., 295, 618
Dworkin, A. G., 581, 586n, 620

Eckland, B. K., 614
Edwards, W. A., 32, 34, 68, 69, 73, 75,
    77n, 114, 116, 117, 133, 134, 136,
    137, 154, 171n, 618
Ehrlich, H., 517, 618
Einhorn, H. J., 77n, 618
Ekeh, P. P., 176, 618
Emerson, R. D., 175, 176, 182, 199,
    220n, 221n, 274, 275, 352, 360n,
    368, 387, 555, 618

Engerman, S. L., 203, 619
Etzioni, A., 349, 619
Eulau, H., 298, 619

Falk, R. F., 544n, 617, 619
Fanon, F., 563, 619
Farkas, G., 23n, 295, 619
Feldman, J., 165, 619
Ferguson, C. E., 75, 619
Firebaugh, G., 297, 619
Fishburn, P. C., 64, 619
Fogel, R. W., 203, 619
Ford, D., 111, 112, 121n, 619
Frazier, E. F., 596, 619
French, J. R. P., 346, 348, 349, 350,
    351, 357, 393, 619
Friedman, A., 243, 257, 259, 260, 263,
    264, 268, 269, 286n, 620
Furnivall, J. S., 518, 565, 619

Gaertner, S. L., 454, 619
Galanter, E., 72, 111, 112, 619
Gamson, W. A., 330, 346, 348, 349,
    395, 396, 619
Genovese, E. D., 286n, 619
Georgescu-Roegen, N., 77n, 620
Gergen, K., 224, 248, 620
Gilman, H., 455, 620
Gist, N. P., 581, 586n, 620
Glazer, N., 521, 620
Glenn, N. D., 419, 620
Goldberg, L., 111, 113, 114, 117, 118,
    629
Goode, F. M., 73, 617
Goodman, L. A., 544n, 620
Goodman, P. S., 243, 257, 259, 260,
    263, 264, 268, 269, 286n, 620
Gordon, L. K., 438, 625
Gordon, M. M., 521, 620
Gordon, R. A., 305, 620
Gouldner, A. W., 205, 224, 620
Graham, N., 172n, 623
Greeno, J. G., 75, 625
Grier, W. H., 563, 620
Guest, A. M., 521, 620
Gustafson, D., 111, 112, 121n, 619
Gwartney, J. D., 454, 455, 620

Halter, A. N., 112, 114, 620
Hamblin, R. L., 43, 72, 73, 74, 75, 469,
    620

Hannan, M. T., 10, 11, 23n, 290, 296, 323n, 544n, 620
Hanselman, W., 454, 627
Hauser, R. M., 23n, 292, 295, 299, 306, 620, 621
Hays, W. L., 78, 621
Heinrich, B. A., 112, 621
Hendon, W. S., 455, 621
Higbee, K. L., 172n, 621
Hitler, A., 167
Holmstrom, V. L., 111, 621
Homans, G., 128, 175, 222, 223, 225, 226, 227, 228, 233, 234, 236, 237, 242, 243, 244, 245, 248, 254, 264, 283n, 554, 605, 621
Hornseth, R., 526, 621
Howell, W. C., 112, 621
Huber, G., 111, 112, 121n, 619
Hurst, P. M., 68, 74, 75, 621
Huson, C., 23n, 295, 296, 297, 617

Irwin, L., 23n, 621

Jahn, J. A., 526, 621
Jiobu, R., 585n, 623
Johnson, C. A., 172n, 621
Johnson, C. S., 520, 621
Johnson, N. R., 454, 621
Johnston, W. B., 470, 622
Jones, E. E., 172n, 621
Jones, L. V., 172n, 625
Jones, M., 172n, 623

Kadushin, C., 324, 621
Kahan, J. P., 172n, 625
Kahn, R. L., 438, 625
Kain, J. F., 455, 621
Kantrowitz, N., 521, 621
Kardiner, A., 563, 621
Karon, B. P., 563, 622
Katzman, M. T., 455, 622
Kaufman, S., 72, 627
Kautz, R., 386, 614
Keeley, S. M., 114, 622
Kelley, H. H., 387, 393, 627
Kennedy, J. F., 449
Kennedy, R. J. R., 521, 623
King, A. T., 455, 622
Komorita, S. S., 68, 74, 617
Koopmans, T. C., 3, 622

Korpi, W., 254, 622
Krantz, D. H., 73, 622
Kruskal, W., 544n, 620
Kuhlman, D., 171n, 623
Kuper, H., 543n, 565, 622
Kuper, L., 565, 585n, 622

Lafferty, T., 172n, 621
Land, K. C., 613n, 622
Lane, I. M., 220n, 622
Langley, C. T., 551, 622
Lapham, V., 455, 622
Lawler, E. E., 284n, 622
Lazarsfeld, P., 295
Lee, W., 59, 71, 75, 111, 112, 113, 114, 115, 154, 172n, 622
Lenski, G. E., 586n, 622
Leventhal, G. S., 224, 229, 285n, 622
Levitan, S. A., 470, 622
Levy, M., 605, 614
Lewin, K., 164
Lichtenstein, S., 71, 121n, 137, 172n, 626
Lichtman, A. J., 23n, 621
Lieberson, S., 520, 521, 528, 544n, 623
Liebow, E., 201, 623
Lindman, H. R., 68
Long, J., 76, 77n, 96, 623
Luce, R. D., 32, 59, 71, 73, 75, 112, 113, 114, 115, 154, 165, 171n, 622, 623
Lupfer, M., 172n, 623

March, J. G., 325, 623
Marple, D. P., 454, 621
Marshall, H., 585n, 623
Marston, W. G., 521, 617
Marwell, G., 252, 626
Marx, K., 224, 225, 247, 285n
Maslow, A. H., 44, 623
Mason, P., 23, 623
Mauss, M., 206, 623
McCaffree, K. M., 454, 620
McCauley, C., 172n, 623
McClelland, D. C., 49, 109, 134, 623
McClintock, C., 32, 59, 165, 171n, 615, 623
McDill, E. L., 294, 625
Mead, G. H., 185
Meeker, B. F., 153, 154, 171n, 220n, 623
Mendelson, M., 386, 614

Merton, R. K., 440, 602, 623
Messe, L. A., 220n, 622
Messick, D. M., 86, 113, 171n, 623
Mieszkowski, P., 455, 622
Miller, A. J., 111, 624
Miller, G. A., 59, 623
Mitchell, G. D., 429, 623
Mitchell, T. R., 165, 172n, 623, 624
Mockovak, W. P., 112, 117, 629
Molotch, H., 546, 624
Moore, B., 225, 624
Morgan, W. R., 284n, 624
Morgenstern, O., 67, 74, 628
Mosteller, F., 67, 68, 624
Moynihan, D. P., 521, 620
Myers, J. L., 172n, 616
Myrdal, G., 406, 408, 448, 557, 596, 608, 624

Nagel, J. H., 325, 624
Nebeker, D. M., 165, 624
Nesset, B., 256, 284n, 285n, 628
Newman, W. M., 529, 624
Nielsen, J. M., 242, 254, 255, 256, 264, 274, 616, 624
Nikolinakos, M., 224, 624
Nixon, R. M., 110
Nogee, P., 67, 68, 624

Ofshe, L., 71, 154, 624
Ofshe, R., 71, 154, 624
O'Neill, D. M., 454, 624
Ovesey, L., 563, 621

Parcel, T. L., 222, 231, 232, 236, 238, 243, 247, 284n, 617
Pareto, V., 75
Parsons, T., 23n, 242, 549, 624
Pascal, A. H., 426, 624
Patchen, M., 236
Payne, J. W., 137, 154, 624
Pepitone, A., 220n, 261, 624
Peterson, C. R., 111, 113, 114, 624
Phillips, L. D., 109, 112, 121n, 615, 624
Pritchard, R. D., 165, 234, 262, 263, 284n, 624, 625
Pruitt, D. G., 71, 154, 172n, 617, 625
Prysby, C. L., 295, 625
Przeworski, A., 23n, 295, 296, 305, 625

Quigley, J. M., 455, 621
Quinn, R. P., 438, 625

Rapoport, Amnon, 73, 164, 171n, 172n, 625
Rapoport, Anatol, 224, 625
Rapping, L. A., 426, 624
Rasmussen, D. W., 455, 625
Raven, B., 346, 348, 349, 350, 351, 357, 393, 619
Reich, M., 419, 625
Restle, F., 75, 625
Richardson, L. F., 366, 370, 392, 625
Rigsby, L. C., 294, 625
Rokeach, M., 34, 625
Roosevelt, F. D., 449
Royden, H. L., 154, 625
Ryan, W., 271, 625

Samuelson, P. A., 589, 625
Sanders, M. S., 165, 625
Sawyer, J., 284n, 624
Schermerhorn, R. A., 23, 330, 625
Schiller, B. R., 455, 626
Schmid, C. F., 621
Schmitt, D. R., 252, 626
Schrag, C., 621
Schuman, H., 271, 626
Sewell, W. H., 295, 626
Shapiro, E. G., 284n, 626
Shapley, L., 325, 626
Shinn, A. M., 58, 72, 626
Shubik, M., 325, 626
Siegel, A. E., 32, 76n, 113, 626
Siegel, S., 32, 50, 68, 69, 71, 74, 75, 76n, 112, 113, 154, 615, 617, 621, 626
Simmel, G., 395, 626
Simon, H. A., 149, 613n, 626
Simon, J. L., 172n, 626
Simpson, G. P., 550, 626
Simpson, R. L., 128, 221n, 253, 275, 285n, 286n, 614, 626
Slovic, P., 71, 121n, 137, 172n, 626
Smith, M. G., 518, 565, 585n, 622, 627
Spaeth, J. L., 23n, 295, 296, 297, 617
Sprague, J., 295, 296, 627
Stack, C., 183, 184, 195, 200, 201, 627
Starr, S. A., 627
Stevens, S. S., 43, 71, 72, 73, 74, 75, 172n, 483n, 627

Stilson, D. W., 111, 624
Stinchcombe, A. L., 147, 585n, 592,
    593, 594, 603, 627
Stonequist, E. V., 586n, 627
Stouffer, E. A., 295, 478, 627
Strauss, A., 22, 627
Sturdivant, F., 454, 627
Suchman, E. A., 627
Suppes, P., 32, 59, 68, 69, 71, 73, 74, 75,
    90, 112, 113, 114, 115, 154, 165,
    171n, 617, 622, 623, 625, 627
Sutton, F., 605, 614
Szymanski, A., 419, 585n, 627

Tabor, J. M., 438, 625
Taeuber, A. F., 520, 527, 528, 544n, 627
Taeuber, K. E., 520, 527, 528, 544n, 627
Taggart, R., 470, 622
Tannenbaum, A. S., 23n, 295, 627
Taylor, M., 77n, 627
Terhune, K. W., 72, 627
Thibaut, J. W., 387, 393, 627
Thomas, K., 265, 627
Törnblom, K., 284n, 285n, 618, 627
Tversky, A., 64, 71, 73, 113, 114, 115,
    116, 117, 136, 151, 154, 164, 165,
    617, 622, 627, 628

Ulehla, L. J., 111, 624

Valkonen, T., 23n, 295, 296, 323n, 628
Valvanis, J., 220, 628
van den Berghe, P. L., 23, 518, 521,
    543n, 565, 628
Vander Zanden, J. W., 420, 628
Veblen, T., 51, 628
Vinokur, A., 172n, 628
Vlek, C. A., 116, 628

von Neumann, J., 67, 74, 628
Vroom, V. H., 172n, 628

Wallster, T. S., 73, 164, 171n, 172n, 625
Walsh, K., 154, 625
Walster, E., 224, 231, 233, 234, 239,
    248, 253, 254, 257, 258, 261, 262,
    264, 265, 266, 267, 268, 269, 270,
    271, 272, 283n, 284n, 285n, 286n,
    458, 615, 628
Walster, G. W., 224, 231, 262, 284n,
    285n, 628
Weaver, R. C., 520, 628
Weber, M., 350, 628
Weed, J. A., 521, 620
Weick, K. E., 256, 284n, 285n, 628
Weinstein, E. A., 257, 268, 616
Welch, F., 455, 628
Wendt, D., 172n, 628
White, H. C., 514n, 628
Wilken, P. H., 6, 76, 77n, 96, 623, 629
Willhelm, S. M., 316, 629
Williams, J., 526, 629
Williams, R. M., 34, 518, 627, 629
Wilson, W. J., 406, 449, 585n, 629
Winkler, R. L., 78, 621
Winship, C., 544n, 629
Winter, D. G., 49, 623
Wirth, L., 520, 629
Wise, J. A., 111, 112, 117, 121n, 615,
    629
Wohlstetter, A., 453, 629
Woofter, T. J., 520, 629
Wyer, R. S., 111, 113, 114, 117, 118,
    629

Yinger, J. M., 430, 431, 550, 626, 629

Zelditch, M., 223, 227, 284n, 614, 615,
    629

SUBJECT INDEX

Achievement, 225, 242
Achievement motivation, 49–50, 109, 134
Action alternatives
    adequacy of, 266
    availability of, 199, 201–202, 217
    compatibility of, 130–31, 133
    selection of, 139–48, 157–58, 161–62, 167, 216; *see also* Choice behavior
    sequencing of, 139, 146–47, 157
Aggregation, 10–12, 167, 175, 214, 290, 307–308, 502, 601
Aggression, 171n, 204, 370–71, 376, 563
Allocation processes, 413–50, 502–12; *see also* Discrimination; Selection criteria
Allocators, 169, 416–18, 437–42
Alternative-outcome matrix, 144–46, 150, 157, 160, 162
Altruism, 153, 155, 196–97, 220n
Ambiguous situations, 518, 563–64, 575, 581
Ambivalence, 363, 368
Anger, 226, 253–55, 262, 278
Anticipated energy exertion, 126, 139, 161
Anti-Semitism, 439
Apartheid, 427
Apathy, 363
Apologies, 268
Applicants, 416–17, 419
Approach, 515, 524
Armaments races, 394
Ascription, 225–26, 242–43
Aspirations, 49–51, 54, 140, 149–50, 162, 183, 186; *see also* Goal fulfill-ment, desired level of

Association relations, 227–28, 231
Attachment, to neighborhood, 594–95, 599
Attribution of merit, 261
Authority, 348–50; *see also* Power; Resources
Avoidance behaviors, 170, 516, 523–24

Bayesian probabilities, 111, 114
"Beetle Bailey" phenomenon, 258, 285n, 286n
Behavior; *see also* Choice behavior; Macro-level theories; Micro-level theory of behavior
    anticipation of consequences of, 30
    causal process theories of, 28–30
    extinction of, 84
    innovations in, 30
    intensity of, 28, 123–27, 133, 142, 144, 146–47, 162, 164, 168, 256–57, 269, 286n
    operant theories of, 81–82, 142, 176, 210–11
    persistence of, 28, 163–64
    purposive action theories of, 28–29, 31–32
Bernoulli paradox, 34
Bias: *see* Allocations; Measurement errors; Discrimination, measure-ment of
Block data, census, 528–35
Boundaries, of groups, 9–10, 166, 541
    and contextual effects, 307–308
    in power contests, 335–39
    and segregation indices, 526–33
Boundaries, of pools, 487, 491, 493–96

Caste, 204
Categorization, errors in, 457–58
Causal chains, 101–102
Causal models, 29, 89; *see also* Working
    theories
Centrality index, 527
Change: *see* Dynamic theories
Change in expected support from others,
    87–88, 162
Choice behavior, 28, 162–63
    inconsistency of, 165, 172n
    simplification of, 31, 202
    transitivity of, 75, 100, 165, 172n
Civil disorders, 118
Civil rights movement, 442–43
Clarity of the situation, 435–36, 443; *see
    also* Ambiguous situations
Coalitions, 327, 359, 364, 394–96, 406–
    407, 436, 448, 468n, 508
Cognitive consistency, 121n
Collectivities, 166
Collinearity, 305, 466, 480
Colonialism, 449
Combined effects, 91, 94–95, 189–91
Commitments, 184, 195, 201–202, 212–
    13, 217, 396–97, 403
Communication, 31, 186, 285n
Communism, 285n
Community power, 362; *see also* Power
Comparisons, relative versus absolute,
    478–83
Competition, 154, 171n, 220n, 511–12,
    550
Competitive race relations, 518n
Compliance, 177, 208
Conditional probabilities, 90–91, 95–97,
    99, 115, 118, 220n
Conflict, 176–78, 254, 315, 326–27,
    365, 368, 370–71, 393–94, 413,
    553–56, 558, 561–62
    regulation of, 366
Conformity, 310–16
Conjoint measurement, 73, 117
Consistency, 390–91
Consistency criterion, 10, 290
Conspicuous consumption, 51, 270
Constant utility models, 165
Constraints, on means, 397–405
Contacts: *see* Interactions, social
Contextual effects, 2, 180, 198–204, 290
    causal mechanisms for, 298–306
    of inequalities, 316–22
    involving deviancy effects, 297–98
    involving group means, 295–96

involving homogeneity measures, 297
involving multiple groups, 298, 306–
    16, 479–83
    models of, 292–98
Control, 332, 346; *see also* Power,
    centralization of
Control variables, in measurement of
    discrimination, 452–67
Cooperation, 171n, 179, 220n
Coping strategies, 256
Costs; *see also* Utility, negative
    of contacts, 552–55
    and equity/distributive justice, 225–
    26, 239–42, 244–49, 251–53, 256–
    60, 266, 269–71
    extrinsic, 554–55, 560
    flexibility of movement, 579–80, 598
    functions for, 566–72, 575–85
    intrinsic, 552–53
    and means, 387
    of segregation, 596–98
    in subjective expected utility model,
        126–33, 137, 151, 155, 161; *see
        also* Utility, negative
Cross-group interactions, 536–41, 546–
    65, 595–97
Cross-modality matching, 75
Cross-pressures, 440–42
Cue similarity, degree of, 86–88, 162,
    187
Cues, 87, 142, 147, 160, 163, 187–88

Decay curves, 84–85
Deception, 183, 389–90; *see also*
    Secrecy
Decision strategies, 123–24, 144, 147–
    57, 180, 184; *see also* Satisficing;
    Subjective expected utility,
    maximization of
    choice of, 151, 155–57, 161
    in exchange, 153–54, 196–98, 202,
        205, 216–17, 220
Deference behaviors, 525, 552; *see also*
    Regulating behaviors
Deferred gratification, 52–53, 152, 184,
    200
Deferred reciprocation, 184
Degree of mobilization: *see* Mobilization,
    of resources
Dependence, 131, 169–70, 387–88, 417
    on contact, 555–56, 559–60, 572–75
    and equity/distributive justice, 223,
        231, 259, 274–75
    in exchange, 180, 198–99, 201–203,

206–10, 212–17, 220n, 221n
  mutual, 552
Deprivation: *see* Utility deprivation
Detachability, of resources, 356
Deviancy effects, 297–98, 310–16
Differences, versus ratios, 467–71, 538
Differential treatment, 419–20, 425–26
Diffuseness of contacts, 549
Dilemmas, of weak parties, 405–408
Diminishing returns, 126, 164, 183; *see
    also* Satiation
Direct effects, 90–96, 101, 121n, 188–89
Disappointment, 226, 228
Disapproval, 286n
Discount rate, of utilities, 52–55, 200,
    321–22
Discrimination, 169–70, 224, 230, 418–
    50
  in business, 438–39
  compromise conceptualization of,
    432–34
  criterion of, 420–27
  double-standard, 425
  existing conceptualizations of, 419–32
  intentionality of, 429, 443
  legitimacy of, 169, 433–50
  likelihood of, 434, 440–41
  measurement of, 419, 429–32, 434–
    35, 451–67, 485–96, 499
  perception of, 443, 445, 449–50
  rank order of, 408
  responses to, 427, 435–37, 442–50
  responses of third parties to, 414, 435–
    36, 438, 442, 448–50
  and selection criteria, 496–512
  types of, 433–34
  utility of, 434, 438, 440–42
  vicious circle of, 418–19
Dissimilar others, 234–35, 237, 241
Distribution rules
  and discrimination, 416, 420, 433–34,
    443
  and equity/distributive justice, 224,
    229, 242–47, 285n
  legitimacy of, 224, 242–44, 285n,
    433–34
Distributive justice, 176; *see also* Equity/
    Distributive justice; Rule of distribu-
    tive justice
Divisibility, of resources, 355–56
Dogmatism, 109
Domains, 182
Dominance, 332, 371–72, 387, 518; *see
    also* Power

Dual institutions, 570, 596–97
"Dull thud" phenomenon, 256, 285n,
    286n
Duplication, of institutions, 570, 596–97
Duration of contacts, 548
Dynamic theories, 20, 340
  of conformity, 310–16
  of segregation, 591–613

Ecological fallacy, 11; *see also*
    Aggregation
Education, 119, 270–71
Efficacy, 78–79, 109, 398; *see also*
    Fatalism
Efficiency, power, 344, 373
  and constraints on means, 397–405
  measurement of, 328
Eligibility pools: *see* Pools, eligibility
Elimination by aspects, 64–65
Emotional identification, 185–86, 217
Energy exertion, 125–27, 131; *see also*
    Anticipated energy exertion;
    Resources, expenditure of
Equal-status contacts, 549–50, 552,
    559–60
Equality, 220n; *see also* Inequalities
Equilibrium, 589, 604–12
  in deviancy models, 311–12
Equity, 71, 153, 169, 176, 179, 478,
    509; *see also* Equity/distributive
    justice
  anticipated, 277
Equity concern, 231
Equity goals, 251, 253–54, 262, 264–67,
    275–77, 285n
Equity theory, 222, 225–27, 233, 237,
    245–46, 251, 284n, 448
Equity with the World, 283n
Equity/distributive justice, 222–87, 431
  components of a theory of, 231–50
  current approaches to, 225–30
  experimental studies of, 240, 286n
  framework for a theory of, 228–31,
    279–83
  relationship of, to other concepts, 223–
    25˙
Equity/distributive justice judgments,
    222, 225, 227, 282, 417–20
  basic variables for characterizing, 230–
    31
  basis of, 230, 232–36, 275–76
  characteristics of, 228–29
  conditions under which they are made,
    231–32

Equity/distributive justice (*continued*)
  criteria of, 230, 236–42
  macro-level, 283
  standard of, 230, 242–47
Esteem, 257, 268
Ethnic groups, 273–74
Etiquette, 525, 552; *see also* Regulating
  behaviors
Exchange, 168–69, 175–221
  balanced, 221n
  direct, 178–82, 188–89, 224, 226,
    228, 230–34, 236, 250, 254, 257
  economic, 175–76, 183
  and equity/distributive justice, 222–
    23, 274–75
  fair rate of, 226, 228, 243
  going rate of, 226, 228
  indirect, 169, 179, 189, 224, 228,
    230–31, 233–35, 254, 417–19
  influence of third parties on, 217
  initiation of, 206–208, 215–16, 275
  macro-level, 175, 177, 214–16, 223,
    283
  maintenance/termination of, 211–16,
    223, 259, 261, 272, 275
  mediated, 179–80, 188, 254
  model of, 216–20
  nature of, 176–80
  and power, 169–70, 175–78, 203, 208,
    214–16, 220n, 413–16
  primacy of, 182, 185, 217, 238–39
  primary, 182–84, 193, 269
  reciprocation in, 207, 209–11, 215–16
  regularization of, 185–86, 188, 193–
    95, 211–13, 215, 217, 231, 235,
    238
  secondary, 182
  terms of, 183
  timing of, 183
  type of, 230, 233–34
Exchange networks, 176, 179–80
Exchange rates, 34
Exchange theory, 128, 222, 225, 228,
  232
Exogenous variables, 19–20
Expectancy, 165
Expectancy theory: *see* Instrumentality
  theory
Expectations, 140–42, 144, 146, 148,
  163, 187, 378–82; *see also*
  Subjective probabilities
Expected utility model, 164
Expected value model, 164
Expected values, 562

Expert power, 351
Expertise, 385
Explicit pools, 486; *see also* Pools,
  eligibility
Exploitation, 153–54, 216, 224–25, 244,
  364, 478
Exposure, 540–41

Family patterns, 183–84, 200–201, 205
Fatalism, 79, 109, 201, 377
Fatigue, 366, 394
Fear, 575–76
Feedbacks, 116, 161–62, 592; *see also*
  Dynamic theories
Field theory, 164
Flexibility of movements, 579–80, 598
Formal organizations, 149, 151
Frequency of contacts, 547, 559–60
Frequency distributions, 78, 145
Friendship, 200–201, 204
Functional explanations, 592, 601–608

Gambles, 67–68, 70, 111, 117, 136–38
  variance of, 71, 136, 171n
Game theory, 171n
Gate keepers, 416, 577
Generalizability of resources, 357
Generalized other, 185, 227–28, 232,
  234–37, 241–42
Gift giving, 206
Gini index, 526
Goal conflict, and discrimination, 427–
  29, 444
Goal decomposition rate, 47–49, 54,
  141, 183, 186
Goal fulfillment, 128–29, 231–32, 239,
  253
  current level of, 38, 45–52, 54, 85,
    140, 148, 157, 160–61, 164, 168,
    183, 200, 217
  degree of, 37–41, 43, 45, 53–54, 59,
    62, 66, 125, 145–46, 159–60, 164,
    171n, 182–83, 200, 217
  desired level of, 38, 46, 48–55, 140,
    149, 157, 160, 162, 168, 183, 200,
    204, 213, 217, 266
  expected degree of, 145–46
  immediacy of, 38, 52–55, 66, 160,
    183–84, 200, 217
Goal fulfillment deprivation gap, 140–
  44, 157, 161–63, 167, 172n, 200,
  217
Goal hierarchies, 44–45, 54, 141, 156,
  167, 211

Goal importance, 38, 41–46, 53–54, 62, 134, 140–42, 150, 156–57, 160, 182, 185–86, 200, 204, 213–14, 217
Goal-objects, 227
Goal-seeking behavior, 29–30, 35, 167
Goals, 16–17, 35–37, 182, 414
  of allocators, 429, 496–503
  biological, 44, 141
  consummatory, 36, 239, 251, 254
  of groups, 167, 496
  incompatibilities among, 374
  instrumental, 36; *see also* Means
  and power, 330–32, 366–74
  social, 44, 141
  status, 239, 251, 254
  versus means, 332, 497–98
  versus outcomes, 361–64
Grievance terms, 370; *see also* Armaments races
Groups, 166–68, 175; *see also* Boundaries, of groups
Group-gain, 154, 220n
Guerrilla warfare, 369
Guilt, 262–63, 265–66, 268, 270–71, 278–79, 448

Hierarchical pools, 488–91; *see also* Pools, eligibility
Historicist explanations, 591–94, 604
  of segregation, 594–601
Homeostasis, 604–605, 608
Homogeneity, 15
  assumptions of, 288
  and contextual effects, 297, 305
  of pools, 495–96
  two kinds of, 11–12
Hope, 285n
Housing, integrated, 517–18

Identification problems, 3, 461, 479–83
Identity, 260, 271
Ideologies, 65–66, 108–110, 155, 167–68, 247
  and power, 374–78, 401
  and reward and cost functions, 570–72
  simplicity of, 375
Ignorance, 575–76
Incentive value of success, 134, 473–76
Independence of utilities and subjective probabilities, 69–70, 85, 113, 123, 133–36
Index of dissimilarity, 477, 520, 526–27
Indifference, 363, 368

Indifference curves, 126
Indifference levels, 609–12
Indifference-point strategy, 67–68, 111
Indirect effects, 90–96, 100–104, 121n, 188–89, 191–93
Indispensability, of resources, 357–58
Individualism, 171n
Inelasticity, 77n
Inequalities, 216, 242, 431–32, 443, 596
  and contextual effects, 316–22
  as independent variables, 471–78
  measurement of, 467–71, 475, 502, 527
  and measurement of discrimination, 451–67
Inequity, 169, 222–24, 235, 278–79; *see also* Subjective expected inequity
  behavioral responses to, 226, 228–29, 231, 250–53, 256–61, 267–72, 278–79, 282–83
  cognitive responses to, 250–53, 256–61, 267–72
  collective, 223, 228
  compensation for, 265–68, 270, 272–73
  congruence of perceptions of, 236, 248–49, 272–74
  consequences of, 227, 250–53
  cost, 248
  degree of, 230–31, 235, 249, 251–52, 254–55, 262, 276, 278
  derogation of victims of, 271
  direction of, 230, 240
  emotional responses to, 226, 229, 231, 250, 253–56, 262–67, 278–79, 282
  intentionality of, 254, 262, 267–68
  investment, 248
  justification of, 265–72
  negative, 230, 236, 248–49, 253–55, 257, 274, 276–78
  positive, 230, 248–49, 253, 274, 276–78
  reduction of, 251–52, 256, 261–65, 274, 285n
  responses of beneficiaries of, 226, 251–53, 257–60, 262–72, 274–75, 286n, 287n, 447
  responses of third parties to, 244, 259, 261, 272
  responses of victims of, 226, 251–62, 274–75
  responsibility for, 254, 257, 259, 262, 267–68, 273, 278–79
  restitution for, 258

Inequity (*continued*)
  retaliation for, 256–58, 263, 265–68,
    270, 272, 285n, 286n
  reward, 247–48
  source of, 230, 257–58, 283n
  total, 248
  types of, 230, 247–48, 278, 285n
Inflation, of subjective probabilities, 84,
    115
  of utilities, 53
  of value of investments, 271
Information, 203, 238; *see also*
    Knowledge; Secrecy
Information integration theory, 172n
Information processing approach, 137
Injustice: *see* Inequity
Input/outcome ratio, 226–27, 232, 237,
    284n, 285n, 448
Inputs, 169, 222, 224, 228, 234–36,
    238–40, 242–44, 246, 250, 253,
    258, 284n, 448
Instrumentality, 165, 172n
Instrumentality theory, 164–65
Insulation, 522–23, 553
Integration, 515, 525, 564
  measurement of, 535–41
  versus segregation, 533–35
Interactions, social, 515, 521, 528; *see
    also* Integration
  cross-group, 536–41, 546–65, 595–97
  equal-status, 533, 536–37, 549–50
  intimate, 536, 548–50
Interchangeability, of resources, 356–57
Interdependence, 177; *see also*
    Dependence
Intergroup relations, 175, 178, 214–16,
    223
Internal states, 29, 31–32, 143, 215
Interval scales, 74–75, 116–17
Intimacy of contacts, 548–50, 552, 556,
    558, 561–63, 581–85
Investments, 225–26, 236–37, 240–42,
    244–49, 251–52, 256, 260–61,
    271–72, 287n
Irreducibility of wants, 77n
Isolation, 522–23, 570

Jews, 438–39
Job security, 269

Knowledge, 110, 201, 210, 253, 261,
    381–85, 402

Labor theory of value, 225
Laboratory research, 31–32, 59, 67–70,
    112–13, 220n, 250–52
Lags, 466; *see also* Time; Dynamic
    theories
Latent functions, 602, 604
Leadership, 344
Learning, 30, 80, 82
Legitimacy, 465
  of contacts, 551, 554, 560–61
  of discrimination, 169, 433–50
  of distribution rules, 224, 242–44,
    285n, 433–34
  of investments, 242
Legitimate power, 348–50, 393
Lexicographic ordering, 64
Life chances, 471, 476–78
Liking, 257, 268, 279
Local comparisons, 227, 233

Macro-level theories, 27, 36
Magnitude estimation techniques, 72,
    74–76
Manifest functions, 602, 604
Marginal men, 581–82
Marginal subjective probability, 93
Marginal utility, 38–42, 45–46, 49, 54–
    55, 85, 125, 134, 140, 148, 159–60,
    200
Marriage, 202–204, 213–14, 235
Martyr response, 258–59
Means
  alternative, 385–97
  consensus on, 401–402
  constraints among, 386–87, 397–405
  and discrimination, 497
  offensive versus defensive, 396–97
  versus goals, 332, 497–98
Measurement
  conjoint, 73, 117
  of discrimination, 451–67
  of inequalities, 467–71, 527
  of integration, 535–41
  of outcomes, 364
  of power, 324–25, 328, 352–54
  precision of, 5
  of segregation, 516, 520, 525–35
  of subjective probabilities, 110–17,
    136
  of utilities, 36, 67–76, 111, 136
Measurement errors, 4, 20, 290, 528; *see
    also* Measurement; Categorization

and contextual effects, 305–306
and inequalities, 468–71, 480
Micro-level theory of behavior, 27, 32,
  164–65, 175
  assumptions of, 29–32
  general model of, 157–64
  goals for a, 28–29, 162–64
  relationship of, to macro-level theories,
    27–28, 166–68
Middleman minorities, 519n, 581
Missing variables: *see* Measurement
  errors
Mixed-blood minorities, 580–81
Mobilization, of resources, 343, 355,
  373, 388, 407–408
Moral indignation, 226, 228, 418
Motivation, 81, 134, 154, 165, 250
  and inequalities, 473–76
Multicollinearity, 305, 466, 480
Multidimensional scaling, 112, 117
Multistage decision-making models,
  172n

Neèd achievement, 49–50, 109, 134
Needs, 47, 183
Negative cause, 90
"Negative" probability, 139
Negative sanctions, 583; *see also*
  Punishing behaviors
Nested groups, 295, 298, 306–16, 479–
  83, 487–88, 526
Nonactions, 121n, 130
Nondiscrimination model, 421–22
Nonutilitarian preferences, 396
Normative conflict, 429–30
Norm of equity/distributive justice, 204–
  206, 226, 242–43, 253, 414, 417–
  18
Norm of reciprocity, 205–206, 210, 221n
Norms, 223
  and contextual effects, 300–303, 310–
  16
  and discrimination, 414, 429–30, 437,
  440–41, 444
  in exchange, 180, 195–96, 199, 204–
  206, 212, 217, 220, 221n, 414

Objective probabilities, 35, 68–69, 80,
  83, 112–15, 134–36, 346–47
Objective properties: *see also* Resources
  conversion into resources, 345, 352–
  54

Obligation, 184
Observability, 382–85
Ordered-metric scales, 68, 74–76, 96
Ordinal scales, 75–76
Organizational goals, 496–97
Outcome/goal matrix, 145–46, 150, 157,
  162
Outcome/input ratio: *see* Input/outcome
  ratio
Outcomes, 16–17, 169, 222–24, 226–
  28, 234–36, 238, 240, 242, 244,
  251, 253, 258, 284n, 415
  allocation of, 179, 253, 415–34, 444–
  45
  compatibility of, 104–106
  consistency of, 83–84, 86, 187
  multidimensional, 56–57, 60–64, 361–
  64
  multiple, 104–106, 133
  patterning of, 83–84, 113, 160
  perceived limits on, 88, 134, 160, 162,
  188
  randomness of, 83–84
  recency of, 84–86, 134, 187
  simultaneity of, 104–106
  versus goals, 361–64
  versus outputs, 398
Outputs, 398

Paired comparisons, 96
Parties: *see also* Boundaries, of groups
  identification of, 15–16, 335–39
Paternalism, 270, 337
Paternalistic race relations, 518n
Pattern variables, 242
Patterned evasions, 437
Perceptions, 378–82
  of efficacy, 78–79, 109
  of inequalities, 473–76, 483
Performance characteristics, 510–12
Performance demands, 500–501
Performance rights, 414
Persuading behaviors, 347–48
Pluralism, cultural, 518–19, 565
Pools, eligibility, 468, 502
  boundaries of, 487, 491, 493–96
  explicit, 486
  hierarchical, 488–91
  potential, 486–87, 496
  qualified, 486, 488, 496
  sequential, 490–93
Positive cause, 90

"Positive" probability, 139
Potential pools, 486–87, 496; *see also*
    Pools, eligibility
Power, 131, 168; *see also* Compliance
    and allocation processes, 417–18
    and discrimination, 418–19, 436, 445,
        447, 449, 508–509
    and equity/distributive justice, 254,
        259, 274–75
    and exchange, 169–70, 175–78, 203,
        208, 214–16, 220n, 413–16
    general model for, 339–45
    measurement of, 324–25, 328
    potential versus kinetic, 324, 326
    punishment, 346–48, 577
    of recipients, 508–509
    scope of concept of, 330–35
    and time, 334–35
Predictability, of contacts, 551–52, 562–
    63
Prejudice, 118–19, 121n, 438–39, 440–
    42, 517
Pressure, 388–89; *see also* Resources,
    pressure and competitive
Prisoners' dilemma, 154
Probabilistic choice models, 59
Probability preferences, 154
Probability of success, 134
Productivity, 260
Profit/cost ratio, 152–53
Profits, 225, 242, 244
Promises, 259
Prothetic continua, 72
Punishing behaviors, 346–48, 372, 393–
    94, 583

Qualified pools, 486, 488, 496; *see also*
    Pools, eligibility

Race, 238, 242, 420–27, 444–45
Race relations, 204–205, 270, 273, 419
Racism, 270
Random utility models, 165
Ratio scales, 74–76, 112, 116–17
Rationality, 6–7, 30, 52, 66, 113, 153,
    200, 220n, 571
Ratios
    of interaction types, 538–41
    versus differences, 467–78, 538
Reciprocity, 154, 171n
Reductionism, 27
Reference groups, 44, 51–52, 226; *see
    also* Contextual effects

Referent power, 348–50, 393
Referential comparisons, 227–28, 233
Regulation of contacts, 524–25, 551–52,
    559–64, 572
Relative deprivation, 52, 223–24, 478
Relevance relations, 228, 231
Residual approach, to measurement,
    453, 455–59
Resources
    apportionment of, 127–28
    conservation of, 129, 373–74
    and discrimination, 414, 417
    and equity/distributive justice, 251–
        52, 261, 274–75
    expending and replenishing of, 123,
        125–27, 129–31, 133, 135–36,
        147–48, 161, 164, 168, 358–60,
        373–74, 378, 392, 400
    in exchange, 193, 198, 201, 203, 216–
        17
    measurement of, 352–54
    pooling of, 354–58
    pressure and competitive, 389, 576n,
        577–78
    supply of, 131, 153, 155–56, 168, 170
    types of, 345–52
    versus objective properties, 329, 343,
        352–54
Response generalization, 82–83
Reverse discrimination, 421, 444
Reward/cost ratio, 152
Reward maximization, 220n
Rewarding behaviors, 346–48
Rewards
    consummatory, 552–53
    of contacts, 552–55
    and equity/distributive justice, 225–
        26, 240–42, 244–49, 252–53, 256–
        60, 266–70
    in exchange, 199
    extrinsic, 554–55, 558, 560
    functions, 566–75
    intrinsic, 552–54, 557–58
    in subjective expected utility model,
        123, 128–33, 137, 151, 155, 161;
        see also Utility, positive
Risk, 109, 154, 171n, 256–59
Risk dimensions, 137
Risk preferences, 154
Role similarity, 234–35
Roles, 176–78, 237
Role taking, 185, 194
Rules
    adherence to, 391–92

clarity of, 392
of distributive justice, 222, 225–28, 236, 243–45, 283n; *see also* Distributive justice; Equity/distributive justice
modification of, 392–93
Runs structure, 86

Sanctions; *see also* Punishment behaviors
and contextual effects, 301–303, 316
Satiation, 38, 40, 42, 45, 49–51, 53–54, 77n, 125, 140, 149, 211–12, 567–68
Satisficing, 65, 147, 149–52, 155–58, 161, 163, 196, 402
Scarcity, 88, 134, 416
Secrecy, 284n, 344, 382–85, 389–90, 393, 509–10
Segregation, 170, 419, 427, 445, 515, 519, 523, 542–43, 545, 554, 576–79
and costs, 578–79, 583
dynamic theory of, 592–613
ecological studies of, 519–22
of fraternities and sororities, 445
measurement of, 520, 525–35
of schools, 436
versus integration, 533–35
Selection criteria, 496–512
biases in, 503–12
secrecy of, 510
vagueness of, 506–507, 509
Self-comparison, 284n
Self-deprivation, 269
Self-esteem, 251, 255, 257–58, 268–69, 271
Self-fulfilling prophecy, 30, 119
Self-interest, 208, 220n
Sequential pools, 490–93; *see also* Pools, eligibility
Sex discrimination, 428
Significant other, 185
Similar others, 234–35, 237, 242
Similarity, cultural, 564–65, 576
Simplifications, 4, 7–8; *see also* Satisficing
and contextual-effects models, 288–91
in estimating subjective expected utilities, 163, 180, 189–93
in estimating subjective probabilities, 106–10
in estimating utilities, 59–67

Size of group
absolute, 572–73, 578–79, 583, 597
relative, 540, 572
Slavery, 202–203, 215–16, 258, 265, 268–69, 275, 286n
Social characteristics
achieved, 225, 242
ascribed, 225–26, 242–43
investment of, 237–39, 246–47; *see also* Investments
substitutability of actions and, 245–46
Social commodities, 34, 176, 178
Social distance, 517, 550, 563
Socialization, 108–109
Sociocultural value context, 242
Specific other, 227, 232–37, 241
Specification errors, 20
Stability, 311–12, 589, 594, 604–12; *see also* Equilibrium
Standardization: *see* Measurement; Control variables
Standards, absolute versus relative, 478–83
States, 227; *see also* Social characteristics
Status, and contextual effects, 300–303; *see also* Inequalities
Status characteristics, 238, 245
Status congruence, 223
Status consistency, 171n
Status inconsistency, 223, 479–80, 580–82
Status loss, 561, 580–82
Status symbols, 254
Status-value theory, 222, 227–28, 232–33, 237, 245–46, 251, 284n
Stereotypes, 438–39
Stimulus generalization, 82
Stochastic utility models, 165
Subgroups, and contextual effects, 306–16
Subjective expected costs, 137, 152, 160–61, 164, 239; *see also* Costs
Subjective expected inequity, 276–79; *see also* Inequity
Subjective expected profits, 137, 152; *see also* Profits
Subjective expected rewards, 137, 152, 160, 164; *see also* Rewards
Subjective expected utilities, 32, 35, 52, 125–26, 129, 147–49, 528–29; *see also* Utilities
and equity/distributive justice, 251, 256, 276–77, 287n

Subjective expected utilities (*continued*)
  estimation of, 33, 55–57, 59, 122–24,
    126–27, 131–32, 136–39, 145–46,
    160–61, 163, 210–211, 240, 276–
    78
  in exchange, 177, 182, 197, 202, 211,
    213–14, 216
  feedbacks on, 161–62
  maximization of, 65, 69, 77n, 147–58,
    161, 163, 171n, 196–98, 202–203,
    205–206, 209, 216; *see also* Utility,
    maximization of
  relative, 56, 59–61, 122, 131–33, 137,
    144, 188–93, 196–98, 216–17, 278,
    282
  representation of, 36, 181
  satisfactory, 149–50; *see also* Satis-
    ficing
  simplifications in estimating, 163, 180,
    189–93
  vicarious estimates of, 194
Subjective expected utility model, 32–36,
    55, 70, 73, 75, 114, 116–17, 136,
    138–39, 148, 164–65, 172n, 176,
    199, 230, 266
  application of, to exchange, 180–98,
    210
  exemplification of, in exchange, 206–
    14
  inclusion of rewards and costs in, 131–
    33
  incorporation of equity judgments in,
    275–79
Subjective expected value model, 164
Subjective probabilities, 17–18, 32–33,
    35, 51, 53, 55, 65–66, 68, 78–121,
    125–27, 148, 150, 159, 165, 169,
    239, 285n, 428, 475, 562
  accuracy of, 110–12
  of aggregates, 114–15, 118–20, 167–
    68, 175
  beliefs and attitudes as, 117–18
  biases in, 112–16, 137, 201
  causal models approach to, 79–80, 89–
    100, 106–108, 115, 120, 188–93
  complications in estimation of, 100–
    106
  confidence in, 118
  derivation of, from actors' causal
    models, 96–100
  determinants of, 79, 106, 115–16, 120,
    162, 216–17
  effects of external stimuli on, 142–44,
    147, 157, 163

  in exchange, 177, 181, 186–96, 199,
    201, 204, 209, 211, 213, 217
  experiential determinants of, 88, 187–
    88
  factors modifying estimates of, 83–86
  feedbacks on, 116
  frequency distribution approach to,
    79–88, 186–88
  interpersonal comparability of, 114–
    15
  measurement of, 110–17, 136
  relationship of, to intergroup processes,
    117–20
  relationship of, to objective probabili-
    ties, 69, 78, 111–15, 121n
  relationship of, to utilities, 65, 75–76,
    107, 124; *see also* Independence of
    utilities and subjective probabilities
  relative, 93–96, 101, 107–108
  revision of, 111, 114
  simplifications in estimation of, 106–
    109, 193–96
  situational determinants of, 86–88,
    188
  in unique situations, 82–83, 187
  vicarious estimates of, 194, 208
Subjective value, 32, 34–35, 76n; *see
    also* Utilities
Sunk costs, 147, 556, 594–95
Surplus value, 224
Surveillance, 258, 393; *see also* Secrecy

Task complexity, 504–507
Task similarity, 504–507
Teleological reasoning, 602
Tension, 576
Theories, 2–5; *see also* Causal models;
    Working theories
Threshold effects, 39–40, 42, 45, 49, 54,
    238, 262
Time; *see also* Dynamic theories
  continuous models of, 609–13
  discrete versus continuous, 590, 601
  perspectives on, 340, 396–97
Tract data, census, 528–35
Trust, 184, 194–95, 217, 383–85

Uncertainty, 35, 75, 110, 117, 149, 154
Unconditional probabilities, 90–91
Unfolding technique, 68, 75, 96
Urgency, 377–78

Utilities, 16–17, 27–77, 125–27, 150, 159, 165, 169, 239, 284n
  as additive functions, 57–58
  of aggregates, 72, 75, 114, 167–68
  axiomatic theories of, 67, 73, 75, 165
  cause indicators of, 36, 73–74
  for choice variability, 71, 113, 154
  complications in estimating, 55–59, 100, 183–84
  constancy of, 71
  determinants of, 37–55, 184–85, 208, 216–17
  devaluation of, 53
  in discrimination siutations, 435, 439, 441, 444–45, 449, 503–12
  effect indicators of, 36, 67–71
  in exchange, 175, 181–86, 199, 205, 209, 211, 213–14, 217
  for gambling, 71, 116–17, 148, 154
  interpersonal comparability of, 44, 76, 167, 172n
  maximization of, 152, 198, 202–203, 205, 252, 256, 261–65, 275, 285n, 286n; *see also* Subjective expected utilities, maximization of
  measurement of, 67–76, 111, 136
  of money, 43, 72
  multidimensional, 36, 64, 70–71
  as multiplicative function, 58–59
  negative, 41, 46, 54, 58, 62–64, 92–93, 123, 128, 136–38, 143–44, 148, 167, 177, 180, 195, 206, 212, 214, 256–58; *see also* Costs
  positive, 46, 123, 128, 136–38, 144, 170, 177, 180–81, 184, 206, 208, 211, 214, 239, 257–58, 414; *see also* Rewards
  as power functions, 42–44, 54, 72–73, 75–76, 160

relationship of, to goals, 35–37
relationship of, to subjective probabilities, 65, 75–76, 107, 124; *see also* Independence of utilities and subjective probabilities
relationship of, to values, 34–35, 76n
relative, 60–64, 76, 93, 108
simplifications in estimation of, 59–67, 185–86
verbal indicators of, 71–72
vicarious estimates of, 180, 184–86, 194, 196–97, 208, 216–17, 220n, 257
Utility curves, 38–39, 42–44, 141, 148, 160, 182–83, 200, 204, 253
Utility deprivation, 141, 144, 199–200, 202–204, 212, 214, 216–17, 239
Utility forgone, 123, 128–33, 148, 153, 170n, 171n

Vacancy chains, 490n
Valence, 134, 165
Values, 34–35, 226, 247
  consummatory, 71, 227, 239–40, 254
  status, 71, 227, 239–40, 251
Variance preferences, 154
Visibility of contacts, 550–51, 554, 559–61, 582–85
Voluntariness, 176–77, 259
  of contacts, 553, 555–58, 560

Wishful thinking, 69, 133–35
Withdrawal, 195, 202–203, 211–12, 515, 524; *see also* Segregation
Workers, 236, 257, 260, 268–69, 286n
Working theories, 36, 80, 89, 378–82, 397, 571; *see also* Causal models